Complete Guide to

FISHING

ACROSS

NORTH AMERICA

JOE BROOKS

Complete Guide to

FISHING

ACROSS

NORTH AMERICA

An Expert's Guide to

Fresh and Saltwater Fishing

in the United States,

Canada, Mexico,

the Bahamas and Bermuda

OUTDOOR LIFE   HARPER & ROW   NEW YORK

To anglers everywhere, with the hope that this book will help you to discover North America's great fishing. Tight lines!

Joe Brooks

ACKNOWLEDGMENTS

I wish to thank the following for their assistance in assembling information about the fishing in their respective areas: Don McCarthy, Fishing Information Bureau, Ministry of Tourism, Nassau in the Bahamas; Pete Perinchief, Director, Bermuda Fishing Information Bureau, Hamilton, Bermuda; Northwest Territory Tourist Office, Ottawa, Canada; Kay Kennedy, Fairbanks, Alaska; Canadian Government Travel Bureau, Ottawa; Lee Straight, The Vancouver Sun, Vancouver, British Columbia; Harvey Dryden, Director, Travel Bureau, Dept. of Industry and Information, Regina, Saskatchewan; W. E. Organ, Director, Travel and Publicity Bureau, Dept. of Industry and Commerce, Winnipeg, Manitoba; Dept. of Travel and Publicity and Dept. of Lands and Forests, Toronto, Ontario; E. B. Bailey, Dept. of Tourism, and Gustave Bedard, Director of Information, Fish and Game Dept., Quebec; Harry L. Garvir, New Brunswick Travel Bureau, Fredericton, New Brunswick; John MacCormick, The Travel Bureau, and S. R. Fraser, Travel Counsel, Halifax, Nova Scotia; Margaret F. Godden and Doug Wheeler, Newfoundland Development Office, St. John's, Newfoundland.

Frank L. Haynes and Jack Lovett, Jr., Dept. of Conservation, Montgomery, Alabama; Walton Lowry, Fishing Editor, *Birmingham News,* Birmingham, Ala.; Mrs. Jack Hazard, Mountain Home, Ark.; Bill Apple, Little Rock, Ark.; George Purvis, Fish and Game Comm., Little Rock, Ark.; Sam Welch, Bull Shoals, Ark.; Bert Coleman, Arizona Development Board, Phoenix, Ariz.; Bill Davidson, *Daily Citizen,* Tucson, Ariz.; C. E. Gillham, Sedona, Ariz.; Tom Rowen, *Mercury-News,* San Jose, Cal.; Ed Neal, Outdoor Editor, *News Call Bulletin,* San Francisco, Cal.; William C. Dillinger, Fish and Game Dept., Sacramento, Cal.; Larry Green, San Bruno, Cal.; John A. Wit, San Gabriel, Cal.; Joe Mears, *Pasadena Star News,* Pasadena, Cal.; Don Domenick, Department of Fish, Game and Parks, Denver, Colo.; Jim Haywood, Outdoor Editor, *Denver Post,* Denver, Colo.; Robert A. Jones, Board of Fisheries and Game, Hartford, Conn.; David S. Hugg, State Development Dept., Dover, Del.; Elgin White, Florida News Bureau, Tallahassee, Fla.; Don Kimsey, Fishing Editor, the *Herald,* Albany, Ga.; Charles Elliott, Field Editor, *Outdoor Life,* Atlanta, Ga.; Jimmy Walker, Manager Okefenokee Swamp Park, Waycross, Ga.; Bob Short, Game and Fish Comm., Atlanta, Georgia.

John Warren, *Moline Dispatch,* Moline, Ill.; Al Lopinot, Dept. of Conservation, Springfield, Illinois; Jim Parsons, Sandpoint, Idaho; Bob Maken, Sports Editor, *Coeur d'Alene Press,* Coeur d'Alene, Idaho; E. Kleiss Brown, Dept. of Fish and Game, Boise, Idaho; Reis Tuttle, Outdoor Editor, *Register and Tribune,* Des Moines, Iowa; Dennis L. Rehder, State Conservation Comm., Des Moines, Iowa; Erwin D. Sias, *The Journal,* Sioux City, Iowa; William M. Toms, Outdoor Editor, *The News,* Indianapolis, Ind.; Tom Buskirck, Outdoor Editor, the *Courier,* Evansville, Ind.; John D. Polson, Fish and Game Comm., Pratt, Kan.; Harry Towles, Fish and Wildlife Resources Dept., Frankfort, Ky.; John E. Murphy, Outdoor Editor, *Post & Times-Star,* Covington, Ky.; Jim Eddleman, Outdoor Editor, the *Herald,* Lexington, Ky.; Grits Gresham, Natchitoches, La.; Frank Adams, Outdoor Editor, the *American Press,* Lake Charles, Louisiana; Bill Burton, Outdoor Editor, the *Sun,* Baltimore, Md.; Burt Dillon, Editor, *Fishing in Maryland,* Baltimore, Md.; Malcolm King, Game and Inland Fish Comm., Annapolis, Maryland; Gene Letourneau, *The Sentinel,* Waterville, Maine; Bob Elliot, Department of Economic Development, Augusta, Maine.

Barry O. Freeman, Game and Fish Comm., Jackson, Miss.; Bryant R. Chaplin, Division of Fisheries and Game, Westboro, Mass.; Frank Woolner, Editor, *The Salt Water Sportsman,* Boston, Mass.; E. B. Kinder, Missouri Recreation and Travel Dept., Jefferson City, Mo.; James F. Keefe, Missouri Conservation Commission, Jefferson City, Mo.; Ray Heady, Outdoor Editor, the *Star,* Kansas City, Mo.; O. I. Rightmyer, Chamber of Commerce, Sault Ste. Marie, Mich.; Ed. H. Caspersen, Chamber of Commerce, Ludington, Mich.; George Labadie, Southeast Michigan Tourist Assoc., Detroit, Mich.; Betty Jane Minsky, Cheboygan Chamber of Commerce, Cheboygan, Michigan; Stanley Lievense, District Fisheries Supervisor, Traverse City, Mich.; Win Kuehl, *News Advocate,* Manistee, Mich.; Helmer E. Olson, Chamber of Commerce, Hibbing, Minn.; Hjalmar O. Swenson, Division of Game and Fisheries, St. Paul, Minn.; Rocky Teller, WDSM-TV, Duluth, Minn.; Jack Kerr, Dept. of Business Development, St. Paul, Minn.; G. F. Kratoska, Cook County Civic Council, Grand Marais, Minn.; Alec Kavink, *The Daily Journal,* International Falls, Minn.; William H. Browning, State Chamber of Commerce, Helena, Mont.; Dan Bailey, Livingston, Mont.; Red Monical, Livingston, Mont.; Frank Rose, Twin Bridges, Mont.; Bruce Elliott, Clinton, Mont.; Russ Ward, Missoula, Mont.

John E. Dodge, Fish and Game Dept., Concord, N.H.; John Brennan, Division of Economic Development, Concord, N.H.; Jules W. Marron, Department of Conservation and Economic Development, Newton, N. J.; L. G. MacNamara, Dept. of Conservation and Economic Development, Trenton, N. J.; Milton Rosko, Jr., Rahway, N. J.; Bill Backus, Outdoor Editor, the *Daily Journal,* Elizabeth, N. J.; Dick H. Schaffer, Editor, *Outdoor Nebraska,* Lincoln, Neb.; Pete Czura, Lincoln, Neb.; Mel Hardman, Fish and Game Dept., Salt Lake City, Utah; "Hack" Miller, *Deseret News,* Salt Lake City, Utah; Hal Welch, Ogden, Utah; Melvin E. McDowell, Fish and Game Comm., Reno, Nev.; David G. Jackson, Editor, *New Mexico Wildlife,* Santa Fe, N. M.; Joe Beamish, Outdoor Editor, the *Herald American,* Syracuse, N. Y.; Art Smith, Outdoor Editor, the *Herald Tribune,* New York, N. Y.; Elmer "Al" Messner, Outdoor Editor, the *Times-Union,* Rochester, N. Y.; Earl Westervelt, Conservation Dept., Albany, N. Y.

Miriam Rabb, North Carolina Travel Information Division, Raleigh, N. C.; Aycock Brown, Manteo, N. C.; Cal Olson, Fargo, N. D.; George Engelter, North Dakota Motor Carriers Association, Bismarck, N. D.; W. E. Shemorry, *The Plains Reporter,* Williston, N. D.; John Ferguson, *The Tulsa World,* Tulsa, Okla.; Lou Klewer, Outdoor Editor, *The Blade,* Toledo, Ohio; Allan W. Eckert, Outdoor Editor, the *Journal-Herald,* Dayton, Ohio; George Robey, Jr., Gahanna, Ohio; William G. Kah, Ohio Dept. of Natural Resources, Columbus, Ohio; Chuck Dell, Outdoor Editor, *The News,* Lima, Ohio; Joe Van Wormer, Bend, Ore.; Charles V. Stanton, Roseburg, Ore.; Milt Guymon, Oregon State Game Commission, Portland, Ore.; George Krause, *The Tribune,* Altoona, Pa.; Seth Myers, Sharon, Pa.; Roger Latham, Outdoor Editor, the *Press,* Pittsburgh, Pa.; Eldy Johnston, McKeesport, Pa.; Eddie Finlay, South Carolina Wildlife Resources Comm., Columbia, S. C.

Bob Roemaker, Sports Editor, the *Daily Journal,* Rapid City, S. D.; F. J. Gilbride, the *Argus-Leader,* Sioux Falls, S. D.; George W. Goodwin, Roanoke, Va.; J. Ed. Campbell, Tennessee Valley Authority, Knoxville, Tenn.; W. L. "Kingfish" Marrs, Johnson City, Tenn.; Bob Witt, Outdoor Editor, *The Banner,* Nashville, Tenn.; Ernest Conner, Jr., Tennessee Game and Fish Comm., Nashville, Tenn.; Curtis Carpenter, Texas Parks and Wildlife Dept., Austin, Texas; Kenneth Foree, Dallas, Texas; Fred Maly, San Antonio, Texas; Leon Kestleoo, Comm. of Game and Inland Fisheries, Richmond, Va.; Claude Rogers, Salt Water Sport Fishing Assoc., Virginia Beach, Va.; Jennings Culley, Outdoor Editor, the *News Leader,* Richmond, Va.; Max Ailor, Outdoor Editor, the *Times-Dispatch,* Richmond, Va.; Perc Angwin, Outdoor Editor, the *Times-Argus,* Barre, Vermont; Stan Fagerstrom, *Longview Daily News,* Longview, Wash.; Jack Henson, Outdoor Editor, the *Evening News,* Port Angeles, Wash.; Frank Haw and Don Reed, Dept. of Fisheries, Seattle, Wash.; Doug Blessenger, Outdoor Reporter, the *Union-Bulletin,* Walla-Walla, Wash.; Gordon L. Palmer, West Virginia Dept. of Natural Resources, Charleston, W. Va; George S. Gutsell, Outdoor Editor, the *Journal,* Martinsburg, W. Va.; W. R. Keyser, Welch, W. Va.; Bill Chaddock, *The News Register,* Wheeling, W. Va.; Syd Herman, Manitowoc, Wisc.; L. P. Voigt, Wisconsin Conservation Dept., Madison, Wisc.

Joe Brooks

CONTENTS

About This Book

This is a guide to the best fishing waters in North America, selected by the author on the basis of personal experience and confirmed reports. It contains forty-eight state maps, prepared especially for this book, which are keyed to the text and show the location of every recommended lake and stream. The reader will note that in the text the names of fishing waters are set in capital letters, followed by a number in parenthesis. This number corresponds to a number on the state map which identifies the water. Nearby towns that are mentioned in the text are usually shown on the map. It is suggested that the fisherman use these maps to determine the location of a lake or stream, and use the travel directions in the text with his own state or county road map to reach a particular water.

North Eastern States

The northeastern states share a common topography resulting from the conjunction of several mountain groups with the marine features of the north Atlantic coastline. New York State has its own distinctive ranges—the Catskills and Adirondacks, extensions of the Appalachians. New Hampshire has its White Mountains, Vermont its Green Mountains. Even low-lying Massachusetts has a share of rolling, wooded country in the Berkshire Hills in the western part of the state. Rhode Island and Connecticut, alone, of this northeastern group of states, do not have mountainous areas.

All the mountain ranges provide a green cover of mixed forests and an extensive watershed to provide lakes and streams suitable for fish of many kinds. In one part or another of this northeastern area, the inland fisherman will have a choice of brown, brook and rainbow trout, lake trout, smallmouth black bass, largemouth black bass, landlocked salmon, walleye, northern pike, muskellunge, yellow perch, white perch, eastern chain pickerel, lake trout or togue, crappie, bluegill and sunfish. At various spots along the coast he may find the big-game species of marlin, swordfish, bluefin tuna and sharks, and the smaller species of tautog or blackfish, pollack, mackerel, weakfish, bluefish, cunner, flounder and codfish. Throughout the length of the coast the anadromous striped bass is taken in numbers, and in a few areas the Atlantic salmon comes into the rivers.

3

MAINE

The State of Maine reaches into a more northerly latitude than any other part of the United States except Alaska. Much of its northern boundary fronts on the Canadian Province of Quebec, separated by the St. John River. Its western borders rise toward the White Mountains of New Hampshire, while its eastern reaches blend into the forests of New Brunswick. The entire coastline on the Atlantic Ocean is rugged, rocky and indented by myriad deep bays. While the seacoast and middle interior have been highly developed, much of the northern part of Maine remains an unspoiled, beautiful wilderness, ideal terrain for the sport fisherman.

Maine lakes and streams offer a wide variety of fishing. It is the only part of the United States whose rivers receive runs of Atlantic salmon, and, almost unique in this field, there is no special license and no rod limit on the waters where this fish is available. Landlocked salmon, regarded by many as just as sporty, are found in some ninety inland lakes and rivers. Brook trout, the native of the eastern United States, are found in hundreds of rivers, lakes and ponds. In some waters they run only from half a pound to 1½ pounds, but in a few places they have been taken up to 7 pounds. Both brown and rainbow trout have been stocked in Maine and are taking well, though they are not found in great numbers. Lake trout occur in some of the same waters as salmon and brook trout.

The smallmouth black bass is found in almost all Maine lakes and ponds from the coast inland to central Maine and is one of the state's greatest piscatorial attractions. This species puts up a particularly hard fight in these northern, cold waters. The same may be said for the largemouth, which, however, is found only in limited waters. The Belgrade Lakes is a hot spot for the species.

The white perch, regarded by many as the top freshwater table fish, is very common. This tasty and hard-fighting fish commonly weighs only from one half to 2 pounds. The world record for the species came from Maine, a 4-pound 12-ounce fish taken in 1949. Pickerel, also highly regarded as a food fish, are very common throughout southern and central Maine and especially in Washington County, at the extreme northeast coast, close to the New Brunswick border. In this area, pickerel are so common that they are sold commercially. The fish usually weigh between 1 and 4 pounds.

The bluefin tuna is the major big-game species of the salt water along the Maine coast. Tuna appear in these waters about the third week in June and are taken from then throughout the summer until the middle of September. Bailey's Island is perhaps the best place to fish for these big, heavy fighters. Another giant of the deep which has been seen in numbers some twelve miles off Cape Elizabeth, near Portland, on the southern coast of Maine, is the swordfish. While extensive angling has not been done for them, some fish have been taken.

The tautog is another species known to occur in some numbers but is not fished for widely. The schools move in about mid-May and fish are taken in many bays and inlets during the summer. Mackerel also arrive in May. Fishing for this species reaches its peak in midsummer. Striped bass, one of the favorite migratory species of the East Coast, begin to arrive in late May and continue on the prod throughout the summer. Other salty species which provide excellent summer coastal fishing are the winter flounder, sand flounder, cunner or sea perch, and pollack. Codfish and haddock work inshore during the spring and are found around offshore banks and in the deeper parts of the harbors during the remainder of the season.

A number of major rivers form the basis of the drainage system in Maine: the St. John, on the north, between Quebec and Maine, the St. Croix on the east, between Maine and New Brunswick; the Penobscot, draining the eastern part of the state; and the Kennebec in the west. But while these are the limited number of large streams, a map of Maine shows almost as much water as land. The rivers already mentioned have innumerable tributaries and a series of lakes and strings of lakes laces the whole countryside, often providing river-like access from one to the other.

The larger lakes are Moosehead, Chesuncook, Pemadumcook, Eagle, in the central area; Grand Lake in the southeast; the Belgrade Lakes in the south-central section; and Mooselookmeguntic, in the northwest.

In spite of the rugged countryside the major part of the state is well supplied with highways. Providing an artery from the Montreal area of Canada as well as northern New York State, U.S. 2 enters from New Hampshire about half way down the western border, crosses about half the state, then curves northward to the New Brunswick border. U.S. 1 provides access to the entire coast, then runs northward parallel to the New Brunswick border, providing entry from the Gaspé area of Quebec. U.S. 201 traverses the eastern part of Maine, as a major highway between Quebec City and Augusta, the capital of Maine, and thence to U.S. 1 at the coast. Quick access from the highly populated eastern sections around Boston is available via the Maine Turnpike, from U.S. 1, north of Boston, to Bangor in south-central Maine.

Highway facilities are not so great in that part of the state which is most important to the freshwater angler—that great rectangle enclosed by the Canadian border on the north, State Highway 11 on the east, State Highway 16 on the south, and U.S. 201 on the west. Many of the fishing camps and resorts in this area are serviced by air from towns such as Greenville at the south end of Moosehead Lake, on State Highway 15, northwest of Bangor. The same area is accessible from U.S. 201 via State Highway 15 near Jackman. Other good jumping-off places for flights to the interior are Shin Pond on State Highway 159, off State Highway 11 at Patten; Portage Lake on State Highway 11, further north, near Portage; and Millinocket, on State Highway 11, further south. Float-equipped planes can readily land on many of the lakes in this isolated area and there are also a number of flying fields suitable for land-based small planes. Some camp owners in the deep interior operate their own flying services to and from their camps.

Some of the flying services through which wilderness outpost service may be obtained are: Holt Flying Service, Greenville, Maine; "Thanny" Coffin, Portage Lake, Maine; Milt Hall's Camp, Munsungun, Maine (address Portage Lake); Dana West and Dana McNally, on Fish River Lake (address Portage, Maine). Plane service may also be arranged by writing the Chamber of Commerce at such towns as Eagle Lake, Jackman, Princeton or Brewer; and even a letter addressed "Flying Service" to almost any Maine town will get a response. Planes also operate to offshore islands on the Atlantic coast from Rockland and other ports. The Federal Aviation Agency at Augusta, Maine, will supply a complete list of aerial facilities, revised annually.

For those adventurous enough to embark on canoe or float trips to reach their fishing, there are unnumbered waters available in this part of Maine, and some in the more southerly areas. In many cases, because of the turbulent nature of the rivers, guides are necessary but some few may be navigated without this service as long as those handling the craft are experienced canoeists or boatmen. The fishing possibilities of the various waters in this group are discussed later in this chapter, but for a basis to start planning such a trip, anglers should obtain the "Map of Canoe Trips" published by the Department of Economic Development, State House, Augusta, Maine. All the streams and lakes covered do not necessarily offer good fishing, but the routes are well described.

The State Forestry Department maintains a series of public camp sites on major canoe routes. Those planning to camp at other places than these must obtain an out-of-doors fire and camping permit from the nearest state forest-fire warden or landowner. This includes fire using such fuels as sterno, gasoline, charcoal, etc., except at state highway picnic areas. A list of authorized camp sites, some 351 of them, of which 263 are in wild territory, may be obtained from the State Forestry Department, Augusta, Maine.

Maine has very cold and snowy winters, a late spring and early fall. Even the summers can be from cool to cold. Anglers should go well supplied with woolens to top lighter summer fishing gear when the weather turns cold, and for evenings even when the days are warm. Good footwear is also a necessity. The famous Maine Bean Boot, made by the renowned L. L. Bean Company at Freeport, Maine, is ideal to withstand dampness when hiking in the woods, and is also good in canoe or skiff. Hip boots are sufficient wading gear for some of the smaller streams but to fish the larger ones you should have chest-high waders. Those planning to camp should take plenty of warm sleeping gear.

Deer are common in most of the wooded areas of Maine. In some places there are also black bear, moose and a few wildcats. However, the angler who leaves them alone will have no trouble. While Maine is not generally considered to be within the range of any poisonous snakes, the timber rattler may occur in the southern part.

Tackle needs in Maine will vary as widely as the fishing. The salmon and trout fishermen lean to fly-fishing gear, though some light spinning tackle is used. The best all-around fly outfit would be an 8-foot rod with HDH (DT6F) line. In bigger rivers an 8½-foot rod should be matched with a GBF (WF8F); and a 9-foot rod with a GAF (WF9F). Many salmon fishermen go to the 9½-foot fly rod, and sometimes use a G2AE line, but usually a GAF (WF9F) will do very nicely.

The best Atlantic-salmon flies include the Jock Scott, Silver Doctor, Silver Grey, Thunder and Lightning, Black Doctor, Black Dose, March Brown, Blue Charm, Cosseboom, Dusty Miller: on hook sizes from number 12 to 1/0 and even up to 3/0 and 5/0 for heavy water. One trout fly, the Muddler Minnow, has proven to be an outstanding Atlantic-salmon fly, and should be carried in sizes number 8, 4, 2 and 1/0. For landlocked salmon in Maine, the Supervisor, tied on a long shank 2, 4 or number 6 hook, is one of the most successful flies, but those patterns mentioned above will also take fish. The best dry flies are the Brown Bivisible, the Grey Wulff, Brown Wulff, and White Wulff, Pink Lady, Grey Hackle and Brown Hackle.

For trout fishing, fly men find that all the old standards pay off in both wet and

While hip boots will do for fishing some of the smaller Maine streams, chest-high waders are best if you want to reach a brownie like this one from the Sandy.

dry flies and nymphs. Hook sizes should be number 16, 12, 8 and some 6.

Spin fishermen use light to medium outfits for all Maine freshwater fishing; and all the standard spoons and lures are successful.

Anglers in the salt will find that on charter boats the skippers will have the right tackle aboard for trolling or bottom fishing. Those who plan to cast for such onshore species as the striped bass use fly, plug or spinning outfits, going to the heavier versions of the gear of their choice. A 9- or 9½-foot fly rod, with GAF (WF9F) line is ideal for fly rodders. Plug casters should have a rod stout enough to work a large lure, because stripers like a mouthful. And spinners go to medium or heavy spinning outfits. Ten- or 12-pound-test line is heavy enough for any striper you will take.

NORTHEAST

Some of Maine's top landlocked salmon and trout fishing is found in the FISH RIVER CHAIN OF LAKES (1) and the adjoining streams, in the northeast corner of the state, named for the river which enters the St. John at Fort Kent on the New Brunswick border. The larger lakes in the group are Long Lake, Mud Lake, Cross Lake, Square Lake and Eagle Lake, lying to the east of State Highway 11; and St. Froid Lake, Portage Lake and Fish River Lake, to the west of the same highway. Because of the northerly latitude, fishermen enjoy a longer season here than in the more southerly areas where the fish are "put down" by the heat of midsummer. The FISH RIVER (2), which parallels State Highway 11 from Eagle Lake to Fort Kent, offers excellent fishing in August.

Further south, the MACHIAS RIVER (3), which can be reached via dirt road west from State Highway 11 at Ashland; the AROOSTOOK RIVER (4) (into which the Machias flows), from there east to the Canadian border; and the ST. JOHN RIVER, are good trout streams.

Extending across the state to the south of this is a vast area of forests, lakes and streams, drained by the St. John and Allagash in the north, and the East and West Branch of the Penobscot in the south. This is good country for the canoeist-angler, the trails through rivers and lakes allowing him to reach dozens of tributaries of the two major streams. There is good fishing for salmon and trout and lake trout. This is a wilderness area and a guide is necessary. Guiding service may be obtained at the many fishing camps in the area. Access by car is over a narrow, private road, which, however, is open to the public, leaving State Highway 11 just north of Ashland, to MUSQUACOOK LAKE (5), where there is a fishing camp. Fishermen using this canoe trail will find an old tavern at Chesuncook Village on the northwest shore of Chesuncook Lake, which has been renovated and where airplane service is available to fly to other lakes. Fishermen may obtain complete details by writing Bert McBurney, Chesuncook Village, Maine.

You may also drive in from the south over a similar road which leaves State Highway 15 just west of Rockwood on Moosehead Lake. This road leads to several of the best fishing spots which can be reached without canoe or plane, notably CANADA FALLS DEADWATER (6); and further north to CAUCOMGOMOC LAKE (7). There are fishing camps at both places.

To the south, a similar road from State Highway 159, running east from State Highway 11 at Patten, provides access to the MT. KATAHDIN AREA (8), named for the mile-high mountain which rises in the midst of this rugged part of Maine. This is a top spot for trout and there are also some landlocked salmon. There are numerous large lakes, the best known to fishermen being Ripogenus, Sourdnahunk Lake and Stream, Kidney Pond, Daicey Pond, Millinocket Lake, Shin Pond, Tongue Pond, Katahdin Lake and Chimney Pond. There are a number of excellent fishing camps to provide accommodations.

From Patten, on State Highway 11, fishermen can reach some good fishing in FISH STREAM (9), not to be confused with the Fish River which lies further north. For eighteen miles, between Patten and Island Falls to the east, Fish Stream offers good trout fishing. Those wishing to take a short canoe trip will find they can travel this stream in one day, with plenty of time for fishing.

MOLUNKUS STREAM (10), a few miles south, between Sherman Mills and Macwahoc, on U.S. 2, is also good.

SOUTHEAST

In the southeastern corner of Maine is one of the most famed fishing areas in the northeastern United States. GRAND LAKE (11), reached via country road from U.S. 1, north of Woodland, is one of the largest bodies of water in this section and is one of the original homes of the landlocked salmon. It still is rated as a top water for this species. The writer well remembers some fine sport there in Grand Lake Stream, which flows out of the lake, with landlocked salmon from 3 to 6 pounds. They slammed into an artificial Green Drake size 12, and before the smoke cleared I had landed and released eight beautiful fish.

The Stream flows into BIG LAKE (12), to the east. The next day I used a small popping bug there and had one of the best days I've ever had for smallmouth, landing and releasing 125 bass from 1 to 4 pounds.

SPEDNIC LAKE (13), on the New Brunswick border, can be reached from U.S. 1 at Brookton. This lake, twenty-three miles long, is also rated as one of the nation's top bass lakes. Its neighbor to the north, GRAND LAKE (14), or Eastern Grand Lake, not to be confused with Grand Lake Stream, is also a top fishing spot for salmon and lake trout. It is adjacent to U.S. 1.

These are only the high spots in an area crammed with outstanding fishing waters, many of which are as yet very lightly fished. U.S. 1 provides complete north-south access; and State Highway 6 from Lincoln, on U.S. 2, crosses the more northern part of the area, while State Highway 9 crosses the southern part. There are numerous woodland camps and resorts.

The outlet of Big Lake to the ST. CROIX RIVER (15) is an excellent spot for smallmouth black bass. It is reached from Princeton on U.S. 1. There is some good casting water among the stumps of trees drowned when the dam was put in near Princeton. Below this, the St. Croix forms the border between the United States and Canada. It offers excellent fishing for brook trout, smallmouth black bass and very occasional salmon. It is possible to wade parts of the river but most of the fishing is from boats. Boats, guides and accommodations are available at Loon Bay Lodge, which is reached via U.S. 1 to Calais, Maine, then across the International Bridge to New Brunswick, Canada. The mailing address is Loon Bay Lodge, St. Stephan, New Brunswick, Canada. Train service is available from Boston to Vanceboro, Maine, and air transportation can be arranged from Bangor to Princeton, where guests will be met.

From the town of Danforth, immediately west of the southern end of Grand Lake, there is some forty miles of fishing for bass, pickerel and trout, the last only in the spring, in the MATTAWAMKEAG RIVER (16), which flows to the Penobscot. The Mattawamkeag may be fished by a long and difficult canoe trip downriver from Danforth to the village of Mattawamkeag on U.S. 2 at the Penobscot River. But parts of the stream may be reached from secondary highways west from Danforth. There are camp sites at several places where the roads approach the river.

Moving west again, the angler will find another concentration of lakes and streams. Enfield, at the junction of State Highway 188 and State Highway 155, just

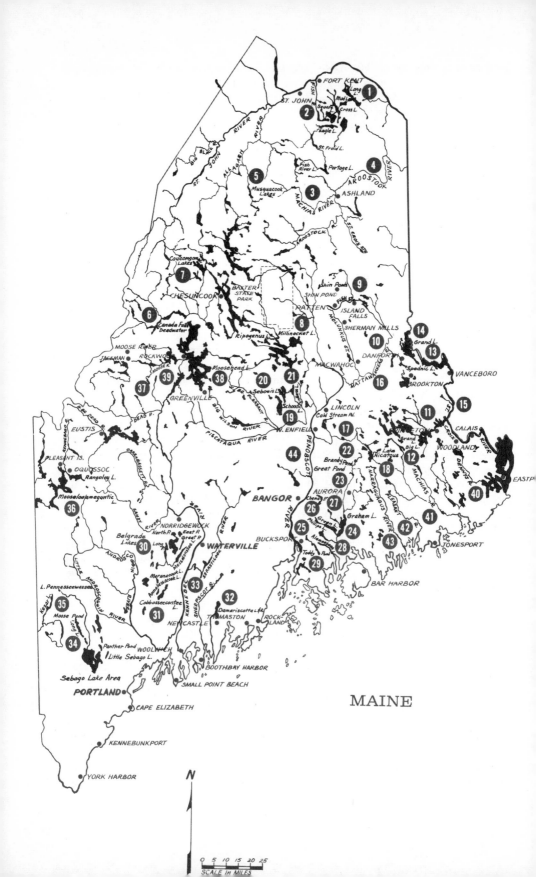

MAINE

off U.S. 2, is a good spot from which to fish COLD STREAM POND (17), a fine lake for lake trout and landlocked salmon. LAKE NICATOUS (18), also renowned for its salmon fishing, is only twenty miles to the east via State Highway 188. Milo, at the junction of State Highways 16 and 11, is the jumping-off place for another excellent salmon spot, LAKE SCHOODIC (19). Nearby LAKES SEBOEIS (20) and ENDLESS (21), and the streams in the area, provide good trout fishing. Guides are available at the several resorts in the area.

Further south, Bangor is the center of some excellent and varied fishing. There is good angling for salmon, lake trout, pickerel, brook trout and brown trout in BRANDY POND (22) and GREAT POND (23), which may be reached via dirt road from State Highway 9, west of Aurora. Via the same road, closer to Bangor, you can fish GRAHAM LAKE (24), GREEN LAKE (25) and PHILLIPS LAKE (26), also called Lucerne-in-Maine; and CHEMO and FLOODS (27) ponds, for salmon, trout and bass. From Bucksport on State Highway 15, about twenty miles south of Bangor, anglers can reach LAKE ALAMOOSOOK (28), TODDY POND (29) and several smaller ponds, all with landlocked salmon, trout and lake trout. Besides the accommodations available in the various towns, there are a number of fishing resorts on the lakes.

SOUTHWEST

To the south and west of Bangor is the renowned Waterville District of Maine, an area distinctive in the compactness of the lakes and streams, so that it is comparatively easy to move from one to the other. There is outstanding fishing for smallmouth, some fine largemouth possibilities. The BELGRADE LAKES (30) off State Highway 8, south of U.S. 2 at Norridgewock, or State Highway 27, north from Augusta, turn up largemouth to 2 pounds regularly, and occasional catches of 7 pounds. The Belgrade group includes Messalonskee, Salmon, Long, Great, East and North Lakes. Messalonskee has some excellent perch fishing and the world's record, weighing 4 pounds 12 ounces, was taken there. The lake also produces occasional brook trout. The Belgrade chain is universally quite good for this species.

Southwest of the state capital of Augusta are several large lakes, including COBBOSSEECONTEE, LITTLE COBBOSSEECONTEE, MARANACOOK and ANNABESSACOOK (31), which offer fishing for bass, salmon, trout and white perch. And from headquarters at the small towns of Readfield on State Highway 41, Fayette on State Highway 17, and Mount Vernon on State Highway 41, anglers may fish several smaller waters for the same species.

East of the Kennebec River, which runs southward through Waterville and Augusta to the coast, is another group of good fishing ponds, lying between State Highway 3 and the coast. The DAMARISCOTTA RIVER and LAKE (32), to tidewater, provide about fifty miles of fishing for bass and pickerel. The lake and river can be reached via secondary roads from U.S. 1 on the coast, and from State Highways 32, 27 and 17, farther north. Between the Kennebec and Damariscotta, the SHEEP-SCOT RIVER (33), which is paralleled by State Highway 218, is gaining an increasing reputation for Atlantic-salmon fishing.

There are excellent highways throughout this area, and numerous resorts, where information as to the best fishing spots can always be obtained.

SEBAGO LAKE (34), in the southwestern corner of Maine, the second largest lake in the state, is one of the original homes of the landlocked salmon and produced the 22½-pound world record. The fishing for this species is outstanding from an early spring opening date till warm weather; then bass take over. The salmon fishing picks up again in the fall. Other lakes in the general area may not have as great a reputation but are good producers of salmon, trout, smallmouth bass and white perch. Some of the better known are Long Lake, immediately north of Sebago, Brandy Pond, Moose Pond and Lake Pennesseewassee. Panther Pond and Little Sebago, to the east, and Peabody and Hancock Ponds to the west, are also good. On the south, Mousam, Crystal, Kennebunk and Bunganut also have good reputations. In the White Mountains, close against the New Hampshire border, LAKE KEZAR (35) is another favorite with anglers.

All these lakes can be reached via excellent roads as this is a highly developed resort area. Accommodations are plentiful.

To the north of this, close to the New Hampshire border, is the Rangeley Lake region, one of the most popular in Maine. RANGELEY LAKE (36) and its neighbor, MOOSELOOKMEGUNTIC (36), are two of the largest and best known lakes in the state and are well supplied with resorts and fishing camps. Trout fishing has always been good here, and the planting of landlocked salmon has resulted in some excellent fishing at times for this species. State Highways 4, 16 and 17 meet at the village of Oquossoc, between the two lakes.

A husky Atlantic salmon from the Narraguagas River.

WEST-CENTRAL

Of special interest to trout fishermen is the DEAD RIVER region to the north (37), reached from Eustis and Stratton on State Highway 27 and via secondary road north from State Highway 16 at North New Portland. The ponds and streams in this area, particularly Tim Pond, Chain of Ponds, Rowe Pond, Carry Pond, King and Bartlett Pond, are at an altitude of more than 1,500 feet and are spring fed, with the result that in the consequently cold water the trout hit well all season. The lakes and ponds are joined by a network of streams.

MOOSEHEAD LAKE (38), in the central zone of Maine, the largest lake in the state, is forty miles long and twenty miles wide. It lies in the center of an exceptionally beautful area and probably offers Maine's outstanding fishing for salmon, trout and lake trout. Dozens of smaller lakes and ponds and a number of streams are readily accessible from the towns of Rockland, Greenville and Moosehead on State Highway 15. Jackman and Moose River, further west on the same road, are also good spots from which to fish the area. There is excellent fishing in the MOOSE RIVER (39) group of ponds, lakes and streams, from Moose River to Moosehead Lake. Resorts of all types are numerous both in the towns and in wooded locations. Wilsons Camp, at Moosehead, at the outlet of the lake into the Kennebec River, is one of the oldest resorts. Trout and salmon are taken in both lake and river, and there are speckled trout in the ponds. There is rail service to Moosehead, and at the same town there are dock facilities for seaplanes. Greenville has an airport for land-based planes.

ATLANTIC SALMON FISHING IN MAINE

The rivers along the Maine coast into which Atlantic salmon make their seasonal runs are mostly those of the southeastern corner, namely the DENNYS (40), MACHIAS (41), PLEASANT (42) and NARRAGUAGUS (43), as well as some lesser streams in the same area. The SHEEPSCOT (33) and PENOBSCOT (44), far down the coast, are host to lesser runs. May and June are the top months, with another good season in September. The fish are taken mostly above tidewater, though some are taken in the estuaries. The average fish will weigh 10 pounds, and they have been taken up to 22 pounds. The minimum legal size is 14 inches. There is good bank fishing on the Dennys and Narraguagus but the Machias is best fished by boat.

No fishing license, other than the regular license for inland waters, is required; but seasons vary on the different rivers, and must be checked with the annual regulations booklet, obtainable from the Department of Inland Fisheries and Game, Augusta, Maine.

Another migrant taken occasionally in coastal rivers is the sea-run brown trout, known locally as the Scotch sea trout. They are taken mostly around Orland, just west of Bucksport, where U.S. 1 crosses the Penobscot.

SALTWATER FISHING

The bluefin tuna is the largest gamefish taken along the Maine coast. These giants move into Maine waters in late June and continue to be taken until the middle of September. They particularly like areas of rips, where wind and tide create opposing currents. The larger fish are taken on whole mackerel or herring bait and chumming is used to bring the big fellows close enough to present a bait. Some smaller bluefins are taken on artificial baits such as feathers, plugs and eels.

Tuna fishermen will find boats suitable for their sport at Boothbay Harbor through Louis Garcelon Jr., phone 910; Pat Elderkin, phone 269-W2; and Harold Wade, phone 953-M. Herbert McIntire can be reached at Small Point, Woolich, phone Hilltop 3-2228; and Lawrence Lewis at Sorrento.

Many charter boats which cater to anglers out for smaller game also carry hand-lines for tuna. Nearly every seaside village and town has some boats available for fishermen, ranging from skiffs to fully equipped charter craft.

Cape Elizabeth is the port to go out from for a chance at swordfish, though this is a long chance. The sport fishing for this species has not been developed in Maine, though quite a few fish have been seen about twelve miles off Cape Elizabeth.

The best catches of tautog, another popular saltwater fish in Maine, are made in the bays along the central part of the coast. Casco Bay, at Portland, is one of the best spots. Boothbay Harbor, reached via State Highway 27 from U.S. 1, near New-castle; and Penobscot Bay at the mouth of the Penobscot River, are also good. The tautog, or blackfish, appear in these waters about the middle of May and are found around rocky areas, shell bars, old wrecks and pilings from then until midsummer, when they go offshore to deep water, returning to the shallows in the fall. Fresh bait, ranging from green worms to crabs, gets the most fish but some few are taken on bullethead jigs bounced along the bottom.

The cunner, often called sea perch, is as common throughout the same waters as the tautog and is taken on the same lures and baits.

The pollack is frequently taken by inshore fishermen. Those caught during the summer in the inshore bays and estuaries are generally small but in spring and fall the larger members of the species often move inshore and sometimes may be seen breaking the surface of the water. When the fish are working on the surface, all sorts of surface plugs, jigs, lures and flies will take them. When they are deeper, sometimes you can stir them up by means of a wooden plug leading a bucktail lure. The noise and commotion of the plug attracts the fish, then they take the lure. In deep water, they are taken on clams, sea worms and cut squid. Since the fish has a large mouth, hooks usually are 1/0 to 4/0 for the smaller fish, and up to 8/0 for the larger.

Mackerel move inshore as early as May but the best fishing is from July through September. They are taken the entire length of the Maine coast and some exciting sport can be enjoyed using artificial lures, shiny spoons, wobblers and jigs, when the fish are schooling or feeding near the surface. Some anglers have even taken the voracious hitters on a piece of white cloth attached to a hook. The sport of casting to these fish can be enhanced by chumming a school of mackerel close to the boat. They'll stay around as long as there's a free meal.

In recent years the striped bass has moved into an important position in Maine's sport-fishing catalog. Although some anglers claim to have taken them for years, it is only recently that they have appeared in great numbers, often being hooked by salmon anglers in tidewater and rivers, as well as by saltwater fishermen. They are taken from June well into autumn, and usually weigh from 4 to 7 pounds. Jigs, lures, sea worms and trolling lures are all successful. The choice spots to fish are the mouth of the Kennebec River near Brunswick and Bath on U.S. 1; the George River at Thomaston and Medomak, reached via secondary road off U.S. 1 at Waldoboro; Belfast, at the mouth of the Penobscot, on U.S. 1; and Machiasport, on Machias

Bay on U.S. 1 near the eastern border of the state. However, the chances are that you can take stripers around every river mouth from Portsmouth to Eastport. Usually they seem to hit earlier in the rivers than in the surf, starting in the former waters about May 20th, but not being ready hitters in the surf until the middle of June.

Despite the generally small size of Maine stripers, some fish up to 60 pounds have been caught at the mouth of the Piscataqua River, north of Portsmouth near Kittery.

All the conventional saltwater flies, popping bugs, streamers and bucktails, and spinning and plug-casting lures take fish. In the surf anglers use block tin squids, large surface plugs, spoons, jigs and rigged eels. Fresh bait is usually native minnows and shiners, and in brackish water the sea worm is a favorite. The best tide is two hours before low-water slack and an hour after the turn of the tide.

Winter flounder and sand flounder, the latter often referred to as sand dab or window pane, are both found in all Maine coastal waters. Winter flounder are also taken in brackish water in the spring and are taken in the salty shallows both spring and fall; then the fish move to the deeper parts of the harbors and offshore waters during the summer. Spreaders are commonly used to present baits to this bottom feeder, short lengths of line being attached to the arms of the spreader and each line baited with a bit of seaworm, clam, crab or squid, on number 6 to 8 long-shanked hook. Sufficient weight must be used to get the baits down in whatever tide is flowing where you fish.

The sand flounder will often be found chasing live bait and at such time will readily hit artificials and puts up a good fight. The mouth of this species is considerably smaller than that of the winter flounder and therefore anglers prefer a smaller hook, usually 1/0.

Codfish and haddock also range the Maine coast and are taken inshore along the rocks and beaches in spring, and offshore during the warmer weather. These are the species that many of the party boats go for. Almost any old bait will do for these voracious eaters. The cod will hit artificials if you find him in the right spot. They are often caught by surf fishermen on the beaches, casting block tin squid or bullheads. The retrieve must be very slow.

Party boats are available at the following ports: York Harbor, at the end of U.S. 1A, the most southern tip of the Maine coast; Kennebunkport, on State Highway 9A, off U.S. 1 at Kennebunk; Boothbay, reached via State Highway 27 from U.S. 1 at North Edgecomb; Spruce Head, on State Highway 131 from U.S. 1 at Thomaston; North Haven, at the mouth of Penobscot Bay, reached via ferry from Rockland on U.S. 1; Cranberry Isle and Isleford, off Seal Harbor, on State Highway 3, on the outer coast of Mount Desert Island; Bar Harbor, on the same road; Jonesport, on State Highway 187, south from U.S. 1 at Columbia Falls; Eastport, at the mouth of Cobscook Bay, facing Campobello Island, reached via State Highway 189 from U.S. 1 at Whiting.

A current list of charter or party boats, with names and addresses of the captains, may be obtained from the Department of Economic Development, State House, Augusta, Maine.

A complete list of hotels, camps and tourist homes may be obtained from the Maine Publicity Bureau, Gateway Circle, Portland 4, Maine.

MAINE FISHING REGULATIONS

Resident Fishing License $2.75
Nonresident Fishing License $8.75
Nonresident 15-Day Fishing License $5.75
Nonresident 3-Day Fishing License $3.75
Junior Nonresident License (10 to 16
    years. No license required under 16) $2.25

SEASONS AND LIMITS

Season opens April 1 in all water naturally free of ice for all species except bass. Season closes August 15 on brooks and streams, September 15 on rivers, and September 30 on lakes and ponds. Season for black bass opens June 21, except that from June 1 to June 20 3 bass per day may be taken on single-hook artificial lures.

Species	Size	Daily Bag Limit
Trout	6″	Not more than 10 fish and not more than 7½ pounds in
Salmon	14″	aggregate unless the last fish caught increases the com-
Togue	14″	bined weight to more than 7½ pounds.
Bass	10″	
White Perch	None	No limit (local exceptions).
Pickerel	None	10 fish. No limit in Washington County.

There are numerous local exceptions to the above: Some ponds and parts of streams are limited to fly fishing only; and in many, the use of live minnows as bait is prohibited.

For complete regulations write: Inland Fisheries and Game Dept., Augusta, Maine.

NEW HAMPSHIRE

With a length of 180 miles sandwiched between Maine and Vermont, the State of New Hampshire has a wide variety of terrain. Most of it is covered with green forests interspersed with blue lakes, and in the middle of the state the White Mountains rise to heights of 5,000 feet. The coast has eighteen miles of seashore.

Consequently there is a fairly wide choice of fishing available to the angler in this area. The mountain streams and many ponds in the northern and central sections hold brook trout, rainbow trout and brown trout. There are smallmouth black bass in many lakes and ponds throughout the state except in the northern part, and largemouth in a few waters in the southern part as well as in the lower Connecticut and Merrimack Rivers. Many larger streams in the south, which ordinarily might not produce much fishing, were at one time stocked with brown trout. This adaptable species has held over to provide some good angling possibilities there. A number of the larger lakes hold landlocked salmon and lake trout, those two usually being found in the same waters, and there is currently some experimentation with splake, a cross between the laker and the speckled or eastern brook trout. In Lake Sunapee and Big Dan Hole Pond near Lake Ossipee, and Tewksbury Pond near Grafton, the angler may also connect with an eastern golden trout, though rarely; and he may also find a cross-breed of this fish with the lake trout. The species is known locally as *aureolus* Sunapee or *Salvelinus aureolus.*

Many of the warm-water ponds and lakes have good populations of eastern chain pickerel, up to 5 pounds. Yellow perch are found in the larger ponds, and the white perch is fairly common in ponds along the southeastern border. While not generally regarded as a sporting species, the horned pout is also taken because of its excellent quality as a table fish.

Walleyes are taken in some lakes and the lower waters of the larger rivers, and the Great Lakes whitefish, locally called shad, is caught through the ice in winter. Another species taken through the ice is the cusk or burbot, a freshwater member of the cod family.

The saltwater species taken offshore include bluefin tuna, striped bass, mackerel, pollack, cod, haddock, cusk and hake.

The largest lake in New Hampshire is Winnipesaukee, lying almost dead center in the state and forming the hub of the renowned "Lakes Region of New Hampshire," long popular with vacationers. Other lakes of considerable size are its neighboring Winnisquam and Newfound; Umbagog, on the Maine border, Ossippee, to the northeast of Winnipesaukee, Squam Lake to the northeast, and Sunapee Lake, well to the southwest.

The major rivers are the Connecticut, which drains the extreme northeastern part of New Hampshire into Maine and forms the western border; and the Pemigewasset and Merrimack, down the central part of the state.

While these larger lakes and streams provide much fishing, many smaller rivers and lesser lakes and ponds offer a great deal more territory to the angler in New Hampshire.

Access to all parts of the state is easy, via an excellent system of turnpikes and state highways. From Massachusetts on the south, Interstate 93 leads up through two-thirds of the north-south length. The New Hampshire Turnpike serves the coastal area between Maine and Massachusetts and the eighteen miles of coast. The Spaulding Turnpike runs from there north to Rochester, and from this point State Highway 16 continues almost to the northern border. Complete highway service is provided along the entire western boundary with Vermont, where Interstate Highway 91 and U.S. 5 bracket the Connecticut River which forms most of the boundary. Many cross-country highways connect these north-south arteries, so that in spite of the rugged nature of much of the state, all sections may easily be reached.

Scheduled airline service operates from various southern cities to Berlin, Concord, Keene, Laconia, Lebanon and Manchester. In addition, there are a number of airfields for private planes. For complete information on such fields, contact the New Hampshire Aeronautics Commission at Concord Airport.

Because its northern latitude is combined with considerable altitude, New Hampshire enjoys cool summers. Anglers should always be equipped with plenty of woolens for cool mornings and evenings. Seacoast fishing also calls for extra garb to don as the day grows cooler, and breezes come in from the Atlantic.

Bear are found in the more northern and mountainous areas and deer will be seen frequently. Wildcat are also common enough to provide some hunting. While New Hampshire is not regarded as snake country, the copperhead and timber rattler both extend their range into the southern part of the state.

Tackle is every man's choice but the trout fisherman in New Hampshire will find that a small, light fly rod or a light spinning outfit is most suitable, and at certain seasons fishing in some rivers and lakes is limited to fly fishing only. In the northern mountain streams, the eastern brook trout seem to prefer bright flies such as the Mickey Finn, Royal Coachman, Parmachene Belle and Montreal. In the more southern waters of the state they like more sober-hued flies such as the Brown Hackle, Black Gnat, Black Ant and Blue Dun. Spinning lures should be small red and white, gold or silver spoons and jig-type lures.

Otherwise, all the standard flies, dries, wets and nymphs and streamer-bucktails pay off. The rainbows seem to prefer a fairly small streamer. Bait fishermen use night crawlers and minnows, and in these hard-fished waters they take a leaf from the fly fisher's book and go light on the terminal end of the line, to at most a 4X tippet. The smaller dimension gets more strikes.

Fly casters take a lot of smallmouth black bass on red and white bucktails, the Mickey Finn, White Marabou and the Dark Tiger, as well as on fly-rod popping bugs with small bodies and a bit of feather or bucktail for a tail. These should be tied on number 2 and 1/0 hooks. These bugs and some of the bigger dry flies do very well at dusk. If you do fish a dry fly on a lake, be sure to impart action to it. Cast it out, let it sit still a moment on the surface, then give a short jerk to make it jump forward a couple of inches, like a natural fly buzzing along the surface. Then give it a longer jerk, let it sit still again, then another jerk. Smallmouth will hit such a retrieve at any stage of the game.

Spinners use both top-water and underwater lures for bass. Play the top-water lures slowly, then finish the retrieve with a series of short jerks. This is the time a smallmouth all but breaks his back as he goes for it.

Some anglers troll for smallmouths with small streamers and others use live

A typical trout stream in New Hampshire's White Mountains.

minnows either drifted or trolled very slowly. Minnows must be handled very carefully so they are not hurt and have lots of pep to attract a bass. When you get a hit, give the fish time to swallow the minnow before striking. And here again, the old saying holds true—the lighter the line and leader, the more strikes you'll have.

In New Hampshire, landlocked salmon fishing is mostly by trolling during the summer when the fish are lying deep. Most trollers use spoons with considerable weight to get down. The real sport with this species comes in the early spring when the fish are in the shallows chasing smelts. At this time fly casters and spinners reap a good harvest. Flies such as the Brown and White bucktail, the Supervisor, Green Ghost, Gray Ghost, Black Ghost, Light Tiger and Dark Tiger are all good. In the spring trollers often use these same patterns to take surfacing fish; and during the spring season they also use a smelt in combination with a spinner. Spin fishermen use goldfish or pearl spoons.

For pickerel, New Hampshire anglers lean to red and white spoons, but the fish will also take streamers, live minnows and worms. Perch will hit the same bait, and are also taken on small spinning lures. Though difficult to scale, these little perch are fine eating.

Because of the long, narrow nature of the state, there is considerable variety in the best fishing season. In general, May and June are the top times for trout, but the farther north you go in New Hampshire, the longer the season of good fishing. There is usually a slump in trout fishing in midsummer, then a spurt of renewed good angling in the fall, especially in some waters now limited to fly fishing only at

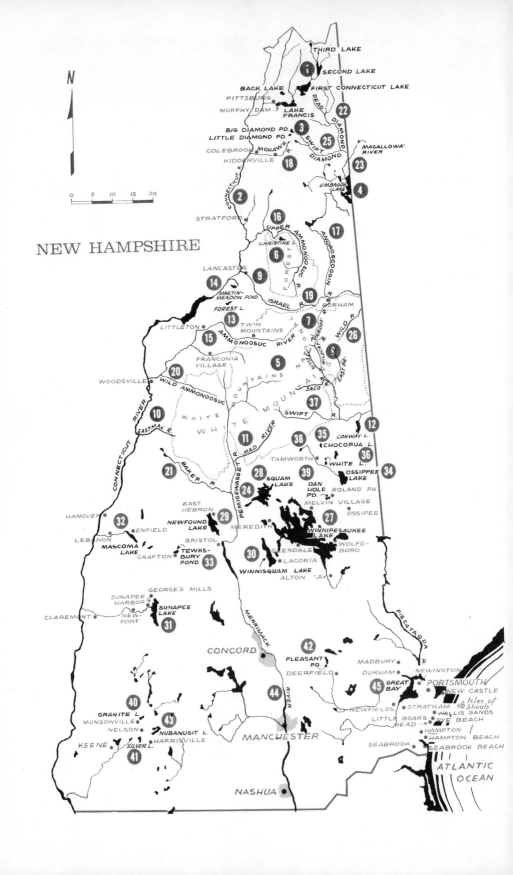

NEW HAMPSHIRE

that time of year. For current details on these streams, anglers should obtain the New Hampshire Game and Fish Regulations for the season in which they are fishing.

June is the top month for smallmouth black bass. As is the case with trout, angling for this species falls off considerably in summer.

NORTHERN NEW HAMPSHIRE

That part of New Hampshire lying north of U.S. 2 is a land of green forests covering rolling hills. Its streams hold brook, rainbow and brown trout, and some of the lakes have landlocked salmon and lake trout. The outstanding waters of this area are the CONNECTICUT LAKES (1): First Connecticut Lake, Second Connecticut Lake, and, to the south, Back Lake; and Lake Francis, formed by the Murphy Dam. This chain of lakes is more or less the headwaters of the Connecticut River. There are a number of cabin resorts on the lakes, and also accommodations at Colebrook, at the junction of the Connecticut and Mohawk Rivers. Brook trout will be found in adjacent Keezer and Ladd Brooks as well as in the Mohawk. The town has a landing strip for small planes.

There is also some good fly fishing water for trouters in the CONNECTICUT RIVER (2) along U.S. 3 around Pittsburg at the junction of State Highway 3 and U.S. 3, near the Murphy Dam on Lake Francis. Fishing is good as far down river as Stratford. Guides and equipment for fishing this area can be obtained through the Pittsburg Guides Association, Pittsburg, New Hampshire.

To the east, BIG and LITTLE DIAMOND PONDS (3), at the head of the Diamond River, can be reached by dirt road from State Highway 26 at Kidderville. There is a chance of taking brook trout, rainbow trout, lake trout and landlocked salmon. In this same area brook trout will be found in Back and Third Lakes, Big Brook, Coon Brook and Scott's Bog, Boundary, Harris, Moose, Round, Middle and Unknown Ponds, East Inlet, Indian and Perry Streams.

On the Maine border, to the east, UMBAGOG LAKE (4), reached from State Highway 26, holds landlocked salmon as well as pickerel, yellow perch and horned pout. From Lancaster, further south, where U.S. 2 crosses the Connecticut River, you can go in to the many streams and ponds of the WHITE MOUNTAIN NATIONAL FOREST (5). At the north edge of the forest near Stark on State Highway 110, there are brown trout in CHRISTINE LAKE (6). Other streams and ponds, and good points from which to fish them are: the PEABODY RIVER (7) at Gorham at the junction of U.S. 2 and State Highway 16; EAST BRANCH, ELLIS, SACO and WILDCAT RIVERS (8) near Jackson on State Highway 16 between Gorham and Conway; the ISRAEL RIVER (9) at Lancaster, at the junction of U.S. 2 and U.S. 3; EASTMAN BROOK (10) at Piermont on State Highway 10; MAD RIVER (11) at Waterville, on a county road east of Interstate 93 at Campton.

There is some bass fishing in the CONNECTICUT RIVER and CONWAY LAKE (12) on U.S. 302 at the Maine border; FOREST LAKE (13) at Whitefield at the junction of U.S. 302 and U.S. 3; MARTIN MEADOW POND (14) at Lancaster, immediately to the north on U.S. 2.

WHITE MOUNTAIN ZONE

The major part of the White Mountains lies to the south of U.S. 2. Motorists will find access from Gorham on the north, via State Highway 16; from Littleton on the west, via U.S. 302; and U.S. 3 cuts down through the western part of the mountains. The larger rivers in the White Mountains which offer trout fishing are the AMMONOOSUC (15), UPPER AMMONOOSUC (16) and CONNECTICUT (2), for browns; the Ammonoosuc, Connecticut, ANDROSCOGGIN (17), MOHAWK (18), ISRAEL (19) and WILD AMMONOOSUC (20), for rainbows; and the same rivers plus the BAKER (21), DEAD DIAMOND (22), MAGALLOWAY (23), PEMIGEWASSET (24), SWIFT DIAMOND (25) and WILD RIVERS (26), for brook trout.

A folder entitled "Outdoors in the White Mountains," published by the White Mountains Region Association, Lancaster, New Hampshire, lists more than 100 other rivers and ponds, along with the name of the town nearest to each, where there is trout fishing of one kind or another. The same folder lists many camps and resorts in the White Mountains area.

Another folder, entitled "White Mountains, New Hampshire," is issued by the White Mountains Recreation Association, also at Lancaster. While limited to tourist items rather than fishing, it features a relief map showing the mountains and highways and indicating where roads run back into the mountain valleys. It would be useful to fishermen who are planning to roam the White Mountains in search of their own fishing.

Good centers from which to fish are Woodsville, on U.S. 302, and Franconia, off Interstate Highway 93. There are also accommodations available at Littleton a few miles to the north, and at Twin Mountains, at the junction of U.S. 3 and U.S. 302. From all of these towns you can fish the Wild Ammonoosuc and many of the other streams already mentioned.

There are a number of public recreation areas in the WHITE MOUNTAIN NATIONAL FOREST (5), where some fishing can be found. A complete list of these, giving what facilities are available and a notation as to possible fishing, as well as the location of about forty privately operated tent camp grounds, may be obtained from the White Mountain National Forest Headquarters, Laconia, New Hampshire.

THE LAKES REGION

South of the White Mountains a series of lakes and ponds stretches across the state. The largest are WINNIPESAUKEE (27), SQUAM (28), NEWFOUND (29), WINNISQUAM (30) and SUNAPEE (31). They offer fishing for lake trout, bass, salmon, pickerel, horned pout and perch. Winnipesaukee and Winnisquam are regarded as the top lakes for salmon and lake trout, especially in the early spring as soon as the ice goes out. At this time they take streamer flies, and the Gray Ghost is a favorite. In the summer the lakers are mostly taken by deep trolling. These lakes offer some fine smallmouth fishing for those who go out in the early morning and late evening. Night crawlers, hellgrammites and crayfish take the most fish.

Accommodations of all kinds are plentiful around Winnipesaukee and there are a number of resorts and fishing camps around Wolfeboro on State Highway 28. Other accommodations will be found at Melvin Village, on State Highway 109 and Mirror Lake, on the same road. On the western shore, Meredith at the junction of U.S. 3 and State Highway 104, and Laconia, at the junction of U.S. 3 and State Highway 106, are both good centers from which to fish.

Aside from those provided by resorts, boats may be obtained at Alton Bay on State Highway 11 at the south end of the lake, and at Wolfeboro, on the east side, where State Highway 109 crosses the outlet from Lake Wentworth. Guides may be obtained at Glendale, on State Highway 11 on the western shore.

In Newfound Lake, lying to the west of Winnipesaukee, and reached from U.S. 3 along the Merrimack River, there is fishing for lake trout, salmon, pickerel and perch. Boats and accommodations will be found at Bristol at the junction of State Highways 104 and 3A, at the south end of the lake; and at East Hebron, on the northeast shore on State Highway 3A. There is a launching ramp at East Hebron at Sleepy Hollow Resort.

Still further west, LAKE MASCOMA (32) offers fishing for brown trout, bass, pickerel, pout and perch. There are some rainbows and browns in the river below the lake. Mascoma can be reached via U.S. 4 to Enfield, near Lebanon. All services are available at these two towns. At the Lakeside Motel on U.S. 4A, which runs along the western edge of the lake, guests have boat privileges for fishing. The telephone is Lebanon 985-W4. On U.S. 4, about half way between Newfound Lake and Mascoma, near the town of Grafton, golden trout are taken in TEWKSBURY POND (33), believed to hold the true pure strain of this rare species.

At the eastern end of this state-wide chain of lakes is OSSIPEE (34), reached via State Highway 25, which runs along two shores of the lake. Fishing is for brown trout, bass, pickerel, pout and perch.

Between Lake Ossipee and the southern edge of the White Mountain National Forest there are two lakes which can produce good catches of brook trout and splake, the latter a cross between lake trout and brook trout. These are CHOCORUA (35) and WHITE LAKES (36), near the town of Tamworth on State Highway 113. The SWIFT RIVER (37), roughly paralleling State Highway 113A north of Tamworth, also offers good fishing; and LAKE TAMWORTH (38) has been stocked with splake. The same is true of BIG DAN HOLE (39), which also has lake trout, golden trout and salmon. Big Dan can be reached from State Highway 16 at Ossipee, west to Roland Park.

Lake Sunapee lies well to the southeast of the lakes already mentioned, near Claremont at the junction of State Highways 103 and 11. There are rainbow trout and the "Sunapee trout," also called golden trout, a native of the lake. Sunapee is the best spot in New Hampshire to try for this one. The golden trout also crossbreeds with lake trout and hybrids are commonly taken. Accommodations and guides will be found at George's Mills on State Highway 11 at the north end of the lake; at Newport at the junction of State Highways 10 and 11; and at Sunapee Harbor.

This lake and the surrounding smaller lakes and ponds are highly developed as resorts and there is considerable water skiing to disturb the fishing. Serious anglers will fare better if they go early in the spring or late in the fall, both because there is less traffic on the lakes and because the fish hit better at this time.

From early December until the middle of March there is excellent ice fishing in these and many other lakes and ponds in New Hampshire. Lakes Winnipesaukee, Winnisquam, Squam and Newfound are very popular, with catches ranging through lake trout, pickerel, whitefish and perch. Ice fishermen use a little hut called a "bob house" and these may be rented in communities near the lakes. One of the best developed regions in this regard is around Wolfeboro on the eastern shore of Lake Winnipesaukee.

SOUTHERN NEW HAMPSHIRE

Although the southern part of New Hampshire is the most heavily populated section of the state there are nevertheless many lakes with good fishing for bass, pickerel and panfish. During the spring and fall, anglers also find some good trout fishing in the many trout ponds and in some streams. A group of lakes west of U.S. 202, east of Keene, provides quite a variety of spring and fall fishing. Early fishermen will take lake trout in GRANITE LAKE (40) near Munsonville on State Highway 9, and in SILVER LAKE (41) at Harrisville, reached by country road from State Highway 9 on the north or State Highway 101 on the south. PLEASANT POND (42), north of Deerfield on State Highway 107, provides both rainbows and salmon. NUBANUSIT LAKE (43), reached from Nelson, off State Highway 9, has salmon and lake trout as well as bass and panfish. Almost every other lake and pond in this southern area has some bass, pickerel, yellow perch, white perch, whitefish, northern pike, horned pout and sunfish.

In addition to smallmouth in the cooler waters, there are largemouth in the lower MERRIMACK (44) and Connecticut Rivers, and in many ponds. Hanover, about a third of the way up the Connecticut River, is the northern limit of the largemouth.

Important in the freshwater fishing scene in southern New Hampshire is GREAT BAY (45), directly west of Portsmouth. Actually Great Bay is a lake emptying into the Atlantic via the Piscataqua River. Accommodations are available at the towns of Newington, Madbury, Newfields, Stratham and Durham. The bay is a favorite spot with ice fishermen in the winter.

SALTWATER FISHING

The New Hampshire coast on the Atlantic Ocean consists of a combination of beaches, rocky promontories and sheltered coves, thus providing more fishing possibilities than would seem apparent at first glance. Access to all coastal areas is easy through many feeder roads from U.S. 1, which parallels the entire shore, and Interstate Highway 95, which follows the same course only a mile inshore.

There is good offshore fishing for a limited number of species, tuna being the largest. This species is taken about one to two miles offshore, the hot spots being off the Isle of Shoals, about a mile out of Portsmouth; and off Hampton and Seabrook. The tuna appear in these waters in mid-June and some stay as late as October 1st. Tuna charters are available at all three cities. At the Wentworth-by-the-Sea Hotel at Newcastle, at the mouth of the Piscataqua River, deep-sea charters are also available and there is onshore fishing from a pier.

The only other large saltwater fish taken generally is the sea pollack, so called because it is larger than the harbor pollack taken inshore, sometimes going to 55 pounds. This species is taken from May to October.

The best inshore fishing is provided by striped bass. While the average in these waters is a school fish weighing only a few pounds, they have been taken up to 65 pounds. The largest fish seem to be in the lower Piscataqua River, hanging out around the bridge abutments below Portsmouth and around Dover Point. School fish usually show up about the end of May and the larger ones are on the scene by mid-June. Some stripers continue in the area through September and occasionally into October.

Hampton Harbor is another good spot for stripers and has some excellent summer fishing for mackerel. Many anglers go for the latter with streamer flies and other cast lures. In this case it pays to use a wire leader to circumvent the sharp teeth of the fish.

Tautog fishing is good in Hampton waters from mid-June to August. The tautog, also called blackfish, is mostly taken on bait, preferably a small crab.

Harbor pollack are also taken on casting gear in the Piscataqua and around Newcastle. Great Bay and Little Bay, backwaters of the river, lying to the west of Portsmouth, get influxes of the anadromous stripers when they are in. Smelt, found in nearly all the large bays and harbors, are taken bait fishing with very small bait.

On the Beach Road, State Highway 1A, anglers will find accommodations and services, and some charter boats as well as skiffs to rent, at Wallis Sands, Rye Beach, Little Boars Head and Great Boars Head. At Hampton Beach there are all seaside facilities including a fishing pier and a dock where charter boats are available for morning and afternoon party-boat trips. Small craft and motors may also be hired here for inshore fishing. The catch will include striped bass, mackerel, pollack, cod, haddock, cusk and hake.

Further south, near the Massachusetts border, Seabrook Beach is regarded as one of the top coastal fishing spots. At the Seabrook end of the Hampton Bridge there are daily party-boat excursions in season, from 8 a.m. till 1 p.m. Bait and line are furnished. During the summer, similar excursions go out on Wednesday nights. Party boats and a fishing pier are also available at Littlefield's Fishing Pier, Seabrook Beach.

The New Hampshire Division of Economic Development, Concord, New Hampshire, has available a list of boat-launching sites, marinas, boat-rental agencies and dealers, which lists many lakes where boats are available, along with rates, size of the lake or pond, recommended limits of boats, if you bring your own, and what services are available. The same organization publishes a list of mobile home and trailer parks and another folder entitled "Tent Camping in New Hampshire," describing both public and privately operated camp sites. The newcomer to New Hampshire fishing should also obtain "New Hampshire Fshing and Hunting."

NEW HAMPSHIRE FISHING REGULATIONS

Resident Fishing License $3.50
Nonresident Fishing License $8.25
Nonresident 3-Day Fishing License $3.75
Nonresident 15-Day Fishing License $5.25

SEASONS AND LIMITS

Species	Open Season	Bag Limit	Size Limit
Trout	Fourth Saturday in April to Labor Day. Then fly fishing only, to Oct. 15	10 trout or 5 pounds	None
Lake Trout	Jan. 1 to Sept. 30	2 (including salmon)	15″
Black Bass	June 1 to June 30	3 fish or 7 pounds	9″
Landlocked Salmon	April 1 to Sept. 30	2 (including lake trout)	15″
Pickerel	Fourth Saturday in April to March 31	10 fish or 10 pounds	None
Golden Trout	April 1 to Labor Day; then fly fishing only to Sept. 30	2	12″
Walleye	May 1 to October 31	10 pounds	12″
Horned Pout (Bullheads)	Fourth Sat. in April to Oct. 31	40	None
Whitefish	Jan. 1 to Aug. 31	6	
White Perch, Yellow Perch, Cusk	No closed season	None	None

For complete regulations write: Fish and Game Dept., 34 Bridge Street, Concord, New Hampshire.

VERMONT

Vermont extends from the Quebec border on the north to the Massachusetts border on the south. Its eastern limit is the Connecticut River, shared with New Hampshire. On the west a full two-thirds of the border is also marked by water. Lake Champlain reaches from the Canadian border more than 100 miles south, then pours its waters into the Poultney River, which forms another fifty miles of border between Vermont and New York State.

The major topographical feature in Vermont is the Green Mountains, which extend the entire length of the state in a series of 4,000-foot-high ridges. Numerous small streams flow down the mountain slopes but the border Connecticut is the only river of real size. However, several medium-sized Vermont rivers are among the historic trout rivers of the East—the Battenkill, White, Mad, Lamoille and Dog all hold long-time reputations among trout anglers. Lake Champlain, shared with New York, and Lake Memphremagog, shared with Quebec, are the only two large bodies of water. Many smaller lakes provide some fine fishing and in the headwaters of the various rivers there are several large groups of ponds which add considerably to the fishing picture.

The species of gamefish found in Vermont waters include brook trout, rainbow trout, brown trout, lake trout, landlocked salmon, smallmouth black bass, a very few largemouth black bass, a few muskellunge, walleye, northern pike, bluegill, yellow perch and bullhead.

In spite of the mountainous character of the terrain, Vermont is well served by highways. The major north-south artery is Interstate 91, running with the Connecticut River for three-quarters of the length of the state, and soon to be completed to the Canadian border at Rock Island. Another Interstate Highway, # 89, crosses the northern part of Vermont, from Burlington, on Lake Champlain, to Barre. Running almost contiguously, U.S. 2 continues from Barre across the balance of the state and into New Hampshire. Further south, U.S. 4 provides the same ready access from New York State to Rutland and then on to Lebanon, New Hampshire. Another important highway, U.S. 7, traverses the entire eastern length of Vermont. Thus, with the many cross roads leading up the mountain valleys, and joining these main thoroughfares, there is no part of even the most mountainous sections of Vermont that is inaccessible.

Northeast Airlines operates daily flights to Newport at the south end of Lake Memphremagog, from June 15 to Sept. 14, and there is also an airport for private planes there. Year-round air service is available to Barre, in the central part of the state.

Anglers visiting Vermont will need the same type of clothing required in most of the northeastern states. Cottons will do at midday, but usually a wool shirt is needed morning and evening, and a Windbreaker is always handy. Those fishing at the higher altitudes will find a wool shirt suitable at almost any time.

Bear and deer may be seen occasionally but present no danger to the angler.

There are a few rattlesnakes along the western slopes of the Green Mountains in the southern part of the state.

While hip boots are sufficient for most of the trout streams, those who plan to fish the Battenkill, White, Mad, Lamoille and Dog should wear chest-high waders. Hip boots will suffice for much of the fishing even on these streams but there are times when position is important in order to put your fly in the right spot and to get a good float, and that often means that you must go into deeper water.

For Vermont trout streams an 8-foot fly rod is ideal and with this the angler should have an HDH (DT6F) line, for light presentation. The leader should be tapered down to a 4X tippet, and for best results even to 5X or 6X. Trout do see the heavier leaders and the finer you go the more strikes you will get, not to mention the greater sport.

All the standard flies pay off, but be sure to check on the size and kind of natural flies coming off the water. Some of these flies, called midges or smuts, are very tiny, calling for a size 20 hook to match them. Remember to strike very gently with these flies, a mere raising of the rod tip.

For fishing the larger lakes in Vermont, fly-rodders usually go to an 8½ - or 9-foot stick, with GBF line.

Spinners fishing Vermont trout waters use a light rod and reel with 4- or 6-pound test monofilament. Small lures pay off. When spin fishermen go after bass and the warm-water species, they sometimes up the line to 8-pound test, but 4 and 6 will do the job nicely. Plug casters should also stay as light as possible.

LAKE FISHING

LAKE CHAMPLAIN (1), Vermont's largest lake, is more than 100 miles long and in some places more than ten miles wide. There is good fishing for walleye, northern pike, pickerel, perch, and bass. A few muskellunge are also taken.

Streamer flies and spinning lures take fish early in the spring and again in the fall, but in general bait is the thing on this large lake. Boats are available at many points alongshore such as Basin Harbor, west of Vergennes on U.S. 7 at the southern end of the lake; Shelburne Bay on the same highway, south of Burlington; the several small towns on Grand Isle, which is reached via U.S. 2, north of Burlington; and Highgate Springs and East Alburg, at the north end of the lake, between Champlain proper and Missisquoi Bay. While not generally required, there is some guiding service available at Highgate. Those who go on Lake Champlain without a guide should always exercise care as the lake can become very rough.

Following the Quebec border due east, you come to LAKE MEMPHREMAGOG (2), which juts down into Vermont from Quebec. This is a top lake for bass and is particularly popular with those who like to cast bass bugs with fly rods, or who use popping plugs on light spinning outfits. There are also brown trout, walleyes, yellow perch, some salmon and some large rainbows in the lake. The rainbows run into WILLOUGHBY RIVER (3) in April and provide some good river fishing at this time. Boats are available at Newport at the southern tip of the lake, on U.S. 5. There are a few guides available, but as with Lake Champlain they are not required to reach the good fishing.

There are innumerable smaller lakes and ponds in the northeastern corner of Vermont, with a great variety of fishing. From Newport you can follow U.S. 5, south to Barton and there take State Highway 16 to Greensboro. From Greensboro a secondary road leads to CASPIAN LAKE (4), with lake trout, bass and perch. A number of small ponds immediately north of the lake offer possibilities for trout.

WILLOUGHBY LAKE (5), from which the river of the same name flows to Lake Memphremagog, is one of the best small lakes in Vermont. Lake trout as heavy as 30 pounds are taken there annually. The lake is reached via State Highway 5A, north from U.S. 5 at West Burke, or from State Highway 58, southeast from U.S. 5 at Orleans.

About the same size, and lying slightly to the northeast, is SEYMOUR LAKE (6), which produces medium-sized lake trout and some landlocked salmon, rainbow, brook and brown trout, and smallmouth black bass. There are several boat liveries on the lake, which is reached via State Highway 114, north from Island Pond, then State Highway 111 to the lake. Or from Interstate 91 at the Quebec border, also via State Highway 111. Guides are not required.

Also reached from Island Pond is ECHO LAKE (6), on State Highway 105. There are rainbows, lake trout, salmon and smallmouth. NORTON POND (6), on State Highway 114 to the north, has brook and rainbow trout.

CRYSTAL LAKE (6), on U.S. 5 at Barton, lies immediately west of Lake Willoughby, at Barton. It holds rainbow and brown trout and salmon.

HOLLAND POND (6), to the north of Seymour Lake, holds brook trout and pickerel; and DERBY POND (6), to the west, at the town of Derby on State Highway 105, has largemouth bass and yellow perch.

Continuing north and east toward the Canadian border, on State Highway 114, you come to AVERILL LAKE (6), especially popular for surface trolling with lures and flies in May and early June, when some nice lake trout and landlocked salmon are taken. During the balance of the season the fish are mostly taken on live bait fished deep, although there are some evening rises to give the light-tackle man a boost. Quimby's Camp on the lake offers accommodations and guide service.

Further north on State Highway 105 is SALEM LAKE (2), at Derby. The Salem Lake Camps provide accommodations, boats and guides to fish for landlocked salmon, lake trout, both large and smallmouth black bass, and big walleyes. There are also numerous ponds in the vicinity where there are brook trout. From the Salem Lake Camps you can also fish the CLYDE (7), BLACK (8), MISSISQUOI (9), and BARTON (10) Rivers for brown and rainbow trout; and also reach Lake Memphremagog. Much of the water during the month of September is limited to fly fishing, and dry-fly fishing at this time is excellent. Rates range from $12 per day to $75 per week.

MAIDSTONE LAKE (11), south of Bloomfield, on the New Hampshire border, can be reached from State Highway 102, which runs along the west side of the Connecticut River. There are lake trout, salmon, brook trout and rainbows in the lake.

Some brook-trout fishing for small fish will be found in a series of ponds and in the headwaters of several major Vermont rivers in the area on both sides of Interstate Highway 91 between Hardwick and St. Johnsbury, in the central part of Vermont. Inquiries should always be made locally to find the waters which are producing best. Some of those which are usually good are in the headwaters of the WELLS RIVER (12), reached by dirt road from State Highway 3A, between Groton and West Groton. The ponds in the Winooski system can also be good. They are reached from Calais, on State Highway 14, or Cabot and Danville on U.S. 2. NELSON POND (13), off State Highway 14, near South Woodbury, holds lake trout and rainbows, as well as northern pike and smallmouth bass. The Marshfield Dam, on U.S. 2, between Marshfield and West Danville, has fishing for brown trout, northern pike,

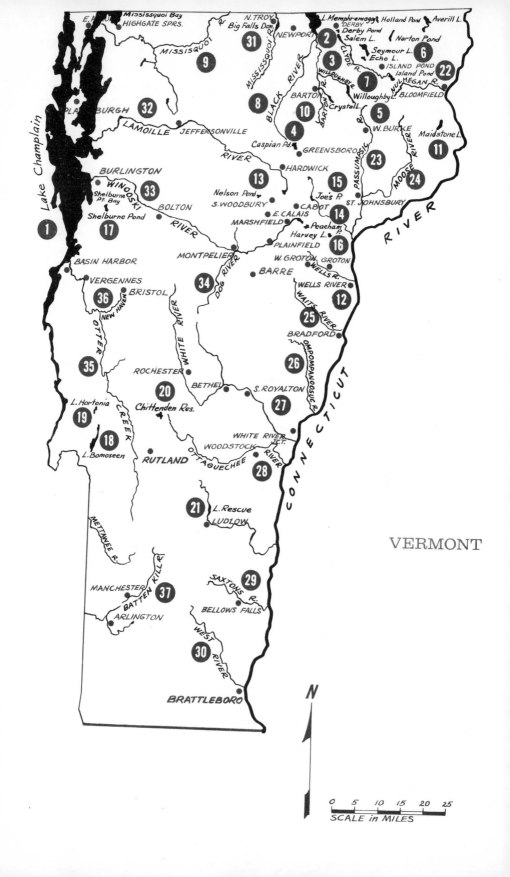

perch and pickerel. Nearby PEACHAM POND (14) has rainbows and browns. JOE'S POND (15), near West Danville, has lake trout, bass, perch and pickerel; while HARVEY LAKE (16) near Groton has lake trout, salmon, rainbow trout and perch. In SHELBURNE POND (17), off State Highway 116, south of Burlington, close to Lake Champlain, there are walleyes, northern pike, bass and perch.

The largest lake in the south-central part of Vermont is BOMOSEEN (18), on State Highway 30, near Rutland. There are northern pike, bass and perch. The same fishing will be found in smaller LAKE HORTONIA (19), immediately to the north. In CHITTENDEN RESERVOIR (20), reached by country road to the north of Rutland, there are rainbow trout; and rainbows will also be found in LAKE RESCUE (21), on State Highway 100, north of Ludlow.

Those interested in seeking out the many smaller ponds in Vermont should obtain a copy of the brochure, "Vermont Fishing Access Areas and Impoundments," from the Vermont Fish and Game Department, Montpelier, Vermont. Ask also for the "Vermont Guide to Fishing," which contains a large-scale map showing both lakes and rivers in the state and indicating what species of fish may be found in each.

RIVER FISHING

The CONNECTICUT RIVER, forming the eastern boundary of the State of Vermont, provides a great variety of fishing. In the northern waters, as far down as the debouchment of its tributary, the Nulhegan River, there are rainbow and brown trout. These may also be taken around the outlets of other tributaries in the northern half of the state, such as the Passumpsic, Wells and White Rivers. Below that the fishing is for smallmouth black bass, largemouth black bass, walleye and northern pike. The fishing is best for these species between the outlet of the Wells River, where U.S. 302 crosses the Connecticut, and White River Junction, where Interstate Highway 89 crosses the river. Below that the fishing is spotty, though occasional good catches are made around Brattleboro, in the extreme south.

The NULHEGAN (22) is one of the most attractive tributaries, flowing through some of the wildest territory remaining in northern Vermont. There is good fishing for rainbows and brook trout. The river can be reached from State Highway 105 as far up as Island Pond, then State Highway 114.

The next large tributary to the south is the PASSUMPSIC (23), entering the Connecticut south of St. Johnsbury. It holds brown and brook trout, as do the smaller creeks flowing into it. U.S. 5 runs along much of the stream.

The MOOSE RIVER (24), one of the better tributaries of the Passumpsic, can be fished from St. Johnsbury via State Highway 18, east from Interstate 91; then by dirt road, which runs for several miles along the river.

Continuing south along the Connecticut, the WELLS RIVER (12), entering the parent stream at the town of Wells River; the WAITS RIVER (25), at Bradford; the OMPOMPANOOSUC (26), along State Highway 113—all hold brown, rainbow and brook trout.

The tributaries which enter the Connecticut south of this usually have brook and brown trout in the higher waters and smallmouth black bass lower down. Among the best are the WHITE RIVER (27), entering at White River Junction, and the OTTAGUECHEE (28), reached from Woodstock, immediately to the south.

The upper White between Royalton and Rochester, where the stream winds beside State Highway 100, then turns east with State Highway 107, is very good, and anglers should explore its several tributaries, too. Midsummer fishing can be fine in this river for fly men. Spinners take their best fish in the spring months. Bethel is a good town to use as headquarters to fish the trout waters around the junction of State Highway 107 and State Highway 12.

The SAXTONS RIVER (29), reached from State Highway 121 off Interstate 91 at Bellows Falls, has fishing for brown trout in the lower waters, brooks in the upper; and the WEST RIVER (30), entering the Connecticut just above Brattleboro, adds walleyed pike and smallmouth bass in the lower waters.

The rivers which flow to Lake Champlain offer many miles of good fishing, often extending almost entirely across the state. The MISSISQUOI (9) starts in north-central Vermont, flows north into Quebec, then south again into Vermont and empties into the lake at Missisquoi Bay at the northern end of Lake Champlain. In the upper waters there are brook trout, and some browns around the BIG FALLS DAM (31), close to North Troy, on State Highway 105, right at the border. From the point where the river comes back into Vermont there are the trouts plus small-mouth, and lower down walleyes and largemouth are added.

The same picture holds true for the LAMOILLE RIVER (32), to the south, though the trout fishing is only fair. Smallmouth black bass, yellow perch and walleyes are at their best around Jeffersonville, where the river approaches State Highway 104, and east of this where it runs along State Highway 15, as far up as Hardwick.

Following the WINOOSKI RIVER (33) upstream from its outlet on Lake Champlain, at Burlington, anglers will find seventeen miles of fishing for smallmouth and large-mouth black bass, as far upstream as Bolton, on U.S. 2. Above that there is another thirty miles of fishing for smallmouth; then from Plainfield up there are brook trout, rainbows and brown trout, the last in limited numbers. Interstate Highway 89 follows the river all the way. The DOG RIVER (34), which flows along State High-way 12, south of Montpelier, is one of the Winooski's top tributaries, with good populations of brown, rainbow and some brook trout.

OTTER CREEK (35), the longest stream in Vermont, flows northward from far down in the southwestern part of the state, to the foot of Lake Champlain. Almost throughout its entire length it can be reached from U.S. 7, and almost everywhere there is fishing of one kind or another. In one of the lower tributaries, the NEW HAVEN RIVER (36), anglers take some good-sized brown trout near the town of Bristol, on State Highway 17, east from U.S. 7 at Vergennes.

From headwaters only a few miles south of where the Otter starts, the BAT-TENKILL RIVER (37) flows south and west. Undoubtedly this is one of Vermont's best-known trout streams. During most of the spring and fall, as well as on summer evenings, fishing can be excellent for brown trout, which come in quite good sizes. In the upper waters there are also some brook trout. The Batten Kill can be reached from U.S. 7, and one of the best stretches of the river is in the Manchester to Arling-ton area, just before the river turns westward to flow into New York State.

VERMONT FISHING REGULATIONS

Resident Fishing License $1.75
Nonresident Fishing License $6.25
Nonresident 14-Day Fishing License $4.25
Nonresident 3-Day Fishing License $2.25

SEASONS AND LIMITS

Species	Open Season	Size Limit	Bag Limit
Trout	Last Saturday in April to Sept. 30	6"	5 lbs. or not more than 12 fish; 2 days' limit in possession
Lake Trout, Salmon	As above	15"	2 lake trout, 2 salmon or 1 each; 4 in possession
Pike Perch, Walleye	Last Saturday in April to March 15	12"	10 daily; 20 in possession
Black Bass	Second Saturday in June to Nov. 30	10"	10 daily; 20 in possession
Muskellunge, Northern Pike, Pickerel	Last Saturday in April to March 15 inclusive	12"	10 daily; 20 in possession

Anglers should consult the annual regulations for exceptions to the above and for regulations governing specially controlled waters.

For complete regulations write: Fish and Game Dept., Montpelier, Vermont.

MASSACHUSETTS

Massachusetts has a full share of all the geographic attractions of the northeast Atlantic coast. Bounded on the north by the states of New Hampshire and Vermont, and by New York on the west, it has some of the low mountain terrain of these states in its Berkshire Hills. On the south it slopes to the rolling agricultural landscape of Connecticut. On its eastern coast it has some of the most attractive territory, from the fisherman's point of view, to be found on the Atlantic coast, in the sandy hook of Cape Cod, south of Boston.

The fish found in this variegated state are eastern brook trout, rainbow trout, brown trout, lake trout, smallmouth black bass, largemouth black bass, walleye, chain pickerel, white perch, yellow perch and panfish: these all in the fresh water. In the salt there are white marlin, blue marlin, swordfish and mako sharks in limited quantities, as well as more plentiful supplies of bonito, bluefin tuna, mackerel, pollack, bluefish, and in season great numbers of the king of them all along this coast, the striped bass. In addition to this, some of the freshwater trouts go to sea and when they return to spawn and are taken in the inlets and rivers, they are known as "salters."

The major river in Massachusetts is the Connecticut, flowing north to south and dividing the higher, western one-third of the state from the lower eastern two-thirds as it slopes to the Atlantic. There are no major lakes but many ponds and a number of reservoirs, of which Quabbin, lying almost dead center in the state, is the largest.

With Boston as the hub, excellent highways traverse every part of Massachusetts, fanning out from that city in all directions. Interstate Highway 90 crosses the state from east to west; Interstate Highway 91, from north to south. State Highway 128 makes a great curve from the tip of land at Gloucester well north of Boston, to the tip of Cape Cod, offering fast, easy movement around the most congested area. Between these, excellent highways provide ready transportation to all good fishing areas. All the major airlines and three railways add their services to the state, and there is excellent bus transport via both Greyhound and Trailways.

The fisherman in Massachusetts will need to vary his clothing to fit the season. Summers are warm, spring and fall cool, and those who go for the striped bass along the Atlantic, and particularly in the Cape Cod area, need Windbreakers at any season, plenty of rain gear, and some warm clothing even in midsummer if planning to do any night fishing.

Anglers will not encounter any game of importance, but the state is within the range of the timber rattler, though it is seldom seen.

Tackle, too, must be adjusted to the fish and the area in which you fish. Trout fishing in the ponds and streams is usually done with a light, 8-foot fly rod, HDH line and standard wet and dry flies in sizes 8 to 20. In bass ponds, the popular rod is a 9-foot fly rod, matching GBF line, and a leader tapered to an 8- or 10-pound-test tippet. When using a popping bug or a large bucktail or streamer on this outfit, the heavy leader is needed for the strike and also because a thinner tippet sometimes becomes weakened and breaks when you are using these larger lures.

Spinners and bait casters use conventional freshwater tackle, leaning to comparatively light equipment.

The popular striper fishing in the Cape Cod Canal and along the beaches calls for specialized gear to meet varying conditions, and this tackle is described in detail in the sections dealing with these areas.

MAINLAND LAKES

The QUABBIN RESERVOIR (1), created by a dam built on the Swift River in 1939, was stocked in 1953 with fingerling lake trout and as a result some fairly good fishing can be enjoyed for this species, the fish ranging up to 10 pounds. Due to planting of smelt as an added food, the trout grow faster here than in most waters, increasing from fingerling to the 18-inch legal size in about four to five years, as compared to seven years in most lakes. Browns, to a 13-pound top weight, and rainbows to 8 pounds, have been taken with comparative regularity, especially around the outlet gates at the dams. In the shallows anglers take largemouth black bass, May being the best month for this species, and there are a few smallmouth in the Pottapaug area on the east side of the lake. Chain pickerel are common throughout the shallower waters; white perch are abundant, hitting best in midsummer; and yellow perch, black crappie and sunfish are also taken.

The lake is reached via State Highway 122 northwest from Worcester, or U.S. 202 northeast from Holyoke. Boats and motors are available and there are three launching sites for those who bring their own craft. Accommodations are plentiful in the surrounding area.

A chart of Lake Quabbin, with complete details as to the services available, may be obtained from the Bureau of Wildlife Research and Management, Division of Fisheries and Game, Westboro, Massachusetts.

Much smaller, but enjoying a good reputation for producing both large and smallmouth black bass, pickerel, perch, bluegills and calico bass, is LAKE CHAUBUNAGUNGAMAUG (2), reached by following State Highway 12, south from Worcester. Due north, near the New Hampshire line, and reached via State Highway 12 near Fitchburg, UPPER and LOWER NAUKEAG LAKES (3) offer good fishing for pickerel and bass.

A large number of ponds throughout the western part of Massachusetts are stocked with trout annually, but the problem with these, as with many other ponds in the state, is access. A list of such waters, indicating where there is public access, may be obtained from the Division of Fisheries and Game, Westboro, Massachusetts. Ask for "Stocked Trout Waters of Massachusetts." In some of these lakes, notably LAKE ONOTA (4), at Pittsfield, on U.S. 7, there is some good ice fishing in winter.

RIVERS

The CONNECTICUT RIVER (5) is the largest in Massachusetts, and the most important to the angler in spite of the fact that through the years it has been badly damaged through pollution and dams. At one time Atlantic salmon ran into the river in great numbers. Then in 1798 a dam was built near Turner's Falls and within twelve years no more salmon were coming up the river. Eventually arrangements were made for fish to bypass the dams but the salmon have never returned. The same thing happened with shad, which also came into the Connecticut on their spawning runs; but after years of experimentation and restocking to encourage a new run, an elevator method was found to help the shad past the dams and as a result it looks as if this species is on the comeback trail. Now there is some excellent shad fishing in April and May. The hot spot is at Hadley, on U.S. 5 near Northampton, but some fish are taken throughout the river as they make their way north all the way to Bellows Falls, Vermont.

The Connecticut also holds largemouth black bass, some to 19 inches in length, and in the more swift-flowing waters there are a few smallmouth. The latter are found mostly from Turner's Dam to the border of New Hampshire. Walleyes and northern pike are taken in the slower waters, especially the bow at Northampton and around Chicopee. There are also pickerel, panfish and channel catfish.

The river can be approached throughout its length from Interstate Highway 91 and U.S. 5; and there are three public access sites, one at Gill on the west bank, one in Sunderland, south of Turner's Falls, and one in Holyoke. Accomodations of all kinds are plentiful all along the river.

Other rivers of size which provide some fishing are the upper HOUSATONIC (6), reached from U.S. 7 in the western corner of the state; the DEERFIELD (7), which can be reached from U.S. 5 south of Greenfield, or State Highway 2, west of the same town; the WESTFIELD (8) along Interstate Highway 90, near the town of Westfield, which offers some of the best trout fishing in Massachusetts; the CONCORD (9), in the far northeastern corner of the state, near Boston; and the TAUNTON RIVER (10), on the southeast, which can be reached from State Highway 138 between Taunton and Fall River. Striped bass fishing in this river begins to be good in late March. The AGAWAM RIVER (11), flowing into the upper end of Buzzards Bay, is another good striper stream, and sometimes brown trout and striped bass are taken in the same waters in this stream. A secondary road follows the river upstream from U.S. 6 near Wareham.

Another good stream is the WEWEANTIC (12), reached from U.S. 6 out of either Wareham or Marion on Buzzards Bay. Boats are available at both towns and there is striper fishing from spring right through to fall. In August and September some snapper blues are taken, often by bridge fishermen. Some anglers also take stripers by wading the shallows, too, and in the lower river these fish are often quite large.

In addition, there are some 483 small brooks and streams, totaling 2,500 miles in length, which are annually stocked with some kind of fish. Annually revised lists of these waters, along with instructions as to means of approach, may be obtained from the Massachusetts Division of Fisheries and Game, Westboro, Massachusetts.

Generally speaking, the trout angler in Massachusetts must get out early, best catches being made immediately after the season opens in mid-April. After that the fish lie deeper and are harder to catch. The best "salter" fishing is also usually early in the season, and again in the fall.

CAPE COD

From all angles, Cape Cod is the top fishing territory in the State of Massachusetts. It boasts a total of twenty-two trout ponds, fourteen trout streams, and an additional forty ponds which are host to at least one other variety of sport fish. In addition, there are the beaches, dunes and offshore waters of the Cape, offering all the saltwater species indigenous to the north Atlantic coast; and the Cape Cod Canal, offering its own special brand of fishing for the ever-popular striped bass.

Buzzards Bay, between the south Cape and the mainland, has good fishing for stripers and weakfish, some up to 10 pounds being taken at Marion on U.S. 6. These, and scup and tautog, are taken all summer.

Anglers reach Cape Cod via State Highway 3 down the coast from the north, or U.S. 6, which comes in from New Bedford on the east coast, then proceeds right out to the end of the Cape. The Cape Cod Canal runs parallel with U.S. 6, across the narrow neck joining Cape Cod to the mainland.

WAKEBY (13), MASHPEE (14) and GULL PONDS (15) are three of the best in the state for trout. Also good are SHEEP POND (16) and CLIFF POND (17) in Brewster; HAMBLIN POND (18) in Barnstable, and LITTLE CLIFF POND (19) in Brewster. Visitors must make inquiries locally to locate these ponds.

The trout in these ponds grow extra large, apparently because of the alewives which provide hearty feeding when they make their spawning runs into the ponds from the ocean. Besides trout, these, as well as dozens of other ponds along the Cape, hold smallmouth black bass, white and yellow perch, and chain pickerel. An excellent list of ponds on the Cape and the species which they hold will be found in the brochure "Sportsman's Guide to Cape Cod," published by the Cape Cod Chamber of Commerce, Hyannis, Massachusetts.

Almost every stream on the Cape may have trout at one place or another. A map showing the streams and the locations of both streams and ponds, most of which will not show on highway maps, may be obtained from the Division of Fisheries and Game, Westboro, Massachusetts. Anglers should also obtain the "Sportsman's Guide to Cape Cod" issued by the Cape Cod Chamber of Commerce in co-operation with the Division of Fisheries and Game. It's important to get current material because these ponds change quickly and the fishing varies greatly from year to year. Those which are reclaimed by cleaning and restocking sometimes suddenly become good producers after years of inactivity.

The main part of Cape Cod is cut off from the mainland by the CAPE COD CANAL (20), extending from Cape Cod Bay on the north to Buzzards Bay on the southwest. The canal produces some sensational fishing for striped bass. Fishing is permitted at all times and at all parts of the canal. The season starts with the arrival of school stripers in May, followed by big fellows late in the month. By June the big ones are really in and from that time through September there is consistently good fishing, and some catches continue to be made in October and November, although most of the fish have moved south by that time.

You'll see very few anglers along the canal in the daytime as the best fishing is early in the morning, late in the evening, and during the night. At these times, fishermen stand elbow to elbow and there are sometimes terrific tangles as a big fish, fighting to get away, crosses the lines of the close-packed anglers. Tackle varies from fly rod to surf gear, but a fellow soon finds that along the canal it generally takes pretty stout tackle to stand up with what the majority are offering, and to throw the big lures that are the best striper takers. When the fish are really in and working hard, you can take them right and left—and again the fishing can be very poor. But those who fish the canal consistently make some wonderful catches. Once in a while a school of blues comes by, too, and they hit everything they see, even the swivels on lines, often chopping the lines in two. You can imagine the aftermath. Besides the air being blue there are the firefly sparks of flashlights gleaming on and off all down the banks of the canal as frantic fishermen desperately try to mend their broken tackle and get back in there for a striper.

While almost every fisherman knows that the night is the best time to fish the

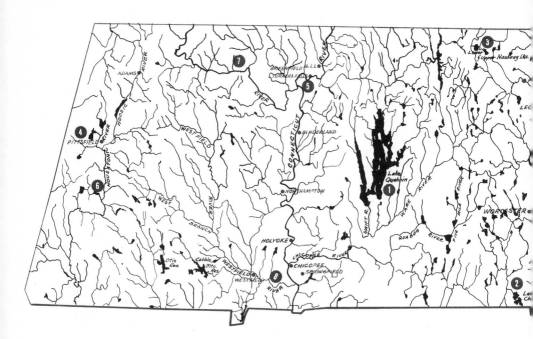

canal, there are many other angles to be considered and inquiries should always be made locally as to what tide is currently the best producer, and what baits. Hal Lyman, publisher of *The Salt Water Sportsman Magazine* of Boston, and his editor, Frank Wollner, know the Massachusetts striper picture better than most, and in their magazine they give an up-to-date account, month by month, of the striper migrations, where they are hitting, what they are taking, and what is the best tackle. A new man in the area can benefit greatly by obtaining a copy of this fine monthly magazine.

The striped bass is also the main species the surf angler seeks on Cape Cod. The fish come in on the beaches in May and are taken through October, with some of the best fishing in late August. Many 50-pounders are taken off the beaches and some have gone as high as 68½ pounds. Those who prefer to fish from boats use large skiffs to fish in back of the breakers, either casting or trolling. Others cast from the jetties, where many good stripers are taken.

Bluefish also come in along the beaches from June through mid-October. Other species are pollack, which run best in May and September but are taken throughout the summer and into October; weakfish, from late June through September; mackerel, from June through September; and flounder, from July through September.

The best beaches are those from Monomoy Island, at the south end of the Cape, along the outside, all the way north to Race Point.

The points at which the surf fisherman will find access to the beaches are Bourne, on U.S. 6, which runs parallel to the Cape Cod Canal; Sandwich, at the

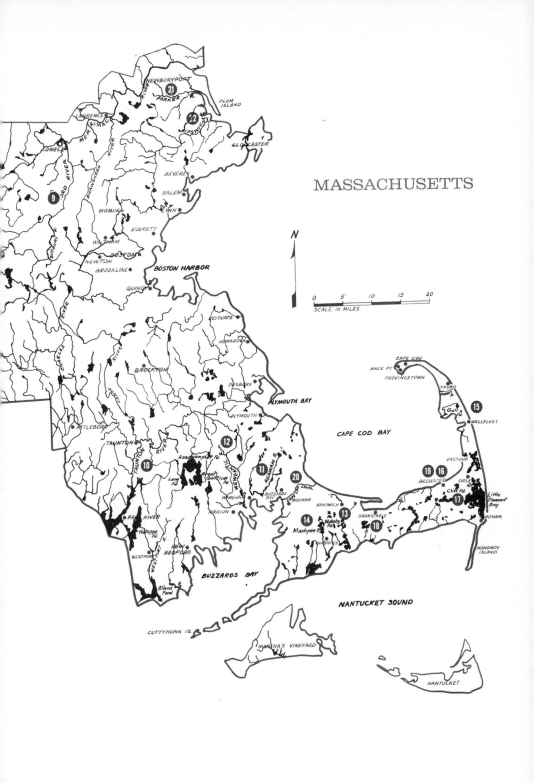

MASSACHUSETTS

N

0   5   10   15   20
SCALE in MILES

NEWBURYPORT
㉑ PARKER R.
PLUM ISLAND

LAWRENCE
㉒ IPSWICH
MERRIMACK RIVER
GLOUCESTER

LOWELL

SHAWSHEEN RIVER

BEVERLY

⑨

SALEM

WOBURN
LYNN

WOOD RIVER

EVERETT
WALTHAM
BOSTON
NEWTON
BROOKLINE
BOSTON HARBOR

SUDBURY R.

QUINCY

CHARLES RIVER

SCITUATE

HUMAROCK

BROCKTON

DUXBURY

PLYMOUTH BAY

ATTLEBORO

CAPE COD BAY

CAPE COD
RACE PT.
PROVINCETOWN

TRURO
PAMET R.

⑮

Gull Pd.
WELLFLEET

TAUNTON

PLYMOUTH

TAUNTON RIVER

⑫

Assawompsett Pd.
Great Quittica Pd.
Long Pd.

⑪ AGAWAM R.

⑳ CAPE COD CANAL

EASTHAM

⑲ ⑯

⑩

WEWEANTIC R.

WAREHAM
BUZZARDS BAY
BOURNE

BREWSTER
ORLEANS

Cliff Pd.
Little
Pleasant
Bay
⑰

MARION

SANDWICH

BARNSTABLE

FALL RIVER
Watuppa Pd.

NEW BEDFORD

⑭
Mashpee Pd.

Wakeby Pd.
⑬

⑱

CHATHAM

WESTPORT

WESTPORT R.

MASHPEE

MONOMOY ISLAND

Allens Pond

BUZZARDS BAY

NANTUCKET SOUND

CUTTYHUNK IS.

MARTHA'S VINEYARD

NANTUCKET

north end of the canal, at the East End Beach Road; Barnstable, on the Sandy Neck Road, off U.S. 6A; Truro, on the Pamet River far out on the Cape, off U.S. 6; Provincetown, off U.S. 6 at State Beach; Truro at Highland Road; Wellfleet via Cross Hill Road; Eastham at Nauset Light via the Cable Road; Eastham at Nauset Beach North, via the Doane Road to the Coast Guard Station; Orleans at Nauset Beach south, via the Beach Road; and Chatham, at Morris Island, off the Morris Island Road. Additional approaches are being constructed each year and a current list may be obtained from the Massachusetts Division of Marine Fisheries, 15 Ashburton Place, Boston. At the same time get a copy of the current regulations governing the taking of shellfish, anadromous fish or eels or sea worms for bait, as these are subject to local regulations.

As far as tackle goes, for school stripers and those who like to "go light," an 8- to 8½-foot squidding rod which can handle line from 25- to 36-pound test, and small lures and metal squids weighing from 1½ to 2 ounces, is a good outfit. Most anglers, however, prefer a 9- to 9½-foot surf rod with 36-pound test line, or even 45-pound test, and lures weighing 2 to 3½ ounces. A few go even heavier, using a 10- to 11-foot stick with 36- to 45-pound test line and 3- to 5-ounce lures. These outfits are used mostly for surf fishing when they really want to get out a long way. To round out the picture for striper tackle there is a very popular rod known as the "jetty stick," widely used in boats and on jetties. This one measures about 8 feet overall. The reels are either good conventional surf-casting reels or big, salt-water spinning reels.

The Atom plugs, first made for stripers, still remain tops in the field for this type of lure. They account for many big stripers and little ones, too. Also outstanding are the Upperman bucktails, made in Atlantic City. They come in many sizes and the two largest, the 8/0 and the Big Ben, are favorites with the writer. A piece of pork rind, Uncle Josh #50, put on the hook, adds to the action of these wonderful jigs which have produced some of the biggest stripers ever taken on rod and reel.

Baits include eelskin rigs, bucktails with pork rind, and others.

Fly fishermen prefer the 9½-foot rod and a single-action reel with GAF line backed with 14-pound test nylon squidding line. The best flies are the big bucktails —white, yellow, blue and white—known as the "blondes," on size 1/0 and 3/0 hooks.

Charter boats for offshore fishing may be obtained by writing or phoning (area code 617) Ken Daly, Barnstable, 362-6389 and 362-3811; Newell Townsend, West Dennis, 398-2018; Karl Sollow, Hyannis, 775-1877 or 775-0035; Goose Hummock Shop, Orleans, Orleans 455, and at Rock Harbor, Orleans 8923; Dennis Marine, Dennis 385-3275.

Beach buggies and guiding service for surf fishermen may be found at Bay-Sea Cabin and Cottages, Orleans, also a good place to stay. It is operated by Dot and Paul Hoffner.

Those who bring their own boats will find many launching sites all along the coast. A list of these is contained in the "Sportsman's Guide to Cape Cod" already mentioned, obtainable from the Cape Cod Chamber of Commerce, Hyannis, Massachusetts.

Beach buggies are the most practical form of transportation for roaming Massachusetts beaches. These vehicles are so popular that the Massachusetts Beach Buggy Association has 1,000 members; and many other unassociated fishermen have their own buggies. Anyone planning to go in for this type of transport should obtain the book *Striped Bass Fishing* by Hal Lyman and Frank Wollner, publisher and editor, respectively, of *The Salt Water Sportsman Magazine,* 157 Federal Street, Boston 10, Massachusetts. The book gives recommendations as to the proper car or jeep to use as a base, what tires give best service, and many other details of construction and operation garnered over years of such fishing by two real experts in the field.

MARTHA'S VINEYARD AND NANTUCKET

Martha's Vineyard, Cuttyhunk and Nantucket Islands are the largest of the group which lies south of the Cape. They are host to excellent runs of stripers from May through October, with the best fishing in the fall. There are boats available at Martha's Vineyard and at New Bedford and Westport on the mainland. There is good surf casting on Martha's Vineyard but most of the fishing at Cuttyhunk is by trolling and casting in the offshore rigs and casting to the rocks near shore.

There is some fishing for white marlin and swordfish between Nantucket and Block Island, July and August being the top months for these species.

COASTAL AREAS

Along the coast north from Cape Cod, Plymouth, at the junction of State Highway 3, the coastal road, and U.S. 44 from Taunton, is a good center for summer fishing. Pollack catches are made in June and early July, mackerel in midsummer, and striped bass are found through most of the spring and summer and into November. There is often excellent striped-bass fishing in Plymouth Bay, out of the two cities of Plymouth and Duxbury. The same is true around Humarock and Scituate, reached by following State Highway 3A north from Plymouth. Some fish are taken in the southern part of Boston Bay, too. The season in all these waters usually starts about the middle of June and continues to about the middle of November.

Plum Island, well to the north, is reached from Newburyport on U.S. 1. There is some excellent fishing at the mouth of the Merrimack River. You can fish from boats in the inlet, or from the beach. The fish are mostly school stripers but there are a few big ones. The season opens in early may and the bigger fish are usually plentiful by late June and at their peak as to numbers in July. Spinning and fly fishing are both popular here but the fish will take anything from top-water lures to sea worms and bloodworms.

Surf fishing is good all along the outer beach and especially near the Coast Guard Station at the mouth of the Merrimack River. All of the beach is fishable except a restricted recreational area at the northern edge of the Parker River Wildlife Refuge. A permit is required to operate a beach buggy in the refuge and another permit is required to fish the beach at night. The permits are free, however, and may be obtainable at the Refuge Office at Plum Island Point.

Inland from the island there's excellent fishing for stripers in the rivers and marshes. The PARKER RIVER (21), which crosses U.S. 1 and Interstate Highway 95, south of Newburyport; and the IPSWICH RIVER (22), near the town of the same name, are both excellent for fly-rod fishing for stripers. You can also fish Broad Sound from small boats launched at Ipswich and the Route 1A Bridge over the Parker River. Charter boats are available at Ipswich for offshore tuna fishing.

While there is not the same amount of big-game fishing as is found further south along the Atlantic coast, some giant tuna are taken out of the ports on Cape Cod, working out of Truro and Provincetown, on U.S. 6, out at the end of the Cape, as well as at the mainland port north of there.

All along the coast summer and winter flounder are taken in inshore waters, according to season. There is fishing for cod and haddock throughout the year.

MASSACHUSETTS FISHING REGULATIONS

Resident Fishing License $4.25
    Minors, between 15 and 18 $2.25
    Women $3.25
Nonresident Fishing License $8.75
Nonresident 7-Day Fishing License $4.25

SEASONS AND LIMITS

Species	Open Season	Size Limits	Daily Bag Limit
All trouts in ponds and lakes	In general, third Saturday in April to third Sunday in Oct.	None	6
All trouts in rivers and streams	As above	None	12
Black Bass	Third Saturday in April to Feb. 28	10″	5
Pickerel	As above	14″	5
All other fish	As above	None	None

No license is required for saltwater fishing, but the taking of shellfish, anadromous fish, eels and sea worms is subject to local regulations. Consult local authorities in coastal communities.

The following size limits apply on saltwater fish: striped bass, 16-inch minimum; pollack, 12-inch minimum; mackerel, 6-inch minimum.

For complete regulations write: Division of Fish and Game, Field Headquarters, Westboro, Massachusetts.

RHODE ISLAND

Rhode Island is the smallest of the states. Situated between industrial Connecticut and Massachusetts, its countryside is largely urban. There are no large rivers of major importance to anglers, and while there are some 200 square miles of fresh water, it is mostly under private ownership. Some of these may be fished with permission of the owner, and the picture is somewhat brightened by a number of public access sites arranged by the State Division of Fish and Game. In such fresh waters as are available there are largemouth black bass, smallmouth black bass, eastern chain pickerel, yellow perch, white perch, bluegill, sunfish and bullheads. Some few streams are stocked annually on a put and take basis with brown, rainbow and brook trout. Though the latter are the local native trout, their numbers would be negligible without the stocking program.

Rhode Island's coastline measures only forty miles on the Atlantic Ocean, as the crow flies, but when you consider all the bays and inlets it adds up to more than 400 miles, providing some excellent inshore fishing waters for striped bass, bluefish, squeteague, sea trout or weakfish, tautog or blackfish, pollack, sea bass, halibut, flounder and cod. Offshore there are bluefin tuna, marlin and now and then swordfish, in addition to the stripers and other inshore species which are also found in the deep.

All parts of Rhode Island are readily accessible via State Highway 146 from Worcester, Massachusetts, and U.S. 1 from Boston. Both lead to Providence in northeastern Rhode Island, at the head of Narragansett Bay. From Providence, U.S. 6 cuts across westward to the Connecticut Turnpike at the Connecticut border. Interstate 95 bisects the southern half of the state diagonally, to accommodate traffic from the Turnpike further south in the New London area; and U.S. 1 skirts almost the entire coast, from the Connecticut border to Providence. The eastern section of Rhode Island, which lies on the eastern shores of Narragansett Bay, is served by State Highway 114 from Providence, to the north and west; and State Highway 177, from New Bedford, Massachusetts, on the east.

Major airlines serve Providence, and there are charter flights available from there to Block Island, Newport and Westerly.

Fishermen visiting Rhode Island will find the spring and summer climate warm and pleasant, tempered by the sea. A light woolen jacket for evenings is all the heavy clothing needed at such times. Coastal fishermen should add a windproof, rainproof jacket, and those who fish the beaches in the spring and fall need heavy woolens, as the weather can then be quite cool at times.

As it is mostly urbanized, the state offers no hazards from wild game or snakes.

Those who fish the ponds and streams which have been stocked with trout will want an 8-foot fly rod with matching HDH (DT6F) fly line, and a leader tapered down to a 4X tippet. Those who go for the other freshwater species with a fly outfit generally use an 8½-foot rod with GBF (WF8F) line, or a 9-foot rod with

43

a GAF (WF9) line. For smallmouth, a 2X tippet is recommended, and for large-mouth, a 1X (9-pound breaking strength).

All the standard fly patterns in small sizes, 14, 16, 18 and 20, will take fish in the small streams and ponds which are stocked with trout. Spinning lures should also be small; and small bass bugs and streamers and small lures are also suitable for the pond fishing.

Plug casters use the standard light plug-casting outfit, and spinners lean to medium or light spinning gear with 4- to 6-pound-test line.

Many surf casters in the salt also use spinning outfits, generally with 10-pound-test monofilament line; and with these outfits find they can handle big stripers nicely. Others still stay with the long-popular surf rod and squidder reel, with 25- to 45-pound-test squidding line. This rig is particularly practical in high surf. The tin squid remains one of the most popular artificials with surf casters, but eelskins and plugs are also good. Inquiries should be made locally as to what natural baits the fish are taking.

FRESHWATER FISHING

In the northwestern corner of the state, WALLUM LAKE (1), reached via State Highway 100 from Bridgeton, is stocked with trout, as are ROUND TOP BROOK and POND (2), immediately to the east, reached via Harrisville. A few miles down the western border of the state, BOWDISH RESERVOIR (3), off U.S. 44 near Glocester, has fishing for white perch. In the same area, PECK POND (4), BRANDY BROOK (5) and the CHEPACHET RIVER (6) are stocked with trout. Similar fishing is found further south near North Foster, between U.S. 6 and State Highway 101, where there is a public fishing area on the PONAGANSET RIVER (7), and HOPKINS MILL POND (8), into which the river flows, and WINDSOR BROOK (9), DOLLY COLE BROOK (10), and SHIPPEE BROOK and POND (11). Below this you will find trout fishing in TURKEY MEADOW BROOK (12) and BUCKS HORN BROOK (13), reached from State Highway 102 near Potterville; and the MOOSUP RIVER (14), off State Highway 14 near Vernon.

BEACH POND (15), on the Connecticut border, is reached via State Highway 165 from Interstate Highway 95. It holds smallmouth, sometimes up to 4 pounds, and crappie. Close by there are trout in BRUSHY BROOK (16) and LOG HOUSE BROOK (17) near Centerville on State Highway 138.

DEEP POND (18), near Arcadia, on Old Nooseneck Road, is limited to fly fishing only. ROARING BROOK (19) can be reached from Millville on State Highway 165; and nearby are MESHANTICUT BROOK (20), near Oaklawn on State Highway 5; FALLS RIVER (21), FLAT RIVER (22), PARRIS BROOK (23) and BREAKHEART BROOK (24), all in the vicinity of the Arcadia State Management Area. There is further fishing in the HUNT RIVER (25), to the northeast, near East Greenwich; and in the PAWTUXENT RIVER (26) between the Scituate Reservoir and the town of Hope on State Highway 16.

Continuing down to the coast you come to CHAPMAN POND (27), near Westerly, which has fishing for white perch and crappie. To the east is WATCHAUG POND (28) in Burlington State Park, off U.S. 1 near Charlestown. The pond has good smallmouth fishing. PERRY HEALY BROOK (29), which flows into it from the south-west, is stocked with trout. WOOD RIVER POND (30), north of Watchaug, has produced chain pickerel to better than 6 pounds. Take the Alton Road from State Highway 112 at Carolina. On the Connecticut border, the ASHAWAY (31) is fishable near Hopkinton on U.S. 84 (New London Turnpike).

Slightly to the east is WORDEN POND (32), at the south end of the Great Swamp State Management area. The pond holds pickerel, yellow perch and white perch. It can be reached from Perryville on U.S. 1, north to the Worden Pond Public Fishing Area near Tuckertown. Continue on up this road and you come to West Kingston. Turn west here for CHICKASHEEN BROOK (33), at the north end of the swamp. It is stocked with trout, as is nearby BARBER POND (34), on State Highway 2. The BEAVER RIVER (35), reached from State Highway 138 near Usquepaugh, to the northwest of the swamp, is considered one of the best streams in the state for trout. South of State Highway 138, to the west of Kingston, BISCUIT CITY POND (36) is another trout-fishing possibility.

In the far northeastern part of Rhode Island, anglers will find trout in ABBOTT RUN (37), which comes in to the PAWTUCKET RESERVOIR (38) near Arnold Mills. To the south of this, close to Providence, in the neighborhood of Saylesville, OLNEY POND (39) offers good fishing for the warm-water species. Close by are GENEVA BROOK (40), running along the Douglas Pike, NORTH BRANCH (41), near Stillwater, and NINE FOOT BROOK (42), near Harmony, all stocked with trout. They can be reached via secondary roads from U.S. 44.

Several ponds in the southeastern part of Rhode Island, on the eastern shores of Narragansett Bay, also provide some trout fishing. BRICKYARD POND (43) is reached from Barrington on State Highway 114, and STAFFORD POND (44), well to the south, can be reached via State Highway 177 at Tiverton. The latter also has a good population of smallmouth black bass and there is no size or creel limit. ADAMSVILLE BROOK (45) and SIN AND FLESH POND (46), immediately to the west on State Highway 177, and DUNDERRY BROOK (47), near Little Compton, are also stocked. The latter also has a good population of smallmouth black bass and there is no size or creel limit on this species in Stafford Pond. Anglers who plan to sample the freshwater fishing in these and various other ponds in Rhode Island, should obtain a copy of the "Rhode Island Fishing Map" from the Rhode Island Development Council, Roger Williams Building, 49 Hayes Street, Providence, Rhode Island. The brochure includes a resumé of most of the public access areas in the state, and a detailed map showing approach roads. It also indicates public and private launching sites for boats.

SALTWATER FISHING

In general the season for each of the popular saltwater species to be taken along the Rhode Island Coast is as follows: striped bass, May to December; bluefin tuna, July to October; white marlin, July to October; swordfish, mid-June to October; bonito, July to October; bluefish, July to mid-October; mackerel, June to October; pollack, April to December; cod, March to late December.

The waters along the coast of Rhode Island provide some of the really great striper fishing on the Atlantic coast. Stripers are found in these waters from April to December but the best fishing times are spring and fall. Big fish are most plentiful in October and November.

The striper season starts when the first fish appear in both surf and river

RHODE ISLAND

inlets about April 15th, from Block Island offshore, to and along the southern part of the mainland. First fishing is usually between Watch Hill, on U.S. Alternate 1, south of Westerly, and Weekapaug, a few miles to the east. Moving up along the coast the fish appear at Quonchontaug and on up the shore to Point Judith at the western entrance to Narragansett Bay. Some of the biggest fall fish are taken at Charlestown Beach and Charlestown Breachway, off U.S. 1. Anglers visiting this area can also get in some good brackish-water fishing in Green Hill Pond, at the town of Charlestown Beach, south of U.S. 1.

Narragansett Bay has been called "the world's best fish trap." School stripers appear there about the first of May. There is good river fishing for the smaller fish, while the big ones concentrate at the entrance to the bay. Out there at all the points of the islands, surf casters have accounted for some whopping striped bass. A 63-pound 12-ounce fish was taken at Sachuest Point, Middletown, by surf caster Joseph Donon. A 65-pounder was taken at Beaver Tail at the middle of the bay mouth, by Arthur Clarke. And a 59-pounder was caught at Point Judith at the western entrance to the Bay by Antonio Bartolomucci. Other hot spots are the islands off Sakonnet on the western side of the Bay, Easton Point, directly west of Sachuest Point, and Narragansett Pier, on the inner western shore of Narragansett Bay.

Block Island, offshore from the coast of Rhode Island, is the center of fishing for big-game species. The island can be reached by charter air service from Providence, by ferry from Providence or Newport, Rhode Island; and by ferry from New London, Connecticut, and Culloden Point, Long Island, New York, during the summer. The biggest bluefin tuna ever taken in Rhode Island waters was caught about two miles off Matunuck Beach, inshore from Block Island. That fish, taken by Henry Brain of New Jersey, weighed 961½ pounds. Big fish will, however, average 100 to 500 pounds, and there are many smaller school fish, often mixed in with schools of bonitos. While not many bluefin are taken, it is believed that with increased fishing more of this species will be found in these waters. A list of accommodations on the island may be obtained from the Rhode Island Development Council, Roger Williams Building, 49 Hayes Street, Providence, Rhode Island, 02908.

Swordfish are also taken occasionally, the biggest of this species being a 321-pounder caught off Block Island by Ray Adams of Wickford, Rhode Island. And while very few blue marlin are taken, one weighing 327 pounds was landed by an angler working out of Block Island, in September, 1955.

The island is one of the most popular spots on the coast for striper fishermen, starting with the schoolfish in mid-April, as mentioned earlier. The big ones usually arrive about a month later and fishing continues good for this species through November, both from boats and from beaches and rocks alongshore.

Some of Rhode Island's best bluefish catches are made at Block Island. Members of this species often go to 7 pounds, and a 12-pound 12-ouncer was taken at Southwest Point by Ben Weissman of Guilford, Connecticut. November seems to be the top month for the big ones, but here, as elsewhere along the coast, schools of hard-feeding blues come rollicking through all summer, providing lots of excitement for light-tackle fishermen. They will hit anything you offer, from artificials of all kinds to whole eels, and they are expert at tearing up tackle.

Boats are available at New Harbor Ferry Dock.

Other saltwater species taken throughout Rhode Island waters include the tautog, a bottom dweller which provides fine angling the length of the coast from late April till the end of November. The tautog is also found in some of the deeper of the saltwater ponds alongshore. The fish gives a good, hard fight, and specimens have been taken up to 21 pounds. Flounders, both the summer and winter varieties, are also favorites with Rhode Island fishermen. The fine flavor of the meat has a lot to do with this but, at the same time, they put up a tough battle and provide good sport in the catching. They are taken mostly on bait from shore or in small boats, and the average is 2 or 3 pounds, though some are taken up to 14 pounds. As elsewhere, you'll hear these big ones termed "doormats." There is some particularly good flounder fishing at Narragansett Pier and Sakonnet Point, but they are taken in estuaries, harbors, river flats and tidal ponds the entire length of the coast.

Long-shore fishermen in Rhode Island will find some great sport using light tackle for sea trout, or weakfish. They hit artificials well and will take many kinds of bait. Regardless of how you fish them, they must be played gingerly because of a soft mouth. The fish average about 3 pounds. An 8-pounder is a large one in Rhode Island.

Although usually caught in deep water, pollack also come into the shallows to furnish fun for casters. They vary in size from 1 pound to 40, and regardless of size, put up a good fight. Another deep-water fish, the cod, is becoming increasingly popular with early-spring and late-fall fishermen who go for them by the jigging method. A heavy, lead-headed jig with bucktail or feather tail is allowed to drop to the bottom, then is worked up and down with hard upsweeps of the rod, to make the lure look alive. This method of working a lure takes lots of cod. And, as a matter of fact, jigging is becoming more and more popular as a way to reach many deep lying fish with artificial lures. The best areas for cod fishing are off Point Judith, Block Island and Sakonnet.

While nearly every oceanside community has some boats available for fishing, certain ones are centers for charter trips. One of the main fleets will be found at Galilee or Snug Harbor, near Point Judith, at the western entrance to Narragansett Bay. Some twenty-four boats are berthed here, including two party boats. Charter arrangements can be made through the Rhode Island Charter Booking Service, Snug Harbor Marina, Rhode Island. Phone Sterling 3-7766.

At Sakonnet Point you can charter trips through Capt. Bud Phillips, Phone Little Compton 650. On Conanicut Island at Jamestown there are boats available through Captain Norman Olson, 116 Avenue B, Phone Jamestown 605; Captain Clyde Parks, Phone Jamestown 713; and Captain Joseph Chesbro, Phone Jamestown 169-M. On the western shore of Narragansett Bay you can get charters at Wickford, just off U.S. 1, about half way up the bay, at Wickford Boat & Tackle Shop, 1 Phillips Street at the bridge.

Anglers planning to fish Rhode Island coastal waters should obtain the Rhode Island Fishing Map mentioned earlier, from the Rhode Island Development Council. It includes a series of detailed maps and charts showing the best fishing areas, and indicates launching sites and many secondary roads to the beaches, which do not show on highway maps.

RHODE ISLAND FISHING REGULATIONS

Resident Fishing License $3.25
    Older than 65 and younger than 18 $.25
Nonresident Fishing License $7.25
Nonresident 3-Day Fishing License $3.25

SEASONS AND LIMITS

Species	Open Season	Daily Limit	Minimum Size
Black Bass	Third Saturday in April to Feb. 20	6	10″
Chain Pickerel	Third Saturday in April to Feb. 20	10	12″
Trout (all species)	Third Saturday in April to Oct. 31	6	No size limit
Trout (all species)	Dec. 1–Feb. 20, thru ice only	2	No size limit
Yellow & White Perch	None	None	None
Bluegill, Sunfish	None	None	None
Striped Bass	None	None	16″

No license required for fishing in salt water.

For complete regulations write: Department of Agriculture and Conservation, 83 Park Street, Providence 2, Rhode Island.

CONNECTICUT

Though Connecticut is essentially a coastal-zone state, with some 250 miles of Atlantic shoreline, nevertheless the rolling countryside as the interior slopes up to Massachusetts on the north and New York State on the west, forms a watershed for dozens of small streams and several large rivers. There are many lakes and ponds, both man-made and natural. The freshwater species found in these waters include brown trout, brook trout, rainbow trout, largemouth black bass, smallmouth black bass, lake trout, rock bass, walleye, eastern chain pickerel, northern pike, yellow perch and black crappies.

Along the coast, anglers take such saltwater species as bluefin tuna, bluefish, tautog or blackfish, mackerel, weakfish, pollack, cunners and white perch. The migratory striped bass and shad work their way into several rivers from the salt, to provide their own brand of fishing, alongshore, in estuaries, and in the streams often quite far inland.

In addition to these native fish, there may be considerable future fishing through some interesting experiments being conducted by the Connecticut Board of Fish and Game. Under the supervision of Robert A. Jones, Supervisor, Fisheries Management, extensive studies have been carried out with European sea trout, a brown trout which goes to sea, then returns to the rivers to spawn, providing some wonderful sport fishing. Some of the fish stocked from eggs obtained from Danish waters have thrived and while it is too early as yet to be assured of results, this program may lead to a fine new sport fishery. Test streams in which the fish have been stocked are Latimer Brook, which runs parallel to State Highway 161, near East Lyme; Eight Mile River, which can be reached from State Highway 156 near North Lyme; the Hammonasset River, entering the ocean near Clinton; and the Saugatuck River, entering the ocean at Westport.

The Connecticut Board of Fish and Game has also stocked landlocked sockeye salmon (kokanee) in East Twin Lake, near Salisbury, on U.S. 44 in the northwest corner of the state, and in Highland Lake, near Winsted, a few miles to the southeast on the same highway. There has been some fishing for this species since 1926, and it is hoped that this fishery, too, will increase.

The major river is the Connecticut, which forms far north in New Hampshire and flows the length of that state, through Massachusetts and thence down through the center of Connecticut. A second major river, the Housatonic, drains the southwestern corner of the state; and on the southeast is the Thames, another stream of good size. Aside from these, a series of smaller rivers extends the length of the coast, many offering some opportunity for freshwater fishing and most having the added attraction of fishing for some of the inshore saltwater species that work into the inlets.

There are no large natural lakes in Connecticut but many small lakes and ponds dot the countryside, and there are a number of sizable reservoirs.

Connecticut is famous for its fine highways leading to every corner of the state. The Merritt Parkway funnels traffic from the New York City area onto the Connecticut Turnpike, which traverses the entire coastal area; and to the Wilbur Cross Parkway, bisecting the state from southwest to northeast. U.S. 5 and Interstate 91 bracket the Connecticut River, as they do in the neighboring states to the north. Besides these main arteries, excellent highways fan out to cover the balance of the state.

Air transportation is probably as good as will be found anywhere in the United States.

The climate is typical of the north Atlantic coastal area—warm in summer, pleasantly cool in spring and fall. As the scene is mostly urban, anglers do not need the northwoods type of clothing such as would be worn in Maine, for instance. Hip boots will usually suffice for fishing the trout streams.

As elsewhere along the Atlantic coast, seaside fishing can be cool, and fishermen should be prepared for rain as well.

Aside from deer the angler will encounter very little wild game. However, as in Massachusetts to the north and New York to the west, there may be copperheads, cottonmouths and rattlesnakes, though they are not common.

Tackle must be chosen according to your fishing plans. Trout fishermen will find an 8-foot fly rod ideal for Connecticut streams and for most lake fishing as well. Those who use spinning tackle should go equally light. All the standard small flies and small lures will take fish.

Saltwater tackle ranges from highly specialized tuna gear, usually provided on the charter boats which cater to this type of fisherman, to bottom-fishing rigs. Those who go for striped bass with light tackle usually prefer a 9-foot fly rod with a GAF (WF9F) line, a reel capable of holding 250 yards of backing as well as the line. Spinners use the regular saltwater spinning reels on a 6½- to 7-foot rod. With both outfits top-water popping lures are good and the deeper-swimming jigs are also popular.

When the shad run is on, spinning is the most popular method of fishing. The small spoons, and in fact, any lure with some flash to it, will take the shad. Some few are also taken by fly-rodders using flies with a tinsel binding.

LAKE FISHING

CANDLEWOOD LAKE (1), on the western border, is the largest body of water in Connecticut. As on so many of the larger lakes in populated areas, fishermen may find themselves surrounded by water skiers, but nevertheless there is some angling for largemouth black bass, a few brown and rainbow trout and fairly good supplies of yellow perch and white perch. The lake can be reached via State Highway 37, north from Danbury, on U.S. 202, as far as New Fairfield, then on State Highway 39 to the west shore of the lake. Boats and bait are available at both New Fairfield and Danbury, and also, during the summer only, at SQUANTZ POND (2) on State Highway 39. This pond has a few trout but is best known for its fishing for largemouth and perch, both yellow and white. Many secondary roads lead in from U.S. 7 to the eastern shore of Candlewood Lake. On this side boats are available at New Milford. Immediately to the south is LAKE KANOSHA (3), immediately west of the town of Danbury on U.S. 202. There is fair fishing for largemouth black bass. BALL POND (4) at New Fairfield also offers some good rainbow-trout fishing at times.

Limited fishing for largemouth black bass and panfish will be found in the widening of the Housatonic River known as HOUSATONIC LAKE (5). There are boats and bait available at Stratford on the coast, and further upstream at Shelton and Derby at the junction of State Highway 34 and State Highway 8.

Still further north along the Housatonic, at LAKE ZOAR (6) there is considerably better chance for the same species plus smallmouth, yellow and white perch. The lake is most easily reached from Southbury on U.S. 6 and U.S. 202, via a secondary road down the east shore. You can also go in from State Highway 34 on the west and there are boats available there at Stevenson.

Continuing north on the Housatonic you come to LAKE LILLINONAH (7), accessible via State Highway 133 from Bridgewater. This lake offers better than average angling for largemouth, smallmouth, yellow and white perch and calico bass.

About the middle of this northwestern part of Connecticut is BANTAM LAKE (8). It can be reached via either State Highway 25 or State Highway 63, south from Litchfield, then, in both cases, over State Highway 109 to the lake. It holds the same species, and boats and bait will be found at Lakeside at the south end of the pond. In nearby MT. TOM POND (9), reached from State Highway 25, there is very limited angling for stocked trout.

Immediately to the west, off State Highway 45, LAKE WARAMAUG (10) has a few largemouth black bass and chain pickerel but the fishing is mostly for perch. Boats are available at New Preston, at the junction of State Highways 25 and 45.

Directly north of Mt. Tom Pond is MOHAWK POND (11), where there is some rather good fishing for brook trout. You can go in from State Highway 4 from Cornwall or State Highway 63 from Litchfield. In the same general area, WEST SIDE POND (12) has good fishing for largemouth and perch plus a few trout. The pond is reached via secondary road off State Highway 63, north of Goshen.

To the west of Goshen, on State Highway 4, boats are available to fish DOG POND (13), where there is good fishing for largemouth and some chain pickerel.

In the extreme northwestern corner of the state, LAKE WONONSKOPOMUC (14) is reputed to occasionally produce some extra-big brown trout, up to 10 pounds, and also some large pickerel. There is public access to the lake in the village of Lakeville at the junction of U.S. 44 and State Highway 41, and boats are available there.

RAINBOW RESERVOIR (15) on the Farmington River, a tributary of the Connecticut, can be quite good. There are largemouth, pickerel and sunfish. The lake is reached from Windsor via State Highway 75 from either U.S. 5A or Interstate Highway 91.

In the northeastern part of Connecticut, WAMGUMBAUG LAKE (16) is the most likely spot for fishing success. It has a substantial population of yellow perch and smallmouth black bass which often run better than 3 pounds. The lake can be reached from South Coventry on State Highway 31, and boats and bait are available.

On the northern state border, 2½ miles north of State Highway 198 just before it joins State Highway 15, is MASHAPAUG LAKE (17), which produced the record Connecticut largemouth in 1961, a fish that weighed 12 pounds 14 ounces. It also produced the state record smallmouth, back in 1941, a fish that weighed 7 pounds 10 ounces. The lake also contains some brown trout and perch. Close by, and reached via the same route, is BIGELOW POND (18), where there is fair fishing only for largemouth and some stocked trout.

A group of lakes in the southeast corner of Connecticut provides fair to good fishing for chain pickerel and yellow perch, with some largemouth black bass and

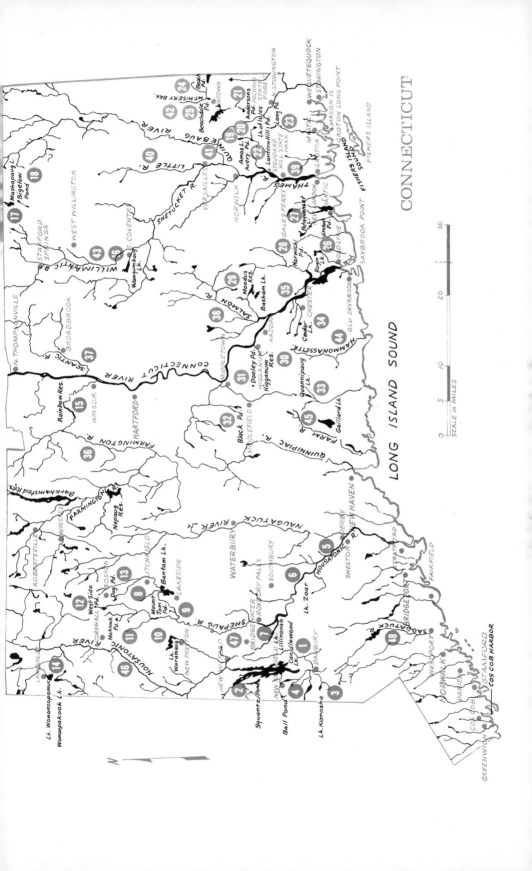

CONNECTICUT

LONG ISLAND SOUND

SCALE IN MILES

0   5   10   20   30

bullheads. AMOS LAKE (19) is reached from State Highway 164 south from Preston City; and AVERY POND (20) is immediately to the south. ANDERSONS POND (21) is southeast of Preston City on a secondary road.

The LAKE OF ISLES (22), reached via State Highway 2, a little south of these three, occasionally provides excellent fishing for the same species. LANTERN HILL POND (23) and LONG POND (23), which lie still further south, in the angle formed by State Highways 2 and 119, near North Stonington, provide fairly good trout fishing. Long Pond is heavily stocked and usually has some holdover trout weighing up to 5 pounds. In addition there are largemouth, pickerel and perch.

On the Rhode Island border, and partly in that state, is BEACH POND (24), east of Voluntown. State Highway 165 crosses the lower end of the lake. This pond holds all three trouts. Immediately to the north is BEACHDALE POND (25), with good possibilities for largemouth and yellow perch.

Yet another group of ponds is found just west of the Thames River inshore from Niantic on the coast. GROTON'S POND (26) is on State Highway 161, off the Connecticut Turnpike near East Lyme. PATAGUANSET LAKE (27) can be reached from the same highway west of East Lyme. Both have good fishing for largemouth and calico bass, which in Pataguanset sometimes run to 3 pounds. There are also chain pickerel and yellow perch. Immediately to the west, accessible from secondary roads off State Highway 156, are ROGER LAKE (28) and NORWICH POND (28). Some fair-sized trout are taken from these two.

To the north again there are two reservoirs, one on each side of the Connecticut River. MOODUS RESERVOIR (29) on the east, can be reached from State Highway 149 near Bashan. The lake is very weedy but can produce some good largemouth bass and yellow perch. On the west side of the river is HIGGANUM RESERVOIR (30), at the village of the same name, off State Highway 81.

From Middletown on the Connecticut you can follow State Highway 17 south to DOOLEY POND (31), where the fishing for largemouth, chain pickerel and perch can be excellent. The same is true of BLACK POND (32), reached via U.S. 6A west from Middletown, or State Highway 147 from Middlefield.

South again, about half way between Middletown on the Connecticut River and Guilford on the coast, is QUONNIPAUG LAKE (33), off State Highway 77. This lake is heavily stocked with trout and holdovers sometimes reach 6 pounds in weight. There are also some largemouth, chain pickerel and yellow perch. CEDAR LAKE (34), off State Highway 148 to the west of Chester, has fine trout fishing for rainbows and brooks.

There are many other ponds in Connecticut which can provide good fishing for one species or another. Anglers planning to really explore what the state has to offer in this regard should obtain a copy of "A Guide to Public Access to Connecticut Fishing Waters," published by the Connecticut Board of Fish and Game. Ask also for a mimeographed leaflet, "Boats for Hire on Connecticut Rivers and Lakes." Those interested mainly in trout should obtain a small map entitled "Where to Go for Trout." While the pamphlet is not a detailed guide, it gives the general location of the major trout ponds and the larger trout streams.

RIVER FISHING

The CONNECTICUT RIVER (35) is the largest stream in the state and while much industrialized still provides a degree of fishing of quite wide variety, ranging from the resident pickerel, northern pike, white perch and yellow perch to the anadromous shad which move in every spring. The run of shad is good and improving each year now that efforts are being made to prevent impediments to the run and, through the imposition of a daily creek limit of six fish, to protect the fish against over-fishing. In 1959 more than 45,000 shad were caught in the Connecticut by sport fishermen, and in 1960 the catch is believed to have been even greater. A fish lift at South Hadley Falls Dam was also added to insure upstream movement of the shad.

Shad will hit small metal spoons, jigs, flies and feathered lures, and even a bare hook with a colored bead added. Many anglers go for them with fly rods, as the sportiest method of taking the species. The shad has a habit of following the lure or fly and striking it several times before being hooked. It also has a strange way of working its mouth open and shut while hooked, evidently trying to get rid of the hook. The mouth is very soft and the cheek covers are tissue thin. Often if a fish is hooked in the cheek the hook will tear down a half inch, giving enough leeway for the shad to shake the hook. They are tough fighters, good jumpers, lots of fun.

They move into the river in late April, and may be taken from Saturday, April 3rd until late June, depending on water levels at Enfield Dam south of Thompsonville on Interstate 91 near the Massachusetts border. The King's Island launching site below the dam can be reached from Interstate 91. There is also access at Windsor Lock Bridge, a couple of miles further south, and boats are available there. Headquarters for a big Annual Connecticut River Shad Derby will be found at Bart's Shopping Center, U.S. 5A, at the Farmington River Bridge at Windsor.

In the extreme northern part of the state there is limited access to the river but anglers will find public entry in the town of Enfield above the Enfield Dam. And one mile northwest of the junction of Interstate 91 and U.S. 5 there is public access to the shad fishing water below the dam. Further access will be found in Wilson, on the northern outskirts of Hartford. In this particular area the fishing is best north of the bridge.

Continuing down river, anglers will find entry at Middletown, just off State Highway 9; and again further south where the river flows between Haddam Island State Park and Haddam Meadows Park. Go in from the village of Haddam east of State Highway 9. At the mouth of the Connecticut there is public access at Old Saybrook.

Shad move from the Connecticut River into some of the tributaries far upstream. In April there is a good run in the FARMINGTON RIVER (36) which enters the main stream at Windsor. There are also some brown and brook trout in the Farmington. The shad also go up the SCANTIC RIVER (37), which enters the Connecticut from the east near Windsor and can be reached from State Highways 140 and 191. The SALMON RIVER (38), near Leesville on State Highway 151, near Haddam Island State Park, gets the spring run of shad, too, and has resident brook and brown trout.

The largest river in the eastern coastal area is the THAMES (39). There is a public access area in Stoddard Hill State Park, a very small park on State Highway 12 on the east side of the river north of Allyns Point. Striped bass come into the Thames. Boats are available at Gales Ferry just below Allyns Point. In the upper waters of the Thames system, the LITTLE RIVER (40), a tributary of the Sketucket, which enters the Thames near Versailles, off State Highway 12, has good fly fishing for browns and brook trout. Similarly, some of the brooks emptying into the

QUINEBAUG (41), another tributary of the Thames, offer some trout fishing. You can get directions as to where to fish Broad Brook at Preston City on State Highway 165, east of Norwich. To the east again there is similar fishing in MT. MISERY BROOK (42) near Voluntown, which is in Pachaug State Forest at the junction of State Highways 138, 165 and 49. Far to the north, in the WILLIMANTIC RIVER (43), another headwater stream in the Thames system, there are brown trout in the area near West Willington to the south of Stafford Springs. The river flows along State Highway 32.

The HAMMONASSETT RIVER (44), which runs parallel to the Connecticut on the west side, has sea-run brook trout and browns, often to 5 pounds. About the middle of the coastline, east of New Haven, is the FARM RIVER (45), which has resident brown and brook trout and also gets sea-run fish, again to 5 pounds.

In western Connecticut the HOUSATONIC RIVER (46) and its tributaries offer some fishing for brown trout, brook trout, rock bass and sunfish. The Housatonic can be reached at many points via dozens of state and secondary roads. Its main tributary, the SHEPAUG (47), can be fished from State Highway 199, south from Roxbury Falls.

The SAUGATUCK RIVER (48), further west, near Westport, on U.S. 1, has the same type of fishing.

These are only a few of the better-known ponds and streams in Connecticut. Names and detailed descriptions of many more will be found in "Hunting, Trapping and Sport Fishing Regulations," published annually by the Board of Fish and Game, State Office Building, Hartford, Connecticut.

SALTWATER FISHING IN CONNECTICUT

Some of the best fishing for schooling striped bass along the Atlantic coast can be found in Connecticut. The big bulls do not seem to come this way, although a few are taken, usually in June. The over-all season is roughly from May to November, though some fish are taken in the rivers as early as February. Trollers well up in the Thames River, for instance, begin to catch resident stripers at this time. As the season progresses, catches are made further and further downstream. By the first of May fish are along the beaches and the coastwise migration is on. Good casting and light trolling begins somewhat earlier in the estuaries—about April 15th. Some of the best coastal spots are the Greenwich–Cos Cob Harbor, the Fish Islands off Darien, the Norwalk Islands off Norwalk, Southport, near Fairfield, and the outlet of the Housatonic River. Fishing can also be excellent in the lower Connecticut River around Saybrook Point, in the Niantic estuary, around New London at the mouth of the Thames River, and at Fishers Island off New London. Facing on Fishers Island Sound, Mystic, Stonington, Groton Long Point, Mason Island and Napatree Point are all hot spots.

There are also weakfish, bluefish, pollack, and blackfish at all these points, the latter mostly around Niantic. The biggest bluefish are usually taken at the mouth of the Thames River.

Boats are available at Mystic, Stonington, Noank, New London, and in fact, every seaside community.

Charter boats fishing out of New London and Stonington also take some swordfish and tuna around Block Island. (See Rhode Island.)

A complete list of boats for hire may be obtained from the State Board of Fish and Game.

Those who wish to launch their own boats along the Connecticut shore will find private facilities at many seashore towns and there are public access sites (fees in some cases) at Seaside Park, Bridgeport, on the west side of Bridgeport Harbor; Fort Hale, New Haven, south of the U.S. Naval Reserve Center; Lighthouse Point, New Haven, in Lighthouse Point Park; East River, Guilford; Great Island, Old Lyme; Black Hall River, Old Lyme; Bayberry Lane, Groton, one mile east of the Coast Guard Station; and Barn Island, Stonington, off U.S. 1 at Wequetequock.

CONNECTICUT FISHING REGULATIONS

Resident Fishing License $4.35
Resident 3-Day Fishing License $1.35
Nonresident Fishing License $4.35
Nonresident 3-Day Fishing License $1.85

SEASONS AND LIMITS

Species	Closed Season	Size Limit	Bag Limit
Black Bass	None	None	None
Northern Pike	None	20″	6 daily
Chain Pickerel	None	None	None
Panfish	None	None	None
Striped Bass	None	16″	None

Trout and shad are subject to certain restrictions annually and according to the waters in which they are taken. Anglers should check carefully in regulations for the season in which they are fishing.

For complete regulations write: State Board of Fish and Game, State Office Building, Hartford 15, Connecticut.

NEW YORK

In the State of New York are found all the salient features of the eastern seaboard of the United States. The Appalachian chain of mountains extends its rugged terrain up through central New York in the form of the Catskills and Adirondacks. The Atlantic Ocean touches a small part of the mainland in the south and encompasses huge Long Island. On the north are two of the Great Lakes, Erie and Ontario, and a goodly length of the St. Lawrence River. Hence the state is ideally situated to have something of everything as far as fishing is concerned. The fresh waters hold smallmouth black bass, largemouth black bass, northern pike, walleyes, chain pickerel, brown trout, brook trout, rainbow trout, lake trout, landlocked salmon, muskellunge, Great Lakes whitefish, bullhead and panfish. In New York State the landlocked salmon referred to includes both a Pacific and an Atlantic salmon. The Pacific is also called red salmon, sockeye, blueback, or "little red fish," and is taken in only a very few lakes. The majority of landlocked salmon taken will be the landlocked descendent of the Atlantic salmon.

In the salt, New York anglers find giant tuna, school tuna, white marlin, blue marlin, kingfish, broadbill swordfish, many varieties of sharks, bluefish, striped bass, and the lesser varieties such as snapper blues, flounders, fluke, porgy, blackfish, sea bass, weakfish, ling, whiting, hake, cod and pollack.

The major rivers are the Hudson, Mohawk, Genessee and Alleghany. The Hudson has its source in Lake Champlain on the Vermont border in the north, and flows the full length of New York state to the ocean. Its tributary, the Mohawk, with its barge canal, flows through the central part of the state from Lake Oneida near Lake Erie, to the Hudson at Albany. The Genessee flows north throughout the western part of New York to Lake Erie at Rochester, and the Alleghany curves up into the southwestern part of the state near Olean, closely followed by State Highway 17. Though not as large, other rivers which are significant in the drainage pattern of New York State are the Delaware and Susquehanna, which find their headwaters in the southeast, near Malton and Margaretville, and flow south into Pennsylvania; and the Chemung, in south-central New York, near Corning, on U.S. 15.

Lake Champlain is the largest lake, lying on the northeast border with Vermont. In the headwaters of the Mohawk is Lake Oneida, another large inland lake, while to the south and west of it lie the Finger Lakes: Seneca, Cayuga, Onandaga, Canandaigua, Skaneateles, Owasco and several smaller ones. Far to the west, close to Lake Erie at the Pennsylvania border, is Lake Chautauqua. While these are the lakes that show large on a map, there are hundreds of others of fine size for fishermen, many of them joined in almost river formation, for easy traveling by boat from one to the other. Anglers planning to fish via canoe trip or other boat transportation should obtain a pamphlet, "Your Outdoor Recreation Map" from the State Department of Conservation, Albany, New York. It gives a composite picture of the water routes throughout the state along with much pertinent information regarding camp sites and services en route. Also ask for the information leaflet on canoe trips.

The whole state is more than adequately serviced by fine highways. Interstate 87 and U.S. 9 and U.S. 4 bracket the Hudson from one end to the other. The New York State Thruway traverses the area from the Hudson at Albany, westward across the south of Lake Ontario to Buffalo, then follows the shores of Lake Erie to the western border. Interstate 81 joins the Thruway at Syracuse with Binghamton on the southern border. Further west, north-south travel is via U.S. 15 to Rochester, and U.S. 62 from Jamestown to the Niagara area. Between these major arteries is a vast network of excellent routes to all parts of the state.

New York State enjoys a typical temperate-zone climate, warm in summer but generally with cool evenings, and anglers who fish spring and fall will need woolens. Rain gear is always necessary for summer showers as well as for the seasonal spring and fall rains. Those who plan to fish the bigger rivers will need chest-high waders, but hip boots will do for most smaller streams.

While much of New York State is urban, the angler who fishes the mountainous areas may encounter deer or bear and small game. The state is within the range of both the copperhead and the rattlesnake.

In general, the fishing season opens as soon as ice-out; but in many waters other than trout waters, fishing may go on through the ice all winter.

Tackle varies widely because of the diversity of fishing. Most lake anglers use spinning gear nowadays, while the majority of stream fishermen in New York favor an 8-foot fly rod, HDH line, and a leader tapered down to a 4X tippet.

All the standard flies are fish takers, but local hatches should always be checked for special flies of the various rivers. A good basic list to start with should include such dries as the Adams, Black Flying Ant, Light Cahill, Royal Coachman, Iron Blue Dun, Mosquito, McGinty, Pink Lady, Gray Midge Hackle, Red Variant, Black Gnat, Gray Wulff, spentwing Blue Dun and Quill Gordon, in sizes 12, 14, 16, 18 and 20. Wet fly patterns which are good producers are Gray Hackle, Yellow Body, Coachman, Royal Coachman, Black Gnat, Woolly Bear, McGinty, Cowdung, Alexandria and Ginger Quill, in sizes 8, 12 and 14. Basic nymphs should include the Alder, Black and Orange, Black and Yellow, Caddis, March Brown, Brown Drake, Ginger Quill and Tellico, in sizes 6 to 12; and in hook sizes 10 to 16, on long-shanked hooks, the Yellow May, Tan May, Black May, Olive May, Brown May and Gray May. Ants and beetles in sizes 8 to 16 are also good. The smaller streamers and bucktails, sparsely tied, are generally better than bulkier flies in New York waters. Patterns should include the Black Ghost, Gray Ghost, York's Kennebago, Lady Ghost, Blacknosed Dace, Mickey Finn, Red and White, Black and White, Black Prince, Prince Charlie and Brown and Yellow.

In the salt the gear again is multiple, from bottom-fishing rigs for inshore to specialized trolling gear for tuna and marlin, and surf-casting outfits for stripers.

FINGER LAKES DISTRICT

In western New York anglers find their best fishing in the Finger Lakes District, where six large lakes fan out in finger form, running southward from just below the New York State Thruway. All hold bass, lake trout, rainbow trout and northern pike. The largest, LAKE CAYUGA (1), is forty miles long. State Highway 90 follows the eastern shore, and State Highway 98 provides ready access to the west. The deepest water, where the majority of the lake trout are taken in summer, is around Varick on the western shore, and King Ferry on the eastern shore. Smallmouth anglers do best at the north end of the lake, in the Barge Canal and around Union Springs on the northeast. This marshy end of the lake is also best for largemouth and northern pike.

LAKE SENECA (2) is almost thirty-eight miles long, produces many thousand lake trout each year as well as some fair rainbow fishing. This is the deepest lake east of the Rockies and seldom freezes in winter. Several spots have earned special reputations among lake-trout fishermen: these are along State Highway 96A on the eastern shore and further south on State Highway 414; but the north shore on the west side can be good, too. The best season for lake trout is from April through June, and again in September. The top fishing for rainbows is at the south end, where Catherine's Creek enters the lake. Watkins Glen entertains dozens of anglers in the spring when the trout season opens. Some fish to 20 pounds are taken here. There is also good fall fishing for smallmouth in Lake Seneca.

Several smaller lakes in the group have earned reputations for special fishing. SKANEATELES (3) is known for big lake trout and rainbows. A 21-pound rainbow was taken in LAKE KEUKA (5) in 1946. But in general the fishing is about the same in all. OWASCO (4), KEUKA (5), CANANDAIGUA (6), CANADICE and HEMLOCK (7) all hold lake trout. All except Canadice also have rainbows. Warm-water fish are found in some of the smaller surrounding lakes such as CONESUS (8), HONEOYE (9), SILVER (10), WANETA and LAMOKA (11), and CAYUTA (12).

The only guide in the Finger Lakes District is Roy Japp at Clark's Point, Geneva, New York. He guides on Lake Seneca. But information about where to fish is available at the dozens of boat docks found throughout the Finger Lakes.

In early spring there is some fairly good stream fishing, mostly for stocked rainbows in the brooks around the lakes. CATHERINE CREEK (13), near Pine Valley on State Highway 14, north of Elmira, has produced some excellent fish in spite of tremendously heavy pressure. GROUT BROOK (14), running into Lake Skaneateles north of Cortland, produces smaller fish but is a fairly good stream consistently, and its condition is maintained by the local landowners. NAPLES CREEK (15) flowing to Lake Canandaigua, and COLD BROOK (16) flowing to Keuka are also good at times.

Not one of the Finger Lake group, but close by, is huge ONEIDA LAKE (17), north of the New York State Thruway and accessible from it via State Highway 81, north from Syracuse; from Bridgeport on State Highway 31; or from State Highway 49, which runs along its northern shores. There are walleyes, yellow perch, smallmouth black bass and northern pike in the lake. Boat docks and all services are plentiful.

Another large lake lies to the southwest of the Finger Lakes. This is LAKE CHAUTAUQUA (18), known as the home of the muskellunge in New York State. There are also bass and panfish, these latter being taken on plugs and live bait, while the muskies are mostly taken trolling big plugs or spoons, though some fly rodders also take their share. Guides are available at Bemus Point, which almost divides the lake in half, on the north shore. Lake Chautauqua is reached via State Highway 17, south from the New York State Thruway at Westfield; or from U.S. 20 at Westfield, or U.S. 62 from Jamestown at the southeast end of the lake. The upper half of the lake is much deeper and clearer than the lower half, and this is where the smallmouth (some to 5 and 6 pounds) hang out, while the largemouth like the lower end, where the water is inclined to be murky. There are lots of docks and cabins around the lake and accommodations of all kinds at Jamestown, Mayville, Bemus Point and Lakewood. There are two public boat-launching sites, one at Bemus Point and another at the Prendergast Point Fish Hatchery. Nearby BEAR LAKE (19), north of Stockton on State Highway 424; and CASSADAGA LAKE (20) on Highway 60, and FINDLEY LAKE (21) to the southwest on Highway 426, as well as CONEWANGO CREEK (22), also have some fishing for muskies.

A few small streams in the general area, such as Cattaraugus, Clear, Ischua, Little Conewango, Mansfield Creeks, and Fenton Brook and Quaker Run also provide a minimum of trout fishing. At CUBA LAKE (23) on State Highway 408 you'll find boats available to fish for walleyes, largemouth black bass, some smallmouth, yellow perch and panfish. RUSHFORD LAKE (24), almost directly north on State Highway 243, has smallmouth, rainbows, a few lake trout and panfish.

There are boat rental docks at almost every community along the south shore of Lake Erie in New York State, and plentiful accommodations of all kinds, on State Highway 5, which follows the shore. Fishing is good for smallmouth black bass all summer, with the peak seasons coming in May and June, September and October.

Several small creeks, including Cassadaga, Cherry, Goose, Mill, Chautauqua and Clear, are stocked with trout each year. Directions as to how to reach the fishable portions must be obtained locally.

Also in northwestern New York State, the GENESEE RIVER (25), a fairly good smallmouth stream, may be reached from U.S. 15 in its lower portion near Lake Ontario (at Rochester); and Highways 5 and 63 cross it further south. OATKA CREEK (26), to the west, running along State Highway 19, is also fishable, while the COHOCTON (27) and CANASERAGA (28) can be reached from U.S. 15 higher up. In the Genesee above Wellsville at State Highway 17 and 19, some trout are found both in the river and the smaller tributaries.

LAKE ONTARIO AREA

LAKE ONTARIO (29) bass fishing can be very productive at times within ten minutes of many onshore ports at the east end of the lake, and around the entrance to the St. Lawrence River. Out of Sacketts Harbor, Pillar Point or Dexter, on State Highway 3; and Chaumont, Three Mile Bay and Cape Vincent, on State Highway 12E, you can fish many shoals and around the islands of Galloo, Charity, Stony, Calf, Grenadier, Fox and California, on the U.S. side, and Wolfe, Ducks, Main, Amherst and Timber on the Canadian side. Guides are available at Hendersonville Harbor near Cape Vincent. In the river, boats, guides and accommodations will be found around Alexandria Bay, at the junction of State Highways 12 and 6.

Nearly all the ponds and lakes bordering on Lake Ontario, both east and west of Rochester, have fishing for pike, walleyes, bass and panfish.

Fishing in the ST. LAWRENCE (30) River is for smallmouth black bass, muskellunge, northern pike, walleyes, perch and panfish. Bass are taken on minnows, softshell crabs, small spinners and streamer flies, according to your choice. Muskies like the large spoons and plugs and it usually calls for deep trolling to take this species. Pike will hit spoons, spinners and plugs, and so will walleyes, if they are fished deep enough. Many walleyes are taken on bait.

Guides in the Cape Vincent area are: Charles Henchen, Henderson Harbor,

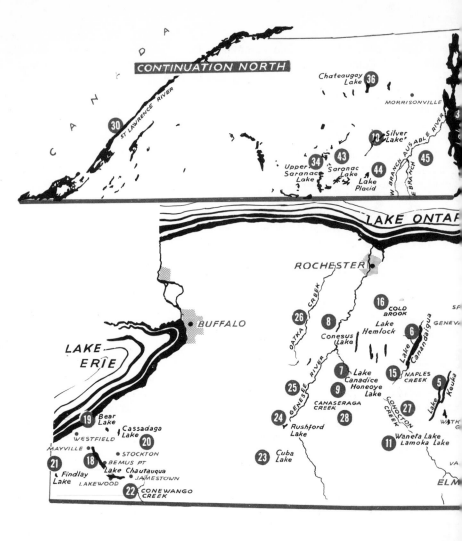

CONTINUATION NORTH

CANADA

Chateaugay Lake **36**

MORRISONVILLE

ST. LAWRENCE RIVER

30

Silver Lake **13**

W. BRANCH AUSABLE RIVER

E. BRANCH

45

Upper Saranac Lake **34**

Saranac Lake **43**

44 Lake Placid

LAKE ONTARIO

ROCHESTER

16 COLD BROOK

OATKA CREEK

26

8 Conesus Lake

Lake Hemlock

6 Canandaigua

GENEVA

SP

LAKE ERIE

BUFFALO

7 Lake Canadice Honeoye Lake

15 NAPLES CREEK

5 Keuka

WATK G

25

GENESEE RIVER

9 CANASERAGA CREEK

COHOCTON CREEK

27

19 Bear Lake

Cassadaga Lake

20

WESTFIELD

STOCKTON

24 Rushford Lake

28

11 Waneta Lake Lamoka Lake

VA.

MAYVILLE

18 BEMUS PT

Lake Chautauqua

21 Findlay Lake

LAKEWOOD

JAMESTOWN

23 Cuba Lake

ELM

22 CONEWANGO CREEK

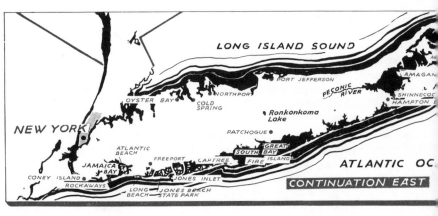

LONG ISLAND SOUND

PORT JEFFERSON

AMAGAN

PECONIC RIVER

SHINNECO HAMPTON

OYSTER BAY

NORTHPORT

COLD SPRING

Ronkonkoma Lake

NEW YORK

PATCHOGUE

ATLANTIC BEACH

FREEPORT

CAPTREE

GREAT SOUTH BAY

FIRE ISLAND

ATLANTIC OC

JAMAICA BAY

CONEY ISLAND

ROCKAWAYS

JONES INLET

LONG BEACH

JONES BEACH STATE PARK

CONTINUATION EAST

NEW YORK

N

0 5 10   20   30   40
SCALE IN MILES

New York; Joe Mezzatesta, Box 335, Cape Vincent, New York; or can be booked through Cape Vincent's Carlton Hotel. At Ogdensburg, Leonard Hartman guides for muskellunge in the St. Lawrence.

Anglers planning to operate their own boats on major New York lakes and in Lake Ontario and the St. Lawrence Seaway, should obtain the necessary charts at $1 each from the United States Lake Survey, 630 Federal Building, Detroit 26, Michigan, For adjacent Canadian waters write Canadian Hydrographic Service, Survey & Mapping Branch, Ottawa, Canada.

NORTHEASTERN AREA

LAKE CHAMPLAIN (31), the largest lake in northeastern New York, is so big that the casual angler would have little chance of locating the walleye, one of the favorite catches, without some help. Charts showing the reefs and shallows and deep parts can be obtained from the U.S. Lake Survey, Corps of Engineers, U.S. Army, 630 Federal Building, Detroit 26, Michigan. The charge is $1 per chart. The best spots in general are around the mouths of the rivers such as the Chazy near Cooperville on State Highway 9B, and at South Bay. As well as the over-all population of walleye, smallmouth, largemouth and northern pike, there are sauger in the southern part of the lake.

In LAKE GEORGE (32), to the south of Lake Champlain, and in some lakes to the northwest, anglers will find landlocked Atlantic salmon. Some of these are SCHROON LAKE (33), on U.S. 9; UPPER SARANAC LAKE (34) on State Highway 30; CRANBERRY LAKE (35), west, on Highway 3; and CHATEAUGAY and LONG POND (36) on State Highway 374, off U.S. 11 at Chateaugay, or north from State Highway 3 at Morrisonville. Some few have been taken in BLUE MOUNTAIN LAKE (37), well to the south, where State Highways 28 and 30 come together.

The HUDSON RIVER (38), running from Lake Champlain and Lake George southward, has populations of white perch, yellow perch, channel catfish, bullheads and a few sturgeon. Perhaps its most interesting possibility, however, is the striped bass which run in from the Atlantic and have been taken as far north as Albany. If the river could be cleared of pollution, a great sport fishery might develop. Anglers should remember that above tidewater they must have a license to fish in the Hudson. In the lower river the stripers are taken on spoons and plugs as well as bait, and the top time is June and July. Haverstraw, at the junction of U.S. 202 and U.S. 9W, is a good center from which to work. While the complete story on these stripers is not known, it is believed that a great many of them winter in this area and occasional catches are made throughout the year.

ADIRONDACK AREA

Such primitive area as remains in New York lies in the Adirondacks, immediately west of Lake Champlain and Lake George. Since the lakes and streams and the mountainous countryside are very popular, even there it is possible to reach all but the most remote spots. Several major highways traverse the Adirondacks, all more or less focusing on Saranac Lake and Lake Placid, in the most highly developed recreational center of the northern part of the Adirondack Park. State Highways 12 and 28 run from Utica to Old Forge and then along the FULTON CHAIN OF LAKES (39) to Eagle Bay Inlet, Sixth, Seventh and Eighth Lakes,

RAQUETTE LAKE (40) and BLUE MOUNTAIN LAKE (41). State Highway 30 leads from southern and eastern points to Blue Mountain Lake, LONG LAKE (42), TUPPER LAKE (43), SARANAC LAKE (43), Paul Smiths, and continues on north to Malone. Railway entry is possible through the Adirondack Division of the New York Central Railway to Saranac and LAKE PLACID (44), with stops at many intermediate points. Both these latter lakes offer some fishing for lake trout and rainbows; and just to the north and east of Lake Placid is the WEST BRANCH OF THE AUSABLE RIVER (45) with its famous Gorge, probably New York's best-known trout stream. The EAST BRANCH OF THE AUSABLE may be reached from U.S. 9N further east.

To reach the more remote areas not served by roads, the angler must turn to the canoe. There are many fine canoe routes in the Adirondacks, with fairly good fishing along the way. Canoes are available at Old Forge, Raquette Lake, Blue Mountain Lake, Long Lake, Saranac Lake and Tupper Lake. Those who bring their own powered craft will find a list of places where they may put into the water on public property in the pamphlet "New York State Boat Launching Sites," published by the Conservation Department, Albany 1, New York. Another publication available at the same source is "Adirondack Canoe Routes," with completely detailed routes, camp sites and suggested itineraries. While they do not necessarily all cover good fishing waters, they are a key to access. A good trip for the canoeist fisherman is the Raquette River trip, starting near the town of Raquette Lake, west of Blue Mountain Lake, on State Highway 28. Those who seek out the ponds a bit off the main course of the route will find some fishing for eastern brook trout. Neighboring Long Lake is good smallmouth water, as is Upper Saranac, and in fact, most of the others along this almost 100 miles of canoe water.

CATSKILL MOUNTAIN AREA

Somewhat similar in terrain is the area of the Catskill Mountains, further south. State Highway 28 leads into this mountainous area from Interstate 87 at Kingston, and several secondary roads provide routes to the interior, both north and south. Comparatively speaking, this is a small area, yet it contains more famous trout rivers than any other region in the east. They include the BEAVERKILL (46), NEVERSINK (47), WILLOWEMOC (48), ESOPUS (49), the top reaches of the EAST BRANCH OF THE DELAWARE (50) and the WEST BRANCH (51) of the same river, where some large brown and rainbow trout are taken each year. All of these streams are capable of giving up some very good-sized trout and many of their tributaries also have good fishing. You will find a lot of waters which are posted, privately owned or reserved for private clubs. Some of the private land can be fished if you request permission. These eastern waters suffer from crowding, and it speaks well for them that they can still give up a basket of trout.

The Beaverkill, Neversink and Willowemoc can be reached from State Highway 17. Anglers fishing the Willowemoc and the Beaverkill can stay at Livingston Manor and Roscoe. South Fallsburg and Woodbourne provide accommodations near the Neversink.

The Esopus runs along State Highway 28 from Boiceville to Shandaken. Accommodations can be found along this route or on nearby Route 212. Rainbow Lodge, on Route 212 at Mt. Tremper, caters especially to fishermen, and owner Dick Kahil can direct you to the best fishing spots in the area.

The East Branch of the Delaware can be reached from State Highway 30, the

West Branch from State Highway 10. Accommodations are available along these routes. Directions should be obtained locally at any of the communities on State Highway 30 as to where to fish the numerous small streams such as Stoney Clove, Batavia Kill, East Kill, Woodland Valley Creek, Catskill River and Fleishmanns Creek.

Trout, bass and pike perch will be found in the ASHOKAN RESERVOIR (52) off State Highway 28; and bass and pike perch in the SCHOHARIE RESERVOIR (53) near the junction of State Highways 23 and 30, north of Ashokan. Smallmouth black bass and some pickerel are also taken in parts of most of the rivers mentioned. Many ponds, which you often have to seek out on your own, also have populations of brook trout.

The WALLKILL RIVER (54), west from Newburgh on the lower Hudson, and reached via State Highway 52, offers fishing for both largemouth and smallmouth black bass. Most of the fish are caught on hellgrammites taken from the stream. Local anglers always carry a small pair of scissors to clip off the claws or the hellgrammite will grab onto the bottom and tear the hook out. The best months for this fishing are July and August.

West again, the top reaches of the SUSQUEHANNA RIVER (55) are available via State Highway 7 from Oneonta southward. There are pike perch, bass and panfish, according to area, and fishing is usually good from June through September.

Those wishing to get guide service in this lower Hudson area should contact Don Mitchell, Station WGHY, Orange County Post Office, Cornwall-On-Hudson, New York 12520. He is a registered guide and if not available himself can advise you where to fish.

From the Conservation Department, State of New York, Albany 1, New York, anglers may obtain a brochure entitled "1001 Top New York Fishing Waters." In addition, the same brochure boils the lakes and streams down to the "50 fishiest"; and adds a "Hiker's Special" list of 300 remote Adirondack trout ponds which are stocked by airplane. To follow the routes it is necessary to obtain an index of United States Geological Survey Quadrangle Maps from the U.S. Geological Survey, Department of the Interior, Washington 25, D.C., and select the required maps from this list and purchase them at 30 cents apiece. For those who require a guide, a very complete list is also available, giving the names and addresses of more than 300 registered guides in the Catskills and the Adirondacks, and indicating the region in which the guide operates.

SALTWATER FISHING

New York's saltwater fishing is basically Long Island fishing. The island is reached by bridge from New York at several points at the east end and also by ferry from near Bayonne, New Jersey; from Bridgeport, Connecticut, to Port Jefferson about half way along the north coast; and from New London, Connecticut, to Orient Point, at the northeast tip. Excellent highways run the length of the island, extending out to the easternmost tip, to Orient Point on the north and Montauk on the south.

Charter boats and skiffs for rent are found at dozens of seaside towns and resorts, especially on the south shore where Coney Island and Fire Island protect miles of good fishing in inshore waters for small boats. Charter boats berth at Coney Island, the Rockaways, Freeport, Jones Inlet, Fire Island, Patchogue, Hampton

Bays, Amagansett and Montauk. Fishermen in Long Island Sound work out of Oyster Bay, Cold Spring Harbor, Northport, Port Jefferson and a few small communities from there out the north shore to Orient Point.

The species taken in the salt around and off Long Island include white marlin, mako shark, striped bass, sea bass, bonito, weakfish, mackerel, tautog, bluefish, pollack, porgy, summer and winter flounder and cod. The marlin are taken from early summer to late fall and range in size from 50 to more than 100 pounds. Mackerel is the favorite bait for this offshore trolling. Offshore anglers also take giant tuna and school tuna, and occasionally swordfish, as well as many species of sharks, including the vicious mako. Shark fishing is especially popular off Montauk. Captain Frank Mundus, aboard the Cricket II, specializes in this kind of fishing. The season for the big makos is from August to October. Catches range up to 300 pounds and over.

Montauk also rates as one of the top striper fishing spots on the east coast of the United States. Many fish are taken in the 40-pound class, some up to 50 pounds, surf casting or trolling the rocky shore reefs. The fish move in in early spring and are taken all summer, with the peak fishing from September into November, as the fish move south again for the winter. At Montauk anglers will find charter boats especially built and equipped to fish close to the surf with its hidden rocks.

In Long Island Sound the best spots to go out from are Manhasset Bay, Glen Cove, Mamaroneck, Little Neck Bay and Flushing, and there's a chance of taking a big one as well as plenty of medium-sized fish any time from May to November. Sometimes the small fish come in even earlier.

There are many charter boats berthed at Montauk and fishing ranges from the inshore striper fishing already described, to trolling offshore for tuna, swordfish and the odd marlin. Mako sharks appear in great schools during the summer months. At Block Island, to the east, you can also surf fish from the rocks. At Orient Point, to the north of Montauk, surf fishermen work the Sound and Gardiner's Bay back of the point without changing position. Inland from this, in Southold Bay, behind Shelter Island, there is good small-boat fishing for weakfish, flounders, porgies, kingfish, blackfish, snapper blues, sometimes striped bass and sea bass, according to season. Pedonic Bay, still deeper in, has flounders, weakfish, blackfish and porgies.

The south shore of Long Island is the surf caster's haven, with many fine beaches where spinning and surf casting are done from May through November. From west to east, Atlantic Beach, Long Beach and Fire Island Inlet, Great South Bay, Shinnecock Inlet and Montauk are the centers where services will be found for all types of fishing. At the extreme western end of the island, in Jamaica Bay and the Rockaways, there is often fine April fishing for school fish, which can be taken along the inlets and from the bridges.

Bluefish move into Long Island waters from the south in late spring and early summer. Trollers take them offshore, casters take them inshore in the bays and inlets, and surf casters get their share along the beaches. They run as high as 20 pounds. Mackerel are taken by trolling and drifting and sometimes by bottom fishermen, too, from early spring to early summer. The tautog also comes into shallow water in the spring, and is taken by bottom fishermen working the wrecks or rocky shallows. The same areas are good for porgies and sea bass from spring to late fall. And the pollack, which can be taken bottom fishing year-round, often works into the surf in the spring to be caught there on all kinds of bait and lures.

The best area for weakfish is in Peconic Bay and Great South Bay, when anglers, usually working from rowboats, chum with live shrimp, then take the weakfish on trolled lures or feathered jigs. The average is about 3 pounds but they have been taken up to 10 pounds.

All the inshore waters have summer and winter flounder fishing. The summer flounder grows to 3 to 5 pounds, and a 20-pounder has been taken. Winter flounder are smaller, weighing only about a pound, but fill the season from February to warm weather and provide some fine eating. Cod are also taken by bottom fishermen in the winter, mostly on skimmer clam bait, used off the reefs and wrecks.

While there are only four fishing piers on Long Island, at Captree and Jones Beach State Park, there are many jetties where fishermen may find good fishing as long as they are careful of their footing. At the west end of the island there are spots where you can fish from the shore right beside the Beltway. Row boats, charter boats and party boats are all available in this area at City Island.

Anglers who like to cast for bluefish will find some suitable water at Great Kills, north of Raritan Bay, on the coast, at Great Kills Park. The area is served by Hylan Boulevard, between Raritan and Interstate Highway 278.

Another spot readily reached from the mainland, and where there is a variety of fishing for smaller species is City Island, at the end of City Island Avenue in the Bronx. There are several piers, boat rental agencies, and many places where you can fish from the shore, for blackfish, flounder, snapper, cod, and a few fluke, butterfish, stripers, porgies and mackerel. The fishing is best from March to November, though a few hardy anglers try their luck there all winter.

Anglers who plan to use their own boats in fishing New York coastal waters should obtain coastal charts, at 75¢ each, from the United States Coast and Geodetic Survey, Washington 25, D.C.

NEW YORK FISHING REGULATIONS

Resident Fishing License $3.25
Nonresident Fishing License $5.50
Nonresident 6-Day License $4.25

SEASONS AND LIMITS

Species	Open Season	Size Limit	Daily Limit
Trout	April 1 to Sept. 30	None	10
Lake Trout and Landlocked Salmon	April 1 to Sept. 30	15″	Lake Trout, 3 Salmon, 2
Black Bass	June 18 to Nov. 30	10″	6
Pikeperch (Walleye)	May 1 to March 1	None	10
Northern Pike	May 1 to March 1	18″	10
Pickerel	May 1 to March 1	12″	10
Muskellunge	June 18 to Nov. 30	28″	None
Bullheads	No closed season	None	None
Whitefish	April 1 to Sept. 30	None	None
Rock Bass, White Bass, Sunfish, Crappie, Yellow Perch, White Perch, Sauger	No closed season	None	None
Striped Bass	No closed season	16″	None

Anglers should consult the annual regulations for exceptions to the above and for regulations governing specially controlled waters.

For complete regulations write: Conservation Department, Division of Fish and Game, Albany 12226, New York.

NEW JERSEY

Sandwiched between Pennsylvania and New York, and itself one of the major industrial states, New Jersey does not look like a promising spot for the angler. However, adequate stocking of rivers and ponds in the interior maintains some degree of freshwater fishing, and the many miles of coastline on the Atlantic provide some excellent saltwater fishing. The freshwater fish include brown, rainbow and brook trout in a few streams and lakes, while the warm-water ponds hold largemouth black bass, pickerel, yellow perch, white perch, sunfish, bluegill, some smallmouth black bass, crappie and channel catfish. In tidewater areas the largemouth and white perch move into the brackish water, as do catfish.

In the salt the Jersey angler will find striped bass, channel bass, bluefish, sea trout or weakfish, flounder, kingfish, occasional croakers, porgies, blackfish, bonito, bluefin tuna, mackerel, white perch, fluke, cod, tautog, dolphin, albacore and snappers, according to the season and method of fishing. White marlin are taken in some numbers offshore; blue marlin occasionally and swordfish very rarely.

The major rivers along the Atlantic coast are the Hudson, which forms the border between New York and New Jersey; the Rahway, south of the city of Elizabeth, the Raritan, entering the Hudson at Perth Amboy; the Navesink at Red Bank; the Manasquan at Point Pleasant; the Mullica just north of Atlantic City; and the Great Egg Harbor, south of the same city. The Delaware River forms the full length of the western boundary and in the northeastern part of the state forms the outlet for some of the better trout streams. In the south its major tributary is the Maurice River, flowing south through central New Jersey to Delaware Bay.

The most important fishing lake is Hopatcong, north of Interstate 80, west of Rockaway. This is the largest of a group of lakes which runs in a southwest to northeast direction in northern New Jersey, just above Interstate 80 and west of U.S. 20, constituting the major lake-fishing area of the state.

All parts of New Jersey are well served by a network of highways fanning out from Interstate 80 on the north and the New Jersey Turnpike in the middle of the state. The Garden State Parkway follows the entire coast and permits access to the beaches all the way from New York to Cape May.

Freshwater anglers in New Jersey will find the summer climate warm enough that heavy clothing is not required, though evenings can be cool along the ocean. For saltwater fishing during the winter season from October through April, when many party boats go for pollack, flounders, codfish, whiting and ling, warm clothing is a necessity.

Though much of the state is heavily populated and industrialized, there are still many areas where deer may be encountered. Dangerous game is nonexistent, but the area is within the range of the rattlesnake and copperheads are common.

NORTHERN NEW JERSEY LAKES AND STREAMS

A glance at the map of New Jersey shows the concentration of lakes mentioned

70

earlier in that area north of Interstate 80 and west of U.S. 202. This is where the New Jersey trout fisherman finds his sport, both in lake and stream; and there are also usually largemouth and smallmouth black bass and eastern chain pickerel. LAKE HOPATCONG (1), near the town of the same name, lies in the angle between Interstate 80 and U.S. 206. It is considered the top fishing lake of the area, with rainbow trout, brown trout and "tiger trout," the latter a cross between a male brook trout and a female brown trout. The fishing in this lake is mostly done by trolling or drifting with live herring, the prevalent food fish in the lake. Walleyes, largemouth black bass, perch and pickerel are also taken, and channel catfish have recently been stocked. The best fishing is from April through June, before the weather becomes too warm. Boats can be obtained at Hopatcong and at Landing, off Interstate 80 at the south end of the lake; and at Woodport, on State Highway 15, which crosses the northern end of the lake.

To the west and north, BIG FLAT BROOK LAKE (2), near State Highway 94, close to the Pennsylvania border, and PAULINS KILL LAKE (3), near the town of Newton on U.S. 206, also hold trout. In these two lakes, while shiners and worms take their share of fish, streamer flies, wet and dry flies are all successful, and a well-fished nymph is deadly.

In the northwest corner of New Jersey several lakes have good reputations for bass fishing. MUSCONETCONG (4), SWARTSWOOD (5), KITTATINNY (6) and CULVERS (7), all lying up close to the Pennsylvania line, are approachable from State Highway 621, which runs between State Highway 94 to the south and U.S. 206 to the north. BUDD LAKE (8), on State Highway 46, southwest of Lake Hopatcong, and CEDAR LAKE (9), near Blairstown, off State Highway 94, are smaller but have good populations of trout, bass and panfish. Another good fishing spot is MOUNTAIN LAKE (10), north from Buttzville on State Highway 69, near the Pennsylvania border. SPRUCE RUN (11), a large new reservoir near the junction of Interstate 78 and State Highway 69, was completed in 1963 and has been stocked with bass, crappie and other suitable gamefish.

Popular both winter and summer is GREENWOOD LAKE (12), astride the New York-New Jersey border, just about the middle of the line. Like Hopatcong, it holds the trouts as well as the warmer-water species. The brown trout grow notoriously large in this lake, some members of the species having been taken up to 8 pounds. In winter there is excellent ice fishing on Greenwood.

The POMPTON LAKES (13), northwest of Paterson, are accessible from State Highways 3, 46 and 23. There are brook trout, brown trout, rainbows and tigers; and at Pompton Dale Acres anglers will find private pay-as-you-fish ponds. This area is only an hour by car from New York.

The bulk of the stream fishing for trout in New Jersey is found in the northwest section. Most of the trout streams also have some other species of fish as well. In the drainage system of the Delaware River along the Pennsylvania border, UPPER and LOWER BIG FLAT BROOK (14) and the MUSCONETCONG RIVER (15) are stocked with trout annually. Big Flat Brook, rising in the Kittatinny Mountains, probably rates as the best trout stream in the state. It can be reached from U.S. 206 near Hainesville and at the villages of Layton, Bevans, Wallpack and Flatbrook. Special regulations apply to the four miles of stream below the concrete bridge on U.S. 206. These are, roughly, when the trout season first opens all methods of fishing are permitted, but a month later this stretch becomes limited to fly fishing only. Anglers should always check the rules when purchasing their fishing license. In the same general area, the PAULINS KILL RIVER (16), flowing out of Paulins Kill Lake and down to the Delaware, can be fished from the towns of Stillwater, Marksboro, Paulina, Blairstown and Columbia, all on State Highway 94.

The DELAWARE (17) itself, in these upper reaches, contains smallmouth bass, walleyes, some pickerel and even a few trout. The bass fishing is best in early July after the fish have spawned. Water Gap is one of the best spots. Anglers will find this part of the Delaware suitable for boats. The fish hit flies, June bug spinners and bait. Below Phillipsburg the Delaware is polluted.

The SOUTH BRANCH OF THE RARITAN RIVER (18), which rises in Budd Lake, is also one of the better trout streams in New Jersey. It can be reached from Morris City on State Highway 46, or from State Highway 24, and then a country road, number 513, near Long Valley. Regulations should be checked before fishing this stream as some parts are annually limited to fly fishing only.

There is also some stocking of trout in northeastern New Jersey, but in many cases this fishing is limited to very early spring as the fish do not hold over in the heat. One of the better rivers is the RAHWAY (19), entering the Raritan above Perth Amboy. Other than those mentioned, streams which are heavily stocked with adult fish, mostly brown trout, are the WANAQUE (20), near Pompton Lakes, on State Highway 511, north of Paterson; the PASSAIC (21), immediately east of Paterson; the WALLKILL (22), between Sparta, on State Highway 15, and Hamburg on State Highway 23; the PEQUEST (23), which can be fished from U.S. 46 near the western border of Pennsylvania, as well as further north, where feeder roads lead in from State Highway 517; POHATCONG RIVER (24), further south, entering the Delaware at Carpentersville, south of Phillipsburg; the PEQUANNOCK (25), near Bloomingdale, just off State Highway 23; the HACKENSACK (26), near Harrington Park, just west of the Palisades Interstate Parkway, near the New York border; the RAMAPO (27), near Mahwah, already mentioned; and the SADDLE RIVER (28) near Upper Saddle River east of State Highway 17, at the New York border. Further south is the MANASQUAN RIVER (29), near Allendale on State Highway 23.

Anglers who must limit their trout fishing to this northeastern area will find a number of other stocked streams listed in the pamphlet "List of Streams," issued by the Division of Fish and Game, Department of Conservation and Economic Development, Box 1809, Trenton, New Jersey. Most of these streams are subject to special closed-day regulations each week, and the areas in which fish are stocked are limited. This information is contained in the New Jersey Fishing Laws.

SOUTHERN NEW JERSEY

In southern New Jersey the emphasis is very much on the coastal fishing along the Atlantic, but there are some possibilities for freshwater anglers, too. Many of the potholes among the cranberry marshes hold pickerel, and there are some good-sized largemouth black bass in these and in all the ponds throughout the low-lying areas. There are also bluegills and white perch in some of the lakes.

There's a concentration of small lakes offering largemouth black-bass fishing just southeast of Camden. These are BLACKWOOD LAKE (30) at Blackwood on State Highway 42; CLEMENTON, PILLINGS and ROWLAND PONDS (31) at Clementon on U.S. 30; COOPER PARK LAKE (32) at Cooper Park, and GRENLOCH LAKE (33) at Grenloch, on State Highway 42. SQUARE CIRCLE LAKE (34), near Gibbsboro off U.S. 30, is stocked with all three trouts, and MUNN'S LAKE (35) at Haddonfield

has both rainbows and browns. HAMMONTON LAKE (36), at Hammonton on U.S. 30, has brown trout and largemouth black bass.

In the same general area several streams receive stockings of trout. They include BIG LEBANON RUN (37) near Turnersville; ELLISBURG CREEK (38) near Ellisburg; MANANTICO STREAM (39) near Millville at the junction of State Highways 47 and 49, and MANAWAY STREAM (40) near Newfield, off U.S. 40.

With few exceptions the lakes across southern New Jersey contain largemouth black bass to some degree. UNION LAKE, (41), off State Highway 47 at Millville, which is south of Vineland, on the Maurice River, is the largest of these. There are smaller lakes at Alloway on State Highway 581, four miles east of Salem, which is on State Highway 49; nearby Aldine, further east on State Highway 581; and Elmer, on U.S. 40, still further east. In the extreme southern part of New Jersey, at the head of Cape May Peninsula, there are similar lakes at Eldora and Dennisville on State Highway 47, and at Belleplain, to the north.

Some very good largemouth fishing can be enjoyed in the NAVESINK RIVER (42) near Red Bank; the MANNASQUAN (29), which enters the ocean at Point Pleasant; the TOM'S RIVER (43) and its tributaries, southwest of Lakewood; the MULLICA AND WADING RIVERS (44) north of Atlantic City; and following on south, in the GREAT EGG HARBOR RIVER (45) and the TUCKAHOE RIVER (46). In all these streams the fishing is scattered, and though some fish are found throughout the length, well up into the state, top spots will only be located by inquiring at local docks or sporting goods stores.

The Mullica and Wading Rivers are considered two of the best for pickerel, also. A canoe, small skiff or car top boat will help in reaching the fishing in remote spots of these rivers. You will need a weedless lure in these slow-moving streams.

Largemouth black bass are also found west of Cape May in rivers flowing into Delaware Bay, notably the MAURICE RIVER (47) below Millville, at the junction of State Highways 47 and 49; the COHANSEY CREEK (48) near Bridgeton, eleven miles northwest of Millville on State Highway 49; OLDMANS CREEK (49) above Harrisonville, west of State Highway 77; and SALEM CREEK (50) above Salem, on State Highway 49.

TIDEWATER FISHING

Largemouth black bass work into the brackish water at the mouths of many of New Jersey's rivers, and there they provide some fine sport. Sharing the tidewater with them in many cases are striped bass, sea trout and bluefish. In many river mouths, as well as alongshore, these species can be taken by casting from the banks, with fly or spinning tackle, or a bait-casting outfit. One of the better spots is the mainland in Barnegat Bay, but most of the islands from there south and, in fact, any shoreline in the state will produce fishing of this kind at some time or other. The Mullica Inlet, Atlantic City and Cape May sections of the coast are all good.

Anglers going in for this kind of fishing must wear hip boots to get through the boggy spots and across narrow coves and inlets. They should also carry insect repellent because the mosquitoes in New Jersey marshes are renowned for their size and ferocity.

Striped bass and weakfish hit best along the banks at evening. Although they can be taken at any time, they usually work the banks on the flood tide.

A saltwater fly-fishing outfit is ideal for this sport. The gear should consist of a 9½-foot fly rod, GAF line, and leader tapered down to 10-pound-test tippet. With this you can throw the big, 5-inch-long bugs and streamers that bring the hits. Best color combinations in the flies are red and white, red and yellow, all white, and the platinum, honey and Argentine blonde bucktails, all on 1/0 and 3/0 hooks. Bait casters like a 5- to 5½-foot casting rod with 200 yards of 15-pound-test line, and the Upperman bucktails, made in Atlantic City, are unbeatable. Spin casters use the Phillips Old Joe and Big Boy for surface fishing for these fish, and the Upperman bucktails when they want to fish deeper.

In all, there are more than 100 rivers along the Jersey coast where there is some form of tidewater angling. In many of these a freshwater license is required above a certain point on the river. A list of streams thus affected, and the point above which you must be licensed, is included in the annual New Jersey Fishing Laws, obtainable from the Division of Fish and Game, Department of Conservation and Economic Development, Box 1809, Trenton, New Jersey.

SALTWATER FISHING

A seasonal timetable for saltwater fishing along the New Jersey coast would show January producing mostly bottom fish. In February there are cod, winter flounder and white perch, and in the rivers some striped bass are taken. The stripers and cod hold over into March, and tautog and pollack are added, plus "snowshoe flounder." In April the striped bass reach considerable numbers in schools on the south coast. Sea bass and porgies show, and there are also pollack, cod and flounder. May is top month for tautog; striped bass keep increasing in numbers, and weakfish and mackerel appear. This month usually also brings the first fluke and bluefish, and some kingfish appear in the surf. By the time June rolls around the striped bass are in great numbers, as are the bluefish. Weakfish and fluke are plentiful and there are good supplies of sea bass, kingfish, tautog, flounder, and, in the south, black drum. School tuna also appear.

The striper fishing reaches a peak in late June or early July, then settles down somewhat through the hot summer weather. Bluefish, weakfish and tuna fishing improve and fluke fishing is at its best. White marlin, blue marlin and some swordfish appear offshore. Fishing for both giant tuna and school tuna is excellent in August and other species continue good. September sees an upswing in the tuna fishing, which reaches its top for the season about the middle of the month. Towards the end of September bluefishing is about as good as you'll find it all year. Offshore anglers take white marlin, blue marlin, swordfish, bonito, kingfish, dolphin, albacore; and inshore fishing is for sea bass, porgies, weakfish and fluke. In October comes the best fishing of the fall season for both striped bass and bluefish. Bottom fishing is very productive for tautog, sea bass and porgies. In the last days of the month pollack and cod appear. November produces good fishing for striped bass, pollack, flounder and tautog and, of course, cod. With December the angler is back to cold-weather bottom fishing.

While all the mentioned species are "big" in New Jersey, the striped bass and bluefish are so popular that some charter boat captains specialize in fishing for these two. One of the top charter boat captains in this group is Captain Otto Reut, 18 Central Avenue, Highlands, New Jersey, who fishes the Sandy Hook area. He furnishes tackle but will also welcome you with your own light gear, which, as many fishermen find, is not always the case with charter boat captains. His rates vary with the fishing. The figures given below are for four people on the striped bass fishing, five people on the other fishing:

Striped bass, spinning tackle & bait. A.M. or P.M., April to Nov. 30—$60 to $75

Striped bass, trolling. A.M. or P.M., May 15 to Nov. 15—$60 to $75

Bluefish chumming. A.M. or P.M., July 10 to October 1—$95

Bluefish trolling. A.M. July 1 to Sept. 25—$75

Fluke fishing. June 1 to August 20—$65

Cod fishing. Nov. 1 to Nov. 30—$65

Mackerel fishing. May 1 to May 30—Oct. 15 to Nov. 30—$65

Charter boats usually fish for bluefish either by trolling or chumming with menhaden (called mossbunkers in New Jersey), from a drifting or anchored boat. Bait is usually menhaden backs or slices of butterfish. The artificials which take blues are feathers, spoons, eelskins and squid. For both stripers and blues, the boats troll up and down along the rocks of inlets, or just out from the surf, or further out when breaking schools are spotted. Both stripers and bluefish, especially the latter, are great travellers, and a guide who knows the water and their habits is essential, unless you are loaded with luck. Those who do plan to use their own boats should remember that navigating can be difficult and dangerous in the inlets and along the jetties.

Almost every port along the New Jersey coast has a marina with a least one or two charter boats available. Those which have good-sized fleets include, from north to south, Hoboken, Atlantic Beach, Atlantic Highland, Seabright, Monmouth Beach, Long Branch, Neptune, Brielle, Point Pleasant, Long Island Beach, reached via State Highway 72 from U.S. 9 at Manahawkin, Island Beach, reached via State Highway 37 at Tom's Harbor on U.S. 9, Barnegat Light, Atlantic City, Ocean City, Avalon, Stone Harbor and Wildwood. Captain Lou Casper, 1130 St. George Ave., West Linden, charters out of Raritan Bay for any kind of fishing. Vince Renzo, Highland Marina, Highland, New Jersey, fishes striper and marlin. Out of Brielle, Marina Captain Sherm Baldwin, captaining the *Albatross,* and Mort Clark, on the *Helen K,* also go for tuna. Another tuna boat, the *Mr. Lucky,* captained by Norm Lakin, operates out of Harbor Inn Basin in the same area. Tuna boats get about $110 per day for a party of six, which figures out to only $18 per person. Some of the boats will fish eight lines at once. In August the big bluefins work in close to the beaches and some are taken only a mile off Manasquan River outlet.

In the Sandy Hook area there are many charter boats, about twenty being berthed at the New Jersey State Marina at Leonardo.

From Atlantic City some of the charter boats fish the Wilmington Canyon, some fifty-seven miles offshore. This great cleft in the ocean bottom lies along the 100-fathom curve, as an offshoot of the Gulf Stream. It is probably the hottest spot in this country for white marlin. Morrie Upperman, manufacturer of the famous Upperman lures at Atlantic City, claims that if you troll more than ten minutes at the Canyon without getting a strike you've had a bad day. On one trip he and some friends caught and released twenty-six marlin in a single day. During the Atlantic City Tournament in 1962, 40 out of 200 boats competing went out to the Canyon and in three days landed 137 marlin. There are also blue marlin, extra-large dolphin, and down deep there are swordfish, catchable when now and then they come top-side. July 8th to September 15th is regarded as the peak fishing time, but the action can run into October.

New Jersey's beaches, stretching down the whole coast, from Sandy Hook to Cape May, offer endless opportunities for the onshore fisherman. There are good beaches for surf casting at Sandy Hook, Seabright, Monmouth, Long Branch, Elberton, Deal, Avon-by-the-sea, Asbury Park, Shark River, Manasquan Inlet, Brielle, Barnegat, Beach Haven, Brigantine, Atlantic City, Ocean City and many other points on down the outer beaches to Cape May. Most of the beaches also have fishing piers, where bait and tackle are available. The catch will range through striped bass, bluefish, sea trout or weakfish, channel bass, flounder, some kingfish, and croaker, depending on the time of the year. Striped bass and channel bass runs are best in June and September, but there is some form of surf and pier fishing from June through October.

From Sandy Hook down to the Manasquan Inlet there are many jetties which have been constructed to prevent beach erosion. Fishing from the jetties is done mostly at night. Those who go out for stripers along the jetties should remember that the fish work in very close to the rocks, so long casts are not necessary, but the lure should be kept in the water right to the rocks. Most anglers fish the high tide at the jetties, but if you're willing to climb over the wet and slippery rocks to the edge, you can get them on any tide.

Party boats carrying large groups of anglers go out daily in good weather from almost every port on the New Jersey coast. Prices range from $5 to $10 per head. All the inshore species may be taken at one time or another, but the porgy is a great favorite. This species, also called "silvers" here, is found all along the coast, with the greatest concentrations in rocky spots such as Tin Can Grounds, off Rockaway, South Channel at Sandy Hook, and the rocks along Long Branch and Sea Bright. The majority of party boats drift fish, and anglers get the most sport from the spunky little porgies with spinning outfits and 12-pound-test line. The porgy has a very small mouth and baits are scaled accordingly.

In Delaware Bay, at the southern limits of the state, there is fishing for weakfish, bluefish, croakers, and the various small bottom fish. Boats will be found at Fortesque, off State Highway 555, north of Fort Norris; at Bivalve, just south of Norris, at the mouth of the Maurice River; and at Reeds Beach, around the curve onto Cape May; as well as at many other small bayside towns. As elsewhere along the New Jersey coast, June and September are the best months, but there is some kind of fishing year-round. A feature of the Shrewsbury and Navesink Rivers which appeals to the skiff fisherman is a run of bluefish in June. These 2- to 4-pound fish are ideal light-tackle quarry.

Those who plan to fish New Jersey waters should obtain a copy of a small newspaper called *New Jersey Angler's News,* published weekly at Bayonne, New Jersey. It costs only ten cents and is loaded with details about what fish are in, what bait they're hitting, and where, both as to freshwater and salt. Its advertisements give you a good clue as to where charter boats are making good catches at the moment. It includes a New Jersey Tide Table, important to all types of fishing.

NEW JERSEY FISHING REGULATIONS

Resident Fishing License $4.15
Nonresident Fishing License $7.15
Nonresident 3-Day Fishing License $3.65
Resident Trout Stamp $2.00
Nonresident Trout Stamp $5.00

Fishing licenses of either Pennsylvania or New Jersey are recognized in the Delaware River from water's edge to water's edge.

Fishing licenses are required in the upper waters of many tidal rivers. The limits should be checked before fishing.

SEASONS AND LIMITS

Species	Open Season	Size Limit	Bag Limit
Trout	April 10 to Feb. 28	No minimum	6
Landlocked Salmon		15"	2
Black Bass	No closed season	9"	5 in aggregate
Walleye (pike-perch),		12"	10
Pickerel (eastern chain)	No closed season	No limit except Hopatcong, 15"	10
Striped Bass	March 1 to Dec. 31	18"	10
Ice fishing for all species	Jan. 1 to Jan. 31		10 pike-perch and pickerel in aggregate
Rock Bass, White Bass, Calico Bass, Crappie, White and Yellow Perch, Catfish, Sunfish, Carp and Eels, Suckers	No closed season	No minimum	No limit

New Jersey has many unusual exceptions, as to hours of fishing, and regulations on certain lakes. Current regulations should be checked carefully.

For complete regulations write: Division of Fish and Game, P.O. Box 1809, Trenton, New Jersey.

Atlantic Coast States

The Atlantic coastal States of Maryland, Delaware, New Jersey, Virginia, the Carolinas and Georgia share a common topography of oceanic features such as the Delaware Bay, the great Chesapeake Bay, Pamlico Sound, and many other lesser inlets of the sea, plus some mountainous or high rolling country in the interior where the land reaches back to the Appalachian foothills. As a result, there is both fresh and saltwater fishing available in great variety, with the salt getting the major part of the attention in most cases. The saltwater angling ranges from giant blue marlin taken offshore in Virginia and North Carolina, to croaker fishing in the shallows of nearly every inlet and bay. Between these extremes will be found almost every sport fish species of the Atlantic coast. In many of the coastal rivers there are seasonal runs of anadromous striped bass and shad, native to the Atlantic coast; and there are also coastwise migrations of cobia and channel bass, interspersed with forays of hard-feeding bluefish and raiding blackfin tuna and false albacore. These seasonal fish add annual spice to the regular, resident species.

Thus the angler in the Atlantic coastal area finds a wide choice of fishing, from skiff or charter boat, from pier, bridge or beach; from bait fishing or bottom fishing, to surf casting for the migratory species, or light-tackle fishing along the shores of the sounds.

The inland fishing is found in the thousands of small lakes and ponds which dot the countryside, augmented by many dam impoundments of the great rivers flowing to the sea, and in those rivers themselves. There is additional limited angling for trout in the mountain streams and in a few lower country rivers where civilization and industry have not altered the nature of the water to make it unfit for survival or stocking of trout. The freshwater species include rainbow trout, brown trout and some brook trout in the mountains; smallmouth black bass in some rivers and lakes; largemouth black bass in most of the warmer fresh waters; and white bass, spotted bass, crappie, bream, walleye, catfish, sunfish and various lesser species in suitable areas throughout the lakes and rivers.

In the middle and southern Atlantic states there is some freshwater fishing all winter long, as the climate is generally mild, with only occasional snow in the higher regions. In the more northern states the season can run into late November if the weather stays fine. Then there is cold and snow until March. The same general seasons apply to the saltwater fishing, the best of it ending with cold weather. Most of the states in the Atlantic group have striped-bass fishing until mid-December.

DELAWARE

The State of Delaware, one of the smallest in the Union, has considerably more fishing available than you would expect from its size and location in the industrial East. Crowded into this three-county state which forms the northeastern one-third of the Delmarva Peninsula is considerable freshwater fishing in numerous ponds, and saltwater fishing for both inshore and offshore species along the coast. The ponds and a few rivers produce largemouth black bass, chain pickerel, black crappie, bluegills, white and yellow perch, catfish, silver chub and trout. Running into the rivers from the sea, in some cases, are shad and striped bass; and in the salt there are white, and some blue marlin, tuna, bluefish, dolphin, kingfish, sea bass, weakfish or sea trout, croakers, porgies and flounder.

The major rivers are the Delaware, which actually is an arm of the sea throughout its course along the border between Delaware and New Jersey; the Murderkill, emptying into the Bay at Bowers Beach; the Mispillion, which empties at Mispillion Light; and the Indian River, which reaches the coast at Indian River Bay. There are no major lakes, but ponds are numerous.

U.S. 13 provides a north-south artery through the state, and two other major highways parallel U.S. 13 to the east: U.S. 113 serves the mid-state area, while State Highway 14 leads to the beaches, all the way from Rehoboth Beach down to Ocean City, Maryland. Entry to Delaware is also possible via U.S. 50 and Maryland Highway 404 from the Bay Bridge over the Chesapeake, and from various east-west highways branching off from U.S. 301 on the Eastern Shore of Maryland.

The climate of Delaware is cool and damp in the winter months, warm and humid in summer, but tempered along the coast by the breezes from Delaware Bay, and in the south from the Atlantic.

The state is highly industrialized in the north. In the south there is considerable area in its natural state, low and swampy, but anglers are unlikely to encounter any wild game except possibly deer. And while Delaware is on the fringe of the range of copperheads and rattlesnakes, these also are not generally a problem. The biggest threat is the mosquitoes which dwell in the moist lowlands, and anglers should always be prepared with repellent.

POND FISHING

There are more than fifty ponds in Delaware to which the public has access. Most of them are very heavily fished throughout the peak seasons, which are April through June and September through November. In most cases boats are available at these ponds. One of the best is NOXONTON MILLPOND (1), at Middleton in northern Delaware near the junction of U.S. 301 and U.S. 13. Fly fishing, spinning and bait fishing are all successful here. At CONCORD POND (2), near Concord on State Highway 20 in the southern part of the state, artificials take largemouth black bass, and there are some pickerel as well. Still to the south, TRUSSEM POND (3), near Laurel, rates as a good spot for both species. TRAP POND (4), in Trap Pond

State Park, off State Highway 24, six miles southeast of Laurel, has a large camp ground and there is some fishing in the pond. Others which have good reputations are SILVER LAKE (5), off U.S. 13 at Dover; LAKE COMO (6), off U.S. 13 at Smyrna; BURTON POND (7), off State Highway 24 at Angola; and TUB MILL POND (8), off U.S. 113 north of Milford. For those who want to take a day out from saltwater fishing at Rehoboth Beach, nearby RED MILL POND (9), off State Highway 14 between Nassau and Overbrook, is good water for fishing with artificial lures for large-mouth black bass and an occasional smallmouth.

A list of ponds which are controlled by the State Game and Fish Department, with public access provided, will be found in the current fishing regulations brochure, obtainable from the Board of Game and Fish Commissioners, Dover, Delaware.

Trout fishing in Delaware is extremely limited, but anglers find some stocked fish in White Clay, Pike and Mill Creeks, north of State Highway 2 between Newark and Wilmington.

SALTWATER FISHING

The northern part of the Delaware coast fronts on Delaware Bay. In many areas the water is shallow, lending itself to such species as the sea trout, or weakfish, flounder, porgies, croakers and tautog. Bluefish make a good run into the bay after the first cold spell in September. They take bait readily and also hit artificials very well, which makes them a favorite with light-tackle anglers.

Skiffs for fishing the upper bay are available at New Castle, just south of U.S. 40; at Delaware Beach, on State Highway 9, at the mouth of the Chesapeake and Delaware Canal; at Port Penn and Bay View a few miles further south on State Highway 9. East of Smyrna, about half way down the state, is Woodland Beach, on State Highway 6. From here south the river widens into the bay. Anglers will find boats at Pickering Beach, off State Highway 9 near Dover, and Kitts Hummock a few miles below.

At Bowers Beach, off U.S. 113, Captain Gummy Faulkner guides anglers for weakfish, croakers and kingfish in the waters around the mouth of the bay. There are several "head" boats, or party boats, at the same port. Rates go about $6 per head per day. There are more party boats at Mispillion Light, on State Highway 36, east of Milford.

From that point south, Delaware boats have ready access to the open Atlantic. From May through September there is always some species making its seasonal appearance in these waters. In May stripers and shad appear. Years ago they used to work into nearly all the rivers but pollution has almost completely destroyed this fishery. Today a few are taken in the lower waters of the Delaware.

Black drum move inshore about the middle of May, and cod, mackerel and bluefish are taken. In June the white marlin and a few blue marlin make their appearance. Fishing for all these species is augmented in August by bonito, false albacore, occasional dolphin and school tuna. There is good bottom fishing inshore for croakers, sea bass, porgies and flounder.

There is a good fishing port at Lewes, within the northward hook of Cape Henlopen, accessible via State Highway 18 from Georgetown. Fishing is for sea bass, porgies, bluefish and dolphin. The Lewes Anglers Club, Lewes, Delaware, will supply a list of the fine charter boats in the fleet based there. Rehoboth Beach, the next port to the south, where State Highway 14 turns inland from the beaches, is

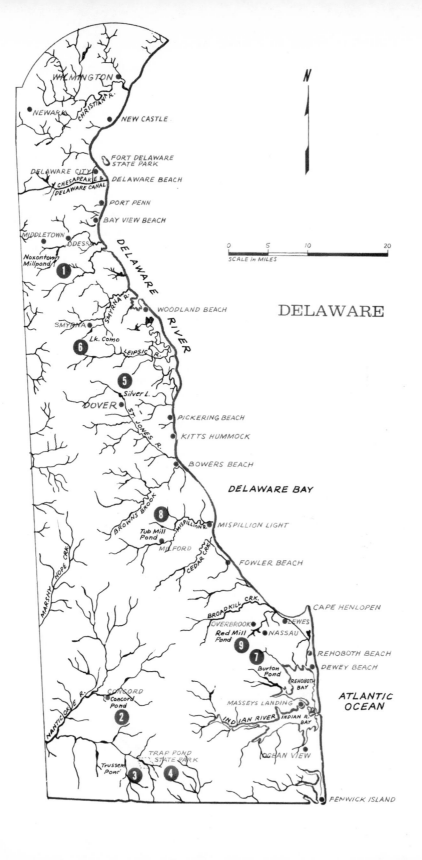

DELAWARE

N

SCALE in MILES
0   5   10   20

WILMINGTON

NEWARK

CHRISTIANA R.

NEW CASTLE

FORT DELAWARE STATE PARK

DELAWARE CITY

CHESAPEAKE & DELAWARE CANAL

DELAWARE BEACH

PORT PENN

BAY VIEW BEACH

MIDDLETOWN

ODESSA

Noxontown Millpond

1

DELAWARE RIVER

SMYRNA R.

WOODLAND BEACH

SMYRNA

Lk. Como

6

LEIPSIC R.

5

Silver L.

DOVER

ST. JONES R.

PICKERING BEACH

KITTS HUMMOCK

BOWERS BEACH

DELAWARE BAY

BROWNS BROOK

8

Tub Mill Pond

MISPILLION R.

MISPILLION LIGHT

MILFORD

CEDAR CRK.

FOWLER BEACH

MARSHY HOPE CRK.

BROADKILL CRK.

CAPE HENLOPEN

OVERBROOK

LEWES

Red Mill Pond

NASSAU

9

7

REHOBOTH BEACH

DEWEY BEACH

Burton Pond

REHOBOTH BAY

ATLANTIC OCEAN

CONCORD

Concord Pond

NANTICOKE R.

2

MASSEYS LANDING

INDIAN RIVER

INDIAN R. BAY

TRAP POND STATE PARK

OCEAN VIEW

Trussem Pond

3

4

FENWICK ISLAND

a well-known seaside resort. Again there are many excellent charter boats. A list may be obtained from the Indian River Yacht Basin, Rehoboth, Delaware; or from Captain Bill Taylor, Odessa, Delaware.

Yet another fine fleet based at the Indian River Inlet between Indian River Bay and the Ocean, goes offshore to fish for bluefish, dolphin, tuna and marlin. The best white-marlin fishing is found between Fenwick Shoals, off the extreme south end of Delaware, south to Ocean City, Maryland. Boats based at Lewes, Rehoboth and Indian River Inlet all fish this area.

Below Rehoboth the coast of Delaware is protected by a strip of sandbanks, forming beaches for some ten miles in front of Rehoboth Bay and Indian River Bay. Summer flounder fishing in Rehoboth Bay is excellent, the choice bait being live bullhead minnows. The flounder can also be taken on artificials. Spin casters use lead-headed bucktail jigs, bouncing them along the bottom. Sometimes these usual bottom dwellers will come well up in the water to take such a lure. The large ones put up a good fight.

Party boats at all these ports fish for sea bass, porgies and flounder, at a charge of around $6 per day, which usually includes bait and tackle. Skiffs are also available for use in the inshore waters and bays. Skiff fishermen find the best baits to be squid, steamed mussel and shedder crab.

There is also some jetty fishing at Lewes and at the Indian River Inlet.

From Lewes, south along the beaches to the Maryland line, there is some surf fishing. At Cape Henlopen kingfish and bluefish are taken. Further south the catch varies through striped bass, channel bass, bluefish, sea trout and croakers. The summer months are the best.

For those who plan to bring their own boats to fish the inshore waters of Delaware, the State Game and Fish Commission operates a number of public access sites. There is one at Fowlers Beach, off State Highway 14, southeast of Milford; one at Lewes, on the Lewes-Rehoboth Canal, off State Highway 18; one at Dewey Beach, on State Highway 14, south of Rehoboth; one at Masseys Landing, off State Highway 24, north from Millsboro. This one gives access to both Rehoboth and Indian River Bays. To the south there is a public access area at Quillens Point, Ocean View, and another at Portsville.

While no license is required to fish salt and tidal waters in Delaware, anglers should obtain the Delaware Sport Fishing Regulations, as they contain a complete tide table, which is of great value when fishing coastal waters.

DELAWARE FISHING REGULATIONS

No license is required for fishing salt water, or tidal water where the tide regularly ebbs and flows, including the Chesapeake & Delaware Canal.

Resident Fishing License $2.20
Nonresident Fishing License $7.50
Resident Trout Stamp $2.10
Nonresident Trout Stamp $2.10

SEASONS AND LIMITS

Species	Open Season	Size Limit	Bag Limit
Bass	No closed season	10"	6
Trout, all species	2nd Friday in April to 2nd Sat. in November	None	4

For complete regulations write: Board of Game and Fish Commissioners, Dover, Delaware.

MARYLAND

The State of Maryland shares so many of the different features of the Atlantic coastal area that in spite of being one of the smallest of the states it has the most variegated of sport-fishing possibilities. The fringes of the Appalachians run through the northwestern part of Maryland where it borders on West Virginia and Pennsylvania. It has vast tidewater areas on both sides of the Chesapeake Bay, on the mainland and the Delmarva Peninsula. On the ocean side of the peninsula are miles of outer beaches, typical Atlantic coastal shoreline.

Several of the most historic rivers of America traverse the state. The Potomac and its North Branch form the entire southern border. The Patapsco comes down through the central area, and to the north and east the Gunpowder River runs the full north-south measurement of the state. In the extreme east the great Susquehanna slices across the narrow wedge bordering on Pennsylvania. Each of these rivers has been dammed at one place or another, adding to the water area within the state, though not always adding to the fishing possibilities since the dams cut off the seasonal runs of anadromous species. However, through these dams, lake fishing is provided at Prettyboy and Loch Raven Reservoirs on the Gunpowder north of Baltimore; in the Conowingo on the Susquehanna River; and the Patapsco Reservoir, east of Baltimore on the Patapsco River.

With all this variety of topography and water, Maryland can offer almost any kind of sport fishing you can name. There are trout streams in the northwest, which are annually stocked with brook trout, rainbow trout and some brown. The largemouth black bass is found throughout most of the lakes and ponds of the less mountainous areas and in some of the brackish waters along the Eastern Shore and the Delmarva Peninsula. Largemouth will average 2 to 3 pounds and some are taken up to 8 pounds. The smallmouth is taken in the cooler rivers of Maryland. They average 1½ pounds but 6-pounders are taken occasionally.

A few of the larger lakes such as Conowingo and Triadelphia, on the Patuxent north of Washington, D.C., as well as several rivers, notably the Susquehanna below the Conowingo Dam and the Potomac below Washington, have walleyes. They will generally run in the 5-pound class though some specimens up to 10 pounds are taken.

The pike or eastern chain pickerel can be taken year-round in Maryland. Like the largemouth, the pike will live in both fresh and brackish water. They average 2 to 6 pounds. They are found in the weedy, shallow areas of the Magothy, Gunpowder, Bush, Seneca, Middle, West and South Rivers, as well as in ponds on the Eastern Shore. Another brackish-water swimmer is the yellow perch, a favorite for the table, found in most ponds around the shores of the Chesapeake as well as in the lower, brackish waters of the rivers just mentioned. Less popular but very numerous in all the brackish waters, is the catfish.

The black and white crappie both frequent numerous lakes, rivers and ponds and have been taken in weights up to 3 pounds, though the average will go only about half a pound, or about 8 inches. The best fishing spots are Conowingo Lake, Loch Raven and Prettyboy Reservoirs, Lake Roland, the Susquehanna and Gunpowder Rivers, and the mill ponds of the Eastern Shore. Many Maryland waters also hold most of the sunfish and panfish, generally classed together as "bream."

Three anadromous fish make seasonal runs into the coastal rivers. The hickory shad comes in from the salt about the end of the first week in April and continues to run till about June 20th. Not as popular as the true shad, the hickory is nonetheless sporting to catch on light tackle and the roe is excellent to eat. The fish average about 1 pound for males, and up to 2 pounds for females. The best runs are in the Susquehanna and Patuxent, but they also appear in the Gunpowder, Winters Run, Octararo Creek and Deer Creek. The true shad appears about a month later than the hickory and continues to run through to June 20th, the end of the season. Their average weight is higher, between 3 and 7 pounds. Since they prefer a little heavier water and stronger current than does the hickory, they are not usually found in the smaller creeks. The main runs are in the Susquehanna, Potomac and Patuxent.

The third, and by far the most popular, member of the Atlantic coast nomads is the striped bass, or "rock" as the fish is commonly called in parts of the Chesapeake Bay. They are taken throughout the bay area and also run into most of the tidal rivers, with the Potomac and the Susquehanna rating as favorite spots. Stripers taken will run from 1 to 5 pounds when they are school fish, though occasionally schools will contain some fish up to 12 pounds. Loners often weigh 15 or 20 pounds.

Wherever these anadromous species are mentioned in the following pages, the reader should recall that fishing for shad is limited to the period of the seasonal runs, and catches of this species are almost nonexistent at other times. Stripers move into the shallows in the spring and fall, and go to deeper water during the hot summer days. There are some around all year, but during the winter they lie doggo in the deep holes in the Bay.

Aside from the anadromous fish, saltwater species generally taken on the Maryland coast include bluefish, cobia, which runs as high as 100 pounds, sea trout, white perch, flounder, spot, or Norfolk spot, and various lesser fry such as the hardhead, croaker, porgy and sea bass. Offshore and along the outer beaches of the Eastern Shore are the bigger ocean swimmers. Ocean City, Maryland, has some of the world's best fishing for white marlin during late June through August. Drum, both red and black, migrate into Maryland waters, appearing in bay waters in May and remaining through the summer. On the ocean beaches they are found in late summer and fall. The top fishing spot on the coast is Assateague Island, near Ocean City. In the Bay, Tangier Sound and the mouths of the Potomac and Choptank Rivers are good.

Bluefish are taken in most saltwater areas along the coast as well as in the Chesapeake. This tasty table fish averages 1 to 5 pounds, with a few larger.

Among the inshore fish, the hardhead and spot are popular. The hardhead is a good table fish and a scrappy fighter, usually taken by drifting and bottom fishing in water about 12 feet deep. They run up to 5 pounds, with most catches more like 3, and are found in nearly all Bay waters during the summer months. The spot is a small fish which occurs almost everywhere in the Chesapeake, regardless of the depth of the water. They are taken in numbers by every angling method, from shore casting to deep trolling, from June until cold weather. Since they are excellent to eat and are taken so readily, they provide a "fill-in" for fishermen when other species are not hitting. The same might be said for the blowfish, stingray and sharks, which are usually taken when anglers are seeking some other species.

Maryland is one of the most heavily-populated states in the country, yet there is much rural country, and especially on the lower Chesapeake and Eastern Shore it is easy to get away from the crowds. There is excellent highway access in all cases. Entrance to the Eastern Shore has been improved in recent years by the construction of the Chesapeake Bay Bridge on U.S. 301 and U.S. 50 from Washington, as well as via the comparatively new Delaware Memorial Bridge which funnels northern traffic into the Delaware section of the Delmarva Peninsula. Numerous crossroads lead to the Eastern Shore of Maryland.

Summer can be very warm in Maryland but spring and fall are delightful, and this is the time when much of the fishing is at its best.

Wild game is not a problem in this well-populated area but along trout streams and around ponds and lakes, anglers must watch for copperheads, rattlers, and a few cottonmouth moccasins. During a hot, dry spell, snakes have a habit of leaving their rocky ledges and working down to water. Both the timber rattler and the copperhead are often seen along mountain streams at such a time. Great care should be used in making your way over rocky ledges, windfalls, or around single rocks.

NORTHWESTERN MARYLAND

The eastern brook trout is the native trout of Maryland but with the encroachment of civilization this species has declined to the point where there is very little natural reproduction today. However, through the planting of rainbows and brown trout, some very good trout fishing has been maintained. Most of the trout streams are in the northwest corner of the state and along the Pennsylvania border, where a number of streams are annually stocked with adult rainbows, and some browns. This is also the area where the few remaining native eastern brook trout are likely to be found. Anglers can get directions to PINEY RUN and PUZZLEY RUN (1) at Frostburg, on U.S. 40, west of Cumberland. They can reach TONOLOWAY CREEK (2) from Hancock, at the junction of U.S. 40 and U.S. 522; BEAR CREEK, BUFFALO RUN, MILL RUN and the YOUGHIOGHENY RIVER (3) at Friendsville, on State Highway 42 in the extreme northwest corner of the state; MUDDY CREEK (4) and SALT BLOCK, at McHenry, further south, on U.S. 219; and the SAVAGE RIVER (5) at Bloomington, on State Highway 135 at the Potomac River.

Further east, the Catoctin area in the Blue Ridge Mountains has some of the best trout streams in the state, most of which can be reached via U.S. 15, north from Frederick. BIG HUNTING CREEK (6) near Thurmont, and FISHING CREEK (7) between Thurmont and Lewistown to the south, are stocked with rainbows and browns from 7 to 12 inches. The LITTLE ANTIETAM (8), with the same kind of fishing, can be reached via State Highway 34 at Keedysville, southwest of Boonsboro.

Via U.S. Alternate 40, northwest from Frederick, you can reach BEAVER CREEK (9), between Boonsboro and Hagerstown, which on occasion can produce some very good-sized brownies as well as stocked rainbows. On U.S. 40 at Ellerton there is the same kind of fishing in MIDDLE CREEK (10).

Very close to the city of Baltimore, two small streams, BEETREE RUN (11) and

LITTLE FALLS are also stocked, but the best fishing close to Baltimore is at Jones Falls River in the Green Spring Valley, where browns are taken from 7 to 14 inches in length. There is also a little trout fishing to the northeast of Baltimore in the James Run near Creswell on State Highway 136, and in Bynum Run near Belair, on U.S. 1.

In northwestern Maryland, DEEP CREEK LAKE (12) can occasionally produce some trout fishing, mainly in the northwest arms of the lake. There's an information booth on the lakeshore road, U.S. 219, on the western shore, and information about where the best fishing is to be found can usually be obtained there. In general, however, the largemouth black bass is the catch in Deep Creek Lake, with pike, perch and catfish as well as all the panfish thrown in. McHenry and Thayerville are the two towns on the lake which offer accommodations. There are numerous bait houses, boat docks, motels and restaurants, and a State Park on the northeast shore, with camping facilities.

All the classic trout flies will take fish in these Maryland waters. A good selection of dries in sizes 12, 14 and 16 should include the Light Cahill, Black Gnat, Flying Black Ant, Red Variant, Ginger Quill, Olive Quill, Light Hendrickson, Royal Coachman and Blue Dun, plus the Jassid in size 18. Wet flies, in the same sizes, which are good fish takers are the Coachman, Black Gnat, Professor, Royal Coachman, Blue Dun, Brown Hackle, Gray Hackle. The favorite nymphs, again in sizes 12, 14 and 16, are the Black and Yellow, Black and Orange, and Gray. When it comes to bucktails and streamers it must be remembered that Maryland streams are small, but even so there are times when a bucktail or streamer will bring a strike from a reluctant trout. The best sizes are 6 and 8, long shank, and the successful patterns include Edson Tiger, dark, Gray Ghost, Blacknosed Dace, Yellow Maribou, Mickey Finn, Black and White bucktail.

During midsummer, when quite good fishing can be enjoyed in the lower reaches of some of the trout waters, it is wise to go to 9-foot long, very fine leaders. Never more than 4X and 6X will bring more strikes. A 7½-foot or 8-foot rod is best for these small streams, with matching HDH line.

Trout fishermen in Maryland should obtain the current "Angler's Guide and Synopsis of Freshwater Fishing Regulations" from the Game & Inland Fish Commission, State Office Building, Annapolis, Maryland. It lists all special regulations concerning trout streams and other freshwater fishing in Maryland.

In northwestern Maryland the UPPER POTOMAC RIVER (13) forms the border between West Virginia and Maryland. This is one of the top spots in the country for smallmouth black bass. It's ideal fly fishing, and much of it is wadable from Hancock, on U.S. 70 at the river all the way down to Great Falls, on State Highway 189, only twenty miles north of Washington, D.C. It is nothing for a good flyman to take 100 fish in a day, fish weighing from 2 to 2½ pounds. Small popping bugs on #2 or 1/0 hooks, with cork or balsa-wood bodies are good, in shades of brown, robin egg blue and yellow. The larger streamer flies and bucktails, on #2 up to 1/0 hooks, also produce. The Muddler Minnow is very effective in fast water. And many fish are taken on dry flies, with the Royal Wulff, Gray Wulff and Brown Hackle, in sizes 6, 8 and 10. This fishing calls for an 8½-foot, slow-action fly rod with GBF line.

Spinners also wade the river, using small lures, and reap a fine harvest. Bait fishermen take the bass on riffle-runner minnows and hellgrammites, making some catches in the 5-pound class.

The wader must beware of rocky ledges, which often extend the full width

of the river. On the downstream side there may be a sharp drop into a 15-foot-deep pool.

Several tributaries of the Potomac also have good populations of smallmouth, rock bass and sunnies, and are also fine to wade. These are the GREAT TONOLOWAY (14), entering the main stream at Hancock; the CATOCTIN (15), which comes in just above Point of Rocks, on U.S. 15; and the MONOCACY (16), reached from State Highway 28 near Dickerson, and State Highway 80 at Buckeystown.

There are two major reservoirs in northwestern Maryland. The Youghiogheny is largely in Pennsylvania but juts down into Maryland at Friendsville, on State Highway 42, off U.S. 219. There are large and smallmouth black bass, northern pike, walleyes, yellow perch, black crappie, sunfish, bluegills and some rainbow trout. There are two small towns on the eastern shore of the Youghiogheny, Selbysport and Friendsville. The boat liveries, however, are mostly further north, in Pennsylvania, on U.S. 40.

At the nearby town of Accident, on U.S. 219, a small community pond is kept stocked with adult largemouth black bass. The fishing is from the bank, with artificial lures only.

Following south along U.S. 219, you come to Deep Creek Lake, mentioned earlier, with all the same species as Youghiogheny, and with a few trout in the northwestern arms. Boat traffic is heavy on this lake.

A smaller reservoir, HERRINGTON MANOR LAKE (17), five miles northeast of Oakland, at the junction of U.S. 219 and State Highway 39, is stocked with largemouth black bass. Close to the Pennsylvania line, near Grantsville, at the junction of U.S. 40 and State Highway 699, SAVAGE RIVER RESERVOIR (18) to the southeast, and PLEASANT VALLEY (19) to the south are used largely by picnic

groups, but there is some fishing for largemouth and smallmouth bass, some rainbows, and bluegills and sunfish in the Savage Reservoir. No motors are allowed.

To the southwest, on State Highway 36 near Lonaconing, DANS MOUNTAIN POND (20) in Dans Mountain State Park is limited to shore fishing only. It contains bluegills and largemouth black bass.

South of Cumberland you can go out from Oldtown on State Highway 51 and fish the old CHESAPEAKE and OHIO CANAL (21) for largemouth, sunfish, yellow perch, channel catfish, bluegills and black crappie. The same kind of fishing is available in a series of pools in the canal. There's a good one about four miles east of Hancock on U.S. 40, just across the river from West Virginia.

The balance of the Potomac River from Oldtown down to Great Falls provides the best smallmouth black-bass fishing in Maryland. There are few access roads but float trips can be started at Oldtown or Pawpaw, both on U.S. 51; or from Hancock; Williamsport, south of Hagerstown; Antietam, south of Sharspburg on State Highway 34; and Harpers Ferry, where U.S. 340 reaches the river, from Frederick. The water is shallow and the bottom rocky in many places and therefore motors are not practical. Besides the smallmouth, anglers take several varieties of panfish and channel catfish.

CENTRAL MARYLAND

Even though Central Maryland is so thickly populated and very much industrialized there are numerous reservoirs, lakes and ponds which provide habitat for largemouth black bass, smallmouth black bass and many panfish. LOCH RAVEN and PRETTYBOY RESERVOIRS (22), to the north of Baltimore, have fishing for largemouth black bass, crappie and catfish. Loch Raven may be fished from sunrise to sunset only, and there is a 50¢ boat charge for everyone over sixteen years of age. Boats and electric motors may be rented at the Loch Raven Fishing Center on the southeast corner of the lake. Take State Highway 146 north from Towson; this becomes Delaney Road, which leads over the Delaney Valley Bridge. The entry to the Fishing Center is on the right, just across the bridge. The best fishing water is from there south to the No. 1 Bridge. The mouth of Hampton Cove is also good.

Prettyboy, which has the same kind of fishing, can be reached via U.S. 83, north from Baltimore. The PATAPSCO RESERVOIR (23), also called Liberty Reservoir, is to the northwest of Baltimore, via U.S. 26 to Wards Chapel, or U.S. 140 to Reisterstown. There is some fishing for bass, crappie and bluegills.

TRIADELPHIA (24) and ROCKY GORGE Reservoirs, the water supply source for Washington, D.C., lie north of that city. Rocky Gorge is reached by U.S. 29, Triadelphia by State Highway 97. Both have bass and panfish. Besides your Maryland fishing license, you must purchase a 50¢ permit at the Brighton Dam at the south end of Triadelphia, or at the Patuxent Filter Plant, or at the office of the Washington Suburban Sanitary Commission in Hyattsville or Silver Spring.

There is some outstanding smallmouth fishing in that stretch of the SUSQUEHANNA RIVER (25) just below the Conowingo Dam in northeast Maryland, down about four miles to the point where the influence of tidewater begins to be felt. There are many fish which weigh 2 and 3 pounds and it is not unusual to take a 4 or a 5-pounder. The writer's largest smallmouth from this spot weighed 6½ pounds. It hit a fly-rod popper that I had thrown in just a foot from shore. Those who know the river well can wade it on Sundays when the water is shut off at the dam. Otherwise, most of the fishing is done from skiffs or from shore. No matter how you fish, you must always watch the water level, as this part of the river can be treacherous because of the varying volumes of water released from the dam at different times. A guide who knows the water well and can take you out for smallmouth as well as stripers and shad in season, is Fred Narvel of Port Deposit, Maryland. You can get instructions at Port Deposit as to how to reach him where he lives on the river. Logan's Wharf, Willow Cove Park and the Port Deposit Marina all have launching ramps, boats and motors for hire. Port Deposit is reached via U.S. 222 on the east side of the river.

The lake above the dam, about four miles of which is within Maryland, has fishing for large and smallmouth bass, the best times on the lake being June to October. There is good spring fishing for crappie, starting about April 15th. The bluegills begin to hit at the first of May, northern pike and walleyes about May 15th. Fishing for chain pickerel is best in June. Catfish are also taken, mostly on frozen herring, shrimp and night crawlers.

Several other species work into the waters below the dam. Walleyes are found close up to the dam and around the mouth of OCTARARO CREEK (26) on the east side of the river. The fish are taken by trolling deep with spinner and worm combination, the bait being bounced off rocks along the bottom by constant jigging. The best time is October, and there is also some good spring fishing.

Around the first of April, white perch run up the Susquehanna from the bay and are taken below the dam. Cast spoons and darts, and minnows, either live or dead, are the most successful baits.

TIDEWATER MARYLAND

The lower waters of the great rivers which flow to the Chesapeake Bay offer a tremendous variety of fishing because they are subject to the influence of tidewater. The largemouth black bass extends its range into almost every backwater, inlet and shallow bay in the brackish-water area, while some saltwater species such as the shad and striper work up into the fresh water. In between these extremes are all the warm-freshwater species, moving down as far as they can accommodate themselves to the salt, and the saltwater species hanging about the river mouths and the lower, salty waters of the rivers themselves.

The brackish-water largemouth is plentiful in all the coves and marshes of the Susquehanna below tidewater, and the whole Havre de Grace Bay area receives so much fresh water from the several rivers emptying into it, that it seems to be ideal habitat for the largemouth who likes his brackish water well flavored with fresh.

Some of the East Coast's top striper fishing is found in the SUSQUEHANNA (27), as far up as the dam, and on the Susquehanna Flats at the mouth of the river. Usually the stripers move into the four-mile stretch of fresh water below the dam about the end of May and stay there until mid-October. They follow the schools of herring upstream and sometimes you can see and hear them as they strike. Often you see a herring knocked kicking high above the water before the ferocious feeding of the stripers. They rest in the pools in the river, spreading out now and then to feed all over the river, often even working within a few feet of either shore. Fly-rodders use big bucktails and streamers tied on 1/0 and 3/0 hooks. The best colors are red and white, red and yellow. The Honey Blonde, a tandem bucktail, and the Platinum Blonde, the same pattern in white, are both great producers. Poppings bugs in the same color combinations bring nerve-tingling strikes.

Bait fishermen use live eels and take stripers up to 25 pounds. Spin fishermen use the Phillips Old Joe with telling effect and both plug casters and spinners use Bob Pond's Atom Striper Popper with great success.

White shad and hickory shad also come into the Susquehanna, the hickories showing in April and continuing in successive runs until the season closes in early July. The white shad, *Alosa sapidissima,* the preferred of the two, shows in mid-May and stays around for about a month. The shads are usually taken on spinning tackle, by casting shad darts, a small, jig-type lure, or small spoons. The retrieve should be very slow. They will also take the same lures trolled. Sometimes it is necessary to use a sinker to get down, as shad usually lie deep.

Both the hickory and the white shad will take small white flies and small fly-rod spoons and spinners. The retrieve should be made in slow, foot-long jerks, and continued right in to the boat. Shad will hit and follow, and hit again, four or five times, before being hooked. Once hooked, the fish must be played carefully as they have a very thin cheek cover and the hook may easily tear out.

Casters should throw their lures into runs, rapids and glides. In slow water the fish will take provided the water is not too deep. While many fishermen confuse the two shads, it is easy to tell them apart. The true shad's jaws come together evenly, while the lower jaw of the hickory protrudes beyond the upper.

Like the Susquehanna, the BUSH RIVER (28), next down the west coast of the Chesapeake, has fine largemouth black-bass fishing. You find them around the old pilings and the foundations of duck blinds, along the face of the marshes and in the guts that penetrate the marshes. There are some good fish back in there. Once the writer took a 6-pounder on a popping bug cast in close to a bunch of tuckahoes. There are also yellow perch in the river. Boat docks will be found on U.S. 40, which runs along the edge of the river.

To the west on U.S. 40, only fifteen miles northeast of Baltimore, is the GUNPOWDER RIVER (29), famous among Maryland anglers, not for the size of the fish but for the magnitude of its run of the tiny gudgeon in the spring. The gudgeon is four to six inches long, and it takes a worm readily. When the run is on in May there are literally thousands of anglers, ranging from tiny tots to life-size adults, lining the banks, snatching these tasty little fellows from the stream. They use spreaders with two hooks and a bobber. The fish are very good fried.

For many years the Maryland State Fish and Game Association of Baltimore has taken a group of a couple of hundred children gudgeon fishing when the season opens. It's a wonderful thing to see, as they fish elbow to elbow, stuffing their pockets with the tiny fish as they bring them in, cramming them into glass jars, even putting them under their hats for safekeeping. On the way home one year, an 8-year-old said to me seriously: "These gudgeon are great game fish!" What more could you ask for?

The river also holds a few white perch, yellow perch and sunfish, and some catfish.

South along the shores of the Chesapeake from Baltimore is the inlet of the MAGOTHY RIVER (30), reached via U.S. 2. There is good fishing everywhere, from the wide mouth of the inlet all the way up the river. Striped bass make spring and fall runs and there is also a resident summer population of the stripers, as well as all-year fishing for perch, pickerel and spot. This is good water for casters as well as bottom fishermen. Boats are available everywhere, from skiffs to large charter boats.

The SEVERN RIVER (31) and the SOUTH (32) are immediately down the coast from the Magothy, easily reached from Washington via U.S. 50 and 301; from Baltimore via State Highways 2 on the east and 3 on the west; and from Annapolis, which stands at the mouth of the Severn. Both rivers are well supplied with docks, and there are several fishing piers. Some of the best pickerel fishing in Maryland can be found in the South River in late fall. The fish weigh up to 3 pounds. Spinner and bloodworm combinations are the most successful baits. There are also occasional runs of stripers around the mouth of the river in the spring and again in the fall. The same fishing is found in the Severn.

The PATUXENT (33) is another great river of this western shore of the Chesapeake, with many miles of good water. Boats and guides will be found at California on State Highway 235; Benedict, where State Highway 231 crosses the river; and at Solomons, on the point at the end of State Highway 416 on the eastern side of the river. Solomons is one of Maryland's favorite fishing spots, with all facilities and fishermen's needs. The river contains stripers, perch, blues, spot, sea trout, hardheads and flounder, and like the Potomac to the west, the lower waters are the most productive.

As mentioned earlier, the Potomac, which forms so much of the western boundaries of Maryland, has excellent fishing in some of its upper reaches. The lower waters are no less attractive to fishermen. There are largemouth black bass in all the shallow bays, inlets, backwaters and marshy areas from Fort Washington, less than fifteen miles south of Washington, all the way to tidewater, and into it. One of the best spots is directly across the river from Quantico, on the Virginia side, around the sunken ships berthed there after World War I. Lower down in the river there are spot, trout, perch, bluefish and hardheads. There is seasonal fishing for shad, and striped bass are all over the Potomac, from the Chesapeake Bay almost to Washington, D.C. The best striper fishing is from where U.S. 301 crosses the river, on down to the Bay. At the mouth of every creek and river there are usually stripers, and they work on up into the rivers. There are also plenty of spot and hardheads and a few blues.

Towards the mouth of the river the fishing is even better. Some of the best cobia fishing in the Chesapeake will be found out of Wynne, which is reached by following State Highway 5 down the peninsula on the east side of the Potomac, to Ridge, then west on Highway 252. The peak season is from early August to late October. There are boats of all kinds available at Wynne and Ridge, from head-boats which charge $5 per person to skiffs. There is some excellent casting water for stripers in Smith Creek near the two towns just mentioned. Another marina and resort will be found at Piney Point, reached by leaving State Highway 5 at Callaway and following 249 to the shore.

Several good rivers enter the Potomac near the mouth. The PORT TOBACCO (34) runs down parallel to U.S. 301, west of La Plata. There is fishing for bass and pickerel, and shad in season. In late March and April there is a wonderful run of yellow perch in the upper waters of the Wicomoco, known as ALLENS FRESH (35). You can catch them right from shore, or from skiffs, which are available where State Highway 234 turns off U.S. 301 and crosses the head of the creek at the town of Allens Fresh.

Along this western shore of the Chesapeake there is much saltwater fishing not directly associated with the great rivers. The Bay is a spawning ground for so many species that almost any time of the year you can take something. The stripers are prime targets, and while the peak season is from April through October, there are some fish in the Bay at all times. Anglers go for them by every known means, trolling the channels and bays and offshore, still fishing with eels, cut bait, bloodworms and shrimp, or floating a soft crab over the surface. They cast with spin poppers and jigs, with fly-rod poppers, bucktails and streamer flies. The fish are taken by every method at some time or other, but during the cold weather when the fish are down deep, trolling is most successful, catches going from 8 to 29 pounds.

Boats go out into the Bay from every 'longshore port. One of the most popular areas, aside from the mouths of the great rivers already mentioned is Herring Bay and Holland Point, almost due east of Washington, via U.S. 4, to the Bristol Road, across 258 to State Highway 2, and south on it to State Highway 423, which leads to Herring Bay. The best season is late summer and fall, and the fish are stripers, bluefish, hardheads and flounder. Skiffs and headboats are available at all the towns along this shore, Deale, Fairhaven, Holland Point, North Beach and Chesapeake Beach.

THE EASTERN SHORE

Maryland's share of the Delmarva Peninsula, which forms the ocean side protection of the Chesapeake Bay, is commonly referred to as the Eastern Shore. The Maryland section runs in an L shape down the eastern shore of the bay, backed by Delaware in the north, with the base of the L running out along Delaware's southern boundary to give Maryland about forty miles of Atlantic coast (as the crow flies). The southern boundary of the state crosses the peninsula at Pocomoke Sound, the narrow portion below that being part of the State of Virginia. Thus the Eastern Shore has all the fishing possibilities of the rest of tidewater Maryland, plus these miles of seacoast to provide added deep-sea species and surf fishing.

At the peak of the Chesapeake Bay, three rivers, the NORTHEAST, ELK and SASSAFRAS (36) all offer excellent casting for largemouth black bass. The Northeast can be reached from the town of North East, just off U.S. 40 at the head of the bay. There are pike and perch as well as the bass, and ice fishing is good in the winter. The Elk also crosses U.S. 40, just south of Elkton, Maryland. This river is best known for its perch fishing, though there are bass in its tributary, the Bohemia, which enters the inlet just south of the main river. The BOHEMIA (37) can be reached from U.S. 213, along the eastern shore of the Bay. Bass fishing can be excellent here. The Sassafras is about twenty miles further south on U.S. 213. Boats are available at Fredericktown and Georgetown on either side of the bridge that crosses the river. Casters like to follow U.S. 213 down two miles past Locust Grove, then turn west on the Bettertown Road. There you can obtain a boat, go upriver and wade the shores and cast when the tide is out. This is a real hot spot for largemouth, for the casting fraternity.

There is some surf fishing along this part of the Maryland coast for stripers and white perch, along the beaches at Sandy Point State Park and Kent Island. Sandy Point is on the west shore, north of U.S. 50 and 301. These roads cross Kent Island, and north-south traffic is on State Highways 8 and 18, on the island. There's a $1 fee to enter the park. Bloodworms are the choice bait, followed by crabs and eels, fished on the bottom.

Every river along this shore has its special reputation with fishermen. The big feature on the CHOPTANK RIVER (38) is fishing for red drum, some of the most substantial sizes of this species being found in Maryland waters. The fishing is best from Cook Point at the mouth of the inlet, up to the point where U.S. 50 crosses the river. Above that there are largemouth bass. Stripers also move into the inlet and lower river in May, and some good fish, 15 pounds and better, are taken from then until the hot weather sets in. In the fall there is a run of small stripers, usually taken by trolling. The fish stay around until December. Hardhead fishing is excellent at the mouth of the Choptank all summer. Many fishermen work out of Tilghman, at the end of State Highway 33, east from Easton, on U.S. 50. Bozman and Neavitt, on State Highway 579, which runs off 33, to the east, are also good fishing ports on this north shore of the wide Choptank Inlet. On the south shore there are boats and all kinds of accommodations at Cambridge, where U.S. 50 crosses the river.

The NANTICOKE (39), WICOMICO (40) and MANOKIN (41) further south all offer the same kind of fishing, and boats are available at small docks along all three. Salisbury, at the junction of U.S. 50 and U.S. 13, is a good headquarters for fishermen. These three rivers all flow into Tangier Sound, one of the top fishing spots on the Eastern Shore for nearly all species. It is a particularly good area for spotted sea trout.

The POCOMOKE RIVER (42) flows into Pocomoke Sound on the Virginia border. Much of the length of the river is paralleled by U.S. 113. There is exceptionally good bass fishing just above Snow Hill at the junction of U.S. 113 and State Highway 12, with some 9-pounders being reported. There are also pickerel, crappie, perch, and some pike, from there all the way down to tidewater and into it. Striped bass and shad come up as far as Pocomoke City at the junction of U.S. 113 and U.S. 13, on their seasonal runs. The stripers as well as occasional bluefish, trout, hardheads and spot can usually be taken around the mouth of the river. There are lots of bays and inlets and coves, ideal for working surface lures for the bass and crappies. Gold or silver spoons plus pork rind will take the pickerel and perch.

Gar are also taken in these waters and carp have been caught up to 40 pounds.

Throughout the Eastern Shore of Maryland there are many ponds and the angler who will do a little exploring can usually find one or more. In the Salisbury area alone there are six ponds well known for bass, crappie, bluegill and pike. PARKER and SCHUMAKER PONDS (43) can be reached via State Highway 350 east from the city. Woodcock, Colborn, Tonytank and Shad Point Ponds are located off U.S. 13 and State Highway 529, to the south. These are more or less backwaters of the Wicomico River. Nearly every river has such ponds in its lower reaches.

Some of the best bottom fishing in the Chesapeake Bay is found along the Eastern Shore. Bottom fishermen take white perch, weakfish or sea trout, flounders, hardhead, black and red drum, and sometimes rockfish or stripers, blues, cobia and sharks. Drum make spring and fall runs into these waters. Tangier Sound is one of the top spots and there are charter boats and bottom boats available at Crisfield, on State Highway 413 at the southern end of the Sound. The Choptank Inlet is another good spot for black drum. A world record at the time—1955— was taken from the bridge on U.S. 50 at Cambridge, Maryland, by James Aaron. The fish is still the record in the 30-pound-test-line class.

The black drum usually appear along the Eastern Shore in May, the red drum a little later. The blacks are usually taken in about 30 feet of water, while the reds move in where it is more shallow. The preferred bait is peeler crab.

Bottom fishing for sea trout is best from July until fall. They will take almost any bait, such as cut-up crab, clam necks, bloodworms, shrimp and pieces of cut-up spot. The last is the best bottom bait for the bluefish which are also found from July through October.

Throughout the Chesapeake, bottom fishing is done in pretty much the same way everywhere. Skiff fishermen use everything from floating shrimp on a fly-rod outfit to deep fishing with a boat rod. Party-boat fishermen usually are equipped with a stout boat rod, about 5 feet long, and a "bay" or "jetty" reel with star drag. Twenty-pound-test monofilament or squidding line is best with this outfit. Saltwater spinning gear with 8- to 12-pound-test monofilament is also popular. The hooks are usually snelled, #4 and #1/0, and sinkers vary from 1 to 6 ounces. The weight is required because there is often heavy tidal flow where the best fishing is found, for example, at river outlets. Every imaginable kind of bait is used. Peeler or shedder crab is tops, cut in chunks for fishing right on the bottom, or without weight for a floating bait. Clam necks, fresh or frozen, are good. The spinner-and-bloodworm combination is highly regarded by many. A lot of bottom fishermen rig two hooks, setting one about 2 feet above the sinker, the other about 18 inches above that. The lower hook is baited with about an inch of bloodworm, the upper with shrimp or a chunk of peeler crab. The theory is that if you make this double-barreled offering you have twice the chance of picking up whatever comes along, and it often works that way. The bait should be kept a little above the bottom in order to avoid eels and toadfish. Let the sinker hit, then raise slightly.

The chum line is widely used in the Chesapeake both by party boats and private-skiff fishermen. Offerings of chopped clams, menhaden and fish of various kinds will troll up everything from cobia to blues and striped bass, as well as the small fry more usually taken.

SURF FISHING

Anglers find stripers in the surf along the Atlantic coast at Ocean City and the length of Assateague Island, which protects the entire coast. Channel bass run north along this coast in May and June, returning southward again about the middle of September through October. They work along the sloughs in the sand, very close to shore. Fish up to 50 pounds are taken during the runs. Cut bait (menhaden) is used mostly by daytime fishermen, while those who go to the beaches at night prefer soft crabs. Cut squid and shrimp are also used, and lures take quite a few fish.

Midsummer beach fishermen at Assateague will usually catch bluefish, stripers, some sea trout and small, eating-size kingfish, which often come in in large numbers. To get to Assateague you rent a boat at Ocean City, at the end of U.S. 50, on the Atlantic; there is also a ferry from South Point, on State Highway 611 about twelve miles south of Ocean City; or you can go from Chincoteague, Virginia, off U.S. 13 via Virginia State Highway 175.

Anglers going to this remote island take food supplies and cook their catch right on the beach. Some set up camps. There's fresh water available at a public pump.

OFFSHORE FISHING

Out of Ocean City, Maryland, deep-sea trollers can find some of the best white-marlin fishing in the world. These scrappy billfish are taken in great numbers from mid-June through September. An annual white-marlin tournament is held at Ocean City in September. The fish range from 55 to 75 pounds, and the top fishing area is known as "the Jack Spot," some twenty-three miles offshore. Trollers use squid, mullet or balao for bait. Most of these great sporting fish are released.

Other offshore species include dolphin, bonito, blue marlin, swordfish, albacore and wahoo. There are some Allison tuna and some bluefin, the latter running up to 100 pounds, though the average is much smaller. Bluefish make a run into these waters in early June and stay around through August. They are caught inshore of the white-marlin grounds, and around the inlets, and in the autumn sometimes come into the surf.

One of the country's finest fishing fleets is berthed at Ocean City, but there are always plenty of fishermen, too, so reservations should be made early. A list of guides may be obtained from Dept. C-3, Information Center, Ocean City, Maryland; or reservations may be made through Captain Talbot E. Bunting, Talbot Street Pier and Ocean City Yacht Basin, Ocean City, Maryland.

The charter boats fish for cod around the reefs off Ocean City during the fall and winter, from December 1st through the middle of March. It's cold-weather fishing but some good catches are made of this excellent table fish.

Headboats, costing about $5 per person, leave the Ocean City Docks every morning during the summer to fish the wrecks for porgies, sea bass and other inshore species.

ONSHORE FISHING ON THE ATLANTIC COAST

Aside from the surf fishing on the outer beaches of Assateague Island, there is good onshore fishing along the whole Maryland coast. Both casters and bait fishermen make good catches from the jetty across the mouth of Sinepuxent Bay, near Ocean City. In the well-sheltered waters of the bay itself you can go in rented skiff and outboard for sea trout (which are found in great numbers in the bay), porgies, sea bass, bluefish and whatever else turns up. One of the most popular species is the flounder, often called "doormat." Thousands of these tasty bottom dwellers are taken in the months from June to September. Minnows or cut pieces of squid are the favorite baits. Sometimes the flounder will also hit a cast bucktail retrieved very slowly along the bottom. Throughout the bay anglers use all kinds of tackle, from light spinning gear to heavy bottom-fishing rigs.

MARYLAND FISHING REGULATIONS

Because of the wide variety of fishing and the difference in seasons in inland and tidewater areas, anglers in Maryland should always check the current Game and Fish laws thoroughly. In general the following regulations hold true:

Resident Fishing License $3.00
Nonresident Fishing License $10.00
Nonresident 3-Day Fishing License $3.00
Special license for residents
    of Virginia, West Virginia and the District of Columbia, to fish the
    Potomac River $3.00
No license required for salt or tidewater fishing.

SEASONS AND LIMITS

FRESH WATER

Species	*Open Season*	*Size Limit*	*Bag Limit*
Black Bass	No closed season	9″ minimum	10 in aggregate (5 in some cases)
Chain Pickerel	No closed season	14″ minimum	5
Northern Pike	No closed season	20″ minimum	2
Muskellunge	No closed season	30″ minimum	2
Striped Bass (Rock)	No closed season	14″ minimum	None
Walleye	March 31–Nov. 16	14″ minimum	5
Trout, all species	April 14–March 15	7″ minimum	7 in aggregate

All other species, no closed season, no minimum size or bag limit.

TIDEWATER

Species	Open Season	Size Limit	Bag Limit
Bass	No closed season	9″ minimum	5 in aggregate
Walleye	No closed season	14″ minimum	None
Pike (Pickerel)	April 30–March 15	14″ minimum	10 in aggregate
Perch, White, Yellow	No closed season	None	None
Hardhead (Croaker)	No closed season	10″ minimum	None
Catfish	No closed season	8″ minimum	None
Sturgeon	No closed season	25 lb. minimum	None
Sea Trout (Weakfish)	No closed season	10″ minimum	None
Bluefish	No closed season	8″ minimum	None
Shad	Dec. 31–July 6	None	None
Striped Bass (Rockfish)	No closed season	12″ minimum, 15 lb. maximum except from June 16 to Apr. 30 inclusive, when one fish over 15 pounds per day, per person may be kept.	None except for fish over 15 lbs.

For complete regulations write: Game and Inland Fish Commission, 516 Munsey Building, Baltimore 2, Maryland; and the Department of Tidewater Fisheries, Annapolis, Maryland. Tide tables, which are invaluable to coastal fishermen, can be obtained from Dillon's Fishing Tackle, 2410 St. Paul Street, Baltimore 18, Maryland.

VIRGINIA

The State of Virginia has an ideal situation for sport fishing. Mountains in the west provide habitat for a limited amount of trout fishing. A wide band of piedmont supports such species as the basses, sunfish, crappie, pickerel, walleye and catfish. And hundreds of miles of coastline on the Chesapeake Bay and the Delmarva Peninsula offer endless saltwater fishing opportunities. There are blue marlin, white marlin, bluefin and yellowfin tuna, wahoo, cobia, dolphin, mackerel, false albacore and bluefish for trollers off the Virginia capes and in the ocean deeps. Along the beaches and in the bays are black drum, channel bass and spotted sea trout, and in various other inshore waters are found tautog, flounder, sheepshead, spadefish, sea bass and lesser species such as white perch, croaker, porgy and spot. Even the tarpon has been taken in the Chesapeake Bay but not enough show up to make it a fishery.

Striped bass, commonly called "rock" or "rockfish" in Virginia, spawn in Chesapeake Bay and its tributaries. In the bay they can be caught almost year-round. In spring and fall they move into the many rivers and are taken in brackish and fresh water. Virginia records show stripers up to 50 pounds. The white shad and hickory shad also make seasonal runs into many Virginia rivers.

The drainage in the State of Virginia is almost entirely to the Chesapeake Bay via the Potomac, Rappahannock, York and James Rivers and their tributaries. The Roanoke system drains the southwestern portion into North Carolina. There are few large natural lakes but thousands of ponds, most of which offer some kind of fishing.

Anglers will find ready access to Virginia fishing waters via Interstate 95 and U.S. 1, throughout the north-south length of the state, from which many cross-country roads lead both to the mountains of the west and the tidewater area of the east. U.S. 301, another major artery, runs up through the state from the southern border, bypassing Washington and turning east across the Bay Bridge at Annapolis to provide entry to the Eastern Shore of Maryland. From the eastern end of the bridge motorists can take Maryland Highway 404 across to U.S. 13, which then runs the length of the Delmarva Peninsula to Virginia's share of the Eastern Shore. There is also a bridge and tunnel to the southern tip of the peninsula, from Norfolk to Cape Charles.

The climate in Virginia is hot in summer, cool enough for snow for a few weeks in winter, and the mountainous areas are cold enough to provide good skiing in some areas. Spring and fall are pleasant throughout, with temperatures fluctuating between 50 and 80 degrees Fahrenheit, ideal fishing weather.

Deer are extremely plentiful and may be seen in the mountains as well as in the farmers' fields and woodlands of lower terrain. Bear and occasionally bobcats are encountered in the mountains and also in the Dismal Swamp in the southeast corner of the state. There are a few elk in southwestern Virginia, where an attempt is being made to build up the herds which once roamed this area.

Anglers should always keep an eye out for copperhead snakes and cottonmouth moccasins in the low-lying ground, and for rattlers in the mountains.

WESTERN AREA

The trout fishing in Virginia is found in the western part of the state where the Blue Ridge, Alleghanies and other ridges of the Appalachian Mountains lie along almost the entire length of the border between Virginia and West Virginia. Here the small mountain streams are free from the silting that takes place in the rivers at lower altitudes. They are stocked annually, mainly with rainbow trout but also with some brook trout. Until recently browns were not included but in the past few years experimental plantings in a few rivers have shown good holdover and many anglers hope that this adaptive species will eventually be added to Virginia's trout list in substantial numbers.

The typical Virginia trout stream is small, calling for light tackle, fine leaders and most of all, careful approach. The suitable fly rod is 7½ or 8 feet long, fitted with an HDH floating line and 9- to 10-foot leader tapered to 5X or 6X tippet. Spinning outfits should be correspondingly light.

All the standard fly patterns are good but in the smaller waters the fisherman must remember that if he is using bucktails and streamers he should go to the smallest in his book. The best bet in late spring and early summer is dry-fly fishing, working upstream slowly and quietly to avoid being seen by the trout, and using as short a line as possible. While Virginia is not a great trout state, a day spent like this can produce a panful of rainbows and brook trout around 9 inches in size and leave pleasant memories of the wonderful scenery of the Blue Ridge Mountains.

The trout streams are located roughly in a long, narrow strip on either side of the mountains. The country is often so rough that it takes both stamina and knowledge of the terrain to get into them. The fishing in each stream is also usually limited to a comparatively small portion of its course. The Virginia Department of Conservation and Economic Development, State Office Building, Richmond 19, Virginia, publishes a "Fresh Water Fishing Map" giving the locations of the various creeks in great detail. However, the following will give a broad picture of the main trout fishing available.

A great deal of the trout fishing is found in the streams lying immediately west of U.S. 11. The NORTH FORK OF THE SHENANDOAH (1) and its tributaries can be good, especially around Bergton, high up against the West Virginia border. The town is reached via State Highway 259, off U.S. 11 at Lacey Spring. The BIG AND LITTLE STONY (2) can be fished from Liberty Furnace, reached via State Highway 42, west from Edinburg on U.S. 11. UPPER CEDAR CREEK and PADDY RUN (3) and close to Strasburg on U.S. 11. PASSAGE CREEK (4), running parallel to, and between the North and the South Fork of the Shenandoah, near Strasburg, has some trout, and so has nearby OPEQUON CREEK (5), in the headwaters only. Cub Run and Pitt Spring join the South Fork of the Shenandoah near Shenandoah on U.S. 340, west of Harrisonburg. There are several unimproved camp sites in this area.

There are a number of trout streams in Shenandoah National Forest, which runs along the mountain ridges, with access via the Skyline Drive, from Waynesboro to Front Royal. BROAD RUN (6) is one of the best. Others are the headwaters of the Rapidan, Hughes, Robertson, Thornton, Jordan and Rush. Information as to where and how to reach them can be obtained from tackle stores at Waynesboro, Harrisonburg and Front Royal. If you have a regular Virginia trout license you don't need a special Park license. But remember that within the Park only artificial baits with a single hook may be used. There is also some commercially operated "pay as you fish" water at Monterey, at the junction of U.S. 250 and 220, close to the West Virginia border. Both streams and ponds are available.

West of Harrisonburg, the headwaters of the NORTH RIVER (7) and its tributary the St. Mary's River, in George Washington National Forest, hold trout, and so does the BULLPASTURE RIVER (8), reached from McDowell on U.S. 250. In the SHERANDO AREA (9), on State Highway 14, off the Parkway east of Waynesboro, there are trout in Sherando Lake as well as Back Creek. Other streams which are regularly stocked are the TYE, ROCKFISH, and PINEY CREEKS (10), which have trout in the upper waters and smallmouth black bass and panfish lower down. Others of this same nature, in the EDINBURG AREA (11), are Moorman's, Pedlar, Stoney Creek, Buena Vista, Rocky Row Run, Shoe Creek, Irish Creek, the Buffalo River, and the tributaries of the Calfpasture, as the Goshen River is called above Goshen.

In 1961 the Virginia Commission of Game and Inland Fisheries, in co-operation with the Shenandoah National Park, opened the headwaters of the RAPIDAN RIVER (12) in Madison County as a "Fish for Fun" area. All fish must be returned to the water unharmed. This is a great step forward in developing trout fishing as a sport, and will result in bigger fish, less money spent for stocking streams, and better fishing for the future. The Virginia Fish and Game Commission is to be commended for this fine effort. To reach the "Fish for Fun" area on the Rapidan, anglers should go to Ruckersville or Madison on U.S. 29, south of Culpeper, then turn up to the Shenandoah National Park on State Highways 230, 231 or U.S. 33. The part of the "Fish For Fun" waters which has the biggest fish is reached via the Skyline Drive to Big Meadow, then a three-mile trail down to the river.

The Rapidan is best fished with dry flies, and small ones. Sizes 14 and 16 are the best. Blue Dun, Iron Blue Dun, Light Cahill, Mosquito, Coachman, Black Gnat, Red Variant and Black Flying Ant, the last in size 18, are all good patterns. Spinning is permitted, but the stream is low and clear and small, and it is difficult to take trout with spoons under these circumstances. Yet you never know what trout will do. Once I fished this stream with Leon Kesteloo and Monk Montague, of Richmond, and watched them take trout on a shad fly. It was the only fly that would get down deep enough that hot day to reach the fish hiding in the holes among the rocks.

In northwestern Virginia there is some exceptional fishing for smallmouth black bass around Riverton, which is near Front Royal, on U.S. 340. Many of the rivers which have trout in their headwaters hold smallmouth black bass and crappie in the lower part of the stream. There is outstanding fishing of this kind in the Shenandoah from Riverton to the West Virginia border. The river crosses U.S. 50 and State Highway 7, providing two points of access. Wading is good and it is fine water for both fly man and spinner, with deep eddies and long riffles. It can also be floated but in shallow boats, as during the dry season there is very little water in the riffles. The nearby South Fork of the Shenandoah is good for smallmouth from Port Republic, off U.S. 340 at Grottoes, all the way downstream to Riverton. U.S.

Many ponds in Piedmont Virginia provide wonderful fishing for largemouth bass, bream, crappie and other small-fry.

340 runs with the river much of the way. The North, Middle and South Rivers which make up the South Fork also hold smallmouth, largemouth and panfish, but don't fish the branch known as the South River, as it is polluted. The above streams also have catfish, which local anglers go for at night with great success. The Fresh Water Fishing Map mentioned earlier will clear up the apparent confusion of names. Nearly all these mountain streams have a North and South Branch or a part called the North River or the South River.

The North Fork of the Shenandoah can be reached from Riverton. There are smallmouth bass and panfish from there up to Fulks Run, and trout above that. In the UPPER RAPPAHANNOCK (13), near Remington, there are smallmouth. The best approach is south of Warrenton on U.S. 15. Further south along the mountains, near Lexington at the junction of U.S. 11 and U.S. 60, the NORTH RIVER (14), also called Maury's River, is a good producer of smallmouth.

The same is true of the tributaries of the James. The COWPASTURE RIVER (15) reaching the James near Iron Gate and Clifton Forge on U.S. 60, can be floated with small boats. The BULLPASTURE (8), a tributary of the Cowpasture, has smallmouth in the lower waters, and, as mentioned earlier, trout in the upper. Another tributary, the JACKSON (16), west of U.S. 220 between Covington and Warm Springs, is actually the top waters of the James. Besides trout in its upper waters, and bass and crappie lower down, there are chain pickerel in that stretch between Bacova and Covington. Unfortunately below Covington it is badly polluted.

PIEDMONT VIRGINIA

The Piedmont is that area stretching the length of the state from the foothills of the mountains down towards the Chesapeake until the influence of the sea is felt.

It is a land of slower-moving rivers and there are many lakes and ponds, some with natural fishing and others which have been stocked. The major species of the Piedmont area are largemouth black bass, crappie, bluegills, sunfish, catfish and carp, and some chain pickerel. Some of the lakes, such as LAKE BRITTLE (17), near New Baltimore on U.S. 211, about thirty miles west of Washington, are extremely heavily fished yet produce good catches of largemouth and bluegills. Lake Brittle is open year-round and there are boats available and live bait for sale.

The largest lake in Virginia is the KERR RESERVOIR (18), also known as the Buggs Island Reservoir. It was formed by damming the Roanoke River on the Virginia-North Carolina line. There are largemouth black bass, smallmouth black bass, walleyes, crappie, sunfish, channel catfish, bullhead, catfish and carp. When the dam was constructed it landlocked a few striped bass which had come up the river to spawn. In the period between 1953 and 1955, the North Carolina Resources Commission further developed this species by stocking a million striped-bass fry. As a result, there has developed some quite good fishing for this species. In 1959 several thousand stripers were caught, both above and below the dam. Fish up to 15 pounds have been taken on rod and reel; and to show the extent of the possibilities, one year, in October, the peak of the season, a group of three anglers took twenty-six stripers and two largemouth black bass for a total of 142 pounds.

A recent regulation places a 12-inch minimum size limit and a creel limit of eight on the stripers in Kerr Reservoir.

The fishing is mostly done by trolling or bottom bumping or jigging with cast lures, either from a boat or from the dam. Fall is the best time, when the stripers are schooling. Below the dam bucktails seem to be the best lures and most catches are made when the water gates are open. Virginia and North Carolina Fishing Licenses are reciprocal in the lake but not in the Roanoke River, where, however, state boundaries are clearly marked. There are many public and private boat docks, concessions and bait houses at the lake. Anglers will find accommodations at Clarksville and Boydton on U.S. 58.

Above the lake, in the DAN RIVER (19), there are largemouth and smallmouth bass, sunfish and crappie, as well as channel and bullhead catfish and carp. At the dam on the Dan River there is great walleye fishing when this species makes its annual run in the spring.

A new lake, GASTON RESERVOIR (20), to the east, is mostly in North Carolina but is also accessible from Virginia near the small town of Bracey on State Highway 637. For boats, most anglers go to Gaston, North Carolina, via State Highway 46 south from Lawrenceville. The lake was stocked with largemouth, northern pike and muskellunge, and should produce good fishing as the fish develop. There are also bluegills, crappie and catfish.

Closer to the Blue Ridge Mountains is the PHILPOTT RESERVOIR (21), on the Smith River. The nearest town is Bassett, on State Highway 57 just off U.S. 220 north of Martinsville. There are largemouth to better than 5 pounds, crappie and sunfish, and a few smallmouth, also of good size, as well as rough fish. Boats are available, and just below the dam there is some trout fishing.

Other lakes of some size, where boats are available, are BEAR CREEK LAKE (22), off U.S. 60 near the town of Cumberland; HOLIDAY LAKE (23), off U.S. 15 on 636 at Sheppards, north of Farmville; or south on State Highway 24 from Mount Rush on U.S. 60; PRINCE EDWARD LAKE (24) near Burkeville, off U.S. 360 at Green

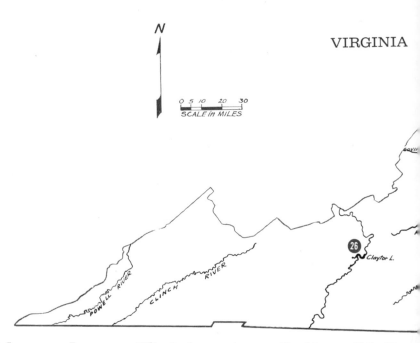

Bay; and LEESVILLE RESERVOIR (25), further west, near Altavista, on U.S. 29. Some striped bass have also been stocked in the latter.

Many other municipal reservoirs and privately owned ponds in the Piedmont have been stocked with various warm-water species and some are open to public fishing. Camp Picket, between U.S. 460 and U.S. 1, west of Petersburg, has four lakes now open to public fishing. Permission must be obtained at the military headquarters there. No boats are available but you may launch your own. CLAYTOR LAKE (26), off U.S. 11 at Radford, west of Roanoke, has some good fishing for smallmouth black bass, largemouth black bass, pickerel, bream, crappie and some brown trout. Still another military reservation where there is fishing is A.P. Hill, off U.S. 301, southwest of Port Royal, on the Rappahannock River. There are ten lakes, several with boats available. A permit must be obtained at headquarters, near Bowling Green on U.S. 301.

A list of many small lakes and ponds where there is some public fishing may be obtained from the Commission of Game and Inland Fisheries, P.O. Box 1642, Richmond 13. They also publish a list of Virginia public boat landings and marinas.

Generally, in these lakes the best lures for bass are the popping bugs and streamer flies. Crappie like a small spoon allowed to sink, then retrieved slowly. Bream, the overall name applied to the many members of the sunfish family, like a small popping bug with rubber legs. Pike will hit both poppers and underwater lures. Bait fishermen prefer live minnows for largemouth bass, with worms running a close second, and take all the other species on the same offering.

A few of the rivers in eastern Virginia provide opportunity for canoe or skiff trips combined with moderately good fishing. The MATTAPONI (27), from Bowling

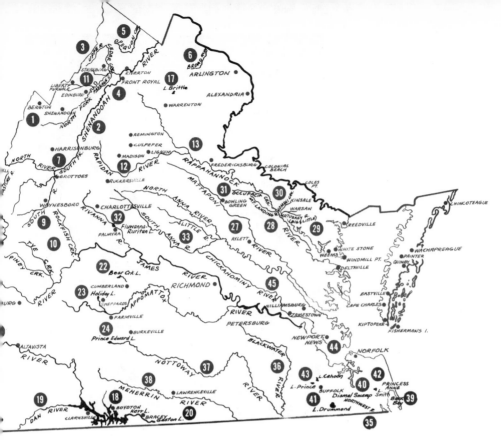

Green to Aylett, is an example. Perch will usually be taken at the mouths of creeks and there's good fishing for pike near Mundy's Bridge. Bass are not numerous but will usually turn out to be extra large. Boats can put in at the State Highway 2 bridge near Bowling Green, the Stephens Run Bridge where U.S. 360 crosses the river, and the Tappahannock Highway Bridge at Aylett, on U.S. 360.

Further inland, the Rappahannock River south of Lake Brittle can be floated either with skiffs or canoes, from Remington, on U.S. 15 and U.S. 29. Smallmouth, crappie, sunfish, catfish and carp will be the catch. There is good wading. Many of the tributaries can also be floated. The main ones are MT. LANDING (28), on the lower river, north of Tappahannock at the junction of U.S. 360 and U.S. 17; BIG and LITTLE TOTUSKEY (29), across the river from Tappahannock, near Warsaw; NOMINI CREEK (30), north of Warsaw; and OCCUPACIA CREEK (31), off State Highway 624 north of Warsaw. Another tributary, the RAPIDAN (12), is best fished by wading or from the bank. It can be reached from State Highway 3, south of Lignum, and U.S. 522, fifteen miles south of Culpeper. There are large and smallmouth bass, bluegills and crappie.

The RIVANNA RIVER roughly parallels State Highway 53 southeast from Charlottsville. The river and FLUVANNA-RURITAN LAKE (32), on State Highway 53, north from Palmyra, produce largemouth and bluegills. There are boats for hire and launching sites.

To the northwest of Richmond the NORTH and SOUTH ANNA and the LITTLE RIVER (33) are mostly limited to bluegills and sunfish but there are a few largemouths.

The JAMES RIVER (34), extending through the entire central portion of the

Leon Kesteloo, of Richmond, Virginia, displays his 55-pound channel bass on the beach at Parramore Island, Virginia. He took the lunker on a 12-pound-test spinning outfit with cut spot for bait.

State of Virginia, can be floated in many places, but always with caution. Fast sections are dangerous, and the river floods heavily after rain. Launching sites for floating the higher portions of the river will be found at Bent Creek where U.S. 60 crosses the James at Bremo Bluff, where U.S. 15 crosses, and near Goochland, on U.S. 522, at Lee. There are also public landings owned by the Inland Game and Fish Commission in Powhatan County and in Fluvanna, Albemarle and Buckingham Counties. Game wardens in these counties are the best contact for visitors who do not know the river.

There is some excellent smallmouth fishing in the seven miles of the James above Richmond. Spin and fly casters have great success with small popping bugs or plugs, and with streamers and bucktails. Robin's egg blue is a good color. Fly fishermen also use dry flies for James River smallmouths, the size 8 and 10 Royal Wulff, Gray Wulff, Adams Hackle, Skating Spider, Gray Bivisible and Brown Bivisible all being successful. Lower in the river, in tidewater, from Jamestown to Norfolk at the mouth of the bay, there are white perch and stripers.

In the southern part of Virginia, the NORTHWEST (35), BLACKWATER (36), NOTTOWAY (37) and MEHERRIN RIVERS (38) all have warm-water species in the upper waters, as well as runs of saltwater species in the tidewater areas.

TIDEWATER VIRGINIA

The influence of the tide is felt far up into nearly every river along the Virginia coast. Saltwater species of fish move in with the tide and the anadromous striped bass and shad make spawning runs into the rivers. The same species are found along the Atlantic coast south of Norfolk, where the shore is protected by a sandy peninsula which forms Back Bay; and along the shores of the Eastern Shore Peninsula. In addition, such freshwater species as can tolerate a certain amount of salinity haunt the inshore waters of this area.

BACK BAY (39), on the coast south of Virginia Beach, is perhaps the best known largemouth black bass water in Virginia, holding myriad fish. The bass run from 1½ to 2½ pounds in weight, with a few as heavy as 6 pounds. It is not unusual to catch as many as fifty a day. Top-water baits are very good for spinning and plug casting, the Old Joe, Devil Horse and Crippled Killer being exceptional producers. The Johnson Silver Minnow with weedless attachment is one of the best lures for fishing below the surface. The bottom is hard sand in many places, so it is possible to wade and cast in to the banks of islands, a good place for bass to be. The best fly-rod producers are the top-water Gerbubble Bug, the 1/0 Skipping Bug, the Twitch 'n' Crawl. Multiwing streamers and the blond flies are also good, all on 1/0 hooks.

Wind controls the fishing in Back Bay, as too much wind muddies the water. If you hit such a period, try the lee shore and the guts and creeks into the Bay. Sometimes it will be clear enough there to produce. The best wind for fishing is from the southwest or southeast, which blows water into the Sound. A north wind blows it out. When there's an east wind you might as well stay home; you seldom get a strike.

The old Trojan Gun Club, reached by Highway 615 and 617, has been purchased by the Virginia Fish and Game Commission for use as a public hunting and fishing area. Near the Club is a canal, some 1,800 feet long. Manager Elwood Waterfield has seen many 6-pound bass come from this canal, which opens into Back Bay. This being tidewater, there is no closed season.

As there are so many marshes and coves and guts of water extending back into the marshes, it's a good idea to have a guide when you fish this water. He can take you quickly to the best fishing, and there's no chance of becoming lost. Supplies, accommodations and guides can be found at Princess Anne on State Highway 615, south of Virginia Beach. There are several public launching sites and boat docks.

The best times are March through May. In June the action begins to slow a bit and in July and August fishing is usually good only early in the morning and at dusk. With the cooler weather of September things pick up again and stay good until the cold of December puts the fish down.

There are also chain pickerel, black crappie, bluegill, white and yellow perch and occasional stripers and flounders in Back Bay.

Guides will be found at several points off State Highway 615 south from Virginia Beach. Some of them are Caleb Cartwright, Rt. 1, Princess Anne, Virginia, on Route 627 at West Neck Creek, phone Princess Anne 3416; Cecil Stevens, Knott's Island, Munden, Virginia, on Knott's Island at the end of Route 664, phone Princess Anne 3280; Albert Henley, Pungo, Virginia, Public Landing, Route 659, North Bay, phone Princess Anne 3502; Roy Lovitt, Rt. 1, Princess Anne at the boat dock at the corner of Routes 603 and 627, phone Princess Anne 3411; Ernest Grimstead, Munden, Virginia, Public Landing on Route 669; Elwood Waterfield, Munden, Virginia, Route 671 at North Land River, phone Princess Anne 3358; Murden's Club, Back Bay, phone Princess Anne 3503; and Willie Davis, Hills Landing, Back Bay, phone Princess Anne, 3063.

On the southern reaches of the Chesapeake and around Norfolk and Virginia Beach there are a number of fishing piers. The charge is usually about $1.10 per person. Tackle, lunches and bait are available in most cases.

To the west of Back Bay in the DISMAL SWAMP (40) is LAKE DRUMMOND (41). The Swamp is bounded by U.S. 17 on the east, State Highway 32 on the west, and U.S. 158 crosses the south end from Elizabeth City, North Carolina, to Sunbury, North Carolina. This is one place you should never venture without a guide. The Virginia Commission of Game and Inland Fisheries, 7 North 2nd Street, Richmond, Virginia, publishes a free leaflet entitled "Tell Me, Warden," which lists the names and addresses of current wardens in the Swamp. They will give you advice on guides for the Swamp.

LAKE SMITH (42), to the east, close to the shores of Back Bay, off State Highway 615, has produced more big largemouth black bass than any other lake in Virginia. A little further to the west and to the north, off U.S. 460, LAKE PRINCE and LAKE CAHOON (43) are reservoirs for the city of Suffolk. They hold largemouth, pickerel, panfish, crappie and white perch. Two new nearby reservoirs, to serve Newport News and Norfolk, opened in 1964, are WEST BRANCH LAKE and DIASCUND LAKE (44). Both are stocked with bass, bluegill and redear sunfish.

The CHICKAHOMINY RIVER (45), emptying into the James on the north shore, has been dammed at Walker's Station to create Chickahominy Lake, which has goodly populations of largemouth black bass and many large panfish. Below the dam there are runs of shad and stripers and above it the river can be waded in many places to produce pickerel, bass and bream. The tidewater also has many old millponds and although most of them are privately owned, a few of them are open to the public and provide good bass and crappie fishing, and the Virginia Commission of Game and Inland Fisheries has constructed a few more for public use. The river is reached via U.S. 60 to Williamsburg and State Highway 5 to Jamestown.

CHESAPEAKE BAY FISHING

Bridging the gap between the freshwater species of lake and stream and the saltwater species are the shad and the striped bass, or rockfish. Both hickory and white shad are taken by trollers and casters using small, bright spoons and spinners, or flies or spinning lures, below dams in tidal rivers and further up in the rivers themselves, at the time of their spring run. Shad and shad roe are great delicacies and each year hordes of anglers go out for these hard-fighting fish. They reach Virginia waters in March and stay around until June. They are caught only on artificial lures, scorning bait altogether, except very rarely, when a shad is taken on a very small hook baited with a tiny bit of worm. But they strike small spoons readily.

This lower part of the Chesapeake Bay has some fine striped-bass fishing. Bait fishermen use soft crabs, peeler crabs, blood worms and grass shrimp. Others use fly, plug and spin gear to cast both top-water and deeper-working lures, working the bars, holes under banks and the channels on the islands and mainland, either wading or by skiff. In the shallow bays they fish over grassy beds in water from 2 to 10 feet in depth. Inlets are good, and spots where the outgoing tide washes out foodstuffs from a bay. Gulls diving and wheeling will often finger schools of stripers in the bay for boatmen. The best fishing starts in April and continues, except for off spells on hot days, through the early summer, dwindles some, then picks up again in the fall. October is usually very good. The cold weather of mid-December usually puts the end to the striper season.

Plug and spin casters use both top-water and underwater lures. They often let the boat drift across a grassy flat, casting ahead or to the side. Sometimes they see stripers breaking, rolling or chasing fish. Other times they cast blind around sand-bars, to shorelines and undercut banks. In the fall the stripers tend to school up and then you may find them anywhere, out in the bay or working inshore waters, and even ascending the brackish water rivers for miles.

One of the best top-water spinning lures is the Old Joe, put out by the Phillips Fly & Tackle Company of Alexandria, Pennsylvania. The blonde pattern bucktail flies are great for stripers. These are also made by Phillips and also by Bill Gallasch, 8705 Weldon Drive, Richmond, Virginia. Gallasch also makes a very effective skipping bug that stripers favor, in the same pattern as that which the writer used to catch the biggest striper known to have been taken on a fly, at Coos Bay, Oregon, in 1948. It weighed 29 pounds 8 ounces.

One of the most popular bay-fishing areas is the area between the Potomac River and the Rappahannock. This section is generally referred to by Virginians as "the Northern Neck." It is well served by U.S. 360 from Richmond and State Highway 3 from Fredericksburg; or you can enter the neck from the south on State Highway 3, via a toll bridge at Grey's Point on the south bank of the Rappahannock. There are charter boats at Weems, Irvington and White Stone, at the end of the Northern Neck; from Reedville, further north, at the end of U.S. 360; from Kinsale, further north at the mouth of the Potomac, and Coles Point, a few miles further north at the end of State Highway 612. Another port is Colonial Beach, well up in the Potomac. From this port, party boats go out for periods as short as three hours during the summer season. In general, the cost of fishing can vary from $12 to $50 per day, depending on the accommodations and number in the party. In many ports and 'longshore communities skiffs with or without motors are available for from $2 to $5 per day. In some, for a small fee the dock owner will tow your skiff to the fishing grounds and call for you again at the end of the fishing day.

From early August until early October there are usually schools of big bluefish around the Southeast Middles, off the mouth of the Potomac, and these are fished from Reedsville and other small communities in the area.

A very complete list of guides and other fishermen's services can be obtained from the Northern Neck Regional Planning and Economic Development Commission, Warsaw, Virginia.

On the neck of land between the Rappahannock and the York there are also many small communities where anglers can find boats for hire, and in some cases commercial fishermen who are willing to act as guides. Urbanna, just off U.S. 17 at Saluda, is a good spot to fish from. Deltaville, at the end of State Highway 33, is another. In fact, at any port along this shore, the angler who can get a skiff or launch his own, in striper season is fairly sure of fish.

Windmill Point, at the northern tip of the Rappahannock outlet, is one of the most popular spots on the Chesapeake for cobia fishing. There's a good marina there, boats for hire, and accommodations at several motels. The fishing is best from mid-July through September, and continues into October. Fishing is conducted on the bars near the Windwill Point Light, fishermen chumming with ground-up menhaden, known locally as "bunker," and baiting the fish with eels and live or dead menhaden. Catches of 40 to 60 pounds are usual. The cobia will also hit artificial lures. In July, 1962, the writer saw a fish swimming free alongside one which my friend Moses Nunnally of Richmond was fighting on a 20-pound-line trolling outfit. I cast a big white bucktail to the free swimmer, using a heavy plug-casting outfit. The fish took, and three-quarters of an hour later I landed it. It went 49 pounds 8 ounces, exactly the same weight as the one that Moses landed in the meantime!

The following provide charter-boat service in this area: Captain Allen Harrow, Deltaville, Virginia; Edmond Harrow, Deltaville, Virginia; Diller Harding, Route 1, Kilmarnock, Virginia; Captain L. M. Sparshott, Kilmarnock, Virginia; Captain Wayson Christopher, Kilmarnock, Virginia; Captain Jimmie Kelley, Kilmarnock, Virginia; Captain G. H. Winstead, Kilmarnock, Virginia; Captain M. K. Thomson, Deltaville, Virginia; Captain Howard McNamara, Deltaville, Virginia; Captain R. F. Shackelford, Irvington, Virginia; and Captain Winnie Abbott, Irvington, Virginia.

There is good bottom fishing throughout the Chesapeake Bay area of Virginia, the catch including croaker or hardhead, spot, gray sea trout or weakfish, flounder, whiting, scup, puffers, pigfish, sea bass and some tautog. Bottom fishing is usually done with two hooks placed a foot apart above the sinker. Peeler crab, cut bait, shrimp, clams or minnows are all good baits. One old-timer advises using three hooks, the two as above, plus a third on 18 inches of line from the sinker and baited with a live minnow. Such a bait is almost certain to get a flounder if there are any in the area.

Many bottom fishermen use chum, lowering a sack of ground menhaden, herring or fish oil and meal mixed together, to coax the fish within their reach.

VIRGINIA BEACHES AND OFFSHORE FISHING

Virginia's outer beaches are reached by bridge and tunnel from Norfolk, or via U.S. 13, south from Delaware and Maryland, down into the Delmarva Peninsula. Anglers coming from the south will find accommodations at Cape Charles and Eastville, and a few other small communities along the highway, but accommodations are limited and arrangements should be made in advance.

The Cedar Island Sports Club, Accomac P.O., Virginia, provides accommodations, meals, boats, bait and beach buggies, on Cedar Island, just east of Accomac. Phone SU 7-1010. There are also accommodations available at the Hotel Russell, Chincoteague, Virginia, proprietor Joe Sparrow.

Surf casters on the beaches of the offshore islands take black drum, channel bass, striped bass, bluefish and flounder. Artificials, cut bait, bunker, peeler crabs and clams are all used. Channel-bass (red drum) fishing is especially good in the summer. The big fish work the sloughs close to shore on Chincoteague, Wachapreague and Cobb Islands. Anglers have most success on the incoming tide, though there are exceptions to this and the best way to figure it is to fish two hours on the incoming and two hours on the outgoing. Surf fishermen should remember that the fish will be very close inshore, so don't put your bait out too far.

The best trolling for channel bass is from Kiptopeke to Fisherman's Island, at the extreme end of the Peninsula. The largest channel bass ever taken in Virginia came from these waters. It weighed 83 pounds. Some very large ones have been taken at Parramore Island, near Quinby, south of Wachapreague Inlet.

There are charter boats available at Quinby, off U.S. 13 on State Highway 182 at Painter; Wachapreague, on State Highway 180 from U.S. 13; and Chincoteague, reached via State Highway 175 from U.S. 13. There are hotel and restaurant facilities on Chincoteague, as well as boat rentals and a marina. Joe Sparrow, Hotel Russell, Chincoteague, will provide all the latest dope on fishing in that area.

In general, rates for offshore trolling are about $70 per day. Offshore reef fishing boats charge about $50, and inside bottom-fishing boats get about $35. There is good striper fishing on the bay side at the Saxis on Pocomoke Sound. Arrangements can be made through Joe Sparrow, at Chincoteague.

Ocean fishing is by trolling the deep water or bottom fishing over the reefs. Offshore fishermen take white marlin, some blue marlin, dolphin, large bluefish, bluefin tuna, mako shark, oceanic bonito and kingfish. Inshore they get scup or porgy, large sea bass, black drum, red drum, and in some oceanside bays large tarpon have been seen and a few have been taken.

White-marlin fishing is best off Chincoteague and Wachapreague, in the blue water some fifteen to eighteen miles offshore. June and July are the best months. Then the fishing dwindles until the first of September. The fish average 60 to 70 pounds, with a top of 85. Some blue marlin have also been taken, up to 286 pounds.

Also in the blue water are dolphin. They often hit marlin baits, and are also taken on feathers and spoons. As in other places where he is found, the dolphin can best be located by sighting any floating debris, even a box or a branch. There may be a dolphin lying in its shade. They average 5 to 15 pounds in these waters, but have been taken up to 35 pounds off Chincoteague. As many as fifty per day have been taken there and out of Wachapreague and Cobb Island.

Though bluefish are most common in the Chesapeake Bay, some are taken off Chincoteague. Normally they appear in April and early May, continue through October, then leave for warmer waters. The average bluefish in Virginia will be 3 to 5 pounds but sometimes they come up to 15 pounds in these offshore waters. Bait fishermen use chum to coax the blues close, then fish with "bunker"—pieces of fish and no sinker—as blues are surface feeders. The bait should be kept moving. And as bluefish usually feed against the tide, the bait should be placed on the down-tide side of the chumline. Remember that the blue has strong jaws and sharp teeth, so be careful when removing the hook.

Guides for the Cape Charles area at the southern tip of the Peninsula and the mouth of the Chesapeake Bay may be obtained through John Crumb, Oyster, Virginia, west of Cape Charles. The phone is Cape Charles 605J11. Also through Willie Crum at Oyster; or Joe Partin, P.O. Box 428, Cape Charles, Virginia.

The Virginia Saltwater Sport Fishing Association conducts an annual saltwater fishing tournament and complete information may be obtained from Claude Rogers, Saltwater Sport Fishing Association, 20th Street and Pacific Avenue, Virginia Beach, Virginia. Much useful information for the prospective saltwater fisherman is contained in the booklet "Saltwater Sport Fishing in Virginia," published by the Virginia

Department of Conservation and Development, State Office Building, Richmond 19, Virginia, the same organization which issues the "Freshwater Fishing Map of Virginia."

VIRGINIA TIDEWATER TIMETABLE

SPECIES	SEASON	PERIOD OF BEST FISHING
Croaker or hardhead	June through winter	May to August
Spot, or Norfolk spot	Year round	August to mid-October
Weakfish or gray trout	Spring and fall	Late April through June; again late August to October
Spotted trout	Fall	Late September through November
Cobia	Summer	July and August
Black drum	Spring	April to mid-June
Red drum	Spring and summer	Late April through June; also on ocean side of Eastern Shore— June and July, September and October
Bluefish	Summer	June and July
Striped bass or rock	May through November	September, October
Marlin	Summer	July through September
Shad	March to May	April and early May
Bluefin tuna	June through August	June and July
Tarpon	Summer	July
Perch	Year round	Year round

VIRGINIA FRESHWATER FISHING REGULATIONS

County or city resident license
    to hunt & fish in county or city
    of residence only $2.00
Resident Fishing License $3.50
Nonresident Fishing License $10.00
Resident or Nonresident, 3-Day Fishing License $1.50
Resident Trout License, in addition to regular
    state fishing license $1.00
Nonresident Trout License, in addition to
    regular state fishing license $5.00
License to fish in National Forests, in addition
    to regular state fishing license $1.00
Sunday fishing is forbidden in some counties.
Any person who fishes on another's property must have permission to do so.

SEASONS AND LIMITS

Species	Open Season	Daily Limit
Black Bass, Spotted, Striped Bass	No closed season	8 daily in aggregate
Pickerel, Walleye	No closed season	8 daily
Crappie, Rock Bass, Bluegill, other Sunfish	No closed season	25 daily in aggregate
Trout	Generally April 7 to Dec. 31 but many exceptions annually	8 daily in aggregate

For complete regulations write: Commission of Game and Inland Fisheries, Box 1642, Richmond 13, Virginia.

NORTH CAROLINA

The State of North Carolina enjoys the benefits of the Appalachian Mountains on the west, providing a watershed which produces a number of streams suitable for trout and sufficient volume of water to create numerous lakes in the midsection of the state. In the east there are vast expanses of shoreline on the Atlantic Ocean. The northern part of this shoreline is protected by one of the greatest natural features of the coast, the Outer Banks, a long strip of sand running from the Virginia border more than halfway down the North Carolina coast, and enclosing two tremendous sounds, Albemarle and Pamlico. Thus North Carolina has a wide variety of waters which support an equally wide variety of fish.

In the mountains there are brook trout, rainbow trout and brown trout. Lower in the streams and lakes there are smallmouth black bass, while the lakes and streams of the Piedmont area, down to the sea, hold largemouth black bass, walleye, white bass, yellow and white perch, crappie and bluegills. In many places the largemouth black bass has moved into tidewater to add brackish water fishing. And in some waters there are also landlocked striped bass, an anadromous species which runs into the coastal rivers and in places has proven adaptable to fresh water.

The saltwater species in North Carolina include most of the game fish of the Atlantic coast. Many blue marlin brought in from offshore waters have weighed in the 400-pound class. A record 810-pounder was boated in 1962. White marlin of 75 pounds and sailfish of better than 70 pounds have been taken; a few swordfish have also been caught. The bluefin, yellowfin, blackfin and Atlantic bigeye tuna move into the offshore waters, too, and current records show weights of 115 pounds, 188 pounds and 195½ pounds, respectively. Also found offshore are bonito, mackerel and false albacore. Amberjack have been taken up to 90 pounds, barracuda to 44; the top dolphin weighed 63 pounds. Wahoo reach good weights, the record being 76 pounds. Cobia have been landed up to 97 pounds and kingfish to 45 pounds 8 ounces.

The species which seasonally move in close to the beaches are equally sporting and substantial in size. The channel bass, or red drum, one of the most popular migrants of the coast, has gone as high as 75½ pounds. The channel bass makes two annual runs, spring and fall. The first fish appear around Cape Fear, on the southern part of the coast, about April, moving north. These early fish are usually small, weighing from 1 to 10 pounds, and are known as puppy drum. As the season progresses, the fish come in waves of increasingly larger fish and start to move in through the inlets between the islands and banks.

Black drum also reach substantial sizes, as much as 82 pounds 4 ounces. Bluefish make phenomenal spring runs, with weights going to 15 pounds 3 ounces. Striped bass move into the sounds and along North Carolina beaches, but although tremendous members of this species are taken in nets each year, the average catch on rod and reel is about 10 pounds. Even tarpon appear off the North Carolina coast. In September, 1958, a 140-pounder was caught in the surf at Baldhead Island, near Southport. In addition to these larger fish, many of the smaller sporting species are found in the bays, sounds and river mouths. These include pompano, croaker, sea trout, flounder and spot.

The major rivers of North Carolina are the Chowan, Roanoke, Pamlico, Neuse, New and Cape Fear, all flowing to the Atlantic shores of the state. The Catawba and Pee Dee are the main drainage arteries flowing southward into South Carolina. The mountain areas along the western boundary feed their waters into the Yadkin, on the north, the French Broad, Tuckasegee and the Little Tennessee, and in the extreme southwest waters flow to the Hiwassee River system.

Because of heavy silting the major lowland rivers do not offer much good fishing, but dams on the rivers have provided a number of large reservoirs which do form habitat suitable for the warm-water species. Gaston Lake, on the Roanoke River, lies on the eastern border with Virginia, and the John Kerr Reservoir is only a few miles to the west, extending well up into Virginia (where it is known as Buggs Island Lake). In the central Piedmont area, on the Pee Dee River, there are two large reservoirs, High Rock Lake and Badin Lake; and above that, on the Catawba River, is a string of river widenings comprising Norman Lake, Hickory Lake, Lookout Reservoir and Rodhiss Reservoir. To the south of this, Lake Catawba forms part of the boundary between North and South Carolina.

Some of North Carolina's finest lake fishing is in the mountain reservoirs: Appalachia Reservoir, and Lake Hiwassee, on the Hiwassee River, in the southern corner between North Carolina and Tennessee. Lakes Santeetlah, Nantahala and Fontana are further north in the same corner of the state.

Like most of the eastern United States, North Carolina is served by excellent highways. U.S. 1, now partially developed into Interstate 95, and U.S. 301 serve the central sector, from Virginia to the South Carolina line. U.S. 17 traverses the entire seaboard; and in the western area the Blue Ridge Parkway, paralleled in large part by U.S. 221, runs the length of the state from the Virginia border to Asheville. From these north-south highways, several major east-west roads such as Interstate 40 and 85 provide fast cross-country travel; and a vast network of lesser arteries lead to the coast on the east and the mountains on the west. The Outer Banks, formerly accessible only by ferry, can now be reached by car, via U.S. 158, at the southern end of Currituck Sound. The main road goes as far as Whalebone, about halfway down Bodie Island. Below that a secondary road follows the banks, with a free ferry at Oregon Inlet, between Bodie and Hatteras, and another between Hatteras and Ocracoke. It is also possible to come onto Bodie Island via State Highways 64 and 264, which cross Croatan Sound between Manns Harbor and Roanoke Island, continue along the island, then cross Roanoke Sound to the Outer Banks.

Climatically, North Carolina is neither "north" nor "south." The fisherman must dress according to the area he will be fishing. Summer fishing along the coast calls for warm-weather gear, but those who go to the Outer Banks from October on must be prepared for wind and cold. The same variety of climatic conditions occurs in the mountains in the western part of the state. The days can be pleasantly warm but the nights will be cool, which is, of course, part of the charm of the region. Throughout North Carolina, fishermen should always pack a rainjacket. All parts of this area, from the Great Smokies to the coast, get enough rainfall to put North Carolina on the list as receiving about the heaviest rainfall of any part of the eastern United States.

Trout fishermen on streams in the mountains will occasionally see bear, which are more common now than they were some years ago. Deer are also plentiful. Both deer and bear also occur in the tidewater swamps. Wild boar were introduced to parts of North Carolina in 1910, have crossed with domestic stock "gone wild," and may be seen in the extreme southwest corner of the state. The state is also within the range of the cottonmouth moccasin, coral snake, copperhead and rattlesnake.

MOUNTAIN STREAMS

The Blue Ridge Mountains and the Great Smoky Mountains, two of the finest groups within the Appalachian Range, extend through the western length of North Carolina. In this rugged section of the state, streams suitable for trout abound. As is usually the case, those which are most difficult to reach provide the best fishing. For anglers willing to work their way through rough terrain there's good trout fishing in HORSEPASTURE (1), TOXAWAY (2) and WHITEWATER RIVERS (3), off U.S. 64 between Rosman and Highlands, near the South Carolina border. A boat trip across Lake Fontana, and then a hike into the hills close to the Tennessee border, will put fishermen on four of the best streams in the Smokies: EAGLE (4), FORNEY (5), NOLAND (6) and HAZEL (7) CREEKS. Another hike up the LINVILLE RIVER (8), which flows into Lake James west of Morganton on State Highway 126, will also produce some real wilderness fishing.

More readily reached are the streams to which you can find access from the Blue Ridge Parkway, which follows the heights of the mountains all the way from the Virginia border to Asheville. Much of this fishing is within Wildlife Management Areas where special regulations apply, including a special $1 permit required in most cases. Regulations limit some streams to fly fishing only. Anglers must check in and out at designated stations. These Management Areas include the Daniel Boone Wildlife Management Area, south of Blowing Rock, with fishing in WILSON CREEK (9), NORTH HARPER CREEK (10) and STEELS CREEK (11), all off U.S. 221 near Linville; the Mount Mitchell Area, between U.S. 19E and the Blue Ridge Parkway north of Asheville, where the streams are ROCK CREEK (12), MIDDLE CREEK (13), NEAL CREEK (14) and the SOUTH TOE RIVER (15); and the Pisgah Game Preserve, off U.S. 276 southwest of Asheville, with fishing in the DAVIDSON RIVER (16), FRENCH BROAD RIVER (17), UPPER SOUTH MILLS (18), NORTH MILLS (19) and LOWER SOUTH MILLS (20).

Similar fishing will be found in the South Mountains, south of Morganton, between U.S. 64 and State Highway 18; in the NANTAHALA RIVER (21) in the Standing Indian Area, off U.S. 64 east of Chatuge Lake; in the Fires Creek Area, west of Hayesville on the same highway; and in WAYAH (22) and RICH LAUREL CREEKS (23) in the Wayah Area, out of Franklin, to the north on U.S. 64.

Special regulations also apply to LAKE SANTEETLAH (24), BARKERS CREEK (25) and BIG SANTEETLAH (26), on the Tennessee border.

Continuing along the Tennessee border to Hot Springs, at the junction of U.S. 25 and 70 and State Highway 209, fishermen will find the Rich Laurel Management Area, with fishing in HICKEY FORK (27), BIG CREEK (28) and CHIMNEY CREEK (29).

Some trout fishing is also available in the Cherokee Indian Reservation near the town of Cherokee, on U.S. 19, close to the Tennessee border. A special license costing $1.03 per day, is required, as well as the North Carolina Fishing License. Among the streams available, and which are regularly stocked by the Cherokees, are Soco Creek, Wrights Creek, Oconalufey River, Big Witch Creek, Ravensfork, and others.

All together there are some thirty streams with trout fishing possibilities in these Wildlife Management Areas. Fishing is limited to certain days of the week, usually Saturday, Sunday and Wednesday, but the regulations can vary from stream to stream and year to year. Current regulations should be obtained from the Wildlife Resources Commission, Box 2919, Raleigh, North Carolina.

Some of the lower waters of the mountain streams produce excellent fishing for smallmouth black bass. The North Fork of the NEW RIVER (30), in the corner between Virginia and Tennessee, holds trout above the town of Creston, on State Highway 88, and from there down it is smallmouth bass water. Smallmouth are also found in the South Fork below Laurel Springs at the junction of State Highways 18 and 88; in the upper YADKIN (31) and ELKS CREEK (32) near Ferguson on State Highway 268; and in several other streams in the same area.

MOUNTAIN LAKES

There are some seventy-five sizable lakes in this mountain region, many of them being part of the TVA system. They can produce anything from trout to muskellunge. FONTANA LAKE (33), in the southwest corner, up close to the Tennessee border, is outstanding for its crop of largemouth black bass as well as plenty of crappie and bream. In winter those who can take the weather also fish for big rainbow trout, some to 14 pounds, at the mouths of the lake's tributaries, particularly Hazel and Forney Creeks. There is a large resort on the lake, Fontana Village, with lots of good accommodations and a dock where boats and guides are available. The address is Fontana Village Resort, Fontana Dam, North Carolina. There are also boats at the eastern end of the lake at Almond Boat Docks near Bryson City. Public lauching facilities will be found near the junction of U.S. 19, which leads to the lake from the south, and State Highway 28, which comes in from the southwest and parallels the southern shore of the lake. There is also access to Fontana via U.S. 441 and U.S. 129 from Knoxville, Tennessee; and U.S. 19 from Asheville on the north.

The three lakes to the south, NANTAHALA RESERVOIR (34), between U.S. 64 and U.S. 19 and 129 where they run together; HIWASSEE (35), near Murphy, on U.S. 19 and 129; and LAKE SANTEETLAH (24), near Robbinsville, on U.S. 129, are all considered among the nation's top bass lakes. Another good spot in the same area is LAKE CHEOAH (36), on U.S. 129 and State Highway 28, south of Lake Fontana.

LAKE CHATUGE (37), near Hayesville, on U.S. 64 on the Georgia border, has largemouth black bass and some extra big crappies, going up to 4½ pounds.

While bass will be taken by deep trolling during the summer, the best seasons are spring and fall, when, in the months of May, June, September and October, the fish move into the shallows within reach of lures. They may also be taken on cast lures on dark days in summer, and at night, when they slip into the shallows to feed.

Most of these mountain lakes have been stocked with walleyes and white bass, and some attempt is being made to bring back the muskellunge. This species was once found in the French Broad and Tennessee River Basins, and under a program of cleaning up pollution, it is hoped they will again thrive in many waters throughout the area.

THE PIEDMONT

As the mountain streams that flow east and south from the mountains of North Carolina reach lower elevations and spread out into the Piedmont, they become too silty to hold the sport species of fish. However, many of these rivers have been dammed and as a result there is some good lake fishing. Rating first in this class is the KERR RESERVOIR (38) (also called Buggs Island Lake) on the Roanoke River on the Virginia-North Carolina border. There are 800 miles of lake shoreline in the two states. This is one of the nation's top bass lakes and in addition there are populations of walleye, bream and crappie. It has also been the scene of experimental stocking of striped bass, and these landlocked sea-goers have done so well that a totally new sport fishery has developed, with fish running as high as 10 to 15 pounds.

U.S. 1 touches the southern end of the lake near Henderson, while from U.S. 15 on the west there are secondary roads leading into one of the arms of the lake at Bullock and Oxford. Above Bullock, just south of the Virginia border, State Highway 39 leads to the lake, crosses back into Virginia, then cuts south again to Townsville, Williamsboro and eventually Henderson. There are plenty of hotel and motel accomodations at Henderson and boats are available at Tar Heel Marina at nearby Satterwhite Point. At Townsville Landing there are boats, launching ramp, gas, oil and water as well as a good tent campground.

Downstream from the Kerr Reservoir is Lake GASTON (39). Boats are available on the south shore near the town of Roanoke Rapids, where U.S. 301 and State Highway 158 come together. At Weldon, about five miles down the river, which is navigable from here to Albemarle Sound, anglers can launch their own boats or obtain rental skiffs. The ROANOKE (40) is a top striper river and some bumper catches are made annually.

On the course of the YADKIN RIVER (41) in central North Carolina there are several large reservoirs which have excellent fishing. HIGH ROCK (42), south of Lexington, between U.S. 29 and State Highway 8, is the largest. To the south are smaller BADIN (43), TILLERY (44) and BLEWETT FALLS LAKES (45). Further west, the impoundments on the Catawba River produce LAKES JAMES (46), RODHISS (47), HICKORY (48) and LOOKOUT RESERVOIR (49), all lying just north of Interstate 40. Two more lakes complete this group: MOUNTAIN ISLAND (50) and CATAWBA LAKE (51), the latter extending into South Carolina. These lakes all offer some fishing for largemouth black bass, bream and crappie, and several of them add white bass. Lake James anglers bring in walleyes up to 10 pounds. An attempt is also being made to introduce striped bass in the Upper Catawba Lakes. All these reservoirs are close to motels and hotels at the many towns in the area. In most cases there are marinas and lauching areas. As with the other large lakes in North Carolina, the top fishing times for fly, plug and spin casters are during the months of May, June, September and October. Those who fish deep in summer and winter take fish at these times, too.

LAKE LURE (52), near Chimney Rock on U.S. 74 about twenty-three miles southeast of Ashesville, is considered one of the best among the numerous smaller lakes in NORTH CAROLINA.

Cities in the Piedmont area which have municipal reservoirs that provide some fishing are Raleigh, Greensboro, Durham, Smithfield, Winston-Salem, Tryon, Benson, Lexington, Hamlet, Asheboro, Aberdeen and Reedsville.

Around Southern Pines in what is known as the Sandhills area there are several lakes which have good bass and panfish possibilities. The main ones are McKINNEY (53) and SALTER (54), in the Sandhills Wildlife Management Area, near Hoffman on U.S. 1.

Throughout the Piedmont, all the way from the mountains down to tidewater, there are numerous farm ponds, many of which can be fished for as little as $1 per day, by permission of the owner. Even the smaller ones have been known to produce good-sized bass, some to 10 pounds. Most of them also offer shellcrackers and crappie.

COASTAL LOWLANDS

The three largest freshwater lakes in the coastal lowlands are the famous MATTAMUSKEET (55), north of Pamlico Sound; PHELPS LAKE (56), still farther north; and WACCAMAW (57), far to the south, almost due west of the city of Wilmington. All three are excellent producers of largemouth black bass and panfish, and boats and guides are available. Mattamuskeet is reached via U.S. 264 to New Holland on the south, and via State Highway 94, which crosses the swamp in a north-south direction, between New Holland and the village of Fairfield on the north shore. Anglers go in to Phelps Lake on a country road from Cresswell, on U.S. 64, along the south shore of Albemarle Sound. Lake Waccamaw is only a mile south of U.S. 74 and 76, on State Highway 214. Other than this, no roads touch the lake.

Adding to his list of these rather heavily-fished lakes, the adventurous angler who is willing to go out and do a little prospecting for his fishing should include ALLIGATOR LAKE (58) and PUNGO LAKE (59), between Mattamuskeet and Phelps; and LONG LAKE (60) and ELLIS LAKE (61), south and west of the Neuse River Inlet in the Croatan National Forest. There are neither guides nor boats, so it takes some hiking; and you are strictly on your own in these isolated lakes, but it is possible to get into some good largemouth black-bass fishing.

The nearer you get to the ocean in North Carolina, the more interesting the fishing becomes. This state is blessed with tremendous areas where the largemouth black bass, scrappy and adaptable, can move into brackish water and provide unparalleled sport. All the way down the coast he works into the sounds back of the Outer Banks, from Currituck to Albemarle to Pamlico. Currituck is especially famous for the quality of the largemouth-bass fishing, with the fish both plentiful and big, and a length of seventy-five miles of Sound to fish. The bass are also found in Albermarle Bay and its tributary rivers, the CHOWAN (62), PASQUOTANK (63) and NORTH (64). To the south they occur in large numbers in the ALLIGATOR RIVER (65), the inlet which almost separates historic Dare County from the rest of North Carolina. The PUNGO (66), PAMLICO (67), NEUSE (68) and TRENT (69) also have bass working down into the brackish water.

Further south along the coast the rivers pour more directly into the ocean and do not have the great areas of Sound to back up the river water and keep it as fresh as it is in the coastal area further north. Nevertheless, anglers will find some fairly good fishing for largemouth in the lower reaches of the WHITE OAK (70), near Swansboro, on State Highway 24, east of Jacksonville; the New River, at Jacksonville; and the CAPE FEAR RIVER (71) below Wilmington.

The best time to fish the Sounds for brackish-water largemouth bass is from May 1st through June; and again in September and October. Midsummer fishing only pays off early and late in the day and there is not too much activity even then, because of the hot weather.

This is ideal fishing for the fly rod and some exceptional catches are made on popping bugs. Plug and spin casters favor the Jitterbug, Old Joe, Crippled Killer, Devil Horse and Silver Spoons, the latter with pork rind.

There are public launching sites at many places along tidewater but anglers fishing this area for the first time will be well advised to take a guide. They are obtainable at Poplar Branch, Grandy, Powells Point and Spot, on State Highway 158. At Bertha on the same road you can get guides, lodging and food through Mrs. Anna Baum, Bertha, North Carolina. Guides' fees vary from $15 to $25 per day for a party of two. Phone Coinjock 453-8131. Guide service is also available through Met Lupton, at Grandy, North Carolina, Phone 453-3914-5.

Even on the Outer Banks there is some good brackish-water fishing for largemouth. Collington, on the Albemarle Sound side of the Banks, just west of the Wright Memorial at Kitty Hawk, is one of the best spots. There are boats available, and guides can usually be obtained at the landings. Further south at Nags Head, near Manteo on U.S. 64, between the mainland and the Banks, you'll find Bob Preston, who is a guide for brackish-water fishing; he can be reached at Box 463, Nags Head, North Carolina. C. P. Nunemaker, of the Nags Head Ice and Cold Storage, can also usually locate a guide, and has tackle, food and ice for sale.

Other species taken wherever brackish water gives way to fresh are pickerel, crappie, white perch, bream and robin. Some of these, as well as the bass, are found in the ponds located on the Banks. A state fishing license is required to fish brackish water. For the convenience of visitors, one- and five-day licenses may be purchased.

SALTWATER FISH IN THE SOUNDS

Almost the entire coast of North Carolina is protected by the long, narrow strip of sand known as the Outer Banks. The wind-swept islands that form the banks are breached here and there by the sea and through these inlets many Atlantic species of fish make their way into Albemarle, Roanoke, Croatan and Pamlico Sounds. Channel bass and striped bass both work in, in the spring and again in the fall. The latter move on up into the tidewater of most of the rivers. For some reason, although very large stripers are taken on nets in the sounds, the average caught on rod and reel will only weigh about 10 pounds. The top month for this migratory species is November but there is another surge of stripers in the spring, as the fish congregate to move into the rivers to spawn.

The cobia is another salty gamester in these inshore waters, the hot spots being back of Ocracoke Island and around Morehead City. In both locations these stalwart fighters are taken by small-boat fishermen, but they must be armed with good stout rods and plenty of weight—as much as 8 ounces—because of the heavy tidal flow. But cobia close to 100 pounds have been taken. The cobia fishing is best in summer.

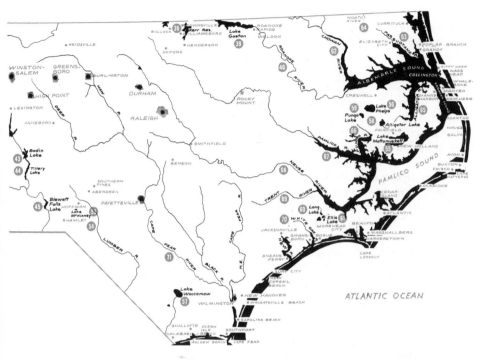

NORTH CAROLINA

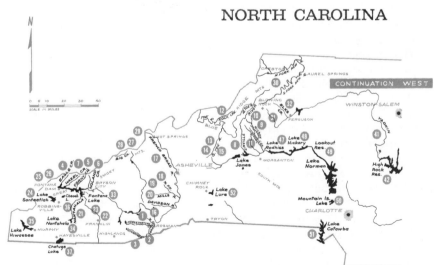

Spotted seatrout also come into the sounds in November and can be taken from that time throughout the winter. Gray trout are taken all summer. The fish will be found in the deeper grassy-bottomed holes, and artificial plugs, fished slowly, are the most successful lures. Fish up to 9 pounds have been taken.

Other species which like the Sounds are the spot, croaker, hogfish, sheepshead, pompano and black drum. Flounders are so plentiful you'd think the bottom is paved with them. Altogether, the Sounds provide a wide variety of excellent fishing for the skiff fisherman in inshore, protected waters.

Charter boats for inshore fishing will be found at nearly every town along the coast. Some of the communities which have large fleets are Manns Harbor, on the mainland at the junction of U.S. 64 and U.S. 264; Manteo and Wanchese, just across Croatan Sound on Roanoke Island; and Ocracoke, at the end of the highway on the Outer Banks. On the mainland east of Morehead City, there are boats available at Harkerstown, Marshallberg and Atlantic, on U.S. 70; and Cedar Island a little further north. From Morehead City south, the sounds are smaller as the banks run close alongshore, protecting the Inland Waterway. While not as good as the sounds to the north, there is still some good inshore fishing. Boat centers where both charters and skiffs are found, are Beaufort, Morehead City, New Topsail Beach, on State Highway 50, on the Banks; Calabash and Shallotte, off U.S. 17 near the South Carolina border.

Boats for a party of six can be chartered for a half day for approximately $35; a full day for $60. Bottom-fishing boats charge about $25 per day. Most of them provide tackle. Skiffs and motors can be rented at most ports, and there are launching sites for those who bring their own boats.

OFFSHORE FISHING

At Diamond Shoals, off Cape Hatteras, the Gulf Stream and the Labrador Current come together and this collision of the two great currents seems to make the coast of North Carolina a meeting place for northern and southern species of saltwater game fish. From May to October you'll almost always find some kind of offshore angling at its peak, either in the Gulf Stream, which varies from 15 to 45 miles out to sea from the coast, or in the shoals and around wrecks closer inshore.

Blue marlin come into these waters in late May and stay around until the end of October. The average blue taken will go about 300 pounds but, as mentioned earlier, an 810-pounder has been landed. The Gulf Stream beyond Diamond Lightship is considered to be just about the hottest spot for marlin along the coast, both as to numbers and as to size, but Morehead City runs it a close second. White-marlin fishing is also good from June through October, though the midsummer months are best. Fish average 60 pounds, go as high as 100. Oregon Inlet boats, fishing Wimble Shoals off the Inlet, are the best bet for whites. Sailfish occasionally go as high as 70 pounds but are usually smaller. The best fishing for this species is from Cape Lookout, off Morehead City, on down the coast to Cape Fear, off Wilmington. To complete the billfish picture, swordfish also appear in the deeps off the Capes, although this species provides only an occasional catch.

Two other top game fish prefer the water just beyond the three Capes. These are the dolphin and amberjack. Anglers look for dolphin around the wrecks and wherever there is driftage along the edge of the Gulf Stream. While occasional members of the species have reached 63 pounds, they average only 5 pounds and a mere 20-pounder is a big one. Regardless of size, the dolphin is a great fish and hits with abandon to almost anything you offer. A trolled feather is a sure thing, and a jig tipped with squid is also good. The dolphin come into North Carolina waters about the same time as the billfish, but stay later and are taken well into December. Amberjack are caught by deep trolling with either spoon or feathers around the wrecks and reefs. The ordinary catch is about 20 pounds in weight but there is a record of a 124-pound amberjack.

The yellowfin or Allison tuna is a May arrival, usually being taken in the Gulf Stream off Cape Hatteras. The largest known to have been landed went 188 pounds. Though fishing for bluefin tuna is still a new venture, this species is also known to occur. The bluefin moves in in midwinter and stays around until April, and authorities believe that when further studies have been made, the bluefin will become an important game fish in North Carolina.

Others of the tuna family which are frequently caught offshore are the oceanic bonito, common bonito and false albacore.

The cero or Spanish mackerel also makes spring and fall runs, the larger fish appearing in the fall, but some good-sized members of the species are taken at all times of the year.

The bluefish, another East Coast favorite, usually puts in an appearance in May and fishing continues to be good until October. The average weight is 2 to 3 pounds, but sometimes schools of unusually large fish appear, weighing as much as 16 pounds and averaging 5. The best catches are made trolling around the various capes—Hatteras, Lookout and Fear,—but sometimes schools of the blues work into the surf, especially around Hatteras, and are taken by surf casters and pier fishermen.

Barracuda are found throughout North Carolina waters. The larger ones haunt the Cape Fear area, where a specimen weighing 44 pounds was caught. On the average, however, barracuda will weigh 10 pounds.

The cobia is also taken by trollers working the offshore reefs. Weights on this increasingly popular species go as high as 100 pounds. Wahoo up to 76 pounds are taken, but are not found in great numbers in North Carolina waters.

While sharks are regarded as pests by many fishermen, the mako is an exception, demanding everyone's respect for his sensational strike and fight. This species is an occasional catch in offshore waters. Hammerheads are common.

There is a fine fleet of charter boats at Hatteras to fish the Diamond Shoals, some twelve miles off the Cape, in the famous Graveyard of the Atlantic, and the Gulf Stream beyond. At Oregon Inlet there are also many fine charter boats, which take their parties mainly to Platte Shoals, Wimble Shoals, and the Gulf Stream. The Morehead City fleet fishes Lookout Shoals, another series of reefs and wrecks similar to that at Hatteras. Further south, off Cape Fear, are the Frying Pan Shoals. Anglers go to this area on charter boats berthed at Southport, Wrightsville Beach and Carolina Beach, all near Wilmington. There are also charter boat fleets at Swansboro, on State Highway 24 at the mouth of Bogue Inlet; Sneads Ferry at the mouth of the New River Inlet; at New Topsail Beach, reached via State Highway 50 to the Outer Banks; at Shallotte, off U.S. 17, about fifty miles south of Wilmington; and Calabash, close to the South Carolina line.

The cost of deep-sea fishing in North Carolina can vary from $75 to $150 per day for a party of six, or less, according to the type of fishing and the time. From most ports the boats leave the dock as early as 5 a.m. and fish twelve hours. But out of Morehead City and Southport, blue-marlin boats often start out at 2 a.m. and don't come in until nearly dark. The fee includes tackle and bait. Anglers fish four at a time, two lines astern and two from the outriggers. With a party of six, the anglers alternate. The deep-sea fishing boats are usually twin engine craft, well equipped, with flying bridge, ship-to-shore radio, Fathometer, and provide excellent tackle for either heavy or light fishing.

Many of the seaside towns along the North Carolina shore also have fleets of party boats, or headboats, which can carry a large number of anglers at very reasonable rates. Morehead City is the main center for this type of fishing, but there will be one or more headboats at nearly every large beach resort along the coast. The fee is usually about $8 per day per person, and this includes bait. You must bring your own tackle, or rent it on board. The fishing is done by drift fishing the reefs. The catch includes a cross section of the Atlantic species of this area, some large, some small, ranging from porgies to 25-pound groupers, from grunts to sea bass, from triggerfish to big red snappers, some in the 30-pound class. In addition, bottom fishermen occasionally find themselves tied to such sea travellers as dolphin and amberjack.

PIER FISHING

There are four piers along the Outer Banks from Nags Head to Kitty Hawk. These can be reached via U.S. 158 from Elizabeth City; from Norfolk, Virginia, via State Highway 168; or via U.S. 64 from Rocky Mount, North Carolina. There's a single pier on the Banks south of Oregon Inlet, and, as mentioned earlier, the ferry from the end of U.S. 158 has now been replaced by a bridge.

A concentration of half a dozen piers will be found along the beaches off Morehead City. They can be reached via secondary roads from U.S. 70. Further south another five piers can be reached via State Highways 210 and 50, off U.S. 17 about twenty miles south of Jacksonville. Two more are located at Wrightsville Beach, reached by State Highway 74 out of Hanover or Wilmington. Below this, piers are strung out at intervals along the coast to the South Carolina border, at Carolina Beach, Wilmington Beach, Kure Beach, Lone, Holden, Ocean Isle and Sunset. All the piers are in resort areas and consequently there are plenty of accommodations of all kinds.

Most of the piers extend a good 1,000 feet out into the ocean so the angler is within reach of a great variety of species of fish which do not move into the 'longshore sloughs. Bluefish, spot and mackerel are frequent catches. Sheepshead hang around the pilings of the piers. There are lots of whiting. In addition, all the fish which work into the sloughs along the beaches can be taken. Tarpon, usually associated with more tropical waters, make their appearance along North Carolina beaches in the late summer, moving as far north as Hatteras. They generally prefer the Cape Fear River Inlet, where they are regularly hooked by pier fishermen, and some quite good ones have been landed. Inshore from Cape Fear, at Southport, a few anglers go for them in skiffs, with spinning gear, using 12- to 20-pound-test line, plus a very heavy leader and large plugs. Many fish are hooked on this gear when the anglers are able to locate a school of feeding silver kings. A great many of them are lost, too, but it's some of the sportiest fishing along the coast, when you find the fish there.

Striped bass come into the reach of pier fishermen, too, and again the Southport area has been a good producer.

It used to be that pier fishermen always used bait but today many cast artificial lures and make good catches, especially when school fish such as the blues and mackerel are in. Some bait fishermen have also extended their scope by "float fishing." The live fish bait is hooked through the back and floated out. It is this method which has added tarpon, kingfish and cobia to the list taken from piers. The rod most used is a strong, 6-foot stick, with 200 yards of 36-pound line, and a 6-foot wire leader and 11/0 hook, plus a reel with a good drag, and capable of holding 400 yards of line.

The cost of pier fishing is minor, the average being about $1 per head. Bait is always there for sale, and you can rent fishing tackle for as little as $1 to $1.50 per day. A deposit of $20 is required, to guarantee return of the tackle.

SURF CASTING ON THE BEACHES

The beaches of the Outer Banks offer surf casting for black drum from May to October; bluefish in two periods, March through June and September through November; channel bass from March through June and September through November; gray trout from September through February; weakfish, or spotted sea trout, from November through February. Of course many lesser species are also taken, but these are the main "run fish" which bring the surf casters to the banks. The striped bass also makes runs up the beaches and are found in the surf at Hatteras in December, January and March, but for some reason they are seldom taken there on either bait or artificials, with rod and reel. For several years now, a number of top New England-striper fishermen have journeyed to Hatteras when the fish were in, to try to take the big stripers of 60 and 65 pounds which are annually taken in nets, and therefore are known to be in the waters. So far, very few fish have been caught. Ralph Gray, of Hatteras, hooked three in one afternoon, but all broke his line. Commercial netters made a haul at the same spot an hour later and swooped up the three fish, each with a lure in its mouth, and trailing the broken line. No one seems to know why they do not hit better; every known lure is tossed at them and all types of bait are offered, yet they rarely take either.

The Outer Banks remain among the most isolated sections of the United States. Only within recent years has it been possible to drive there by car. Today the beaches can be reached via U.S. 158 from the north and U.S. 64 and 264 from the west, across Croatan Sound to Roanoke Island, then across Roanoke Sound to the Banks. These two roads join up with U.S. 158 at Whalebone. Above that the banks extend up the coast, enclosing Currituck Sound and the Intracoastal Waterway, or Inland Waterway. Although there is no doubt there is good fishing to be enjoyed along this part of the beach, there is no access other than by beach buggy and it is seldom fished.

South of Whalebone a system of secondary roads and ferries allows fishermen to make their way down the Banks as far as Ocracoke. There is also a daily ferry to Ocracoke from Atlantic, on the mainland, which is on U.S. 70 about forty miles north of Morehead City. A new bridge has recently been constructed at Oregon Inlet at the north end of Hatteras Island, where travellers used to depend on a ferry. Ferry is still the means of crossing Hatteras Inlet at the south end of the island, in order to reach Ocracoke. A landing strip on Hatteras can handle small and medium-sized craft.

With the improvements in roads and the addition of the bridge, there has been a corresponding increase in the number of good, modern motels and other accommodations, at the villages of Rodanthe, Waves, Sala, Avon and Buxton on Hatteras Island, and at Ocracoke on Ocracoke Island.

The Cape Hatteras area is one of the most popular with the surf fishermen. Accommodations can be found at George Fuller's Motel, Box 187, Buxton, North Carolina, or at the Beach-Haven Motel, under the same management, on the beach between Cape Hatteras and the village of Frisco. The Buxton Sportsman's Center has bait and tackle for sale as well as groceries and ice, and can give visitors information about the fishing.

Bill Dillon's Outer Banks Motel also is a very popular spot with surf fishermen, and is open all year. Bill Dillon can provide the latest information as to fishing conditions. His telephone number is 995-2351.

Other accommodations at Buxton will be found at the Sea Gull Motel, the Cape Hatteras Court, the Falcon Motel, Town Circle Motel, Burrus' Motel, Oden's Harbor, and the Gen. Billy Mitchell. There are also several restaurants. Beach buggies can be rented at most of the communities along the beaches for about $15 per day; or with a guide, for $25 per day for a party of four.

From Okracoke south to Cape Lookout there is no highway, ferry or bridge. The banks are as they have always been, wild and undeveloped. Some anglers go by boat across the sound from Atlantic, on U.S. 70 on the mainland, to Drum Inlet, where there are some simple housekeeping cabins. Visitors must bring their own bedding and food. Beach buggies can be hired, however, and they are also obtainable on the Banks to the south, opposite Davis.

A few fishermen fish Portsmouth Island to the north by driving up the beaches at low tide, the only time it is possible to cross Swash Inlet between Drum and Portsmouth. Even then there are sometimes impassable sloughs cut by recent storms. Although there is a small town of the same name on Portsmouth Island, this is almost a ghost town and there are no accommodations of any kind.

There are four public camping areas in Hatteras National Seashore Recreational Area, which extends along Bodie, Hatteras and Ocracoke Islands. They are on the south shore of Bodie, near the bridge; on the north shore of Hatteras, near the Bodie Ferry; near the Lighthouse at Cape Hatteras; and on Pamlico Sound near the town of Ocracoke. Detailed regulations about camping should be obtained from the Superintendent's Office, Cape Hatteras National Seashore, Manteo, North Carolina.

From Cape Lookout, opposite Morehead City, southward, the islands of the Outer Banks have been much more highly developed. There is a bridge from U.S. 70 to Atlantic Beach on Emerald Isle, and a road runs almost the entire length of the island. A free ferry operates from the town of Bogue on State Highway 24 on the mainland, across Bogue Sound to the southern end of Emerald Isle. Further south, below the outlet of the New River, State Highway 50 crosses the Inland Waterway and leads to Del Mar Beach, Surf City and New Topsail Beach. On U.S. 17, near New Hanover, U.S. 74 leads out from the mainland to Wrightsville Beach.

Surf casters require special clothing. In the summer something should be worn on the legs and feet to prevent sunburn. In the cooler weather chest-high waders, or at least hip boots, will keep you dry and warm. A rainjacket is essential for rain and spray protection. Surf casters usually carry a collapsible chair for comfort, and a sand spike to protect the reel from the sand when set down. Those who plan to fish at night should also have a flashlight.

The popular gear is either the conventional surf-casting outfit or big saltwater spinning gear, with 27- to 36-pound-test braided line or 16- to 20-pound-test monofilament. Those who do their surf casting with bait usually use a "fishfinder," which utilizes a 2- to 4-ounce lead, depending on the current, attached by a swivel. This allows the bait to work freely on the bottom. Artificials are used, too, and are particularly successful when schools of drum come into the surf.

For serious fishermen there's an unusual opportunity to sample all the varieties of fishing available on the Outer Banks through an Annual Sport Fishing Short Course, held in June each year at Cape Hatteras. Sponsored by the North Carolina State College, the course is designed to interest both novice and expert, and includes classroom instruction in tackle and techniques. There are expeditions into the field in the form of a day's trip to the Gulf Stream, another trip to waters not so far offshore, and two days of inshore and sound fishing, plus a nighttime beach expedition for sharks. The $150 fee for the course includes room and board, boats, baits, fishing trips and instruction. Application forms may be obtained from the Division of General Extension, Box 5125, State College Station, Raleigh, North Carolina.

Anglers planning to visit North Carolina should obtain a booklet entitled "Let's Go Fishing and Hunting in North Carolina," from the Department of Conservation and Development, State Advertising Division, Raleigh, North Carolina.

NORTH CAROLINA FISHING REGULATIONS

Resident Freshwater Fishing License
    All species except trout $4.25
One-Day License $.85
Nonresident Freshwater Fishing License
    All species except trout $8.25
Nonresident 1-Day $1.65
Nonresident 5-Day $3.75
Resident Trout Fishing License $1.25
Nonresident Trout Fishing License $3.25

SEASONS AND LIMITS

Species	Open Season	Size Limit	Bag Limit
Trout	April 7–Sept. 3	None	10
Muskellunge	Year-round	24"	1
Chain Pickerel	Year-round	None	12
Walleye (pike perch)	Year-round	None	8
Bass (largemouth, small-mouth, Kentucky)	Year-round	10"	8
White Bass	Year-round	None	None
Sea Trout (weakfish)	Year-round	None	25
Striped Bass	Year-round	12"	25
Panfish	Year-round	None	None

In some trout streams and in John Kerr Reservoir there are exceptions to these regulations. Rules should be checked annually.

For complete regulations write: Wildlife Resources Commission, Raleigh, North Carolina.

SOUTH CAROLINA

The State of South Carolina shares a few features of the Appalachian Range, which pokes into the northwest corner, but in general it consists of piedmont and coastal topography. As a result there is limited habitat for the cold-water species, a wide range of waters suitable to hold the warm-water species, and many miles of coastline where a great variety of saltwater fish are found.

The fresh waters of the state hold largemouth black bass, bluegill, crappie, yellow perch, white bass, channel catfish, rough fish and some trout. These are augmented by the striped bass in the Santee-Cooper waters, where stripers have been landlocked and now provide some excellent fishing. Saltwater species taken along the South Carolina coast include blue marlin, tarpon, tuna, sailfish, amberjack, mackerel, bluefish, striped bass, channel bass (or red drum), sea trout, snapper, sea bass, sea bream, cobia and grouper, according to the location and season you fish.

The drainage of the state is entirely from northwest to southeast, through such major rivers as the Pee Dee, Santee-Cooper, Edisto, Salkehatchie, Coosawhatchie and the Savannah, which forms almost the entire southwestern border with Georgia. The headwaters and tributaries of these major streams have been dammed to produce some tremendous lakes: Lakes Moultrie and Marion and Wateree Pond on the Wateree and Lake Wylie in its headwaters on the North Carolina border; Lakes Murray and Greenwood on the Saluda, which drains into Lake Marion through the Congaree River; and the Clark Hill and Hartwell Reservoirs on the Savannah River along the Georgia border.

There is ready access to all parts of the state. South Carolina is on the way to almost anywhere in the southeastern United States and is consequently equipped with a vast network of highways. Interstate 85 crosses the northwest corner and from it Interstate 26 then cuts diagonally southeast all the way to the coast at Charleston. U.S. 17, the main seashore highway, parallels the beaches for the full length of the coast, while U.S. 1 and U.S. 301 provide inland arteries in a general north-south direction, from the North Carolina border to the Georgia border.

The climate of South Carolina ranges from very warm in summer to pleasant in spring and fall. In winter it is cold enough to call for woolen clothing for fishermen.

The angler will not be likely to encounter any big game, but should always watch for snakes. The water moccasin, copperhead and coral snake are all indigenous to this area.

TROUT FISHING

South Carolina's trout fishing is confined to a few mountain streams in the northwest corner of the state, well up against the Georgia and North Carolina borders. The largest of the trout streams is the CHATTOOGA RIVER (1), which forms the Georgia border at this point. The river is annually stocked with rainbows, brown and brook trout, and provides good fishing for both fly fishermen and spinners. The stream can be reached via U.S. 76 between Clayton, Georgia, and Westminster, South Carolina; or from State Highways 28 and 102, both of which cross the river near the border.

A few miles to the east is the KEOWEE RIVER (2), formed by two smaller streams, the TOXOWAY (3) and the WHITEWATER (4). There's no road paralleling these streams and it's tough getting to the fishing but it can be quite good. The lower Keowee can be reached from State Highway 183, west from Greenville about thirty-four miles, while the upper reaches and the two tributaries can be approached from State Highway 11 at Eastatoe.

The CHAUGA RIVER (5), also a fair trout stream, can be reached from the town of Walhalla on State Highway 28, west of Seneca.

In this northwestern corner of South Carolina there are two State Parks, Oconee, between State Highway 107 and State Highway 11, near Salem; and Table Rock, further north on State Highway 11. Both parks have several small trout lakes and there are a number of creeks which provide a minimum of stream fishing. In their lower reaches the same streams have good fishing for largemouth black bass and bream.

FRESHWATER LAKES

The SANTEE-COOPER RESERVOIR (6), northwest of Charleston, is the largest and most important fishing water in South Carolina. It consists of two enormous reservoirs, Lake Moultrie on the Cooper and Lake Marion on the Santee River. The two lakes are joined by a narrow channel just south of the Santee Dam which controls the flow from Lake Marion into the Santee. This is the top fishing water in the state and, in fact, is one of the greatest anglers' attractions in the southeastern part of the country.

Interstate 26 between Columbia and Charleston parallels the two lakes and numerous state highways lead to the small communities on the shore. U.S. 301 and U.S. 15 provide access from the north and east, crossing Lake Marion west of Summerton.

Striped bass which became landlocked in the Santee-Cooper development have made the system famous among fishermen. The fish average about 5 pounds. Several weighing 40 pounds have been taken and the top catch went 55 pounds. Fishing deep it is possible to take them consistently all summer, but fishing picks up in the fall and rises to a peak in late winter and early spring when the fish are running upstream to spawn. Some run far up the tributaries, and large fish are taken in the CONGAREE (7) right in the shade of the State Capital at Columbia. Some of the best spots for action in the spring are the DIVERSION CANAL (8), reached via State Highway 45 from St. Stephen; and the Santee River bed from around Eutawville, on State Highway 6, at the southwest corner of Lake Marion, right up to the head of the lake, at the conjunction of the Wateree and Congaree. The rest of the year the best action will be found in Lake Moultrie, although Marion can be quite good on occasion. Bait fishermen use either live or cut bait, fished deep. Trollers also go deep, with slow-trolled baits of all kinds. The most productive fishing with lures seems to be casting bucktails to shoals of feeding stripers.

The several other kinds of fishing to be found in the Santee-Cooper are too often overlooked because of the interest in the stripers. There is especially good

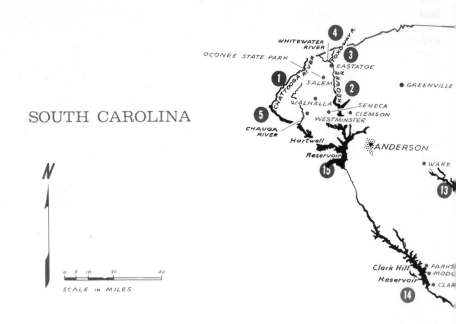

SOUTH CAROLINA

fishing for largemouth black bass, crappie and catfish. The bass average about 2 to 3 pounds and are very plentiful. The world-record crappie, a 5-pounder, came from the Santee-Cooper, as did the world-record channel catfish, weighing 57 pounds. Other fish which are taken are white bass and many species of panfish, all dubbed "bream" and pronounced "brim."

The largemouth fishing, in particular, can be sensational. The spring is the peak season but fishing can be very good during warm spells in winter. February and March are usually good and the fishing builds into spring, then dwindles with the arrival of hot weather. At the many flats near Russellville, off State Highway 45 at the northeast corner of Lake Moultrie, the lower end of the Diversion Canal, and various other spots around the shores of the upper lake, it is possible to wade and cast. However, most of the fishing is done from boats. Fly-rod poppers and standard plugs and weedless spoons are all good. Two of the best top-water lures are the Phillips Old Joe, Crippled Killer and Rainbow Runner.

Especially in Lake Marion, crappie fishing is excellent around brush and old trees in the lake. Both black and white crappie are common, averaging about half a pound; and ten a day is a normal catch. Small minnows, the favorite bait, can be purchased at most docks. Spinners also take their share with small spoons. The best spots to fish for crappies on the west shore of Lake Marion are around Santee, at the junction of U.S. 301 and State Highway 267; near Elloree where State Highways 6 and 267 come together; and at Lone Star, further north on State Highway 267. On the eastern shore a good location is Rimini, on a country road out of Pinewood, on State Highway 261. The top months are May through August.

Carp, gar, warmouth, pickerel, yellow perch and a sprinkling of white bass round out the fishing population of these two big lakes. Several white catfish weighing 60 pounds have been taken. The best catches of this species are made just above

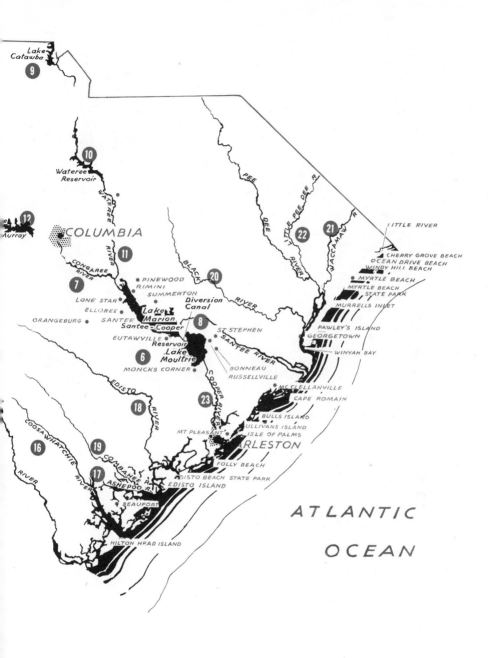

ATLANTIC

OCEAN

Low-country swamp fishing in Carolina is a peaceful, rewarding sport.

the Lake Moultrie powerhouse, south of Bonneau, off U.S. 52, at the south end of the lake. Catfishermen favor cut shad as bait, fished near the bottom.

Anglers will find plenty of accommodations of all kinds around both Lake Moultrie and Lake Marion. Chief headquarters is Moncks Corner, where U.S. 52 crosses the southern tip of Lake Moultrie. Bait, tackle and fishing licenses may be obtained there at the Thornley Motor Company, along with information and details about the best places to fish at the moment and what baits or lures are proving most successful. Eutawville, on State Highway 45, on the southwest shore of Lake Marion is another good headquarters; and the larger cities of Summerton and Manning, on U.S. 301 as it approaches Lake Marion from the northeast, both cater to anglers with all kinds of motel and restaurant services. Tackle shops in all these centers can help in obtaining a guide if you need one. Numerous fishing camps and boat landings alongshore offer skiffs for hire.

The northeastern part of South Carolina is drained into Lake Marion through the Catawba-Wateree River system. A dam near the state line between North and South Carolina forms LAKE CATAWBA (9), and another north of Camden, at the junction of U.S. 1 and U.S. 521, forms the WATEREE RESERVOIR (10). Both are good producers of largemouth black bass, crappie and bluegill. Some striped bass are taken below the dam on the WATEREE (11).

On the Congaree River, to the west, are two more large reservoirs, LAKE MURRAY (12) and LAKE GREENWOOD (13), and on the border between the two Carolinas, north of Augusta are CLARK HILL (14) and HARTWELL RESERVOIRS (15), formed by dams on the Savannah River. All these lakes hold largemouth, white bass, bream and crappies, and a few stripers have also worked in. As in Lakes Marion and Moultrie, the fishing is good year-round, but best in spring and fall. Boats are available at several small communities along Lakes Murray and Greenwood, and both are approached by many state highways off U.S. 76 and Interstate 26, to the north, and U.S. 378 and U.S. 25 to the south. Accommodations are to be found also in many communities, from Columbia, the capital, which is close to the eastern end of Lake Murray, to Ware Shoals, at the western tip of Greenwood Lake. At Clark Hill Reservoir there are boat docks at Modoc, Clarks Hill and Parksville on U.S. 221, which runs along the eastern shore. To fish Hartwell Reservoir fishermen go out from the small town of Clemson, where U.S. 123 crosses the lake.

COASTAL RIVERS

The best stream fishing in the coastal area is not in the large rivers but in such smaller ones as the COOSAWHATCHIE (16), ASHEPOO (17), EDISTO (18) and COMBAHEE (19). Of these four that enter the ocean to the south of Charleston, the Edisto and Combahee are the best. Further north, the BLACK RIVER (20), which empties at Georgetown, and the WACCAMAW (21), which parallels the coast from the North Carolina border down to the head of Winyah Bay Inlet at Georgetown, are both rated as top streams of the coastal area. The LITTLE PEE DEE (22), immediately inland of the Waccamaw, is also very good; and the COOPER RIVER (23) from Lake Moultrie down to Charleston is excellent. All have fishing for largemouth black bass and bream, and in most cases there are spring and fall runs of striped bass.

There are a number of ponds and lakes in the swampy areas around the larger rivers where there is some good fishing for bass and bream. In many cases, however, these waters are on private land. Most of the lower waters are muddy, which makes for poor fishing, but some fair catches of catfish, bream and bass are made when the water is clear enough.

SALTWATER FISHING

South Carolina has a considerable expanse of coast on the Atlantic Ocean, with fishing opportunities varying from piers to surf casting along sandy beaches to offshore trolling. The northern coast is favored because of the fact that the Gulf Stream swings in a little closer there. Consequently most of the sport fishing is centered in the north, particularly around Myrtle Beach, Ocean Drive Beach and Little River, just south of the North Carolina line. At almost any seaside spot along here you can find charter boats to fish the offshore waters, and party boats and skiffs for inshore angling. There are also numerous fishing piers. Hotels and motels are available everywhere along U.S. 17, which parallels the coast.

There is year-round fishing from bottom boats for snapper, sea bass, sea bream, grouper and cobia, at a cost of about $6 per head, including bait and tackle. The offshore fishing season is from April to Thanksgiving. The fishing is for amberjack, mackerel, bluefish, blue marlin, tarpon, tuna and sailfish. Boats which go fifteen to twenty miles offshore charge about $60 per day for a party of six or less. Those which work out to more productive waters forty miles offshore, and to the Gulf Stream, charge $90 to $150 per day. This also includes tackle and bait. For complete information about this fishing, and the names and addresses of boats currently fishing the area, write Jimmie Casey, News Bureau, Chamber of Commerce, P.O. Box 1317, Myrtle Beach, South Carolina.

About thirty-five miles further south on the coast, where U.S. 521 and U.S. 701 come out to U.S. 17, Georgetown is another favorite fishing center, with a good port on Winyah Bay. One of the features here is bottom fishing with mullet from anchored boats for big channel bass which work in along the jetty. The fish run from 15 to 45 pounds. Rates for this fishing are $65 per day for six persons, plus $10 for each additional person. There is also a variety of offshore trolling and some still fishing, about twelve miles offshore at the "Hector Wreck." Species taken include bluefish, amberjack, cobia, Spanish mackerel, king mackerel, albacore, angelfish and bonito. At the offshore shipping lane, about eighteen miles out, fishing is for the same species with the addition of false albacore, barracuda and dolphin. This is an all-day trip, and the boats leave the docks between five and seven in the morning, according to the tides. The cost can vary from $100 for up to six people to $125. There is an extra charge of $10 per person above the number of six. The ideal fishing group for trolling is four, as only four lines are fished at a time. If there are more in the party, the lines are rotated. The number of boats available is limited, and reservations should be made in advance, through Litchfield Inn, Litchfield Beach, Pawleys Island, South Carolina. Telephone Georgetown 3-1326.

Anglers in the Charleston area, about halfway down the coast, can find year-round saltwater fishing to combine with fishing in Lakes Moultrie and Marion a few miles to the north. Charter trips are available out of the Municipal Yacht Basin at $75 per day, with a limit of fifteen persons per party. Reservations can be made through Captain Burn, "The Tiki," Municipal Yacht Basin, Charleston, South Carolina. Phone Raymond 3-1279. There is also deep-sea fishing at Blackfish Banks, offshore, at $5 per person, on the Captiva, an eighty-passenger, 65-foot diesel yacht. The boat sails from the Fort Sumter Hotel at 9 a.m. and returns at 4 p.m. each Wednesday, Saturday and Sunday, from the end of May to the first of September. The price includes a hot sea-food lunch, and bait. Reservations can be made by phoning Raymond 2-4444 at Charleston.

In the Charleston area there is good pier fishing at both Edisto, to the south, where State Highway 174 comes out to the ocean; and to the north of Charleston at Isle of Palms, where State Highway 703 reaches the ocean. The species are croaker, spot, sheepshead, flounder, whiting and some bass. The same fishing will be found along the old causeway bridge to Mount Pleasant on U.S. 17, five miles east of Charleston, and the Breach Inlet Bridge. Local anglers claim that fresh shrimp is the best bait, overall, but that sheepshead will take only fiddler crabs and flounder will take only live minnows.

Some excellent surf fishing for channel bass or red drum can be found at Bulls Island, inshore from Cape Romain, near the town of McClellanville, which is on U.S. 17 and 701 about forty miles north of Charleston. The big reds start to come in here early in October and can usually be found until the end of November, working into all the sloughs and creeks between the islands. There is an excellent fishing camp on Bulls Island, operated by Mr. and Mrs. Charles Mills, McClellanville. Phone 3045 or 3211.

There is small-boat fishing throughout the Charleston area, either trolling or bottom fishing, for all the common saltwater species of the coastal waters. Boats are available at many docks in the harbor.

Surf casters find many beaches on which to practice their skill. They catch bass, spot, sea trout, bluefish, black drum and whiting, the favorite baits being shrimp or mullet. Catfish and sharks are also taken. The Rock Jetty at the west end of Sullivans Island, on State Highway 703 at the ocean, is a favorite spot; but such fishing is to be found at many beaches alongshore. At Folly Beach, where State Highway 171 reaches the ocean, ten miles southeast of Charleston, boats and fishing equipment may be rented at Andre's, on the Folly River.

Lying only a few miles north of the Georgia border, the large island known as Hilton Head provides the top fishing of the southern coast of South Carolina. The island is reached via State Highway 462 from U.S. 17, or State Highway 170 from Beaufort. There is also commercial and private air service, and an excellent marina for yachts travelling the Intracoastal Waterway. The bays offer much sheltered water for skiff fishing and offshore trolling is also available at approximately $75 per day. The catch will be bass, flounder, sheepshead, bluefish, trout, cobia and mackerel, according to season.

SOUTH CAROLINA FISHING REGULATIONS

Resident Fishing License $1.10
Nonresident Fishing License $10.25
Nonresident 10-Day Fishing License $3.10
Special permits, usually costing about $1.00, are required in a number of South Carolina Lakes, such as Santee-Cooper, Lake Murray, Lake Greenwood, Catawba-Wateree, Clark Hill and Hartwell.

SEASON AND LIMITS

No closed season except for trout: October 1 to March 1.

Size Limits
None

Bag Limits
10 bass, rockfish or trout, in aggregate, plus 25 other game fish.

For complete regulations write: Wildlife Resources Dept., 1015 Maine Street, Columbia, South Carolina.

GEORGIA

Because of an extended coast on the Atlantic Ocean plus a projection of the Appalachian Mountains into the northwestern part of the state, Georgia enjoys the same wide variety of fishing as its northern neighbors, North and South Carolina. Its unique feature is the width of the piedmont which extends from the narrow swatch of mountains on the northern border through many miles of high piedmont, piedmont and planes to tidewater.

Georgia fresh waters hold brown, brook and rainbow trout, largemouth black bass, spotted bass, white bass, yellow perch, crappie, bluegill, shellcracker, pumpkinseed, chain pickerel, redfin pickerel, green sunfish, warmouth, channel catfish and white catfish, as well as a number of nonsporting species.

In the salt, along the Atlantic coast, will be found albacore or little tuna, amberjack, blackfish or common sea bass, tarpon, sailfish, jack crevalle, mackerel, kingfish, cobia, bluefish, black drum, channel bass, sheepshead, whiting, winter trout or speckled sea trout, summer trout or weakfish, barracuda, flounder and croaker. To round out the picture, striped bass cruise the shallows and move up into some rivers; and shad make spring runs into many sounds, inlets and rivers.

While at first glance it might seem that the drainage of the State of Georgia is to the Atlantic, there are actually three watersheds of importance: The Atlantic watershed embraces the Savannah which forms the border with South Carolina; the Altamaha, entering the ocean in the middle of the coastline; the Satilla, a little further south; and the St. Marys, on the Florida border, and many smaller, intermediate rivers. The Chattahoochee drainage system carries waters picked up throughout the western part of the state southward along the Alabama border and to the Gulf of Mexico. In the extreme north a few streams flow northward to the Tennessee River, and eventually to the Mississippi.

There are fifteen major reservoirs in Georgia, plus many thousands of small lakes and ponds. Clark Hill and Hartwell Reservoirs, half way up the South Carolina boundary on the Savannah River, are shared with that state. Tugalo, Burton and Rabun lakes are just inside the border in the same system. Three larger lakes are found in the north: Chatuge, on the North Carolina border; Nottely Lake to the southwest of this; and Blue Ridge Lake still further west. In the north-central part of the state, Lake Sidney Lanier is a reservoir on the upper waters of the Chattahoochee. Another large reservoir in central Georgia is Sinclair Lake, on the Oconee River, a branch of the Altamaha, near Milledgeville, at the junction of U.S. 441 and State Highway 49. Large reservoirs on the Chattahoochee, in the west, are Bartlett's Ferry, or Lake Harding, and its companion lakes to the south, Goat Rock and Lake Oliver. In southern Georgia the Jim Woodruff Reservoir, or Lake Seminole, sprawls in the corner between Alabama, Florida and Georgia. Blackshear Lake, to the north, between Americus and Cordele, is the only other large lake in the southern part of the state.

Transportation facilities are good throughout Georgia. U.S. 41 enters northern Georgia at Chattanooga, Tennessee, and runs the complete length of the state into

Small mountain streams in the northwest corner of Georgia provide some excellent trout fishing.

Florida. U.S. 1 enters on the eastern border at Augusta and curves out toward the middle of the state, then back towards the east to Jacksonville, Florida. Between this and the seacoast are two other important north-south highways, U.S. 301 and U.S. 17. Major east-west roads also bisect the state: U.S. 278 through Augusta to Atlanta, U.S. 80 from Savannah to Macon and Colubus, and U.S. 82 from Brunswick on the southern coast to Valdosta and Bainbridge in the west. Besides these main highways there are more than adequate secondary roads leading to all the good fishing areas.

When you're in Georgia, you're in the South. While there are spells of frost in winter, in general the angler here needs only lightweight cottons during most of the fishing season, with a heavier jacket for morning and evening, and for fishing coastal areas, where the wind can be cool.

Deer are fairly plentiful and hogs, although of domestic stock, run free in many sections of Georgia and have become quite wild. There are bears in the mountains and swamp sections.

The main wildlife the sportsman needs to keep an eye out for is the snake. Water moccasins are common and there are both copperheads and coral snakes, as well as the eastern diamond-back rattler.

TROUT FISHING

Northern Georgia, where the Appalachian Range juts down into the state, has a number of excellent trout streams, producing rainbows, brook trout and brown trout. Some of the fishing is for resident fish but in the more heavily used waters there is considerable annual stocking. Altogether, authorities estimate that there are 700 miles of trout streams in northern Georgia. The same streams, in their lower reaches, produce smallmouth black bass, redeye and bream.

While the smaller streams are subject to an annual closed season, usually beginning about September 15th, a number of the larger ones are open year-round. These include: the HIAWASSEE RIVER (1) below Rice Bridge on State Highway 75, near the town of Hiawassee; the NOTTELY RIVER (2) below the bridge on U.S. 129 and 19, below Blairsville; the TOCCOA RIVER (3) below Butts Bridge, near Blue Ridge on U.S. 76; the TALLULAH RIVER (4) below the dam at Lake Rabun, off U.S. 23 and 441; the CHESTATEE RIVER (5) below Garnet Bridge and the ETOWAH RIVER (6) below the State Highway 52 bridge. These last two are north of Gainesville. Others are MOUNTAINTOWN CREEK (7), below the U.S. 76 Bridge, east of Chatsworth; and the CHATTOOGA RIVER (8) in the extreme northwest corner, roughly paralleled by U.S. 27 and State Highway 114. The Chattooga is open year-round throughout its entire length.

There are many other trout streams in the same general area, which, however, are so small as not to appear on maps. These, being headwaters, often offer the best trout fishing. Information about these streams and roads leading to them can be obtained from the Georgia Game and Fish Commission, 401 State Capitol, Atlanta 3, Georgia.

LAKE FISHING

You can pretty well take your choice of the type of lake fishing you prefer in Georgia, from deep, clear, spring-fed Lake Sidney Lanier, to small, backwater ponds without names. The common species are largemouth black bass, crappie, bluegill, redbreast, and warmouth. Some of the lakes have white bass populations, others yellow perch and channel catfish, according to the nature of the water. In general the fishing for bass is best from April through June and from September through November. Crappie start to hit well earlier in the spring.

LAKE SIDNEY LANIER (9), in the northern part of the state, near Gainesville, is fed by the cold, clear headwaters of the Chattahoochee and Chestatee Rivers. The lake has innumerable arms and inlets and is well serviced by U.S. 129 and U.S. 23 in the east, and U.S. 19 on the west, with access to the lake shore via many secondary roads. There are some fishing camps along the east and south shores.

Crappie fishing is good in spring and fall, with emphasis on the period from September through November. The favorite baits are doll flies and live minnows, fished deep. White bass move into the feeder streams from the lake in April and May and are fished successfully with spinners and small spoons. The largemouth bass fishing starts in May, is at its best in June, and the fish continue to hit fairly well all summer in this cold lake. There is another peak in October and November. Bass average 2½ pounds.

North of Sidney Lanier is a group of smaller reservoirs. BLUE RIDGE RESERVOIR

(10), on U.S. 76, close to the South Carolina border near the town of Blue Ridge, is an impoundment of the Toccoa River. Its deep, cool waters harbor the only muskellunge found in Georgia. Fish up to 36 pounds have been taken. There are also smallmouth and largemouth black bass, crappie, bream, bluegill, channel catfish, shellcracker, warmouth and walleye. Two fishing camps on the lake provide boats and bait. One is on the west side on State Highway 2 and the other almost directly across the lake near Morganton. Midsummer fishing is better than in most Georgia lakes because of the cool water.

Following U.S. 76 eastward you come to NOTTELY LAKE (11) and CHATUGE RESERVOIR (12), holding the same species as Blue Ridge, with the exception of muskellunge. You can go in to fishing camps at the northern end of Nottely from Ivy Log, on U.S. 11; or the south end from Blairsville. Access to boat docks on the western side is via an unmarked road which joins Ivy Log and U.S. 76 a few miles east of Morganton.

Chatuge lies on the border between Georgia and South Carolina, about half in each state. There are a number of fishing camps along U.S. 76, which cuts across the southern end. Chatuge has a reputation for producing big bass. You must have a North Carolina Fishing License to fish across the state line.

Also in the northeast corner of Georgia are LAKE BURTON (13), LAKE RABUN (14) and TUGALO LAKE (15). Lake Burton has been stocked with rainbow and brown trout and its cool waters have proven good habitat. Trout are frequently taken up to 8 pounds on deep-running spoons and slow-fished spinners. It is also an excellent bass lake. The bass fishing is best in spring and fall, but the trout hit well year-round. Two fishing camps are located on State Highway 197 on the western shore of Lake Burton. There are also two camps on Lake Rabun, on U.S. 23 out of Lakemont. The fishing is for trout, walleye, bass, bluegill and bream.

One of the top fishing lakes in Georgia is LAKE SINCLAIR (17), formed by a dam on the Oconee River in the central piedmont area. There are fishing camps off State Highway 16 on the north, State Highway 212 on the south, and U.S. 441, which crosses an arm of the lake. Accommodations of other kinds will be found at Milledgeville and Eatonton, on U.S. 441. Sinclair has the name of growing bigger crappie faster than any other lake in the state. Many are taken weighing 2 pounds. Largemouth black bass are plentiful, and white bass make an early spring migrational run. Bream are also numerous. Channel catfish have been taken weighing better than 20 pounds. The one disadvantage of this lake is that it is generally muddy in the spring, when the Oconee River is flowing at full flood. Aside from this, the best crappie fishing is in March and April as the fish are spawning in shallow water at that time. In April the white bass make their run and are taken in the headwaters of the lake and the tributary rivers. May is the top month for bass. So the spring fisherman has a busy time on this lake. The autumn months are also good. Casting with fairly deep-running plugs is particularly good in the coves and across the many points in the lake.

CLARK HILL RESERVOIR (18), on the Savannah River between South Carolina and Georgia, was formed by damming the Savannah River about thirty miles upstream from Augusta. Largemouth black bass are the major target for anglers here, the average weight being about 2 pounds. Crappie are taken in numbers, averaging less than one pound. There are also catfish, some white bass, and the lake has been stocked with striped bass but so far has not produced sport fishing for this species.

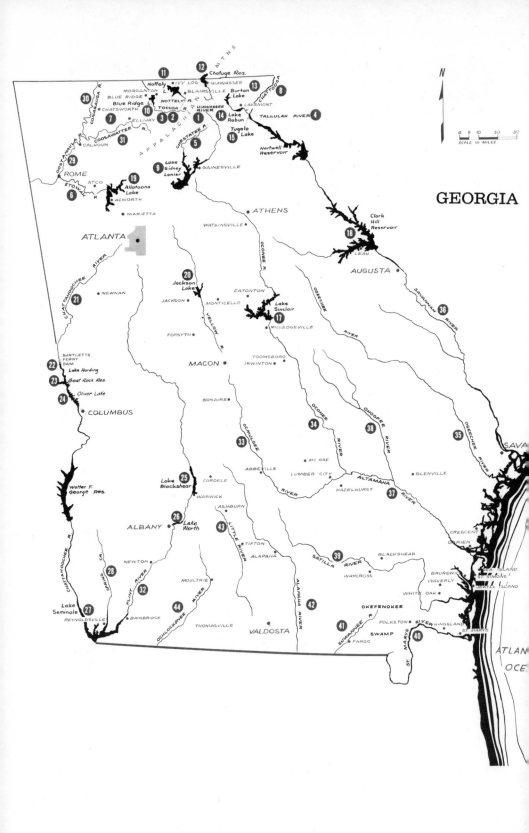

N

GEORGIA

0 5 10   20   30
SCALE IN MILES

MTNS

Chatuge Res.

Nottely   IVY LOG   HIAWASSEE
MORGANTON L.
BLUE RIDGE   BLAIRSVILLE   Burton
Blue Ridge L.   NOTTELY R.   Lake
CHATSWORTH   TOCCOA   LAKEMONT
ELLIJAY   HIAWASSEE   RIVER
RIVER   Lake
Rabun
COOSAWATTEE   CHESTATEE R.   TALLULAH RIVER
R.   Tugalo
CALHOUN   Lake

Hartwell
Reservoir

Lake
Sidney   GAINESVILLE
Lanier

ROME   ATCO
Allatoona
Lake
ACWORTH
MARIETTA

ATLANTA   ATHENS

WATKINSVILLE

Clark
Hill
Reservoir

LEAH
AUGUSTA

CHATTAHOOCHEE   Jackson
Lake   EATONTON
RIVER   MONTICELLO   Lake
JACKSON   Sinclair
NEWNAN   MILLEDGEVILLE

OCONEE R.

OGEECHEE

SAVANNAH

FORSYTH
YELLOW R.
RIVER

BARTLETTS   MACON   TOOMSBORO
FERRY   IRWINTON   RIVER
DAM
Lake Harding
Goat Rock Res.   BONAIRE
Oliver Lake   OCMULGEE
OCONEE   OHOOPEE
COLUMBUS   RIVER   RIVER   OGEECHEE
MC RAE   RIVER   SAVA
Walter F.   Lake   ABBEVILLE   LUMBER CITY
George Res.   Blackshear   CORDELE   GLENVILLE
WARWICK   RIVER   ALTAMAHA
ASHBURN   HAZELHURST   RIVER
ALBANY   Lake   CRESCENT
Worth   TIFTON   DARIEN
NEWTON   ALAPAHA   BLACKSHEAR
SPRING CR.   SATILLA   BRUNSWICK   SEA ISLAND
MOULTRIE   RIVER   WAYCROSS   WAVERLY   ST SIMONS
FLINT RIVER   RIVER   JEKYLL ISLAND
Lake   OCHLOCKONEE   WHITE OAK
Seminole   RIVER   ALAPAHA   OKEFENOKEE
REYNOLDSVILLE   BAINBRIDGE   RIVER   FOLKSTON   RIVER   KINGSLAND
THOMASVILLE   VALDOSTA   SUWANNEE R.   ST MARYS
SWAMP   ATLAN
FARGO   ST. MARYS R.   OCE

The bass fishing is best in May and June, October and November. Crappie fishing is best in the fall, though some good catches are made in April and May. Artificials are the most successful lures in Clark Hill. Fish are taken all over the lakes, as wide expanses in the middle are only 8 to 10 feet deep, so anglers should fish the open water as well as the coves. There are several fishing camps where boats can be obtained, on U.S. 378, which crosses the northern part of the lake, and on State 104, at Leah, on the southern shore.

In northwestern Georgia, LAKE ALLATOONA (19) is famous for its fishing for spotted bass. There are also some largemouth, white bass, crappie and lots of blue-gills, as well as minor populations of redbreast, warmouth and log perch. The spotted bass hit best in October, but good catches are made in the spring months. Spring and fall fish are taken in the shallows; summer fishermen usually must troll deep. The crappie fishing is best in March, but like the bass fishing swings up again in the fall after a summer layoff. However, summer fishermen make some very good crappie catches at night, during the month of August. The white bass make their spawning run in March and April and are taken mainly in the headwaters of the lake. There are fishing camps at many spots along the shores of Allatoona. Over-night accommodations may be found at Acworth on U.S. 41, which crosses the southern end of the lake about ten miles north of Marietta.

JACKSON LAKE (20), to the southeast of Atlanta, is not large, but produces some good-sized bass as well as crappie, bluegill, yellow perch and channel catfish. In general the fish are smaller than in the other lakes of the piedmont area. There are several fishing camps off State Highway 36, north of Jackson. Accommodations are available at Jackson, or to the east at Monticello.

The best white-bass fishing in Georgia will be found in the string of dammed lakes along the CHATTAHOOCHEE RIVER (21), on the central Georgia-Alabama border. Bartletts Ferry, also known as HARDING LAKE (22), is the largest. It produces largemouth black bass, white bass, crappie, bream and channel catfish. In spite of the fact that the water is usually discolored, good catches are made, both spring and fall. The fishing is particularly good if you are lucky enough to hit clear water in the fall. The white bass make their usual spring spawning run up to the headwaters and into the river but in Bartletts Ferry they also school out in the lake all summer and are taken by casters using surface lures. The channel catfish bite best in June. Twenty-pounders are common. Harding Lake is reached via U.S. 29 southwest from Atlanta, or State Highway 103, north from Columbus.

The next downstream widening of the Chattahoochee is GOAT ROCK LAKE (23), usually muddy, but productive of the same species as Bartletts Ferry. Many anglers regard this as the top water in all Georgia for both white bass and channel catfish. The choice spot is the tailrace of the Bartletts Ferry Dam. In April and May many white bass are taken here by casting across current and into the eddies with spinners, small spoons and doll flies.

The Oliver Dam at Columbus backs up the third in this series of reservoirs. LAKE OLIVER (24) is the most recently completed and while fishing is still in the process of development, it promises to be as good as its neighbors to the north. To fish these two lakes, anglers go north from Columbus on State Highway 103. There is a fishing camp at the Oliver Dam, another where the highway crosses an arm of the lake further upstream.

Directly to the interior of the state from these three reservoirs are smaller LAKE BLACKSHEAR (25) and LAKE WORTH (26), both on the Flint River. U.S. 280

crosses Blackshear and accommodations will be found at Cordele, only seven miles away. Fishing camps are operated on both sides of U.S. 280 on the western shore and there's another one at the southern end of the lake, near the town of Warwick. There is some excellent early-season fishing in this lake, the crappie starting to hit in February. The bass come along in April and the bream in late April and May. There is also good fall fishing in October and November. The white bass make their spawning run in mid-April and are taken in numbers at this time below the power dam, in the upper waters of the lake and in the Flint River. In the fall, anglers make their best catches around the mouths of the several creeks which enter the reservoir, casting small, flashy lures or spinners.

Lower on the Flint River is LAKE WORTH (26). There are lots of bluegills, good populations of bass and shellcrackers. Around the sawgrass and in the streams which feed the lake anglers take chain pickerel, crappie and catfish. The latter offer some extra-good fishing in this lake. The best times for bass and bream are April and May. Unfortunately this lake is so extensively used by pleasure boats that fishermen are pretty well crowded into the coves and streams. The lake is only about two miles from Albany, where all kinds of overnight accommodations and services can be obtained. There is a fishing camp on U.S. 19 at the western end of the lake.

In the southwestern corner of Georgia both the Chattahoochee and Flint Rivers have been backed up by the Jim Woodruff Dam to form LAKE SEMINOLE (27), on the tri-state border between Georgia, Alabama and Florida. Seminole is big and shallow, ideal for bass, bream and crappie. It has a greater variety of fish than any other Georgia lake, including bluegill, shellcracker, blue-spotted sunfish, dollar sunfish, orange-spotted sunfish, warmouth, black crappie, white crappie, chain pickerel, grass pickerel, channel catfish, white catfish and an assortment of rough fish. In addition the striped bass move in on their spawning runs and are caught in the Flint River below Albany and the Chattahoochee near Columbus. The stripers get up through the navigation locks of the Jim Woodruff Dam but cannot go above the dams at Albany and Columbus. It is hoped that as a result the striper will develop into a landlocked species in the lake. Currently an occasional fish up to 40 pounds is taken in the lake. The best fishing is in the SPRING CREEK (28) arm of the lake, near Reynoldsville, on State Highway 253, on the north shore. Chain pickerel, commonly called jack in these waters, run to 30 inches and are plentiful around the grassy flats in the lake. Bass have been taken up to 15 pounds. April and May mark the peak of the season but excellent catches are made year-round. This is one lake where top-water lures are always good, though deep trolling also takes bass in midsummer. Late in the summer they school all over the lake and surface lures are best again. Bream fishing is good all year, with a peak in April, May and June. Crickets are the top bait, fished on the bottom. Crappie fishing is best very early, in February and March, with another season in October and November.

Guides will be found at Wingate's Camp, RFD, Bainbridge, Georgia. The camp also provides some accommodations and boats on the Flint River arm of the lake. There are two more fishing camps off State Highway 253 on the Spring Creek Arm, and two more off State Highway 39, west of Reynoldsville.

RIVER FISHING

The mountain streams of Georgia warm quickly as they flow to the lower levels of the hills and on to the piedmont. Trout give way to smallmouth black bass, redeye and spotted bass. These will be found in the majority of trout streams mentioned in the extreme northern part of the state. Then as the course continues to the lower piedmont, the smallmouth disappears and the largemouth takes over.

Among the better northern streams for spotted bass, redeye bass, largemouth, crappie, redbreast sunfish and bluegills is the OOSTANAULA RIVER (29), which can be reached out of Calhoun on U.S. 41, south of Chattanooga. The Oostanaula itself also has some walleye and flathead catfish and is known to have produced sturgeon up to 50 pounds. Its tributaries, the CONASAUGA (30) and COOSAWATTEE (31), are considered two of the best rivers in Georgia for redeye bass, especially in the fall. The Conasauga curves around in roughly the same arc as State Highway 2, crosses U.S. 411 in Tennessee, just north of the Georgia border, then proceeds across U.S. 76 down to U.S. 41 near Calhoun. The Coosawattee rises near Ellijay on U.S. 76, flows across country to Calhoun, crossing U.S. 411 en route.

The ETOWAH RIVER (6), which, as mentioned earlier, has trout in the upper waters, is further south and is easily reached from U.S. 411 between Atco and Rome. It is also good for spotted bass, redeye, redbreast sunfish, bluegill and crappie, as well as some walleye and catfish. Spring and fall are the best seasons.

The same is true of the CHESTATEE (5), entering the north shore of Lake Sidney Lanier, and reached via State Highway 60 as well as several country roads from U.S. 19. This stream has the additional attraction of the spring run of white bass from the lake.

The great river of the southern interior part of the state is the FLINT (32), flowing due south of Atlanta down to Lake Blackshear, then on to Lake Seminole on the Florida border. This is one of the top streams in Georgia, with excellent angling for redear bass, which are known locally as smallmouths, as well as largemouth black bass. These two species are at their best when the water is low and clear, from October through January, but some are taken all summer. The fishing for bluegills and redbreast is good year-round. U.S. 280 crosses Lake Blackshear west of Cordele. The Flint River can be reached by many roads off U.S. 19 and State Highway 91. In the lower part of the river, striped bass move up from Lake Seminole as far as Newton, fifteen miles southwest of Albany on State Highway 91.

The OCMULGEE RIVER (33) makes a great curve to the southwest below Jackson Lake, to eventually flow into the Altamaha east of Lumber City, on U.S. 23 south of McRae. Near the junction is the spot where the world-record 22-pound largemouth black bass was taken. This river is very muddy in spring but even so the fishing can be good, and later in the season it is excellent in the backwaters and shoal areas. By fall it is in really good condition and the largemouth fishing is really productive. A few striped bass are also caught in the Ocmulgee and there are bluegill, redbreast sunfish and channel catfish.

One of the best stretches is from Jackson Lake down to Macon. There are numerous public access spots and two boat-launching sites, one where State Highway 18 crosses the river east of Forsyth, and one at Macon. Another good part of the river is south of Macon. Boats and a couple of fishing camps will be found near Bonaire at the junction of State Highways 96 and 247. Similar facilities are available near Abbeville, to the south, at the junction of U.S. 280 and U.S. 129.

The OCONEE RIVER (34) flows from the highlands down to Lake Sinclair, then on south to reach the Ocmulgee north of Hazelhurst on U.S. 221. Like the Ocmulgee, the Oconee River suffers from heavy silting in the spring but for the rest of the year the fishing is fair for largemouth, redbreast sunfish, bream and channel catfish.

The river above Lake Sinclair also produces spotted bass, and white bass make good runs out of the lake in April and May. Very occasional striped bass are taken as far upstream as Milledgeville, only a few miles south of the lake.

Some of the best fishing in that part of the river which is north of Lake Sinclair will be found between Athens and the spot where State Highway 15 crosses the river southeast of Watkinsville. There are boat-launching sites here. South of Lake Sinclair there are boat-launching sites where State Highway 57 crosses the river east of Irwinton to the town of Toomsboro.

The OGEECHEE RIVER (35), running parallel to the Savannah, some miles west of that border river, has the reputation of being one of the best black-water streams in the United States. In the piedmont area it is a small stream with good fishing year round for largemouth, chain pickerel, redbreast sunfish and channel catfish. One of the top spots is where State Highway 102 crosses the river at the junction of the Little Ogeechee and the main stream, due west of Sinclair Lake. As the river reaches the lowlands along the ocean, the fishing is even better, extending out into many backwaters and swamps. In March the shad come in from the ocean and striped bass make spring and fall runs into the lower waters. Both these species will be taken mostly in the area below the U.S. 17 bridge, though a few do move higher in the stream. Striped bass up to 40 pounds are taken. From the bridge north there are many boat docks and fishing camps.

The upper waters of the SAVANNAH (36), which forms the border between Georgia and South Carolina, offers fishing for largemouth black bass, redbreast sunfish, chain pickerel and bluegill throughout the year. The spring is the peak season, and at this time the river also has a run of white bass from Clark Hill Reservoir. U.S. 378 from Columbia, South Carolina, crosses Clark Hill Lake, as State Highway 72 does further north. Above that the river can also be reached via many interstate roads. There are numerous launching sites along the shore.

Lower in the stream certain areas are affected by pollution but there is some fishing for the same species. In the extreme lower end, near the Atlantic, shad move in on their seasonal runs in March and April. In Savannah Inlet anglers also take winter trout, redfish and tarpon.

One of the great rivers of central Georgia is the ALTAMAHA (37), entering the Atlantic Ocean a few miles north of Brunswick. All the midstate species such as largemouth, redbreast sunfish, bluegill and channel catfish are found. At the outlet to the ocean, below the U.S. 17 bridge, the angler will find some excellent tarpon fishing on occasion, with the fish going up to 125 pounds. During the winter some trout and redfish also move in. There are several fishing camps along that stretch of river from the entrance of the Ohoopee, about ten miles west of Glennville (on U.S. 301), via State Highways 144 and 178. The OHOOPEE RIVER (38) itself is off the beaten path and produces some good fishing. There are numerous public access sites and a fishing camp at its junction with the Altamaha.

Nearing the southern border of Georgia we come to the SATILLA RIVER (39). Redbreast sunfish are the most popular species, being taken all year. There are also bluegill and warmouth. Bass fishing improves as the river clears in spring. Fall is the best time for this species though some good catches are made year-round. Chain pickerel are also numerous. From State Highway 252, northeast of Folkston, down to the sea there are the brackish-water species. This is just about the best area in Georgia for striped bass, the stripers concentrating in the many canals found in this section of the state, from November through the winter. Winter trout and redfish also move in during the winter, being taken from October through March. The peak is in December and January, which months seem to produce some extra-large members of this species.

To balance the picture with regard to the influx of saltwater species, summer sees tarpon appearing on the scene. Angling for this much sought species is particularly good in the White Oak and Waverly Rivers, two tributaries of the Satilla. Information as to boats and guides may be obtained at the small towns of White Oak and Waverly, on U.S. 17.

Last of the coastal rivers, is the ST. MARYS (40), forming the border between Florida and the southeastern corner of Georgia, just above Jacksonville. There is some topnotch spring fishing for largemouth, redbreast sunfish, bluegill and crappie throughout the river. Down towards tidewater there is some very fine fishing for several saltwater species. Shad are taken by casters using jigs and small spoons, from January to April. Striped bass make their upstream migrations starting in November, and continuing on until spring, sometimes going as far as fifty miles upstream, though the best fishing is in the sound area. Throughout the winter, from October through March, redfish or channel bass, and winter trout, may be taken in the inlet. There is a fishing camp on State Highway 40, a couple of miles east of its junction with State Highway 110. Accommodations will be found at Kingsland on U.S. 17, within easy reach of the river.

The rivers of southern Georgia which flow south into Florida are in general clearer streams than the coastal rivers. There is good fishing for redbreast, bluegill and warmouth in most of them throughout the year, and some fine angling for largemouth black bass. Most of the rivers have many sloughs and ox-bow lakes, and swamps are everywhere, including vast Okefenokee, in the southeast, extending into Florida.

Furthest east of these southward-flowing rivers is the SUWANNEE RIVER (41), which makes up in Okefenokee Swamp. The Okefenokee is one place no fisherman should go without a guide. There are few roads, far apart, and no conveniences. At Fargo, on U.S. 441, which runs along the western edge of the swamp, arrangements may be made to go to two locally operated fishing camps well up in the swamp. Access to the northern part of the swamp is from Waycross, at the junction of U.S. 1 and U.S. 84 and 82; and from Folkston, on U.S. 1 near the Florida border. Guides may be obtained through tackle stores at either town. Arrangements for day trips into the swamp may be made through the headquarters of the Okefenokee Swamp Park, P.O. Box 860, Waycross, Georgia, phone AT 3-0483.

About half way between U.S. 41 and U.S. 441, the ALAPAHA RIVER (42) runs down through southern Georgia to join the Suwannee in Florida. Although it is a comparatively small stream it is excellent for boat fishing. The water is nearly clear, but can be very low in the fall. At all times the fish are concentrated in the numerous deep holes and backwaters. All the local species are taken and there is some excellent fishing for jacks in the fall. There are numerous points of public access from U.S. 29 and U.S. 221, in the southern part of the river. At Alapaha, at the junction of U.S. 129 and U.S. 82, there is a fishing camp; and another at the junction of State Highways 32 and 125 north of Tifton.

Immediately east of U.S. 41 and Interstate 75, is the LITTLE RIVER (43), an excellent small stream, particularly noted for warmouth fishing but also with an abundance of largemouth, sunfish, chain pickerel and bluegill. The fishing is best in the more northerly part of the stream. There are many boat landings and plenty of accommodations at Ashburn and Valdosta, as well as smaller towns along the two highways mentioned above.

The OCHLOCKONEE RIVER (44), the next river of size as you move westward, can be reached from U.S. 319 at many points between Moultrie and Thomasville. The stream holds good populations of most of the freshwater fish of the area but unfortunately is badly polluted.

SALTWATER FISHING

Georgia's offshore fishing is best in midsummer. Charter boats work the Gulf Stream waters twelve or more miles off Brunswick and Savannah for sailfish, barracuda, amberjack and little tuna or albacore. Closer inshore they take jacks, Spanish mackerel, cobia, kingfish and bluefish, and around pilings and old wrecks are drum, flounder, croaker, sheepshead and other lesser species. Tarpon move into Georgia waters to some degree about the last of May and stay around until cold weather. They are taken by trolling, still fishing and casting around the sounds and inlets and also in offshore waters. In midsummer some tarpon move into the tidal waters of nearly all the rivers along the coast. Party boats will be found at the ports mentioned above, and also at St. Marys, on the Florida border.

Around the mouths of the sounds, surf casters have excellent sport with big channel bass, averaging 5 to 20 pounds, but an occasional one going as high as 50 pounds. The fish stay around sloughs and sandbanks along the beaches, at the mouths of rivers, and around oyster beds, all summer. They are taken on everything in the books—cut mullet, shrimp, crab, squid, plugs and spoons.

Winter trout, or speckled trout, spark the fall fishing season, appearing in October in the sounds, inlets and river mouths. From that time on through winter they hang around the oyster beds and can be taken on shrimp or cast plugs. The peak of the season is in December and January. The weakfish, called summer trout in these waters, is found year-round.

Bluefish make two runs annually into Georgia waters, the spring run in April and May, the fall run in August and September. Mostly they are taken by offshore trollers, but quite frequently they appear in sounds and inlets, usually on a flood tide. Then they can be taken on cut mullet, squid and spoons.

The two anadromous species of the Atlantic coast, the striped bass and the shad, also provide some outstanding sport in inshore waters and in some of the rivers. The striped bass run into sounds, rivers, inlets and along the beaches during the spring. They are taken trolling, casting and still fishing. The shad enter the St. Marys, Altamaha, Ogeechee and Savannah Rivers in January and usually may be caught on into March. Flies and spoons cast with spinning outfits are used for this fishing, and some are also taken by trollers using small spoons.

Besides the main fishing ports of St. Marys, Brunswick and Savannah, skiffs and outboards can be obtained at Darien at the mouth of the Altamaha; just north of there at Crescent on State Highway 99; and at numerous docks on Sea Island, St. Simons and Jekyll Island, off Brunswick, and Tybee Island near Savannah.

An excellent description of Georgia's fishing lakes and streams entitled "Georgia Fish and Fishing" may be obtained from the Georgia State Game & Fish Commission, 401 State Capitol Building, Atlanta 3, Georgia.

GEORGIA FISHING REGULATIONS

Resident Fishing License $1.25
Resident Combination Hunting and Fishing License $3.25
Nonresident Fishing (3-day) License $1.25
Nonresident Season Fishing License $6.25

SEASONS AND LIMITS

All streams, lakes and ponds of Georgia are open to fishing throughout the entire year with the exception of the mountain trout streams of north Georgia.

Species	Size	Daily Creel Limit
Bream (Bluegill, Red Breast, etc.)	None	50
Crappie, Yellow Perch	None	40
White Bass and Yellow Bass	None	30
Black Bass, Redeye Bass, Spotted Bass	None	15
Striped Bass or Rockfish	None	15
Eastern Pickerel or Jack	None	15
Trout	See below	8
White Shad, Hickory Shad	None	8
Sauger, Walleye	None	8
Muskellunge	None	2
Channel Catfish	None	None

Note: There is no size limit on trout, except in Noontootley Creek in the Blue Ridge Management area, where all trout under 16 inches must be released unharmed; and in the Chattahoochee River below Buford Dam to Old Jones Bridge, where all trout under 10 inches must be released unharmed.

For complete regulations write: State Game and Fish Commission, State Capitol, Atlanta 30303, Georgia.

Clark Hill Lake on the Savannah River, one of the largest reservoirs in the South, holds largemouth bass, bream and crappie.

Appalachian
States

The states of Tennessee, Kentucky, West Virginia and Pennsylvania derive their fishing opportunities from the Appalachian chain of mountains which runs from south to northeast. Roughly, the ridge of the range forms the border between the first three states and the Atlantic Coast states of Virginia and North Carolina. Then the mountains fan out into rolling hills that cover much of the state of Pennsylvania.

In Tennessee the heights slope off quickly to the plains of the Mississippi River Valley and the drainage is mainly to this river or its tributary, the Ohio. In Kentucky the Ohio forms the entire northern border of the state, picks up most of the drainage and delivers it to the Mississippi. Many West Virginia rivers also flow eventually to the Ohio, but those of the northeastern part of the state flow to the Potomac and thence to Chesapeake Bay; as does the Susquehanna, which drains the whole central portion of Pennsylvania through its many tributaries. To the east, the Delaware forms the border between Pennsylvania and New Jersey and New York, draining the eastern part of Pennsylvania into Delaware Bay.

While there are few major natural lakes in this Appalachian area, a number of dams have created reservoirs which have been highly developed for recreational purposes and some of these now produce excellent fishing. These are the impoundments of the Tennessee Valley Authority on the Tennessee and Cumberland Rivers and their tributaries, in Kentucky and Tennessee.

Originally many of the mountain streams of the Appalachians held native eastern brook trout, but with the encroachment of civilization these have disappeared except in a few remote areas. They have been replaced by heavy stocking of rainbows, and some browns, particularly in Pennsylvania.

Many of the warm-water streams also have native populations of smallmouth black bass and rock bass in their cooler sections. These soon moved into the great lakes of the TVA system. The lakes are now also the home of vast populations of white bass and crappie, as well as several varieties ot catfish. And the Kentucky bass is common in many waters.

Some trout have also proven adaptable to certain waters of the TVA system, doing especially well in the cold water which is released from the bottom of the various dams.

PENNSYLVANIA

The main ridge of the Appalachian Mountains runs through the central part of Pennsylvania, from south to northeast, and is flanked on the west by the Alleghenies. Cutting through both ranges, from north to south, is the great Susquehanna River, which drains northeastern Pennsylvania through its main branch, and north-central Pennsylvania through its west branch. Another major river, the Allegheny, traverses the entire western part of Pennsylvania from north to south, and the Delaware River forms the border between Pennsylvania and New York and New Jersey.

These are the only large rivers in the state but there are hundreds of smaller ones, both tributaries of these and independent streams. In addition, Pennsylvania has a number of limestone streams, rising from springs, calm, serene waters filled with food for trout. There are few natural lakes of great size, but a number of rivers have been dammed to form reservoirs, both large and small, which provide additional habitat for various sporting species.

Brown trout do especially well in the limestone springs, rainbow and brook trout in the higher mountain waters. Smallmouth black-bass fishing can be excellent in some of the larger rivers and the same streams produce some fishing for large-mouth black bass. In many rivers bass and trout live together in the lower waters of the stream. Various rivers also hold muskellunge and walleye. These species, along with trout, the two basses, bluegill, crappie, pike, eastern chain pickerel and occasionally lake trout, are found in reservoirs at one place or another. In addition there is seasonal fishing for shad which move up the Delaware River on the eastern border on the state in April, May and June.

Like West Virginia, Pennsylvania has suffered greatly before the onslaught of pollution from mines and industry, but nevertheless considerable good fishing has been preserved and increasing efforts are being made to improve conditions where damage has been done in the past, and to prevent it in the future. All the popular warm-water species are being introduced in suitable reservoirs and ponds, and trout are stocked in considerable numbers in the mountain trout streams as well as cold-water ponds. The range of the muskellunge is being greatly extended, with stockings in many reservoirs and rivers, and this species is already becoming increasingly important on the fishing scene. Pennsylvanians have also been leaders in the field of "Fishing for Fun" projects, encouraging anglers to return their fish to the water unharmed, to live and fight another day; and several streams have stretches designated annually as "Fish for Fun" areas.

Pennsylvania is highly developed industrially; hence there are more than adequate roads to every part of the state. The Pennsylvania Turnpike crosses the entire southern half, with ready exits to some of the best fishing spots, while the Northeast Extension of the Turnpike provides the same service to the eastern part of the state and its Pocono and other mountain areas. Excellent highways service the balance of the state.

Springtime fishing in Pennsylvania calls for light-weight woolens. Though sum-

153

mer days are frequently very warm and cottons are the order of this time, you still need a sweater to don at evening, especially in the mountains.

Game is very plentiful in the mountain regions. There are a few bear, many deer, and much small game such as rabbits, squirrels, ruffed grouse, pheasants, wild turkeys, quail and doves. Anglers should always watch for snakes; there are copperheads and rattlers in most parts of Pennsylvania.

All kinds of tackle are used in Pennsylvania fishing, but this is especially the land of the fly-rodder, where much of American fly-fishing lore has been developed. The best all-around fly rod for trout here is an 8-foot stick with slow action. An HDH (DT6F) fly line and a 12-foot-long tapered leader rounds out perfectly matched equipment. Standard flies, both wet and dry, and nymphs as well, will all take trout; and streamers and bucktails are also successful on most Pennsylvania streams. The limestone streams, however, such as Penns Creek, the LeTort, and many others, call for special flies known as terrestrials, tied on small hooks. During the early season, flies tied on number 16 and number 14 hooks will do well, but after the aquatic fly hatches are over and summer comes into view, the trout seldom rise to anything but land insects such as ants, grasshoppers, beetles, jassids, leaf worms and daddy long legs. To meet this condition, Pennsylvanians developed a whole series of these terrestrial flies which have proven extremely successful. The angler going to fish the limestone streams should have the Black Jassid, tied on size 18, 20 and 22 hooks; Black Beetle on size 16 hooks; Black Ants on size 14 and 16 hooks; and Grasshoppers on size 12 hooks. The size 20 Black Flying Ant is always a good dry fly on limestone streams, and the Spentwing Blue Dun, size 14, pays off.

Another point to be remembered in fishing these small flies on limestone streams is that the leader tippet must be very fine—5X and 6X. Nothing heavier will fool the sharp-eyed old brownies.

DELAWARE RIVER DRAINAGE

In the northeastern part of Pennsylvania, the DELAWARE RIVER (1) offers fishing for smallmouth black bass and there are also walleyes, chain pickerel and very occasional trout which have strayed from tributaries. It is possible to float this river, and fishing can be very good as far down as Phillipsburg; below that it is polluted. Anglers put in with their boats at Port Jervis or Milford on U.S. 209, or further down at Dingmans Ferry and Bushkill. Some of the best fishing is around Water Gap, just to the south.

One of Pennsylvania's most famous trout streams, the BRODHEAD (2), is in the northeastern part of Pennsylvania, rising in the Pocono Mountains and flowing to the Delaware River near East Stroudsburg. Very little of this historic stream is now open to public fishing, the only two such areas being in the town of Canadensis and approximately seven miles between Analomink and East Stroudsburg. Both areas are easily reached from State Highway 290, which runs along the river valley. There are accommodations plus a mile of private fishing water reserved for guests at the Old Red Barn, south of Canadensis. This is limited to fly fishing only. Similar accommodations are available at the Log Cabin Farm, R.D. 2, East Stroudsburg, Pennsylvania.

On the PARADISE RIVER (3), a tributary of the Brodhead, coming into the main stream above Canadensis, there are accommodations and private fishing for guests at Henryville Lodge. Most of the trout in the Brodhead and Paradise are stocked fish, running from 8 to 18 inches in length.

SUSQUEHANNA RIVER DRAINAGE

It is to the SUSQUEHANNA (4) and its tributaries that Pennsylvanians mainly look for their fishing for species other than trout. Through its two branches, the main stream and the WEST BRANCH, the Susquehanna drains the whole central part of the state. Throughout its length through Pennsylvania, down to Conowingo Lake on the Maryland border, some four miles above the Conowingo Dam, this great river plays host to myriads of game fish, with the fighting smallmouth black bass the most numerous. This is one of the country's greatest smallmouth rivers. There are also largemouth, some muskellunge, walleyes, rock bass, fallfish and sunfish.

The Susquehanna is a mile wide in places and quite shallow over most of its length, with many rocky ledges. In spots it is easy to wade, in others impossible, and its length is broken up by the lakes above the Holtwood and Safe Harbor dams, as well as the Conowingo. But whether you step in and wade the shallows, or go by boat, or fish from the bank, practically the only thing to stop you from taking fish is a muddy river. Unfortunately during the spring months, after heavy rain, the river is frequently muddy for a few days.

Poppers, dry flies and streamers all take the smallmouths for fly men; small plugs and spoons for plug casters and spinners. The best baits are hellgrammites, night crawlers, and, when you can get them, soft-shell crawfish. Stonecats, riffle runners and chubs are fine live bait.

The river can be reached at many points from U.S. 11, which follows the west bank of the main fork, and from State Highway 147 on the east bank. The West Branch is paralleled by U.S. 15 from the forks up to Williamsport; then by U.S. 220 and U.S. 120 for many miles. West of Cooks Run, access is through secondary roads from State Highway 879.

One of the larger tributaries of the Susquehanna is the JUNIATA (5), also an outstanding bass stream. It can be reached from State Highway 26 south of Huntingdon, or from U.S. Highway 22, which follows the river down to its juncture with the Susquehanna, north of Harrisburg.

Boats are available at several spots and there are public access sites at Millerstown, Newport and Mexico, off U.S. 22. There is excellent wading and many anglers prefer to fish the Juniata this way. The catch may also include walleyes, channel catfish, fallfish and panfish; and muskies have been stocked and are beginning to take hold.

SPRUCE CREEK (6), which joins the Juniata at Spruce Creek on State Highway 45, north of the town of Water Street, is a fine little trout stream. Much of this river is private water but there are open stretches in Colerain State Forest between Spruce Creek and Franklinville; between Pennsylvania Furnace and Rock Springs; and near Spruce Creek. There is also some open water on its tributaries, Warriors Mark Creek and Half Moon Creek. Spruce Creek has been known to produce browns to 6 pounds, and brook trout to 14 inches.

TROUT STREAMS OF CENTRAL PENNSYLVANIA

Central Pennsylvania is fortunate in having a number of the top trout streams of eastern United States, streams on which American fly-fishing history was made.

The YELLOW BREECHES (7), flowing to the Susquehanna, south of Harrisburg, is one of America's historic streams. It provides thirty-five miles of fishing for rainbows and browns, as well as largemouth black bass, smallmouth black bass, pickerel and walleyes. Because of heavy silting, which results in a low rate of reproduction, the trout fishing is mostly on a put and take basis. Fly men find that the best fishing is in early spring because of the fact that on this stream the spring fly hatches are unusually early. There is always a problem of high and murky water if there is rain, but if you get a fairly dry spring the fishing can be hot from early April on into late May. The most used flies here are the No. 14 Dark Hendrickson, No. 18 Adams, Pale Evening Dun and Tup's Indispensible, according to the hatch of the moment. The Yellow Breeches has produced some good fish, including brook trout to 4 pounds, browns to 10 pounds, largemouth to 6 pounds and smallmouth of better than 4 pounds.

State Highway 174 follows the river's course, and can be reached from the Carlisle exit of the Pennsylvania Turnpike, or from U.S. 15 at Dillsburg, south of Harrisburg.

The LOYALSOCK (8) enters the Susquehanna from the northeast at Williamsport. This is the biggest water the trout fisherman will find in Pennsylvania. Chest-high waders are essential in order to reach the best spots. And then extreme care should be taken, as this is a difficult river to wade, with many boulders and slippery spots. While it is not productive as to numbers, it does turn out some fish of good size, even in the 5-pound class. Fly fishermen find the fishing best when there is a hatch on, as many of the pools are so large and deep that fish cannot be reached.

Williamsport is a good headquarters from which to fish the Loyalsock; or you can follow State Highway 87 upriver to World's End State Park and camp right on the stream. Mid-May is usually the best time to fish the Loyalsock, but mid-summer anglers should not be too discouraged. On the Loyalsock and other big Pennsylvania trout streams the brownies stay deep while the sun is hot and bright, but when dusk comes they swim up and cruise the tails of the big pools, snatching insects as they go. This calls for some spectacular casting and good timing to get a fly in front of the fish, but lunkers can be caught in this way and keen anglers look forward to this sporty fishing.

The many tributaries of the Loyalsock also provide good fishing. From Williamsport up, they are Mill Creek, which enters the Loyalsock between Williamsport and Montoursville on State Highway 87; Wallis Run at Butternut Grove; Little Bear Creek, a couple of miles further up; Big Bear Creek at Barbours; Pluncketts Creek, another couple of miles up; and Elk Creek, two miles north of Hillsgrove. You may get browns and rainbows up to 20 inches, and some brookies as well.

KETTLE CREEK (9) was at one time the top brook-trout water in Pennsylvania. Today this once fine stream, entering the West Branch of the Susquehanna near Westport, has warmed considerably and as a result the fishing is not what it used to be. However, there is still some brook-trout fishing in the upper waters and in the several tributaries; there are also a few browns. Two tributaries, Trout Run and Hammersley Fork, are still regarded as just about the best in Pennsylvania for fly fishing for brook trout. Access to the river is via State Highway 144, which leaves U.S. 120 between Shintown and Renovo. There is also an unimproved road which runs most of the length of the river from Westport up. Anglers also take smallmouth in the lower part of Kettle Creek.

Big Spring Creek, near Newville, offers three miles of chalk stream trout fishing.

To reach BIG SPRING CREEK (10), the protoype of limestone streams, you take U.S. 11 south from the Pennsylvania Turnpike near Carlisle, to State Highway 233 to Newville, then south on State Highway 891 for three miles. There are brook trout in the upper waters, browns lower down. The stream is open to all kinds of fishing but flies are most generally used, the top-rated pattern being the Slate Drake, to match a natural early-season hatch. The Pale Evening Dun, size 18, is good a little later. And after that, in midsummer, the terrestrials mentioned earlier come into their own, imitations of beetles, cress bugs and tiny duns, as well as nymphs. While daytime fishing is slow in summer, there is usually an evening rise. Check for special regulations on Big Spring.

On the outskirts of Carlisle, anglers will find the LETORT (11), also the perfect limestone stream, and the one on which the terrestrial flies were first developed. While most of the river flows through private land, access can be gained by request at several farms along the way. The Letort calls for all the skill of the fly man's art, but some fine fish are taken from it.

PENN'S CREEK (12), which enters the Susquehanna at Selinsgrove, at the junction of U.S. 15 and U.S. 522, is another classic limestone stream. From Selinsgrove westward to the mountains there is smallmouth-bass fishing for about twenty miles upstream from the mouth, then trout and bass for another twenty miles, and finally

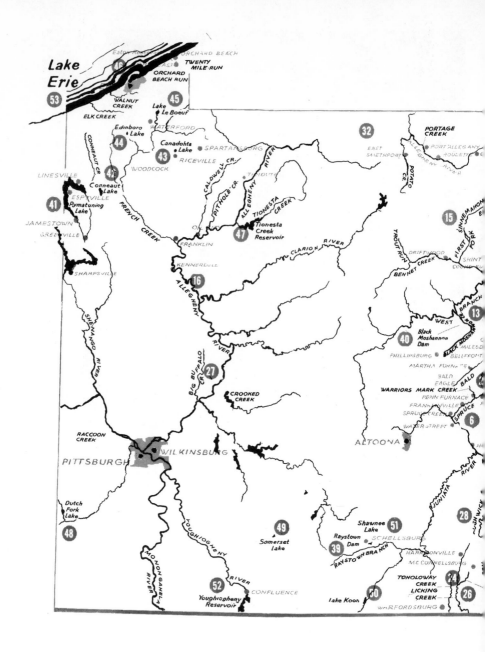

Lake Erie

53

ORCHARD BEACH
EATON ROAD
18
TWENTY MILE RUN
ORCHARD BEACH RUN

WALNUT CREEK
45 Lake Le Boeuf
ELK CREEK

Edinboro Lake
14 WATERFORD

CONNEAUT CR. 43 Canadohta Lake
LINESVILLE RICEVILLE SPARTANSBURG
42 WOODCOCK
Conneaut Lake
ESPYVILLE CALDWELL CR.

41 Pymatuning Lake FRENCH CREEK PITHOLE CR. ALLEGHENY RIVER TIONESTA CREEK
JAMESTOWN TITUSVILLE
GREENVILLE OIL 47 Tionesta Creek Reservoir
FRANKLIN

32 PORTAGE CREEK
PORT ALLEGANY
EAST SALETHPORT ALLEGHENY RIVER POTATO CR.
COUDERT

15 SINNEMAHON...
FIRST FORK
SHINT COUDER...

SHARPSVILLE KENNERDELL CLARION RIVER DRIFTWOOD
SHENANGO RIVER ALLEGHENY 16 BENNET CREEK TROUT RUN WEST BRANCH 13

RACCOON CREEK
PITTSBURGH WILKINSBURG

27 BIG BUFFALO CR.
CROOKED CREEK

40 Black Moshannn Dam BLACK MOSHAN...
PHILLIPSBURG BELLEFONT WEST MILES...
MARTHA FURNA...E
BALD EAGLE BALD 4
WARRIORS MARK CREEK
PENN FURNACE
FRANKLINVILLE SPRUCE
SPRUCE CREEK 6
WATER STREET

ALTOONA H...

Dutch Fork Lake
48 MONONGAHELA RIVER YOUGHIOGHENY RIVER 49 Somerset Lake Shawnee Lake 51 SCHELLSBURG
39 Raystown Dam JUNIATA 28 ...WIC...
RAYSTOWN BRANCH HARRISONVILLE MC CONNELLSBURG 24

52 Youghiogheny Reservoir CONFLUENCE Lake Koon 50 TONOLOWAY CREEK LICKING CREEK 26
WARFORDSBURG

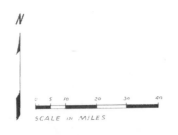

N

0 5 10   20   30   40

SCALE IN MILES

PENNSYLVANIA

YOUNG
WOMAN'S
CREEK

CREEK

LITTLE
PINE CR.
PINE CR.
14
PLUNKETTS
CR.
SLATE
WALLIS
RUN
LOYAL
SOCK
ELK CR.
CREEK
RIVER
MILL
CREEK
BEAR CR.
MIDDLE
CREEK
36
HAWLEY
8
BIG
Lake
Wallenpaupack
PAUPACK
FORT JARVIS
MONTOURSVILLE
Harveys
Lake
Promised
Land Lake
MILFORD
CHERRY
RUN
WILLIAMSPORT
38
SCRANTON
37
SEY-SHORE
LOCK
VEN
CLEMINGTON
VILLE
12
LITTLE FISHING CR.
FISHING CR.
PENN'S CREEK
WEST
4
WILKES BARRE
3
CANADENS
2
ANALOMINK
EAST STROUDSBURG
PARADISE RIVER
BRODHEAD CREEK
COBURN
MIDDLEBURG
BRANCH
SELINSGROVE
REL
WEIKERT
SUSQUEHANNA
RIVER
MIDDLE
30
MAHANTANGO
CREEK
29
SUSQUEHANNA
RIVER
BETHLEHEM
5
JUNIATA
ALLENTOWN
RIVER
DELAWARE
1
HARRISBURG
LEBANON
READING
CARLISLE
LETORT
CR.
17
HAMMER R.
NEWVILLE
BIG SPRING
CREEK
11
RIVER
LITITZ
YELLOW
10
7
BREECHES
CONEWAGO
RIVER
YORK HAVEN
LANCASTER
PHILADELPHIA
AMBERSBURG
31
COLUMBIA
Safe
Harbor
Lake
35
OCTORARO R.
YORK
SAFE HARBOR
18
34
BUCK
Lake
Conowingo
HOLTWOOD
Holtwood
Lake
33
19
MUDDY CREEK
DRUMORE

the pure trout stream above. The trout are mostly browns, but a tributary, CHERRY RUN (12), also has brook trout.

PENN'S CREEK is the largest limestone stream in Pennsylvania and also probably offers the greatest challenge of any. There are miles of pools and riffles and you can fish them all without catching a fish—and again you can make bumper catches. The best fly-fishing stretch for trout is from Coburn up; June and July fishing is usually good. Size 18 nymphs are probably the most successful flies. Bait fishermen like the water above Weikert.

State Highways 304 and 104 run with the river to a junction with State Highway 235 at Gleniron. Above that an unnumbered secondary road provides means of access to some miles of stream within the Joyce Kilmer-McConnell Narrows State Forest. You can come in to the top waters of Penn's Creek from Penn Cave on State Highway 45; or from U.S. 32 at Potters Mills.

BALD EAGLE CREEK (13) has its source near U.S. 220 between the villages of Hannah and Bald Eagle, and flows nearly fifty miles alongside the road to the West Branch of the Susquehanna at Lock Haven. This stream has produced brown trout weighing as much as 12 pounds. Fish from 22 to 26 inches are fairly common. The best fishing is in early season. Later the water warms and drops considerably and the fish are then concentrated in the deep holes and pools at the mouths of tributaries. One of the favorite early-season stretches on Bald Eagle is that part of the river between Port Matilda and Martha Furnace, immediately adjacent to U.S. 220. However, many of the bigger fish are taken near Milesburg, where, although the fishing can be spotty, some real whoppers are taken on midsummer nights. Though Bald Eagle is a freestone stream, many of its tributaries are limestone streams. Most of them have brown trout in the lower reaches, brook trout in the upper waters and some stocked rainbows. Marsh Creek, which enters the Bald Eagle at Eagleville, also has bass in the lower waters. Another tributary which is well worth fishing is Fishing Creek, entering the Bald Eagle at Flemington, near the junction with the Susquehanna. This creek has a reputation for producing many trout in the 3-pound class and some browns to 10 pounds. Fishing Creek has many good tributaries of its own, which add many miles to the fishing possibilities. These are Cherry Run, Cedar Run, Little Fishing Creek and Long Run. Other good tributaries of the Bald Eagle are Laurel Run, at Port Matilda; Wallace Run at Wingate; Spring Creek at Milesburg; Nittany Creek at Curtin; Lick Run at Howard; and Beech Creek at Beech Creek Station, just below Eagleville. From Eagleville to the Susquehanna there is thirteen miles of fishing for pickerel, muskies and bass, as well as for some big trout in that stretch of river between the dams at Howard and Eagleville.

PINE CREEK (14), another good stream, enters the West Branch of the Susquehanna near Jersey Shore. The lower part, Pine Creek Gorge, has some fishing for smallmouth black bass. In the upper part the deeper pools will produce brown trout up to 20 inches and the several tributaries such as Little Pine Creek, Slate Run, Cedar Run and the West Branch, are all good streams for browns and brook trout. Pine Creek flows through wild country and the angler may expect to see many deer and frequently may encounter bear. The river is reached via State Highway 44 north from U.S. 220, near Jersey Shore; then State Highway 414 up as far as Morris. At Waterville on State Highway 44 Little Pine Creek branches off to the east and is roughly paralleled by State Highway 284.

Continuing up the West Branch of the Susquehanna, you come to another good tributary trout stream, SINNEMAHONING CREEK (15), which crosses U.S. 120 just east of Driftwood. The lower part, known as the First Fork, parallels State Highway 872 for considerable distance to Wharton, where it is joined by the East Fork. The First Fork is good early in the season and can be good all summer, but like Penn's Creek, it is a tough one to figure. It's big water in many places, hard to read and hard to fish. There are a couple of hatches nearly every day, and if the angler watches for these, he'll soon discover where the fish are. There are brown trout up to 25 inches and the stream is heavily stocked for the opening of the season with trout from 8 to 12 inches. Many anglers prefer to fish this water at night in midsummer, and then they take some big fish on size 6 wet flies. Many anglers consider the water from Conrad down to Wharton as tops in both size and numbers of brown trout. Further up there is good fishing for brookies.

The East Fork is a smaller stream. It has a good population of brook trout, and is popular with dry-fly fishermen. There are also brook trout in the numerous tributaries of both the First Fork and the East Fork.

During the hatches, the choice fly on the Sinnemahoning group seems to be a size 16 or size 18 Blue Dun; but in May there are hatches of several naturals so you should be well supplied with such favorites as the Quill Gordon, Adams, Cahill, Stonefly and March Brown. Later in the season the East Fork is usually more productive than the First Fork, for flies, while the First Fork produces well for bait and spin fishermen. Smallmouth bass are found in the lower waters, and also in the Driftwood Branch, a few miles to the north on U.S. 120. Anglers will find a small hotel at Wharton, and some cabins a few miles north.

North of the Sinnemahoning, anglers can find some good trout fishing in the headwaters of the ALLEGHENY (16), which rise east of Coudersport on U.S. 6. The upper waters can be reached from State Highway 6 out of Coudersport and this part of the river is good for brook trout. Below Coudersport the stream is larger and there are brown trout of considerable size as well as rainbows and some brook trout. Some browns have been reported up to 8 pounds, rainbows as high as 10. There is some particularly good fly water between Coudersport and Roulette. Bait fishermen take quite a few brown trout from the flood-control channel of the Allegheny right in the town of Coudersport. The tributaries, Fishing Creek and Dingman Run, in the lower part, and Woodcock Creek, higher up, are good for brook trout.

Below Coudersport the river warms and takes on more of the nature of its course through western Pennsylvania. There are muskies, pike and bass, though some big trout hold on in the pools. They are mostly taken by spinners bouncing a lure along the bottom. There are also usually trout around the mouths of such feeder streams as Portage Creek at Port Allegany on U.S. 6, and Potato Creek at East Smethport, and even below that in several tributaries.

By the time the Allegheny enters New York State its population consists entirely of the warmer-water fishes. The balance of the river, after its return to Pennsylvania, is dealt with later in this chapter.

There are many other trout streams in central and eastern Pennsylvania, varying greatly in productivity. Most of them are stocked before the season opens and thus produce fair fishing for the early-season crowds. Then things slow down, though there is still good fishing for the trout fisherman who will spend the time to study his stream. Such possibilities will be found in the HAMMER (17) near Schaeffertown, east of Lebanon and near Lititz, further south, both on State Highway 501, north of Lancaster; the OCTORARO (18), from the Maryland border up; MUDDY

CREEK (19), near York, which lives up to its name, but nevertheless has twenty-two miles of fair trout fishing, some reserved for fly fishing only.

Pennsylvanians have led in the development of "Fish For Fun" areas on streams; and many of the rivers, especially the limestone streams, have areas limited to fly only, to fly with barbless hook, or to "put 'em back alive" regulations. One of the top attractions in this regard is Fishermen's Paradise, on SPRING CREEK (20) on State Highway 545, three miles south of Bellefonte on U.S. 220. Here the angling is limited to fly fishing only and all fish must be returned to the water. This part of the stream is open year-round, providing trout fishing for Pennsylvanians when the season is closed otherwise in the state. Another such area is found on YOUNG WOMANS CREEK (21), on U.S. 120, northwest of Lock Haven.

Other streams which have certain areas designated for fly fishing only are Penn's Creek, the First Fork of the Sinnemahoning, Slate Run, the Loyalsock, Laurel Hill, Muddy Creek and others. The areas are usually clearly marked along the stream.

Some streams have been developed commercially, also. One of these is the Limestone Springs Trout Hatchery, on State Highway 2 out of Lebanon, where the angler can find year-round fishing under natural stream conditions for large, stocked trout. Registration fee is $1.50 and you pay $1.40 per pound for your fish. There's a hotel at Millardsville, only half a mile away, on State Highway 422.

Besides the already mentioned streams which hold trout and bass, there are many streams in central Pennsylvania which harbor large numbers of warm-water fish. The CONOCOCHEAGUE (22), which can be reached from Chambersburg on U.S. 30, has forty miles of fishing for bass and panfish. BACK CREEK (23), near St. Thomas, a few miles to the east, is also good.

Good fishing for bass, pickerel and panfish is available in BIG TONOLOWAY CREEK (24) near Warfordsburg, on U.S. 522 immediately north of the Maryland border; in COVE CREEK (25), to the east, near McConnellsburg, on U.S. 30; and LICKING CREEK (26), near Harrisonville, between McConnellsville and the Pennsylvania Turnpike. Further northwest, BIG BUFFALO CREEK (27) has twenty-two miles of fishing for bass and pickerel, with starting point at Newport on U.S. 22. AUGHWICK CREEK (28), near Orbisonia, on U.S. 22, also has bass and panfish.

At Pleasant Mills on State Highway 35, southwest of Selinsgrove, anglers will find bass fishing in MAHANTANGO CREEK (29); while due north, at Middleburg, on U.S. 522, MIDDLE CREEK (30) is fishable for twenty-five miles, and produces good bass catches. The CONEWAGO (31), south of Harrisburg, can be fished near York Haven on U.S. 111 for the same species.

WESTERN PENNSYLVANIA

The ALLEGHENY RIVER (32) rises in central Pennsylvania near Coudersport, travels north and west into New York State, then returns to Pennsylvania to flow across the northwest corner and then south to join the Monongahela at Pittsburgh. From the point where the river returns to Pennsylvania, all the way through its meanderings down to Kittanning on U.S. 422, halfway between Youngstown and Altoona, the river produces some good fishing for bass, northern pike, walleyes and some muskies. Unfortunately, below that, the river is so badly polluted that fishing is impossible.

In the upper part, near the border, where the river traverses the Cornplanter

The author and champion caster Bruce Brubacher admire a fine trout from Limestone Springs, near Lebanon, one of Pennsylvania's "pay" trout streams.

Indian Reservation, there used to be some excellent fishing for rainbows and some of North America's best smallmouth black-bass fishing. However all this is about to disappear before the onslaught of the Army Engineers now constructing a dam below Kinzua. While it's fishable, this remains one of the few places in Pennsylvania where you can get a guide. The Indians on the Reservation will provide this service and also have boats for rent and bait for sale.

The really good muskie fishing on the Allegheny—and it's some of the best in the state—is in the stretch of river between the town of Tidioute and Tionesta Creek. The river runs beside U.S. 62, and there are boat landings along the way and several public-access spots. The fish also work into the water below the dam in Tionesta Creek, as do walleyes, bass and occasional trout. Above the dam on the Tionesta, the reservoir holds all these species. There are boats available above the dam. Following down the Allegheny, there is some good fishing for big catfish between Franklin and Kennerdell, then the angler is into walleyes and bass again.

Though this river is limited to the warm-water species, some of its tributaries have pretty good trout-fishing possibilities. From north to south, they include the Brokenstraw, which enters the Allegheny at Irving, from the west, and is adjacent to State Highway 77; Pithole Creek, further south; and Caldwell Creek, which travels beside State Highway 27, then State Highway 8, to enter the Allegheny at Oil City. The Caldwell is temperamental, but a very pretty stream to fish.

One of the largest of the tributaries of the Allegheny is French Creek, rising up near Lake Erie and flowing south to enter the parent river at Franklin. U.S. 322 runs beside the river nearly all the way, and there is good fishing for bass, walleyes and muskies the length of the stream. There are public access sites near Cambridge Springs, Saegertown and Meadville.

LAKE FISHING

In Pennsylvania there are a number of fair-sized lakes which provide good fishing for the warm-water species, plus a great many smaller lakes, ponds and reservoirs which have been stocked with the same species, and an increasing number of trout ponds. In addition, Pennsylvania has some fifty miles of shoreline on Lake Erie.

Three large dams on the Susquehanna River have created three lakes in south-central Pennsylvania, just above the Maryland border. LAKE CONOWINGO (33), above the Conowingo Dam, HOLTWOOD LAKE (34) above the Holtwood Dam and SAFE HARBOR LAKE (35) above the Safe Harbor Dam can all be reached from secondary roads leading off State Highway 222 on the east and State Highway 74 on the west. U.S. 30, between York and Lancaster, also crosses the top of Safe Harbor Lake. All three have fishing for walleyes, largemouth black bass, smallmouth black bass, crappie and fallfish, and the latter two have also been stocked with muskies. There are many miles of shoreline, ideal hangouts for bass, providing really great fishing for casters, where they can drop their flies and lures into pockets beside the tree trunks or under overhanging banks and tree limbs.

Boats are available at Drumore, off U.S. 222 at State Highway 272, at Holtwood, off U.S. 522 at Buck, on State Highway 372, at Safe Harbor, and at Columbia on U.S. 30. There are accommodations at all the towns in the area, plentiful around York and Lancaster.

A large natural lake, LAKE WALLENPAUPACK (36) can be reached from U.S. 6 at Hawley, directly east of Scranton. There are all the warm-water species except muskies. Walleyes up to 14 pounds have been taken in Lake Wallenpaupack. All services and accommodations will be found at Hawley and also at Paupack, on State Highway 507. You can continue on south on State Highway 507 to the Promised Land State Park where there are camping facilities. PROMISED LAND LAKE (37), on State Highway 390, also has fishing for largemouth black bass, pickerel, yellow perch, bluegill and smallmouth, and Lower Promised Land Lake has been stocked with muskellunge.

Also in northeastern Pennsylvania, west of Scranton and Wilkes-Barre is HARVEYS LAKE (38), which offers fishing for trout and lake trout as well as smallmouth perch and walleye. The lake can be reached via State Highway 118, turning north on State Highway 415, east of Lapman; or from Beaumont, on U.S. 309.

There are some accommodations at Beaumont and at Dallas, at the junction of U.S. 309 and State Highway 118.

There are two fairly large dams in central Pennsylvania which provide some fishing. RAYSTOWN DAM (39) on the Raystown Branch of the Juniata River, southwest of Huntingdon on U.S. 22, has a good reputation for substantial catches of largemouth black bass and there are also smallmouth, walleyes and panfish. Muskellunge have been stocked but as yet the results are not known. Boats are available on the lake and there are launching sites as well. This lake is much used by pleasure boaters, which sometimes interferes with the fishing.

Further north, near Phillipsburg, is BLACK MOSHANNON DAM (40), reached by State Highway 504 between Phillipsburg and Bellefonte. This lake has a wide range of species, from muskies, which have developed well from stock planted some years ago, to largemouth, smallmouth, pickerel, walleyes and various panfish. No motors are allowed on the lake, but there are boats for hire, or you can launch your own for $1.

The largest lake in Pennsylvania is PYMATUNING (41), on the Ohio border only about twenty miles south of Lake Erie. While Pymatuning is shared with Ohio, the major portion of the lake is in Pennsylvania and Pennsylvania fish regulations apply except along the Ohio shore. The lake is 18,000 acres in size and has seventy-two miles of shoreline. The northeastern part is a game refuge, with no fishing permitted, but the rest of the lake is wide open, with no closed season, no size or daily limits. Pymatuning is best known for its walleyes but there are also muskellunge, largemouth black bass, crappies and catfish. Those who fish the lake a lot follow a regular schedule: starting in April they fish the run of crappies, followed almost immediately by the walleyes, which are taken on deep-running trolled lures or bait consisting of nightcrawlers or minnows; later come the bass. Fishing for this species is especially good around the stumps in the northern part of the lake.

Pymatuning Lake can be reached via U.S. 6, which skirts the north shore, and there are boat rentals and accommodations at Linesville; or you can go in from the south, from U.S. 322, at Espyville or Jamestown. At Jamestown there are camping facilities in a state park.

The Shenango River flows out of the south end of Pymatuning Lake on the Pennsylvania-Ohio border. The river is generally murky because of driftage of algae from the lake, but from June to September some fairly good catches of muskellunge are made with live minnows, particularly in the area between Greenville and Sharpsville.

South of Lake Pymatuning, on the northeast (Ohio) border there is some early-season fishing for stocked trout in the Little Shenango River, which can be reached from State Highway 58. There are also largemouth and smallmouth black bass; and one of the tributaries, Sandy Creek, holds pike.

A number of smaller lakes to the east of Pymatuning also offer some fair angling possibilities. CONNEAUT LAKE (42), on U.S. 322, is 928 acres in size, and has a good population of largemouth black bass, smallmouth black bass, northern pike, walleyes, crappies, yellow perch, bluegills and catfish. Lake trout have been stocked, and so have muskies. From June through September the latter are taken with some regularity by anglers using live minnows for bait. A 52-pounder, the largest ever caught in Pennsylvania, came from Conneaut Lake. The bass fishing is best around the weed beds, and surface plugs and poppers are most successful. There is a public access area a couple of miles south of Harmonsburg, on State Highway 618, where you may launch your own boat; and there are several boat liveries along the lake shore.

CANADOHTA LAKE (43), to the northeast, is much smaller, but also has fishing for bass, walleyes, northern pike and muskies. The lake is near the town of Riceville on State Highway 77 between Meadville and Spartansburg. There are lots of boat liveries on the lake.

Another small one which can be surprisingly good is EDINBORO LAKE (44), at the junction of U.S. 6 and State Highway 99, southwest of Erie. Though only 120 acres in area, and only an occasional producer, Edinboro does turn out some good-sized muskies and there are also walleyes, largemouth and crappies. In the same area LAKE LEBOEUF (45), near Waterford on U.S. 19, is populated with large-mouth, walleyes and panfish. In the northeastern tip of the state, near the town of Northeast, EATON RESERVOIR (46) also produces some good fishing.

TIONESTA CREEK RESERVOIR (47), on the Tionesta Creek, also has all the warm-water species as well as some trout. The lake can be reached from U.S. 62 at Tionesta, via State Highway 66.

In southwestern Pennsylvania there are a number of small lakes which are worthy of the angler's attention. DUTCH FORK LAKE (48), near Claysville, off U.S. 40, has largemouth, walleyes and muskies, as well as panfish. SOMERSET LAKE (49), near the town of the same name, on U.S. 219, at the Pennsylvania Turnpike, has largemouth, walleyes, northern pike and panfish; and LAKE KOON (50), off U.S. 220 just above the Maryland border, adds trout and smallmouth to the list. These are all small lakes and in most cases motors are not allowed, but boats are available. Koon Lake may be fished from the banks only.

To the north of Koon is SHAWNEE (51), reached via Schellsburg, on U.S. 30. There are both large and smallmouth black bass, walleyes and panfish.

The largest lake in this part of Pennsylvania is the YOUGHIOGHENY RESERVOIR (52), which extends from southern Pennsylvania down into the northeast corner of Maryland. This lake produces excellent catches of big northern pike as well as largemouth black bass. There are also crappies, panfish and yellow perch. The reservoir is accessible from Confluence, on State Highway 53, on the north; or from U.S. 40, which crosses the centre of the lake.

While the State of Pennsylvania has limited access to LAKE ERIE (53), there is some excellent year-round fishing to be had along this shallowest of the Great Lakes. Crappies and northern pike move inshore in the spring, followed by bass, walleyes and rock bass. Fishing for muskellunge and northern pike picks up in the fall, as does deep fishing offshore for smallmouth black bass. In the winter the bay at Erie looks like a housing development, with hundreds of ice fishermen's little shacks. The catch of perch, smelt and crappies, along with some northern pike and walleyes, is tremendous.

During the warm seasons there is good wading in parts of Presquile Bay at Erie; and then fly, spin and plug casters make some fine catches in the shallows. Others go by skiff and cast in to the weed beds which abound in the bay and provide fine habitat for fish.

There are boats available at Leo's Livery and Denmark's Lagoon Livery on the Peninsula facing Erie; and Erie sporting goods stores always have the latest dope on where and how to fish the lake at the moment.

As a result of stocking of rainbows, there is some fishing for this species in several streams which run into Lake Erie along the Pennsylvania shore. While this is not a very consistent fishery, the rainbows appear to have run out into Lake Erie to feed, then return to the rivers in the early spring. Anglers who get in on the fishing at opening date, April 15th, may come up with some better than substantial rainbows, running as high as 11 pounds. Few small ones are taken, and the majority of fish are caught on salmon eggs drifted through the pools. Some are taken on worms and minnows, and a few on spinners.

From east to west, the streams in which you may find these lake-run rainbows are: Twenty Mile Run, near the New York State line; Orchard Beach Run, near the town of the same name; Twelve Mile Run, east of Erie; then west of Erie you find Walnut Creek, Trout Run at Avonia, Silk Creek, Crooked Creek, Raccoon Creek and Conneaut Creek, which flows from Pennsylvania to its outlet on the Ohio shore of Lake Erie.

As mentioned above, this is spotty fishing and of short duration. The best possibilities are from April 15th to mid-May.

The Pennsylvania Department of Commerce and the Fish Commission have recently published a very complete list of nearly every fishable lake, pond and stream in Pennsylvania; and this is available through either department, at Harrisburg, Pennsylvania. The booklet gives very complete descriptions of the species found in each water, and directions as to how to reach the lake or stream. It also includes some very good information on fly hatches, special regulations, and public access to certain waters provided by the Fish Commission.

In addition to the many lakes described above, and listed in the booklet just mentioned, there are some "Pay and Fish" lakes in Pennsylvania. Krystal Kleer Trout Fishing Lake, half a mile south of Newmanstown, near Schaefferstown, is just north of the Pennsylvania Turnpike where it crosses State Highway 322, north of Lancaster. There is fishing for brooks, browns and rainbows of substantial size, at $1 per person and $1.40 per pound of fish. Flies, artificial lures and bait, except live minnows, are allowed.

PENNSYLVANIA FISHING REGULATIONS

Resident Fishing License $5.00 plus 15¢ fee
Nonresident Fishing License $9.50 plus 15¢ fee
Trout stamp (in some waters) $5.00
Nonresident 5-Day Fishing License $5.00 plus 15¢ fee

Their is some kind of fishing available year-round in Pennsylvania. For instance, bass and pickerel seasons are open year-round in the Conowingo and Youghiogheny Reservoirs and the Delaware River; but there are closed seasons on other species. Bass, pike and muskellunge may be taken year-round in Lake Erie, but there is a closed season on rainbow trout. In inland waters, all the panfish may be taken year-round, but there are two closures on bass, pickerel, walleye, muskellunge and pike. Special license regulations also apply in Pymatuning Lake, on the Ohio border; in the Delaware River on the New Jersey-New York border, and the Youghiogheny Reservoir on the Maryland border.

For complete regulations write: Fish Commission, P.O. Box 1673, Harrisburg 17120, Pennsylvania.

WEST VIRGINIA

West Virginia is almost wholly mountainous, with the backbone of the Appalachian Range filling the eastern and central part of the state and the slopes sliding down to the Ohio border on the west. As is the case with many mountainous areas, rivers are much more numerous than lakes, and the fish to be found in West Virginia are those most suitable to such conditions. The brook trout was once prevalent in natural state, but so many of the state's streams have been ruined through pollution and the encroachment of other uses on forest and stream, that today's trout are mostly stocked fish—brooks, rainbows and browns. A fourth trout, the "Centennial Golden Trout," may also be encountered as the result of the stocking in some 130 lakes and rivers in 1963 of a breed developed in the state hatcheries from California golden trout stock.

The two basses, the largemouth and smallmouth, occur in many rivers, the smallmouth in particular providing some outstanding fishing. Walleye, channel catfish and bullhead occur in the more sluggish streams as well as a few lakes and reservoirs; and the muskellunge has been stocked with considerable success in suitable rivers and lakes.

Several historic rivers form the backbone of the drainage of the State of West Virginia. The Potomac and a network of its tributaries drain the eastern area which juts out between Maryland and Virginia. The Monongahela, with many tributaries, drains the north-central border area. And the Ohio and the numerous rivers, both large and small, which pour into it, drain the northwestern part of the state. On the south the New River picks up water from many streams along the slopes of the mountains and carries it north and west across the state to the Kanawha, and finally the Ohio. The bulk of the fishing in West Virginia is found in these rivers and their tributaries. There are no natural lakes of major proportion, though there are a few reservoirs which are of importance to fishermen.

A glance at the map will indicate that in West Virginia no road goes straight to its destination. In this mountainous area, while the highways are good, they wind back and forth through the hills and many areas are served only by secondary roads. However, access to the main ridge of the mountains is provided along the east by U.S. 219 from Pennsylvania and Maryland, all the way down the state, through White Sulphur Springs, and this highway is paralleled to the west by U.S. 19. The major east-west highway is U.S. 33, which traverses the widest part of West Virginia, from Pomeroy on the Ohio border to Harrisonburg, Virginia. U.S. 60 provides parallel transportation across the narrower southern part of the state.

From these major highways state roads lead to the less highly developed mountain regions. In many such areas accommodations are limited but state authorities have made efforts to overcome this by assembling a list of West Virginia farms where food and lodging will be provided for sportsmen. This list, including location of the farm, and what fishing is available nearby, may be obtained without charge from the Department of Natural Resources or the Department of Agriculture, Charleston, West Virginia.

169

As in most mountainous areas of the temperate zone, daytime temperatures will allow for cotton fishing clothing, while evenings call for warmer gear. On most West Virginia mountain streams hip boots are adequate for wading, but those who wade the lower levels of the rivers for smallmouth black bass prefer chest-high waders, in order to reach the choice spots.

Trout fishermen will find the 8-foot rod suitable in all cases. The standard trout flies also are all good. A basic selection should include the Black and Orange Nymph and the Black and Yellow Nymph, on size 16 hooks; wet flies in Black Gnat, Coachman, Royal Coachman, and Blue Dun patterns, size 12 hooks; dry flies in Royal Coachman, Black Gnat, Blue Dun, Mosquito, Light Cahill patterns, on hooks number 12 and 14. Small streamers and bucktails on size 12 long-shank hooks should be carried in Muddler Minnow, Blacknosed Dace, Black Marabou, White Marabou, Mickey Finn and Black Prince patterns.

Fishing for all sport species except trout is open year-round. The trout season opens in April and there are regular stockings throughout the spring and until the middle of June; then, as the hunting season approaches, there is a closed season for two weeks in certain areas, for a repeat stocking. Fishing in these streams re-opens with the hunting season, thus providing a combined attraction for the hunter-fisherman in the fall. Complete details on annual changes in the dates of this program should be obtained from the West Virginia Department of Natural Resources, Division of Parks and Recreation, Charleston 5, West Virginia.

The same department published a "Centennial Guide to Trout Fishing in West Virginia" to celebrate the State Centennial in 1963. It gives a list of streams which are stocked regularly with trout, and detailed instructions on how to reach them. The list may be obtained by writing the department.

The mountains of West Virginia are renowned as the home of much wild game. Bear are common in some parts. Deer are plentiful. Small game includes rabbits and raccoons, and there are grouse and turkeys. Anglers should watch for snakes, as rattlers and copperheads are both found in this area.

POTOMAC RIVER WATERSHED

The POTOMAC RIVER (1) offers some of the best smallmouth black-bass fishing in the eastern United States. Through that stretch of river along the West Virginia border there is fine wading, or the angler may fish from shore or go by boat. Fly fishermen usually pick up a boat at a local rental and go to the spot where they wish to fish, then anchor and wade. Three good spots to start such a junket from are Harpers Ferry on U.S. 340, between Frederick, Maryland and Charles Town, West Virginia; Berkeley Springs, on U.S. 522, south of Hancock, Maryland; and Shepherdstown, on State Highway 45, off U.S. 11 at Martinsburg.

The smallmouth are thick through this area and always seem hungry. It is possible to take fifty to seventy-five in a day, mostly weighing from 1 to 1½ pounds, but with some 2- and 3-pounders. Now and then 4- and 5-pounders are caught but this is the exception.

Fly rods for this bass fishing should be 8½ or 9 feet in length, and with this you need a forward-tapered fly line. A GBF (WF8F) will match the 8½-footer, and a GAF (WF9F) will match the 9-foot rod. Nylon leaders should be 12 feet long and tapered from a 20-pound-test butt section to a 6-pound-test tippet. Small popping bugs are the top-rated lure, and the colors that bring strikes are red and white, red and yellow and robin's egg blue. Streamers which also produce are the Phillips multiwing flies in red and yellow and red and white, on 1/0 hooks. The black and white, red and white and all yellow bucktails are good, as is the Muddler Minnow, all on size 10 long-shank hooks. Sometimes it is fun, and productive, too, to use dry flies for the smallmouths. Best flies, in sizes 6 and 8, are the Grey Wulff, Royal Wulff, and Grizzly Wulff.

Spinners take their share of these Potomac bass, using small spoons, plugs and even surface-popping plugs. Bait fishermen use hellgrammites, rifflerunners, and small catfish, called Mad Toms. When using the catfish, the pectoral fins should be cut off so the bass can swallow the Tom more easily.

Catching the hellgrammites is something of a fishing trip in itself. Fishermen wade out in the fast water, place a net downstream from a rock, then lift the rock up. As the current washes the hellgrammite from his cover, he rolls himself into a ball and floats into the net. When fishing with a hellgrammite—and this is by far the favorite bait of bass fishermen—the bait is hooked under the collar, that band of hard shell that goes around the back of the neck. This keeps the bait alive, so it squirms on the hook and provides the bass with a tasty-looking dish.

When a bass takes one of these baits, the fisherman should be sure to give him plenty of time. Generally they make one run, stop, turn the minnow, and swallow it head first, then take off on another run, and that's the time to strike.

Bait fishermen use all kinds of rods, fly, spinning or plug, but best results will be found with an 8½- or 9-foot fly rod. It allows you to cast the bait with stiff-arm action so as not to snap it off, and with the long rod it is easier to control the bait and keep it off the bottom.

You find the smallmouth black bass in the rapids, in glides along shore, in front of and in back of protruding rocks, and in pools, too. Along the slower backwaters of the Potomac you will also find the largemouth, increasing in numbers and size further downstream.

In September channel cats are found in the same waters, and can frequently be taken in the rapids on flies. Some years back, in September, during a big hatch of white miller flies, I took many channel catfish on a matching dry fly. They are fighters and a welcome addition to the smallmouth. They are also good on the table.

The Shenandoah, a major tributary of the Potomac, flows through the eastern corner of West Virginia; but this river has suffered so greatly from pollution that it supports mostly catfish, and is not very attractive to fishermen. Nevertheless those who know the river manage to find good smallmouth fishing wherever the condition of the water permits this fine species to live.

The CACAPON RIVER (2), one of the Potomac's most easterly tributaries, is highly regarded by those who like to use flies or spinner-and-fly combinations for smallmouth. The river has many small tributaries which are stocked with trout.

The Cacapon flows northeast along the border between West Virginia and Virginia, and can be reached from Berkeley Springs, close to the Pennsylvania line on U.S. 522; or further south, anglers can approach the river from State Highway 259 between High View and Capon Springs. A number of the afore-mentioned small tributaries come in on the west side of the river and country roads cross them all close to their junctions with the Cacapon. A larger tributary, the NORTH RIVER (3), also comes in on the west side. It can be reached from Slanesville on State Highway 29, and also far upstream, from Moorefield on U.S. 220. A second large tributary, the LOST RIVER (4), runs close to State Highway 259, on a line with the border, all the way up to Wardensville and Lost City.

The major tributary of the POTOMAC is its SOUTH BRANCH (5). From Old Fields on U.S. 220, twenty-one miles to Romney on U.S. 50, the South Branch can be float-fished for smallmouth. The section of the river between these two towns is known as "The Trough" and should not be attempted by any but expert boatmen. All who are planning to float this part of the river should first contact the District Conservation Officer at Romney. Boats are available at both towns. There is also good fishing for channel cats in the South Branch.

Many of the tributaries of the South Branch of the Potomac receive substantial stockings of trout. Going south from Petersburg on secondary roads, you can cross South Mill Creek, Spring Run and Dumpling Run, all emptying into the South Fork of the South Branch. There are also trout in the NORTH FORK (6), accessible from Seneca Rocks on U.S. 33 and Cherry Grove on State Highway 28.

Another fairly good stream in this northeast sector of the state is MILL CREEK (7), which can be reached via State Highway 51, east of Gerrardstown, U.S. 11 at Bunker Hill, and State Highway 36 near the mouth of the creek. ROCKY MARSH (8), accessible from State Highway 45, west of Shepherdstown, is also stocked.

MONONGAHELA WATERSHED

A myriad of small tributaries flowing in from the highlands in the east form the CHEAT RIVER (9), a tributary of the Monongahela. There are many miles of fishing readily accessible from country roads running off U.S. 50 at Macomber and U.S. 219 at Parsons. The upper part of the Cheat is known as the Shavers Fork, and extends far down into the central part of the state, so far that in an area west of the junction of U.S. 219 and U.S. 250, the headwaters of the north-flowing Shavers Fork, and those of the south-flowing Greenbrier, run parallel to each other for some miles. This upper part of the Shavers Fork is comparatively inaccessible except at Cheat Bridge, where U.S. 250 crosses the river. The small towns of Bartow and Durbin, on U.S. 250, provide fishermen's accommodations and can direct anglers as to where to fish the streams. Those planning to fish this area should write Dick Huffman's Rock Inn at Bartow, or the Pocahontas Hotel at Durbin. There are also accommodations further north at Elkins, at the junction of U.S. 219 and U.S. 33.

SENECA CREEK (10), another stream which is regularly stocked with adult fish, can be reached from the town Mouth of Seneca on U.S. 33.

There is some good fishing to be found in the Bruceton Mills area, in the corner of West Virginia which is bounded by Pennsylvania on the north and Maryland on the east. The Cheat River and three smaller creeks, especially BIG SANDY CREEK (11), offer some angling for natural trout as well as stocked fish, including some of the 1963 Centennial Golden Trout. Fish can run as high as 17 inches.

The Sandy is best below the dam, usually producing an assured catch. Above the dam for about two miles the water is slow moving but from there up for about five miles, to the Pennsylvania border, there are again pools and riffles. The Big Sandy also holds bass, bluegills and catfish. To get directions as to the best places to fish these rivers, anglers should stop at the Cabin Way Inn, two miles south of Bruceton Mills, on State Highway 26.

THE OHIO DRAINAGE AREA

The waters which flow to the Ohio in West Virginia are generally more sluggish than those nearer the mountain ridges and consequently this is where the muskel-

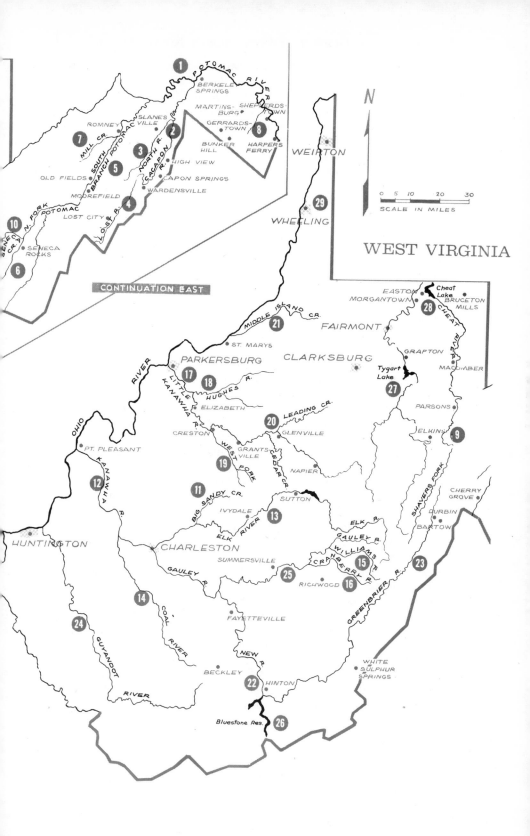

lunge, walleyed pike, largemouth black bass, catfish and bullheads are most common. The unexpected quality of the muskellunge fishing is the main feature of these rivers; and there is also some excellent fishing for channel catfish, which are found in the lower reaches of all the larger steams wherever there is fairly swift water. In some places enormous shovelhead, or mudcat, are also taken. The bullhead are found in the more heavily polluted waters.

Channel cats are commonly taken on artificial lures, small bucktails and streamers, fished very slowly and deep, but on occasion they can be taken on flies and other surface lures.

The KANAWHA RIVER (12), which enters the Ohio River at Pt. Pleasant, is fed by a number of large rivers, making up well into the center of the state. The New and the Gauley are the first source of the Kanawha, and they are augmented by the ELK (13), a big river in itself, and the COAL (14). In spite of a major pollution problem, the Kanawha supports good populations of largemouth black bass. Its tributary the Elk is a top muskie river, and the Coal also produces good fishing for this species. The Kanawha, Elk and Coal all have channel catfish averaging 5 pounds but going as high as 15 pounds. Around Sutton, at the Junction of U.S. 19 and State Highway 4, you can fish the Elk above the Sutton Reservoir for warm-water species; and there are trout in the tailwaters of the dam. Just to the south of this are two good tributaries of the Gauley, the WILLIAMS (15) and CRANBERRY RIVERS (16), both fairly good trout streams. They can be reached from State Highway 39 and 20 between Summersville and Richwood.

Entering the Ohio further north, at Parkersburg, the LITTLE KANAWHA (17) provides the same kind of fishing as the Kanawha and its tributaries.

The Little Kanawha is probably the best for muskellunge and is fishable for many miles right beside the road. State Highway 47 follows the north bank of the river for about twenty miles upstream from Parkersburg; or anglers can use State Highway 14 to Elizabeth, then take State Highway 5, which cuts back and forth across the river from there up to Napier on U.S. 19, in the middle of the state.

The river here is fine for float trips, especially between Glenville at the junction of State Highway 5 and U.S. 33, and Grantsville, where State Highways 5 and 16 both cross the river. Muskies to 25 pounds are taken regularly in the Little Kanawha.

Some of its tributaries which also hold muskies are the HUGHES RIVER (18), along State Highway 47, north of the main stream; WEST FORK (19), off State Highway 5 at Creston; CEDAR CREEK and LEADING CREEK (20), near Glenville on U.S. 33 at the junction with State Highway 5.

Entering the Ohio at St. Marys, north of the Little Kanawha, MIDDLE ISLAND CREEK (21) is a meandering stream with the banks lined with willows. It is ideally fished by boat as in several places the stream wanders far back from the road. At "the jug," in particular, near Middlebourne on State Highway 18, boatmen can traverse some four miles of river in virtual wilderness country.

Most muskie fishermen in West Virginia use bait-casting rods and reels with Creek Chub Pikie muskie plugs or other large, jointed plugs. The Pflueger Tandem Bucktail Spinner is also good. Some anglers also take muskies by trolling live bait such as suckers or chub. Such bait should be large in size.

THE NEW RIVER

A dam near Hinton, at the Junction of State Highways 20 and 3, backs up the

New River (22) almost all the way to the Virginia border. Below the reservoir there is fishing for bass and walleyes, and the waters right below the dam rate as one of the best spots in the state for channel catfish. There is also some muskie fishing in the New, the muskies being taken mostly in winter on deep-fished bait.

The outstanding tributary of the New is the Greenbrier River (23), which flows for many miles along the Alleghenies just a few miles inside the West Virginia border. The upper waters of the Greenbrier hold trout, as do most of its tributaries. Lower down in the river, especially around its junction with the New, smallmouth bass fishing can be very good. The same waters produce walleyes which regularly go to 5 pounds and occasionally to 10. For much of its length the Greenbrier is paralleled by U.S. 219; and from White Sulphur Springs south to the New, by State Highway 63. This is one of the most highly developed sections of West Virginia and accommodations of all kinds are plentiful.

Half a dozen lesser tributaries of the New can be fished from Beckley, on U.S. 21; and further north, from Fayetteville on U.S. 19 and 21. Directions as to how to reach the tributaries should be obtained from sporting goods stores in these towns.

In Beckley at Keatley's Sports Store, or in Princeton, at Douglas Sporting Goods Store, information can also be obtained about some limited muskie and bass fishing which is available in the Guyandot River (24), the southernmost tributary of the Ohio, to the west of Interstate Highway 77.

Still another tributary of the New is the Gauley River (25), which joins the New at Gauley Bridge, in the middle of the state. The Gauley has some walleyes, and is fishable from Summersville on U.S. 19, north of White Sulphur Springs. Several small tributaries which flow into the Gauley from the southwest also offer limited trout fishing.

LAKE FISHING

Lake fishing in West Virginia is pretty well limited to reservoirs and other impoundments. The larger reservoirs are Bluestone (26), in the south on the New River, on State Highway 20 near Hinton; Tygart Lake (27), in the north near Grafton, which is at the junction of U.S. 119 and U.S. 50; and Cheat Lake (28), still further north, off U.S. 119 at Easton near the town of Morgantown.

Tygart and Cheat Lakes are stocked with bass and panfish. There are camping facilities in a state park at Tygart, and other accommodations at Webster and Grafton on U.S. 119. Anglers fishing Cheat Lake can stay at Morgantown or Easton on U.S. 119, or over to the east at Bruceton Mills on State Highway 73.

The Bluestone Reservoir has bass, crappie and bluegills plus some pike, and as mentioned earlier there is good fishing for catfish in the river below the dam. Both indoor accomodations and camping facilities are available at nearby Bluestone State Park, as well as at the town of Hinton.

In the long, narrow strip of West Virginia which juts up between Ohio and Pennsylvania, there are several small lakes or ponds where there is good fishing for channel catfish. Oglebay Park Lake (29), at Wheeling, is one, and the Bear Rock Lakes, a series of ponds in the same area, produce panfish and catfish. The latter are also stocked with trout early in the season. Special regulations apply in these lakes, and should be checked in the annual fishing regulations.

A number of smaller impoundments, many of them under control of the

Department of Natural Resources, provide a degree of fishing for both trout and warm-water species. The "West Virginia Fishing Regulations" pamphlet lists these ponds annually, with the type of fishing currently available, and the open and closed dates, which vary greatly both as to season and daily fishing hours. The regulations and location of these ponds should be obtained annually from the Department of Natural Resources, Charleston 5, West Virginia.

WEST VIRGINIA FISHING REGULATIONS

Resident Fishing License $3.00
Nonresident Fishing License $10.00
Nonresident 6-Day Fishing License $3.00

SEASONS AND LIMITS

Species	Season	Bag Limit
Trout	Late April to Dec. 31	8 daily, 16 in possession No size limit
Black Bass, Spotted Bass	Open year-round	8 daily, 16 in possession No size limit
Muskellunge	Open year-round	No possession limit Minimum size, 26 inches
Other Species	Open year-round	No limit, no size limit

For complete regulations write: Department of Natural Resources, Capitol Building, Charleston 25305, West Virginia.

KENTUCKY

Like Tennessee, the State of Kentucky stretches nearly 500 miles east and west. It's eastern border is formed by the rugged ridges of the Appalachians, providing abundant, cool, clear mountain streams suitable for smallmouth black bass, rock bass and bream. On the north the Ohio River winds its course the full width of the state, the river itself and its many tributaries providing slower-moving, warmer waters for suitable species. Largemouth black bass thrive, and in many areas the bass fishing is augmented by the Kentucky or spotted bass, found to some degree in almost all the waters of the state. Other species found are white bass, crappie, perch, northern pike, walleye, chain pickerel, a few muskellunge and catfish. In some few places, as below the dams of the large reservoirs, rainbow trout have been stocked.

In Kentucky, for one species or another, there is year-round fishing. In the dead of winter jig fishing for bass is practised in the major impoundments. In February there is excellent walleye fishing as the fish make their annual runs into the headwaters of Lake Cumberland. Crappie, white bass, bluegill, catfish and some muskies can be taken throughout the rest of the year.

The larger rivers in Kentucky are the Ohio, Kentucky, Cumberland, Licking, Green, Big and Little Sandy, Elkhorn Creek, Dix, Rockcastle, Nolin and Chaplin. The major lakes are man-made, and include Dale Hollow, on the southern border, shared with Tennessee; and Kentucky Lake, in the western part of the state, one of the largest man-made lakes in the world.

Other large lakes within the borders of Kentucky are Lake Cumberland, on the Cumberland River; Herrington, in the bluegrass country; and Dewey Reservoir, in the east, near Prestonburg. In all there are nine major lakes and four more under construction. There are also some thirty-six state-owned lakes which are managed from the fisheries standpoint by the Kentucky Department of Fish and Wildlife Resources. To this are added more than 50,000 farm ponds which have been stocked with warm-water species.

There are very few parts of Kentucky which cannot be reached by good highways, the major routes being Interstate 64 through Lexington in the north, and Interstate 65, which now runs from Louisville on the Indiana border, south through Kentucky as far as Nashville, Tennessee. State Highway 80 winds through the southern width of the state. From these major arteries a network of roads fans out to cover the entire state.

The latitude of Kentucky is far enough north, and the altitude is sufficient to ensure definite summer and winter seasons. Summer temperatures go high enough that cotton sports clothes are all the angler needs except in the mountains, where a wool jacket for evenings will suffice. However, some of the best fishing is in the winter—for example, the walleye run in Lake Cumberland, and some cold-weather jigging for bass in deep water. At such times the temperature may be below 50 degrees, and warm clothing is needed.

Anglers will not encounter any dangerous game in Kentucky but should always watch for snakes, as Kentucky is within the range of the rattler, cottonmouth and copperhead.

EASTERN AND CENTRAL AREA

The largest lake in eastern and central Kentucky is CUMBERLAND LAKE (1), situated just north of the Tennessee border. Cumberland measures 105 miles long and is as much as 90 feet deep in places. There are largemouth black bass, smallmouth black bass, walleyes, which sometimes run as much as 20 pounds, as well as white bass, catfish, bluegill and crappie.

The walleyes run up from the lower section of the lake in mid-February and at that time, for about two weeks, are taken in the upper part of the lake as well as in the rivers which are tributary to it—the SOUTH FORK OF THE CUMBERLAND (2), the LAUREL (3) and the NORTH FORK OF THE ROCKCASTLE (4). Heavy jigs are generally used, to get down to these deep dwellers, and to buck the heavy currents.

Some striped bass have been stocked in Cumberland Lake, but to date there is not sufficient result to guarantee this species will make a fishery.

Rainbow trout have also been stocked in the river below the dam, providing some good fishing spring and fall, the choice months being November into December, and March into April.

You can get guide service on Lake Cumberland through Irvine Moffet at Jamestown on the west side of the lake; and through Andy McIntyre at Beaver Lodge, Monticello, on the east side. There are resorts at Albany, Corbin, Burnside, Somerset and Cumberland City, and a few right on the lake.

Lying just to the south, on the Tennessee-Kentucky border, DALE HOLLOW LAKE (5) is backed up by a dam on the Obey River in Tennessee. The main body of the lake is in that state, but it extends somewhat into central Kentucky west of Albany on U.S. Highway 127. It can be reached from State Highway 90, south on State Highway 61 from Burkesville. There are a couple of dozen boat docks and fishing camps at this Kentucky end of the lake, and while there are no established guides, the dock operators can tell you where the fishing is best at the moment.

This is considered one of the best lakes in the south for smallmouth black bass and walleye pike. The world-record smallmouth, weighing 11 pounds 15 ounces, was caught here in 1955. There are also white bass, crappie and bream. The bluegills are large, often being taken up to 12 ounces.

In general, it can be said that the best seasons for casters are spring and fall, when good bass catches can be made from shore. In the early summer "jump fishing" for both black and white bass is excellent—that is, casting surface lures to fish which are rising as they feed on minnow schools. As the water warms up with the summer heat, the bass generally move to deeper water and some very good catches are made at great depths.

A few muskellunge were stocked in Dale Hollow some years ago, and currently a few catches are being made of fish up to 6 pounds.

Dale Hollow is a more natural-looking lake than many reservoirs and has some pleasant camping areas.

Another reservoir which has more than the usual wilderness look, for a reservoir, is HERRINGTON (6), on the Dix River. This thirty-one-mile-long lake can be

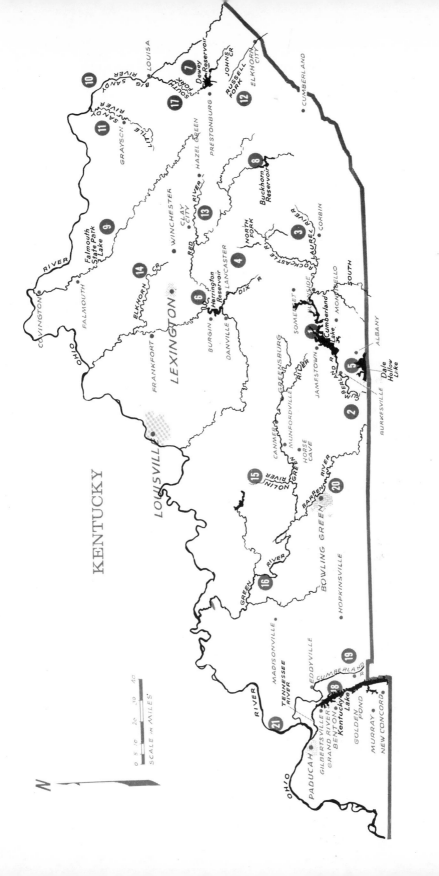

reached from Danville, at the junction of U.S. Highway 52 and State Highway 52, in the central part of the state.

The lake produces largemouth black bass, white bass, bream, crappie and a few walleyes. There are also some enormous catfish among the submerged tree stumps. As at Lake Cumberland, rainbow trout have been stocked below the dam, and there is good fishing for this species in November and December, and in April and May.

White bass run out of the lake and up the Dix River in April and spark three weeks of fishing excitement. In early summer the white and black bass are taken "jump fishing" in the lake; and when the weather becomes very hot, some anglers continue to make good catches of bass by fishing the very deepest parts of the lake. Lead-headed jigs with pork rind and rubber night crawlers are popular baits in this lake.

There are not many guides available on Herrington Lake but the dock operators at Burgin, Lancaster and Danville will give fishermen all the dope they need about where to fish. There are plenty of accommodations at these three towns, too.

DEWEY RESERVOIR (7), formed by damming Johns Creek, is reached via U.S. 23 and 460, at Prestonburg, in the extreme eastern part of Kentucky. This scenic lake, sixteen miles long, lies up near the West Virginia border, in the mountains. There's good bass fishing in early spring and late fall and there are bluegills and crappie year-round. You can stay at Prestonburg and fish out of the Brandy Keg Dock at the lake.

BUCKHORN RESERVOIR (8) lies to the southwest of Dewey, just north of the junction of U.S. 421 and State Highway 80. This smaller lake offers the same general kind of fishing, plus some occasional muskellunge. It is probably the only lake in Kentucky where this species can be taken, though it is found in a few rivers.

As mentioned earlier, there are some thirty-six state-owned lakes in Kentucky. One of the better ones, located off Interstate Highway 75 about forty miles south of Cincinnati, Ohio, is FALMOUTH STATE PARK LAKE (9). It is stocked with bass and provides good early-season fishing.

There are several fine smallmouth streams, and not overfished, in the mountain section of eastern Kentucky, and more in the bluegrass area. The BIG SANDY (10), forming part of the West Virginia border, and accessible from U.S. 23 north of Louisa, is highly regarded by fly fishermen. Slightly to the west, the LITTLE SANDY (11), off U.S. 60 near Grayson, has muskies, bass and rock bass.

Along the Virginia border anglers would be well advised to try the RUSSELL FORK OF THE LEVISA (12), out of Elkhorn City, on State Highway 80. There are largemouth black bass, walleye and channel catfish.

In the Cumberland Mountains the RED RIVER (13) and ELKHORN CREEK (14), both tributaries of the Kentucky, are also good bass streams. The Red River is reached from Clay City on State Highway 15, southeast of Winchester, or from Hazen Green, upriver on State Highway 191 (north from State Highway 15 at Pine Ridge). Elkhorn Creek is near Elkhorn, off U.S. 127 north of Frankfort.

The NOLIN RIVER (15) is also a fine smallmouth black bass river, especially close to the Mammoth Cave National Park. It can be reached from Interstate Highway 65 at Munfordville or Horse Cave. There are also sauger, walleye and catfish in the Nolin. The GREEN RIVER (16), to the east, has the same species. It crosses a number of highways where anglers can gain access: State Highway 88 at Munfordville, 31E at Canmer, and U.S. 68 at Greensburg.

The SOUTH FORK OF THE BIG SANDY (17), which roughly parallels the eastern border of Kentucky, has all three basses—the smallmouth, largemouth and Kentucky bass—as well as rough fish. This river is best in the late fall when it is low and clear.

WESTERN AREA

The outstanding fishing feature of western Kentucky is KENTUCKY LAKE (18), formed by the damming of the Tennessee River at Gilbertsville, south of Paducah, where the Tennessee River enters the Ohio River. The lake extends some sixty miles southward to the Tennessee border. It can be reached via U.S. Highway 68 from Hopkinsville to Aurora, or U.S. 62 from Paducah. This is the last in the TVA chain of lakes.

There is good fishing of one kind or another year-round. Fly, plug and spin casting are all successful in taking bass in the early spring to midsummer. Deep bait fishing takes bream, white bass and catfish in the summer; and there's deep trolling for walleyes all the time.

Boats may be obtained at Grand Rivers, Gilbertsville, Golden Pond, Eddyville, Benton, New Concord, and Murray. There are plentiful accomodations all around this popular lake.

There is also some good river fishing in western Kentucky. The CUMBERLAND RIVER (19) flows north from Tennessee, roughly following the shores of Lake Kentucky. This section of the river has bass, perch and channel catfish.

The GREEN RIVER (16), flowing northwest from the central part of the state, empties into the Ohio near Evansville, Illinois. The late spring is good for white bass, white perch and catfish. Late fall sees an upswing in fishing for sauger, largemouth and smallmouth black bass, crappie and the already mentioned species. The Green and its tributary the BARREN RIVER (20), are also known as good muskellunge rivers, the fishing being best in the fall when the water is low and the fish concentrated in pools. Underwater lures are used, and bait fishermen take muskies on large minnows. Bowling Green, a good center from which to fish, provides all accommodations.

The OHIO RIVER (21), around Evansville, has been producing some exceptionally large catfish in recent years, some over 50 pounds, and immediately across the river from Evansville anglers have been finding a few smallmouth black bass around the dikes.

While the Mississippi forms the western border of Kentucky, it does not add much to the fishing scene, the take being largely limited to catfish; and this part of the river is rather highly polluted, thus making it unattractive to anglers.

KENTUCKY FISHING REGULATIONS

Resident Fishing License $3.25
Nonresident Fishing License $5.50
10-Day Nonresident Fishing License $2.25
Ohio River Fishing License for residents of Ohio, Indiana and
    Illinois, only $3.25

CREEL AND SIZE LIMITS

Species	Daily Limit	Possession Limit
Black Bass	10	20
Rock Bass	15	30
Walleye	10	20
Sauger	10	20
Muskellunge	5	10
Northern Pike	5	10
Chain Pickerel	5	10
White and Yellow Bass	60	60
Rockfish	1	1
Crappie	60	60

There is an 11-inch minimum size limit on bass in Elkhorn Creek and its tributaries; a 12-inch limit in all state-owned lakes, Buckhorn, Rough River, Herrington and Dewey Reservoirs and their tributaries. There is a 15-inch size limit on walleye in these lakes and a 24-inch limit on musky and northern pike.

For complete regulations write: Department of Fish and Wildlife Resources, State Office Building Annex, Frankfort 40601, Kentucky.

TENNESSEE

Tennessee is only a little more than 100 miles wide in a north-south measurement, but it is close to 500 miles from east to west borders. Thus it covers a wide range of topography—from the 6,000-foot altitudes of the Great Smoky Mountains on the eastern border, to the plains of the Mississippi on the west. The fishing varies from small native brook trout in the sparkling clear mountain streams to the catfish and other warm-water species of the Mississippi River system. In between these two extremes, fishermen will find almost every game species of the temperate zone. Rainbow trout have been added to the native brook trout in suitable cold streams and have also been successfully stocked in some of the lakes and in the waters just below the TVA dams. There the temperature is low enough in the flow from the turbines at the base of the dams to provide suitable habitat for this trout.

Brown trout are found in all of these places, with some exceptional fishing just below the dams. Browns of 5, 6 and 7 pounds are not unusual. The largest brown ever known to have been taken in the U.S.A. was a monster weighing 26 pounds 2 ounces landed by George Langston in the waters immediately below the Dale Hollow Dam.

Brook trout are generally of the small, pan-size variety, but on occasion go to 2 pounds. Rainbows will average a pound, quite a few go a little heavier, and in the big lake outlets may run as high as 8 pounds.

The smallmouth black bass is the most widespread of the native game species, being found in practically all clear, cool streams and having spread out into many suitable lakes. A 5-pounder is a very heavy smallmouth anywhere. Quite a few this size are taken in Tennessee, and on occasion in such lakes as Dale Hollow, Watauga, Norris and Center Hill, they run much higher. In 1955 a world-record smallmouth weighing 11 pounds 15 ounces was taken by D. L. Hayes at Dale Hollow.

The largemouth black bass is equally popular with fishermen and in Tennessee will average a little larger than the smallmouth, reaching a top weight of 14 pounds. The largemouth is more adaptable to warmer waters and is found in the shallower parts of the lakes, in bayous and backwaters of rivers. Reelfoot Lake, in the low, western part of the state is one of the best spots for largemouth. Both basses may be taken year-round but fishing is generally best in spring and fall when the water is cooler.

Cousin of the two better known basses is the Kentucky bass, also called spotted bass and yellow bass. This member of the family frequents the waters between the habitats of the largemouth and smallmouth, liking water not quite so warm and sluggish as the former, and not quite as cool and rocky as the latter. For this reason they are often taken in the streams of western Tennessee. The Kentucky is a good fighter, and provides some of the best fishing in Tennessee. One of the largest specimens known to have been taken was a 4-pounder from Norris Lake in northeastern Tennessee. They are highly regarded as table fish.

So also is the white crappie, one of the most common catches in the large reservoirs. This species averages about a pound, with a few going as high as 3 pounds. The species is most abundant in the late spring months.

Also abundant in the reservoirs, and equally good to eat, is the white bass, also called "stripes." This is a school fish, weighing up to 1½ pounds, with occasional catches up to 3 pounds. During the summer the white bass can sometimes be found near the surface and can be taken on flies and spinners. Most of the time, however, the schools lie deep, or swim deep, and fishermen must go down to them with minnows and worms. In the spring months of March, April and May the fish make spawning migrations and are taken in streams and tailwaters of dams.

Bream, which includes practically all of the south's pan-sized fish—sunnies, stumpknockers, ring perch, flyers and other small swimmers, are thick and are found in the reservoirs and in many farm ponds and smaller lakes.

Dale Hollow Lake, formed by damming the Cumberland River, Center Hill Lake on the Caney Fork River and Norris Lake on the Clinch and Powell Rivers, turn up walleyes, which, though in limited numbers, often run to substantial sizes, some to 15 pounds. A 21¼-pounder was taken in Center Hill Lake.

The sauger, also called jack, makes winter runs into several of the impounded rivers, providing good fishing from November to March. French Broad and the Little Tennessee are the best in this regard. Sauger may be taken year-round in Watts Bar Lake, on the Tennessee River, southwest of Knoxville, but fishing for the species reaches a peak during the spawning run in September, and then follows on into October and November in the lower part of the lake.

In a very few areas there are some muskellunge and pickerel; while in nearly all the man-made lakes and most of the waters of the Mississippi basin there are catfish, both channel and yellow.

The summer angler in Tennessee will need only cottons and such light gear. For fall and winter a sweater, woolen jacket and rain coat are necessary. A pullover rain jacket with a hood is a good idea at all times, not only to keep you dry in case of a sudden shower, but also to break the wind and provide warmth.

You see plenty of small game as you fish Tennessee waters, and now and then a deer. Bear are few and scattered. In the Tellico Wildlife Management Area there are wild boar but these do not usually constitute a problem to fishermen. But keep a wary eye for snakes. There are rattlesnakes, copperheads and some cottonmouth moccasins.

TROUT STREAMS

The mountains of eastern Tennessee and the piedmont section to the east are the center of the stream trout fishing. U.S. Highway 411 from Johnson City, near the North Carolina border, runs parallel to the mountains for the full length of the state and from it almost every transverse highway leads up to the trout fishing waters. To the east of Johnson City are LAUREL BLOOMERY, DOE, GENTRY and UPPER BEAVER DAM CREEKS (1), all holding small rainbows. Gentry also has brook trout in the upper waters. Other creeks in the area which offer some brook-trout fishing are BIRCH, FAGALL and CHALK (2), all reached via country roads from Mountain City on U.S. 421.

Further southwest in the Hampton area, DOE RIVER, ELK RIVER and STONEY and LITTLE STONEY CREEKS (3) have rainbows, while the higher streams such as CAVE CREEK, GEORGES and ROARING CREEKS have brookies. They can be fished from Elizabethton, south on State Highway 194.

One of the best fishing areas can be reached from the town of Erwin, on U.S.

Highway 23. Here the SPIVY, GRANNY, NORTH and SOUTH BROAD SHOALS, ROCKY FORD, LOWER HIGGINS and ROCK CREEKS (4) all hold rainbows and some of them have brook trout in the upper waters. In addition, DEVILS and FLINT BRANCH CREEKS have brook trout.

Moving south again you come to HORSE, CAMP and JENNINGS BRANCH (5) for rainbows, Horse and Jennings also for brook trout. These tributaries of the Nolichucky River come down out of the mountains from the south, at the upper end of Davey Crockett Lake. They can be reached by State Highway 81 between Jonesboro and Erwin.

Going east from Cleveland on U.S. Highway 64, around Ducktown, the angler can find another series of creeks which hold trout. They are SMITH, BIG LOST, GEE, RHYMER GAP and WOLF (6). There are also some rainbows in LITTLE RIVER (7), near the town of Maryville on U.S. Highway 411.

There is some very good trout fishing in the Tellico Wildlife Management Area in the headwaters of the LITTLE TENNESSEE and TELLICO RIVERS (8). These streams are under Wildlife Area management and a special license is required in addition to the regular state fishing license. U.S. 411 and U.S. 64 form an angle enclosing much of this water and leading to Lake Ocoee. Rouen Creek and Big Creek, entering the south shore of this lake, also have rainbows.

To the northeast of Lake Ocoee, BIG LOST CREEK, SMITH, WOLF, SPRING and SEE CREEKS (9) have trout, and the larger CONASAUGA has smallmouth black bass and rock bass.

While all the standard trout flies are good, the famous Tellico Nymph is one of the best in this area. Also good are the Black and Yellow Nymph and Gray Nymph. All these should be on number 12 and 16 hooks. Other good wet flies, on number 12 hooks, are the Black Gnat, Coachman, Light Cahill, Ginger Quill and Mosquito. Good dries are the Black Gnat, Royal Coachman, Red Variant, Blue Dun, Iron Blue Dun, Light Cahill, Quill Gordon and Mosquito, all in sizes 12 and 14.

There's an interesting side trip for trout fishermen in the spring in those streams in the northeast corner of Tennessee, up against the mountains. At this time the "hornyhead," also called "stoneroller" and "steelback," schools up in the trout streams. This fish grows to a maximum length of 9 inches and a weight of about 5 ounces, but is a very fine table delicacy. The hornyhead has a sucker-like mouth, but very small, so that it can take only the tiniest bait. Anglers go for them with fly rods in the larger streams with a bit of bread or worm on a very small hook. In the smaller streams, cane poles are called for. They are very ready hitters and if you get into the schooling time you can take them almost as fast as you can bait your hook. These are the fish the kids in this area cut their teeth on.

A little further west, some of the streams of the Cumberland River drainage are also capable of supporting trout. These are fished pretty much on a put-and-take basis but with regular stocking of keeper-sized fish, the angling in these rivers holds up fairly well. Best known as good producers are the streams that feed into Center Hill Lake—PINE, MOUNTAIN BARREN and CHARLES CREEK (10) on the west, and ROCK RIVER and CALF KILLER on the east. They are easily reached from either Smithville at the Junction of State Highways 26 and 56, or McMinnville, at U.S. Highway 70S and State Highway 56.

There are also rainbows in the top waters of the SEQUATCHIE RIVER (11) reached from either Dayton or Spring City, on U.S. Highway 27, north from Chattanooga. Nearer to Chattanooga (12), in SWEDEN CREEK, BATTLE CREEK and

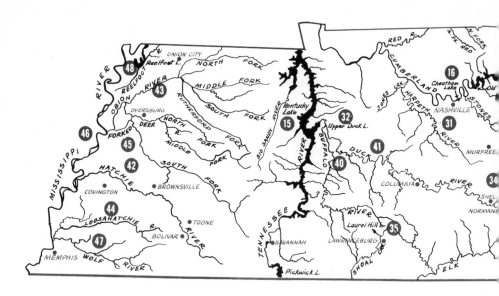

the LITTLE SEQUATCHIE, and just north of the city, in FALLING CREEK and CHICKA-MAUGA CREEK there are also some trout.

From Manchester, on U.S. 41, twenty-six miles northwest of Chattanooga, you can reach the headwaters of the DUCK RIVER (13), and here, and in a small tributary, CRUMPTONS CREEK, there are also rainbows. Just to the south, in the LITTLE HURRICANE (14), which flows to the Elk River, there are also a few.

THE TENNESSEE LAKES

The great lakes of the TVA System are the major feature of today's fishing in Tennessee. In West Tennessee, KENTUCKY LAKE (15), renowned for its white bass, 184 miles long and with 2,300 miles of shoreline, sprawls across almost the entire north-south mileage of the state, narrows somewhat in the south, then widens to form Pickwick Lake on the Mississippi-Alabama border. Six major highways cross the lake; U.S. 62 at the dam at Gilbersville at the north end of the lake, in Kentucky; State Highway 80 at Aurora, Kentucky; U.S. 79 at Paris Landing, Tennessee; U.S. 70 from Nashville, at Johnsonville, Tennessee; State Highway 100, also from Nashville, at Perryville; and ,U.S. 64 at Savannah, from Chattanooga.

Across the north-central part of the state the Cumberland River has been dammed to form CHEATHAM LAKE (16) at Nashville; OLD HICKORY LAKE (17), reached by either U.S. 31E or U.S. 70N, also from Nashville; and the renowned DALE HOLLOW LAKE (18) on the Kentucky border. Dale Hollow, which is tops for smallmouth and has some muskellinge also, can be reached from many county roads from State Highway 52 at Celina or 42 at Byrdstown.

To the south, one of the Cumberland's tributaries, the Caney Fork, has been

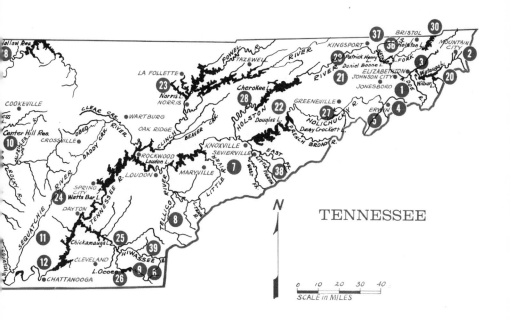

TENNESSEE

SCALE in MILES

dammed to form CENTER HILL RESERVOIR (19), on U.S. 26 at Smithville. And in a long string across the entire eastern part of Tennessee are WATAUGA LAKE and WILBUR LAKE (20), DANIEL BOONE LAKE (21), DOUGLAS LAKE (22), on the course of the Holston River. This series of lakes is accessible in many places from U.S. 11E and U.S. 11W from Knoxville. Watauga offers the greatest variety of fishing, with walleye, rainbow trout, brown trout, kamloops trout, smallmouth, largemouth, kokanee salmon, silver salmon, crappie, bream and rough fish.

Still another river, the Clinch, has been dammed at its joining with the Powell to form NORRIS LAKE (23), a good lake for black bass, which can be approached from State Highway 33 south of Tazewell, U.S. 441 at Norris, or U.S. 25W at La Follette.

On the Tennessee River are WATTS BAR LAKE (24) and CHICKAMAUGA (25), with OCOEE LAKE (26) on a tributary, the Hiwassee. The first two can be reached from U.S. 27 on the west, and from State Highway 58 on the east. Ocoee is accessible via U.S. 64 east from Cleveland on U.S. 11.

DAVEY CROCKETT LAKE (27), on the Nolichucky River, is close to the Smoky Mountain National Park. It can be reached via U.S. 70 south from Greenville. Nearby CHEROKEE LAKE (28), on the Holston River, is noted for its white bass fishing, while, further north, in the corner of the state, PATRICK HENRY LAKE (29) and SOUTH HOLSTON LAKE (30) offer good fishing for black crappie.

The Kentucky bass is most common in the middle of the state in the HARPETH RIVER (31). Another occasional catch is the pickerel, occurring in Tennessee lakes in limited numbers throughout middle and western Tennessee, in UPPER DUCK LAKE (32) and the eastern tributaries of Kentucky Lake.

Fishing methods in the great reservoirs cover the whole field of the sport. In spring and fall, when the fish are near the surface, fly, spin and plug casting are successful for the basses. Walleyes are usually taken by trolling over submerged reefs or points, or by deep bait fishing with minnows at the same kind of location and in the boils below dams. Minnows are also used for bass and sauger and for white bass when the schools are working deep. For crappie and bluegill many Tennessee fishermen use roaches, crickets and worms.

W. L. Marrs, the "Professor Kingfish" of radio broadcasting at Johnson City, Tennessee, believes strongly in the plug-casting outfit for this lake fishing. His own gear, on which he's caught plenty of fish, is a 6-foot plug-casting rod, custom made for him by Frank White of Elizabethtown, a 15-pound-test line, Ambassaduer 5000 or Shakespeare sport cast reel. For top-water fishing he likes the Creek Chub Darter, Phillips Crippled Killer, Heddon Lucky 13, Dalton Special, Skip Jack and the Injured Minnow made by Creek Chub. For semi-surface and deep-running lures he favors the Bomber, River Runt, red and white spoons, Helldiver and the Shannon Twin Spinner.

From April through early fall, "lantern" fishing is very popular for white bass and sometimes for crappie. The equipment consists of a Coleman lantern, which can be rented at most docks, a dip net and your tackle. The lantern is aimed so its light hits the water near your skiff. The light attracts hundreds of tiny silvery minnows, which provide one of the main foods of the white bass. With the dip net you dip up a bucket full—and it's easy, because the minnows seem to stick their heads right out of the water to look at the light. Then you bait your hook with one of the minnows and fish for the white bass, which in turn have been attracted by the school of minnows. The best fishing is usually around the drop-offs from sandy points.

Besides these large lakes there are many smaller ones that provide excellent fishing of one kind or another. BURGESS FALLS LAKE (33), near Center Hill Reservoir, south of Cookeville in central Tennessee, is famous for its excellent largemouth black bass angling, some fish being of substantial size. There are also smallmouth below the dam.

Burgess is one of a group of state-owned lakes managed especially for fishermen. Another good one is BEDFORD LAKE (34), near Normandy, fourteen miles east of Shelbyville. A couple of 13-pound largemouth black bass have come from this lake.

In one of the larger state lakes, LAUREL HILL (35), fourteen miles west of Lawrenceburg, off Highway 64, muskellunge have recently been stocked.

Most state-owned lakes are equipped with various facilities such as docks, boats (at $1 per day), launching sites for private boats, fishing piers and picnic facilities. A complete list of state lakes is included in the folder "Guide to Tennessee Fishing," published each year by the Tennessee Game and Fish Commission, Cordell Hull Building, Nashville 3, Tennessee.

Accommodations of all kinds can readily be found along the Tennessee Lakes. A folder which you can obtain from the Tennessee Division of Information, 2174 Cordell Hull Building, Nashville, Tennessee, lists 284 fishing docks on twenty-two lakes. Some of the smaller lakes, such as Davey Crockett, have limted accommodations, with only one dock, Scotty's Dock, out of Greenville. Others have many services. For instance, Kentucky Lake has sixty-nine docks. At all of them you will find boats for rent; most have motors, bait, tackle and lunches. Close to many lakes there are cabins in state parks, and where this is not the case there are numerous establishments in nearby towns. In most cases overnight accommodations can be had for from $2 to $5 per person. Boats range from $1.50 to $2 per day. Motors are $3 to $7.50. And guides vary from $5 to $10, according to location and season.

Those who bring their own boats will find many public access points; and can obtain maps of the lakes from the TVA offices at Knoxville, at very small cost.

RIVER FISHING FOR BASS

Tennessee has its share of one of the choicest features of the lower elevations of the Appalachians—river fishing for smallmouth black bass. The NORTH and SOUTH FORKS OF THE HOLSTON (36), near Kingsport on U.S. 11W are loaded with smallmouth and there are many miles of wadable stream. The WATAUGA RIVER (37), near Johnson City on U.S. 23 and U.S. 321, is good. The LITTLE PIGEON (38), out of Sevierville, on U.S. 411 and U.S. 441, near Gatlinburg; the Little Tennessee near Calderwood on U.S. 129 south of Maryville; the HIWASSEE (39), near Charleston, on U.S. 11 north of Cleveland, are all good smallmouth streams in the foothills. Furtherwest, the BUFFALO RIVER (40), which runs beside State Highway 13, east of Kentucky Lake, is another good one, and can be fished from Napier; and the DUCK RIVER (41), flowing for miles across country between Manchester, on U.S. 41, south of Murfreesboro, and Kentucky Lake, is best near Columbia, on U.S. 31 and near Shelbyville, on U.S. 231. Most of the Tennessee smallmouth rivers are readily waded and in a few stretches it is possible to use a canoe or skiff. There are no guides available, so you must be a capable riverman. The same rivers will also produce largemouth bass.

Bass bugs, streamers and bucktails are all good on fly gear while spinners like the Injured Minnow, Darter, Lucky 13, and Dalton Special.

The Buffalo River, in that part in the southern portion of middle Tennessee is especially good water for a summer float trip for bass and bluegills.

As an indication of the still-natural state of the streams, the Buffalo, Cumberland and French Broad are all on the Wild River Study List, with an eye to preserving them without further damming or alterations that might change their nature.

WESTERN AREA

In western Tennessee all the large rivers drain to the Mississippi, which forms the border between Tennessee, Missouri and Arkansas. The HATCHIE (42), OBION (43), LOOSAHATCHIE (44) and FORKED DEER (45) all produce catfish, as does the mainstream of the MISSISSIPI RIVER (46). The tributaries also offer fishing for Kentucky bass, bluegills and some largemouth. The North Fork of the Obion, which is one of the best of this group, can be reached from Union City on State Highway 22. Below this, U.S. 51 crosses the main Obion, and access can be found from gravel roads on either side of the river. The fishing is mainly for catfish, witth some largemouth black bass. The Hatchie is reached by country roads from U.S. 51 at Covington, U.S. 70 and U.S. 79 south of Brownsville, State Highway 100 at Toone, and U.S. 64 at Bolivar. The Forked Deer has only carp in its lower reaches but the North and South Forks add largemouth, channel catfish and bluegill. The Forked Deer wanders all over the central part of western Tennessee and almost every north-south highway crosses it at one point or another. Dyersburg, on U.S. 51, is a good headquarters from which to work upstream.

The Loosahatchie and the WOLF (47), which join the Mississippi near Memphis, have fishing for catfish, some Kentucky bass and bluegills. The Wolf is reached from State Highway 57 north of Collierville; the Loosahatchie from U.S. 51 and U.S. 70 north of the city of Memphis.

REELFOOT LAKE (48), the only large natural Lake in Tennessee of any size, was created in 1811 by an earthquake. The lake, which is eighteen miles long by two and a half miles wide, lies in the extreme northwest, close to the Mississippi River. The water is shallow, making for good casting possibilities, and the fish are the species that appeal to casters too—largemouth black bass, Kentucky bass, yellow bass, crappie, bream and catfish.

The fly fishing with popping bugs is particularly exciting when you push your boat among the weeds and cast to the cypress knees where the trees stick up, and into lily pads. A slow play of the surface bug pays off. The fish will usually hit before you have retrieved the bug a foot and a half. Heavy underwater flies and lures are not good here because of the shallow water, upjutting cypress knees and sticks and grasses. A weedless spoon or plug is a necessity. There are plentiful picnic and camping facilities around the lake.

TENNESSEE FISHING REGULATIONS

Resident Annual Sport Fishing & Hunting $3.00
Nonresident Sport Fishing only, same as applicant's home state nonresident
     license, with a minimum of $5.00
Nonresident, State-wide Sport Fishing Trip (3 consecutive days) $1.50
Nonresident, as above, 10 consecutive days $2.00
One-Day Nonresident State-wide Fishing License $.50
Trout Stamp, Resident and Nonresident $1.00
License not required for children under 16.

SEASONS AND LIMITS

In Tennessee there is year-round open season on all the warm-water species in all waters; and on all species in TVA waters. In the cold-water streams the trout season opens on March 15th and runs through September 30th; but there is no closed season on trout in TVA and Army Engineers Reservoirs or the main outlet from such reservoirs. However, anglers must remember that the closed season regulations does apply to all streams *entering* the reservoirs.

No limits on crappie, white bass (stripes), yellow bass (striped jack), bluegill, bream, warmouth, all non-game fishes.

All muskellunge under 25 inches must be released with least possible injury into the water from which taken.

Length limit on trout: rainbows and browns, 9 inches; brook, 7 inches.

Anglers planning to fish in Tennessee should obtain "Guide to Tennessee Fishing," issued by the Tennessee Game and Fish Commission, Cordell Hull Building, Nashville, Tennessee. This pamphlet gives current complete information on open and closed waters, seasons, cost of license, stocked streams, etc. Also ask for "Tennessee Fish and Where to Catch Them."

Great Lakes States

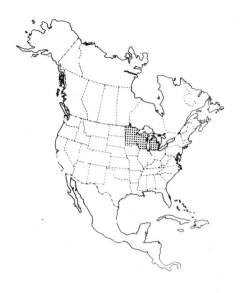

The Great Lakes States of Minnesota, Wisconsin and Michigan consist of thousands of square miles of beautiful forest land dotted with a multitude of lakes—clear, cold, blue and fresh. These lakes, resulting largely from the glacial history of the countryside, are the main features of the area from the fisherman's point of view, but there are other sides to the angling scene. The Mississippi River, which influences such a vast drainage area down the center of the continent, rises in central Minnesota and forms part of the border between Minnesota and Wisconsin, providing its distinctive brand of fishing. All three states have the additional angling opportunities of thousands of miles of shoreline on the Great Lakes, varying from the rocky bluffs of Lake Superior to the shallower shores where Michigan touches on Lakes St. Clair and Erie.

In spite of great industrial and agricultural development of many part of the Great Lakes area, there are still vast reaches which retain their natural beauty, and consequently these three states stand out as a green island along the northern central border of the U.S.A.

The native fish are: largemouth and smallmouth black bass, walleyes, northern pike, the mighty muskellunge, trout and bluegills, as well as catfish and some of the warmer-water species in the more southern areas.

191

MICHIGAN

Michigan holds the unique position among the states of bordering on four of the five Great Lakes. As a consequence there is more of the deep-sea type of fishing than is the case with its neighboring Great Lakes states of Wisconsin and Minnesota. Nearly every lakeside town can offer charter boats or skiff service of some kind to reach the longshore fishing or the reefs and islands offshore.

In addition, this situation on the Great Lakes permits of some unusual fishing in the connecting waters such as the St. Mary's River at Sault Ste. Marie; and Lake St. Clair, between Huron and Erie.

However, the bulk of Michigan's fishing is in the many thousands of lakes scattered throughout the state and in a considerable number of rivers which provide some excellent trout fishing, along with angling for a few other species that like river waters.

The species to be found are numerous and widely scattered. They include largemouth black bass, common from 2 to 5 pounds and with a state record of 11 pounds 15 ounces; smallmouth black bass, common from 1 to 3 pounds, and with a record of 9 pounds 4 ounces; northern pike, probably the most wide-spread of all the native fish, averaging 1 to 3 pounds, with occasional 10-pounders and a state record of 35 pounds; and walleyes, also common, with the usual weight from 2 to 4 pounds, and a top one on the lists weighing 17 pounds 3 ounces. Muskellunge, one of the most eagerly sought species, are on record up to 62 pounds 8 ounces, but a fish in the 10- to 20-pound class is currently a good one. The trouts include the rainbow, brook or speckled, brown and lake trout.

Brook trout taken in streams usually run only 9 inches but an occasional 2- or 3-pounder is taken. Brown trout average a pound, with frequent catches of 2- and 3-pounders, and a whopping 21-pound 12-ounce fish the best ever known to have come from Michigan waters. The rainbows vary greatly according to habitat. Stream fish will run 8 to 12 inches, lake fish from 1 to 2 pounds, while those coming in from the Great Lakes on spawning runs may go up to 6 pounds. The state record for the species is 21 pounds 7 ounces. Lake trout also vary, with an ancient record of 88 pounds, a current record of 53 pounds, both from the Great Lakes; and common catches of 3- to 4-pounders in a few inland lakes. Today they are taken only in Lake Superior of the Great Lakes because of the depredations of the lamprey eel in the other lakes.

In general the trouts are found north of a line drawn midway across the main part of the state from Ludington to Bay City. South of this, however, trout have been stocked in many waters to provide some fishing in lakes and ponds. These are mostly rainbows. Under such conditions they do not reproduce but nevertheless have resulted in some good fishing as they frequently grow to fairly substantial size. The Conservation Dept., P.O. Box 8, Publications Room, Lansing 26, Michigan, issues a brochure on such lakes entitled "Five Ways to Fish Trout Lakes," giving their locations and size.

Michigan waters also provide excellent fishing for goodly populations of bluegills, up to 2 pounds 10 ounces, black crappie to 4 pounds 2 ounces, yellow perch to 3 pounds 12 ounces, rock bass to 3 pounds 5 ounces and catfish and bullheads.

The climate in northern Michigan, both in the top part of the mitt and the Northern Peninsula, is typical northwoods climate as far as the angler is concerned. He will need woolens for evening, though cottons will do for most days. Those who go in early spring or in September will find that woolens are almost entirely in order.

Tackle should be chosen according to the fish you are going for, and, again, the season. During spring and fall there is plenty of opportunity for fly fishing and light spinning. During midsummer, when the fish are likely to be lying deep because of the heat, trollers have their day, though evening will often bring opportunities to use light tackle. Throughout the year the fly is popular on the trout streams. Some of the famous old rivers such as the Pere Marquette, that hold brown trout, are most successfully fished at night, and old-timers claim their best catches are made on very large, spider-type flies. Aside from this, flies that take trout include all the standard patterns used on both eastern and western streams in other parts of the country—dry, wet and streamers.

Fly-rodders who go for smallmouth black bass in Michigan lakes and rivers have good success with surface poppers during the warmer parts of the year. They play them slowly, interspersing pops with half minute waits, casting the bugs beside fallen logs, trees, rocks, and against weed patches along the shores of lakes and rivers. They play them along any known drop-offs, and avoid any flat water that shows there would be neither food nor resting place for fish. In the fall, when the water and air cool off, the bass like a faster retrieve with both plugs and streamers and bucktails. Best colors, in all cases, are all white, all black, all yellow, red and white and red and yellow.

Spinners and plug casters use both top- and underwater lures, the Phillips Crippled Killer being a very hot bass bait. Silver spoons weighing ¼ to ½ ounce are also very good. These lures are cast into the same spots as flies would be, and the fish co-operate equally well. During the heat of midsummer bass go deep and during the daytime hours it will pay to fish deep, out of the glare of the light. And at such time, the best fishing will be early in the morning and again from dusk into the night.

As throughout the northern Great Lakes area, there are bear and moose as well as deer in certain parts of the country and anglers should go quietly about their own business and leave such animals alone. Campers should leave supplies which might attract a bear in a safe place. Snakes are not generally a problem in Michigan.

Michigan divides naturally into two parts, the Upper Peninsula, jutting out from Wisconsin and running in an east-west direction between Lake Superior and Lakes Michigan and Huron; and the main body of the state, shaped like a great, mittened hand, with the thumb forming the eastern shore of Saginaw Bay.

The whole of the main section is served by a network of excellent highways and there is good rail service to most of the larger cities. There are also numerous airports in this section. The Upper, less populated peninsula is traversed by U.S. 2, from Rhinelander, Wisconsin, across to Sault Ste. Marie, and so into Canada; and by State Highway 28, providing entry from or exit to Ashland, Wisconsin, and covering the entire northern part of the Upper Peninsula. It joins U.S. 2 south of Sault Ste. Marie.

A toll bridge now makes it possible to cross from the northern tip of the mitt to the Upper Peninsula, between Mackinaw City and St. Ignace. The toll charge is $4.25 per car, with as many passengers as you wish. A single-axle boat trailer and car goes for $5.75, and the fee for a car towing a double-axle trailer is $8.

The Upper Peninsula is also served by rail through Sault Ste. Marie, and there are commercial airfields at Escanaba and Menominee on the south shore and at Marquette on the north shore.

In addition to these land methods of transportation, there are numerous passenger and car ferries between lake ports in Wisconsin and those in Michigan; and also between Michigan ports and the various islands along shore and well offshore. Details about these will be given in describing such areas which are of interest to fishermen.

SOUTHERN MICHIGAN

In the more southern part of the Michigan mitt the trouts are found only in lakes and streams where they are regularly stocked, but there is a substantial number of these described and located in the brochure "Five Ways to Fish Trout Lakes," mentioned earlier. There is also considerable good natural fishing for other species.

The GRAND RIVER (1) and its tributaries, the THORNAPPLE (2) in particular, can be very good for walleyes, smallmouth black bass and pike, and there are also some catfish. The Grand is considered best between Lyons and Grand Rapids; while the Thornapple is best fished from State Highway 66 at Nashville, or State Highway 37 at Hastings and Middleville.

Ferries operate regularly in the summer between Manitowoc, Milwaukee and Kewaunee, Wisconsin, and Ludington, Michigan. The fishing in the famous Pere Marquette River, which enters Lake Michigan at Ludington, is described later in this chapter. There is also some angling in several lakes which have outlets to Lake Michigan, and into which the smallmouth black bass and northerns make autumn migrations and provide extra-good fishing at this time. One of these is PERE MARQUETTE LAKE (3), right at the city of Ludington, and another is PENTWATER LAKE (4), on U.S. 31 about ten miles south of Ludington. However, marinas and power-boating activities have almost destroyed this fishing, partly by the boating activity in itself, and partly because the bass habitat has been destroyed through removal of so many old slabs and other debris which formed bass hideouts. Nevertheless, those who fish late—both late in the season, and late in the day—sometimes make good catches.

There is also steamer service between Milwaukee and Muskegon, midway up the western shore of Michigan. This district was once one of the finest fishing sections of Michigan, but is now so highly developed that naturally the fishing has suffered. Nevertheless there is still some good angling for bluegills, black bass, perch and sunfish in ROUND LAKE (5), three miles north of Walhalla on U.S. 10; for walleyes, northern pike, bass and rainbows in FORD LAKE (6), eight miles north of Walhalla on U.S. 10. One of the oldest resorts in the Walhalla area is Barothy's Lodge; and guides can be obtained there for trips to various other worthwhile lakes and streams in the neighborhood.

This is only one of many such resorts in this part of Michigan, which offer a combination of cabin-type accommodations, some fair fishing in the immediate vicinity, and the opportunity to make trips to less heavily populated and less heavily fished waters for some better fishing.

Another lake which has a good reputation for northern pike, pickerel, walleye, largemouth black bass, smallmouth black bass, trout, bluegills and sunfish, as well as some muskellunge, is HAMLIN LAKE (7) reached via State Highway 116 north from Ludington along the shore of Lake Michigan. In winter this is a favorite ice-fishing spot. There are numerous resorts of all types along the lake.

Tucked in between Lake Huron and Lake Erie is LAKE ST. CLAIR (8) the smallest of the Great Lakes chain. Lake St. Clair has good populations of all the Great Lakes species except Lake trout, but its chief claim to fishing fame lies in the number and size of muskellunge which are taken in these urban waters, practically on Detroit's doorstep.

There are two varieties of muskies found in Michigan: one lives in the inland lakes, and a slightly different type in the Great Lakes. The difference is so slight that the average angler will not be aware of it—he'll know he has a muskie, and that's enough. The largest muskie taken here in 1963 weighed just over 40 pounds. Fifteen- and 20-pounders are common and the average is about 12. The season runs from mid-May to mid-October.

Most muskie fishermen leave from the area between Nine and Ten Mile Roads at St. Clair Shores, on State Highway 29, north of Detroit. Two full-time guides operating there are Al Lesh Charter Boat Service, 3233 Los Angeles, Warren, Michigan, phone: Area 313-754-7689; and Homer Le Blanc, 23323 Liberty, St. Clair Shores, Michigan, phone: PR 5-3300. There are also half a dozen other guides who operate only on weekends. Rates, which include boat, guide and all tackle, are reasonable. Unless you know the water, a guide is a great help, as Lake St. Clair is more than 400 square miles in area, and you have to know the spots to catch fish.

The short stretch of Lake Erie shore which lies in the southeast corner of Michigan, between Toledo and Detroit, also offers good fishing for typical Lake Erie species, walleye, perch and the black and white basses.

To the north, on Lake Huron, is Saginaw Bay, one of the most popular spots on the Great Lakes for walleye fishing. This whole Lake Huron coast is also good smallmouth black-bass water, while the tip of the thumb at the mouth of Saginaw Bay is a famous spot for perch and bass both, along the sandy beaches.

Along the shores of Lake Huron, here, as throughout Michigan, there is very good fishing for yellow perch in the bays, rivers mouths and around piers and breakwaters. The fish school up in April and May and at that time can be taken in great numbers. This species is generally caught on bait, preferably small minnows 1 to 3 inches in length, but also on crayfish, worms and grasshoppers. The fish move to deeper water in the summer, then return for another flurry of fast fishing in the fall.

North from Midland, the TITTABAWASSEE RIVER (9) flows south, roughly following the curve of Saginaw Bay. It can be fished from Edenville, which is reached via State Road 30 from U.S. Highway 10, about seven miles northwest of Midland.

The renowned AU SABLE RIVER (10) enters Lake Huron at Oscoda, just north of this, and continuing up U.S. 23 anglers will find good fishing in Thunder Bay at Alpena, where there are several resorts which cater especially to anglers. The THUNDER BAY RIVER (11), which has its outlet here, has been obstructed with several power dams and reservoirs, but there is some fairly good rainbow and brook-trout fishing in the headwaters. In between the dams there are muskies, occasionally up to 35 pounds, and pike, smallmouth black bass and largemouth black bass. Though this river falls off in production during the summer, it is very good both spring and fall and is a popular stream with casters.

A November afternoon catch from a western Michigan trout lake.

Inland from Oscoda, halfway across the state, at the junction of U.S. 27 and State Highway 55 is one of the state's largest bodies of water, HOUGHTON LAKE (12). Fishing here is for northern pike, walleyes, perch and bluegills, while neighboring HIGGINS LAKE (13) has smallmouth black bass and lake trout. This is a well-developed area with plenty of tourist and fishermen's accommodations of all kinds.

FAMOUS TROUT RIVERS OF MICHIGAN

The streams which made Michigan's name famous in the earlier days of trout fishing in North America are in the northern part of the mitt section of the state. Though they are not what they used to be, the thorough-going trout angler can still find some exceptional fishing in them. They are the Au Sable, Big Manistee, Little Manistee, Pere Marquette, the Boardman and the Sturgeon. The Manistee, Pere Marquette and Boardman flow into Lake Michigan on the west, north of Ludington. The Sturgeon flows up the center of the state into Mullet Lake; and the Au Sable flows east from Grayling to the shores of Lake Huron above Saginaw Bay.

In the AU SABLE RIVER (10), for 200 miles from Frederic, on U.S. 27 north of Grayling, all the way southeast to Lake Huron, where the river enters the bay at Oscoda, on U.S. 23, there is good trout fishing wherever you find fast water. The best part of the river is probably the stretch upstream from the Mio Dam near Grayling, and in the tributaries. In the lower part, for the twenty one miles up from the lake to the first dam there is some steelhead (rainbow) fishing in October and also in the spring. In the backwaters at the various dams which have been constructed from Grayling down, there are also pike, bass and bluegills.

From Grayling east, the stream may be reached from several country roads off State Highway 72. This is a highly developed tourist area and accommodations are plentiful.

Starting in almost the same area but flowing to Lake Michigan, the BIG MANISTEE RIVER (14) runs west, to enter the lake at the town of Manistee. Although this river has also unfortunately been dammed in many places, there is nevertheless some 200 miles of fishing, producing rainbows in the downstream area, northern pike, smallmouth bass and walleyes elsewhere. Below the last downstream dam, known as the Tippy Dam, the Big Manistee is regarded as Michigan's best "steelhead" stream—the steelhead being a rainbow trout which runs into inland rivers from the Great Lakes to spawn. The devastations of the lamprey eel have greatly reduced this species but the work now being done to try to eliminate the lamprey may eventually return the Big Manistee to something of its former choice position in the angling world. Fishermen used to take the big rainbows up to 20 pounds and very occasionally they are still caught up to 15 pounds. In 1956 Frederick Clement of Flint took one that weighed 16 pounds 10 ounces in the Big Manistee. The average is more likely to be from 2 to 3 pounds.

The best fishing is in May and again in October and November. In the lower part of the river a boat is almost required, although some few spots can be fished from shore. Very little wading is feasible. In this lower part of the river anglers lean to bait, though the Flatfish, River Runt and Daredevle are also popular. The baits in most common use are salmon eggs, Mayfly larvae, nightcrawlers, and spawn from the female rainbow, this latter being tied up in little, marble-sized bags made from nylon hose. Those little sacks are fished on a Number 4 or Number 6 salmon egg hook, with a split shot or two added. The summer fishing is good for bass, walleyes and northerns.

The Manistee is one of the rivers listed on the Wild River Study List and it is to be hoped that it will be preserved from further human depredations, at least in its present state, and perhaps even improved a little, rather than being subjected to more dams, as seems to be the trend before the onslaught of the Army Engineers.

State Highway 55, between Manistee on the lake shore and Cadillac, inland, crosses the Manistee at the Tippy Dam Lake. State Highway 115 crosses it above the second dam, at Mesick, and U.S. 131 also crosses it, well up in the top waters, near Walton Junction. The upper part is ideally fished via canoe trip and there are many good camping spots along the banks. There are also some camp grounds in the lower section: Redbridge Camp Ground at the Tippy Dam Lake, Horseshoe Bend Camp Ground below that, and Seaton Creek Camp Ground at the Seaton Creek Dam.

Those who require a guide in the Manistee area should contact Bill Friedrich, U.S. 31 and Filen Street, Manistee. Guides are also available at the several resorts in the Manistee environs, notably, Charles Wise at the Wellson Inn, Wellson; Larry Gunia at the Riverview Resort, Wellson; and Earl Hellman, Wellson.

From Manistee, at the mouth of the river, and from Onekama, on Portage Lake, about twelve miles north on State Highway 22, anglers also fish Lake Michigan waters for yellow perch, just about the tastiest fish on the books. The peak of the season is in spring and fall—the month of May, and the months of October and November. The average perch runs from 9 to 12 inches but some are taken up to 16 inches. The fishing is mostly from boats. Favorite baits are small minnows and the Mayfly larvae.

Offshore fishermen also find smallmouth black bass in these waters almost anywhere they can locate a boulder-strewn area; and while the take is inconsistent, in midsummer this fishing can be very good on occasions.

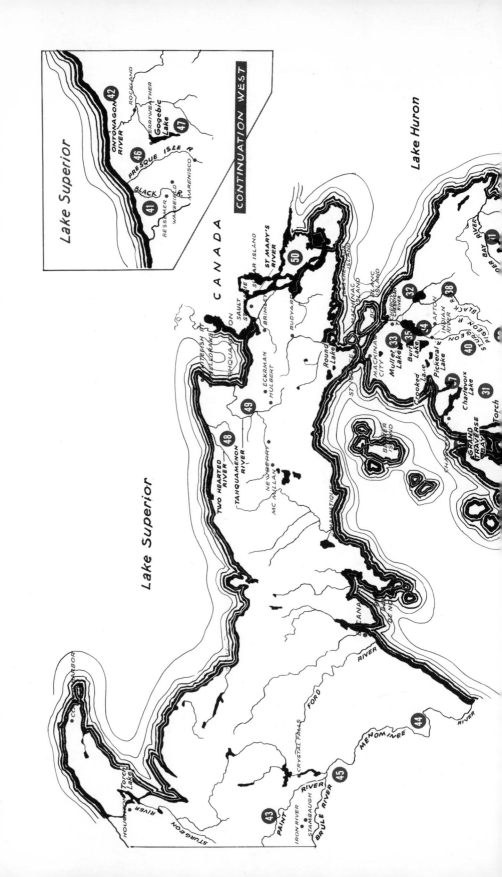

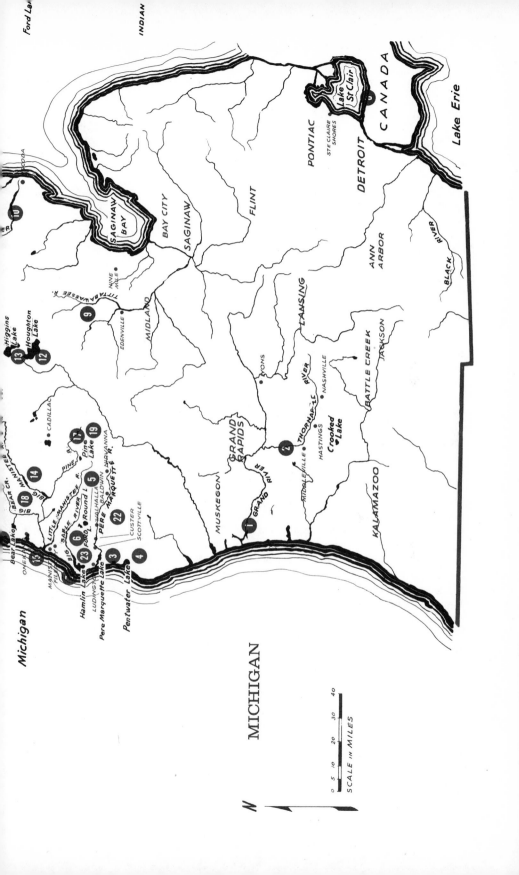

South of the Big Manistee is the LITTLE MANISTEE (15), a smaller river, faster in pace, with some excellent trout fishing for rainbows, browns and speckled trout. The lower waters of the Little Manistee can be reached from U.S. 31 at Filer City. Further up, a number of secondary roads lead in to the river from State Highway 37. This whole area is highly developed from the tourist point of view.

Near Manistee, the BETSY RIVER (16), PINE CREEK (17) and BIG BEAR CREEK (18) also offer some fair trout fishing, while PINE (19), ROUND (20) and BEAR (21), LAKES have trout, bass, perch and walleye populations.

Still further south is the famous PERE MARQUETTE RIVER (22), one of the nation's historic trout streams. Brown trout is the principal species, and are currently taken up to 8 pounds. The lower reaches also produce some good northern pike. Walleyes come into the river to spawn, but are taken mostly in Pere Marquette Lake; and smallmouth black bass are also taken in the marsh area next to the lake. They do not seem to migrate very far up the river. A few steelhead also come into the Pere Marquette in spring and fall to spawn. Fortunately there are no dams on this river, to stop the fish from running in.

All together, the Pere Marquette offers some ninety miles of river, alternately shallow stretches and deep pools. Like the Manistee, it is a good fly-fishing river, with possibilities of an extra big fish. Much of the river can be reached from Baldwin, Nirvana and Walhalla on U.S. 10, east of Ludington. There are many resorts in the area and guides are available at most of them. One of the oldest is Barothy's Lodge, near Walhalla.

The Mason County Tourist and Resort Association, Ludington, publishes a map entitled "Pere Marquette River Canoe Trails," showing some 75 to 100 miles of the river, corresponding to about twenty eight miles of U.S. 10 which parallels it on the north bank. Overnight camp sites are shown as available at most bridges; and there is drinking water at Scottville at the junction of U.S. 31 and U.S. 10; at Custer, Walhalla and Upper Branch, all on U.S. 10, to the east.

From about April 15th through May there is a migration of perch from Lake Michigan into the basin and harbor of the Pere Marquette, and anglers come from miles around to enjoy fishing for this fine table fish. Miller Marina at Ludington supplies bait and boats for fishing Pere Marquette Lake and the lower reaches of the river. There are plentiful accommodations in the city and surrounding areas.

Another river lying just to the north is the BIG SABLE (23) or Sauble, not to be confused with the Au Sauble in the eastern part of the state. The Sable is good for a two-day trout fishing canoe trip, putting in at Lake County Bridge on State Highway 669, or at U.S. 31 Bridge south of Manistee. Canoes are available at Manistee Canoe Cruises, at Manistee.

The BOARDMAN RIVER (24) circles the end of Grand Traverse Bay on Lake Michigan, and crosses U.S. 131 at Kalkaska. There is currently some forty miles of fishing for bass, pike and panfish. This was once a top brown-trout stream, and there are still some good brownies in the river, though they are not plentiful. The stream is wadable for almost its entire length, though caution must be used in the lower part, where there are some deep runs.

GRAND TRAVERSE AREA

The Grand Traverse area is in general an excellent point from which to try some of the best smallmouth black-bass fishing in Michigan. Smallmouth of 5 and 6 pounds are taken occasionally and 2 pounders are common. Nearly all the lakes contain this species. LONG LAKE (25) which can be reached by country road to the southwest of Traverse City; and LITTLE GLEN LAKE (26), on State Highway 22, northwest of the city, are two of the best.

The hottest brown-trout fishing in the locality is LAKE LEELANAU (27), northwest of Traverse City. Brown trout of better than 15 pounds have been taken here. The largest in 1963 weighed 15 pounds 5 ounces. However, the general run will be more like 17 inches. Like all brown trout, Leelanau fish are smart and after a good flurry of hitting at the opening of the season in May, anglers generally have to work hard for their catch. The two favorite methods of fishing for the brownies in this lake are trolling with a "cowbell" followed by a fresh minnow, and still fishing with a free-swimming live minnow off a weedbed or point. The lake also contains smallmouth black bass, northern pike, yellow perch and lake trout.

Leelanau is reached via State Highway 22, then country roads to several spots on the lake. Two resorts offer facilities and cater especially to the brown-trout fisherman. These are Perrin's Landing, at the southeast end of the lake, and Au-She-Gon Landing, on the middle east side of the South Lake. Boats and motors are available, and guides can be hired for $2 per hour.

GRAND TRAVERSE BAY (28) itself can be very good on occasion, though like most of the fishing in the Great Lakes, success seems to depend on hitting the cyclic peaks the fish allow in these waters. In Grand Traverse Bay the best fishing is in July and August, and anglers do best around those areas where they can locate a lot of boulders. The inland lakes of this area produce their top catches in June.

There are a few places in the lakes and bay where wading is possible and there fly rods and poppers are used by some anglers, but in general the spinning outfit is most popular. The Mepps and Shyster spinners and the Shannon spinner all do well, and a very successful bass taker popular with local anglers is the Jig-A-Doo plus a night crawler, fished along the bottom, especially around logs.

CRYSTAL LAKE (29), a large lake to the southwest of Traverse City, just inshore from Lake Michigan, is planted annually with rainbow trout, as are several other smaller lakes in the neighborhood. The fishing is best in early spring and in the fall, and the lake can be fished either from shore with minnows, or from a boat, either with minnows or by trolling artificial lures. U.S. 31 touches Crystal Lake at Beulah and State Highway 22 runs around the western shore. Accommodations of all kinds are plentiful. The fish run as high as 10 pounds, average from 2 to 6; and, of course, many smaller ones are taken.

The TORCH CHAIN OF LAKES (30), accessible from U.S. 31 north of Traverse City, also offer some good angling. Torch Lake itself, from which the group takes its name, is fifteen miles long. It is possible to go by canoe or other water craft from Torch Lake to Round, Intermediate, Clem, Bellaire, Six Mile and Elk, all in the same chain. Elk Lake is particularly well known for its rainbow fishing as it is heavily stocked annually. This particular lake is known for "temperature fishing" in August and September, and near-surface fishing in the fall. The temperature fishermen anchor their boat where the bottom temperature is 50 degrees Fahrenheit, and still-fish with live minnows. The minnow is hooked ventrally behind the anal opening and a small split shot is pinched in about 2 feet above the minnow. The bait is then cast well away from the anchored boat. Fall fishing is mostly by trolling with Flatfish, Daredevle and other spoons.

From Traverse City U.S. 31 leads north past the Torch Chain of Lakes to CHARLEVOIX LAKE (31), almost an inlet of Lake Michigan. Here there is fishing for lake trout, bass, pike and some brook trout, as well as crappies.

Those who wish to explore the lakes of the Grand Traverse region can do so on their own by renting boats on trailers at Murrays Boat Supply, in Traverse City.

To the northeast lies another waterway system of considerable length and one on which the boatman can penetrate from Lake Huron well into the state. Beginning at Lake Huron and following the CHEBOYGAN RIVER (32), it is possible to go through MULLET LAKE (33), INDIAN RIVER (34), BURT LAKE (35), CROOKED LAKE (36), to PICKEREL LAKE (37), a distance of some eighty seven miles. Mullet Lake has fishing for walleyes, rainbows, muskellunge, pike, perch and sturgeon as well as smallmouth black bass. The same species are found to some degree in the other lakes of the chain. The Cheboygan Chamber of Commerce publishes a "Sportsman's Guide to Cheboygan County," showing the lakes and rivers and indicating what species are likely to be found, as well as public access spots and camp grounds. Cheboygan, at the junction of U.S. 23 and State Highway 27 (from Interstate 75) is a good central point from which to explore this fishing, and is well supplied with hotels, motels and all services. There are also many resorts and waterside facilities along the lakes and streams.

South of Cheboygan, the BLACK RIVER (38), flowing from Black Lake to the Cheboygan River, offers some excellent trout fishing and also smallmouth, walleyes and muskellunge. You can reach the Black from the Alverno Road, or from Manning Road, off U.S. 27 south of Cheboygan.

To the southwest again, the PIGEON RIVER (39) flows due north to Mullet Lake, roughly paralleled by U.S. 27, from which highway it can be reached via several country roads. This river has all three stream trout. The town of Afton on State Highway 68 provides all facilities. Still further west is the STURGEON RIVER (40), flowing to Burt Lake. Anglers will find services of all kinds at Indian River, at the intersection of Interstate 75 and State Highway 68.

These are the only lakes in Michigan where sturgeon fishing is legal and they are extremely popular in the winter when there is some fine ice fishing for this species.

Seventeen miles northwest of Cheboygan is Mackinaw City, on the northern tip of the main part of the state. This is the jumping-off place for the northern or Upper Peninsula, via the world's longest suspension bridge over the Straits of Mackinac, to St. Ignace on the Upper Peninsula. From both St. Ignace and Mackinaw City there is ferry service to the famous Mackinac Island, which lies due east of St. Ignace. There are smallmouth black bass, walleyes and some rainbow trout or steelhead in the waters around Mackinac. The island can be reached from St.Ignace by skiff in fine weather, being only a half-hour run by outboard. But all such trips on the Great Lakes should be undertaken only after consulting the weather probabilities as the situation can change very quickly in these waters. The same thing applies to those who wish to fish Bois Blanc, another island in Lake Huron, northeast of Mackinaw City, or Beaver Island, which lies thirty miles offshore from Charlevoix, to the southwest in Lake Michigan. There is summer ferry service to Beaver Island, and this is highly recommended, rather than attempting the trip in a small skiff.

There is limited accommodation on Beaver Island, at St. James; Bois Blanc, on which there are several good fishing lakes, has a hotel and an air strip; and Mackinac

Trout fishing on the Tobacco River in northern Michigan.

Island has a luxury hotel. No cars are allowed on this island.

Around the north shore of Lake Huron, east on State Highway 134 from St. Ignace, anglers can reach another group of islands, known as Les Cheneaux, famous for a fine spring run of perch and smelt, and also for some good brook trout and walleye fishing. Guides are available at the two small towns of Hessel and Cedarville.

Those who wish to use their own skiffs and outboards at any of these islands can arrange to have them carried across on commercial boats to avoid the risk of crossing this possibly treacherous open water.

Persons planning to tow their own boats on trailers in Michigan should obtain the very complete "Boat Launching Guide" from the Michigan Tourist Council, Lansing, Michigan. This brochure includes all the necessary information about boat-launching sites plus a brief clue in each case as to the fishing possibilities.

THE UPPER PENINSULA

A glance at the map of the Upper Peninsula of Michigan shows a network of rivers running predominantly north and south, either to Lake Superior on the north, or Lake Michigan on the south. Nearly all hold fish of one kind or another. In most cases these rivers can be reached only by canoe trip or, occasionally, via county roads from the main cross-country highways U.S. 2 and State Highway 28.

In the extreme west, the BLACK RIVER (41), which holds trout and smallmouth black bass, can be reached from Bessemer on U.S. 2, via a county road which runs parallel to the river all the way down to Lake Superior. Further east, the ONTONAGON RIVER (42), which has some excellent trout water, can be approached from U.S. 45 at Rockland; and the upper branches cross State Highway 28 in several places.

On the opposite watershed, the PAINT RIVER (43), which is regarded by some as an outstanding bass stream, can be fished out of the towns of Iron River on U.S. 2, or Crystal Falls, at the Junction of U.S. 2 and U.S. 141. There are accommodations at both towns.

Along the Wisconsin-Michigan border, the MENOMINEE (44) and BRULE (45) RIVERS provide good fishing for walleye, pike, smallmouth black bass and perch. Iron River, Stambaugh and Crystal Falls are good headquarters for fishing these two as well as the Paint. A little further west, where U.S. 2 and State Highway 28 come together at Wakefield, you will find the PRESQUE ISLE RIVER (46), with fishing for all three stream trout.

GOGEBIC LAKE (47), in the same western part of the Upper Peninsula, is the largest lake in the State of Michigan. Much of the surrounding area is wilderness and privately owned but State Highway 64 runs up the west shore from Marenisco on U.S. 2 and Merriweather on State Highway 28, and there are two public launching sites, one at the south end and one on the west side, where there is also a camp ground. The fish are brook trout, rainbows, bass and panfish, and Gogebic is justly famous for its fine walleye fishing.

Near Gogebic Lake there are several chains of smaller lakes of a very isolated nature, wonderful for canoe-fishing trips.

The Michigan Tourist Council, Stevens T. Mason Building, Lansing 26, Michigan, will provide a brochure entitled "Michigan Canoe Trails," which gives details about the requirements and the services which will be found.

Some of the canoe trips available, such as a thirty-mile float on the Black River, are rough and rugged and for experts only. A canoe trip through the Cisco Chain of lakes near Gogebic, is less rugged and there is excellent fishing. In both cases you must bring your own canoe. In other trips outlined in the brochure it is indicated where there are resorts which can outfit canoeists, where to put in and take out, where supplies can be obtained enroute, and the type of fishing to be expected.

From the Keweenaw Peninsula, which juts out on the north shore of the Upper Peninsula, there are ferrys at Houghton, Hanock and Copper Harbor for Isle Royale. This island, which is entirely a National Park, lies close to the Canadian shore, sixty miles across Lake Superior, but is a part of Michigan. There are twenty eight inland lakes, with fishing for walleyes, smallmouth black bass, rainbow trout, brook trout, and perch and whitefish in Lake Superior itself. There are also lake trout in Siskiwit Lake, one of the larger lakes on the island, and in Lake Superior. Isle Royale may also be reached by steamer from Sault Ste. Marie.

The small towns along the Keweenaw Peninsula provide accommodations of all kinds for anglers who wish to fish for the Great Lakes species along those shores; and further east, at Grand Marais, deep-sea fishing boats go out daily all summer, to fish for lake trout though Great Lakes fishing is at best a spotty venture these days.

TWO HEARTED RIVER (48), lying a few miles to the east, is good for rainbows and brook trout. Anglers can go in on a country road from McMillan, on State Highway 28, or from Newberry on State Highway 123.

Beyond this, Whitefish Points curves around to shelter Whitefish Bay at the entrance to the Sault Ste. Marie area. Whitefish Bay abounds in northern pike, perch and walleye. Skiffs and a few charter boats will be found at Whitefish Point, Shelldrake and Tahquamenon. The fishing is good all summer in this area and around Tahquamenon there is some especially good fishing for large walleyes in the spring. The TAHQUAMENON RIVER (49), running parallel to State Highway 28, then north to Tahquamenon Bay, frequently produces good muskies, and there is also some fishing for this species in the bay. Local people can direct trout anglers to several small streams in the neighborhood of Tahquamenon Paradise; and the same is true further south around the small towns of Hulbert and Eckerman. Hulbert Lake, on State Highway 28 and State Highway 123, also produces some fine catches of smallmouth.

Fishing in the ST. MARY'S RIVER (50) at Sault Ste. Marie has been very bad for some years because of the work in progress of deepening the navigation channel; but the job is now almost finished and conditions are improving. In the river anglers take largemouth black bass, smallmouth black bass, perch, walleye, northern pike and muskellunge. Rainbow and speckled trout are found in the St. Mary's Rapids. The walleye fishing is generally best in August and through October, while muskies are taken from July through October. Both muskies and northern pike are also speared through the ice in winter, especially in the upper St. Mary's.

While there are few guides in this part of Michigan, there are many resorts and most resort operators can direct anglers to the best spots. There are many resorts on Sugar Island, the first large island of the group that is strung out through the narrows between Lakes Superior and Huron. A ferry operates from Sault Ste. Marie to Sugar Island, and a road runs the length of the island to the small community of Homestead. Sugar Island is best known for its spring and fall runs of jumbo perch, but walleye and pike fishing are good all season. The next island in the line is Lower Neebish, which enjoys a reputation for good fishing for northern pike and walleyes. Lake trout fishing has also begun to pick up again after many years of being almost nonexistent because of the depredations of the lamprey eel. There is a ferry from State Highway 129 on the mainland to the island at Oak Ridge.

Munuscong Bay, south of Neebish, and Potagannissing Bay, north of Drummond Island, offer good fishing for smallmouth black bass, walleyes and pike, and this whole inland waterway system can produce some excellent muskie fishing. There is limited accommodation on the island, which is reached by ferry from the small town of De Tour at the end of State Highway 134 on the mainland.

There is also some good fishing in inland lakes around Detour, for perch, bass and walleyes. Information, cabins and boats may be obtained from Kent Hamilton, Detour, Michigan.

The Lake Michigan shore of the Northern Peninsula also has some excellent fishing for walleyes, pike, rock bass and perch. The walleye catch is particularly good in the Escanaba to Manistique area, especially in Little and Big Bay de Nocs. This whole shore is served by U.S. 2, but there are few towns and accommodations are limited. Anglers should make reservations in advance if they plan to stay at any of the small towns, which are limited both in size and number. There is more plentiful accommodation at Escanaba, where U.S. 2 and U.S. 41 touch the lake at Little Bay de Noces, and also at Manistique, and northeast of there in the Blaney Park area, on State Highway 77.

In a state as widely visited by tourists as Michigan is, even with its 36,000 miles of rivers and 11,000 lakes, there is need for public access to fishing waters and this matter has been well taken care of by state authorities. There are close to 500 such public access sites, where the visitor may launch his boat free of charge to reach otherwise inaccessible waters. A list of these sites may be obtained from the Michigan Department of Conservation, Lansing 26, Michigan. County maps may also be obtained, showing the exact location of the launching sites. The maps are free up to a quantity of seven; from seven to twenty, send $1. And for a complete set of the entire list, send $2.50.

MICHIGAN FISHING REGULATIONS

Resident Annual Fishing License $2.00
Nonresident Annual Fishing License, except trout $5.00
Nonresident, 15-Day, except trout $4.00
Resident and Nonresident Trout Stamp $2.00
The trout stamp is required of everyone over 17 years of age.

SEASONS AND LIMITS

Open seasons vary greatly in Michigan because of the numerous species of sporting fish and the fact that many of these species occur in the same lakes and streams. For instance, the muskellunge season is different in lakes and streams where there are trout than it is in the Great Lakes. Therefore anglers must always check the season for the water in which they plan to fish. In general, however, it can be said that the trout, muskellunge, northern pike and walleye seasons open on April 27th and extend, with exceptions, to September 8th. In non-trout waters muskellunge, northern pike and walleyes may be fished throughout the year except for a brief period in March. The season for largemouth and smallmouth black bass is from June 1st to September 8th in trout waters; to December 31st in others. There is no closed season on white bass or the various panfish.

Species	Limits
Trout	5 from lakes or 10 from streams but not more than 10 pounds & 1 trout
Mackinaw or Lake Trout	2
Muskellunge	No limit
Northern pike, Walleye, Black Bass	5, singly or combined
Bluegills, Crappie, Sunfish, Rockbass	25, singly or combined

The Michigan Fish Law Digest, obtainable from the Michigan Department of Conservation, Box 8, Lansing 48926, Michigan, also lists a large number of trout lakes where special provisions are in force.

Those planning to fish the border waters between Wisconsin and Michigan, on the Northern Peninsula, should also obtain special regulations from the licensing agent when they obtain their fishing licenses. This applies in Dickinson, Gogebic, Iron and Menominee Counties.

WISCONSIN

The State of Wisconsin has three distinct types of fishing: that of the Great Lakes, in some 500 miles of shoreline on Lake Superior and Lake Huron; that of the northwoods country of the northern part of the state, with its thousands of lakes and rivers; and the fishing provided in the more urban southern part of the state and in the Mississippi River, which, with its tributary the St. Croix, forms much of the western border. The species to be found include muskellunge, largemouth and smallmouth black bass and northern pike, all found in most of the rivers and lakes. Many of the larger lakes and some rivers in northern Wisconsin also have walleyes, either native or introduced, and in addition the walleyes are taken along the shores of the Great Lakes. The largest walleye ever caught in Wisconsin came from the Namekagon River and weighed a substantial 16 pounds 8 ounces. The average will be 2 or 3 pounds and a 10-pounder is a very big fish. Walleyes are generally taken on deep-fished lures or bait but in the spawning season, which in northern Wisconsin can vary from mid-April to the first of May, you can occasionally catch them on cast lures.

The trouts, brown, rainbow and brook trout, lake trout, and some "splake," a cross between brook trout and lake trout, are also found in Wisconsin. The brook trout is native to the waters of the northern part of the state but due to deforestation, pollution and general warming up of the waters, plus the fact that this species is such a ready taker of flies and lures that it is easily fished out, the brook trout is not as widespread as it once was. It is now confined mostly to the upper parts of the streams in the well forested areas of the extreme north. In many of the more southern rivers and creeks its place has been taken by the hardier and less easily caught brown trout, stocked from German brown and Loch Leven strains. The rainbow has also been introduced and is the most common "put and take" trout. There is some natural reproduction of rainbows in the streams of central and northern Wisconsin. The rainbow also produces a special type of fishing as a seasonal migrant out of Lake Superior into the coastal rivers, where it is called the "steelhead."

In the warmer waters of Wisconsin the largemouth bass provides some fine fishing. Wisconsin is near the northern limit of this species, yet it is found to some degree in most lakes throughout the state, in the shallow, weedy areas and in the backwaters of rivers. The average fish will go about 2 to 3 pounds, with the state record of 11 pounds 3 ounces. This fish was taken from Lake Ripley in the northwestern part of the state, near the town of Trego, at the junction of U.S. 53 and U.S. 63. In early spring anglers make top catches of the largemouth with flies and light spinning lures, but from the middle of July through August the most successful fishing is with underwater baits and lures.

Perch are found in some larger inland lakes and in the Great Lakes while nearly every lake and stream has its share of panfish, including rock bass, sunfish and bluegills. Catfish occur in the Mississippi River drainage area, and sturgeon are also taken in a few places.

As is the case with its neighboring Great Lakes States, there is some kind of fishing year-round in Wisconsin, from the opening of the trout season right on through summer and fall into winter, when there is ice fishing in many lakes throughout the state.

While there is still considerable natural forested land, and there are numerous national forests and wilderness areas, the state is thoroughly laced with a network of highways both north and south, so that access to the good fishing waters is excellent. There is also better than average rail transportation available, with the Soo Line, the Chicago, Minneapolis and St. Paul, and the Chicago and Northwestern all providing numerous main and side lines, many covering those areas of particular interest to the angler.

To provide still another entry to the good fishing areas, there are several car and passenger and railway ferries, notably those between Muskegon, Michigan and Milwaukee, Wisconsin; Ludington, Michigan and Milwaukee, Wisconsin; Ludington and Manitowoc, Wisconsin; Frankfort and Manitowoc; Ludington and Kewaunee; and Frankfort and Kewanee. There is also a ferry between Frankfort, Michigan, and Menominee, Wisconsin, which goes through a passage in the Green Bay Peninsula but it does not stop there, making its landing at Menominee on the Wisconsin-Michigan border.

To add to the transportation conveniences, the resort industry is very highly developed, particularly in northern Wisconsin, and there are resort hotels, fishing camps and motels available almost everywhere; as well as camp sites, boat launching facilities, and other conveniences.

The summer climate in Wisconsin is typical northwoods climate. You need cotton shirts for the warmer part of the day, woolens at night. Those who plan to do any stream fishing should have chest-high waders in order to reach the best parts of the rivers.

In the more remote parts of the state the angler may encounter deer and possibly bear. The swamp rattler and the timber rattler are the only two poisonous snakes, and are readily identifiable. They are limited to the central, western and southwestern part of Wisconin.

NORTHERN WISCONSIN

Of all Wisconsin fish the muskellunge gets the most attention, not because of his numbers but because of the fact that the species is scarce everywhere, but more numerous in Wisconsin than in most places. Wisconsin has two varieties of the muskellunge, one, generally called the Wisconsin muskie, a hybrid between the northern pike and the true muskellunge; the other often locally referred to as the "tiger muskie," which is the true muskellunge.

The majority of waters in which the muskie occurs lie roughly in an east-west band across the northern part of the state along the drainage area of three rivers, the CHIPPEWA (1), which enters the Mississippi below Eau Claire, and drains the north-central part of the state; the UPPER WISCONSIN RIVER (2), further to the east, running from Rhinelander southward, also to eventually reach the Mississippi; and the AMINCON RIVER (3) which flows into Lake Superior east of the town of Superior, in the upper northwest corner of Wisconsin. These are believed to be the original natural habitat waters of the fish within Wisconsin. Now they have been planted in a number of lakes outside this range, mostly in the eastern part of the state.

In all there are some 600 lakes which are considered possible muskie waters from the angler's point of view, and some fifty four rivers. Occasionally they are also taken in Green Bay, but this is a catch-as-catch can proposition.

Even in waters which are regarded as muskie habitat the take is spotty and it speaks highly for the fighting qualities of the fish that in spite of the relatively few caught, as compared to the take of other species, the muskellunge is still the top-rated fish that anglers say they would like to go for in Wisconsin.

Muskies in lakes prefer to hang out in the bays near weed beds and usually in rather shallow water. Out in the lakes they will haunt the edges of channels and rocky shoals. In rivers they like the slower water. Plug casters and spin casters drift or row quietly along, casting to the edges of the weed beds or the channel edges, or to overhanging branches alongshore. All the classic spoons, plugs and spinners are good, and bucktails have also proven out, but for real sport and bigger fish, try an oversize plug. Fast action rouses the fish, too. Strike immediately on the hit.

Trollers use 20- to 30-pound-test line and stout bait-casting reels. Muskies are frequently taken accidentally on large lures trolled for walleye or largemouth or smallmouth black bass. Those who fish with live bait usually use a sucker about 12 inches long.

The biggest muskellunge ever taken in Wisconsin weighed 69 pounds 12 ounces. It came from the Chippewa. This was the world record for the species until it was surpassed by a mere 3 ounces by a fish taken from the St. Lawrence River in 1952. The lower part of the Chippewa is reached via State Highway 85, south from Eau Claire and State Highway 25, south from Durand. Accommodations are plentiful at both towns. Above Chippewa Falls, the many rivers of the vast Chippewa drainage also hold muskellunge.

One of the best bets is the LAC DU FLAMBEAU region (4), up towards the Michigan border. This area can be reached from Rhinelander via U.S. Highway 8 west to U.S. Highway 51, then north. Indian guides are obtainable at the Lac Du Flambeau Indian Reservation, as well as through the many resorts in the neighborhood. In this small section of true northwoods country there are several hundred lakes which hold muskies, two of the top producers being Escanaba and High Lakes. The EAGLE CHAIN OF LAKES (5), near Eagle River, at the Junction of U.S. Highway 45 and State Highway 70, also hold good reputations; as do PELICAN and RICE LAKES (6), south of Rhinelander on U.S. Highway 45.

The Lac du Flambeau region, with its hundreds of lakes, also has excellent fishing for smallmouth black bass and walleyes. Worthy of special mention is the MANITOWISH LAKE AND RIVER SYSTEM (7), within the Flambeau group, which presents fine canoeing opportunities to get to some of the best fly fishing and other casting for smallmouths in the state. Fly fishermen use small popping bugs and the best color combinations are red and yellow, all brown, red and white, and perhaps the tops of all is robin's egg blue. Spin casters have great success with the Phillips Crippled Killer, a surface lure that really makes the bass flap their scales. Entry to the Manitowish group can be found at Mercer, on U.S. 51; at Manitowish Waters, further south on the same highway; or from Springstead, on State Highway 182 between Manitowish Waters and Park Falls, to the west.

Besides the Manitowish river and lake and the adjacent waters, the fighting smallmouth is widespread throughout the northern part of Wisconsin. They thrive in rivers wherever there is fairly fast water, and in lakes wherever there is a fairly rocky bottom. In some places their habitat overlaps that of the trout, with the bass taking over the lower waters of the river, where it may be a little too warm for trout. The angler who wants to try his luck for smallmouth in rivers will find many miles of suitable streams in northern Wisconsin.

In the Ashland District the BAD RIVER (8), the MARENGO (9), the POTATO (10) and the WHITE (11) are all good. Part of the Bad, Potato and White Rivers run through the Bad River Indian Reservation. The Bad River can be reached from U.S. 2 at Odanah, about ten miles east of Ashland; the Potato from State Highway 169 at Gurney. The Marengo is a tributary of the Bad, flowing in from the west at the town of Marengo on State Highway 13. The White is reached from State Highways 112 and 13, outside the Reservation; and also higher upstream where it crosses U.S. 63 near the small town of Mason.

Along the eastern edge of the state, the MENOMINEE (12) between Michigan and Wisconsin, is also a good smallmouth river, with sixty five miles of fishing. Anglers can go in from U.S. 8 and U.S. 141, via a number of country roads. Another famous smallmouth river, the PESHTIGO (13), lies just to the south. It crosses U.S. 141 at Crivitz.

Wausau is the center of another well-developed fishing resort area, with more than average fishing for smallmouth black bass in a series of rivers around the city. The BIG EAU PLEINE RIVER (14) lies to the southwest of Wausau via U.S. 51 as far as the Eau Pleine Reservation at Mosinee, then west on State Highway 153 about ten miles. The BIG RIB RIVER (15) can be reached via U.S. 51, north from Wausau to Merrill, then west on State Highway 64 to the river. Anglers can also find access to less heavily fished parts of the river by several country roads leading in from State Highway 64 on the south and State Highway 13 on the west. The headwaters of the Wisconsin River can also be fished from Merrill. And further to the east, the EAU CLAIRE (16) crosses State Highway 52 and State Highway 64, as well as U.S. 45. The Wausau Chamber of Commerce can supply information about resorts throughout the area. Those who are particularly interested in river fishing for smallmouth black bass should also write for a pamphlet entitled "Smallmouth Bass Streams" issued by the Wisconsin Conservation Department, Madison 1, Wisconsin.

One of the most interesting places in the state to fish for smallmouths in both lake and stream is currently that section around the small town of Keshena (17) at the junction of State Highway 55 and State Highway 47, about 100 miles east of Wausau. This used to be the Menominee Indian Reservation and used to be closed to fishing, but is now open to the public. It abounds in picturesque atmosphere, with many Indians still wearing the colorful native dress. In addition to smallmouth bass there are muskies, walleyes, and a bonus of many miles of trout streams newly open to fishing.

Of special interest, also, is the area around the town of Hayward (18), at the junction of U.S. 63 and State Highway 27 in the northwestern part of the state. There is good fishing here for all the northern species, with emphasis on the muskellunge. The same situation holds good a few miles to the south, where the small towns of Cumberland and Turtle Lake on U.S. 63 are the centers from which to reach the fishing. Similar opportunities will be found around RICE LAKE (19) and Haugen, on U.S. 53. There are many woods resorts in the neighborhood of all four towns.

Still another good center from which to fish in this northwestern part of Wisconsin is the town of Minong, where State Highway 77 branches off westward from U.S. 53, leading to a large group of lakes both north and south of the road, and to the headwaters of the St. Croix River (20).

In these upper waters of the St. Croix, along the border with Minnesota as far south as St. Croix Falls, on U.S. 8, there is excellent fishing for smallmouth bass. Lower down in the river anglers take northern pike and walleye.

The famous Namekagon River (21), from which the state's largest walleye was taken, flows through a vast area of this section of the state, roughly following U.S. 63 south through Hayward and Trego, then cutting across country to its junction with the St. Croix. You can go in to the lower part of the river via a country road north from State Highway 77, just west of where the latter crosses the river.

There are many areas all across northern Wisconsin which offer some fishing for brook trout, most of the streams being small in size and not too long. North of Eagle River on U.S. 45, north of Rhinelander, there is considerable good fishing of this kind. Information as to resorts having access to them can be obtained through Herman M. Smith, Secretary, Vilas County Chamber of Commerce. To the west, on U.S. 51, the town of Woodruff is a center for other small stream trout fishing, and information here can be obtained through John E. Zillmer, Secretary, Chamber of Commerce, Woodruff.

Further northwest on U.S. 51 is the town of Hurley, in whose neighborhood there are several trout streams. The Montreal River (22), one of the best, can readily be reached from U.S. 51 in its upper waters, and from a country road north from Saxon on U.S. 2, in its lower waters. The fishing can be very good for both brook and brown trout in spring and fall. During the summer the river warms considerably and the fish then congregate at the spring sources and are not so easily taken. Information as to accommodation and services in the area can be obtained from H. W. Kinney. Secretary, Iron County Advertising Commission, Hurley, Wisconsin.

Traveling U.S. 2 from the Michigan border to Ashland, the angler is within reach of another group of similar streams, while in the extreme northwest corner there are additional creeks, plus the Little Amnicon River, which latter has some nine miles of brook-trout fishing. The Little Brule in the same area, holds all three stream trout, as does the nearby Nabagamon Creek. For information as to accommodations in this sector, write Blanche Friermood, Secretary, Eau Claire Lakes Association, Solon Springs, Wisconsin. The Eau Claire Lakes should not be confused with the city of Eau Claire location. The lakes lie in the northwestern part of Wisconsin, between U.S. 53 and U.S. 63.

It is in the rivers along the shores of Lake Superior, in this northern part of Wisconsin, that anglers find their fishing for "steelhead," rainbows which run from the lake into the rivers to spawn. There are good runs of these fish into the Bois Brule (23), Iron (24) and Flag (25), all three flowing into the lake east of the town of Superior, Wisconsin. There are lesser runs in some of the smaller streams, and in addition, all these rivers hold resident browns, rainbows and brook trout. While U.S. 2 crosses the upper reaches of some of the rivers, there is very little highway access to them and few communities in the area. Those who fish them usually work up from State Highway 13, which skirts the coast. Anglers planning to try these streams should contact Lyle Cowley, Secretary, Lions Club, Port Wing, Wisconsin, for information as to accommodations and guides.

A number of small trout streams are also to be found in the northeast, bordering on Michigan, just north of U.S. 8 and east of State Highway 139. Here the POPPLE (26), BRULE (27) and PINE RIVERS (28) provide excellent fishing for all three trout and there are numerous small creeks with populations of brook trout. Detailed information may be obtained from the Florence County Chamber of Commerce, Florence, Wisconsin. Spread Eagle is a good headquarters resort town.

Anglers planning to fish Wisconsin's trout streams should obtain the pamphlet "Wisconsin Trout Streams" from the Department of Conservation, Madison 1, Wisconsin. Ask also for "Wisconsin Trout Lakes," as a great many lakes in the areas where there are trout streams have also been stocked.

In the northwestern part of Wisconsin, near the small town of Hiles on State Highway 32, immediately east of U.S. 45, and close to the city of Rhinelander, the renowned WOLF RIVER (29) finds its beginning. It flows southward draining much of northeastern Wisconsin, flowing some 400 miles to Lake Poygan, west of Lake Winnebago. The fishing in the Wolf varies from the primitive fishing of the wild and scenic Dalles of the Wolf, near Keshena, to the quieter angling in the marshy waters of the lower reaches. Some excellent catches are made in the faster waters and the stream around Langlade, at the junction of State Highway 64 and State Highway 55, is particularly good, with brown trout running to 5 pounds. The slower-moving, wider windings of the river near the lake are the scene of a tremendous run of walleyes in the spring, as these fish travel more than 100 miles from Lake Winnebago to spawn in the Wolf. The river can be reached from State Highway 55, which follows it closely as far south as Shawano. Below that access is via State Highway 187 as far as Stephensville. There the Wolf turns west and crosses U.S. 45, then flows south again to Fremont and across U.S. 10 and so to Lake Poygan. There is a public boat launching site at Langdale.

The tributaries of the Wolf also provide some excellent trout fishing. The RED RIVER (30), north of Shawano, can be reached by country road from Gresham, west of Keshena. The EMBARRASS (31), entering the Wolf at New London, at the junction of U.S. 45 and State Highway 54, is also considered excellent, but in addition to these two major tributaries, all the small streams in the Wolf River Watershed are good possibilities. Accommodations are available at all the towns along State Highway 55, and there are many resorts in the Rhinelander area from which the river can easily be reached.

Also included in northern Wisconsin is the Green Bay Peninsula, jutting northward along the Wisconsin-Michigan shore. Some of the best smallmouth waters in the Midwest are those of Green Bay, enclosed by the peninsula. Door County, extending from half way up to the end of the peninsula is a well-developed and attractive resort area with several plush golf courses and resorts, but nevertheless plenty of the type of accommodation anglers prefer. There are state parks for campers, public beaches, free boat ramps, and, most important, plenty of room in the waters of Green Bay for everyone to fish.

For the smallmouth fishing in the Bay no license is required as these are considered outlying waters of Lake Michigan. Anglers have little trouble taking their daily limits of smallmouth up to 5 and 6 pounds. The style of fishing seems made to suit everyone. In the spring, usually about mid-June, during spawning season, fly fishermen and light-spinning-tackle enthusiasts have their day, wading the shorelines and casting into the pickerel grass and weeds. Bonuses of huge rock bass and jumbo perch may come their way while they work over the smallmouth. In late summer

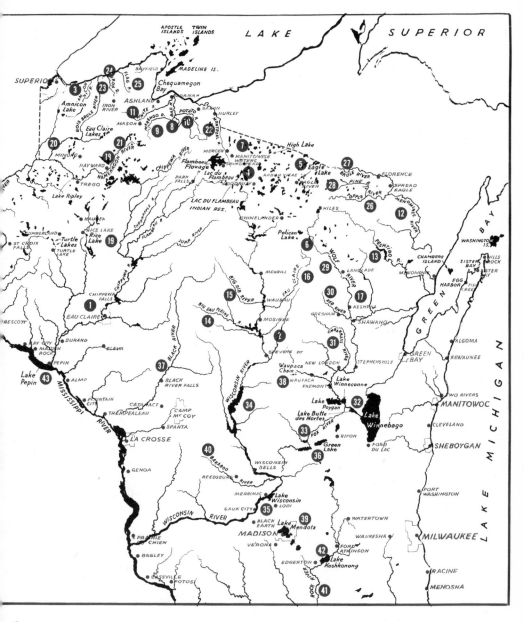

WISCONSIN

the bait fishermen come into their own, with excellent catches made on dragon-fly nymphs, locally called hellgrammites, and on soft-shell crabs.

In addition to the excellent angling for smallmouth black bass there is some outstanding fishing for perch and northerns; and in the fall trollers take walleyes up to 12 pounds along the reefs.

There are also many small bog lakes where adventurous anglers find some outstanding bass fishing. This is an angle you pretty well have to develop for yourself as those who fish these small "ponds" are understandably reluctant to reveal their favorite fishing holes.

At the town of Fish Creek there is good fishing from piers or by boat, and charter boats also operate out of this port to fish for bass and perch. Charter boats also take parties offshore to Chambers Island, a picturesque place with a lake on it that is loaded with big northerns and bass. On one trip in 1963, Syd Herman, outdoor writer for the Manitowoc *Herald Times* reported that his party took sixty-three northerns, the biggest 14 pounds, and a 23-inch smallmouth black bass. They were casting Daredevles for the northerns, plugs for the bass. The charter boat company at Fish Creek has boats on the lake and the cost is included in that of your trip to the island. The charge is about $3 per head for the works.

Other good spots to make your headquarters on the peninsula are Egg Harbor, Sister Bay, Eagle Harbor and Gills Rock, at all of which there are accommodations and services. This whole area is ideal for camping.

From Gills Rock there is a ferry to another interesting island, Washington Island, off the northern tip of the peninsula. The trip takes about half an hour. While there are roads on the island, accommodations and services are scarce, though there are campsites. Light-tackle enthusiasts will find some wonderful wading and casting territory in the shallows between Washington and Hog Island, where smallmouth like to hang out.

Almost anywhere you touch on the shores of the Great Lakes, in Wisconsin, there is good perch fishing, with emphasis on two great bays—Chequamegon, on the Lake Superior coast; and Green Bay on Lake Michigan. There is good perch fishing out of practically every town down the Michigan shore, some of the ports where anglers will find boats available being Algoma, at the base of the Green Bay Peninsula, Two Rivers, north of Manitowoc, Cleveland, half way between Manitowoc and Sheboygan, Sheboygan, and Port Washington; as well as the large cities of Milwaukee, Racine and Kenosha.

Jutting out above Chequamegon Bay are the Apostle Islands, where there is some trolling for lake trout. There is a ferry from the town of Bayfield on State Highway 13 on the mainland, to Madeline, the largest and closest inshore of the islands. There are limited accommodations on Madeline, and a road the length of the island. There are also some accommodations on Twin Island, the farthest out of the group. Boats are available at Bayfield. Anglers planning to fish here should write the Chamber of Commerce at Bayfield for complete details as the region is little developed.

SOUTHERN AREA

Just below the Green Bay Peninsula is LAKE WINNEBAGO (32), one of the largest inland lakes of the Midwest. This is a wonderful walleye lake, and fishing is open year-round. Trolling is excellent summer-long, while winter brings out the ice fishermen by the thousands to construct their huts on the frozen surface and take their share of this tasty fish. They also catch sand pike and northerns. Live bait and jigs are the medicine for this winter fishing. All the popular trolling lures take fish in the summer. Accommodations of all kinds are available at all the towns along U.S. 41, which skirts the western shore of the lake, and State Highway 55, which follows the eastern shore.

Winnebago and the lakes and streams to the northwest, in the Wolf River drainage basin are a bonanza for light-tackle fishermen in the spring. During the spawning season the fish run as much as 100 miles up the river and the chain of lakes which includes BUTTES DES MORTS, WINNECONNE and POYGAN, and the FOX RIVER (33). This run usually comes from mid-April to May 1st. At this time, during the Mayfly hatch, they are taken on flies and poppers all up and down the river system. There is also a similar run in the WISCONSIN RIVER (34) in the central part of the state. LAKE WISCONSIN (35), a widening of the Wisconsin River, has good populations of both walleye and sauger, and also some smallmouth black bass and panfish. The lake is reached via State Highway 78 or State Highway 60. Accommodations will be found at Sauk City, Merrimac and Lodi. The lower Wisconsin River system, like Winnebago, offers year-round fishing. Besides the walleyes there are shovelnose sturgeon and flathead catfish.

While not to be classed as angling, there is a spring season when the spearing of sturgeon is legal on Lake Winnebago, and many enthusiasts fly in onto the ice with their planes, to try for these monsters which run up to 100 pounds.

Southern Wisconsin can produce some very good trout fishing. There are three areas of concentrated trout lakes to the west of Winnebago. One group is around Stevens Point at the junction of U.S. 10 and U.S. 51; another in the area of Cataract on State Highway 27 near Camp McCoy. The third group is in the southeast corner near Waukesha. Most of the lakes in these areas have rainbow, brown or brook trout, but a few also have splake, and Kamloops or Lake Trout. GREEN LAKE (36), just southwest of Winnebago, on State Highway 23, west of Ripon, has produced some fairly good lake-trout fishing.

A pamphlet entitled "Wisconsin Trout Lakes," issued by the Wisconsin Conservation Department, Madison 1, gives detailed instructions on how to reach the numerous lakes, and what fish will be found in them.

Stream trout fishing in southern Wisconsin will be found concentrated in an area south of U.S. Highway 10 between Durand and Eleva, and bounded on the east by the new Interstate 94 and on the west by the Mississippi River. Here there are a surprising number of small trout streams each offering anywhere from one to fifteen miles of fishing. Anglers can get detailed information on where to fish them from the pamphlet "Wisconsin Trout Streams" issued by the Conservation Department, Madison 1, Wisconsin.

Several lakes in southern Wisconsin are also known as good muskie waters. These include GREEN LAKE, BIG TWIN LAKE, LITTLE GREEN and SPRING LAKES (36), all near Ripon on State Highway 23, west of Fond du Lac. The BLACK RIVER FLOWAGE (37) and POTTER FLOWAGE (38), near Black River Falls on U.S. 12, north of LaCrosse, also produce some good muskellunge fishing; as do the WAUPACA LAKES (38) near Waupaca, north of U.S. 10, west of Lake Winnebago.

LAKE MENDOTA (39), at Madison, Wisconsin, is considered to be the best perch lake in the state; and nearby at Black Earth, there is good fishing for stocked trout, while just to the south at Verona, on U.S. Highway 18 there are several small, spring fed trout streams.

To the north around Wisconsin Dells, and to the west of them, there are various waters providing fairly good trout, bass and panfishing. Sparta is a good center from which to fish the Hiawatha Valley; while from Reedsburg, you can reach the BARABOO RIVER area (40).

East of Wisconsin Dells, around the town of Waupaca, there is some fine fishing for panfish, bass, northern pike and an occasional muskellunge in a string of twenty-three spring-fed lakes; and there are also stocked trout streams in the neighborhood.

In the extreme south-central part of Wisconsin the ROCK RIVER (41), though a very sluggish river, produces quite an assortment of fish. In the upper portion, above LAKE KOSHKONONG (42), where the river winds down along State Highway 26 from Watertown, there are seasonal runs of walleyes and white bass out of the lake. Year-round anglers take northern pike and crappies as far down as Jefferson on U.S. 18. Below that the bullhead and catfish take over. Anglers who fish Lake Koshkonong for the walleyes and bass stay at Fort Atkinson on the northeast corner of the lake, on U.S. 12 and State Highway 26; or at Edgerton, on U.S. 51 at the southwest corner.

In the Mississippi River, which forms so much of the western border of Wisconsin, there is an endless variety of fishing, usually overlooked by all but those who live adjacent to the river. Largemouth black bass and many varieties of panfish are taken in the backwaters and sloughs. Smallmouth are frequently found around the rocky revetments and rip-rapped wing dams. Walleyes and sauger haunt the tailwaters of the many big dams. Northern pike like the weed beds. And in the spring there are runs of white bass in the main channel. Freshwater drum and sheepshead are also taken around the dams, and almost anywhere you may find channel catfish, flathead catfish or mudcat, bullheads, and occasional shovelnose sturgeon.

The problem with fishing the Mississippi is that it is so big, two miles wide in many places. The only way to successfully fish it is to choose your location somewhere along the 230 miles of Wisconsin border and make enquiries there as to the best spots and the type of fishing in that locality. It can vary from fly-rod casting with poppers to "ker-chunking," that is, bouncing a heavy sinker, a spinner and a gob of worms along the bottom for sauger or walleyes. You are almost certain to find some fishing for every species within easy reach of your headquarters. In general, old-timers on the river say to fish below the dams in the spring, fish the wing dams in the summer, and the backwaters in the winter.

La Crosse, where U.S. 16 crosses the Mississippi, and Prairie du Chien, on U.S. 18 are two good cities from which to fish the river. There are also many small, picturesque towns which provide the necessary services and are on good parts of the river. These are Potosi, just off U.S. 61 north of Dubuque; Cassville, a few miles further north, on State Highway 81; Bagley, south of Prairie du Chien; and the small town of Genoa, on State Highway 35, near Dam Number 8. North of La Crosse, a series of good headquarter towns on State Highway 35 includes Trempealeau, Fountain City, Alma, Pepin, Maiden Rock and Bay City, all convenient to the big waters of LAKE PEPIN (43), one of the major widenings of the Mississippi. Still further north, Prescott, on U.S. 10 at the river, is also a good fishing center. All these towns provide the necessary services such as accommodations and boats.

Fishing licenses for the Mississippi are reciprocal between Wisconsin and Minnesota and Wisconsin and Iowa.

Those who plan to bring their own boats to fish in Wisconsin should obtain a list of boat launchings, ramps, etc., telling how to reach them, the cost, if any, and other details from the Recreational Publicity Section, Wisconsin Conservation Department, P.O. Box 450, Madison 1, Wisconsin.

WISCONSIN FISHING REGULATIONS

Resident Fishing License $3.00
Nonresident Fishing License $5.00
Temporary 15-Day Family License $6.00

SEASONS AND LIMITS

Species	Open Season	Bag Limit	Size Limit
Black Bass	June 20–Jan. 15	5 in aggregate	None
Northern Pike	May 17–Jan. 15	5	18″
Walleye	May 17–Jan. 15	5	13″
Muskellunge	May 25–Nov. 1	1	30″
Trout	10 a.m. May 3–Sept. 7	10	6″
Lake Trout	April 1–Sept. 30	5	17″
Panfish	No closed season	25 each species	None

For complete regulations write: Conservation Department, P.O. Box 450, Madison 1, Wisconsin.

MINNESOTA

Minnesota's claim to 10,000 lakes is something less than the truth. There are actually 14,215. Add to this its shoreline on Lake Superior in the north, and the waters of the Mississippi River which has its headwaters in Lake Itasca in northern Minnesota, and flows south to form part of the border between Minnesota and Wisconsin, and you have a picture of the endless opportunities and the variety of the fishing available. In addition, the northern boundary between Canada and Minnesota is almost entirely water, comprised of a series of primitive, unspoiled lakes and streams in the Lake Superior National Forest on the United States side and Quetico Park Wilderness Area in Canada.

It all boils down to the figure that in Minnesota there is more fresh water than in any other state in the Union. Fortunately much of this water has been maintained in condition to support populations of the numerous native species of fish as well as a few which have been added through stocking. In all, the roster includes smallmouth black bass, largemouth black bass, walleyes, northern pike, muskellunge, bluegill, black crappie, white crappie, lake trout, brown trout, rainbow trout, brook trout, some brook trout which run out into Lake Superior and are known as "coasters," and landlocked salmon. The latter have been stocked in a few lakes in the state. The Minnesota Department of Conservation, Division of Game & Fish, also operate a series of "managed lakes" for trout. These are centered in four areas: between Bemidji, at the junction of U.S. 2 and U.S. 71, and Brainerd, to the southeast, at the junction of U.S. 210 and U.S. 371; in the extreme northeast point of the state, above Grand Marais on U.S. 61; in the area immediately west of Duluth at the western tip of Lake Superior; and in a number of quarries around Waite Park and St. Cloud, on U.S. 10, northwest of Minneapolis-St. Paul. A complete list of these waters and directions on how to reach them may be obtained by writing the Department, at St. Paul 1, Minnesota.

Channel and blue catfish are also taken in southern Minnesota and bullheads are found almost everywhere except in the cold, northeastern waters of the Lake Superior drainage.

Three major east-west highways cross Minnesota. U.S. Highway 2 provides access to the northern part of the state via Duluth; U.S. Highway 10 cuts through the center part of the state; and U.S. Highway 14 runs across the south. Many north-south highways bisect these roads in such a way that access can be had to even remote areas by car. From road's end the adventurous angler may go by canoe, rail or plane, or on foot, to many lakes and streams which have all the attributes of primitive wilderness. Those who fly will find that the Minneapolis-St. Paul area is served by seven major airlines, and besides the airport there, regarded as one of the best in the United States, there are 220 other airports throughout Minnesota, equipped to handle either commercial or private craft.

Along with the other Great Lakes States, Minnesota enjoys an ideal summer climate with warm, usually bright days and cool, clear nights. Fishermen should always carry jackets for the evenings and campers should have sufficient warm clothing to be comfortable in case of a possible "cold spell," which can occur even in midsummer. Fishermen should also carry rain gear.

Tackle used in Minnesota fishing varies greatly according to the species sought. In either lake or stream, the smallmouth black bass will hit just about anything you offer him, but, as with the largemouth, the greatest sport lies in light tackle and a top-water lure. For this kind of fishing the early and late seasons and the early and late parts of the day are best. When you can find the smallmouth taking near the surface, as is the case in many of the shallow lakes in northern Minnesota, or along rocky shores, you can have unexcelled sport with surface poppers, on either fly rod or spinning rod.

Fly casters usually find an 8- to 8½-foot fly rod adequate for either wet or dry-fly fishing in the rivers, and a 9-foot fly rod is fine for fishing the fly-rod poppers and streamers for largemouth and smallmouth bass in the big rivers and lakes. This outfit is also used by many Minnesota anglers to fish for northern pike. Almost any-where you fish in northern Minnesota you may run into this species and he is a ready hitter either to surface poppers or such underwater lures as the jointed lures and flashy wobblers. Casters work the weed beds and outlets from rivers but the northern may be found almost anywhere. In these waters they average 3 to 6 pounds and commonly run as high as 15 pounds.

Since walleyes dwell deep, the live minnow, fished deep, is the most popular method of going for this species. But casters take them, too, on yellow and orange plugs of the darter type. Jigging with a spinning outfit is also successful. The best spots to find the fish are over sandbars and reefs, and the fish is a notorious night feeder, though walleyes are also taken in the daytime, particularly on dull days. The average walleye in Minnesota will run from 2 to 4 pounds and they have been taken up to 16 pounds 8 ounces.

Lake-trout fishing also calls for deep fishing, generally a very heavy lure trolled deep on a metal or other sinking line. In summer the lakers seek the cool holes of the deepest parts of the lakes and you really have to get down to find them. Those who can be on hand in early spring or late fall, however, have unexcelled sport taking lake trout on cast lures and flies around rocky ledges and the shores of islands and wherever else they can be found feeding on the surface.

Plug-casting tackle is widely used in Minnesota both for bait fishing and for casting for muskies, northerns and bass, as well as general trolling. The most suc-cessful lures with the bait-casting outfit are the spoons and the jointed plugs with plenty of action. Spinners find that the same type of lures work well on a 7½-foot rod and conventional reel, with 6- to 8-pound-test line.

While most muskie fishing is done with trolling gear, they can frequently be taken by casters, especially in the spring and fall, in the shallow bays with which Minnesota lakes abound. Muskies can grow very large and old records show that many in these waters used to reach 40 pounds. The average today is considerably smaller but every muskie fisherman fishes with the idea that he may come up with a tiger. There have been many stories told about the untamable qualities of the muskellunge, and some anglers have even recommended shooting the fish before attempting to bring it aboard. However, all that is necessary is a short-handled gaff to land the fish and a sharp knock on the head to subdue it; those who are thinking of carrying a gun should remember that the use of firearms on a fish is strictly illegal in Minnesota.

The typical northern species of big game may be encountered in certain areas of Minnesota. Especially in the north, one may meet moose, deer and black bear, all of which, however, will leave you alone if you leave them alone. The only poisonous snakes whose habitat extends into the area are the smaller rattlers and these generally occur only in the southeastern corner of the state.

NORTHERN MINNESOTA

Northern Minnesota divides naturally into several regions according to watersheds. One of the most famous is the Arrowhead Country, which is, roughly, that portion of the state which juts out in a point between Lake Superior and the Canadian border. This area has been highly developed from the tourist point of view, yet aside from U.S. 61, which parallels the shore of Lake Superior northeastward from Duluth, only a few roads penetrate the wilderness and these only to a limited degree, thus assuring some excellent wilderness fishing. The towns of Schroeder, Tofte, Lutsen, Cascade, Grand Marais, Hovland and Grand Portage, all on U.S. 61, offer motels and other accommodations and also serve as headquarters and mailing address for the numerous resorts back in the wilderness.

There is some lake-trout fishing along the shores of LAKE SUPERIOR (1) but unfortunately this species, once so common in the Great Lakes, has been seriously depleted in numbers by the lamprey eel, so that today only a few are taken. The largest ever known to have been caught was a hefty 43 pounds 8 ounces, and was taken near the port of Hovland, once a commercial fishing center for the species. Efforts are now being made to control the eel by mechanical means and bring back a substantial population of the very desirable lake trout.

The lake trout from the Great Lakes is usually red-fleshed, almost like salmon, while those found in the inland lakes have lighter flesh, varying from deep pink to almost white.

Aside from Lake Superior, the lake trout likes the deeper lakes inland and in such waters can be taken throughout northern Minnesota. The Arrowhead Country and the lakes just to the west are recognized as tops for the laker. Motorists can go inland via woods roads romantically named the Gunflint Trail, from Grand Marais; the Arrowhead Trail from Hovland; the Caribou Trail from Lutsen; and the Sawbill Trail from Tofte, all on U.S. 61. From the Arrowhead Trail the angler has access to many waters of the famous Pigeon River watershed encompassing many lakes and streams on the Canadian border. The longer Gunflint Trail leads far into the interior, to GUNFLINT (2) and SAGANAGA LAKES (3), further west on the Canadian border.

Throughout the area fishing is for walleyes, smallmouth black bass and northern pike as well as lake trout. The latter occur in the larger lakes, one of the best being CLEARWATER (4), on the Gunflint Trail. Accommodations, boats and guides are available nearby at Forest Lodge, twenty-nine miles north of Grand Marais. Nearby WEST PIKE LAKE (5) is also rated as a top lake-trout spot.

GREENWOOD LAKE (5), reached from a spur road running east from the Gunflint Trail, also has some good lake-trout fishing and Greenwood Lake Lodge offers additional fishing for landlocked salmon, speckled, brown and rainbow trout, as well as walleyes, northern pike and bass. From this point anglers may also reach several streams which are regularly stocked with brook trout.

Two of the best walleye lakes in this section lie to the northeast, along the Canadian border. These are NORTH and SOUTH FOWL LAKES (6), on the path followed by the exploring voyageurs centuries ago. These two lakes produce good catches of walleyes even in midsummer, and there is good fishing for bass, northerns and trout within an easy canoe or outboard trip. Anglers can stay at Wilderness Retreat Lodge on McFarland Lake, which is reached via the McFarland Road, off the Arrowhead Trail. Seaplane service to some of the inland lakes is available at the lodge, at a cost of about $10 per person.

The farthest you can drive into the interior is via the Gunflint Trail, to Chik-Wauk Lodge. (Mailing address is Grand Marais, Minnesota.) There you can get outfitted for canoe trips still deeper into the wilderness or from the lodge you can fish Big Saganaga Lake for walleyes, northerns and lake trout. There is also good smallmouth fishing in outlying lakes, and for those desiring real seclusion, the resort operates a system of rustic outpost cabin camps in the neighboring Canadian wilderness of Northern Ontario. The same general services are available at Gunflint Lodge on Gunflint Lake, which straddles the border.

This whole Arrowhead area is more water than land, and nearly every lake, as well as the many rivers joining the lakes, has its quota of fish. Rustic resorts are numerous. For complete details about what each has to offer, anglers proposing to visit the area for the first time should obtain a folder and map entitled "The Tip of the Arrowhead" from the Cook County Civic Council, Grand Marais, Minnesota.

Besides the universal lake fishing, some resorts also feature stream fishing for trout. Rainbows have been stocked in three miles of stream controlled by the Lutsen Resort, north of the town of Lutsen. And stream fishing for brook trout can be enjoyed in the POPLAR LAKE (7) area, twenty-eight miles up the Gunflint Trail, at Balsam Grove Lodge. The lake itself is well known for walleye, northern pike, bass and panfish. Guides are available for several excellent canoe-fishing trips into the interior.

Moving west along the Canadian border the angler finds himself in some outstanding waters for smallmouth black bass. BASSWOOD LAKE (8), half in the Quetico Provincial Park in Ontario, and half in Minnesota, is regarded by many as the top smallmouth lake on the continent. Certainly it and the adjoining string of lakes running east to Lake Superior and west to Rainy Lake produce more than their share of this species, and to substantial size. There are many 2- and 3-pound fish, while the top weight known to have been taken is 8 pounds. Perhaps one reason for the continued production of such excellent fishing is that many of the lakes are within the Superior National Forest Roadless Area and can be reached only by canoe or plane from distant resorts.

A good jumping-off place for a trip into the wilderness area of northern Minnesota is Ely, reached via U.S. 53, north from Duluth, then northeast on State Highways 169 and 1 to Ely, where arrangements can be made through Bill Rom or Wilderness Outfitters. Similar well-organized canoe trips can also be arranged through Cliff Wold, at Bovey, on U.S. 169 west of Hibbing. Such trips can be taken with or without guides, according to the abilities of the canoeists, and the outfitters will supply everything except your clothing and fishing tackle. Cost of such a trip varies with the number in the party. A large group can go for as little as $32 per person per week if the group is self-sufficient—that is, needs no guide. Parties of two run about $36 per person per week. Guides cost about $28 per day. There can be additional charges for the use of a motor the first day to get away from civilization in a hurry and to reach the first portage quickly. Anglers also need a Canadian nonresident fishing license, costing $6.50, since some of the traveling will be through Canadian waters. However, even with these extras, this can be an extremely reasonable trip in some of the best fishing waters in the country. The season is from June to September, and the species found will be walleyes, northern pike, smallmouth black bass and lake trout.

An unpaved road leads through the bush from Ely and curves back west to join U.S. 53 just north of the town of Gheen, at Orr (not shown on maps). About forty-nine miles from Ely a side road leads to CRANE LAKE (9), which is another starting point for trips to more remote waters. There are more than twenty resorts and a trailer park on Crane Lake. A list of the resorts may be obtained from the Crane Lake Commercial Club, Crane Lake, Minnesota. The fishing in the lake itself is for lake trout and walleyes in the spring, while midsummer usually produces bass, crappies, perch and some walleyes. In the fall anglers take trout, walleyes and northern pike. Canoe junkets to the interior may be arranged through Handberg's, at Crane Lake.

Just to the northwest is RAINY LAKE (10), the largest along the chain between Ontario and Minnesota. This is considered to be one of the continent's best lakes for smallmouth, and its smaller neighbors, NAMAKAN (11) to the east and KABETOGAMA (12) to the south are also very good. Kabetogama has extra rating as one of the best walleye lakes in Minnesota, and has good fishing for northern pike, muskellunge to 25 pounds, and crappies.

This has long been one of the most popular sections of the north with sportsmen and there are many services, ranging from resorts to houseboats. A complete list may be obtained from the Chamber of Commerce at International Falls, Minnesota. Outfitting canoe and camping trips from International Falls are The Sportsman's Service, operated by Wayne Judy; and Canoe Voyageurs, operated by Don Trompeter.

Fly-in trips to remote waters can be arranged through the Rusty Myers Flying Service or the Vern Jones Flying Service, both headquartered at Fort Frances, Ontario, just across the border from International Falls. Another interesting fishing holiday on Rainy Lake can be arranged through Northernaire Floating Lodges, International Falls. These are houseboats, powered by big outboard motors, which serve as your hotel as you travel around to fish the more remote parts of the lake. With cook and guide the cost runs about $130 per week per person. On a "do-it-yourself" basis the cost can be cut to as little as $8 per person per day.

There is also some interesting float-fishing on the Big Fork River, southwest of International Falls. Both the Big Fork and the Little Fork, as well as the Rainy River, offer some very good muskie fishing. Guides and boats for the trip can be obtained at the small town of Grand Falls, on U.S. 71 between Bemidji and International Falls.

Less primitive waters may be found by anglers who follow U.S. 53 south from International Falls to PELICAN LAKE (13), near the towns of Cusson, Glendale and Orr (not on maps). Pelican is large, 13,000 acres in size, with many islands and a very irregular shoreline, making lots of fishing. It produces some exceptionally fat

Fishing in the more remote wilderness areas of northern Minnesota often calls for canoe trips through the hundreds of adjoining lakes and rivers.

and hard-fighting northern pike and in recent years has been noted for fine catches of both largemouth and smallmouth black bass. The lake is ideal for fishing with artificials. In the neighborhood there are a number of beautiful little walleye lakes, notably ELEPHANT and BLACK DUCK.

These waters can all be fished without the aid of a guide, making this a very popular spot for family vacations. For more serious fishermen, most of the resorts can also guide their guests to less frequented inland lakes for muskellunge and lake trout. For a list of resorts in the Pelican Lake area write Trenton C. Fry, Jr., Secretary, Orr Pelican Lake Civic Club, Orr, Minnesota. Addresses of resorts and guides in the dozens of lakes around the town of Hibbing should be obtained from Helmer E. Olson, Manager, Chamber of Commerce, Hibbing, Minnesota. These lakes are universally good for walleyes, northerns and crappie.

Continuing westward we come to the LAKE OF THE WOODS (14), which lies mainly within the boundaries of the Canadian Province of Ontario, though some miles of the southern shore are in Minnesota. The lake may be reached there by State Highway 11 from International Falls west to Warroad. Lake of the Woods is big and shallow, perfect water for many species of fish which readily hit cast lures, and is a favorite with light-tackle men. It produces some wonderful smallmouth-bass fishing, and some excellent muskellunge. Most of the resorts and services are on the Canadian shore. For further details see the Ontario chapter in this book.

Well to the south of the Lake of the Woods, via State Highway 72, lies a string of very large lakes, extending well down into the center of the state. The most northerly are UPPER and LOWER RED LAKE (15). Upper Red Lake is a good spot for walleye fishing. State Highway 72 touches the eastern end at Waskish and boats may be obtained there. Much of the remainder of the shoreline lies within the Red Lake Indian Reservation.

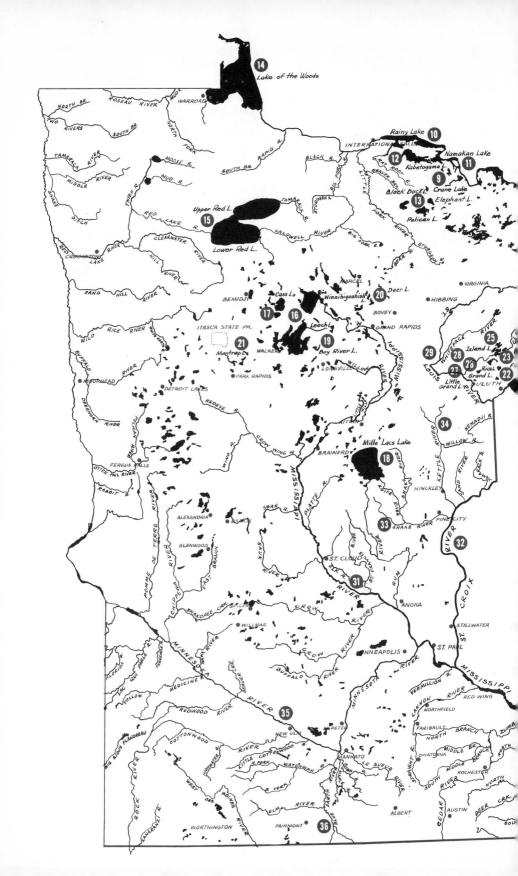

Saganaga L. ③

② Gunflint L. West Pike L.

④ N.⅌S.Fowl Lks.

Clearwater L. ⑤ Greenwood L. ⑥

BRULE GRAND PORTAGE •

HOVLAND

⑦ GRAND MARAIS •

Poplar L. LUTSEN

TOFTE

SCHROEDER

LAKE SUPERIOR

5 10   20   30

SCALE in MILES

NESOTA

WINONA

LA CROSS •

RIVER

Not as large, but offering generally better fishing, are WINNIBIGOSHISH and LEECH LAKES (16), which are most easily reached via U.S. 2 from Bemidji or Grand Rapids. These lakes are both producers of fine walleye fishing. CASS LAKE (17), a few miles to the west on U.S. 2, is another good lake. All have fishing for muskellunge and pike. The town of Walker at the southwest corner of Leech Lake is a favorite spot from which to fish these lakes.

The most southerly in this string of big lakes is MILLE LACS (18) which can be fished from the many resorts in the Brainerd area, at the junction of U.S. 10 and U.S. 210. Because of its location in the midst of an extremely popular resort area, Mille Lacs gets very heavy traffic, yet its shallow waters are ideal habitat for walleyes and northerns and it continues to produce some fine catches of good-sized fish. Immediately north of Mille Lacs is a string of lakes where there is good fishing for bass, pike, walleyes, crappie and sunfish. The town of Aiken, at the junction of U.S. 169 and U.S. 210, is a good headquarters.

CENTRAL AREA

The smallmouth black bass extends its range as far south as Grand Rapids at the junction of U.S. 2 and U.S. 169; and Park Rapids, at the junction of U.S. 71 and State Highway 34 from Detroit Lakes. However, from a line roughly on a level with the Detroit Lakes, southward, it is really the largemouth which makes the fishing. Most of the lakes in this section of Minnesota have many weedy bays ideal for casting surface lures, a favorite way of taking the largemouth. Many are taken in the 5-pound class, and the largest ever known to have come from Minnesota waters weighed 9 pounds 14 ounces.

Towns which serve as good centers for fishing the central part of Minnesota are Alexandria and Osakis, on U.S. 52, and Glenwood, on State Highway 55, south of Osakis; Detroit Lakes, at the junction of U.S. 10 and U.S. 59; Park Rapids, to the east of Detroit Lakes, on State Highway 34; Longville, on State Highway 84, southeast of Leech Lake; Spicer, on U.S. 71 north of Willmer; Brainerd, on U.S. 210; Aitkin, at the junction of U.S. 210 and U.S. 169. Further north, around Grand Rapids, where U.S. 2 and U.S. 169 meet, there is also some good largemouth fishing, and the writer has enjoyed some excellent sport fly-rod fishing for largemouth in the lakes around the small town of Marcell, north of Grand Rapids on State Highway 38.

From Bemidji eastward towards Grand Rapids, encompassing part of the Mississippi River, there is good muskellunge fishing in BOY RIVER (19) and DEER LAKE (20), as well as many of the smaller, less known lakes in the group. The MANTRAP LAKES (21), west of Walker and north of Park Rapids, number a total of sixteen, in one small group, with fine fishing for muskellunge, smallmouth, largemouth, crappies and sunfish. There are many resorts in the area and every accommodation. The lakes can be reached from U.S. 71 between Park Rapids and Bemidji; and from two transverse secondary roads, joining U.S. 71 and State Highway 34 between Walker and Park Rapids.

Duluth anglers can reach some good fishing lakes only fifteen miles northwest of the city via U.S. 53. FISH LAKE (22) has excellent angling for walleyes and northern pike; and in the same area RICE (23), CARIBOU (24), ISLAND (25), GRAND (26), LITTLE GRAND (27) and AMINCON (28) are good. Besides the other species Amincon also has muskellunge. Duluth fishermen can also quickly reach a total of twenty-three trout streams flowing from the highland west and north of Lake Superior. Some of this fishing is found within the city limits, while for some you must travel close to one hundred miles, following U.S. 61 east towards Grand Marais. Almost every river flowing into Lake Superior has some trout fishing. The catch will mostly be rainbows but there are some brook trout and browns. Rainbows and browns of better than 14 pounds have been taken, and the Minnesota record for brook trout is a hefty 9 pounds.

As in other rivers flowing into the Great Lakes, the trout sometimes run out into the lake. There they feed heavily and when they return to the stream, fat and strong, they provide excellent fishing. In the lake these brookies are usually referred to as "coasters." They work along the shallows of the big lake, hide under the rocks, feed sometimes in only a foot or so of water. At such times they will take flies and small spoons, and put up a fine fight.

Some few brown trout also live in Lake Superior, moving into the river mouths to spawn in the fall, but they are not frequently taken by anglers.

To the west of the city, Duluth fishermen take bass, walleyes and catfish in the St. Louis River (29), which crosses U.S. 2 in several places on its way to Lake Superior from the Fond du Lac State Forest; and in its tributary the Cloquet (30), which touches U.S. 33 at several spots north of U.S. 2.

SOUTHERN AREA

Where the topography of Minnesota breaks away from the rocky, forested Lake Superior drainage and slopes southward to the more rolling, though still green-covered, central and southern part of the state, bluegills appear. These little fish are good fighters in the cool waters of Minnesota lakes and a growing clan of admirers goes for them with small poppers, hair bugs and dry flies. Since the fish have very small mouths, the lures must also be very small. This is the species youngsters usually go for when they make their first try at fishing, but that is no indication that they are easy to take. Casters must remember to stay well back from the edge of the weed bed or brush pile where the fish like to hide out, and make long, careful casts.

Another dweller of most Minnesota lakes, aside from the cold-water area of the Lake Superior drainage, is the crappie. The black crappie is found almost universally in the central and southern lakes, while the white crappie is limited to the southern area. These fish like weed beds and in spring are also found around sand bars and gravel reefs. They take more readily than any other fish in Minnesota, and grow to sizes up to 1½ pounds. Like the bluegill, the crappie is becoming more popular every day with those who use extra-light spinning tackle.

Aside from the lakes, there is some good river fishing in southern Minnesota. The main river is, of course, the Mississippi (31), which has its source in Lake Itasca, on State Highway 31, southwest of Bemidji, winds eastward and then south to Minneapolis and St. Paul. There it joins with the St. Croix, and forms the balance of the border with Wisconsin. In the central portion, from St. Cloud, at the junction of Interstate 94 and State Highway 23, down to Anoka on U.S. 10, northwest of St. Paul, the Mississippi is known for good fishing for muskellunge and smallmouth. Other parts of the upper river produce smallmouth, largemouth, pike and walleye. As you proceed south the stream widens and becomes slower, with many sloughs and backwaters, in which there is often outstanding fishing for largemouth black bass. The fly-rod popper is very good for this fishing, the popper being cast in around stumps, weeds, and along shorelines. Sunfish, walleye and sauger, northern pike, white bass, crappie and catfish are also found, and in some areas paddlefish and sturgeon are taken occasionally. The Mississippi is so large and variegated that anglers often find it difficult to find the fishing. It's a safe bet that enquiries at the tackle shops in any town along the river will elicit details on where and what to fish for locally as well as what is the best method. It is also a general condition along the river that there is good fishing of some kind below the dams and wingdams; and in every backwater there are almost certain to be panfish.

The ST. CROIX RIVER (32) which forms a considerable amount of the eastern border of Minnesota offers about the same conditions as the lower Mississippi— there is some fishing almost everywhere, and occasional good fishing "where you can find it." Two of the tributaries of the St. Croix offer very good angling for smallmouth black bass, largemouth black bass, walleyes, northerns, bluegills and crappie. These are the SNAKE (33), which crosses U.S. 61 at Pine City, and the KETTLE (34), which is accessible from State Highway 48 from Hinckley on U.S. 61. East of U.S. 61 both rivers flow through primitive country and it takes some hiking to get to the best water.

The MINNESOTA RIVER (35), a major tributary of the Mississippi, flows across much of southern Minnesota. Its fishing is pretty much limited to channel catfish and blue catfish. The same kind of fishing is found in the BLUE EARTH RIVER (36), flowing into the Minnesota near Mankato, at the junction of U.S. 14 and U.S. 169.

Near the southern limits of the Mississippi within Minnesota, is the WHITE-WATER RIVER (37), entering the big river about sixteen miles north of Winona. This is considered one of the state's best brown-trout streams. Much of the Whitewater is paralleled by State Highway 74.

By the very nature of the countryside, Minnesota is ideal camping territory, and recognizing this, state authorities have provided a fine system of campsites in state forests. The angler who plans this kind of fishing vacation should write for the pamphlet "Camping in Minnesota," which is obtainable from Minnesota Vacations, State Capitol, St. Paul 1, Minnesota. It lists all the state parks, wayside parks, recreational areas and state and national forests, along with information about what camping and fishing facilities are available. While a check mark under "fishing" on such a list doesn't necessarily mean that the fishing will be good, it can mean just that in Minnesota, more often than not.

Those who tow their boats behind their cars should also obtain "Water Fun in Minnesota" from the same source. This gives the Minnesota boat-and-water safety laws, and lists public access spots to many Minnesota lakes and streams.

MINNESOTA FISHING REGULATIONS

Resident Fishing License $2.25
     Combination, husband and wife $2.75
Nonresident Fishing License $5.25
     Combination, husband and wife $8.25

SEASONS AND LIMITS

Species	Open Season	Limits Daily	Possession
Northern Pike or Pickerel	May 12–Feb. 15	3	3
Walleye, Sauger	May 12–Feb. 15	6	6
Muskellunge	May 12–Feb. 15	Minimum size limit 30″ except in Little Shoepack, Shoepack, St. Louis County, minimum limit 26″.	
Black Bass, all waters east and north of U.S. 53 from Duluth to International Falls	May 26–Feb. 15	6	6
All other waters	June 9–Feb. 15		
Trout, except Lake Trout	April 28–Sept. 15	10	10
Lake Trout, Lake Superior only	Dec. 30–Sept. 25	3	3
	Nov. 5–Oct. 10	3	3
Crappie	Continuous	15	30
Sunfish, Bluegill	Continuous	30	30
Rock bass, White Bass	Continuous	15	30
		either, or in aggregate	
Grayling	No open season except by special regulation		
Splake	No open season except by special regulation		

Special regulations apply in Minnesota-Wisconsin Boundary waters; and in Minnesota-Dakota, and Minnesota-Canada boundary waters, and must be checked when you purchase your fishing license.

For complete regulations write: Department of Conservation, Saint Paul 1, Minnesota.

Central
States

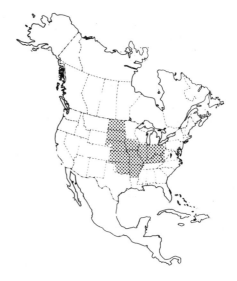

The states which lie in a broad belt down the center of the United States belong basically to the drainage system of two great rivers, the Missouri, which traverses North Dakota, South Dakota, then forms the boundary between Nebraska and Iowa and a part of Kansas and Missouri; and the Mississippi, which comes down out of Minnesota in the Great Lakes area, to form the boundary between Iowa and Illinois and Illinois and Missouri and then forms the eastern boundary of the southernmost of these central states, Arkansas.

While on a relief map this central area of the continent shows as the wide trough of the Great Plains, there is much variety to the topography. The Dakotas have their Badlands, Nebraska and Kansas the rolling prairies, Oklahoma its vast, flat fields, Iowa its lush farm lands and Missouri and Arkansas the rolling wooded hills of the Ozarks.

This is the agricultural heart of the continent yet every state in the belt has its own variety of fishing, some of it in natural waters, but more of it in impoundments controlling the great rivers. Thus the fish vary from the warm-water species native to the Mississippi and Missouri and their tributaries, to those species which require cooler waters, the basses, and even in many cases, the trouts. Fishing can vary from the pleasant wading in the small streams of the Flint Hills of southeastern Kansas to a trip to the waters of the Rosebud Indian Reservation, on the border between South Dakota and Nebraska, from floating the famous Ozark streams to fishing in an air-conditioned in summer, heated in winter fishing dock on one of the vast reservoirs found in most of these states.

231

OHIO

The State of Ohio feels the influence of Lake Erie on the north, where the rivers flow through typical Lake Erie flatlands, and the Ohio River, on the south, which drains most of the hilly southern part of the state to the Mississippi. In general, the terrain is ideally suited to agriculture and by the same token it is not particularly good from the fisherman's point of view. Most of the lakes are soft-bottomed and muddy, as well as very shallow. The largest lake in the state, Grand Lake St. Mary's, 15,000 acres in size, has a maximum depth of 6½ feet. To the further detriment of good fishing, many of the streams which should provide sport have been heavily polluted by industrial waste. Under pressure from Ohio sportsmen, efforts are now being made to restore these streams, particularly the Ohio itself, but to date very little progress has been made.

In spite of this situation, Ohio anglers have a considerable number of lakes and farm ponds to fish in, and these have been augmented by numerous reservoirs, and the picture is greatly improved by the fact that almost the entire northern border touches Lake Erie, where fortunately there is some outstanding fishing to be had.

The species commonly found in the inland waters are largemouth black bass, smallmouth black bass, white bass, "blue pike" (which is probably merely a color phase of the walleye), walleye, northern pike, crappie, bluegill, channel catfish, bullhead and carp. All three trout, rainbows, browns and eastern brook trout, are found in very limited waters; and the muskellunge, a species anglers generally expect to find in colder, more northern waters, has been planted and is doing well in a few streams and lakes, to the extent that fish up to 30 pounds have been caught.

In Lake Erie the species are smallmouth black bass, white bass, also called locally "stripers," walleyes, yellow perch, crappie, sheepshead, bluegills, catfish and carp. The largemouth black bass is the most widespread of all the species, adapting itself admirably to the shallow, warm waters of the lakes and ponds. In the larger lakes they go as high as 9 pounds, and 5-pounders are fairly common. In smaller lakes and ponds the average is more likely to be two pounds. The top weight for smallmouth black bass in Ohio is 5 pounds, while northern pike go as high as 16 pounds. Walleyes run from 3 to 10 and the top weight taken in Ohio was a 15-pound fish taken from Lake Pymatuning in 1955. The crappie and panfish are average in size throughout the state; while in Lake Erie yellow perch are taken up to 2½ pounds and white bass to better than 3 pounds.

Those who fish the Ohio and its tributaries come up with substantial members of the catfish family. The top blue catfish weighed 92 pounds, but fish of this size are not caught nowadays, that one being taken away back in 1911. Channel catfish can run to 30 pounds, and a shovelhead or flathead catfish weighing 58 pounds was caught in the Muskingum River in 1958.

The waters of both the Lake Erie and the Ohio River drainage areas turn up a sizable number of muskellunge every year, and Ohioans claim there are two varieties, the northern, which is spotted, and the southern, which wears stripes. In either case, he is a hard-fighting gamefish, and enough of them have been caught to encourage the Fish Management authorities to continue stocking the species. Some lakes which have been stocked are Deer Creek Reservoir, and Piedmont Lake, near Piedmont, on U.S. Highway 22 west of Steubenville; Clendening Reservoir, near the town of Tippecanoe on State Highway 8, in the same area; Hoover Reservoir, immediately north of Columbus; Lake White, near Waverly, on U.S. Highway 23, south of Chillicothe; Leesville Lake, near Palermo, off state Road 39 east from New Philadelphia; Rocky Fork Lake, near Hillsboro, at the Junction of U.S. 62 and U.S. 50; Lake Jackson, near Oak Hill, off U.S. 35 west from Gallipolis. They have also been planted in the Shade River, Leading River and Muskingum River in southeastern Ohio, east of Zanesville. The largest muskie ever taken in Ohio, a 30-pounder, came from Wills Creek in this area.

In the northern part of the state most muskies caught are taken at the mouths of the various rivers running into Lake Erie, especially in the marshy areas.

While this sounds like a lot of muskie fishing, actually the fish is a little unpredictable anywhere, and even more so in Ohio. Nevertheless, the species may be taken in widely different waters, and even as recently as 1963 George Robey, Jr., outdoor writer for the *Columbia Citizen,* reports tangling with seven muskies, up to 36 inches, in one afternoon in Dillon Lake, on Route 146 north of Zanesville.

The fisherman in Ohio has no trouble reaching the fishing waters of the state. A network of major highways covers the whole area. Fast east-west transportation can be found on the Ohio Turnpike in the north, and several connecting Interstate Highways provide the same easy access north and south. A tremendous network of excellent highways ties these all together.

As far as the fisherman is concerned, the climate is at its best in the spring, when it is neither cold enough to demand heavy clothing, nor hot enough to down the fish. The summer weather is definitely hot, with consequent poorer fishing, at least till the cool of the evening. In the fall the days are cool enough for angling to pick up again. Winter is cold enough for freezing of the ponds and lakes, and there is some excellent ice fishing in these as well as in shallow Lake Erie.

The fishing in Ohio is varied enough that every angler must be his own judge as to what tackle he will choose, but because of the shallowness of much of the fishable water, the various forms of the fly-rod outfit are highly regarded here. Bass, and panfish, in particular, come up to surface or just-under-the-surface lures, and even the muskie will come up to big plugs played on or close to the surface. It should be remembered that most inland waters are small in size as well as shallow, and tackle therefore need not be big. An 8½-foot fly rod with GBF is ideal for throwing bass poppers or streamers, and can also handle lighter flies when suitable; and the lighter plug and spinning outfits are also the order here.

In most of Ohio's lakes, fishing for largemouth black bass is usually at its best in the early spring, in March, April and May. Ohioans recommend fishing deep at this time, on the theory that the fish are still sluggish from the cold of winter; but bait and fly casters take their share with top-water lures, too, especially among the weed beds and lily pads. The top-water outfit is definitely the most successful for evening-fishing later in the summer when the heat keeps the fish dormant during the daytime. After the summer lull of June, July and August, largemouth fishing picks up again in September and remains good through November.

In general, there is little to watch for with regard to potentially dangerous game or reptiles. However, much of Ohio is within the range of the eastern Massassauga rattler as well as the copperhead, and fishermen must watch for these two, even though they are so rarely seen.

LAKE FISHING—NORTHERN OHIO

Three of the best known fishing lakes in Ohio are in the extreme northeastern corner. They are PYMATUNING (1), MOSQUITO (2) and BERLIN RESERVOIRS (3). Pymatuning lies on the border between Pennsylvania and Ohio, shared by the two states. Anglers holding an Ohio fishing license may fish from a boat anywhere except in the Wildlife Sanctuary at the northeast side of Pymatuning. But the islands are under Pennsylvania's jurisdiction, and to fish from an island a Pennsylvania license is required. The lake is reached on the Ohio shore via State Highway 7, north from Youngstown to Williamsfield, then turn east on U.S. 322 to the lakeside town of Simons; or further north a gravel road leads in from State Road 7, four miles north of Andover, to Padanaram, again on the lake.

Mosquito Lake is about five miles north of Warren and Interstate 5 crosses the southern end. There are boats available at the town of Cortland on Interstate 5, and also further north at Mecca, where State Highway 88 crosses the lake. Berlin Reservoir is north of Alliance, the outskirts of the city extending almost to the lake. State Highway 14A from Salem to Ravenna, and State Highway 183 from Alliance to Atwater both cross narrow parts of the lake. Boats are available at Alliance and North Benton on the south shore, and at Limaville on the west.

LAKE MOGADORE (4), which is only about five miles from the eastern outskirts of Akron, can be reached from State Highway 43, south from State Road 18 at Brimfield. There are bass, crappie, bluegills, catfish and some muskies. NIMISILA RESERVOIR (5), fifteen miles south of Akron on State Highway 93 offers the same fishing, minus the muskies.

In the central part of northern Ohio, CLEAR FORK RESERVOIR (6) has bass, bluegills and walleyes. The lake can be reached via State Highway 97, northwest of Lexington, which is seven miles south of Mansfield on U.S. 42. Another lake, to the northeast of Mansfield, which offers good fishing at times for crappie, bluegills, bass and catfish is CHARLES MILL RESERVOIR (7), at the junction of Interstate 71 and U.S. 30. Further south, at Fredericktown, at the junction of State Highways 95 and 13, KNOX LAKE (8) has the same kind of fishing.

The HOOVER RESERVOIR (9), northeast of Columbus, is reached by State Highway 161 from Central College, or from Galena, on the lake shore a mile east of State Highway 3 at the north end of the lake. Boats are available at all three of these lakes and accommodations are plentiful in the surrounding towns.

Two other well known fishing lakes lie in the northwestern part of the state. GRAND LAKE, or ST. MARY'S LAKE (10), or, as it is sometimes called, Grand Lake St. Mary's, is near the town of St. Mary's, about twenty-five miles southwest of Lima. U.S. 127 skirts the western end and State Highway 29 extends along the entire north shore. Anglers will find accommodations at St. Mary's and Celina. INDIAN LAKE (11) is about the same distance southeast of Lima, via State Highway 196 to New Hampshire, then U.S. 33 to the lake. The towns of Lakeview and Russells Point both offer accommodations and boats.

Grand Lake has the distinction of emptying its waters into both of the major Ohio watersheds. The outlet at the eastern end is to the St. Mary's River and thence to the Maumee and Lake Erie, while that to the west is through Beaver Creek to the Wabash and eventually to the Mississippi. This lake, built as a feeder reservoir for the Miami-Erie Canal System, is generally regarded as the best largemouth black-bass lake in Ohio. The fishing is good all spring and summer, with best spring-time catches on live bait, while in the summertime the fly fishermen and those who use other forms of surface lures score the best catches.

Both Grand Lake and Indian Lake have good populations of largemouth black bass, crappie, walleye, sunfish and channel catfish. Indian Lake also offers some fishing for smallmouth black bass but it is best known for its sometimes exceptionally good panfishing. Artificials produce the best catches and the spring is the top time, though fishing remains good all summer. In this lake small white wet flies are highly productive of crappie, both black and white varieties.

LORAMIE LAKE (12), near Minster, between State Roads 119 and 705, south of Grand Lake, is also very good at times for bass, bluegills, catfish and crappie. Boats are available at Minster.

LAKE FISHING—SOUTHERN OHIO

In southern Ohio, along the eastern side of the state, anglers will find the ATWOOD RESERVOIR (13) eight miles west of Carrollton, on State Highway 39; and LEESVILLE RESERVOIR (14), to the south, which can be reached via State Highway 332 from Carrollton. Besides largemouth black bass, crappie, bluegills and catfish, which are common to both lakes, Leesville has some muskellunge.

Three other major lakes in eastern Ohio are TAPPAN (15), CLENDENING (16) and PIEDMONT RESERVOIRS (17), located roughly in that area between Liverpool and Cambridge. All these lakes have good fishing for largemouth, crappie, bluegills, channel catfish and carp. Clendening also has some good smallmouth fishing and on occasion a few muskies are taken. Tappan is known for good bank fishing for bass, walleyes and panfish, while Piedmont's reputation is for big muskies, bass, panfish and catfish. Motors are limited to 6 horsepower on Piedmont and Clendening. Tappan Reservoir is on U.S. 36 and 250 between Cadiz and Dennison. Boats are available at Tappan. To reach Piedmont you take U.S. 22 southwest from Cadiz to the town of Piedmont; and from the same highway you can turn north at Smyrna, west of Piedmont, and follow State Highway 8 to Tippecanoe on Clendening Reservoir.

In central Ohio BUCKEYE LAKE (18) is a good bass-fishing spot and also has panfish and catfish. This is one of the state's most popular ice-fishing spots in winter. The lake is only three miles off U.S. 40 (Interstate 70) halfway between Columbus and Zanesville. It can be reached via State Highway 13 from Linnville on U.S. 40, then west on a gravel road at Thornville to Millersport on the lake. Or you can come in from Lancaster to the south, on State Highway 37, to the Millersville road. Another means of approach is via State Highway 79 south from Hebron to the village of Buckeye Lake on the north shore.

On State Highway 146 immediately northwest of Zanesville, DILLON RESERVOIR (19) has also developed into a muskie lake of some repute, the fish hitting well to such lures as the bombers and L.S. Bass Masters. There are no hotels as yet, but accommodations are readily available at Zanesville. A limited number of boats will be found at Pleasant Valley, halfway up the lake.

Well to the south is JACKSON LAKE (20), two miles via gravel road west of the town of Oak Hill, which is on State Highway 93. This lake has quite good fishing for largemouth black bass and sunfish, and boats are available at the lake.

Another lake of major size in southern Ohio is ROCKY FORK (21), reached via U.S. 50 between Chillicothe and Hillsboro. State Highway 124 runs from Hillsboro to Marshall, where a gravel road covers the rest of the distance to the lake; boats are available. There are some bass and crappie, but this lake is especially known for its good bluegill fishing.

Over towards Cincinnati, where U.S. 68 and State Highway 32 come together, GRANT LAKE (22), although small, is an excellent producer of big bluegills and anglers also make some fine catches of largemouth black bass. Rubber spiders are very good on this lake, but all the popular bass lures will take fish.

In addition to the larger lakes and reservoirs, there are numerous farm ponds in Ohio, many of them very small, but most of them good producers of panfish and some largemouth black bass. There are also many pay lakes, where costs range upward from $1 per day. In the pay lakes the fishing is generally for channel catfish, bullheads, crappie, bluegills, yellow perch and walleyes, in that order, plus some largemouth black bass. Some of these lakes can provide excellent fishing, as for instance CHOPPER LAKE (23), at Beverly, on the Muskingum River, on State Highway 60, north of Marietta. This small pond, operated privately by the Lakeside Motel, has produced largemouth black bass up to 8 pounds, as well as good-sized bluegills. Lakes of this type are becoming more common in Ohio every year.

A list of public fishing areas, both free and pay, and some ponds which are fishable with permission of the landowner, can be obtained from the Ohio Department of Natural Resources, Division of Wildlife, Columbus, Ohio. The list gives complete details as to the types of fish to be expected and indicates whether there are camping and boating facilities, as well as giving detailed highway directions on how to reach the lakes. Another very complete folder entitled "Ohio State Parks" lists all lakes and ponds under the jurisdiction of that organization, with details as to availability of boats, the use of motors and such pertinent information. Those who bring their own boats or motors should remember that because of the small size of the lakes motors are not permitted in many cases.

LAKE ERIE

The main sport-fishing species in LAKE ERIE (24) are the white bass, perch, walleye and smallmouth black bass. While some boat-rental agencies can be found in most of the ports along the entire Lake Erie shore, the concentration of these services is in the area around Sandusky Bay, and east as far as Lorain, the boats running out to fish the islands north of the mouth of Sandusky Bay. Out here the angler has a fine choice of fish, almost year-round. The smallmouth fishing starts in May around the well-named Bass Islands. From May through September many party boats operate in the area, carrying from six to ten anglers. Party-boat angling is most often done with minnows in 20 feet or more of water, around the small islands. Minnows take the bass when nothing else will. However, as they school up to spawn, they come nearer the surface and can be taken on casting gear, too. Popular in this Lake Erie fishing are the Mepps, and plugs from ⅛ to ½ ounce. Even when the fish are in comparatively shallow water, the lure should be allowed to get down to the rocks.

As summer warms the water up, the fish again retreat to the deeper holes and

A typical smallmouth black bass stream in Ohio. Such streams are highly productive, especially in spring and fall.

again deep-fished minnows are the best bet. In September the smallmouths again move to the shallows and for a brief spell the casters again 'have their day.

Following right on the heels of the smallmouths when they arrive in May are the white bass, which move in about May 20th. They use the same water as the smallmouths. The white bass is a school fish and when a school is located the activity can be fantastic as the eager fish hit almost anything that is offered. Early in the season the best white bass grounds are around the Bass Islands, then they move northward toward the Canadian shore. During August the great schools can often be located far out in the lake, and provide the same exciting fishing.

The best table fish of them all, though Lake Erie is favored in the edible types available, is the walleye, caught mainly by trolling over the reefs in Lake Erie. Vying with it for flavor, and probably exceeding it for popularity with sportsmen, is the yellow perch, a very abundant school fish. If you locate one, your chances of a good catch are reasonable. They hang out in schools around the reefs in fairly deep water and are mostly fished with two hooks on a spreader, each baited with a minnow.

This shore of Lake Erie also offers some good shore fishing. There are good locations on the docks at Sandusky Battery Park, Sandusky Bay Bridge, and also at Crystal Rock, Danbury, White's Landing, Cedar Point and many other spots on both sides of the bay. The water in Sandusky Bay is very shallow, but skiffs can be used, and there are boat launching facilities at Sandusky at the Municipal Ramp. There are also launching sites and boat-rental agencies at East Harbor on the Marblehead Peninsula which encloses Sandusky Bay. There's good fishing for largemouth and panfish in East Harbor and the whole lake is at the harbor's mouth.

Yellow perch and white bass are taken year-round, and catfishing enthusiasts find this the choice spot in Ohio, particularly during the spawning run in May and

June. The best areas are at the mouths of the rivers and around the bridges where there is added current in the bay water.

Crappie, sheepshead, bluegills, walleyes and occasional smallmouth and large-mouth black bass are also taken; and there are bullheads and carp and a variety of other coarse fish.

On summer nights, the visitor to Lake Erie's shores will often see the flash of dozens of lanterns bobbing out in the lake—these are the lights used by anglers who are after "blue pike," a local variation of the walleye. The lanterns are used to attract minnows, which are then dipped and used for bait; and the lights also attract the blue pike. This species doesn't grow as large as the yellow walleye, but provides good eating, and is found alongshore off almost every city along the southern shore of the lake.

Boat-launching facilities may be found at many points alongshore. Those listed by the Division of Wildlife of the Ohio Department of Natural Resources are found at Conneaut, Ashtabula, North Ferry, Cleveland (3), Lorain, Sandusky, East Harbor, Catawba, and one each at the mouths of Little Portage River, Portage River and Turtle Creek. There is also a launching facility on South BASS ISLAND (25).

Those who plan to operate their own boats on Lake Erie should obtain the Department's sheet showing the launching sites and giving storm-warning information for the complete Ohio shoreline. Lake Erie can blow up rough very suddenly and fishermen must watch the weather closely.

Guides for this area can be obtained through Nate Ladd, Postmaster at Put-in-Bay, who can give addresses for the Bass Island area, Gem Beach, Catawba Island, Port Clinton. Operating out of Toledo, Glenn Lau, 378 Millard Street, provides a service for both fishermen and duck hunters, guaranteeing "no fish, no pay."

During the winter there is excellent yellow-perch fishing through the ice in Sandusky Bay, December and January being the top season.

RIVER FISHING

River fishing in Ohio is very spotty, largely because of the pollution problem. The rivers flowing into Lake Erie which are fishable in one place or another are the ASHTABULA (26), at Ashtabula; the GRAND (27), at Fairport Harbor; the CUYAHOGA (28), at Cleveland; the BLACK (29), at Lorain; the HURON (30), at Rye Beach; the VERMILION (31), at Vermilion; the SANDUSKY (32), at Sandusky Bay; the TOUSSAINT (33), at Locust Point; and the MAUMEE (34), at Toledo. In the lower waters of these rivers there is usually some good fishing in the spring when fish move in on high water from Lake Erie. This situation holds up until early summer, then fades. The catch will generally include bass, walleye and panfish. South of Conneaut, in the extreme northeast corner of Ohio, CONNEAUT CREEK (35) has some muskies and smallmouth black bass, and these are found in limited numbers also in the Grand River.

Some Ohioans float the rivers in a few places but this fishing is not good enough nor consistent enough to be anything more than an occasional venture.

On the east-central border the MUSKINGUM RIVER (36) provides some smallmouth fishing, but again, it is very spotty and it takes a lot of traveling from place to place to locate the fishable and productive water. Far upstream, in the central part of the state, some of its tributaries also hold bass, and, in spite of their small size, have a few muskies. The main tributaries of interest to the angler are the MOHICAN

Lake Erie

TOLEDO

CONNEAUT
Conneaut Cr.
ASHTABULA

GRAND R.

Pimatuning
Lake
ANDOVER
WILLIAMSFIELD

MECCA

CLEVELAND

Mogadore Res.
CORTLAND
WARREN
Youngstown

AKRON
ATWATER
LIMAVILLE
Berlin Res.
N. BENTON
ALLIANCE · SALEM
Nimisila Res.

TUSCARAWAS
JEROMESVILLE
WOOSTER

Grand Lake or
St Mary's Lake
LIMA

CELINA
ST MARY'S
LAKEVIEW

Indian
Lake
HAMPSHIRE
RUSSELLS POINT

Loramie
Lake

MINSTER

Clear Fork Res.
Charles
Mill Res.
Clear Fork Res.
LEXINGTON
MANSFIELD

Knox
Lake
FREDERICKSTON
BRINKHAVEN

Atwood Res.
CARROLTON
Leesville Res.

DENNISON
Tappan
Res.
CADIZ

Clendening Res.
TIPPECANOE
PIEDMONT
SMYRNA
Piedmont
Res.

COSHOCTON

GALENA

Hoover
Res.

Dillon
Res.
PLEASANT VALLEY

COLUMBUS

HEBRON
Buckeye Lake
MILLERSPORT
THORNVILLE
LINNVILLE
LANCASTER

LICKING R.

ZANESVILLE
Senecaville
Res.

STILLWATER R.

TWIN CR.

DAYTON

CAESAR CR.

CAESAR CR.
ANDERSON CR.
RATTLESNAKE CR.
PAINT CR.

MIAMI R.

LITTLE

HILLSBORO
MARSHALL
Rocky Fork Lake

WEST BRANCH

Lake
Grant

CINCINNATI

OHIO RIVER

OHIO BRUSH CR.

SCIOTO R.

Jackson
Lake
OAK HILL

Chopper
Lake
BEVERLY

MUSKINGUM R.

MARIETTA

PORTMOUTH

N

OHIO

0   5   10   20
SCALE of MILES

(37), KILLBUCK (38), TUSCARAWAS (39) and LICKING RIVER (40). U.S. 36 runs along the Tuscarawas east of Coshocton; the Killbuck can be reached from State Highway 76 between Coshocton and Wooster; and the Mohican, further west, is crossed by U.S. 30 at Jeromesville, and U.S. 62 at Brinkhaven, as well as by several county roads. The Licking River wanders across country from Utica to the Muskingum system at Dillon Reservoir just north of Zanesville. The Licking is probably the most attractive of the group, with much of the rocky and gravelly bottom the smallmouth bass prefers, and some quite good fishing for this species can be enjoyed.

The SCIOTO RIVER (41), which enters the Ohio on the southern border, at Portsmouth, has some reputation for occasional good muskie fishing. U.S. 23 parallels the river for many miles upstream and the balance can be reached from U.S. 35 to the east. In the Dayton area there are a number of rivers which, although heavily fished, do produce smallmouth black bass. These are CAESAR CREEK (42), ANDERSON FORK (43), OHIO BRUSH CREEK (44), PAINT CREEK (45) and RATTLESNAKE CREEK (46). However, the fishing is limited in scope and anyone planning to fish these streams should first spend a little time in any tackle shop in Dayton, finding out if they're worth trying at the moment, and obtaining directions as to exactly where to fish the creeks. When these streams are producing you may also catch largemouth black bass, shovelhead catfish and channel catfish. And nearby LITTLE MIAMI (47), TWIN CREEK (48), great MIAMI (49) and STILLWATER RIVER (50) also produce largemouth.

Those who fish with live bait will have the best luck with minnows for the largemouth black bass, and craws for the catfish. The best of the artificial bass lures seems to be the Yellow Shyster.

Anglers planning to visit Ohio should obtain the Ohio Outdoor Map and list of Public Hunting and Fishing Areas and Camp Sites from the Ohio Department of Highways, 1500 Dublin Road, Columbus 12, Ohio.

OHIO FISHING REGULATIONS

Resident Fishing License $2.25
Nonresident Fishing License $5.25
Nonresident 15-Day License $3.25

SEASONS AND LIMITS

With few exceptions there is no closed season, no length, bag or possession limits. While regulations may change from year to year, currently the only exception is Pymatuning Lake, where the following bag limits hold:

Species	Daily Bag Limit	Possession Limit
Yellow Pike, Perch (Walleye)	10	Maximum total possession
Black Bass	10	Limits not to exceed two days'
Muskellunge	2	legal bag limit
All other fish	none	No maximum bag limits

For complete regulations write: Department of Natural Resources, Division of Wildlife, 1500 Dublin Road, Columbus 12, Ohio.

INDIANA

Lying as it does in the industrial heart of the country and having neither a mountain range, a series of hills nor a prominent string of lakes within its boundaries, the State of Indiana would seem to be among the least blessed, from the sportsman's point of view. However, certain topographic features provide more fishing water than would be apparent at first glance, and, in fact, if it were not for the problem of pollution due to the high industrialization of the state, there would be some very fine fishing.

A small portion of the northern border faces on the southern tip of Lake Michigan, providing a limited Great Lakes fishery for large perch; and the southern and southwestern borders are marked by the Ohio and Wabash River. Their tributaries drain the state from far up into the interior. There are also numerous small lakes, especially across the northern part of Indiana. These vary from fresh, clear, glacier lakes (in the northeast) which are excellent habitat for the basses and pikes, to small, warm-water ponds more fitted for panfish varieties. In addition, some suitable waters have been stocked with trout. Thus, according to the nature of the water, in Indiana the fisherman may find largemouth black bass, smallmouth black bass, redear sunfish, rock bass, walleye pike, northern pike, brown, brook or rainbow trout.

Because of its geographic location, Indiana is readily reached from almost any part of the eastern half of the United States. The Indiana Expressway skirts the northern part of the state, providing easy access to the lake area of the northeast; and U.S. 30 passes just to the south. U.S. 40 bisects the central part of Indiana, and U.S. 31 (Interstate 65) supplies direct north-south travel from Louisville, Kentucky, to South Bend, near Lake Michigan.

The state enjoys a typical Great Lakes climate—warm summers, usually with moderately cool nights. Since it is so completely industrial and agricultural, there is no wild game of importance to the fisherman, but snakes should always be watched for, especially in the southern half of the state.

Since the streams are small, the trout fisherman will want an 8-foot rod, HDH line, and a fine, tapered leader. Bass fishermen can use an 8½-foot rod with GBF line to throw popping bugs and streamer flies. All the standard patterns are used with success on Indiana rivers and lakes.

Spin fishermen will also find a small outfit sufficient; and the smaller spinners, jigs and top-water lures are all successful, both on lake and stream.

Indiana's two largest rivers, the Wabash and the Ohio, are so warm and have been so adversely affected by the industrial nature of the state that fishing in them is limited to catfish. However, the northern tributaries of the Wabash are considerably better, particularly the TIPPECANOE (1) and the EEL (2), where there are largemouth black bass, smallmouth black bass, northern pike, and catfish. The Tippecanoe has long been a favorite stream for canoe-trippers, and there are a number of good fishing lakes along the way, and especially at the northern, or upper end of the stream. This rectangle, bounded by lines drawn from Goshen to Warsaw

242

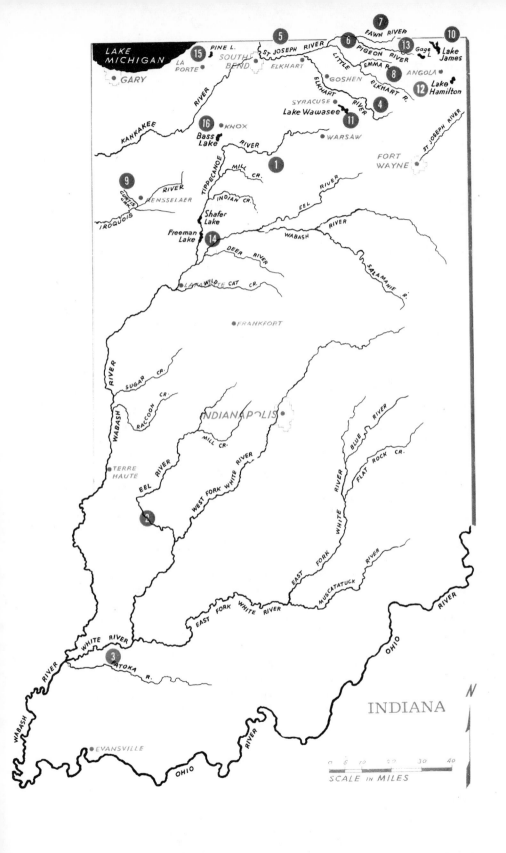

to Fort Wayne, to the Michigan-Ohio corner of the state, holds a great many of the best natural lakes of Indiana. All of them are extensively used for water sports, but nevertheless there is good fishing for bluegills, walleyes, perch and some pretty good-sized bass.

A large tributary of the Wabash, the WHITE RIVER (3), flows southwest through the center of the state to join the Wabash at Mt. Carmel, Illinois. This river is known for its white perch, and in the lower, wider reaches there is some excellent catfishing.

Among the rivers in the northern part of Indiana, the ELKHART (4), east of the city of Elkhart, provides good spring and fall fishing for smallmouth black bass, northern pike and rock bass, while the nearby ST. JOSEPH'S RIVER (5) offers small-mouth black bass, northern pike, rock bass and channel catfish. The PIGEON RIVER (6), near Angola, has trout, bass and pike.

River fishermen in Indiana should remember that the waters here carry a heavy load of silt and are often not clear enough for good fishing until June.

Of some forty-four streams and lakes stocked by the Indiana Department of Conservation with brown, rainbow and brook trout, the top spots are in the north-east, too. You cross the FAWN RIVER (7), one of the best, several times as you drive the Indiana Turnpike. The EMMA and the ELKHART (8) in the Goshen-Angola area. Far to the west, almost on the Illinois line, CURTIS CREEK (9) is also highly regarded as a trout stream. Ask advice on where to fish it at the town of Rensselaer.

The northeastern part of Indiana also has the state's best lake fishing. LAKE JAMES (10) and LAKE WAWASEE (11), near Syracuse, just south of U.S. 6 are the largest. The fishing is for largemouth black bass and smallmouth black bass, northern pike, walleye and crappie, and in spite of the fact that the lake is much used, the fishing remains fairly good year-round.

In the northeastern corner of Indiana, sandwiched between U.S. 6 and the Turnpike, and accessible via U.S. 20 near Angola, HAMILTON LAKE (12) supports a good population of largemouth, northern pike, bluegills and crappie. GAGE LAKE (13), in the same area, adds walleyes and some rainbows.

Directly across the state there is fishing for white bass and catfish in the Monticello area at FREEMAN and SHAFER LAKES 14); PINE LAKE (15), near LaPorte, has largemouth black bass and bluegills; and BASS LAKE (16), near Knox, has the same species plus walleyes.

All the waters of Indiana are easily reached from towns of sufficient size to assure plentiful accommodations of all kinds. Most of the larger lakes have boat-rental agencies at the lakes, and as Tubby Toms, Outdoor Editor of the Indianapolis News, puts it, "The only guide you need in Indiana is a street guide." Get yourself to the lake or stream, and you'll catch the fish without help. However, there are some guides available at Schaffer and Freeman, a favorite resort area.

There are also a great many smaller lakes and ponds, where public access to the fishing water is assured by the Division of Fish and Game. You can obtain this by writing the Commission at the State House, Indianapolis, Indiana, and asking for "Guide to Indiana's Lakes."

INDIANA FISHING REGULATIONS

Resident Fishing License $2.50
Nonresident Fishing License $3.50
Nonresident 14-Day Fishing License $2.50
Trout Stamp $2.00

SEASONS AND LIMITS

On all species except catfish and trout, the open season for fishing in Indiana is from June 16 to April 30. The trout season extends from May 1 to August 31. There is no closed season on catfish.

Species	Bag Limit	Size
Bluegill		
Redeared Sunfish		
Crappie	25	5"
Rock Bass or Goggle-Eye		
Silver or Yellow Bass	6	10"
Black Bass, White Bass, Kentucky Bass		
Walleye (Pike Perch)	6	10"
All Trouts, in aggregate of all kinds	15	7"
Pike or Pickerel	6	

For complete regulations write: Department of Conservation, State Office Building, Indianapolis 9, Indiana.

ILLINOIS

Though the State of Illinois has considerable coastline on Lake Michigan from Chicago north to the Wisconsin border, the sport fishing in these waters is mainly limited to yellow perch which make a seasonal run in the spring and summer. It is to the Mississippi basin that the Illinois fisherman looks for his sport. The Mississippi forms the entire western boundary and into it drain all the major rivers, many of them winding the entire width and others almost the entire length of the state. These include the Rock River on the north; the Illinois, which crosses the north-central area on a northeast to southwest course to empty into the Mississippi far down below St. Louis; and the Ohio, fed by its tributary the Wabash, which pulls all the water from the southeastern part of the State; and many lesser rivers.

The species most commonly caught in Illinois, therefore, are those associated with this great "river road," as Illinois people call it—the basses, sauger, walleye, sunfish, northern pike, crappie and catfish. In addition, in the Mississippi itself the angler may occasionally encounter the paddlefish, known to occur only in the Mississippi, the Missouri, a few of their tributaries, and the Yangtze River in China. The rare hackleback sturgeon is also sometimes found in the Mississippi.

The major lakes of Illinois are also mostly associated with the Mississippi and its tributaries. Even the group of lakes in the northeast corner of the state, known as the Fox Chain-O-Lakes, near the Wisconsin border, and within a few miles of Lake Michigan, sent their waters to the Mississippi through the Fox River and the Illinois.

The state of Illinois is largely urban, with many great cities such as Chicago, Peoria, Springfield and East St. Louis. Hence highway travel is no problem. Interstate Highway 80 joins Chicago and Moline on the western border. Interstate Highway 70 runs from Terre Haute, Indiana, across the south-central area to East St. Louis. And many lesser roads fan out from Chicago like the spokes of a wheel, to provide easy cross-state routes. North-south highways also bisect Illinois only a few miles apart, so the angler can find access to every part of the state.

Fishing is mostly in semi-urban areas, with no problems of wild animals. There are water moccasins, copperheads, and rattlesnakes in some places. The climate is equitable throughout the spring and summer, being considerably warmer in the south and along the Mississippi, however, than in the northeast, where the climate is comparable to that of the southern part of Wisconsin, in the influence of the Great Lakes.

Almost any kind of casting tackle can be used at one time or another. Regulation plug casting and spinning gear is widely used to cast surface plugs for bass, as well as small underwater spoons and plugs. The bait-casting rod is popular with those who use bait, too, live or dead. Minnows, worms, grasshoppers and chunks of fish are all good, but it is always wise to ask at the nearest tackle store as to what is the favorite local bait.

Fly casters are limited to those waters which are reasonably clear. They generally use an 8½-foot fly rod with GBF (WF8F) line or a 9-foot rod with GAF

(WF9) line. Surface bugs and poppers, and bucktails tied on number 2 or 1/0 hooks will take both largemouth and smallmouth bass; while the smaller bucktails and streamers are good for crappie and bluegills. Occasionally, even when the water is muddy, a fly man can coax a big bass up by popping a big lure across the surface, making plenty of noise.

LAKE FISHING IN ILLINOIS

As mentioned earlier, there is some excellent late spring and early summer fishing for yellow perch along the shores of LAKE MICHIGAN (1). Anglers in this area use a distinctive outfit called a "trolley line" when they go for yellow perch. The gear consists of a series of hooks, all baited, and a string attached to a bell which signals when there is a hit. Not exactly a purist's way of angling, but it gets results from this excellent eating fish.

The best fishing in natural lakes in the interior of the state is probably to be found in the FOX CHAIN-O-LAKES (2) in northeastern Illinois. It includes Channel Lake, Lakes Katherine and Marie, Bluff Lake, Petite Lake, Grass Lake, Nippersink Lake, Pistakee Lake, Long Lake and Fox Lake, the largest, and the one for which the group is named. A series of lesser ponds runs southwest from the chain, and the whole group drains through the Fox River to the Illinois and hence the Mississippi. All the lakes in the string have populations of largemouth black bass and a few have smallmouth. Crappie, channel catfish, bluegill, redear, occasional northern pike, walleyes and white or yellow bass, make up the balance of the catch. Grass and Pistakee Lakes are particularly noted for northern pike, a species which is not common elsewhere in Illinois. They also have good spring fishing for bluegills. Fox Lake is noted for some excellent deep trolling with minnows, which produces some whoppers of fish. The other lakes are not quite as deep; anglers get results trolling in the channels and casting to the edges of the channels and in the shallower water. Fly fishermen especially like the spring fishing in the shallows for bluegill and crappie. Throughout the lakes the fishing is at its best in early spring and late fall.

The Fox Chain-O-Lakes is highly developed as a resort area and there are plentiful accommodations everywhere. Boats are always obtainable. Highway access is via State Highway 175 to Antioch, or via the Tri-State Tollway north of Chicago, or via U.S. 1A to the town of Fox Lake. The Chicago, Milwaukee and St. Paul Railway also serves the Fox Lake region.

In Illinois there are two U.S. Department of the Interior Wildlife Refuges which have fishing lakes within their boundaries. These are LAKE CHAUTAUQUA (3), at Havana, on the Illinois River, where U.S. 136 crosses it just south of Peoria; and CRAB ORCHARD LAKE (4), at Carterville, near Marion, at the junction of State Highway 13 and State Highway 37, in the extreme southern part of the state. Crab Orchard has two good sized lakes, Crab Orchard and LITTLE GRASSY (5). Boats are available at both, and there are camp sites at Crab Orchard and Little Grassy. Species include largemouth bass, bluegill, sunfish, crappie, channel catfish, bullhead and white bass.

Also in southern Illinois near Cairo is HORSESHOE LAKE (6), an oxbow of the Mississippi, reached via U.S. 5. There is excellent fishing for bluegill and crappie among the cypress and tupelo trees. The crappie go to 4 pounds and there are occasional catches of smallmouth.

An interesting development for fishermen is the conservation work being done on the diggings left by strip mining for coal. These can produce some fine fishing for largemouth black bass. They are mostly situated in the central part of the state, those around Coal City on Interstate Highway 55, south of Joliet, being rated as among the best. Other strip-mine lakes which have established reputations for producing bass are found near Joliet; Danville, on Interstate Highway 74 close to the Indiana border; Marion, near Crab Orchard Lake on Interstate Highway 57 in southern Illinois; and Galesburg, in the west-central area, on U.S. 150 west of Peoria. Inquiries should be made at local tackle stores as to how to reach the lakes.

The fishing picture is augmented by a considerable number of state and city owned or supervised lakes. Most of them hold largemouth bass and a few have smallmouths. Crappie, channel catfish, bluegills, redear and bullheads make up the balance of the species, along with occasional northerners, walleyes and white bass.

The conditions and facilities around these lakes may vary from year to year. A complete list and current details as to availability of camping sites, boats, bait and supplies, may be obtained from the Division of Fisheries of the State of Illinois, Room 102, State Office Building, Springfield, Illinois.

RIVER FISHING

Even those who live in Illinois—in fact, especially those who live there—do not fully take advantage of the fine fishing of many different types which can be enjoyed in the waters of the Mississippi River. Each area has its specialty but in general the 375 miles of navigable water along the western border of Illinois stacks up as good bass water in all the sloughs and lakes, good habitat for sauger, drum, walleye, channel catfish, blue catfish and flathead catfish in the currents below the dams, and at times good fishing for crappie and white bass in these same waters.

Next to bass, the sauger and white bass have the most appeal for the sports fisherman. These three are found in abundance in the upper waters of the MISSISSIPPI (7). There are thirteen Federal Locks and Dams in this area and each dam has created a lake which may be from ten to forty-five miles in length, and so wide in places that the many islands and bays are confusing. It is hard to believe that this is really a river rather than a large lake. Each dam also provides many spots which are suitable for fish to congregate in, because of the flow of water from the dam, thus adding considerably to the natural habitat they would find along the river.

In general, fishing is best in the spring when the fish make their spawning runs. It dwindles with the heat of July and August, then picks up again in September.

At the dams the sauger and walleye are generally taken on worms fished a couple of feet from the bottom. This usually calls for considerable weight, to get the bait down in the heavy current. Artificial lures are also used successfully, the weighted spinners rating among the favorites. These must be fished very slowly to assure that they get down and stay down.

When the crappie and white bass come in in the spring, they prefer a minnow fished near the surface. Lures fished on or just under the surface are also good fish getters at this time.

In the sloughs and backwaters of the Mississippi fly fishermen come into their own with some terrific catches of largemouth black bass, crappie, bluegills and sunfish. Some of the best results come from casting among the stumps and coves in the shallow backwaters, an exciting and sporty way of fishing. Standard popping bugs

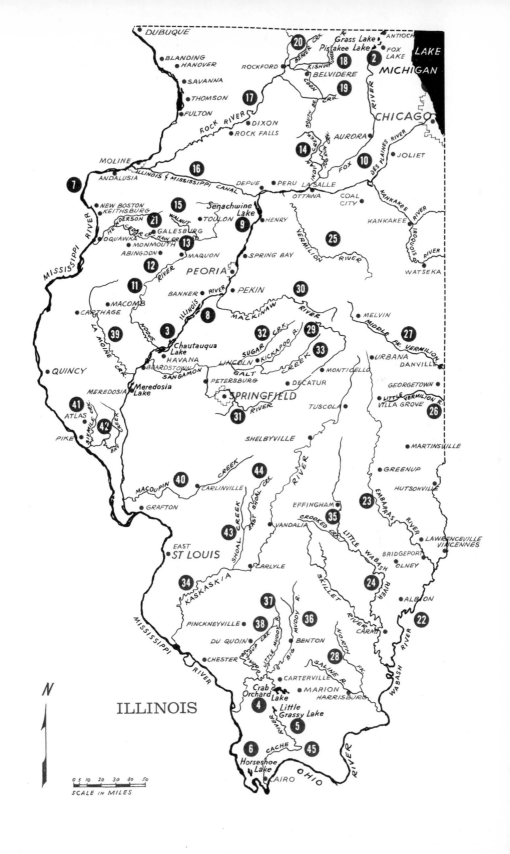

take the bass, and the smaller ones are used for bluegills. A 9-foot fly rod and matching GAF (WF9F) fly line makes a good overall outfit and can throw the larger poppers easily. For sunnies and bream and such smaller fish, an 8-foot rod with HDH (DT6F) line and small wet flies, small bugs and streamers, will do the job.

Boats are available at many cities and towns along the Mississippi and there are many launching sites for those who bring their own craft. However, everyone who plans to go on this river in a boat should pay careful attention to the rules of navigation. The river can be very dangerous, particularly near the dams, and signs should always be heeded as to where to go and where not to go. Boats on the river must have a U.S. Coast Guard Approved Life Preserver for each passenger, and proper running lights if the boat is 16 or more feet in length. Another item every boat fisherman on the Mississippi should have at hand is a 5- to 10-pound anchor, as that much weight is necessary to hold the boat in the strong current. Incidentally, anglers should always anchor from the bow. The current is such that a stern-anchored boat may readily take water.

River charts of the middle and upper Mississippi may be obtained from the Corp of Engineers, U.S. Army, for $1.50, at the District Offices in Rock Island or Chicago; or at St. Louis, Missouri.

Another point which anglers on the Mississippi must remember is that an Illinois fishing license permits fishing on the Mississippi only providing you are not on or anchored to part of another state and are fishing in running water. That is, lakes and backwaters on the other shore, even though you have come by boat, are regarded as part of that state to which they are adjacent, and a suitable license is required.

Some of the best fishing on the Mississippi is in the area of the big bend at the northwest corner of the state of Illinois, south of Dubuque. Here the river widens considerably to form Spring Lake. Guides in this area may be obtained through Richard Brown, Spring Lake Resort, Savannah, Illinois; or Bob Traum, Fin n' Feather Club, Thomson, Illinois.

Other spots along the Mississippi where fishing possibilities are good are Blanding, in the northwest corner of the state, off U.S. 52 near Hanover; Fulton, at the spot where U.S. 30 crosses the river, and where there are several bayous and sloughs; Andalusia, on State Highway 92, west of Moline; Oquaka, immediately to the south, reached via State Highway 164 from Monmouth on U.S. 67; New Boston, immediately north of Savannah; Keithsburg, reached by county road from U.S. 67, northwest of Monmouth; Quincy Bay at U.S. 24 and the river; Pike, at U.S. 54 and the river; Grafton, at the junction of the Illinois and the Mississippi; Chester, on State Highway 3, seventy-five miles south of St. Louis.

Most of the tributaries of the Mississippi provide fishing for the same species as the big river itself. The ILLINOIS RIVER (8), crossing the state from northeast near Chicago, to Grafton, just north of St. Louis, Missouri, is the largest of the tributaries. Favorite fishing spots will be found at Henry on State Highway 29, southwest of LaSalle; Spring Bay on State Highway 87, north of Peoria; Banner, on State Highway 29; Havana, where U.S. 136 crosses the river; Beardstown at U.S. 67 and the river; Meredosia, at State Highway 104 and the river, west of Springfield; DePue, immediately west of Peru on State Highway 29; GOOSE LAKE (9), a few miles further south on State Highway 29, at Henry; French Pass, Grass and Buck, further south, off U.S. 24; and Grafton, at the junction of the Illinois and Mississippi Rivers.

The Fox River (10), a tributary of the Illinois, can be fished from Aurora, on U.S. 30; Ottawa, on U.S. 6, west of Joliet; Olney, on U.S. 50, west of Vincennes; as well as many other places.

The Spoon River (11), entering the Illinois from the north side, at Havana, can be fished at Maquon, south on State Highway 97 from Galesburg on U.S. 34. In the same area, Brush Creek (12), near Abingdon, eleven miles south of Gales-burg on State Highway 41, and Haw Creek (13), six miles east of Galesburg on State Highway 150, can offer some good possibilities, too. The Spoon can also be good north of Peoria around Wyoming on State Highway 17, and nearby are Jug Run Creek and Indian Creek (14) at Toulon on the same highway, and Walnut Creek (15) at West Jersey on State Highway 78. The Spoon River can also be fished from Duncan's Mills, at the junction of U.S. 24 and 136.

The Illinois and Mississippi Canal (16), also called the Hennepin Canal, joins the upper Illinois and the Mississippi. In the canal, between Moline and Peru, there is top fishing for bass, walleye (up to 10 pounds), white or yellow bass, drum, catfish, large crappie and bluegills. The canal is about 80 feet wide and is readily fished by casting from the banks.

In the northern part of the state the Rock River (17) extends from the central Wisconsin border down through Rockford, Dixon and Rock Falls to the Mississippi at Moline. The Rock is noted for some excellent smallmouth black-bass fishing in the spring and also produces walleyes, river perch, channel and flathead catfish. In the Rockford area the Kishwaukee River (18), north of U.S. 20, is heavily fished around Belvidere and in the same neighborhood the Coon River (19) is good. Slightly to the north, near Poplar Grove on State Highway 173, Beaver Creek (20) also provides some fishing.

There are smallmouth bass as well as the other species common to Illinois waters in Elk Horn, Coon, Rock, Green, Buffalo, Cattail, Little Rock, Deer and Howland Creeks near Fulton, where U.S. 30 crosses the Mississippi River, north of Moline. About the same distance to the south on U.S. 67, Henderson and Cedar Creeks (21), near Little York on State Highway 94, also provide some small stream fishing.

In the southeastern part of Illinois, the Wabash River (22), forming part of the eastern state border, provides some good fishing around Hutsonville on State Highway 1, and again further down the same highway at Carmel.

One of its tributaries, the Embarrass (23), flowing for many miles on a line with the parent river to finally enter it south of Bridgeport, produces spotty fishing, one of the better areas being near Lawrenceville on U.S. 50. Other spots to fish the Embarrass are Charleston on State Highway 16, Greenup on U.S. 40 to the south of this, and Villa Grove, north of Tuscola on U.S. 36.

The Little Wabash (24) follows relatively the same course as the Embarrass, but is further to the west. In the upper reaches there are white and black crappie and in the lower part there is good fishing for channel catfish. It may be fished from Golden Gate near Albion on State Highway 15; and Carmi on U.S. 460 is also a favorite spot. From Carmi you can also reach the Skillet Fork. The best part of the river is generally conceded to be fairly far north around Wayne City at the junction of State Highway 142 and State Highway 15.

Another tributary, the Vermilion (25), flows to the Wabash in Indiana, east of Danville, which is a good central point from which to fish its waters; and a little further south the Little Vermilion (26) may be reached from Georgetown on

U.S. 150. The MIDDLE FORK OF THE VERMILION (27) is accessible from Melvin on U.S. 54, northeast of Decatur.

Continuing south along the eastern border of the state, you come to the SALINE RIVER (28), where there is some fishing around the town of Equality off State Highway 13, east of Harrisburg.

Moving northward, anglers will find fishing for all the state species except smallmouth in the KICKAPOO RIVER (29) near Peoria; the MACKINAW (30) around Goodfield on U.S. 150, east of Peoria and near the town of Mackinaw, off State Highway 9, seventeen miles east of Pekin.

The SANGAMON RIVER (31) crosses almost the entire central part of the state, providing fishing at many places. Two popular spots are Monticello, on State Highway 47, and a little further north, Mahomet on U.S. 150, west of Urbana, and Chandlerville, far to the west on State Highway 78, near the Illinois River. There is also some fishing around Petersburg on State Highway 97, northwest of Springfield and Decatur on U.S. 51.

Other fishable streams in the central part of Illinois include SUGAR CREEK (32) and SALT CREEK (33), all near Lincoln on U.S. 66; Salt Creek near Farmer City at the junction of U.S. 54 and U.S. 150 west of Urbana, and the same creek near Greenview on State Highway 29 northwest of Springfield.

The KASKASKIA (34) is another river which traverses the entire state, flowing from northeast to southwest to enter the Mississippi well down on the western border. Some of the most popular areas with fishermen are Shelbyville, on State Highway 16 west of Mattoon; Tuscola, on U.S. 36 in the east-central part of the state; Vandalia, on U.S. 40 at its junction with U.S. 51; New Athens, on State Highway 13 south of St. Louis; and near the dam at Carlyle on U.S. 50, some forty-five miles east of St. Louis.

The East Fork of the Kaskaskia can be fished from Fairman on U.S. 51, south of Vandalia; and there is some fishing in CROOKED CREEK (35) near Central City about nine miles to the south on U.S. 51.

From State Highway 37, a few miles to the east, anglers can reach approximately twenty-eight miles of fishing along the BIG MUDDY RIVER (36) from Benton, and there's ten more miles on the Middle Fork of the Muddy near Orient, to the east. The LITTLE MUDDY RIVER (37) can be fished from DuQuoin, on U.S. 51. BEAUCOUP CREEK (38), to the west, can be fished from Pinckneyville, on State Highway 127.

Along the western border of Illinois, anglers will find some fishing in LA MOINE CREEK (39), which can be reached from Carthage on U.S. 136 or from Macomb on U.S. 67. MACOUPIN CREEK (40) crosses both U.S. 66 and U.S. 67 on its way to the Mississippi, north of St. Louis. Some of the best fishing is around Carlinville, on State Highway 4, halfway between the two major roads.

In the triangle between the junction of the Illinois with the Mississippi there are several streams which have all the local species. These include the SNY RIVER (41) at Atlas on U.S. 54 and BAY CREEK (42) at Nebo, on a secondary road to the south. SHOAL CREEK (43) can be fished for some thirty-three miles from Pocahontas on U.S. 40 to the east of St. Louis. EAST SHOAL CREEK (44) also has all the species common to the state. The CACHE RIVER (45), entering the Mississippi near Cairo, at the extreme southern tip of the state, provides some fishing for all species near its outlet and also further north around Ullin.

Current details as to availability of boats, camping grounds and other facilities at these and many additional fishing spots along the rivers will be found in the booklet "Official Fishing Guide," published by the Illinois Department of Conservation, Springfield, Illinois.

ILLINOIS FISHING REGULATIONS

Resident Fishing License $2.00
Nonresident Fishing License $4.00
Nonresident 10-Day Fishing License $2.00

SEASONS AND LIMITS

Species	Open Season	Bag Limit	Size Limit
Largemouth Bass	No closed season	10	None
Smallmouth Bass	Varies with areas	10	10″
Walleye and Sauger	May 1–Feb. 15	8	16″
Northern Pike	May 1–Nov. 30	None	None
Trout (except in lakes)	April 1–Sept. 30	8	7″
Catfish	Year-round	None	None

For complete regulations write: Illinois Department of Conservation, State Office Building, Springfield 62706, Illinois.

IOWA

The drainage system of the State of Iowa is based on three great rivers, the Missouri, which forms the western border, the Mississippi, which forms the eastern border, and the Des Moines, a tributary of the Mississippi, which flows through the center of the state in a north-south course. In the Mississippi waters the Iowa fisherman catches catfish, walleyes, white bass, sheepshead and northerns as well as suckers, bullhead and carp. In the Missouri he is pretty well limited to catfish, bullhead and carp, and a few northern pike. The Des Moines, above the city of Des Moines, carries walleyes and smallmouths as well as northerns.

However, the best river fishing is in the tributaries rather than in the main streams. The Upper Iowa, Turkey, Yellow, Volga, Maquoketa, Wapsipinicon and Cedar, and their tributaries the Shellrock and Winnebago, in the northeastern part of the state are considered to be among the better streams.

The major natural lakes of fishing interest are in the north-central area, bordering on Minnesota. These lakes have walleye, northern pike, bass and panfish as well as catfish and bullheads.

Scattered throughout the state are many artificial reservoirs which have been stocked with the same species and provide the bulk of the fishing. Trout have also been stocked in a number of streams, mostly in the northeastern corner bordering on Minnesota and Wisconsin, in waters flowing into the Mississippi and its tributaries. The State Conservation Commission, East 7th and Court Streets, Des Moines 8, Iowa, issues a very comprehensive mimeographed brochure giving approach roads to each stream, nearest towns, and complete details about where to fish each stream, and this is well worth having for anyone who is going to fish trout in Iowa.

All of Iowa's fishing waters are easily reached via an excellent road system, as the state is almost a true rectangle and is crisscrossed by many of the major east-west and north-south highways of the nation.

Anglers will find most of their sport in spring and fall. During the summer the climate is warm and successful fishing is limited mostly to early morning and late evening hours. But there are numerous public camp sites in a comfortable atmosphere of park and greenery, where the visiting fisherman can fill in the heat-of-the-day hours when the fish are lying low.

Game is not a problem because of the fact that the state is almost entirely agricultural. Fisherman should give special attention to closing of farmers' gates, avoid trampling crops and disturbing cattle. In all cases where you are not fishing at a public access spot, be sure to get permission of the landowner before going on his land.

While snakes are not generally regarded as a threat in Iowa, the state is within the range of the copperhead, moccasin and rattlesnake.

Lake and river fishermen in Iowa use a wide assortment of gear ranging from the plug-casting outfit popular with bait fishermen, to the ever-present spinning outfit many casters now use. For the trout fishing in the northeastern streams, anglers will find the 8-foot rod just about right, with matching HDH line. In general, the standard flies will suffice—the Light Cahill in sizes 12, 14 and 16, Royal Coachman in sizes 12 and 14, Grasshopper, size 12, Brown Bivisible, size 14 and 16, Gray Bivisible, 14 and 16, and Light Hendrickson, sizes 12 and 14. During the midge hatches you can go down to an 18 and 20 matching midge.

Spinning lures should be small, ⅛ or ¼ ounce, and the spinner will do well with a bubble and weighted fly.

For the bait fisherman, minnows, crayfish and worms are good in summer, while in the fall, grasshoppers and crickets head the list.

MISSISSIPPI RIVER FISHING

The catch here will be northern pike, walleyes, sauger, largemouth black bass, bluegill, crappie, yellow bass, white bass, channel catfish and flathead catfish. Walleyes, black bass, crappies and sunfish are the most numerous and most popular, and fishing is open in the MISSISSIPPI (1) year-round for all species. The walleyes are taken during the warmer weather below navigation dams and around submerged wing dams, and the best catches are made in cooler weather. When winter comes there is excellent walleye fishing through the ice in backwaters. Bass fishing is also good in the backwaters in spring and fall, and continues excellent through the summer if you fish the cool part of the day.

One of the hot spots for walleyes is below the dam at Harpers Ferry, and another is below the dam at Lynxville.

From New Albin to Keokuk there is some kind of angling that is good at any time of the year you choose. You can catch sauger and walleyes below the several dams, and at times the white bass will rise to flies. As mentioned above, there are largemouth black bass and panfish in the sloughs. A writer for the *Iowa Conservationist*, Roger Fliger, reports that he caught better than 100 white bass one morning on white streamer flies. He kept fishing for a week and took a total of 900! He marked them and returned them to the water, and since he never caught the same one twice, he says "You could make some wild mathematical calculation on the number of fish there."

All together the Mississippi in Iowa has 300 miles of possible fishing. The best location in all cases is the first mile below each dam. Top pools are at Lynxville, Guttenberg and Dubuque, and from Harpers Ferry to Bellevue. A Mississippi statistician has estimated that the catch is a fish every hour—good fishing anywhere.

Walleye and sauger like deep water and strong current, so they should be fished accordingly. Deep-running plugs and jigs are best, while bait fishermen use nightcrawlers and minnows and get them down with a considerable amount of weight. However, floating or drifting a bait is very successful when the water is only about 10 feet deep. And in almost any water the bait man will find it a good trick to "bounce" a gob of nightcrawlers.

Baitfishermen often take sheepshead in the channels, and a few are also taken on plugs and spoons. One of the little sidelights to Iowa fishing is to hear the sheepshead croaking on a summer night.

MISSOURI RIVER FISHING

Since upriver dams have controlled the flow of the MISSOURI (2), which used to be so full of silt that only species known as "silt strainers" could survive, there is much clearer water than used to be the case, and the river is consequently much more attractive to fish and fishermen. The population of sauger and crappies has increased tremendously and there are also catfish. In the oxbows there is excellent fishing for black bass.

The best areas on the river are between the mouths of the BIG SIOUX and FLOYD RIVERS (3) in Sioux City, and at Snyder Bend, Winnebago Bend, Decatur Bend, Blackbird Bend, BROWN'S LAKE (4), BLUE LAKE (5) and LAKE MANAWA (6), but there are fish all the way from Yankton, South Dakota, to Omaha. Spring and fall are the best times for sauger; crappie are taken year-round off the rock revetments and wing dams. In addition to these species there are northern and catfish. Artificial lures work well for casters, and of course the baitmen take their share, too.

One of the tributaries of the Missouri, the LITTLE SIOUX (7) in western Iowa, from Correctionville south to its confluence with the Missouri, offers some excellent catfishing.

In the extreme northeastern corner of the state, the UPPER IOWA RIVER (8) has both smallmouth black bass and catfish. This is a very scenic stream and is popular with float fishermen.

LAKE FISHING

The major fishing lakes in Iowa are the OKOBOJI LAKES (9), CLEAR LAKE (10) and SPIRIT LAKE (11). The Okoboji Lakes lie up near the Minnesota border, and have a population of largemouth black bass, smallmouth black bass, northern pike, crappie, bluegill, yellow perch, walleye and bullhead, and also some white bass and yellow bass. If you catch a "silver northern" in these lakes, it is just a variation of the northern. West Okoboji is over 100 feet deep in places and is a fine bluewater lake. The lakes are well supplied with lodges and camp sites, and boats and guides are available.

Clear Lake, near the town of Clear Lake, just west of Mason City, in the north-central part of Iowa, has largemouth black bass, northern pike, walleyes and yellow bass. There are a few bluegills, crappie, channel catfish and white bass. This is in a state park and there are camp sites, a trailer park and boat dock, as well as a lodge.

Spirit Lake, just north of the Okobojis, is on the Iowa-Minnesota border, but lies mostly within the state of Iowa. The species are the same as in the Okoboji lakes, and there are plentiful accommodations in the neighborhood.

In all these lakes, fishing is best in the spring and fall, although during the summer anglers continue to make excellent catches of smallmouth black bass by fishing lead-head jigs over the deep rock reefs. Winter fishing is also very good.

Walleyes in the Okoboji-Spirit Lake group are commonly taken up to 12 pounds. Perch run to a pound and a half, and are best in the autumn.

The small, lead-head jigs, known locally as the "Warden's Worry" and "Jim Stone" patterns, are the best producers for these little fish, and the larger sizes are used for bass and walleyes. You can get them at Cap's Tackle Shop, Arnold's Park, Iowa, on West Okoboji. Cap Kennedy is an expert fisherman and guide.

A number of smaller lakes in Iowa provide excellent fishing at one season or another. STORM LAKE (12) is at the town of the same name, where U.S. Highway 71 makes an eastward jog; and BLACK HAWK LAKE (13) is a few miles further

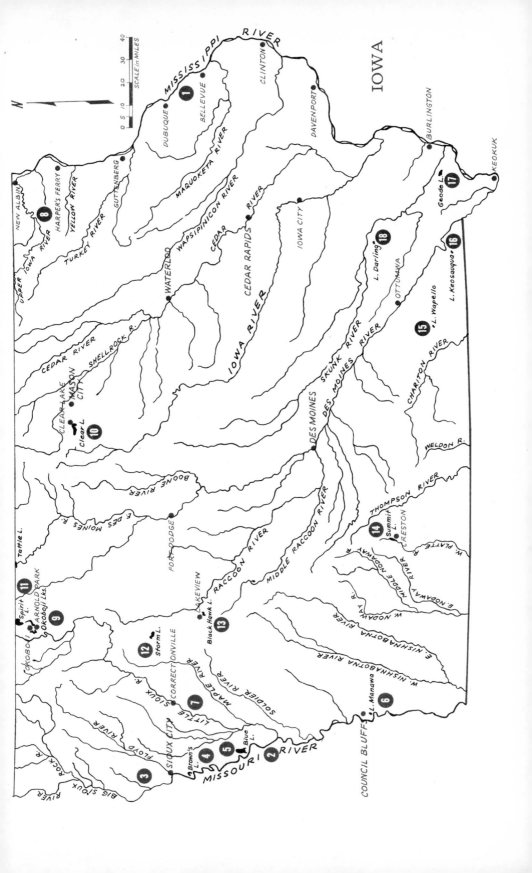

south along the same road, at Lakeview. Storm is considered by many anglers to be the best walleye lake in Iowa, and there are also white bass, crappie, channel cat and bullheads. This lake is shallow, and its name is well earned—it can be quite rough. Boats are available at several docks. Black Hawk is not as good a walleye lake but has crappie, some largemouth black bass, panfish and bullheads.

A string of fishable lakes running across the southern part of the state includes SUMMIT LAKE (14), LAKE WAPELLO (15), LAKE KEOSAUQUA (16), GEODE LAKE (17) and LAKE DARLING (18), as well as some others. Anglers who plan to explore lake fishing in Iowa, should obtain two leaflets, "Iowa's Public Access Fishing Areas," and "Iowa's 100 Best Fishing Spots," from Ries Tuttle, Outdoor Editor of the Des Moines Register and Tribune, Des Moines, Iowa.

IOWA FISHING REGULATIONS

Resident Fishing License $2.50
Nonresident Fishing License $3.00

SEASONS

Species	Open Season
Inland waters:	
Walleye, Sauger, Northern Pike (pickerel)	May 8–Feb. 15
Smallmouth Black Bass	May 29–Feb. 15
Muskellunge, Rock Sturgeon	Closed
Other fish	All year
Special season in designated lakes:	
Walleye, Northern Pike, Sunfish, Catfish	May 8–Feb. 15
Smallmouth and Largemouth Black Bass	May 29–Nov. 30
Special seasons in boundary waters—Mississippi Missouri and Big Sioux Rivers, and inland waters of Lee County:	
Largemouth and Smallmouth Black Bass, Walleye, Sauger, Northern Pike (pickerel)	All year
Other fish	Same as in inland waters
Special seasons in all streams; Missouri and Mississippi River oxbow lakes; and artificial lakes:	
Walleye, Sauger, Northern Pike (pickerel)	All year
Other fish	Same as in inland waters

For complete regulations write: State Conservation Commission, E. 7th Street and Court Avenue, Des Moines 9, Iowa.

MISSOURI

The State of Missouri feels the influence of two great rivers, the Missouri, which forms part of the western border, then flows across the middle of the state; and the Mississippi, which forms the entire eastern border. Within the state are found three different types of topography, the agricultural, rolling hills of the north, the prairies of the northeast and southwest, and the mountains of the Ozarks, in the south-central part of the state. In addition to the major Missouri-Mississippi River, there are several important streams in the north, the Modaway, Fabius, Salt, Chariton, Platte, Vuivre and Grand; and in the south, the cooler, fresher St. Francis, Osage, Black, Eleven Point, White, Current and the Meramec.

As a result of dams on the Missouri and Mississippi, there are a number of large reservoirs and these and some smaller natural lakes, as well as artificially developed ponds, offer fishing for one or more of the warm-water species: crappie, white bass, goggle-eye, paddlefish, catfish and carp; some of the slightly cooler waters adding walleye, known locally as jack salmon.

The walleye is most common in the upper Mississippi where the water is clearer, but also in the Lake of the Ozarks, and the Lower St. Francis River, the Meramec, Current, and the Black River below Clearwater Lake. Some fish up to 16 pounds are taken each year. Largemouth black bass, smallmouth black bass and pike are also found. In the Missouri there are hackleback or shovelnose catfish, and both the Missouri and Mississippi have white sturgeon and lake sturgeon, though these are seldom seen except in the spring. At that time, when they are running, they can be taken on rod and reel.

Trout are not native to Missouri but have been planted in a few springs and lakes where water can be maintained at a low enough temperature. The Missouri Conservation Commission stocks and maintains several trout-fishing areas, notably in the Montauk, Bennett Spring and Roaring River State Parks. (Special daily tags are required in addition to the state license and trout stamp.)

Trout are also fished in some waters of the Ozarks, and on these same streams there are twenty-five popular float trips combining a scenic camping and fishing tour.

All together, in Missouri the angler has a wide choice of fishing, from wilderness stream to popular lake, from wading and casting, to trolling from boats, from fishing from the bank of a quiet lake to fishing from the air-conditioned docks provided at some of the lakes.

Missouri was on the main track of westward exploration and settlement of the continent, and many of its good highways and well-kept byways follow or cross some of the routes of pioneer times. Even in the most rugged sections of the Ozarks there are roads to most of the good fishing waters and in most places there is good rail service and airplane facilities.

The climate varies considerably with the topography, but in general it is quite warm in summer except in the mountains, and comfortably cool the rest of the year. There is little seriously cold weather at any time. As far as summer heat is concerned, anglers do their fishing early in the morning and late in the evening, to beat the heat. Midsummer heat does not interfere with fishing below the dams or trolling deep in some of the reservoirs.

In the most remote sections of Missouri, the angler may encounter black bear, especially in the Ozarks. Deer are plentiful, and so is small game. Missouri is within the range of nearly all the poisonous snakes of North America, and anglers should govern themselves accordingly. Don't step over a log or into brush without looking. In other words, conduct yourself as a woodsman should at all times, whether there are snakes or game or not.

LAKE FISHING

The largest lakes in Missouri have resulted from the construction of dams on the various tributaries of the Missouri-Mississippi system. The LAKE OF THE OZARKS (1), in the foothills of the mountains, is the largest. This lake was formed by damming the Osage River, a tributary of the Missouri. It lies square in the middle of the state, and is reached via U.S. Highway 54 and U.S. Highway 63, and also Missouri Highways 5 and 52. The 1,372 miles of shoreline has been highly developed and there are many resorts, restaurants and boat marinas lining the shore.

In the rocky bays in the upper part of the lake there are a few smallmouth black bass but the main fishing is for largemouth black bass, spotted black bass, walleyed pike, bluegill, channel catfish, white bass, and crappie of unusual size. The fishing for white bass is very popular in the Camdenton area, while for walleyes anglers favor the water just below the dam, or, during February and March, the mouths of the various rivers, especially the OSAGE (2), LITTLE NIANGUA (3) and GLAIZE (4).

One of the most highly developed lakes in Missouri is comparatively new TABLE ROCK RESERVOIR (5), south of Springfield, on the southwestern border between Missouri and Arkansas. The dam releases cold water into the river below and into Taneycomo Lake, producing a suitable atmosphere for trout, which promises to make this a great area for this species as well as for the more common species of crappie, bluegill, largemouth black bass, channel catfish, drum, sunfish and white bass. Excellent trout catches are made at the foot of the dam.

March through June is the best time for white bass as they move into the shallows heading for rivers on their spawning runs at this time. That is the cue to fish them around the mouths of rivers. As the run dwindles, and again in the fall when they are schooling out into the lake, a small shad minnow or an artificial lure aping the same will take plenty of these tasty little fish.

Table Rock has also been stocked with walleyes and the best months are January, February and March, with a few lasting into April. Fishing for this species picks up again in the fall. Bottom lures and minnows fished deep take the walleyes.

While winter fishing on a big lake like Table Rock can be cold, this is the time to take the big bass. A catch of six bass brought in in February, 1963, to Baxter's Boat Dock near Lampe, weighed 25 pounds and that was only part of the day's bag.

In June a good day will produce forty-odd white bass—some people get sixty—half a dozen really good bass, and twenty or more crappie. June is also a good top-water fishing month, and a sample day at Baxter's shows fifteen bass from 1½ to 4 pounds taken on top-water baits and fly-rod poppers.

For information about Table Rock Lake write Bob Bright, Baxter Boat Dock, Table Rock Lake, Lampe, Missouri. There are half a dozen top-notch motels and resorts within walking distance of the dock, and he has 100 boats at $2.50 per day. Motors are $5, guides $12.50. There is a free campground there, too. The motels have a standard rate of $8 for air-conditioned kitchenette apartments for two persons.

Bob gets out a weekly news letter and if you are thinking of going there it's a good idea to have him send you a few copies for the time of year you are planning on, and you'll get a pretty complete picture of what to expect at Table Rock. He has also fished for years at Bull Shoals and can give you information on that.

Immediately to the east is LAKE NORFOLK (6), formed by a dam on the White River in Arkansas, and backing water up eight miles into Missouri. There is excellent fishing for crappie, white bass, largemouth black bass, smallmouth black bass, bluegill and channel catfish. The lake is most easily reached from Springfield, via U.S. Highway 160, and there are all types of accommodations and services at the lake.

On Lake Norfolk there is considerable good casting water, and it is popular with the light-tackle fraternity. Fly fishermen make good catches on bright-colored bucktails and streamers and popping bugs, while spinners use small, light and bright lures.

A part of BULL SHOALS LAKE (7), formed in Arkansas, juts up into Missouri just east of Taneycomo, and provides a lot of good fishing for the species found in this lake. It can be reached from Lutie or Isabella on U.S. Highway 160, and there are several resorts in the Theodosia area to the west of the main arm (see Arkansas). The biggest bass in this lake are usually taken in winter.

The white bass taken in these lakes is also called striped bass or silver bass. This freshwater species likes deep, still water with a sandy or gravel bottom. They grow very fast and live short lives, seldom more than four years, but they often reach a length of 12 inches in a two-year period. The white bass makes an ideal light-tackle fish, readily responding to fly and spinner combinations, small spoons and small plugs. You're more likely to pick them up at the narrows in a stream, or along the edges of channels in the lakes. They are most readily taken during the spring run from February through May.

When the fish are surfacing, or are in shallow enough water to reach them with a fly, fishermen claim they like a fly with some white in it, and in general they lean to white bucktails and marabou streamers.

LAKE WAPPAPELLO (8), in the southeast corner of the state, was created by a dam on the St. Francis River in the southeastern Ozarks, near the town of Poplar Bluff on U.S. Highway 60 just north of the Arkansas line. The crappie in this lake will run as high as 2½ pounds, with some to 4 pounds. There are also some black bass. Cabins, boats, bait, boat-launching sites and all conveniences are available at the lake.

Just to the west is CLEARWATER LAKE (9), on the Black River. As the name suggests, this lake is normally clear and therefore very popular with those who like to fish with artificial lures. There are crappie, bluegill, largemouth black bass and catfish. It also is well supplied with resorts and all facilities for fishermen.

FLOAT FISHING

The float trip is probably the most unique feature of Missouri fishing and in no other state is there a comparable number of floats available. Float trips have been

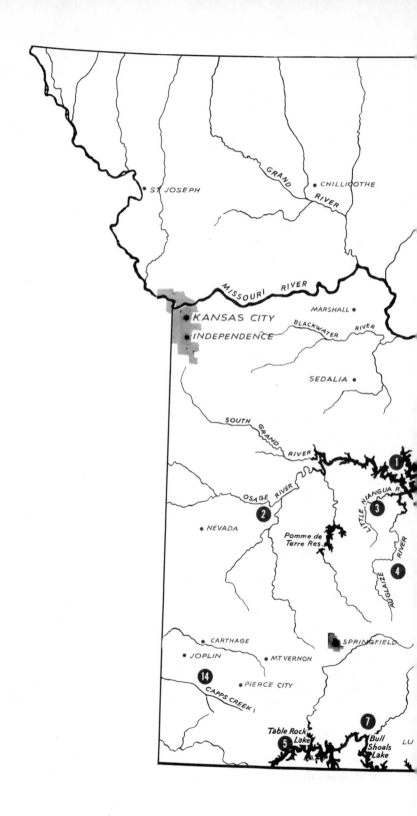

N

0 5 10   20   30   40
SCALE in MILES

MISSOURI

KEOKUK

HANNIBAL

MISSISSIPPI RIVER

RLY

MEXICO

INDIAN CR
11

LUMBIA
FULTON

ST CHARLES

MISSOURI RIVER

CLAYTON ST LOUIS

GASCONADE RIVER

BOURBEUSE R.

MERAMEC RIVER

ROLLA

DRY CREEK

13

MISSISSIPPI RIVER

WHITE WATER

CAPE GIRARDEAU

CURRENT

9
Clearwater Lake

8
Wappapello Lake

15

RIVER

SIKESTON

CUBIDOCK CREEK

ELEVEN

10

POINT

BLACK

ST FRANCIS

POPLAR BLUFF

RIVER

6

Lake Norfolk

RIVER

RIVER

popular in the waters of the Ozark region since they first originated in the James River area in 1904. The trips vary from half a day to almost as long as the angler chooses to make them, and there are twenty-five streams on which such trips can be made. Generally it is wise to hire a professional guide if you plan to travel where there is white water, and this is usually the case if you want to reach the best fishing. However there are a few trips that anglers can make on their own, as long as they are experienced river travelers.

Generally the fish will be largemouth black bass, smallmouth black bass, goggle-eye, walleye, (often locally called jack salmon), channel catfish, and, in some cases, trout.

Float trips are feasible on Beaver Creek, Big River, Flat Creek, Elk River, Dry Creek, Bourbeuse, Gasconade, Osage Fork, Niangua, Big Piney, Little Niangua, Meramec, Huzzah, Courtoi, Osage River, Kings River, Long Creek, Flat, James, Upper Taneycomo, Kings, White, Elk, Indian, Bryant, Lake Norfolk, North Fork of the White River, Current, Jacks Fork, Eleven Point, St. Francis, Black, Sac River and Swan Creek.

If one were asked to make a choice, the Gasconade would probably rate as the best fishing river. The current is regarded as the finest for float trips with good fishing thrown in. And the Jacks Fork and Eleven Point also rate high.

The Missouri Division of Resources and Development, Jefferson City, Missouri, publishes a pamphlet entitled "Floating and Fishing in Missouri," which lists the names and addresses of a number of guides, and the rivers on which they float. It is important to get the pamphlet issued in the year in which you plan to float as some of the rivers shown in earlier publications may have been dammed.

On these float trips the angler need only bring his own tackle—and he can rent that if he prefers. The outfitter supplies the boat, guide service, sets up overnight camps, provides the meals. Bass is the main fish and they can be taken on flies, spinning gear or plug outfit, or by bait fishing. In addition there are goggle-eyes and walleyes, the latter frequently running up to 12 pounds, and some having been taken to 17 pounds. In some waters there are also trout, and flies usually take these.

The cost of a float trip may vary from $15 to $20 per person per day, though this is entirely according to the outfitter and the water in which you will be fishing. The boats are flat bottomed John boats, about 18 feet long, with a midship width of 3 feet, and are about 16 inches deep. They are usually comfortably equipped with chairs, ice box—all the comforts of home, and of course, a motor for upstream or inshore pulls.

TROUT FISHING

Trout are not native to Missouri but are now found in a goodly number of rivers in state parks, thanks to a program of heavy stocking of suitable streams. Even so, natural reproduction cannot maintain a population and the trout fishing in Missouri is largely on a put and take basis.

The commission also stocks a few streams on private land in co-operation with the landowners, who permit "reasonable" fishing on their land, without charge. These are: GREER SPRINGS BRANCH and ELEVEN POINT RIVER (10) as far down as Turner's Mill; INDIAN CREEK (11) from Rocky Comfort down to Rosenberry Bridge; ROUBIDOUX CREEK (12) from Roubidoux Spring down to the Gasconade

View of Table Rock Lake above the dam, Lake Taneycomo below it where cold water provides good fishng for trout.

River; DRY CREEK (13) from the mouth of the Westover Spring Branch downstream for about 1½ miles (Near Johnson Ford); and CAPPS CREEK (14), South of Pierce City.

Since most of the trout are raised, planted and caught all within one year they are stocked in good size, a minimum of 10 inches.

ODD FISH IN MISSOURI

The waters of Missouri harbor quite a few fish not commonly encountered elsewhere and these provide some exotic fishing if not always of the most sporting type. The bowfin is an example. This species is not really classifiable as a game fish and is usually taken by accident when fishing for other fish. They are found in the "bootheel" area of the state in the Mississippi River, down near the Arkansas and Tennessee border, where they like the weed-grown shallower lakes and slow-moving streams. This strange critter has many admirers and some anglers will travel regularly to "swampeast" Missouri to try for him. Indicating their high regard, they call them "cypress trout" and "prairie bass." Actually, the bowfin does give a good account of itself when taken on light tackle.

There are also four species of gar which, though not generally regarded as a sport fish, are sought by a few. Others go for the paddlefish, found in the Mississippi, Missouri and Osage and St. Francis River, but these are taken by snagging, which is not fishing and will not be dealt with here.

In many Missouri markets—for it is a commercial species—you'll see drum listed as white perch or just perch. Many years ago these drum, variously called sheepshead, perch, white perch, stone croaker, thunderpumper, gray perch and gasperou, grew to enormous sizes in the Missouri area. There are reports of fish as heavy as 60 pounds, and even nowadays an odd 20-pounder is caught in the Lake of the Ozarks. An interesting sidelight is that the bones of the species found in old Indian camp sites suggest that this fish may originally have reached 200 pounds!

Distantly related to the saltwater drums, croakers and yellowtail, the freshwater drum is found the length of the North American continent in the 35-degree-latitude range, indicating that it may have originated from stocking from the Gulf of Mexico at some early time in geological history. In Missouri they are mainly taken in the Lake of the Ozarks and a few of the larger lakes, as well as in the Missouri and Mississippi Rivers. As they are basically bottom feeders it usually takes bottom fishing with worms and crawdads to reach them, though in the fall they are regularly caught on live minnows.

A local variety of smallmouth bass is also found in the north-flowing Ozark streams and the tributaries of the Mississippi. In the south-flowing rivers of the Ozarks is still another variety, known as the Neosho smallmouth. They are so similar as to be almost indistinguishable and in the Whitewater River, St. Francis, Current and the Black, the two bass have crossed and formed a hybrid.

The spotted bass is also found in some Missouri waters, mostly in the southeast lowlands in the Gasconade, South Grand, Whitewater, St. Francis and Meramec watersheds.

And filling out the picture of occasional catches is the grass pickerel, taken usually in the weedy sloughs of the Current, Black and Meramec, usually on small lures when fishing for other species.

Another species not too highly regarded by the sporting fraternity has a wide audience of fans in Missouri. This is the channel catfish, certainly not as flashy as the bass or trout, nor as long fighting and stubborn. But they make surprisingly good runs and in shallow water will wage an exciting surface fight. The meat is white and firm, and I have known anglers who live in the heart of the trout country of Montana who go east every year or so for "a little catfishing" on either the Missouri or the Mississippi.

The catfish makes its nest in a hole under a bank and as a result of this one of the popular ways of fishing for them in Missouri is with a "bank pole," an outfit consisting of a willowy green pole, a 3-foot line and a 2/0 hook. The pole is butted into the bank so the bait bobs just beneath the surface. This brings them up, even in deep water around brush piles. Bait ranges from minnows to dough balls, one of the best of the latter being made of a half and half mixture of cotton seed meal and flour, moistened with just enough water to ball up nicely.

A 2- to 3-pound catfish makes the best eating. Five pounds is considered large, but on occasion they have been taken up to 25 pounds. They are also called spotted eel, white, fiddler, Fulton and Mississippi cat.

MISSOURI FISHING REGULATIONS

Resident Fishing License $3.25
Nonresident Fishing License $5.25
Nonresident 14-Day Fishing License $3.25
Trout Fishing Permit $2.25 in addition to regular license
Trout Permit in Management Areas $1.00 daily in addition to regular
  license

SEASONS AND LIMITS

Missouri has year-round open season with the exception of bass, on which there is a closed season from March 1 to the following May 28, *except in impoundments,* where they may be taken year-round.

Trout fishing in the Management Areas is limited to sunrise to 30 minutes after sunset, from March 1 through October 31.

Species	*Limits*
Largemouth Bass, in streams	6 daily, 12 in possession
Largemouth Bass, in impoundments	10 daily, 20 in possession
Walleye	4 daily, 8 in possession
Crappie	30 daily, 60 in possession
Goggle-Eye, Warmouth, White Bass	15 daily, 30 in possession
Channel Catfish	10 daily, 20 in possession
Trout	5 daily, 10 in possession

For complete regulations write: Conservation Commission, Jefferson City, Missouri.

ARKANSAS

The State of Arkansas, because of its latitude, has many of the qualities of the southern states, plus the advantage of the Ozark Plateau which comes down from Missouri in the northwest corner of the state, where the Boston Mountains supply an eastward flowing watershed. A similar formation to the south, around Little Rock, is the basis of another series of streams. All of these eventually reach the Mississippi, which forms the major part of the eastern border of Arkansas.

The waters of the Mississippi itself are too warm and muddy to support anything but coarse fish, but the many tributaries hold substantial populations of largemouth black bass, smallmouth black bass, white bass, Kentucky bass, rock bass, bluegill, crappie, and, in some cases, alligator gar, long-nosed gar, walleye and channel catfish. In the cooler waters of the north-central mountains, there is some excellent fishing for rainbow and brown trout. In addition, the numerous lakes, both natural and man-made, hold largemouth black bass and the cooler ones add smallmouth black bass.

This brief description of the fish life of the state does not give a true idea of the varied and unusual fishing to be found in Arkansas. For instance, it is claimed that there is no body of water in Arkansas that does not hold some kind of bass. The largemouth grows to 10 pounds regularly. The smallmouth is less widespread, but is found in many of the cooler lakes and streams. The float trips available on some Arkansas rivers are almost unique; and the trout fishing around some of the dams, such as Bull Shoals, is certainly without equal in many similar waters.

The White River below Bull Shoals Dam, Spring River below Mammoth Springs, the North Fork below Norfolk Dam, Little Missouri below Narrows Dam, Ouachita below Blakely Dam, all produce unusual trout fishing because of the cold water that is released from the dams. Trout like the cooler water, there is an unlimited supply of baitfish, and consequently the trout which are stocked there grow in record time to record sizes. It is believed that these fish can grow to three times their stocking weight in a single season. Both browns and rainbows are planted, though the emphasis is on the rainbows.

Browns as heavy as 15 pounds 9½ ounces have been taken and 4- to 6- pounders are fairly common. Rainbows go to 15 pounds and regularly run around 10.

In most of the waters below these dams there is no closed season but there are certain local regulations which should always be checked; for instance, in some seasons, only artificial lures are permitted.

In the deep water below the dams, most of the fish are taken on spinning lures such as Al's Goldfish and the Mepps spinners. Bait fishermen use worms, crawfish tails, grubs, small minnows and grasshoppers.

Both bait fishermen and casters should use line no heavier than 4-pound test or at most 6-pound-test monofilament.

Probably the most sensational fish in Arkansas waters is the alligator gar. This is the largest freshwater species in North America, a great, armor-plated monster that grows to weights close to 200 pounds. Fish up to 50 pounds are taken regularly by anglers.

The alligator gar is found in the lower White River, the Ouchita and St. Francis, the Red River and the Arkansas River. The fish usually frequent the places where sand bars drop off to depths of 12 feet or so. The best time of the year to fish for them is from late June through the middle part of September. While mostly they are taken deeper, sometimes they can be seen surfacing in substantial numbers, adding considerably to the excitement.

Gar fishermen use large saltwater-style rods or very heavy boat rods, 5½ or 6 feet in length, plus a big star-drag reel with at least 250 yards of 50-pound test or better nylon line, and add a stainless-steel leader testing 90 pounds or even more. The bait is usually the head of a fish and the bait itself will weigh up to a pound, and is put on treble 8/0 hooks. This gigantic bait is heaved out into the center of the river and allowed to sink to the bottom. When a gar picks it up, the angler must pay out line to give the fish time to mouth the bait and even swim a little with it. Then when he really has it, the angler sets the hook. Standard equipment to finish off these bruisers when they are finally brought to shore is a .38. Nothing else will penetrate that armor-like hide.

The state of Arkansas is well located for easy access from every part of the U.S.A. U.S. 67 cuts diagonally across from the corner of Tennessee and Missouri in the northeast to Texarkana in the southwest. Paralleling it, U.S. 79 bisects the southern part of the state, from Memphis, Tennessee, to Shreveport, Louisiana. U.S. Highway 62 runs across the entire northern width, covering the main great reservoirs, and with feeder roads to every other part of Arkansas.

The summer climate can be very warm, and at this time anglers fish early and late, and many of them all night. Spring and fall bring ideal fishing weather, and the fish hit better then, too. And even wintertime is good fishing time in Arkansas, with no freeze up, and this being the time when the real lunkers are taken.

Fishermen will not find wild game a problem anywhere in Arkansas, but must always watch for snakes. And of course jiggers are a constant nuisance, as are horse-flies or deer flies, and mosquitoes.

LAKE FISHING

The seven great reservoirs which provide most of the lake fishing in Arkansas today are Bull Shoals and its neighbor, Norfolk Reservoir, on the upper waters of the White river, straddling the Arkansas Missouri border, about half way across the state; Table Rock, which juts into Arkansas west of those two, on the same border; Lake Ouachita on the river of the same name, near Hot Springs; Lake Nimrod at Fourche Junction on State Highway 10, west of Little Rock; Blue Mountain Lake still further west on State Highway 10 and Lake Greeson, on U.S. Highway 70, southwest of Hot Springs.

In general, reservoir lakes are subject to fluctuations of the water level, result-ing in denuded shores and a quick dropoff to deep water. But they can be fished from shore by spinners using heavy (though small) lures. And trollers also use this type of lure and work it very slowly, in short jerks, to take many fish. Leadheaded jigs with bucktail skirts are also very popular with casters, as are plastic worms. Trollers like weedless lures in those areas where there's lots of drowned brush or stumps on the bottom.

The major reservoirs in Arkansas suffer much less from the common reservoir faults than do those in many other places. Bull Shoals and Lake Norfolk, for instance, are renowned for their scenery; but even if they weren't beautiful, the fishing would bring the fishermen.

LAKE NORFOLK (1) has produced largemouth black bass up to 12 pounds and smallmouth black bass to 6 pounds. White bass run as high as 4 and crappie of substantial weight are taken regularly. Other species found in the lake are Kentucky bass, walleyes, bream and catfish.

This great reservoir has a shoreline of more than 500 miles and its many inlets and bays provide fine habitat for fish. Many people regard it as the best bass lake in North America. As mentioned earlier, the winter is the time the experts say you should go for the really heavy largemouth black bass, and the recommended method is slow, deep trolling with plastic worms, or jig and eel. In spring and early summer there is good casting, the deeper-running lures being favored, though surface poppers and fly-rod lures will also produce. Phillips Weedless Popper and Crippled Killer are both very good.

In the spring the fish everyone wants to go for is the white bass, and at all times of year this fish is sought eagerly by nighttime anglers. The sight of the lake aglow with the lights of lantern fishermen is a common one. The anglers anchor their boats off a sandy point or a bluff, set up a lantern, and this attracts the fish to the minnow bait. Catches are tremendous and it's great nighttime sport. In fact, almost any time except during the winter, nighttime fishing with a fly-rod popper and streamer flies can pay off.

In the summer all the basses like to go to deeper water, but as things cool off in the fall, they move into the shallows again. Then the white bass school up, to provide some really fast fishing; the big largemouths and the sporty smallmouths are found more frequently in the shallows and under shoreline brush, where casters can reach them, and, in fact, things really look up at Lake Norfolk.

In addition to the already mentioned species, sauger were introduced to this lake in 1961 and should be producing shortly.

With so many miles of shoreline, there are innumerable communities on the lake, the outstanding ones being the fishing colonies at Mountain Home, Tracy, Cranfield, Buzzard Roost, Gamaliel, Panther Bay, Henderson and Newton-Hand. There are resorts at all of them, and boats and guides are available.

BULL SHOALS LAKE (2) offers the same kind of fishing as Lake Norfolk, for the same species of fish. There are also rainbows in Bull Shoals, and it is reported that in 1962 more than fifty trout in the 4- to 8-pound class were taken. In the same period, over half of all the largemouth black bass caught weighed between 6 and 11 pounds. The big fish are usually taken during the winter, but in the spring, in March, April and May, many big fish are in the shallows and some fine catches are made. Black seems to be a good lure color, eels, jigs, and combinations of jigs and eel all producing.

A point to remember during the winter is that the shad minnows on which so many of the fish feed, die of the cold in mid-winter, and these dead fish are the favorite food of the game fish—hence a slow played, lifting and falling silver spoon, looking like a dying or dead shad, is a good strike-getter. Surface lures come into their own in May.

Crappie fishing is at its peak in May, too, and this species grows commonly to 2 pounds and occasionally to 3.

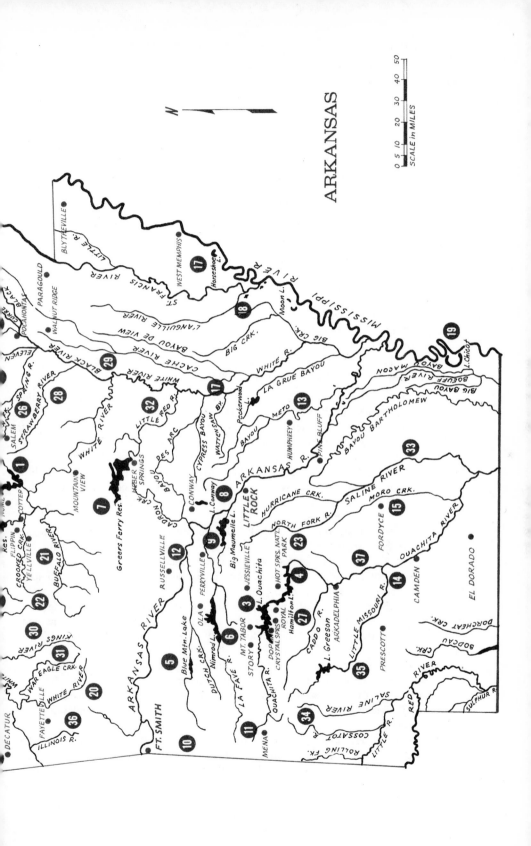

ARKANSAS

N

SCALE in MILES
0 5 10 20 30 40 50

Deep fishing will bring up the walleyes, especially at the upper end of the lake, and these fish will go from 4 to 11 pounds.

Some of the famous fishing spots on Bull Shoals are the Jimmie Creek Arm on the west side, the White River area on the east, and the main channel in the northern end of the lake.

There are many resorts, centered around the towns of Mountain Home, Lakeview, Flippen, Fairview and Theodosia. Lakeview, on U.S. Highway 178, has docks on both the lake and the White River, and at this town most of the guides are quartered who outfit float trips on the White River.

Guides for lake or river fishing or both may be obtained through the following:

State Park Trout Dock, Bull Shoals, Ark., Jerry McKinnis, operator.
Bill Newland Fishing Service, Bull Shoals, Ark.
Al Gaston's Resort, Lakeview, Ark.
Wildcat Shoals Resort, Flippin, Ark.
Forest Wood Fishing Service, Flippin, Ark.
Rack Pace, Flippin, Ark.
Sportsman's Trout Dock, Flippin, Ark.
Floyd "Big" Treat, Flippin, Ark.
Johnson Coral Cabins and Dock, Cotter, Ark.

Ira E. Matheny, of Bartow, West Virginia, covers the White River within Arkansas, and the Greenbrier in West Virginia.

LAKE OUACHITA (3), ten miles north of Hot Springs, lies in the scenic Ouachita Mountains and Ouachita National Forest. The lake is fifty miles long and has over 600 miles of shoreline, and the first time out it is advisable to go with a guide, to help you locate the best fishing areas. The species are largemouth and smallmouth black bass, crappie, bream, redear and bluegill. Striped bass have also been planted, the first in the late 50's. Only two have been caught to date, but the largest of those went 17½ pounds and was ready to spawn. Plantings have been made since then and it is hoped that the species will do as well here as it has in some of the Carolina reservoirs.

Trees were left standing when Lake Ouachita was flooded, and consequently there are plenty of snags—another reason for taking a guide. He will know the best trolling spots, the sand bars and drop-offs. The flooded brush, of course, provides plentiful cover for fish and some of the best catches are made where you also stand the best chance of snagging your lure.

The best fishing is usually from March through the month of June; things slow up for the hot weather, then pick up again in September and fishing remains good into December. After that the fish are down very deep but they are still there, if you can go for them.

Two of the times anglers enjoy most on Lake Ouachita are June, when the black bass often school on the surface; and the earlier spring months when the walleye fishing is good on the South Fork. The smallmouth record taken here in 1963 by Mr. A. F. Beckham of Little Rock, weighed 5 pounds 11 ounces, and was taken in the winter.

Towns which offer complete service for fishermen, are Brady Mountain, Crystal Springs and Royal, all on U.S. Highway 270; or you can go north on State Road 7 from Hot Springs, and just north of Jessieville turn west on a dirt road to Mount Tabor, Avant and Story.

HAMILTON LAKE (4), only five miles from Hot Springs, west on U.S. Highway 70, is twenty-five miles long with 240 miles of shoreline. The same fish are found here, with the bass going to 11 pounds and averaging 3 and 4 pounds. Walleyes are taken up to 16½ pounds, and there are plentiful bream. In 1957 rainbow trout were stocked in the upper end of Hamilton Lake, and within a couple of years some fish up to 5 pounds had been caught. But as in so many lakes, during the hot weather all these species like to go deep and summer fishing is best by trolling deep with slow-working lures. The exception is the school bass, which feed on the surface from late May on through till midsummer, and then surface casting pays off.

There are some excellent resorts along the lakeshore with boat docks and all services.

BLUE MOUNTAIN LAKE (5), on the Petit Jean River, and NIMROD LAKE (6), on the Fourche La Fave River, lie on a line drawn diagonally between Little Rock and Fort Smith. Blue Mountain is usually murky but there is some good crappie fishing. Nimrod is better, with some huge crappie, big white bass, and an increasing number of largemouth black bass.

You reach Nimrod by following State Highway 7 north from Hot Springs; then to reach Blue Mountain go on north to Ola, and there go west on State Highway 10.

GREERS FERRY RESERVOIR (7), the latest addition to the system of reservoirs in Arkansas, lies to the northeast, and can be reached by U.S. Highway 65 north from Little Rock, the east on State Highway 25 to Heber Springs. This lake was filled in 1963, and should produce some fishing within a few years.

There are also a number of public owned fishing lakes in Arkansas, many of which provide excellent fishing. Of these, LAKE CONWAY (8), twenty miles north of Little Rock, and accessible off U.S. Highway 64, is probably the best bream water in Arkansas. The lake is full of cypress trees, gum and oak, and among them the fly-rod exponent can have great fun casting and catching these sporty little fish. Boat lanes have been cut through the timber and these also produce some trolling possibilities with chances of catching some nice bass.

HARRIS BRAKE (9), forty miles west of Little Rock, near the town of Perryville, was formed by damming Coffee Creek. There are bass, big bream and catfish. This lake is reached via State Highway 10 from Little Rock.

In the Fort Smith area, SUGAR LOAF LAKE (10), just off State Highway 45, eighteen miles south of the city, has black bass, crappie, bluegill and channel catfish. In addition to other facilities it has a heated fishing dock capable of taking care of thirty anglers at one time. Catfish in this clear water reach 8 pounds.

Just to the south is LAKE WILHELMENA (11), five miles from the town of Mena and reached by State Highway 8. This is a typical mountain lake and features pleasant shore fishing.

Particularly known for crappie, bass and bream is ATKINS LAKE (12), southwest of the town of the same name, on U.S. Highway 64 northwest of Little Rock.

Boats, bait and tackle, and boat launching sites are available on all these lakes.

Other lesser lakes, where in most cases boats are not available, are HALOWELL RESERVOIR (13), reached from U.S. 79 via a gravel road half a mile south of Humphrey, near Little Rock; WHITE OAK LAKE (14), between Camden and Prescott; TRI-COUNTY LAKE (15), in Calhoun, Dallas and Cleveland Counties, near Fordyce; and CRYSTAL LAKE (16), a spring fed lake near Decatur, between State Highways 59 and 102. The latter has good fishing both from shore and boat, for redear, bluegill, bass and channel catfish that go better than six pounds.

In the eastern part of the state, HORSESHOE LAKE (17), about twenty-nine miles southwest of West Memphis, is an old Oxbow of the Mississippi which has been cut off from the mainstream. This is considered to be one of the best bass fishing lakes in the south, and there are also bream, catfish and crappie. The bass run to 8 pounds on occasion.

In the same area, BEAR CREEK LAKE (18), fifty miles from West Memphis, is a man-made body of water, and very deep. There is excellent bass and crappie fishing.

LAKE CHICOT (19), another oxbow of the Mississippi is 125 miles south of Little Rock. This is the largest natural lake in Arkansas, and while there are some areas set aside for fishing, and good catches of bream, crappie and bass are made, the lake is used so extensively for recreational purposes as to interfere with the fishing.

RIVERS

The best fishing rivers in Arkansas are the WHITE (20), the BUFFALO (21), CROOKED CREEK (22), and the NORTH FORK (23), the first two being known for rainbow trout, the latter two for smallmouth black bass, plus bluegills, sunfish and channel catfish. The Crooked Creek and Buffalo River fishing is best in May and June but the others are good all summer long.

There are many fine float trips on these and other rivers, and the John boat, as the craft used in Arkansas are called, is widely known among fishermen. This is a boat about 17 feet long, low sided, and with upturned ends, and when you fish in one of these, "Arkansas style," you sit in a comfortable chair, with a bottle of Coke by your side, as you lazily drift down the river. A float trip may last a single day, or may be of a week's duration, with camps set up on suitable sand bars or lake shores, or overnight lodging arranged at resorts along the way when possible. Most of the rivers on which floats operate are fed by mountain springs and consequently are pure and cool and clear.

The main rivers which are floated are the White and the Buffalo, though parts of many others offer limited floats of equal attraction. They are the CURRENT (24), ELEVEN POINT (25), SPRING (26), CADDO (27), STRAWBERRY (28), BLACK (29), KINGS (30), WAR EAGLE (31), LITTLE RED (32), SALINE (33), CASSATOT (34), LITTLE MISSOURI (35), ILLINOIS (36), and the OUACHITA (37).

The catch is mostly smallmouth, also called "brownie" in these waters. There are also spotted bass, green sunfish, rock bass, walleye and channel catfish. Below Bull Shoals Dam on the White River, Norfolk Dam on the Norfolk, Narrows Dam on the Little Missouri, Blakely Dam on the Ouachita, and in Spring River below Mammoth Spring, you may also take some tremendous rainbows. Six-pounders are often taken and they can run as high as 15 pounds. Floating makes for particularly pleasant fly fishing because there are no brush and trees to hamper the caster.

The cost of a float is between $30 and $35 per day per person. You can float a single day, returning to the same starting point at evening, or your guide will arrange for a commissary boat to go ahead, set up camp and have dinner ready when you reach your destination each evening. As noted earlier, the guides are generally obtainable in the Bull Shoals, Flippen and Cotter area. See list earlier.

A map of the state showing seventy-four fishing waters and giving details of the fishing, as well as the nearest centers from which access is made, is obtainable from the Information-Education Division, Arkansas Game and Fish Commission, Little Rock, Arkansas.

ARKANSAS FISHING REGULATIONS

Resident Fishing License $3.50
Nonresident Fishing License $6.00
Nonresident 14-Day Fishing License $3.50

SEASONS AND LIMITS

Species	Open Season	Daily Limit
Black Bass	All year	10
Crappie	All year	20
Catfish (other than bullhead)	All year	10
White Bass	All year	25
Bream, Goggle-Eye, Pickerel, Sunfish or any Perch	All year	50
Trout		6
With artificial bait	All year	
With natural bait	March 1–Oct. 31	
Walleye, Northern Pike, Sauger	All year	6

Not over 75 game fish in the aggregate may be taken during one day, and two days' catch may be possessed except when fishing or returning from a one-day fishing trip.

For complete regulations write: Game and Fish Commission, State Capitol Grounds, Little Rock, Arkansas.

NORTH DAKOTA

The State of North Dakota is part of the area once covered by the prehistoric Lake Agassiz. The great glaciers which scooped out lakes in Minnesota on the east had no effect here. At the same time, North Dakota is far enough from the Rockies to be deprived of the benefits of streams flowing down from them. Natural lakes are few in number, small in size, and have many disadvantages from a fisherman's point of view. Among these is the fact that they are inclined to shrink in size; the water is sometimes unsuitable for game fish because of mineral content; and the heavy ice cover in winter sometimes kills fish by cutting off the oxygen supply.

The rivers have similar problems, often being fairly well loaded with silt, and sometimes also having a high mineral content. In the spring and summer they are still high and muddy, carrying the waters off from the distant mountains to the Mississippi.

Nevertheless, there is sufficient variety of topography that with a little help from man some very fine fishing has been developed in North Dakota. The landscape is generally one of rolling plains, with some hills in the Turtle Mountain area on the Canadian border. Flat agricultural plains line the Red River Valley, and along the Missouri the land is spotted with potholes in the plains. On the Little Missouri, the Badlands provide still another scenic change. The Pembina Hills in the north are well timbered, and the lakes hidden therein are suitable for trout, bass, perch and pike.

The drainage of the state is tied in with the great Missouri River which flows from north to southeast through the central part of the state; and with the Souris and Red River, flowing to Canada, the latter forming the eastern border. Lakes of any size are mostly reservoirs on the Missouri and its tributaries, the largest being Garrison Lake and Heart Butte or Lake Tschida.

The main tributaries of the Missouri are the Yellowstone, which enters near Fairview and flows north to the Missouri; the Little Missouri, flowing from the southwest corner to the Missouri near Elbowoods; the Knife, in the west-central area, reaching the Missouri near Stanton; the Heart, rising near Dickinson and flowing to the Missouri near Mandan; the Cannonball in the southwest central area; and the James, which rises in the east-central part of the state and flows south into South Dakota before reaching the Missouri.

The Red River rises from the joining of the Ottertail and Bois de Sioux Rivers near Wahpeton, in the southeast corner of North Dakota, and forms the border between that state and Minnesota before flowing on into Canada. The Souris rises in Canada, enters North Dakota near Kenmare in northwestern North Dakota, flows north again, and leaves the state north of Westhope, about midway along the northern border.

North Dakota is primarily bird country and the fisherman will see many pheasants, Hungarian partridge and ruffed grouse as well as waterfowl. There are also deer, mostly in the southwest and in the northeast in the Pembina Hills. Anglers may also very occasionally see elk, bighorn sheep, coyotes, bobcats, wolves, and perhaps buffalo in preserves. North Dakota is outside the common range of poison-ous snakes.

The climate is northern, quite hot for a short period in summer, cool in the spring and fall, and cold as winter approaches. Woolens are always in order. Those who plan to wade either lake or stream will find chest-high waders comfortable both for getting out far enough and for the extra warmth.

The fish that are native to the waters of North Dakota are northern pike, wall-eye pike, sauger, rock bass, yellow perch, sunfish, crappie, and a long series of rough fish including suckers, carp, ling, bullheads, buffalo fish, tullibee and catfish.

In spite of the many natural difficulties, the planting of trout and some other species has been undertaken by the North Dakota Game and Fish Department with considerable success.

Those who go out for panfish during the summer use fly rods and regular trout flies, and some of the streamer flies in the spring and fall when the fish are in deeper water. Spinners use small, bright lures and sporty, light tackle, 4-pound-test monofilament line being standard. This same equipment then fills the bill when they get around to their trout fishing.

When fishing for the large trout at the face of the dams or in the Yellowstone and Missouri Rivers, where the water is big and rough, they go to slightly heavier leaders or line. With both these outfits, and for all kinds of fishing, especially in summer and fall, you can't beat imitations of the grasshopper.

LAKE FISHING

From north to south in North Dakota the Missouri River is a series of reser-voirs, starting with GARRISON LAKE (1), which extends all the way back from the dam at Riverdale to the town of Williston on the Montana border. The lake is actually about 200 miles in length and has numerous arms, providing a great extent of shoreline.

In the tailrace below the dam there is good fishing for walleye and sauger. In the lake itself there are large rainbow trout and northern pike, plenty of walleyes, sauger, perch, crappies, goldeyes and channel catfish. The latest state record for northerns was taken at the outlet of the Snake River, on the west side of the embankment, in June of 1963. It weighed 32 pounds 2 ounces, upping the top weight by about 4 pounds over the previous record there. Sauger also run heavy, having been taken up to 8 pounds 3 ounces, the world record for the species.

Accommodations are available at a number of small towns along the lake, from Riverdale and Garrison on the east to New Town on the northern shore of the lake, and Williston at the western end.

Much of the Lake lies within the Fort Berthold Indian Reservation and a great deal of the shoreline is entirely undeveloped. Anglers new to the lake should check with Pangus Sportsman Shop, 109 Main Street, in Williston, for advice on the best spots and lures of the moment.

Good waters around Williston include the BLACKTAIL DAM (2) and SPRING-BROOK DAM (3). Tributaries of the Missouri which also bring good catches of walleye, northern pike and channel catfish are the KNIFE (4), TOBACCO GARDEN CREEK (5), LITTLE MISSOURI (6), HEART (7) and CANNONBALL (8) on the west and south; and the LITTLE MUDDY (9) and WHITE EARTH (10) on the north.

In the middle-eastern part of the state, just west of Fargo, the SHEYENNE RIVER

(11), a tributary of the Red, has been dammed to form LAKE ASHTABULA (12). This reservoir holds northern pike, walleye and sauger as well as perch and crappies. Muskellunge have also been stocked. The pike go to 30 pounds, and fishing for this species is good early in the season, while the walleyes are taken later. Many anglers consider this the best perch lake in the state.

A few miles further west is JAMESTOWN RESERVOIR (13), where there are plentiful 3- and 4-pound northerns, and walleyes and bluegills as well. SPIRITWOOD LAKE (14), a much smaller body of water to the east is also good for northerns, fair for walleye, yellow perch and catfish; and has recently been planted with muskies, with extremely satisfactory results.

South of U.S. Highway 10 at Glen Ullin is LAKE TSCHIDA (15) or Heart Butte Reservoir, on the Heart River. There are pike, walleye, largemouth black bass, perch, silver bass, and it's also considered the best crappie lake in the state. The walleyes run up to 13 pounds and better. This lake is short on facilities, so go equipped with everything you need.

There is a string of lakes along the Canadian border where good fishing can be found for largemouth black bass, walleye, northern pike, crappies, sunfish and perch. LAKE METIGOSHE (16), reached via State Highway 5 to Bottineau, then State Highway 14 to the lake, is one of the best, but occasionally suffers from drought conditions, and you should make enquiries before going there. There are a number of resorts and boat-rental agencies on the lake.

Further west is LAKE DARLING (17) on the Souris River, an excellent lake for northern pike, catches ranging from 4 to 25 pounds. There are also some very big perch, and plenty of walleyes and sauger. There are some fish in the river below the dam.

Other lakes which have established reputations with North Dakotans are STRAWBERRY LAKE (18), south of Minot on State Highway 41; GORDON LAKE (19), near St. John, north of Rolla on State Highway 5; LAKE JESSIE (20), near Williston, on U.S. 2; LAKE ILO (21), west of Strawberry, which provides some very good fly-rod fishing for bass, bluegills and crappie; and LAKE TEWAUKON (22), off State Highway 11 near Geneseo, in the extreme southeast corner of the state. Here there is good pike fishing in the lake and some fishing in the tributaries of the Red River.

Most of the trout lakes are in the south-central and southwestern part of the state, and a few in the Turtle Mountain country. Some of the lakes are McVILLE DAM (23), BOWBELLS COAL MINE LAKE (24), WELK DAM (25), NIEUWSMA DAM (26), HAMMAN LAKE (27), near Amidon; SPRING LAKE (28) near Rhame; JENSEN LAKE (29) near Killdeer north of Dickinson on U.S. Highway 10, and DAWSON POND (30), near St. Anthony.

Many of the lakes are so small that they suffer badly from winter kill and the fishing is mostly on a put and take basis, but there are some good catches made. However, the best catches are the browns and rainbows taken in the Garrison Dam, the YELLOWSTONE RIVER (31) and parts of the Missouri, though it is spotty fishing at best.

Anyone who is planning to fish North Dakota for the first time should obtain a copy of "North Dakota Fishing Guide" issued by the North Dakota Game and Fish Department, Bismarck, North Dakota. It gives exact details of where to fish and what to expect.

RIVER FISHING

The RED RIVER (32), on the eastern border of North Dakota, can on occasion

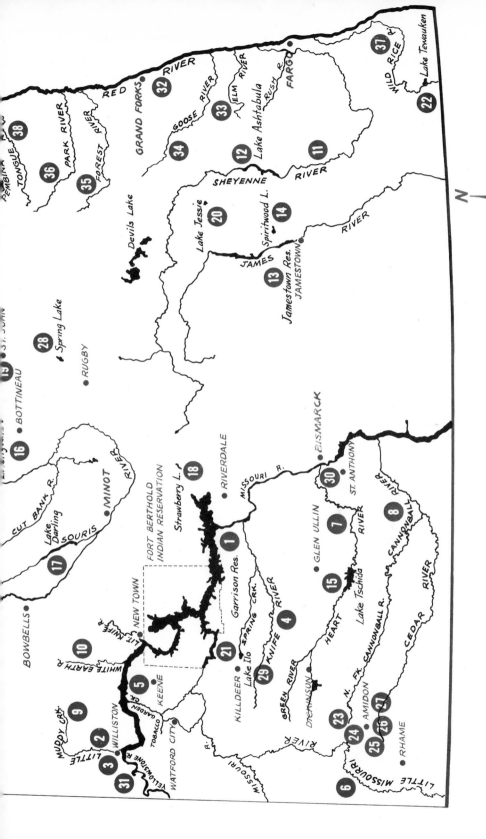

NORTH DAKOTA

produce some excellent fishing for walleyes, northerns and crappie. Anglers find that the best catches are made where smaller tributaries pour their water into the main river. In such locations a top-water plug or a popper will often take fish when the water is quite murky, as it often is. Some anglers go so far as to use phosphorus plugs, in their effort to let the fish see their offering, and on these they have made some very good catches of walleyes and northerns.

Tributaries of the Red include the SHEYENNE (11) near Valley City on U.S. 10, and the ELM (33), GOOSE (34), FOREST (35), PARK (36), WILD RICE (37) and TONGUE (38) RIVERS, each with some degree of the same fishing as the Red itself.

WINTER FISHING

North Dakota is increasingly a state where you really can fish year-round, as long as you are brave enough to face a little cold. That North Dakotans do not find it too cold is evidenced by the tremendous increase in ice fishing over the past ten years. Many anglers fish without benefit of shelter of any kind—but last year nearly 2,000 ice-fishing houses were licensed.

Such shelters, even those made of canvas, which you can move around as you please, must be licensed, but the fee is only $1.

The catch when you fish through the ice can cover everything from crappie (rarely) to trout, though northerns and perch are the most frequently taken, and most popular. Sauger and walleyes are also taken. The most widely used bait is the minnow, live and wiggling. Big ones are used for northerns, small ones for lesser species.

Those who go in for winter fishing find that the hourly catch is higher than in summer fishing; and in many species the fish are also larger. The largest ling (burbot) and sauger are usually taken at this time and by this method.

NORTH DAKOTA FISHING REGULATIONS

Resident Fishing License $2.00
Nonresident Fishing License $5.00
Nonresident 7-Day Fishing License $1.00

SEASONS AND LIMITS

Species	Open Season	Size and Bag Limit
Northern Pike	Jan. 1–March 17	18" minimum length 3 in possession
Walleye	May 11–Dec. 31	5 walleye or combination of walleye, northern and sauger
Sauger	Check annual regulations	Same as above
Trout	Check annual regulations	No limit, size or quantity

No closed season on other species

For complete regulations write: State Game and Fish Department, Capitol Building, Bismarck, North Dakota.

SOUTH DAKOTA

South Dakota lies dead center in the United States and as a result shares a number of the characteristics of east and west, north and south. Most of the natural lakes lie in the northeast corner, adjacent to the lake country of Minnesota. In the southwestern corner, the Black Hills blend into the topography of neighboring Wyoming. And running north to southwest through the middle of the state, the mighty Missouri River covers territory comparable to the plains of North Dakota and the rich agricultural lands of Iowa and Nebraska.

The fish found in the natural lakes of the northeast are walleyes, northern pike, bass, yellow perch, bluegills, crappies, sunfish and bullheads. In the Black Hills a number of rivers harbor brown, brook and rainbow trout, with extensive stocking annually adding to the supply of catchable-sized fish.

The Missouri River, where it traverses South Dakota, used to be a dead river, heavy with silt, so that few fish could live in it. With the system of dams now created on the river, much of the silting has been overcome, the aquatic growths and plankton on which fish feed thus being able to survive. As a result there is some limited river fishing in the Missouri, and some extremely good reservoir fishing for northerns, which now reach a weight of 12 pounds in three years of growth. Anglers can expect to take them weighing as much as 35 pounds on occasion. Walleyes will run to 10 pounds, while the paddlefish, found in some of these waters, has been taken up to 69 pounds in weight. In addition, a great many other warm-water fishes are found in these man-made "Great Lakes of the Missouri," in South Dakota. These include rock bass, channel catfish, yellow perch, bullhead, bluegill, pumpkinseed, green sunfish, goldeye, sauger, white bass, blue catfish, white crappie, drum and black crappie.

Several of the major east-west highways of the nation cross South Dakota, U.S. Highway 10 and U.S. Highway 12 leading into the northeastern lake section from Minnesota; while U.S. Highways 14 and 16, both top-rating travel roads, cross the state from one side to the other, providing access to the Missouri system en route. All the main highways have plentiful motel service, and the main fishing areas also have resorts and fishing camps. In addition there are innumerable resorts in the "tourist attraction" areas of the Black Hills. Anglers planning to drive to South Dakota would be well advised to obtain a copy of a very complete brochure called South Dakota Vacation Guide, published by the Black Hills, Badlands and Lakes Association, Sturgis, South Dakota. It is strictly a listing of hotel and motel accommodations, but has enough details of the surroundings of each area covered to give a good idea of the fishable nature of the surrounding country, in the case of each scenic or historic attraction.

The summer climate of South Dakota is pleasant, warm and dry in the daytime, cool enough for a blanket at night. The days are warm enough that fishing in midsummer will be better early and late; and overall, the best catches will be made in the spring and the autumn.

Since the trout streams of South Dakota are small, the trout angler will find his best weapon a small fly or spinning outfit. Flies and lures should be small, too. All the standard flies, in sizes 14 and 16 are successful, and spinners need the ⅛ ounce small spoons. For the warmwater species, fly men will want an 8½- or 9-foot rod, any single-action or automatic reel, and a GBF or GBG fly line to match the 8½-foot stick, or a GAF for the 9-footer. Streamers, bucktails and popping bugs will all get fish, depending on the condition of the water and the season.

Spinners in the lakes, larger river waters and reservoirs, will find the medium-sized spinning outfit just right, an 8-foot rod and a reel capable of holding 100 to 200 yards of 4-, 6- or 8-pound-test monofilament line. Both underwater and surface lures pay off. This outfit can also be used for bait fishing; or the standard plug-casting outfit is equally good.

Game is not a problem to the fisherman in South Dakota. Deer will be seen in the Black Hills, antelope in the Wind Cave National Park and its vicinity, and there is a buffalo herd in Custer State Park. Besides these he may see mountain goats on Harney Peak and the surrounding mountains. Care should always be exercised to watch for rattlesnakes.

EASTERN AREA

As in the neighboring state of Minnesota, the group of natural lakes in the northeast corner of South Dakota were formed by glaciers centuries ago. They are clear, fresh and spring fed, and abound in crappies, bluegill, perch, walleyes and northern pike. This is an ideal family vacation spot with plenty of good casting or bait fishing from the shores of the numerous lakes and enough good-sized fish to make it worthwhile for the more experienced angler. The largest lakes in the group are LAKE TRAVERSE (1) and its neighbor to the south, BIG STONE LAKE (2). These two form a major part of the border between South Dakota and Minnesota and are fished by anglers from both shores. There are largemouth black bass, northern pike, walleye, bluegill, crappie and bullhead. The lakes are reached from U.S. 81 and interstate Highway 29, via several county roads. The area is well supplied with hotels, motels and resorts and there are plenty of boat docks at the lakes.

To the west of U.S. 81, a lake with the fascinating name of "ENEMY SWIM" (3) has the reputation of turning out some of the best catches of the group. ROY LAKE (5), west of Sisseton on State Highway 10 is also good. Following U.S. 81 south-ward you come to Watertown, where, in nearby LAKE KAMPESKA (6) there is good angling. About fourteen miles south of this, LAKE POINSETT (7) is known for excellent angling for walleyes and panfish in winter and spring. And continuing on U.S. 81 to Madison, anglers will find bass, perch, walleyes and northerns in LAKE HERMAN (8) and MADISON LAKE (9). There is also some good fishing in the upper waters of the BIG SIOUX RIVER (10) which crosses the highway in several places. One of the favorite spots is at Dell Rapids, fifteen miles north of Sioux Falls.

This fishing is best after the spring runoff has subsided, allowing the water to clear somewhat. Bait or bright lures or fairly heavy plugs are the best producers, although when the water is right you can take the fish on small, bright fly-rod spoons.

THE GREAT LAKES OF THE MISSOURI

Most of the Missouri River fishing is in a series of great reservoirs which have been constructed along its length, slicing right down through the center of South Dakota. The Missouri is a muddy river because of the fact that its sediment content is mostly clay. The water released from the various dams which impound the reservoirs is clear for a few miles downstream, then picks up another load of sediment from tributaries along its course, so anglers try to choose the clear stretches for their sport.

The completion of the dams and the subsequent stocking of the lakes has created a sharp increase in fishing possibilities for South Dakota anglers. The OAHE DAM (12), six miles northwest of Pierre, the capital of South Dakota, backs up water for many miles to the north and will eventually form a lake 250 miles in length, extending into North Dakota. U.S. 212 crosses it about fifty miles north of Pierre and U.S. 12 crosses at Mobridge at the north end of the lake. Access roads lead in from U.S. 83 on the eastern side and from many points on the western side. The reservoir produces some excellent fishing for northerns, best in April, May and June; and for sauger, satfish and panfish year-round. During the winter months paddlefish are sometimes caught in the tailwaters of the dam.

Paddlefish occur throughout this stretch of the Missouri. This is a rare species known only here, in the Mississippi watershed, and in the Yangtze River in China, and in a very few lakes in Iowa. Its name is an adequate description; it is sharklike in shape, with a long flat bill, and is often also called spoonbill cat, boneless cat, shovel-nose cat, spoonbill sturgeon and flatbill sturgeon. There is no known sporting way to take the paddlefish, as it feeds on plankton and does not take bait. Fishermen take them by "snagging," which will not be covered in this book.

To the south of the Oahe Dam, the BIG BEND RESERVOIR (13) at Fort Thompson is also a good producer of northerns and walleyes. It is reached by State Highway 34 on the east, or via a secondary road which follows the course of the river on the western side.

Still further south, FORT RANDALL RESERVOIR (14) has some areas of shoreline which are wilderness in character. Species of fish found in its waters include northern pike, walleye, sauger, sheepshead, crappie, perch, channel catfish, sturgeon and bullheads. It can be reached from U.S. 281 on the east or U.S. 18 on the west, via secondary roads. The towns of Lake Andes and Pickstown, just above the Nebraska border, provide good accommodations.

Here the river curves around to the east, forming the state border. Near Yankton the GAVINS POINT RESERVOIR (15), also known as Lewis and Clark Lake, is subject to the least water-level variation of any of the chain and thus provides a pleasant atmosphere for fishing, with partially wooded slopes and rugged cliffs, and much wild terrain. Access is via U.S. 81 to Yankton, and State Highway 50 to various secondary roads along the north shore.

BLACK HILLS

A third area in South Dakota which is attractive to anglers is the Black Hills, northwest of Rapid City, on the western border. The altitude here is approximately one mile above sea level, providing the most pleasant summer climate in the state. There are approximately 250 miles of fresh, cool streams flowing through forests of ponderosa pine and these streams are regularly stocked with keeper-sized brown, rainbow and brook trout. The main trout streams are SPEARFISH (16) and SPRING CREEKS (17). You'll hear reports of real lunkers being taken occasionally but most

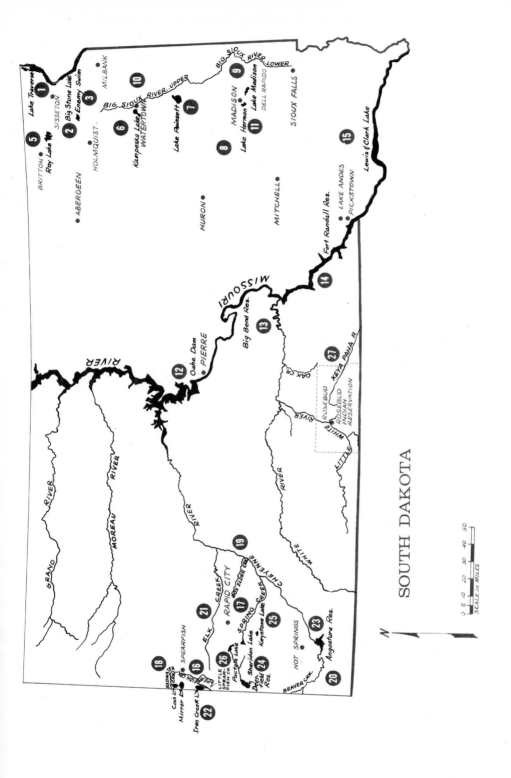

SOUTH DAKOTA

SCALE in MILES
0 5 10 20 30 40 50

N

fish will go under a pound. Many tributaries of these two, and some other small streams in the neighborhood, also offer good fishing and are known to have 4- and 5-pound fish in the less accessible waters. The best creeks are REDWATER (18), BOX ELDER (19), BEAVER (20), ELK (21) and LITTLE SPEARFISH. The latter produces catches to 2 pounds year-round. Anglers must obtain information at either Spearfish or Sturgis, on U.S. 14, as to where to fish these creeks. Wherever the water is open enough for casting, the best fishing is with flies, especially imitations of the grasshopper, floated dry. The #4 muddler is very good. When it is impossible to use a fly rod because of the extremely heavy overhang of bushes, anglers usually have to use bait, and in some of the dark pockets inaccessible by other means, they take some very good trout. Lakes in the same area which provide trout fishing are Cox's LAKE (18), IRON CREEK LAKE (16) and MIRROR LAKE (18). Since this is all in the general area of the Mount Rushmore Memorial, there are plenty of accommodations of all kinds.

In the same general area, the DEERFIELD RESERVOIR (26), reached from U.S. 385 west of Rapid City, is known for excellent catches of rainbow trout to 5 pounds. Fishing is good year-round.

Following U.S. Highway 385 or State Highway 79 south to Hot Springs, you find yourself near ANGOSTURA RESERVOIR (23), with the state's best largemouth black-bass fishing, for fish from 3 to 6 pounds. There are also walleyes, northerns, catfish and panfish. Boats are available at the lake, motels and hotels and restaurants at Hot Springs, and there are numerous resorts in the neighborhood.

SHERIDAN LAKE (24), KEYSTONE (25) and PACTOLA LAKE (26) also have some fishing possibilities.

Anglers who like to try something new and different will enjoy a trip into the waters of the ROSEBUD INDIAN RESERVATION (27), just to the east of the Black Hills, on the border between South Dakota and Nebraska. This reservation of the Sioux Indians has now been opened, under their control, as a recreational area, and includes a lot of wilderness country which can be reached only by pack trip, canoe trip or long hike. It's accessible by U.S. Highway 18, east and west, and you get your Reservation Fishing Permit and guide service at the tribal offices at the town of Rosebud. The fish are trout, bass, pike and panfish, according to the waters fished.

SOUTH DAKOTA FISHING REGULATIONS

Every person 16 years of age or older must have a license, except when fishing on own premises.

Resident Fishing License $2.00
Nonresident Fishing License $5.00
Nonresident 3-Day Fishing License $1.00

SEASONS AND LIMITS

Season and possession limits vary in three different areas in South Dakota, and regulations must be checked at the time you purchase your fishing license. In general, the limit on walleye is 6 daily, 12 in possession; northern pike, 6 daily, 12 in possession; largemouth black bass—varies, check regulations; white bass, 50 daily, 100 in possession; rock bass, varies, check regulations; crappie, 50 daily, 100 in possession; perch, 50 daily, 100 in possession; catfish, varies, check regulations; trout, varies, check regulations; bluegill, catfish, sturgeon, varies, check regulations; bullhead, 50 daily, 100 in possession.

There are no size limits on fish taken by hook and line.

For complete regulations write: Game, Fish and Parks Commission, Pierre, South Dakota.

NEBRASKA

The State of Nebraska has a wider variety of topography than is apparent from first glance at a map. On the west it is similar to the Wyoming landscape. To the south it flattens to the plains of Kansas and on the east it feels the influence of the Missouri River which forms the eastern border. The mighty Platte River traverses the entire central part of the state. While these rivers in themselves are negligible from the angler's point of view, the many tributaries and some impoundments as well as such minor streams as the Niobrara and the Blue and their tributaries, give Nebraskans a total of 11,000 odd miles of stream fishing; and to this is added a total of 3,000 lakes in which can be found some kind of fishing.

The cool streams of the piney northwestern section of the state along the borders of Wyoming and South Dakota, are a suitable habitat for trout. In the south-central area great reservoirs supply the living quarters for walleyes, northerns, white bass and crappie. The Sand Hills lakes are well supplied with northern pike, bass, crappie and bluegills. And the paddlefish, catfish, sturgeon and sauger are found in the waters of the Missouri and parts of the Platte.

The main artery of travel is U.S. 30, the first coast-to-coast paved highway. U.S. 20 also crosses the northern part of the state, and from the framework of these two major roads, Nebraska is well served by a network of north-south highways which cover every part of the state.

In addition there are numerous major airfields and more than 200 landing strips for sportsmen who fly their own planes. Information on these can be obtained from the Nebraska Department of Aeronautics, State Capitol, Lincoln 9, Nebraska. An aeronautical chart of the entire state costs $1.75; and a directory of airfields is $2 per copy. The department will also send you free radio facility data cards.

There are no dangerous wild animals in Nebraska. Mule deer will often be seen in open country and in the pine hills of the northern part of the state. White-tail deer are found in the creek and river bottoms. There are also antelope in the more arid areas. These are the largest animals but the fisherman will see plentiful small game and birds. Anglers should always watch for rattlesnakes.

The summer climate in Nebraska is very warm, and the fisherman must always be prepared for a shower, particularly in the afternoon.

While that part of the Missouri which forms Nebraska's eastern border is of little value to the angler, there is some excellent fishing in LEWIS AND CLARK LAKE (1), in the northeast corner, shared with South Dakota. This lake has the least water variation of any of the series on the Missouri and is therefore all the more attractive to fishermen. There are northern pike, walleye, sauger, channel catfish, sturgeon, crappie, perch and paddlefish. Anglers stay at Yankton or Springfield, on the South Dakota side of the lake, although there are now a few cabins near Santee on the Nebraska side. There are numerous boat marinas at the lake. The world-record sauger came from the Missouri above the Lewis and Clark Reservoir and chances of taking a big one are very good.

Another big reservoir which is attracting thousands of fishermen to Nebraska is LAKE McCONAUGHY (2), in the south-central part of Nebraska on the North Platte, just west of its juncture with the South Platte. Lake McConaughy is probably the top fishing water in Nebraska, holding eight of a total of twenty-two state records for various species taken on hook and line. There are rainbows, brook trout, brown trout, smallmouth black bass, white bass, walleyes, northern pike and crappie.

Trout fishing is best in the spring, fair in the summer and good again in the autumn. Flies and nymphs are the most popular offerings but bait fishermen make good catches on salmon eggs, worms and cheese.

For northern-pike fishing the spring months of April and May are tops. These fish are daytime hitters, ready to sock top-water lures as well as the deeper-running ones, depending on weather conditions. A 27-pound 8-ounce northern was taken in Lake McConaughy.

March to July are the months for walleyes, and they are more inclined to take well in early morning, late evening and at night. Deep-running lures and bait are most successful.

The white bass is a midsummer fish, good all the way from June through September, and the favorite lure is a shiny, silver-plated spoon.

The largemouth black bass can be taken in Lake McConaughy from July to December. Like their species anywhere, they prefer a surface lure, popper or floater, when in fairly shallow water; a deeper-running, lively but slow-working lure in deeper water.

The stilling basin below the Kingsley Dam is the place to go for trout, and officials at the dam have a schedule posted daily which will give you an indication of the level at which the fish are most likely to be found. It's worth a reference because this can vary greatly, the fish rising to flies, or again taking nothing but deeper-placed lures. Some very substantial browns and rainbows are taken here with regularity.

Ogallala is a good place to stay while fishing Lake McConaughy, and you can get good guide service and all the latest information about what is hitting and on what, from Earl Cogil at his Sportsman's Service Cafe, at the lake. There are two airplane landing strips at the lake, well used by fishermen; and a few resorts, as well as numerous camping sites.

SUTHERLAND RESERVOIR (3) and JOHNSON RESERVOIR (4), just to the south of the Platte River near the town of North Platte, produce the same fish but not as substantial in size. However, Johnson is particularly noted for turning out good catches of white bass, perch and catfish all summer, and of walleye until mid-July.

The same type of fishing is available at the ENDERS (5), SWANSON (6) and HARLAN (7) Reservoirs further south on the Republican River system.

The BIG BLUE RIVER (8) and its tributaries, with emphasis on the WEST BRANCH (9), are regarded as among the top catfish waters of the state.

Though the reservoirs along the Missouri and the Platte systems provide the major fishing in Nebraska, many smaller bodies of water are producers of good catches of smaller fish. The Sand Hills district, described in state brochures as an area of barren sand and gravel hills likened to "swells of the ocean which have become motionless or frozen," is dotted with lakes which provide excellent northern-pike fishing and also have a population of largemouth black bass, perch, crappie, bluegills and bullheads. South on U.S. 83 from the town of Valentine, in the Valentine National Wildlife Refuge, WATTS LAKE and HACKBERRY LAKE (10) offer good pike fishing, and PELICAN, DEWEY and DUCK LAKES (10) all have their share of

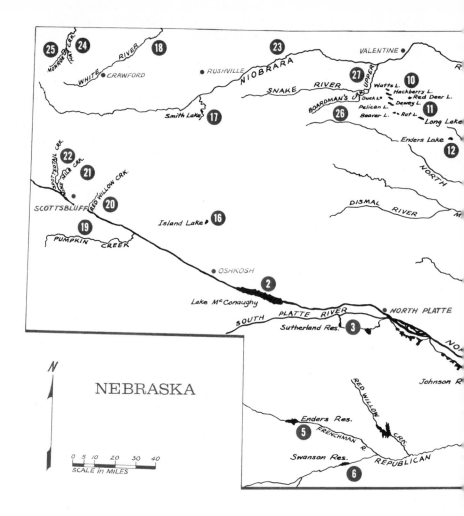

the other species found in the Sand Hills. Bait fish are prohibited in these lakes, and motors are not allowed, so it's ideal fishing for the contemplative type. Other well-known fishing lakes in the area are BEAVER, RAT and RED DEER.

Two other lakes which earn special note are LONG LAKE (11), which has plentiful bass from 2 to 3 pounds, and the ENDERS OVERFLOW (12), southwest of Ainsworth on U.S. Highway 20. The angler who gets to this water early in the season before the midsummer growth of weeds, can expect some outstanding fishing for northerns and crappie.

Other small lakes noted for good action are Ogallala, Burchard, Verdon, Grove and Fremont #2.

Near the town of Chambers, BRUNNER LAKE (13) has good pike fishing, and a food supply that makes for quick growth to large sizes. SWAN LAKE (14), south of Atkinson, and WILLOW LAKE (15) are also good. These three are on private land and permission to fish must be obtained from the land owner.

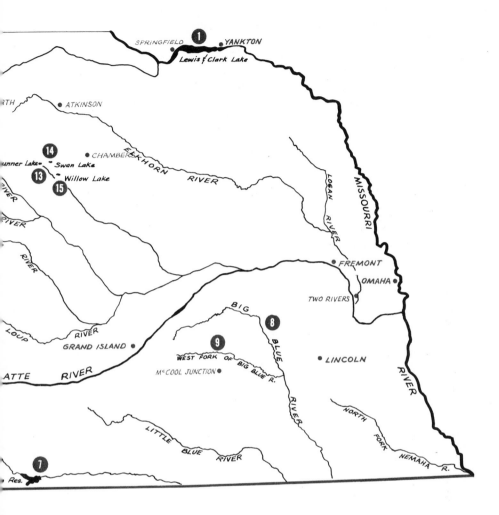

In the western Panhandle, ISLAND LAKE (16), near Oshkosh, in the Crescent Lake National Wildlife Refuge, is stocked regularly. (No bait or motors here, either.) Farther north, near Rushville, on U.S. Highway 20, SMITH LAKE (17) produces better than average fishing for bass, northern crappie, bluegill, channel catfish and bullheads. And a little further west, in the WHITE RIVER (18) below Crawford, there are black bass.

It's in the cold-water streams in the Panhandle in this northwestern part of Nebraska that the trout fisherman will find his sport. In the Scottsbluff area there is excellent trout fishing early in the season in PUMPKIN (19), RED WILLOW (20), NINE MILE (21) and SPOTTED TAIL (22) CREEKS—in fact, in all tributaries of the Niobrara. As the season progresses the NIOBRARA RIVER (23) itself, and the upper waters of the WHITE RIVER (18), above Crawford, on U.S. 20, are fair, and HAT CREEK (24) can be quite good.

MONROE CREEK (25), BOARDMAN'S CREEK (26) and the UPPER SNAKE RIVER

(27) also have some trout fishing; and in the extreme opposite end of the state, at Two Rivers, near Omaha, there is some fee fishing for trout, at $1.50 per day plus the regular Nebraska Fishing License.

The Nebraska Game, Forestation and Park Commission puts out a small guide, "Where to Fish Nebraskaland." It's well worth having. As is the "Nebraskaland's Modern Motels" folder put out by the Nebraska Motel Association. If you plan to camp, ask for the "Guide to Nebraskaland Camping," published by the Parks Division of the Nebraska Game Commission, Lincoln 9, Nebraska.

NEBRASKA FISHING REGULATIONS

Resident Fishing License $3.00
Nonresident Fishing License $5.00
Nonresident 5-Day Fishing License $2.00

DAILY BAG AND POSSESSION LIMIT

Species	Daily Bag	Possession Limit
Trout	7	7
Black Bass	10	10
Walleye	6	12
Northern Pike	6	6
White Bass	50	50
Sauger	10	10
Catfish	10	10
Crappie	50	50
Bullheads	50	50 with exceptions, for which see your regulations.

No limits on rock bass, bluegill, sunfish, freshwater drum.

In some areas a daily trout tag is required as well as the regular Nebraska Fishing License. The trout season extends roughly from April 1 to December 1, but annual regulations must be checked before fishing.

For complete regulations write: Game, Forestation and Parks Commission, Wildlife Building, State Fairgrounds, Lincoln 68509, Nebraska.

KANSAS

The State of Kansas lies squarely in the middle of the United States. On the west are the high plains sweeping down from the Rockies; on the east the wooded hills rolling back from the Missouri River, which forms part of the northeastern boundary. The major rivers, aside from the Missouri, are the Kansas and its tributaries, the Big Blue, Republican, Buffalo, Salmon and Smokey Hill; the Arkansas and its tributaries, the Rattlesnake, Minnescah, Whitewater and Walnut; and the Neosha and its tributaries, the Fall and Cottonwood.

The state is largely agricultural and the emphasis as far as the sportsman is concerned has been on shooting, which is outstanding for waterfowl and other game birds.

The lowly catfish comes into his own in Kansas, where he supplies sport in places where there are few other native species, and where he is also highly valued as a food fish, especially in the western half of the state. The flathead, also called yellow cat or mud cat, is considered the best table fish. They are found in most of the larger streams and some of the smaller ones, though they are not as common as the channel catfish. The blue catfish occurs mostly in the Missouri, with a few also in the Kaw and the Marais des Cannes. The only other fish found in the large rivers, which are generally slow moving and usually muddy, are the very occasional sturgeon and paddlefish, and the coarse species such as carp, buffalo fish, burbot and bowfin. The clearer headwaters of tributaries and small streams also have populations of largemouth black bass, a few smallmouth, crappie, sunfish, perch and walleye. These latter species are also found in most of the lakes and ponds of the state. There are few natural lakes but that situation has been improved by the addition of numerous impoundments on the larger rivers, and a state-wide network of state- and county-owned lakes. They have been stocked with the above mentioned species and also hold coarse fish such as bullhead and carp. In addition to the already mentioned species, many of these have been stocked with white bass, also called sand bass and striper in Kansas. This fish usually stays in deep water, but in May can be taken in many of the major reservoirs wherever there are rocky and weedy patches, and around river outlets.

There are no wilderness fishing areas in Kansas, all waters being easily reached via transcontinental highways Interstate Highways 70 and 33, running east and west, and then on lesser arteries; and via Interstate Highway 35, running north and south through the central part of the state. Campers will find camp sites and picnic grounds in the neighborhood of most of the fishing lakes. Those who plan to stay at motels or hotels should make reservations at the larger towns as such services are limited in small Kansas communities.

In general, the summer climate is hot and cotton clothing is sufficient. After the first of September woolens are called for, and winter fishing, which can be quite good, calls for plenty of warm clothing.

While wild game is never a problem, Kansas is one state where anglers may see buffalo in more or less wild state, as there are several herds on enclosed land. Kansas is within the range of the rattlesnake, water moccasin and the coral snake.

Anglers in Kansas use all the standard favorite tackle, the only more or less local outfit being that used for catfish. These are very often taken on 18-foot poles and heavy line. However, rod-and-reel fishermen get their share using plug- and spin-casting outfits baited with worms, chicken entrails, various home-concocted "stink baits," and even such improbable come-ons as Octagon soap and corn kernels. The catfish has taste buds all over him and all he needs to do is bump against something with a strong flavor and he immediately knows it's edible. Occasionally they are also taken on spoons trolled slow and deep, and on jigs, worked up and down in the water. The casting fraternity usually find their best fishing from mid-March through November, but catfishing remains good year-round.

Federal reservoirs, state lakes and city lakes make up the lake-fishing picture in Kansas. As is usually the case, reservoir fishing fluctuates with the water level, but most of them are maintained at sufficient depth to permit fishing throughout the summer. Occasionally state lakes are drained and cleared of rough fish and then restocked, and during this process are not fishable. Anglers should always check with the Fish and Game Commission on the condition of state lakes in the season in which they are fishing.

Aside from reservoirs and state lakes, there are thousands of farm ponds which are stocked with fish from state and federal hatcheries. Permission of the landowner can usually be obtained to fish such ponds.

Another significant addition has been made to Kansas angling through the development of "strip-mine lakes," mostly in the southeastern part of the state. Here mine operators and the Fish and Game Commission have united to restore the large areas devastated by the strip method of mining for coal. As a result a number of very fine lakes have been developed, with pleasant tree plantings to provide shade and picnic areas. The waters have been stocked with bass, crappie, bluegills, green sunfish and channel catfish. Some of the largemouth black bass taken from these ponds have run as high as 8 pounds. They respond readily to lures as well as bait. Many of the strip-mine lakes are equipped with boat launching ramps as well as picnic and camping facilities. One of the best areas is near Columbus, at the junction of U.S. 160 and U.S. 69; and another is near Pittsburgh, a few miles further north on U.S. 69.

NORTHEASTERN AREA

TUTTLE CREEK RESERVOIR (1), on the Big Blue River north of Manhattan on U.S. 24, is the largest lake in the state. It holds all the standard species and has also been stocked experimentally with northern pike. This species seems to be doing very well, and spoons, surface plugs and spinners have all been successful in taking them. Since the pike frequent shallow waters they can also be taken here on flies and very light spinning lures cast along weed beds and in holes among the weeds. There are camping facilities and boat-rental services at the lake, and a limited number of cabins.

Another large lake in this general area is KANAPOLIS RESERVOIR (2), some 3,550 acres in area when full. In 1961 this lake produced a state-record walleye weighing 10 pounds 8 ounces. There are also white bass, largemouth black bass, channel catfish, crappie, bluegill and coarse fish.

Due north, near the state border, LOVEWELL RESERVOIR (3) is 3,000 acres in size. It is stocked with all the native species and is equipped with camp ground and boat launching ramp. Food, boats and bait are available. The lake is reached by country road from Belleville, at the junction of U.S. 36 and U.S. 81.

Immediately east of Tuttle Creek Reservoir lie two state lakes which have earned a good reputation with anglers. POTTAWATOMIE COUNTY STATE LAKE No. 1 (4), reached from Westmoreland on State Highway 99, is only twenty-four acres in size but is known for good catches of bass, bluegill and some channel catfish. No boats are available but there are good picnic and camping facilities. Seventy-five-acre POTTAWATOMIE COUNTY STATE LAKE No. 2 (5) is four miles northeast of Manhattan, which is at the southern tip of Tuttle Creek Reservoir on U.S. 24. It has the same species as above, camping and picnic areas are available, and there is a concession renting boats and selling bait and food.

In the extreme northeastern corner of Kansas, BROWN COUNTY STATE LAKE (6) is reached from the town of Hiawatha, on U.S. 36. There is good fishing for bass, channel catfish, crappie and bluegill. Boats and bait are available and there is a camping area. The lake is sixty-two acres in size. Nearby ATCHISON COUNTY STATE LAKE (7) is about the same size and offers the same species and services. It is reached from Atchison at the junction of U.S. 73 and U.S. 59.

SHAWNEE COUNTY STATE LAKE (8), 135 acres in size, is reached from Silver Lake, on U.S. 24, eleven miles west of Topeka. Both Shawnee, and WASHINGTON COUNTY STATE LAKE (9), northwest of Tuttle Creek Reservoir, are comparatively new lakes, stocked with bass, channel catfish, bluegill and crappie. At time of writing there were no facilities.

LEAVENWORTH COUNTY STATE LAKE (10) has 175 acres of water and excellent camping, boat and bait facilities. It is reached from the town of Tonganoxie on U.S. 24 and U.S. 40, west of Kansas City.

LONE STAR LAKE (17), fifteen miles southwest of Lawrence, which is at the junction of U.S. 59 and U.S. 40, is used Wednesdays and Fridays for pleasure boating and water skiing, but at other times usually offers good fishing.

OSAGE COUNTY STATE LAKE (18) is nineteen miles south of Topeka, off U.S. 75. This is a very popular lake and there are all facilities.

In the same eastern sector of the state there are currently several more lakes under construction. A number of lakes are also operated by counties and cities, usually with some small (25¢ to $2) daily or annual fee charged for use. One of the largest, 434 acres in size, and regarded as a top bass lake, is LAKE COUNCIL GROVE (11), three miles west and one mile north of the city of Council Grove, on U.S. 56. There are also bluegill, ring perch, crappie and channel catfish. Camping is permitted and live bait and food are available.

Smaller lakes with similar services, on some of which, however, no fee is charged, will be found at Herington City, on U.S. 56 immediately west of Council Grove; LAKE WABAUNSEE (12), five miles west of Eskridge, on State Highway 4, southwest of Topeka; SABETHA CITY LAKE (13), five miles west of Sabetha, on U.S. 36; HORTON CITY LAKE (14) at Horton, on U.S. 159; and WYANDOTTE COUNTY LAKE (15) about twelve miles northwest of Kansas City. The latter usually provides good fishing and there are boats available and plenty of tourist courts nearby.

Close to Kansas City are OLATHE LAKES (16), near the city of Olathe on Interstate Highway 35. The old lake is reached via U.S. 50 and is stocked with all species but considered especially good for bass. There are picnic and camping facilities, boat ramps and docks. The new lake is three miles west of Olathe and is stocked with crappie, bass, bluegills and channel catfish. Facilities also available here.

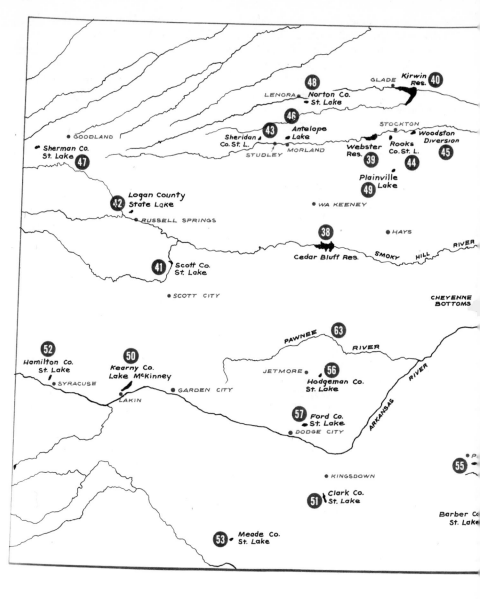

GLADE
48 Norton Co. St. Lake   Kirwin Res. 40
LENORA
46
43   Antelope Lake   STOCKTON   Woodston Diversion
GOODLAND   Sheridan Co. St. L.   Webster Res.   Rooks Co. St. L.   45
Sherman Co. St. Lake   STUDLEY   MORLAND   39   44
47
Plainville Lake
49
42 Logan County State Lake
RUSSELL SPRINGS   WA KEENEY
38   HAYS
41 Scott Co. St. Lake   Cedar Bluff Res.   SMOKY   HILL   RIVER
SCOTT CITY   CHEYENNE BOTTOMS
PAWNEE   63
52   RIVER
Hamilton Co. St. Lake   50   JETMORE   56 Hodgeman Co. St. Lake   RIVER
SYRACUSE   Kearny Co. Lake McKinney   ARKANSAS
LAKIN   GARDEN CITY
57 Ford Co. St. Lake
DODGE CITY
KINGSDOWN   55   P
51 Clark Co. St. Lake   Barber C St. Lake
53 Meade Co. St. Lake

KANSAS

N

0   10   20   30   40
SCALE IN MILES

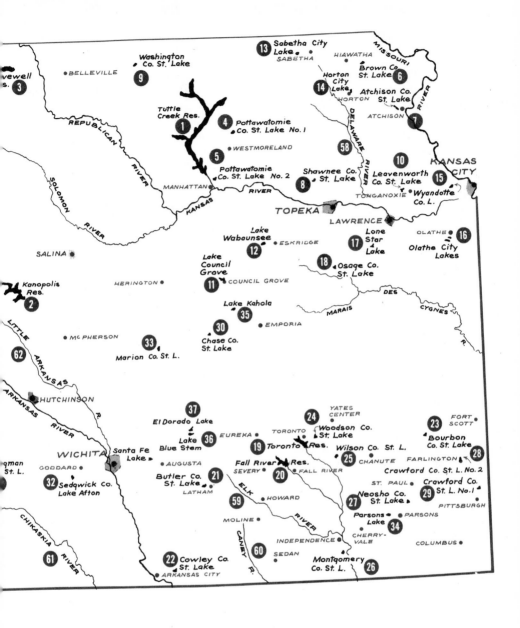

SOUTHEASTERN AREA

There are a number of large reservoirs in southeast Kansas. TORONTO RESERVOIR (19) and FALL RIVER RESERVOIR (20) are close together, between U.S. 54 and State Highway 96, halfway between Wichita and the eastern state line. Each is slightly more than 2,500 acres in size, and they are heavily stocked with walleyes, white bass, channel cats, largemouth black bass, crappie and bluegill. The towns of Toronto and Fall River have some tourist accommodations and camp sites are available at the lakes. Boats are also available.

Another lake in southeastern Kansas which offers fishing for the above mentioned species is BUTLER COUNTY STATE LAKE (21), 124 acres in size, which lies two miles west and one mile north of Latham, near Augusta, on U.S. 54. Bait, food and boats are available. COWLEY COUNTY STATE LAKE (22), thirteen miles east of Arkansas City on U.S. 166, is eighty acres in size. This clear, deep lake usually produces well. Boats, food and bait are available and there are camping facilities. At BOURBON COUNTY STATE LAKE (23), nineteen miles west of Fort Scott, on U.S. 54, near the eastern border of the state, there are camping facilities but no boats or other concessions. WOODSON COUNTY STATE LAKE (24) covers 179 acres, and is located five miles east of Toronto Reservoir. There is good fishing for largemouth black bass, crappie, channel catfish and bluegills. Food, bait and boats are available and there is a heated fishing dock.

WILSON COUNTY STATE LAKE (25) is thirteen miles south of Yates Center on U.S. 75. The lake is 119 acres in size, and there are camping facilities. Reached via U.S. 169 to the town of Independence, is MONTGOMERY COUNTY STATE LAKE (26), 105 acres, with camp sites, boats, motors and bait available. There are neither boats nor bait at NEOSHE COUNTY STATE LAKE (27), near Parsons, at the junction of U.S. 160 and 59, but the lake is provided with fishing docks for night fishing. Another lake which has a fishing dock is CRAWFORD COUNTY STATE LAKE No. 2 (28), one mile north and one mile east of Farlington on State Highway 7 near the eastern border of the state. A heated dock, privately operated, is open all winter for crappie fishing. Other species in the lake are bass, channel catfish and bluegill.

This is the general area of some of the best strip-mine lakes. CRAWFORD COUNTY STATE LAKE No. 1 (29), four miles north of Pittsburgh, covers about sixty acres and produces bass, crappie, bluegill and channel catfish. A 3 pound 4 ounce white crappie was recently taken from this lake. In this southeastern corner of the state are hundreds of other strip-mine lakes which have produced such good catches as a 2 pound 2 ounce green sunfish, a 10½-pound walleye and a 20½-pound carp.

CHASE COUNTY LAKE (30), 109 acres in size, can be reached from State Highway 13, south of Cottonwood Falls, near Emporia, on U.S. 50. It holds bass, crappie, bluegill and channel catfish.

Towards the middle of the state, KINGMAN COUNTY STATE LAKE (31) about fifty miles west of Wichita off U.S. 54, offers lake fishing with the added attraction of fishing in the Ninnescah River below the lake.

There are three shallow lakes in the Marais des Cannes Waterfowl Management area, close to the eastern state border, reached via U.S. 69. In spring and early summer fishing is good, with many bass in the 4-pound class. Later in the season there is too much vegetation for good fishing. Similar possibilities will be found in the Neosho Waterfowl Management Area near St. Paul on State Highway 57.

Numerous other small lakes in southeastern Kansas are controlled by either the city or county in which they are located. In many cases there is a small daily, weekly or annual fee charged to fish these lakes. At SEDGWICK COUNTY LAKE (32), also known as Lake Afton, near Goddard, on U.S. 54, west of Wichita, there are some cabins as well as boats and bait available. The lake is 240 acres in size. MARION COUNTY LAKE (33) is near the town of the same name, on U.S. 56. Besides the above mentioned facilities there are several fishing piers. PARSONS LAKE (34), off U.S. 160, at Parsons, also has fishing docks and boats. It is 980 acres in size. LAKE KAHOLA (35), nineteen miles northwest of Emporia City, on U.S. 50, produces some good fishing for all the local species and there is a camping area.

Another fairly large lake is BLUESTEM (36), reached by State Highway 13, northeast of the town of El Dorado. Boats, motors and food are available. Only a quarter of a mile away is Old EL DORADO CITY LAKE (37), 315 acres in size.

The Lake at Cherryvale, on U.S. 169, just north of the Oklahoma border, though only forty-five acres in size, has produced bass up to 8 pounds, on artificial lures, and is popular with the casting fraternity.

NORTHWESTERN AREA

Three major reservoirs in northwest Kansas are CEDAR BLUFF (38), WEBSTER (39) and KIRWIN (40). Food, boats and bait are available at all three. Cedar Bluff, 6,600 acres in size, is reached from U.S. 40 at Ogallah, near Hays; or south on U.S. 283 from WaKeeney. There are largemouth black bass, channel catfish, crappie, bluegill, sunfish, walleyes, bullheads, carp and white bass. Some of the latter run to 3 pounds. Webster Reservoir, located immediately west of Stockton on U.S. 24, is 4,000 acres in size. It has been stocked with channel catfish, largemouth bass, walleyes, crappie, bluegill and bullheads. The Kirwin Reservoir is on the Solomon River, near U.S. 183 at the town of Glade. It has the same fishing as the other two.

To the east of these, about the middle of the state, are the Cheyenne Bottoms, immediately north of Great Bend, at the junction of U.S. 281 and U.S. 56. While this is mainly a wildfowl area, it has been stocked with channel catfish and bullheads. There are no boats or services available, but accommodations will be found at Great Bend.

SCOTT COUNTY STATE LAKE (41) at Scott City, at the junction of U.S. 83 and State Highway 96, contains largemouth black bass, crappie, bluegill, channel catfish and bullheads. Boats are available and there is a campground.

Other state lakes which provide good fishing for the above mentioned species, but on which boats are not available, are LOGAN COUNTY STATE LAKE (42), seventy-five acres, found four miles northwest of Russell Springs on State Highway 25; SHERIDAN COUNTY STATE LAKE (43), eighty-seven acres, which is two and a half miles west of Studley on U.S. 24; ROOKS COUNTY STATE LAKE (44), three miles southwest of Stockton at the junction of U.S. 24 and U.S. 183; and the WOODSTON DIVERSION (45), east of Stockton.

City and county lakes in northwest Kansas, where there is some fishing, are ANTELOPE LAKE (46), eighty-five acres in size. It is located two and a half miles north of Morland, on U.S. 24; SHERMAN COUNTY LAKE (47), twelve miles southwest of Goodland, on U.S. 24 near the Colorado border; NORTON COUNTY LAKE (48), near Lenora on State Highway 9; and PLAINVILLE LAKE (49), two miles west of Plainville, on U.S. 183. This lake is one of the few city lakes in northwestern Kansas that has boats available.

SOUTHWESTERN AREA

The largest fishing lake in southwestern Kansas is LAKE McKINNEY (50), of Kearny County State Lake, two miles east of Lakin on U.S. 50. This 3,000-acre impoundment is limited to channel catfish, bullheads and carp. Further east, CLARK COUNTY LAKE (51), 337 acres in size, is reached from Kingsdown on U.S. 54. This is one of the deepest lakes in the state. There are no concessions, but a camp ground is available.

HAMILTON COUNTY STATE LAKE (52), three miles west of Syracuse on U.S. 50, is ninety-four acres in area. There are camping facilities and boat-launching ramp. The lake is stocked with bass, crappie, bluegills and channel catfish. The same species are found in MEADE COUNTY STATE LAKE (53), on U.S. 160. This 100-acre lake is highly developed, with boats, bait and food available.

Well to the east, at Medicine Lodge, on U.S. 160, is BARBER COUNTY STATE LAKE (54), seventy-seven acres in size, with fishing for bass, channel catfish, crappie, bluegill and bullheads. There is a boat-launching ramp.

PRATT COUNTY LAKE (55), three miles southeast of Pratt at the junction of U.S. 281 and U.S. 54, holds all the native species, and there are camping facilities. There are out-of-county fishing fees and also a boat fee.

HODGEMAN COUNTY LAKE (56), five and one half miles east of Jetmore on U.S. 156, is thirty-three acres in size when full. There are no boats or bait available. The same is true of seventy-six-acre FORD COUNTY LAKE (57), three and one half miles northeast of Dodge City on U.S. 50, but there is a boat-launching ramp.

Throughout the state are a number of similar lakes and ponds, some of which vary in fishing quality from year to year; and on those described, facilities also change annually. Anglers planning a visit to Kansas should write the Information Division of the Kansas Forestry, Fish and Game Commission, Pratt, Kansas, for current details.

RIVER FISHING

As mentioned earlier, fishing in the larger rivers is pretty well limited to catfish; but in the tributaries and headwaters and some of the smaller streams such sporting species as crappie, largemouth black bass, sunfish and white bass provide sport for light-tackle casters. The angler must seek out his own fishing on this score, as it varies widely in each river, according to the conditions at the time. However, some of this type of angling will be found in the headwaters of the DELAWARE (58), north of Topeka, accessible from U.S. 75 via State Highways 4, 16 and 9; in the ELK (59), immediately to the south, reached from Elk Falls on U.S. 160, west of Independence; the CANEY (60), which crosses U.S. 160 about six miles further west, and also crosses U.S. 166 further south; the CHIKASKIA (61), which crosses U.S. 281, State Highways 14 and 2, southwest of Wichita, and U.S. 166 near the Oklahoma border; the LITTLE ARKANSAS (62), which crosses U.S. 56 about fourteen miles west of McPherson, at the junction of U.S. 81 and U.S. 56, and also crosses State Highways 61, about ten miles north of Hutchinson on U.S. 50; and the PAWNEE (63), which roughly parallels U.S. 156 to the north, between Garden City and Larned.

The Flint Hills section of south-central Kansas has numerous clear streams which are ideal for fly-rod fishing and light spinning for green sunfish, spotted bass, channel and other catfish. Fly-rodders have real sport here, taking the game little sunnies and bass on top-water lures or streamers, while wading as in a trout stream. The fish are small but it's lots of fun amid pleasant surroundings. Early fall is best, though the fishing is good throughout most of the year. The hair bugs and hair flies are most successful. Permission should be obtained from landowners before going on the land. The Flint Hills lie east of Arkansas City on U.S. 166. They are rolling, grass-covered hills and the small streams which form a network across the valleys are marked by lines of low trees, the only tall growth on the landscape.

KANSAS FISHING REGULATIONS

Resident Fishing License $3.00
Nonresident Fishing License $5.00
Nonresident Trip Fishing License, 10 days $3.00

SEASONS AND LIMITS

Species	Open Season	Bag Limit	Size Limit
Black Bass	No closed season	10	None
Channel Catfish, Blue Catfish, Flathead Catfish	No closed season	10 in aggregate	None
The daily creel limit of the above species, in combination, is 10 fish.			
Walleye, Sauger	No closed season	5	None
Crappie	No closed season	Not to exceed 30 lbs.	None
Northern Pike	No open season		

For complete regulations write: Forestry, Fish and Game Commission, P.O. Box 581, Pratt, Kansas.

OKLAHOMA

The State of Oklahoma is a plateau sloping down from a height of 4,900 feet in the northwest to the southeast, where in the Texarkana corner the altitude is only 400 feet above sea level. All the drainage is from the northwest to the southeast via such major streams as the Arkansas, Cimarron, Canadian Washita and the Red, the latter forming the southern border of the state between Oklahoma and Texas. However, within the state none of these rivers are of much importance to fishermen, though several reservoirs on the rivers provide most of the lake fishing in Oklahoma.

While the area is a plateau, nevertheless it has some mountain elevations in the Wichita Mountains and the Arbuckle Mountains which run across the southern part of the state; and in the Ozarks which jut into the northeastern sector.

Owing to the nature of the country, natural lakes are few but those that do exist have been highly developed, and a number of man-made lakes have improved the fishing scene considerably over the conditions supplied by nature. To further develop the use of available fishing water, some of the lakes feature covered fishing docks which can be heated in cold weather and are air conditioned in hot weather.

The species of fish found in Oklahoma are largemouth black bass, smallmouth black bass, white bass, crappie, bluegill, channel catfish, flathead catfish, bullhead, and some rainbow trout.

Wild animals are not much a part of the Oklahoma scene. The outdoorsman may see coyote, fox, wolverine, and very occasionally antelope in the northwestern corner of the state, and whitetail deer and bison on preserves. However, as throughout the South and West, the angler should at all times guard against poisonous snakes.

The winter climate in Oklahoma is pleasant for fishing most of the time. In midsummer, when the days are very warm, anglers tend to go out in the early morning and late evening. During the winter, the daytime fishing is excellent.

The major east-west highway enters the state from Joplin, Missouri, and as Interstate Highway 44 travels southwest to Oklahoma City, then on west as U.S. 66. The main north-south highway is Interstate Highway 35, slicing through the middle of the state from the Kansas to the Texas boundary, on a line with Oklahoma City and Fort Worth.

The GRAND LAKE OF THE CHEROKEES (1), on the GRAND RIVER (2) in the northeastern corner of Oklahoma, is the largest body of water in the state. It is sixty miles long, with so many arms and inlets that there are close to 1,000 miles of shoreline. The fish are largemouth black bass, white bass, sunfish, crappie and rough fish. This lake is heavily fished both by Oklahomans and Missourians, being only forty miles from Joplin, Missouri, but it is so large and winding that there is no feeling of crowding. There are plenty of accommodations around the lake, and boats are available at numerous docks.

The white bass is generally regarded as the prime favorite, and is very popular as a table delicacy. Two successful lures are the jigs and the Fle Flys, but don't let that hamper your own inventiveness. These scrappy little fellows will take a wide

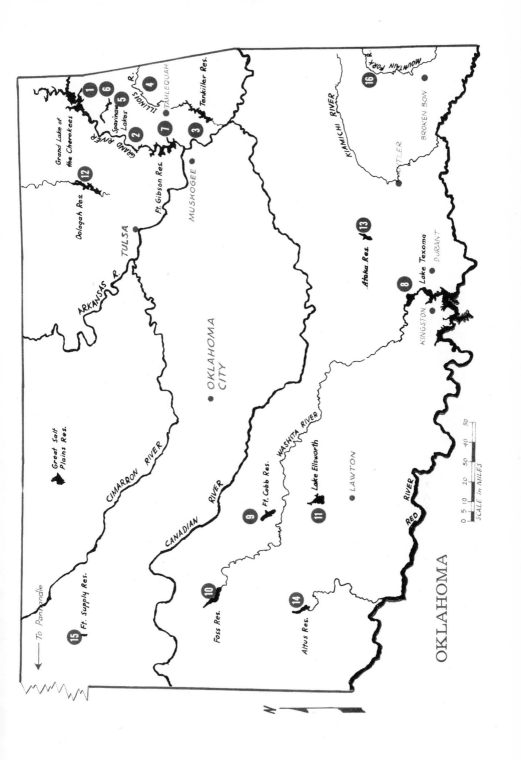

OKLAHOMA

variety of lures under a wide variety of circumstances, and it is better to follow your own intuitions. They may very well pay off.

To the south of this lake, east of Muskogee, TENKILLER LAKE (3), on the Illinois River, offers the same kind of fishing: good catches of large and smallmouth black bass, white bass, bluegills, crappie and channel catfish as well as flathead catfish. The lake is thirty miles long and only three miles wide at its broadest point, providing plentiful shoreline for fishermen to work. There are some rainbows in the river below the dam.

Just to the north, the town of Tahlequah is a good headquarters from which to plan a float trip on the ILLINOIS River (4), one of the few clear, floatable streams in the state, where the catch will be largemouth and white bass.

Immediately to the south of the Grand Lake of the Cherokees are the SPAVINAW LAKES (5) and LAKE EUCHA (6), where the bass fishing is usually good. Spring and fall are the best times and the favorite lure is the plastic worm.

South again, and only thirty miles east of Tulsa, is FORT GIBSON LAKE (7) on the Grand River. Crappie fishing is very good here and there are several covered docks or fishing barges, air conditioned or heated as required. For a guide in this area try Joe Kreiger, Jr., who was 1961 World Series of Fishing Champion. His address: 5132 East 25th Place, Tulsa. Or Francis (Little Doc) Bauder, Langley, Oklahoma; or Carl Potter, Spavinaw, Oklahoma. All are good fishermen and know the area thoroughly.

Ninety minutes from Dallas and Fort Worth, two and a half hours from Oklahoma City, formed by a dam on the Red River on the Oklahoma-Texas border, vast LAKE TEXOMA (8) is the outstanding fishing feature of the state. The dam backs up both the Red River and the Washita to form a vast, sprawling lake with great variation and many miles of shoreline. The north shore, in Oklahoma, is generally sandy and sloping, while the Texas shore is steeper and more rocky. The lake is 140 square miles in area and there is more than 1,000 miles of shoreline. Fishermen should check with local authorities about fishing licenses, as there are variations in both price and legal limits between the two states.

The largemouth black bass is the chief quarry here, and is taken in weights up to 9 pounds with satisfying regularity. There is good bass fishing year-round, with a high time for the big ones in the spring and again in the fall. The largest taken to date went 12 pounds 4 ounces. In addition there are white or sand bass, known locally as "sandies," and there are also crappie, blue, yellow and channel catfish, bream, goggle-eye and perch.

The sandy is a popular favorite with casters because it surfaces in schools at times, and casters can take their limit in record time when they find such a school. Again, anglers should watch the local regulations. Texas allows a limit of twenty-five per day. Oklahoma sets no limit on the number that can be taken.

When the sandies are not surfacing they still run in schools and then anglers must go deep for them, using minnows. Once you have located a school, you can catch your limit readily. These fish average about 1½ pounds.

There are as many as fifteen fishing barges on Texoma, some heated in winter, air conditioned in summer, all provided with all the comforts of home. Usually they are built in the style of a runway around a fishing well, and are equipped with comfortable chairs where the angler may sit and drop his bait overboard. Lazy man's fishing, if you like, but some good catches are made and there is always the assurance of some fish, as the waters in the area of the barges are baited.

The Roosevelt Bridge on which Highway 70 between Durant and Kingston crosses the Washita waters of the lake, in the northeast, is the only bridge in the state where fishing is allowed—and here you will sometimes think that fishing has taken over and the passage of vehicles is of secondary importance. On a spring or summer night, a car can hardly get by the hundreds of anglers, completely equipped with bait buckets, flashlights, and deck chairs, who scramble for places and set up shop from one end of the bridge to the other. Many good bass are taken from the bridge. Hooking an 8-pounder calls for a long hike to shore and a descent to the riprap to land it. White bass are also taken in great quantities, and occasionally catfish running from 12 to 28 pounds.

Lights suspended close to the water draw the fish, and then the multitude of anglers offer a multitude of baits and lures. Minnows are by far the most popular and successful bait. They sell for $1 for three dozen, and this is one place you get your full money's worth, for nearly every dollar's worth you buy will turn out to be closer to five dozen.

On a Saturday night there will be between 300 and 400 people at the Roosevelt Bridge, and it is natural that a great many sinkers and lures, as well as lines and even rods, are lost overboard. Rumor has it that one salvage man makes a very good living dredging up tackle from under the bridge. Anglers who fish Lake Texoma can count on ten months of fishing, January and February being the off months, although some fish are taken then.

Other Oklahoma Lakes which have a more or less local reputation for fishing are the FORT COBB RESERVOIR (9) in the southwest; the FOSS RESERVOIR (10) in the same area; LAKE ELLSWORTH (11), north of Lawton; OOLOGAH RESERVOIR (12) in the northeast; LAKE ATOKA (13) in the southeast; ALTUS-LUGERT RESERVOIR (14) in the Wichita Mountains; and FORT SUPPLY RESERVOIR (15) in the northwest near Fort Supply.

As mentioned earlier, the Illinois River can be floated, in the Tenkiller area, and the MOUNTAIN FORK RIVER (16) in eastern Oklahoma is also good for floating. The fish are smallmouth black bass, channel catfish, crappie and bluegill.

Most of the stream fishing is in the extreme southeast corner of the state, where the Kiamichi and Mountain Fork Rivers are fine little streams, the latter being floatable. Headquarters for fishing in this area is Broken Bow, at the Junction of U.S. 70 and State Highways 3 and 7. Or you can fish the river higher up, from the town of Antlers, at the Junction of U.S. 271 and State Highways 3 and 7.

The Kiamichi and Winding Stair Mountains give a watershed here to fill a number of small streams such as the Sallisaw, Big Lee's, and Barren Fork, the Mountain Fork, Little Beaver, Glover, Anderson and Bear, Black Fork, Breakdown, Little and the Coal.

The only fishable river in western Oklahoma is the Washita, which enters from Texas, then goes southeast to the Red River. However, there are a few sweetwater streams in the area of the Great Salt Plains National Wildlife Refuge in north-central Oklahoma, almost on the Kansas border, and these have black bass, bluegill and crappie. The lake itself has only catfish as the water is too salty for others to survive.

OKLAHOMA FISHING REGULATIONS

Resident Fishing License $2.00
Nonresident Fishing License $5.00
Nonresident 10-Day Fishing License $2.25

SEASONS AND LIMITS

Species	Open Season	Daily Bag Limit
Black Bass	All year	10 in aggregate
Channel and Blue Catfish	All year	15 in aggregate
Walleye	All year	5
Trout	All year	6
Crappie	All year	37

For complete regulations write: Department of Wildlife Conservation, State Capitol, Oklahoma City 5, Oklahoma.

Gulf Coast States

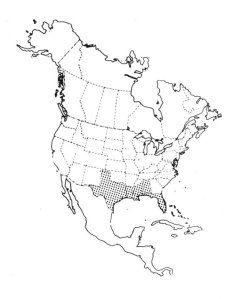

The Gulf States all take the major part of their nature from the fact that they border on the great, shallow, warm Gulf of Mexico and share in the benefits of its major feeder stream, the Mississippi. Almost the entire area, as far as the fisherman is concerned, is low, swampy bayou country. In the northeast the remnants of the southern Appalachians give some height to northern Alabama, while in the south and west Texas marks the transformation from bayou country to the great dry plains of the New Mexican desert.

The inland, fresh water provide fishing for largemouth black bass and some few smallmouth, and panfish of myriad variety, including Kentucky spotted bass, stripes or white bass, crappie, bluegills, redear bream, shellcracker, rock bass or goggle eye, and so on. There are also channel and blue catfish, as well as sturgeon and coarse fish.

The saltwater species are also many and varied, including sea trout, channel bass, snappers, groupers, sea bass, flounder, cobia, tarpon and sailfish. In addition, some few rivers have annual migrations of the striped bass usually associated with more northern waters.

FLORIDA

The State of Florida represents the United States' share in the subtropical zone of the Northern Hemisphere. Its landscape is almost wholly marine, the exception being the mid-state area from Lake Okeechobee north to the Georgia border, where citrus groves cover the gently rolling hills marking the state's only uplands. Even here the influence of the sea is felt in tidal movement in almost every stream. In south-central and western Florida the vast Everglades swamps slant to Florida Bay and the Gulf of Mexico, providing a scene unknown elsewhere in the United States; and to the south, a long string of islands, the Florida Keys, juts out 160 miles, with the Gulf on one side and the Atlantic Ocean on the other.

More than 600 species of fish are found in the salt waters that lap Florida's shores. The main species of interest to the sport fisherman are the African pompano, **Allison tuna, amberjack, barracuda, blackfin tuna, bluefish, black drum, bonefish, bonito, cobia,** false albacore, dolphin, grouper, jack, jewfish, kingfish, ladyfish, **mackerel, mako** shark, blue marlin, white marlin, permit, pompano, redfish, sailfish, **various sharks,** snapper, cobia, snook, swordfish, tarpon, spotted sea trout, gray trout, bluefin tuna, wahoo and Warsaw grouper. In the fresh waters of the many inland lakes, ponds and rivers there are largemouth black bass, crappie, bluegills and numerous other panfish; and into some of the lakes and ponds, and into most of the streams which have outlets to the sea, move tarpon, snook, jacks, redfish, ladyfish and others, according to the tide and the season.

The major highways leading into Florida are U.S. 1 at Jacksonville and its parallel Interstate Highway 95, now complete almost all the way from Jacksonville to Miami. U.S. 17 from north-central coastal points also feeds traffic to these two highways at Jacksonville, and itself goes on across and south all the way to Punta Gorda on the southwest coast. U.S. 301 enters the state along with U.S. 1, below Folkston, Georgia, then branches westward to serve the north central and Tampa area. U.S. 41 comes in from south of Valdosta, Georgia, and proceeds down through the center of the state as far as Tampa, then east to Miami as the Tamiami Trail. U.S. 27 and U.S. 19 pick up traffic from Tallahassee and west to funnel it down to the Florida Peninsula. The only part of Florida in which there are not good access roads is the Everglades and even these may be penetrated to some degree via the Tamiami Trail on the southern fringes, U.S. 27 to lake Okeechobee on the east, and State Highway 80 from Clewiston to Fort Myers on the north. Between Fort Myers and the Trail, near Ochopee, there are now two roads, State Highway 82 and State Highway 29, providing deeper penetration into this Everglades area, and a number of secondary roads work well back into the northern part of the Glades.

Florida is also well served by two railways, the Florida East Coast and the Seaboard Line; and practically every major airline in the country.

The climate in Florida is semitropical. Daytime temperatures in summer average between 80 and 90, evenings go down to about 75. In the winter, while many days register temperatures in the 80's, there are cold spells, especially in the northern part of the state, and at this time light woolens are pleasant to have. At all times fishermen should have rainsuits, both pants and jackets, as a protection against squalls. The rain in Florida usually comes in buckets when it comes. Standard footgear is the rubber-soled sneaker, safe on both sand and boat decks. Anglers should always wear long-sleeved shirts and long slacks until they have acquired a good coat of tan, and even then, if they are to be out for long periods of time. The sun and salt wind together can cause severe burns even to those who think they are inured to them. Sunglasses are also essential, and a hat with either a wide brim or a peak. Those who plan to wade along the beaches in search of shallow-water fish should carry an extra pair of sneakers for that. Be sure they have laces to tie them on, as the other kind come off in sand or mud. Barefoot wading can result in bad cuts from shells, and there's always the possibility of stepping on a sea urchin with its sharp spines.

Needless to say, use lots of sunburn lotion; and if you get a cut or an abrasion in Florida, treat it immediately. The warm, damp air is conducive to infection.

With all its charms, there are many pests to beware of in Florida. While there are some bear and wild cat and cougar in the Everglades, these are never any danger, fleeing from man faster than he flees from them. But at all times, even on the road as you step from your car, you should watch for snakes as the Florida rattler is deadly, the cottonmouth moccasin extremely dangerous. There are also coral snakes, though these are not so great a danger because of their small mouths. A coral snake must literally chew its way in to bite, and you would almost have to be asleep to have this happen.

All the lakes and potholes in Florida may have populations of alligators, and crocodiles are spotted here and there in salty stretches. Anyone wading in such waters should be extremely cautious.

Bugs are another serious pest. As is often the case, where the fishing is good, the insects are bad. Use lots of repellent.

Perhaps the most feared "critter" in Florida is the shark. While there are not many records of people being attacked by these vicious marauders, there are some. Anglers who are wading in the salt should keep a wary eye out for them and if you see one, get into shallow water immediately. Sometimes a 9- or even 14-foot shark will come into water only 4 or 5 feet deep. If you should cut yourself, and blood is getting into the water, get out quickly, as there's nothing draws a shark like blood. Another watery hazard is the Portuguese man o' war. Always watch for them when wading, and if there are many in the water, it's better to stay on shore. They can cause serious stings and many bathers who have encountered them have had to be hospitalized. This is another reason for wearing long trousers rather than shorts when wading without hip boots or waders.

Whatever type of tackle an angler likes to use at home, he will usually find suitable for some kind of Florida fishing. In the lake areas bass bugging with a fly rod is very popular and the same 9- or 9½-foot rod used there is suitable for many of the saltwater species which can be taken on flies. The rod should be lined with a GAF or G2AF forward-tapered line, and 200 yards of 18-pound-test nylon squidding line for backing, for smaller, inshore fish. The backing can be upped to 30-pound-test Dacron for 100-pound tarpon and bigger offshore fish.

Plug casters will find the most useful rod in the salt is one about 6 feet 1 inch in length, equipped with a good stout reel with cub drag, and 15-pound-test monofilament line. A smaller outfit will do for freshwater fishing. Spinners in fresh water generally use a medium spinning outfit with 4-pound-test line if you want to go really light, and a maximum of 8-pound test. The rig with the 8-pound test is also used in the salt for most of the smaller species, and this outfit will also handle some quite big fish. Tarpon up to 90 pounds have been landed on 8-pound-test line. However, if you plan to be using big, heavy lures such as 7-inch-long surface plugs, and jigs weighing 3 to 3½ ounces, they can be worked better if you use a heavier rod and 12-pound-test line.

As far as lures and flies are concerned, anglers can work on the principal that saltwater fish like a brighter lure, a faster retrieve, and mind commotion less than do the freshwater species. This does not mean they mind noise less. It must be the right kind of noise to attract them. Spinning and plug-casting lures which attract such voracious feeders as the jacks, barracuda, tarpon, ladyfish, redfish, spotted sea trout and others, include the top-water popping plugs (with stout, salt-resistant hooks), and lead-headed jigs with tail of feathers or deer hair. The latter can be cast and retrieved just under the surface, or allowed to sink, then worked in a jigging way, in fast or slow upward pulls, to make the lure dance up and down through the water.

The fly fisherman going into the salt will need a considerable variety of flies, according to the fish he is seeking. For bonefish and other shallow-water swimmers, the small Phillips pink shrimp fly on hook sizes 6, 4 and 2, and the various bonefish bucktails on 1/0 and 3/0 hooks are what is needed. For snook, redfish and other such species, the breather type flies, with flaring wings of feathers, on hooks ranging from 1/0 all the way up to 5/0, will serve, according to the depth of the water you are fishing. The famous "blonde" patterns of saltwater bucktails are excellent. In many cases a saltwater popper is also very successful. The skipping bug made of balsa wood is light to cast and buoyant in the water. It should be tied on 1/0 and 3/0 hooks, and have a tail of deer hair, not feathers. The 1/0 is fine for ladyfish, spotted sea trout, mangrove snapper, small tarpon, small snook, small jacks and small redfish. The larger popper is good for tarpon, snapper, snook, barracuda, redfish, amberjack, jack crevalle and dolphin.

In Florida there are many party boats, also called bottom boats and head boats, on which anglers may fish for anything from $1.50 per person up to $10 per person, depending on the type of boat and the number of anglers in the party. In most cases you should query the captain as to what to use in the way of tackle. Sometimes it is provided, and in such case is usually quite heavy gear. If you bring your own, a stout spinning rod and reel with 12-pound-test monofilament line will usually fill the bill.

While prices vary somewhat according to location and service, anglers will find that in general, a day trolling offshore for big-game fish will cost about $75 plus tip for a party of three or four. Spin and fly fishermen and plug casters fishing two from a skiff, with guide, will pay about $50; or you can rent a skiff for $5 to $7.50 and a motor for $7.50 to $10 and go it on your own.

NORTHEAST

From the fisherman's point of view, Florida divides naturally into specific areas: the northeastern section, the southeastern including the Keys, the west coast, and the Gulf Coast. The northeastern part of the state has endless opportunities for freshwater, as well as saltwater, fishing. In the hundreds of ponds, lakes and potholes that dot the interior, and in the rivers, there are largemouth black bass and a selec-

Big tarpon move into Florida waters in the early spring and provide some of the world's most exciting fishing. This 148½-pounder was taken by the author (left) on fly tackle.

tion of bream ranging from stumpknockers to red-breasted sunfish. The two major rivers, the ST. MARY'S (1) and the ST. JOHN'S (2), also have the same species. There's excellent bass fishing in the St. Mary's above Baldwin, at the junction of U.S. 90 and U.S. 301, west of Jacksonville. And the same is true of the St. Johns everywhere above tidewater. One of the top spots is at Welaka, on State Highway 309 just north of Lake George. Guiding and accommodations are available through A. P. Oliver, Sportsman's Lodge, Welaka, Florida.

LAKE CRESCENT (3) and LAKE GEORGE (4), both reached from Crescent City on U.S. 17; and LAKES HARRIS, DORA and ORANGE (5), reached from Leesburg on U.S. 27 or Tavares on U.S. 441, all hold fine reputations for their bass production. The same is true of LAKE APOPKA (6) at Orlando, which while highly developed from the resort point of view, is still good fishing water. But the visiting fisherman need not limit himself to these larger lakes. Every pothole and river throughout the area may produce good bass fishing and at every turn there are motels, hotels, restaurants and boats for hire. Much of the fishing is done with cast lures, but there is usually bait available for those who want it. Bass in these waters may run up to 5 and 6 pounds.

Another group of similar freshwater lakes and ponds is centered around Frostproof and Sebring, just off U.S. 27, south of Winterhaven. Complete details can be obtained from the Lake County Chamber of Commerce, at Leesburg.

Vast LAKE OKEECHOBEE (7), in south-central Florida, is the top freshwater fishing spot in the state. It is a shallow, weed-choked lake in which bass grow to substantial sizes and all kinds of bream, crappie and catfish do equally well. Ten-pound bass are common, especially during the months of January and February. The best fishing is in the weedy areas, not in the open lake. Okeechobee can become very rough and if you are not familiar with it, it is advisable to take a guide. They can be obtained through the Clewiston Inn at Clewiston, on U.S. 27 on the south-west shore of the lake; at Port Mayaca on U.S. 441 on the east shore; and there is a fine lodge at Sportsman's Village, eight miles northeast of Moore Haven on U.S. 27, where guides are also available. There are other fishing camps on State Road 78.

In all the canals around Lake Okeechobee, and as far south as Andytown on U.S. 27, there is also fine fishing to be found.

Coastal fishing in the northeastern part of Florida has many variations. Striped bass and shad are both taken in the St. Marys and St. Johns Rivers, when these two anadromous species make their seasonal runs into the rivers. Some stripers to 15 pounds are taken in the sounds and creeks and along marshes. While much of the fishing is done in the lower sections of the streams, some of the best shad fishing is far upriver, near DeLand where U.S. 92 and U.S. 17 meet; and near U.S. 520, north of Cocoa. The fish are mainly taken on small bright spoons, fished deep and jigged. The shad run starts in November and usually continues through the winter.

Along the ocean here, there's almost no time when there is not some species of fish available. Spotted sea trout move in in the fall, out again in the spring. Weakfish appear in August, large black drum in February and the puppy drum from spring to fall. Bluefish like the spring and fall, too, while tarpon appear in midsummer. Jacks, Spanish mackerel and various bottom fish all are found throughout the year. Along the northeastern coastal strip there are many fishing camps on U.S. AIA; and there's good fishing around the mouth of the St. Marys River and from all the jetties from there south. Three miles south of the town of Fernandina there is a pier at Fernandina Beach. At Mayport, south of the entrance to the St. Johns River, there is some fishing for snappers, very deep, at offshore banks; while from there south along the beaches there are channel bass. These are also commonly taken further south along the beach, to St. Augustine.

Around St. Augustine the sea trout and black drum fishing can be very good. The drum appear in great numbers in late February and stay till late spring, then the puppy drum come in to replace them. Heavy tackle is usually used, as these fish can be very large. Around Matanzas Inlet, however, spin and fly casters have their innings fishing for the weakfish in the many protected areas there.

Along this coast there are numerous fishing piers, the main ones being at Fernandina Beach, already mentioned, at Atlantic, Jacksonville, Anastasia Island, reached via AIA from St. Augustine; on the beach fourteen miles below Marine-land; at Flagler Beach, and Daytona.

There are several at the latter city, and also many charter boats and bottom boats. Charter boats fish offshore for dolphin, sailfish, bonito, king mackerel, while the party boats fish the offshore reefs for bottom fish. There's lots of fishing from the bridges over the HALIFAX RIVER (8) and the TOMOKA RIVER (9). Anglers there come up with channel bass and tarpon at the inlets; snook and spotted sea trout upstream; and freshwater bass above the U.S. 1 bridges.

Further south the onshore fishing is for sea trout, snook, channel bass, snappers and sheepshead, and light-tackle fishing is good, especially from New Smyrna down in the Indian River (10) area, where Mosquito Lagoon at Ponce de Leon Inlet is particularly popular with casters. At Titusville, anglers often catch tripletails, which are not common elsewhere. There is a fishing pier here as well as a charter-boat fleet, and a fisherman's walk on the bridge over the Indian River.

The INDIAN RIVER (10) and BANANA RIVER (11) at Cocoa, Florida, are two of the really great places for spotted sea trout. The fish hang out in channels and in the cuts among the flats, and over stretches of grassy bottom and sand. They are often taken from causeways, as well as by skiff fishermen and those who wade. The latter should remember that there are many rays in this area and if you step on one you may get a slap from its tail, on which there is a sharp barb. A wound from such a slap can put you in the hospital for a while. Waders should slide their feet, rather than stepping down, as in this way you can usually flush a ray rather than come down on him and risk being hit by a lashing tail. The writer has waded a great deal in this area, and never been hit, but it always pays to be careful.

The best season is from January 1st to April 17th. The most popular bait is live shrimp although cut bait is also used. Casters like Boone's needlefish lure, mirrowlure, jigs and plugs. Fly fishermen use big streamers and bucktails and take lots of fish.

Besides the fishing for spotted sea trout at Cocoa, there is great surf fishing on the ocean side for channel bass, bluefish, snook, permit, flounder, sea trout, pompano, black drum and tarpon. In the bays and rivers you may also tangle with a tripletail, sea bream, sheepshead, mangrove snapper and an occasional cobia. Offshore there are the oceanic swimmers, including sailfish, mackerel, false albacore, wahoo, the odd blue and white marlin, dolphin, oceanic bonito, yellowfin and blackfin tuna. All facilities for going for these great species are found alongshore, and there are numerous motels and hotels.

SOUTHEAST

Continuing south to Melbourne, at both beach and inlet and along the cause-way over the Indian River the angler finds the same fine fishing for all the inshore species, with emphasis on sea trout. More big sea trout are taken here than any-where else along the coast. As a result this is one of the most popular areas with light-tackle men who go for this species. From Melbourne freshwater anglers can also go inland to LAKE HELEN BLAZES (12), renowned bass waters in the headwaters of the St. Johns River, and the beginning of the Everglades country. Those who wish to make this trip should contact the St. Johns Fishing Camp at Lake Washington; or the Sweetwater Camp, east of the bridge at Melbourne.

A few miles further down Interstate Highway 95 or U.S. 1 is Vero Beach, on the Indian River, which is really a tidal lagoon. There is good casting for sea trout along the shallows and there are also channel bass or redfish, drum and sheepshead. From the beach, which is reached via a causeway off U.S. 1, anglers get pompano, bluefish, croakers and whiting.

From this point south there is less shoal water and more offshore fishing as the deep waters of the Gulf move closer to the beach. Out of Fort Pierce anglers take sailfish. There are also wahoo, dolphin, kingfish, cobia and some marlin, as well as black-tipped sharks, amberjack, snapper, grouper and barracuda. At the harbor inlets tarpon, snook and jacks are caught, the tarpon hanging around the jetties from early summer until fall, while the snook are around the jetties and generally wide-spread through the other inshore waters. There are some bluefish from late Septem-ber until spring, with the best fishing for this species at the latter time. For beach fishermen there are pompano in the winter, and some are taken in the surf up until May. Also blue runners, channel bass, whiting and croakers, while spotted sea trout, often in good size, are taken over the weed beds. There is good shelter for casters and small-boat fishermen. A few miles south at Jensen Beach is also a good spot for sea trout and snook, and in winter there are sometimes blues and mackerel.

Stuart, on the south bank of the St. Lucie, is known as "The Sailfish Capital of the World" because more sailfish are taken there year-round than anywhere else in Florida. Big numbers arrive in January and boats from surrounding ports all congregate to fish the waters off Stuart. Some white marlin and an occasional blue marlin are also taken.

From Hobe Sound, ten miles south of Stuart, you can go out to Jupiter Island, where there are two good annual runs of bluefish. The blues come in for several weeks in September, then return again in the spring. Beach fishermen also take pompano from January to May, and around the jetties there are snook, mackerel, jack crevalle and Spanish mackerel. The same situation will be found on Singer Island, to the south again.

From Juno Beach pier, ten miles below Hobe Sound, anglers take a wide variety of fish, including king mackerel, barracuda, snapper, grouper, amberjack, bluefish, Spanish mackerel, jacks, blue runners and snook.

From Stuart southward the angler finds it hard to make up his mind what he will fish for. Along the Atlantic coast swim dozens of species of fish, some resident, some coming to Florida, like the tourists, for the winter, and making a short but telling annual invasion of these waters. Every hamlet from Palm Beach south has its boat dock or marina with every type of craft available, from skiff to party boat to charter boat for offshore trolling. At Stuart there's good snook fishing in spring and summer, with fish being taken both by trollers and casters. Ladyfish and jacks are common throughout the year and in winter the bluefish come in. The largest tarpon ever taken in Florida, weighing 222 pounds, was taken near Port Sewell.

From the St. Lucie Inlet you can go in on the South Fork to Lake Okeechobee via the St. Lucie Canal, to enjoy the fine freshwater fishing in this lake, as described earlier. County roads give access to the South Fork in many places. In the North Fork there are spotted sea trout, snapper and snook in winter, and baby tarpon stay around all year.

In the Lake Worth-Palm Beach area, there are all the same species with special attractions for skiff fishermen at Lake Worth itself, which is usually calm. Bluefish are found all winter and Spanish mackerel and pompano are also taken on casting gear from small boats, as well as some snook, spotted sea trout, ladyfish, tarpon and jack. There is also good bottom fishing along the beaches, and at the Lake Worth Pier, where on occasion sailfish have been taken. At Palm Beach is berthed probably the finest fleet of charter boats on the Florida coast and the big event of the year is the Silver Sailfish Derby in January. Many other important tournaments are held here each winter to take advantage of the fabulous fishing for sails in the Gulf Stream just offshore. There is also excellent party-boat fishing, with kingfish being the main catch; and there is surf fishing for bluefish, kingfish, big jacks and other species.

While every community along this shore has some charter boats, the next big concentration is at Fort Lauderdale, where many are berthed at the famous Bahia Mar Marina, and several downtown docks. There are also a number of bottom boats. All the offshore species are taken, and one of the highlights of the fishing

Fishing for spotted sea trout is excellent in the area around Cocoa, Florida. The author took this beauty on spinning gear, using the needlefish lure so popular in these waters.

scene here is the number of big blue marlin taken, to the point that the city sponsors an annual marlin tournament in November. Inshore anglers find good fishing for snook in the many inlets and canals of the area.

Similar fishing fleets are also found at Hollywood, Hallandale and North Miami Beach.

Miami Beach marks the beginning of another string of sand beaches, islands and keys which eventually turn into the Florida Keys. At Miami Beach anglers have a choice of many marinas, from Bakers Haulover in the north end of the city to Government Cut along the causeway between Miami Beach and Miami. There's good offshore fishing for all the Atlantic coastal varieties of game fish, and inshore, in the waters of Biscayne Bay, along the causeways, bridge abutments and jetties and on the beaches, there is excellent angling for all the inshore species. Fishermen should remember that the best fishing season is from April to November for many species, and this is the time when off-season rates can be enjoyed, so that a comparatively cheap fishing vacation can be spent at Miami Beach in the summer months. There are major boat docks at Haulover Beach in North Miami Beach; at the 79th Street Causeway; Gulf Docks at the end of the MacArthur Causeway; and the Chamber of Commerce Docks at the same location.

Government Cut, the channel which leads from Miami out into the ocean at Miami Beach, is one of the great concentration points for tarpon during the winter. The average tarpon taken here weighs 70 pounds and almost all fishing for them is done at night. Junior Ellis, of Junior's Tackle Shop, Miami Beach, knows this water very well and can advise you on times, tide and tackle, and can find a guide for you. There is also some summer fishing for snook and permit, and some fishing for big kingfish in winter.

In the city of Miami there are also many charter boats for Gulf Stream fishing and for bottom fishing. Most of them are berthed at Pier 5 in downtown Miami, but there are also some at South Bay and other docks in the Coconut Grove section. As is the case at Miami Beach, anglers in Miami find the same excellent light-tackle fishing for casters in Biscayne Bay and South Bay, all the way down to Sands Key and Elliott Key, the first of the long string which runs off to the southwest to Key West. Around Norris Cut, and around the east bridge on the Rickenbacker Causeway which spans Bear Cut, there is good winter fishing for blues and mackerel. Back of Norris Cut over the shallow flats and the guts between them there are bonefish, ladyfish, trout, jack, bluefish and pompano. Bill Curtis, Key Biscayne, Miami, guides parties for permit, bonefish, jacks and other inshore gamesters in these waters.

Miami's many causeways and bridges offer fine opportunities for anglers to fish from shore. In the north part of the city at Sunny Isles Pier at 163rd Street and the Causeway, there is good fishing year-round for the species of the moment, and in late September there is a good run of bluefish and Spanish mackerel. Some fish stay over all winter. Kingfish to 40 pounds have been taken from this pier, and also some good bonito.

Following U.S. 1 southward from Miami towards the Keys, then turning east at the sign indicating Card Sound, just a half mile below the town of Homestead, anglers will find some good sheltered small-boat fishing for mackerel and blues in season, and trout, snapper and grouper all the time.

West of Miami there is spectacular fishing in the TAMIAMI TRAIL CANAL (13) along U.S. 41, starting with largemouth bass in the fresh waters nearest Miami (you need a freshwater license), and then going into tarpon, jacks and snook as the influence of the salt is felt as you approach the coast. The snook move in in numbers in March and April and some tremendous fish, up to 30 pounds, have been taken by fly casters and spinners working from the banks, as you might fish a trout stream. The best snook water lies between Ochopee, about 63 miles west of Miami, and Royal Palm Hammock, fifteen miles further west. The system is to drive along the canal looking for working fish which signify their presence by a slash as they feed or a wave as they swim. When you spot such fish, you park your car and run ahead of the fish in order to put your lure in front of them. At other times they can be taken by casting the lure or fly right against the far bank, letting it sink, then retrieving it. The best flies are the breather-type streamers tied on 1/0 hooks. All blue is a favorite color. The honey blonde on a 3/0 hook will sometimes get a heavyweight. Many lures will also take snook in this canal and a word with Meece Ellis at the Royal Palm Hammock Service Station will get you advice on the ones which are currently most successful. But in general, flies pay off better than plugs and lures in these confined waters.

Trail fishermen should watch carefully for snakes, which are common here.

THE KEYS

From Miami Beach southward to Elliott Key and on down to Key Largo and for another 100 miles to Key West is the long string of islands known as the Florida Keys. The islands are traversed by U.S. 1, also called the Overseas Highway. Here you'll find some of the world's best saltwater fishing, in the Atlantic Ocean with its Gulf Stream, on the east, and the warm Gulf of Mexico on the west.

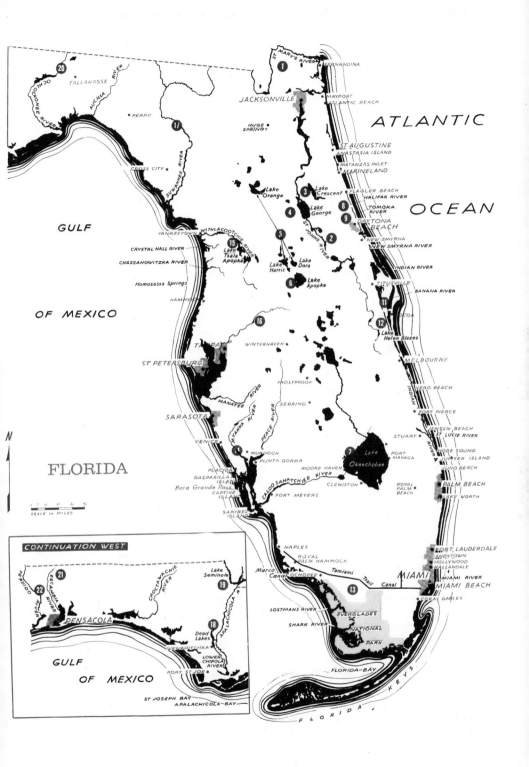

A fairly complete roster of fish that are found year-round in Key's waters would include amberjack, mackerel, grouper, snapper, barracuda, muttonfish, albacore, bonito, dolphin, jack, permit, ladyfish, yellowfin tuna, African pompano, cobia, spotted sea trout, snook, mako shark, some sailfish, redfish, bonefish and tarpon. The added high spots provided by season migrations start in November when the sailfish move in in numbers, from more northern waters. They are followed by kingfish and wahoo, hitting the high season through the months of December and January and on into February and March. In April all the shallow-water species begin to work better. The bonefish move in on the flats in increasing numbers and there are more redfish or channel bass on the Gulf side of the Keys. There is an inshore migration of muttonfish. About the same time the fabulous migration of big tarpon, from 50 to 200 pounds, starts, and runs through May and into June. In June white marlin appear in the Gulf Stream, big dolphin appear in increasing numbers, and there are plentiful supplies of albacore and bonito. In July and August sails, bonito, albacore and some blue marlin work the schools of bait in the Gulf Stream, the activity dwindling into September, when the calendar lists great bottom fishing and inshore angling for bonefish, ladyfish and some snook. By November the cycle is complete.

Though you don't have to look very far for fishermen's services on the Keys, where everything is tuned to fishing, certain communities are the main centers of activity. At Key Largo, Mandalay, Tavernier, Islamorada, Marathon, Big Pine Key, Sugar Loaf Key and Key West, and at many smaller places in between, there are charter boats and guides for skiff fishing, or you can rent a boat and motor and go out on your own. Launching sites are provided at most fishing camps. Accommodations are also available, ranging from modest fishing camps to luxury resorts.

Trollers fish the Gulf Stream waters along the Keys for sailfish, some marlin, dolphin, kingfish, amberjack, and the various other species listed earlier. The dolphin offer a special kind of fishing in the spring when trollers search out the line of "driftage," patches of sargassum weed floating with the stream, and cast their lures in to the edges, to coax out the dolphin that nearly always hide under there. Some anglers try to hook a dolphin on trolling gear, keep the fish on and in the water, and other dolphin will join it and swim along with it, offering fine targets for casters to try their luck. Many dolphin are taken in this way, some up to 30 pounds.

The choice prey of the inshore fishermen is the bonefish which come in on the shallow flats along the Keys with the incoming tide and feed in water from 6 inches to 2 feet in depth. Bonefish like finny crabs, worms, even minnows, for live bait, but they have a special weakness for live shrimp. Many anglers cast live shrimp with spinning gear to take these fine game fish; others use artificial lures such as the Phillips Wiggle Jig and the Hampson lure, another great bonefish bucktail. Casters go after the bonefish by skiff, with a guide to pole the boat through the shallow water; or you can go by wading. When a fish is sighted, the lure or bait is dropped in front of him, or beyond and ahead of him, then brought back across in front of him. The thing to remember is never to drop the lure or bait back of a fish or in the midst of a school. It will spook them for sure.

Plug casters use small plugs for bonefish, and while this manner of fishing is rarely done, there are those who would rather go for the wily ghost of the flats with this rod. Spinners use 1/8- and 1/4-ounce lead-headed jigs tied on #2 hooks and 1/0's. Fly fishermen favor the Frankee-Belle bucktail fly and the Phillips Pink

Shrimp fly, although any small bucktail will take them. Hook sizes should be #4 for very shallow water, #1 for water to 2 feet in depth, and 1/0 for water over that depth.

Another fish frequently found on the flats is the channel bass or redfish. Their favorite hangout is the "back country" of the Keys, the area west of the islands, and over by Everglades National Park. Channel bass are notoriously blind and they like a big streamer fly tied on a 1/0 or 3/0 hook. Red and orange and red and yellow are fine color combinations. Even with this brightness, it pays to slap the fly down hard on the surface to attract the attention of the fish. They will also take a popping bug in 4 or 5 feet of water and many are taken by spinners using lead-headed jigs backed up with bright-colored feathers. Some are also caught by trolling the channels.

Inshore fishermen can have great fun with ladyfish in the waters of the Bay of Florida on the west side of the keys. The ladyfish is just about the quickest fish on the books, and they are great jumpers. Although they average only about a pound and a half, they often come in large schools and so provide plenty of action for light-tackle men. They are good night hitters. Spin casters take them on underwater jigs and top-water plugs; fly fishermen on both poppers and streamers, on 1/0 and 3/0 hooks.

Casters along the mangrove edges on the Gulf side of the Keys and along channels, over grassy flats and around stumps and sandy beaches may connect with snook. They are often found in the same places as redfish and will hit the same lures. They are very strong fighters, often make several jumps, and have a sharp place on the gill covers which can easily slice through a leader. Many anglers tie on an additional leader tippet of 12 inches of very heavy nylon, 40- or even 60-pound test, to avoid this.

The glamor fish of the Keys is the permit, a spooky, flashy, hard-fighting member of the pompano family. They are most commonly taken on crabs, crawfish and shrimp, but are also caught on jigs by spinners; and although very few have been taken on flies, this method of going for them is so challenging that an increasing number of fly fishermen try their luck at it. The Content Key area, southwest of Marathon, is the top permit territory, and Captain Johnnie Cass operates a houseboat out there right on the fishing grounds, catering to parties of two or four. Fishing is for bonefish, tarpon and permit. You stay on the Yachtel Cassamar and fish from skiffs. Rates are $150 per day per couple, two persons to a stateroom. Single occupancy is the same price. For further information write Captain Johnnie Cass, Yachtel Cassamar, P.O. Box 40, Summerland Key, Florida. Or phone Miami or Tampa Marine Operator, Yachtel Cassamar.

There is also some fine permit fishing closer to Marathon, in much the same areas where big tarpon come in in the spring, to provide some of the most fantastic light-tackle fishing on the Keys.

For guides for all this fishing, anglers may contact Captain Stu Apte, Big Pine Key, Florida. He specializes in fishing for tarpon, permit and bonefish, especially with a fly, although he guides for all types of casting. Other guides at Marathon are Captain Harry Snow, Sr. and Captain Harry Snow, Jr., also both famous among light-tackle anglers. Still other guides may be found through the Marathon Guides Association, Marathon, Florida.

The big tarpon, fish weighing from 50 to 200 pounds, which move into Keys waters in February and stay through June, provide some of the most sensational fishing available to light-tackle men anywhere. Some tarpon stay all winter, moving into shallow water periodically during warm spells, and some stay all summer, too, but the peak season is April, May and June. At this time, guides are so heavily booked that you usually must make a reservation well in advance. This fish is a fantastic jumper, a terrific fighter, and readily takes flies, lures, bait—anything you care to offer. Guides may be booked through the Marathon Guides Association, Marathon, Florida; and the Islamorada Guides Association, Islamorada, Florida, these two towns being the main headquarters for this type of fishing.

The same associations can provide information as to charter boats for offshore fishing for sailfish and other Gulf Stream species.

One of the great attractions of the keys to many anglers is the succession of bridges, offering opportunity to fish both from catwalks on many of the spans and from the abutments approaching them. From the Keys bridges, with the tide running through from ocean to bay or the reverse, you may catch many species. Huge tarpon and giant jewfish have been taken. On the other hand, many anglers fish for smaller panfish. There are annual runs of bluefish and mackerel, starting in the fall and continuing all winter. Bridge fishing generally means bait fishing. Those who plan to fish deep for some of the giants of grouper, snapper, jewfish, big sharks and so on, use a big, stout rod and a chunk of meat or a mullet head or whole fish. Those who do this kind of fishing regularly, usually try to figure the tides so they are fishing on a slack tide and thus are able to get the bait down better. Those who like to fish near the surface use everything from small fish to shrimp, and they take mackerel, snapper, grouper, bluefish, jacks, and many others.

Light-tackle anglers cast lures of all kinds, and take the same species of fish. Around the bridge abutments they take many snook and also hook many tarpon when the season is on—but it is difficult to land these fish from either bridge or abutment.

Some anglers "troll" from the bridges, putting their bait over, then simply walking along, jigging the bait or lure as they go, and many fish have been taken this way. It must be remembered, however, that the bridges are highways, and very narrow at that, and this kind of fishing can be extremely dangerous. If an angler is on the roadway when he has a strike, he may automatically pull back into the path of a car. A number of fishermen have been killed in this way. Night fishermen should also carry a flashlight both for use in handling tackle, and for protection. To overcome the hazards, catwalks have been added to many of the bridges, and here anglers may fish in safety. However, it is still necessary to remember to watch your backcast, as cars will be passing behind you, less than a rod length away. Some serious wrecks have been caused when a fisherman brought his rod back to make a cast and shattered a windshield with lure or weight.

Around Key West, the most southerly of the Keys, there are some tarpon all year but the peak season starts about the middle of February. Amberjack are common year-round, and there is a good spring influx of cobia and jacks. In midwinter kingfish appear in great numbers. Most of the other Keys species are also taken in the seasons already mentioned, and there is some excellent bottom fishing in channels and around shoals and wrecked ships. Anglers will find a fine fleet of charter boats stationed close to U.S. 1, as you enter Key West, at Garrison Bight.

Anglers who want to fish the Marquesas, the few small islands off to the southwest of Key West can get guides at the latter city, or instructions as how to get out there on their own. There is no habitation of any kind on the islands and no water.

The path out to the islands, known as "The Trail Through the Lakes" is difficult, and boats should always make the trip in pairs. Fishing can be very good for permit, snapper and barracuda.

Still further out is the Dry Tortugas, and the National Monument of Fort Jefferson, under the care of the Park Service. It's too long a trip for an outboard but larger craft make the trip regularly. A motel is currently being constructed there.

Anglers who want to fish the "back country," as the water around Flamingo on the north shore of Florida Bay is known, either go in with guides from the Florida Keys, or drive via U.S. 1 from Miami to Homestead, then southwest on State Highway 27 to Flamingo in the Everglades National Park. There is a good motel there, skiffs for hire, and some guides for skiff fishing (write Capt. Walter Mann) as well as several charter boats. There are also camping sites and boat-launching facilities. From Flamingo you can fish for sea trout, tarpon, ladyfish, channel bass, jacks, snook and various lesser species throughout the guts and channels among the flats that surround the keys offshore. Some of the finest casting for all these species is found here and one of the "lakes" among the flats, within easy sight of Flamingo, is a favorite hangout for large schools of big tarpon in the spring.

On the way to Flamingo you pass the Ranger Station at Little Coot Bay, where charter boats are available to fish big Whitewater Bay, whose entrance is on the west coast, and on up into Shark River. Boats may also be launched here and small craft can go through the creeks and channels into the inner end of Whitewater Bay. There is fine light-tackle casting for snook, ladyfish, sea trout and tarpon. Anglers should not venture out in these waters without charts unless they know the territory thoroughly. Even old-timers get lost. Also, the bay can blow up very rough in a hurry, and extreme care should always be observed not to get caught out in the middle of the bay in a blow.

WEST COAST

Fishermen following U.S. 41, or the Tamiami Trail, as it is known, westward from Miami may turn off at State Highway 29, and go south to Everglades, the western gateway to the Everglades National Park, and entrance to the Ten Thousand Islands, with tremendous variety of fishing in lakes, canals and salt, and in mangrove rivers. This is Florida's last frontier. There is varied accommodation at Everglades City, including the Everglades Rod & Gun Club, with dockage for cruisers, charter boats and skiffs for hire, and air-conditioned cottages. Rates are from $15 to $22 including meals. At the Rod & Gun Club, Guide Rocky Weinstein, a fly-rod enthusiast, can get you into lots of light-tackle casting for tarpon, snook, jacks and redfish. Just outside the town, Ted Smallwood, long-time guide in the Everglades area, has a fishing camp where you can get cabins for $5 to $7 per day, skiffs from $4 to $6. Ted himself will guide you to fish in a fine sea skiff, for $65 per day. He also has a 55-foot cruiser for hire. It is air-conditioned, will accommodate six persons plus crew, and can be chartered for cruises for $175 per day for two persons, $250 per day for four; $300 per day for six, everything included.

There is much fine fishing for snook and tarpon around Everglades, as well as for trout and many other species. Some of the most intriguing sport is to go up the narrow rivers and cast for snook among the mangroves. All kinds of casting tackle is used but because of the hazards of the mangrove roots, Ted Smallwood recommends a fairly short plug outfit with heavy line. Surface lures make for more sport and do not so easily become snagged, but the fish are taken on all kinds of lures. The tarpon fishing at Everglades usually starts in March if the weather is moderately warm.

Continuing up U.S. 41 from the Everglades turnoff, you come to State Highway 92, leading to Marco, where there is fishing for snook, tarpon, sea trout, and most other inshore species, in season. The tarpon appear in numbers from March through April. In May and June, snook show along Marco Beach and then fly and spin casters can have a field day walking along the sandy beach, looking seaward for cruising snook. Sometimes they will be seen practically onshore, in 6 to 12 inches of water. The mosquitoes and sand flies can be very bad so go prepared with your favorite insect repellent.

The Marco Canal, which runs from the Gulf inland to the Tamiami Trail Canal, can furnish a lot of action from jacks, tarpon and snook. At times you may go hitless, but the next time may get fast and furious action. Offshore from Marco there is great cobia fishing around the buoys in the summer months. They come as heavy as 100 pounds and are taken on artificials as well as live bait such as small snappers. In the fall there is a run of mackerel and blues off Marco. And at almost any time the inshore fisherman may pick up small redfish, snapper and sheepshead on either live or dead shrimp. Practically all the passes nearby, such as Caxambas and Big Marco Pass have big snook in May and June. Permit, jacks and redfish are also taken.

Marco Island Inn and Cottages provides excellent accommodation and can supply guides at the following rates: outboard skiff with guide, two persons, $35 per day. Inboard, three persons, $40 per day. Cabin cruiser, four persons, $65 per day. Rooms are about $12 to $20 per person, depending on the season. The address is Marco Island Inn, Marco, Florida.

Along U.S. 41, from Naples to Fort Myers, there is good inshore fishing for spotted sea trout, redfish, snook and tarpon. Offshore are groupers, kingfish, mackerel and blues. The famous Naples free fishing pier plays host to thousands of fishermen each year and most of them make some good catches, some even latching into a buster of a tarpon or snook. Fort Myers itself has more than its share of tarpon, snook, redfish, snapper, sheepshead and sea trout. Accommodations are plentiful here, and boats of all kinds will be found at the town docks.

To the north and west of Fort Myers is one of the most renowned tarpon fishing spots in Florida, the famous Boca Grande Pass, often called the Tarpon Capital of the country. Fishing in the pass is by trolling or drifting, sometimes in water from 40 to 80 feet in depth, with lines marked so they may be fished just off the bottom; and again with flat lines without any weight, depending on how the tarpon are coming. Baits vary, too, from one time of day to another, and from one season to another. At dusk and at night a small blue crab about 4 inches long is tops, but bream, mutton minnows and squirrel fish are all popular. Lines are usually 20-, 30- or 50-pound test, and hooks 7/0, 8/0 and even 9/0. Fish range from 50 to 160 pounds. Most anglers fish Boca Grande "early and late," as the tarpon seem to be there in greatest concentrations from about 5 in the morning to 9; and again in the afternoon from 4 until 8 p.m.

To reach Boca Grande, take State Highway 771 from U.S. 41 at Murdoch, or State Highway 775 from U.S. 41, south of Venice, to Placida, then by toll bridge to

Gasparilla Island. There are several motels, including the Waterfront Motel and Tarpon Inn, both on the bayou, and catering especially to fishermen. There is also the fine old Gasparilla Inn and Golf Course, a more elaborate resort. Boats and guides will be found at the dock opposite the Pink Elephant, a good place to eat.

Tarpon, mackerel, bluefish, redfish, snook, trout, pompano and many other species are also taken around the beautiful islands of Sanibel and Captiva, offshore from the mouth of the Caloosahatchee River. Quite often boats from Boca Grande cruise up here to fish, a comfortable two-hour run. You can drive to Sanibel by taking State Highway 867 from Ft. Myers to Punta Rassa, then a ferry (every half hour from 8 to 5) thirty minutes to Sanibel. There are some accommodations on the island but it isn't safe to go without a reservation. South Seas Plantation, Captiva, will meet Atlantic Coast Line Trains at Fort Myers, and a mail boat leaves Fort Myers for Captiva at 9 a.m., arriving at noon. Transportation is $1. Or you can arrange plane service from Fort Myers to the lodge. For further information write DeClinton Nichols, Manager, South Seas Plantation, Captiva, Florida.

At Punta Gorda, where U.S. 17 comes to the Gulf from inland, and U.S. 41 along the coast, there are several charter boats and lots of skiffs available to fish for all the usual coastal species as well as in the fresh water of the Peace River for bass and panfish. Further up U.S. 41 there are a number of fishing camps on the MYAKKA RIVER (14) and you can camp in Myakka State Park.

Around Sarasota there are many spots with well-sheltered water where the inshore fisherman will catch all the Gulf species and there is lots of bridge fishing on the numerous causeways and spans over the inlets. A tarpon fishing fleet is berthed at three city docks and they also fish for amberjack, channel bass, barracuda, cobia, Spanish mackerel and bluefish. There are also miles of beach from which casters ply their sport.

Although St. Petersburg and Tampa are both enormous cities, excellent tarpon fishing can be enjoyed right under the shade of the big buildings in Tampa Bay. Boats and guides are available at the bridges for fishing for all the species of the Gulf coast; and a large fleet is berthed at the Municipal Pier in downtown St. Petersburgh. St. Petersburgh anglers have two other "best times" for fishing: in March, when there's a good run of mackerel, and in October, when there's a run of small redfish.

Continuing north on U.S. 41, you come to LAKE TSALA APOPKA (15) where there is some good bass fishing as well as angling for perch, bream and crappie. The same is true in the WITHLACOOCHEE, CRYSTAL HALL and CHASSAHOWITZKA RIVERS (16), near Homosassa Springs on U.S. 19. In the river mouths there are also redfish, sea trout, snapper, sheepshead, snook and some tarpon. Yankeetown, to the north, near the mouth of the Withlacoochee River on U.S. 19, has limited accommodations for fishing that area.

GULF COAST

The SUWANNEE RIVER (17) is more or less the demarcation point between peninsular Florida and the northwest section along the north coast of the Gulf of Mexico. The river can be floated and there is a camp ground well down toward the mouth at the Manatee Springs State Park in the corner formed by the river and U.S. 19 and 98, a few miles from Cross City. State Highway 349 runs up the west shore of the southern part of the Suwanee. Further up it can be reached via

State Highway 340 from High Springs at the junction of U.S. 27, 41 and 441. Far in the interior, as it winds down from the Georgia border, it can also be reached from many secondary roads from U.S. 27, 90 and 41 and 441. The fishing is for bass and bream as well as catfish. From the mouth of the river you can run south to Cedar Key by boat.

As you round the bend into northwestern Florida and its Gulf Coast, there is some good fishing for bass in the DEAD LAKES (18) on the lower part of the Chipola River near Wewahitchka.

Probably the outstanding bass fishing in this part of Florida, however, will be found in LAKE SEMINOLE (19), formed by the damming of the Apalachicola River on the Georgia-Florida-Alabama border. It can be reached from U.S. 90 at Sneads, at the southern tip of the lake; and by secondary road which runs up the west side of the lake. Ten-pounders are common, and some larger ones are taken from time to time. There is excellent fishing for speckled perch, bream, chain pickerel and catfish.

From Perry, in northern Florida, where U.S. 27, U.S. 221 and U.S. Alternate 27 all come together, you can take U.S. 98 westward along the coast to the OCHLOCKONEE RIVER (20). State Highway 375 follows the river from Tallahassee south to the west side of Apalchee Bay. There is good bass and bream fishing in the fresh water, and some of the saltwater species work into tidewater around the mouth of the river.

Continuing west on U.S. 98 you pass Appalachicola Bay, where there is some inshore fishing, then reach Port St. Joe on St. Joseph Bay. This is a good center from which to fish surrounding waters both fresh and salt. There are some accommodations and instructions as to where to fish must be obtained from local people.

The next major fishing center is Panama City, without a doubt the biggest attraction along this part of the coast. There is a tremendous variety of species and type of fishing, from beach fishing on miles of sand beach to pier fishing. There are tarpon in late spring to summer, a fantastic run of big cobia in the spring, sea trout in early spring and again in the fall, king mackerel from April through June, flounder in fall and early winter. There is practically no season when some species is not making a special appearance in these waters. Charter boats and skiffs are available and there are plenty of accommodations. In addition to the saltwater fishing some new angling possibilities have been added through the construction of a dam across the bay to provide fresh water for growing industrial development. The big lake thus created has been stocked with bass, crappie, bream, chain pickerel and catfish, and is now providing excellent fishing along some 285 miles of shoreline. Anglers can often cast from the causeway into fresh water to take the above species, then turn around and on the other side take sea trout, snappers, redfish, amberjack, tarpon, very large ladyfish, flounder or various other shallow-water swimmers of the salt.

Those wishing detailed information about accommodations and fishing should contact Roy Martin, Mayor, Panama City, Florida.

U.S. 98 continues around the north shore of the Gulf to Choctawhatchee Bay, enclosed by a strip of beach which is traversed by the highway. Santa Rosa and Destin are two centers offering accommodations. There is excellent fishing from April through October. More than thirty charter boats are berthed at Destin, many specializing in reef fishing for red snapper and Warsaw grouper, which is very good in February. Spanish mackerel appear in March, then cobia, redfish and sea trout. May is the peak month with nearly all species in, including ladyfish, jacks and tarpon; while offshore there are dolphin, bonito, barracuda and sharks.

Two rivers, the ESCAMBIA (21), reached via U.S. 29 from the Alabama line to Pensacola Bay, and the PERDIDO (22), on the Alabama-Florida line, both offer good bass fishing and there are numerous fishing camps along the rivers, where boats are available. Accommodations are also plentiful in the Pensacola area.

FLORIDA FRESHWATER FISHING REGULATIONS

Resident Fishing License $3.00
Nonresident Fishing License $8.00
Nonresident 14-Day License $3.25
Nonresident 5-Day License $2.25

SEASONS AND LIMITS

There is no closed season on any fish in Florida's inland waters.

Species	Daily Bag Limit
Black Bass	10
Chain Pickerel	15
White Bass	30
Panfish	35

Special limits in designated waters. Total possession limit: two days' bag limit after the first day of fishing.

For complete regulations write: Game and Fresh Water Fish Commission, 646 W. Tennessee, Tallahassee 32304, Florida.

ALABAMA

From the piedmont on the Georgia border to the east and the Tennessee Hills on the north, the topography of Alabama slopes down in a southwesterly direction towards the Gulf of Mexico. The country varies accordingly, from rolling hills to bayou to sandy seashore where the State has a Gulf coast of some sixty miles as the crow flies but much more actual shoreline because of the indentation of Mobile Bay.

In the freshwater lakes the species to be found are mostly the warm-water varieties, including largemouth black bass, Kentucky spotted bass, stripes or white bass, crappie, shellcracker or redear bream, blue catfish and channel catfish. While the smallmouth black bass is not commonly found, there are a few, and a one-time world record weighing 10 pounds 8 ounces was taken in 1950 at Wilson Lake formed by the Wilson Dam at Florence. Evidence that bream grow to good size is given by a 4¾-pound bluegill taken at Katona Lake near Birmingham, also in 1950.

In the salt along the Gulf Coast anglers find snapper, spotted sea trout, redfish or channel bass, sea bass, grouper, cobia and flounder. Offshore are tarpon and sailfish in season.

The largest river in northern Alabama is the Tennessee, which comes in from Tennessee in the northeast corner, curves down through a series of dams and impoundments, then flows back up to the Alabama-Tennessee border on the northwest. Rising in the north-central part of the state, the Black-Warrior and the Coosa Rivers and their tributaries flow to the southwest. The Black-Warrior joins the Tombigbee about halfway down the Mississippi border and the Tombigbee in turn becomes the Mobile, flowing to Mobile Bay. Further east the Alabama picks up the waters of the Coosa and its far-eastern tributary the Tallapoosa, from the central part of the state. The southeastern and south-central areas drain into the Gulf of Mexico through the State of Florida, via the Escambia, Conecuh, Pea and Choctawhatchee. The western border from the middle of the state down is formed by the Chattahoochee River.

Alabama's lakes range from tremendous impoundments to small lakes and ponds, totalling some 16,000 in number. The lakes of major size are in the Tennessee system in northern Alabama: Guntersville Lake in the northeast, Wheeler and Wilson Lakes in the northern mid-state, and Pickwick Lake, shared with Mississippi and Tennessee, on the northwest. In central Alabama there are lakes of considerable size at Lake Martin on the Tallapoosa River; Lake Mitchell on the Coosa, both in the eastern area; and Demopolis Lake where the Tombigbee and Black Warrior come together.

Further south there are hundreds of small ponds and lakes; and there is added fishing in the brackish waters of many streams at tide level, especially on the Mobile Delta.

The angler has no trouble finding access to Alabama's fishing waters. Interstate Highways 65 and 59, the latter in conjunction with Interstate Highway 20, form a big X with Birmingham as the center and the legs stretching out to provide entry from the various neighboring states. U.S. 43 follows the western border due north and south from the Tennessee border to Mobile on the Gulf. From Florida on the south, three main highways lead up into Alabama: U.S. 231 from Cottondale, Florida to Montgomery, Alabama; U.S. 84 from De Funiak Springs to Opp; U.S. 29 from Pensacola north to the border; and Interstate 90 from Pensacola to Mobile.

The various national airlines serve Decatur and Huntsville in the north, Birmingham in the central part of the state, Montgomery in the south-central section, Dothan in the southeast and Mobile in the southwest.

Humidity is the main point to remember about the Alabama climate. In summer when the weather is hot, you'll want the lightest of cottons, with rain gear for wet days and a light Windbreaker. In late fall, winter and early spring, the dampness can be quite cool and then it's well to be equipped with light woolens, such as a Viyella shirt, topped by your Windbreaker, and of course, your rain gear. Always have slip-on rubber boots for getting in and out of boats or walking in boggy places. Most anglers who wade, wade wet; long trousers and tennis shoes are accepted gear for this way of fishing.

Wild game will not present any problem to the Alabama angler but snakes will. There are rattlers and cottonmouth moccasins, both very dangerous. There are also alligators, which present a menace only if you should step on one or go too close to one at night. Gnats, mosquitoes and sandflies can be very numerous, so go well-supplied with insect repellent.

While as everyone knows, each angler has his own favorite tackle, the inland lakes and ponds of Alabama are ideal for the bass-bug enthusiast. The best all-around fly rod is the 9- or 9½-foot, slow-action stick, plus a reel capable of holding a GAF (WF9F) line. Poppings bugs will get you bass and bream, the size of the bug depending on which fish you are after. The large poppers bring up old busters of bass and the small popping bugs, usually with rubber legs, take bream. Once in a while a big bass will strike your bream bug and usually get away because of the small hook straightening out. But some 4- and 5-pound and even bigger bass are caught on these peewee bugs. Streamers and bucktails also bring hits and when the fish are down these lures often save the day. These flies represent minnows. They should be tied on number 6, 2 and 1/0 hooks.

The best times for fly-rod fishing are from March through May and again in October and November. In the very hot weather the fish go deep and are not so readily taken in this manner.

Bait casters also find fine sport with light casting rods and 10- or 12-pound-test line, with surface poppers. Underwater plugs and spoons also take plenty of bass. Spin fishermen use medium-weight outfits and just about the same lures as plug casters, although somewhat on the lighter side. The artificial black or purple worm or eel is a top bass taker.

In general it may be said that there is fishing throughout the year in every part of Alabama, and there is no size limit. However, not more than fifty fish in aggregate may be taken daily. Individual bag limits should be checked at the end of this chapter.

TENNESSEE RIVER FISHING

The TENNESSEE RIVER (1) gives northern Alabama its fame among fishermen.

The river holds crappie, stripes or white bass, bluegills, largemouth black bass, rock bass, sauger, walleye, sturgeon and rough fish. This is the only part of Alabama where the smallmouth black bass is taken. There is some fine fishing for the species in the Tennessee system, especially in October and November. As mentioned earlier, a one-time world record weighing 10 pounds 8 ounces was caught near the Wheeler Dam. In the tailwaters of all the dams anglers find some sporty fishing for blue catfish and channel catfish, sometimes up to 70 pounds. The standard procedure in fishing for catfish is to launch a good, strong boat with fast motor, move well up into the tailrace, then drift back, using light deep-sea tackle.

With all this variety, extending through the river waters as well as those of PICKWICK (2), WILSON and WHEELER (3), and GUNTERSVILLE LAKE (4), the Tennessee chain provides just about as fine freshwater fishing as an angler could ask. There are access points at many places off U.S. 72 to the north and U.S. Alternate 72 to the south, as well as U.S. 231, south of Huntsville, and State Highway 79 which runs along the north shore of Guntersville Lake. Accommodations are available at Huntsville at the junction of U.S. 231 and U.S. 72; Decatur on Wheeler Lake at the junction of Interstate Highway 65 and U.S. Alternate 72; Athens, immediately north of this on Interstate Highway 65; Florence, at the junction of U.S. 43 and State Highway 2, on Pickwick Lake just below the Wilson Dam; and at many smaller communities along the way. Some fifty-odd fishing camps provide boats and motors, launching sites, bait, and in some cases, cabins. A complete list of these and other fishing camps throughout the state, including location, name of operator and what he has to offer, may be obtained from the Fisheries Section, Alabama Department of Conservation, Montgomery, Alabama.

CENTRAL AREA

To the south, in the headwaters of the BLACK-WARRIOR RIVER (5), are two more good fishing reservoirs. They hold the same species, plus some spoonbill or paddlefish. The same fishing will be found in BANKHEAD RESERVOIR (6) on the Locust Fork tributary, to the west of Birmingham. The river and lake can both be reached via State Highway 61. Boats and cabins are available at Inland Lake on the Blackburn Fork, north of Birmingham. This is the city's water supply.

The Coosa River, further east and to the south, has been dammed in three places to produce LAKES LAY (7), MITCHELL (8) and JORDAN (9). They can be reached from Interstate Highway 65 on the west and U.S. 231 on the east, via many country roads. The river itself can be fished from entry on many roads running off U.S. 411 between Birmingham and the Georgia border. The Coosa is best from Jordan Dam down to Wetumpka on U.S. 231. It can be reached here via State Highway 11 on the west, and State Highway 29 on the east. Some striped bass work up the Alabama River and into the Coosa and are occasionally taken at Wetumpka. Late April to mid-June is the time.

MARTIN LAKE (10), on the Tallapoosa, to the east of these three, is reached from U.S. 280 between Opelika and Alexander City. The river extends from the Georgia border at U.S. 78, southward, and can be reached throughout its course by many secondary roads. Striped bass also occasionally work into the Tallapoosa.

The CAHABA RIVER (11), to the west, also has good fishing from Birmingham to Selma. From State Highway 5, you can go in to the river at many places.

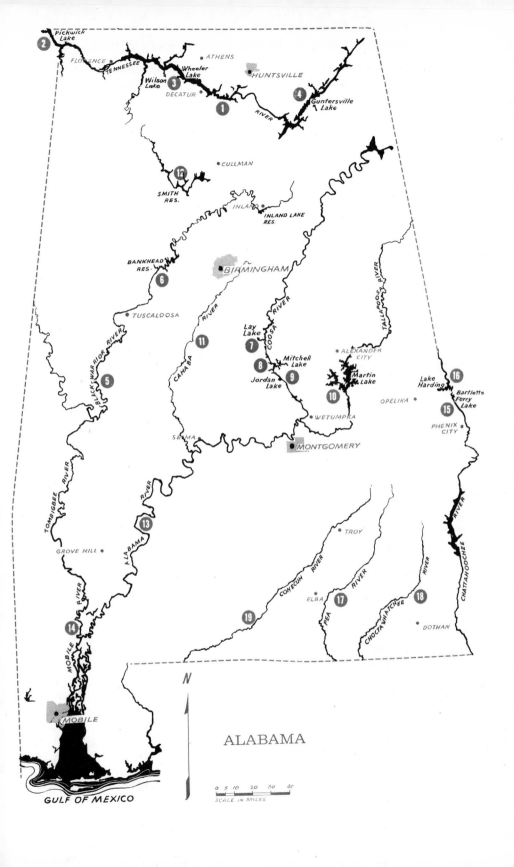

PICKWICK LAKE

FLORENCE

TENNESSEE

WHEELER LAKE

WILSON LAKE

DECATUR

ATHENS

HUNTSVILLE

GUNTERSVILLE LAKE

RIVER

CULLMAN

SMITH RES.

INLAND

INLAND LAKE RES.

BANKHEAD RES.

BIRMINGHAM

TUSCALOOSA

BLACK WARRIOR RIVER

CAHABA RIVER

RIVER

LAY LAKE

COOSA RIVER

MITCHELL LAKE

JORDAN LAKE

ALEXANDER CITY

MARTIN LAKE

LAKE HARDING

OPELIKA

BARTLETTS FERRY LAKE

TALLAPOOSA RIVER

PHENIX CITY

WETUMPKA

SELMA

MONTGOMERY

TOMBIGBEE RIVER

ALABAMA RIVER

GROVE HILL

TROY

CONECUH RIVER

PEA RIVER

ELBA

CHOCTAWHATCHEE RIVER

RIVER

DOTHAN

CHATTAHOOCHEE RIVER

MOBILE RIVER

MOBILE

N

ALABAMA

0 5 10   20   30   40

SCALE IN MILES

GULF OF MEXICO

SMITH RESERVOIR (12), a comparatively new lake, lies about the center of this northern part of the state. It promises to be an excellent producer. Access is via Interstate 65 at its junction with U.S. 278 at Cullman.

SOUTHWESTERN AREA

Throughout its course through the southwestern part of Alabama towards Mobile Bay, the ALABAMA RIVER (13) is wide and winding. It holds all the local varieties of freshwater game fish, but there are few fishing camps along its route and access is by dirt road in most cases, either from U.S. 43 on the west or from other secondary roads which wander up the east bank. U.S. 84 also crosses the river near Grove Hill, and further north U.S. 80 crosses it at Selma, west of Montgomery.

After the Alabama and Tombigbee Rivers unite to form the MOBILE (14), the river weaves through many channels and backwaters before emptying into Mobile Bay. Numerous fishing camps can be reached from U.S. 98 on the east side of the river and bay, and from U.S. 90 on the west side, as well as from U.S. 43 north of Mobile. In Mobile Bay the saltwater species appear, so that the angler in this area has a choice of largemouth black bass, crappie, rock bass and bream, plus the sea trout, channel bass, tarpon, white trout, red snapper, ling, bluefish, sheepshead, mackerel and flounder that work up into the water where river and sea meet. A 1,000-acre freshwater lake in Gulf State Park offers fishing for largemouth, shellcracker and bluegill.

SOUTHEASTERN AREA

The same kind of fishing is found in BARTLETT FERRY LAKE (15) or LAKE HARDING (16), on the Chattahoochee River, twenty miles north of Phenix City, on the Georgia border.

In southern Alabama the PEA (17), CHOCTAWHATCHEE (18) and CONECUH RIVERS (19) all flow southward into Florida, thence to the Gulf of Mexico. All have good fishing for the various Alabama species. The Choctawhatchee can be reached from U.S. 84, west of Dothan, and the Pea is fished from the same highway a little further west, near Elba. The Conecuh is accessible for many miles from U.S. 29, west from Troy, down as far as the Florida border.

SALTWATER FISHING

Saltwater species found along the Alabama coast include king mackerel, little tuna, kingfish, bluefish, barracuda, bonito, blackfin tuna, cobia, dolphin, snapper, sea trout, ladyfish, pompano, drum, whiting and flounder. Tarpon and sailfish also make migrations into these waters and striped bass are sometimes taken around the mouths of coastal rivers.

In January, while the weather is cool, the main fishing is in inland waters where the sea trout and redfish hide out in the holes in creeks and rivers. But as soon as things start to warm up they begin to move, and in February they are taken in most inshore waters. Fishing continues to improve in March and by April these two species are found in great numbers over the grassy flats along shore. In April, offshore trolling is under way for mackerel and cobia begin to appear. By May the migration of this latter fish is in full swing. Meantime, anglers along the beaches and piers are taking jacks, pompano, ladyfish, blue runners, croakers and sheepshead.

Late in May tarpon appear in great numbers and these, along with kingfish and sailfish, stay around all summer. In July there is also good fishing for little tuna, dolphin, bonito, barracuda and tripletails. Amberjack are taken on the reefs year-round but August is the peak month for the species. September sees a big influx of big blackfin tuna and also of big sharks. By mid-October the channel bass and sea trout are starting to move back into the shallows to begin the cycle all over again.

Skiffs and motors will be found at nearly every shore-side town, but the main centers for charter boats are Dauphin Island on the west shore of Mobile Bay, reached via State Highway 163 from Mobile; Orange Beach and Gulf Shores, in the east, reached via U.S. 98 to Foley then south on secondary roads. In the same areas anglers will find pier and bridge fishing and can get directions to the artificial snapper banks which have been constructed offshore.

ALABAMA FISHING REGULATIONS

Resident Fishing License $2.00
Nonresident Fishing License $5.00
Nonresident 7-Day Fishing License $2.00

SEASONS AND LIMITS

There is no closed season on game fish in Alabama. Not more than 50 fish in aggregate may be taken in one day, and the possession limit is the creel limit of each species.

Species	Daily Limit
Walleye (jack salmon)	15
Pickerel (jack)	15
Black Bass (trout or green trout)	15
Yellow Bass	30
White Lake Bass (striped bass)	30
Crappie or White Perch	30
Bream in aggregate of all kinds	40
Rock Bass or Goggle-Eye	30
Saltwater Striped Bass	30

Anglers planning to fish in Alabama should obtain the pamphlet "Alabama Sportsmen's Guide" from the Game and Fish Division, Department of Conservation, Montgomery, Alabama.

MISSISSIPPI

Of all the Gulf States, Mississippi is the one which most truly takes its full character from the river for which it is named. It is a country of low-lying land, slow-flowing streams, oxbows, bayous and backwaters. The Mississippi flows the full length of the western border except for a few miles close to the Gulf. Several other large rivers follow the same north-south direction. Nowhere is there any elevation to speak of. The countryside is agricultural and woods, mixed together, with vast areas of cypress swamp. Many of the streams in the northern and eastern part of the state are muddy most of the time, but in the western section and the south, while brownish in color, the waters are fishable. The main rivers are the Mississippi on the western border; the Pascagoula, near the eastern border, with its tributaries the Singing, Chickasawhay and Black, draining the country from the far north-central interior; and the Wolf in the south-central part.

The largest freshwater lake is Pickwick Lake, shared with Tennessee and Alabama. Other large lakes are Sardis, on the Tallahatchie River in north-central Mississippi; and the Granada Reservoir on the Yalobusha River, a few miles further south. There are many smaller lakes along the winding Mississippi with its endless oxbows and throughout the state there are a myriad ponds and bayous.

The freshwater fish found in these waters are the largemouth black bass, white bass, bluegill, crappie, walleye pike, channel catfish, gar, sunfish and rough fish.

In the Gulf waters along Mississippi's southern border on the coast are the endless variety of Gulf of Mexico saltwater species, including such favorites as sea trout, redfish, croaker, whiting, drum, pompano, sheepshead, snapper, flounder, cobia, mackerel, bluefish, jack crevalle, dolphin, bonito, tripletail, little tuna, bluefish, kingfish, gafftopsail catfish, snapper, grouper, and some tarpon and striped bass.

Mississippi is served by two Interstate Highways. Interstate Highway 55 enters the northwestern corner, from Memphis, Tennessee and provides a good artery all the way south to the border of Louisiana. Interstate Highway 59 comes in about the middle of the eastern border with Alabama at Meridian and cuts southeastward to New Orleans, Louisiana. Crossing both highways, U.S. 49 provides travel from the far northwestern corner of the state through Jackson, and Hattiesburg to Gulfport on the central coast of Mississippi. Another major highway, U.S. 61, follows the entire eastern bank of the Mississippi throughout the state. Besides these highways, myriad secondary and county roads permit access to every corner of Mississippi.

All the major cities such as Gulfport, Hattiesburg, Meridian, Laurel, Jackson, Vicksburg, Columbus, Tupelo and Greenville are on the routes of scheduled flights of several of the nation's airlines, and there are many small private flying fields.

Mississippi's climate is warm and sultry in summer, moderate and damp in winter. Cotton clothing is sufficient most of the time for fishermen. Rain gear is always essential and good, waterproof footgear is necessary for any hiking in marshy areas.

332

Poisonous snakes are common, including the rattlesnake, cottonmouth and coral snake. Especially during high water, watch your step on all projecting land or around logs.

Mississippi is ideally the fly fisherman's and the bait man's country. The fly outfit is ideal for fishing for bass and panfish in swampy, shallow water in the cypress swamps, while bait fishing is best in the murkier streams, where artificials are not so readily seen by the fish. A 9- to 9½-foot fly rod with GAF (WF9F) line and a good collection of popping bugs pays off. Streamers and bucktails also take many fish. Plug and spin casters use top-water plugs, spoons, and various underwater lures. Baits commonly used in Mississippi are minnows, worms, red worms, crickets, and in some waters near the Gulf, shrimp.

LAKE FISHING

As mentioned earlier, PICKWICK LAKE (1), in the northeastern corner of the state, is Mississippi's largest freshwater lake. It can be reached via State Highway 25 from U.S. 45, to Iuka, where there are some accommodations available. Fishing is mainly for panfish in the Mississippi portion of the lake, but there are also large-mouth black bass, striped or white bass, walleye pike and crappie.

Reached from Interstate Highway 55 and U.S. 51 at Sardis, is SARDIS RESERVOIR (2), where a state park provides facilities for camping. There are boats available at the lake and fishing can be excellent for bass, bream, crappie and catfish. The crappie in this lake are noted for their size. Accommodations will be found at Sardis and also at the town of Oxford, to the south of the lake at the junction of State Highway 6 and State Highway 7. The latter highway cuts across the top end of the lake. There is similar fishing in the TALLAHATCHIE RIVER (3), which flows out of the lake.

ENID LAKE (4), about twenty-five miles south on Interstate Highway 55, offers the same type of fishing. Accommodations will be found at the small town of Water Valley at the east end of the lake, where State Highways 315 and 32 come together.

Continuing down Interstate Highway 55 you come to the GRENADA RESERVOIR (5). There are some cabins at the lake and further accommodations in Coffeeville on State Highway 7, to the north, and at Grenada, at the junction of U.S. 51 and State Highway 8. Crappie, bass and bream are taken and as evidence of the extent to which this lake is fished, there are 300 skiffs available for hire.

At the ARKABUTLA RESERVOIR (6), in the northwest corner of Mississippi, there are no boats available. The lakes lies just to the west of U.S. 51 near the Tennessee border. HORN LAKE (6), only a couple of miles further north, offers both cabins and boats for hire.

Near the town of Tupelo, off U.S. 78 and U.S. 45, near the Alabama border, is TOMBIGBEE STATE PARK LAKE (7), where there are a few boats and cabins, and additional accommodations in the town. To the south on U.S. 278, the town of Amory provides accommodations for those who fish LAKE MONROE (8). There are boats for rent at the lake. Directly to the west, reached via State Highway 32, a 200-acre LAKE AT HOULKA (9) can provide some good fishing at times. There are cabins on the lake.

In the east-central part of Mississippi there are dozens of small lakes, all offering fair-to-good fishing for the native species. Some which have earned good reputations among fishermen are CHOCTAW LAKE (10), near Ackerman, reached via U.S. 82, south at Eupora to State Highway 9. Boats are available and there is a fishing camp on the lake. LAKE TIAK O'KHATA (11), is about sixteen miles south on State Highway 9, near Louisville. Boats with electric motors are used on this lake. ADAMAC and ADAMS LAKES (12), far to the west near Jackson, on U.S. 80, have boat-rental facilities, but no accommodations.

Close to the eastern border near Meridian, two lakes provide boats for rent. JASPER COUNTY LAKE (13) at Rose Hill, is reached via State Highway 513, which runs off U.S. 11, south of Meridian. From Meridian you can also reach CLARKO PARK LAKE (14), via U.S. 45 to Quitman.

Along the course of the Mississippi River there are innumerable lakes, ponds and backwaters with fine fishing for bream, bass and catfish. Among the better ones are a group lying south of Greenville at the junction of U.S. 82 and U.S. 61. The lakes, located between U.S. 61 and the Mississippi, include Lakes BEULAH and BOLIVAR (15), and there are many lesser oxbows of the river. Immediately to the south another group of lakes can be reached by State Highway 1 which follows the river. These are LAKE LEE (16) at Avon and LAKES JACKSON and WASHINGTON (17) at Glen Allan. The latter is one of the best. At Vicksburg you can get directions as to how to reach three good lakes, ALBERMARLE (18), CHOTARD (19) and EAGLE (20). The latter is a fine oxbow, twenty miles long. Largemouth and stripers grow large, some of the former to 10 pounds. The best fishing is in May, June, September and October.

Two good lakes further inland are BEE LAKE (21) near Thornton U.S. 49, north of Yazoo City, and HORSESHOE LAKE (22), a little further north near Tchula.

Well to the south, at McComb at the junction of U.S. 51 and U.S. 98, LAKE TANGIPAHOA (23) is in Percy Quin State Park. There are cabins and a lodge.

By following State Highway 48, west from McComb, or U.S. 61 south from Natchez, you can reach Woodville, where there are two good fishing lakes, LAKE MARY (24) and FOSTER LAKE (25). A limited number of boats are available, and there are accommodations at Woodville.

RIVER FISHING

Mississippi is laced with rivers and in general they have common features. Those in the east, in the farming areas, are discolored by silt, but in the lower areas near the Mississippi and towards the Gulf Coast the water is clear. Most of the fishing in the past has been done from the banks, but with the increasing number of anglers who use their own boats, good angling is being found by floating, most of the streams being navigable. The PASCAGOULA (26) in the southeast, plus its several tributaries, including the CHICASAWHAY (27) and the LEAF (28), can produce excellent bass catches. Those who venture down to the mouth of the Pascagoula will find the salt-water species working into tidewater. The Pascagoula can be reached at many points from State Highway 63, while the Chicasawhay runs close to U.S. 45. The Leaf crosses several highways on its progress through the central part of the state, then runs parallel to U.S. 98, from Hattiesburg down to its juncture with the Chicasawhay.

Similar fishing will be found in BLUFF CREEK (29) at Wiggins on U.S. 49, north of Gulfport. The catch will include bass and bream, plus catfish and crappie in the former.

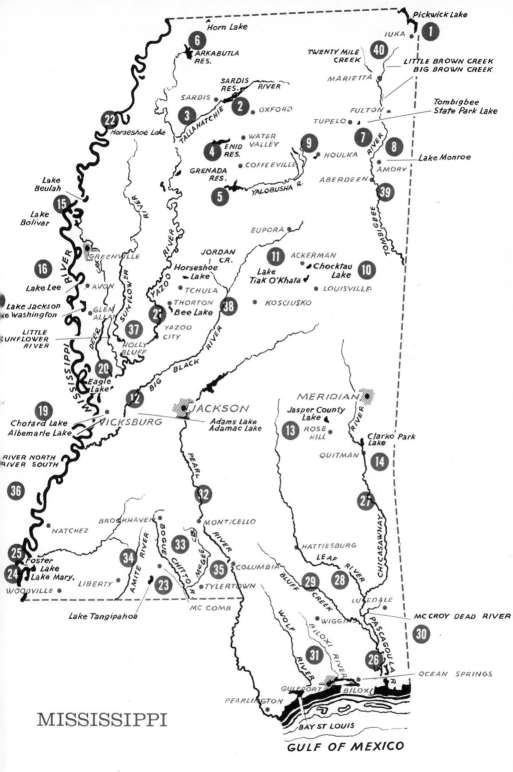

Pickwick Lake
1
IUKA
TWENTY MILE
CREEK
40
LITTLE BROWN CREEK
BIG BROWN CREEK
MARIETTA
Horn Lake
6
ARKABUTLA
RES.
FULTON
SARDIS
RES.
RIVER
Tombigbee
State Park Lake
SARDIS
2
OXFORD
TUPELO
7
8
Lake Monroe
22
3
TALLAHATCHIE
RIVER
HOULKA
Horseshoe Lake
WATER
VALLEY
9
4
ENID
RES.
AMORY
COFFEEVILLE
ABERDEEN
Lake
Beulah
GRENADA
RES.
YALOBUSHA R.
39
15
5
Lake
Bolivar
RIVER
EUPORA
TOMBIGBEE
JORDAN
CR.
ACKERMAN
11
GREENVILLE
Horseshoe
Lake
Lake
Tiak O'Khata
Chocktau
Lake
10
16
SUNFLOWER
YAZOO
AVON
TCHULA
LOUISVILLE
Lake Lee
GLEN
ALLAN
THORTON
Bee Lake
38
KOSCIUSKO
Lake Jackson
ke Washington
37
RIVER
YAZOO
CITY
LITTLE
SUNFLOWER
RIVER
2
HOLLY
BLUFF
DEER
RIVER
MISSISSIPPI
20
BLACK
MERIDIAN
Eagle
Lake
BIG
RIVER
12
JACKSON
Jasper County
Lake
19
VICKSBURG
Adams Lake
Adamac Lake
13
ROSE
HILL
Chotard Lake
Albemarle Lake
Clarko Park
Lake
RIVER NORTH
RIVER SOUTH
PEARL
QUITMAN
14
36
32
BROOKHAVEN
MONTICELLO
2
Natchez
BOGUE
RIVER
HATTIESBURG
CHICASAWHAY
25
Foster
Lake
34
33
CHITTO
LEAF
RIVER
Lake Mary.
35
COLUMBIA
29
28
24
LIBERTY
AMITE RIVER
TYLERTOWN
BLUFF
WOODVILLE
23
MC COMB
LUSEDALE
MC CROY DEAD RIVER
Lake Tangipahoa
CREEK
WIGGINS
PASCAGOULA R.
30
WOLF
BILOXI
RIVER
31
26
OCEAN SPRINGS
RIVER
PEARLINGTON
GULFPORT
BILOXI
BAY ST LOUIS

MISSISSIPPI

GULF OF MEXICO

0 5 10   20   30   40
SCALE IN MILES

Other rivers where boats will be found are the McCROY DEAD RIVER (30) near Lucedale on U.S. 98 near the Alabama border; the BILOXI (31) near the city of Biloxi, and the WOLF RIVER (31), flowing through the western part of this area. The PEARL (32), traversing almost the entire western area, can be floated in most places, but usually you must bring your own boat. It crosses U.S. 84 at Brookhaven, U.S. 98 at Columbia, then forms the border between Mississippi and Louisiana. The best place to put in is at Monticello on U.S. 84 near Brookhaven.

Near Gulfport there are many bayous which are ideal for casting. Directions as to how to reach them should be obtained from local tackle stores.

The BOGUE CHITTO RIVER (33), which can be reached from U.S. 51 between Brookhaven and McComb, is a good fishing river but there are no boats available and you must put in where you can. You can put in to the AMITE RIVER (34), near Liberty, reached by State Highway 48, west from McComb, and there is good fishing for bluegill, bass and catfish.

Just southeast of McComb, at Tylertown on U.S. 98, McGEE CREEK (35) is very popular with casters. And in the Natchez area to the west, you can fish OLD RIVER NORTH and OLD RIVER SOUTH (36) for a total of twenty-six miles.

In the northern part of Mississippi two of the best rivers are the SUNFLOWER and LITTLE SUNFLOWER (37), which between them provide about twenty miles of fishing, and boats are available at several spots along the rivers. The Little Sunflower can be reached from Rolling Rock on U.S. 61, south of Greenville. The Sunflower is just to the south at Holly Bluff, on State Highway 16, out of Rolling Fork. Nearby there is also good fishing in Ten Mile Bayou. Ask directions to Spanish River Fork.

Running cross-state, in the central part, is the BIG BLACK RIVER (38), flowing to the Mississippi. The best place to put in is at Kosciusko, and there is some forty-four miles of river between there and the Mississippi.

The TOMBIGBEE RIVER (39) which flows down through the northeastern corner of Mississippi is best fished between Fulton on U.S. 78 and Aberdeen on U.S. 45. State Highway 25 follows the course of the river. North of Fulton, near the little town of Marietta on State Highway 4, anglers can fish BIG AND LITTLE BROWN CREEK and TWENTY MILE CREEK (40), all good producers.

Location of approaches to these streams and to hundreds of lesser waters in the state will be found in a leaflet entitled "Mississippi Angler's Guide," available from the Mississippi Game & Fish Commission, Post Office Box 451, Jackson, Mississippi.

SALTWATER FISHING

The coastal zone of Mississippi has a more variegated fishing than the rest of the state. All the usual Mississippi species are taken, plus redfish, speckled trout, flounder and mullet which move in with tidewater. Back Bay at Biloxi, on coastal route U.S. 90, is a good spot to find almost all these species. Boats are available and there are some cabins, and plentiful accommodations in the city. Fort Bayou near Ocean Springs, Bay St. Louis, and Mulatto Bayou to the west, near Pearlington, all on the coastal highway, are other good spots.

The coast is protected by a string of islands which form Chandeleur Sound and Mississippi Sound. To the west the Mississippi Delta hooks out to provide further protection, so that the coast is more or less enclosed, providing lots of sheltered inshore fishing. In the delta, which is part of Louisiana, the marshes provide excellent breeding grounds for shrimp and other food, and this in turn attracts fish to the coastal area. The species taken include sea trout, channel bass, sheepshead, blue runners, jack crevalle, lemon fish, tarpon, sea bass, blackfish, sharks, flounder and whiting. As is the case along the Alabama coast, they seem to work on a time table. In January there is fishing for channel bass, sea trout, sheepshead and croakers in the inshore waters and up into the bayous and brackish water in the early part of the year. The sea trout start to move out to spawn in February, and at this time best catches are made around the islands offshore. The other species are taken from this time, in increasing numbers, through the summer. In April tarpon appear on the scene, how early depending on the weather, and they continue to be taken until October and a few even later. Spanish mackerel and bluefish appear in June and fishing for these two popular species is good all summer. Sea trout and blackfish also hit well all summer.

Some of the best fishing spots are the mouth of the Pascagoula River, the mouth of the Biloxi, Wolf and Jordan, and all the bayous alongshore. Skiffs are available at every community for inshore fishing, and charter boats will be found at Gulfport and Biloxi.

For information about the Mississippi Deep Sea Fishing Rodeo at Gulfport, contact Bob Rice, Phone 71, Gulfport, Mississippi.

MISSISSIPPI FISHING REGULATIONS

Resident Fishing License $3.00
Nonresident Fishing License $6.00
Nonresident 3-Day Fishing License $1.00

SEASONS AND LIMITS

There is no closed season.

Species	Size Limit	Bag Limit
Black Bass	None	15 daily
Panfish	None	15 daily
Crappie	None	20 daily

Aggregate on all species, 50 per day.

For complete regulations write: State Game and Fish Commission, P.O. Box 451, Jackson, Mississippi.

LOUISIANA

Louisiana typifies Mississippi River country. Half the eastern border is formed by this great river and then it flows through the balance of the state, winding and twisting through the delta till it finally reaches the sea. In general the country is low-lying, with many ponds and lakes, and laced with bayous and rivers, most of which have as many windings as the Mississippi itself. The coast is ragged and indented deeply in places, providing hundreds of miles of shoreline on the Gulf of Mexico. In the south, the landscape is almost tropical while in the north there is some higher ground. Throughout the state vast cypress swamps add to the beauty of the fishing scene.

Freshwater species found in Louisiana waters include largemouth black bass, spotted or Kentucky bass, white bass, yellow bass, goggle-eye, bream, white perch, locally called sac-a-lait, and channel and blue catfish. In the salt there are white marlin, sailfish, bonito, dolphin, giant sea bass, Spanish mackerel, tarpon, jack crevalle, channel bass or redfish, barracuda, red snapper, spotted weakfish or sea trout, pompano, barracuda, sheepshead, flounder, yellowfin tuna, bluefish, cobia, pompano, jewfish, ladyfish, and some tripletail, wahoo and amberjack.

There are several great river systems. The main one, the Mississippi, flows down most of the eastern border, then cuts through the balance of the state to the Gulf. The Pearl River forms the southeastern border and the Sabine marks the state line on the Texas side. The Red River, a tributary of the Mississippi, crosses the northwestern part of the state. Most of the large streams are heavy with silt, but smaller streams in higher locations can be clear and produce good fishing.

The main lakes of size are concentrated in the northwest corner around Shreveport, along the Red River Route, and in a band across the coastal area, from Sabine Lake on the Texas border to Lake Pontchartrain at New Orleans. But there are literally thousands of smaller lakes, often associated with bayous, which provide excellent fishing in every part of Louisiana. "Borrow pits" are also found in great numbers wherever levees have been constructed. The pits take their name from the fact that when earth was dug out to form the levee, the hole that was left filled with water. These now provide some excellent fishing. Borrow, or barrow, pits are found along the Mississippi levees, the Atchafalaya, Morganza and Red Rivers. Take your own boat. One of the best areas is the Ramah Pits, near Maringouin, west of Scotlandville. There is some accommodation at the towns of Marigouin, Ramah and Rosedale, on State Highway 411. The water in most Louisiana lakes is dark in color from tannic acid seepage and many of them seem like vast swamps with stands of cypress rising from the water.

Each late winter and early spring the runoff from a vast area to the north pours into Louisiana streams, causing them to overflow their banks and flood the adjoining low-lying timberland. Fish move into the overflow, and when the water recedes and these lakes become low and clear fishing can be good in the ponds and backwaters.

Access to all but a few remote areas is comparatively easy. U.S. 1 and U.S. 71 run along opposite sides of the Red River from the Texas-Arkansas border, eventually leading well out onto the Delta at Grand Isle. U.S. 80 provides complete cross-country thoroughfare in the north and U.S. 190 in the south. A network of lesser highways follows the rivers and in remote spots you can frequently travel along the narrow tracks atop the levees built along the rivers. Anglers who venture onto these roads should remember that a heavy rain can make them too slick to travel and you may find yourself stranded on the other side.

Louisiana enjoys a very warm, humid climate, so that the angler seldom needs heavy clothing. A Windbreaker is useful on the coast and on the larger lakes. Rain gear should always be carried. For those who plan to wade, cotton pants and sneakers are all you need.

Wild game is never a problem, snakes may well be, especially during the summer. Watch where you step and always carry a snake-bite kit. Never step over fallen trees or logs, avoid brushy places and rock piles. And never reach up with your hand or arm to a river bank or ledge. Alligators are also common in some swampy areas.

Here, as elsewhere, every man likes to choose his own tackle, but undoubtedly Louisiana offers outstanding fishing for those who like to use surface lures on either fly rod, light spinning rod or plug outfit. Largemouth black bass, and crappies, the two most prevalent species, make ideal targets and the surface lures are fine for working among the cypress tree roots and obstructions found in the flooded areas where you often fish. Louisianans use surface lures in all three classes—poppers, chuggers and sliders. If they decide to go under, they usually use a weedless bait.

The ideal fly rod is a 9- or 9½-foot stick and GAF (WF9F) line. An 8- or 10-pound test tippet is about right. All the poppers, bass bugs, streamers and bucktails take fish. Spinners like a 7-foot stick and usually use 6- or 8-pound-test monofilament line. And you should have a selection of weedless baits if you decide to go deep.

Baits correspond to the fly-rod poppers—any of those that make a noise, stir up a little water, and chunk along, will waken old largemouth. Plugs such as the Devils Horse and Crippled Killer are excellent. And there are times when a weedless spoon, preferably gold in color, and as shiny as possible, will be what is needed.

For the plug caster, a 6-foot 2-inch stick will fill the bill, and any of the good bait-casting reels, along with plugs similar to those suggested for spinning.

LAKE FISHING IN LOUISIANA

Along the course of the Mississippi lies a string of lakes formed mostly in old channels of the river. These include LAKES PROVIDENCE (1) and EAGLE (2), YUCATAN, BRUIN and ST. JOSEPH (3), ST. JOHN and CONCORDIA (4), and FALSE RIVER (5). All hold plenty of largemouth and crappie as do the numerous borrow pits along the same route. Lake Providence is on U.S. 65 close to the northern border of the state. It is one of the most highly developed from the point of view of recreation, and resorts are numerous. Eagle Lake, to the south, is more easily reached from U.S. 61 on the east side of the river, just north of Vicksburg, Mississippi. Yucatan, a great oxbow of the river, lies immediately east of U.S. 65 near Newellton, and Lakes Bruin and St. Joseph can also be reached from that town. A few miles further south are Lakes St. John and Concordia. Ferriday is a good headquarters from which to fish them both. Lake St. John offers excellent bass fishing year round, with a peak from March to October. Concordia also has good bass and bream fishing. There are accommodations at the lake as well as in Ferriday.

False River, another old oxbow, is on State Highway 1 at New Roads, well to the south. Below this are LAKES CATAOUATCHE and SALVADOR (6), well out on the delta, reached via State Highway 18. Fishing camps and other accommodations as well as boats for hire will be found at all these lakes. Some make a feature of "raft fishing," with floats set out in the lake equipped with shelter, rest room and bait, all for the cost of $1 per person.

A similar string of lakes marks the upper course of the Red River near Shreveport. CROSS LAKE (7), right at Shreveport, has all the freshwater species but fishing is best for barfish or striped bass and channel catfish. CADDO LAKE (8), to the north of Shreveport, extends across the Louisiana-Texas line. Like Reelfoot Lake, it was formed by an earthquake. There is excellent fishing for crappie plus some fishing for bass, barfish and bream. BLACK LAKE (9) lies to the south, off U.S. 71 near Campti. The northern part is called Black Lake, the southern part Clear Lake, and is connected with Saline Lake by bayous. There is good bass fishing. The lake is particularly noted for the way the white and yellow bass, locally called stripers or barfish, school up in fall and winter. In the cypresses alongshore there are some outsize bluegills, mostly taken on worms. Accommodations are available at Meyers Black Lake Lodge and several other resorts in the area.

Lying to the east of the Red River, LAKE BISTINEAU (10) can be reached from U.S. 71 via State Highway 154 at Elm Grove, or State Highway 7, south from Minden. This is one of the top lakes for bass, crappie, stripers and sunfish. There are numerous lodges and fishing camps to provide accommodation.

Just northeast of Alexandria on U.S. 71 and U.S. 165, LAKE CATAHOULA (11) can be reached via State Highway 8 or U.S. 84. You can find accommodations at Jena on U.S. 84 and Jonesville on State Highway 8. Fishing for all species can be very good in this area from March or April until November. The bass are mostly taken on top-water lures, plastic worms and spinners. Crappie seem to like live minnows or jigs. Bluegills are taken on popping bugs, pecan worms and earthworms. This is "overflow" country, and the fishing varies widely with the state of the water. Two good lakes nearby are TEW and LARTO.

Well to the north, near Bastrop, where U.S. 165 and State Highway 2 meet, BUSSEY LAKE (12), a 2,200 acre impoundment of the International Paper Company, is open to the public. It has excellent fishing for bass, bluegills and crappie, and has a record of a 9-pound bass. The lake lies over flooded forest so obstacles are many, making it ideal for top-water fishing. March to November is the time, with the spring being the best season. Immediately to the south, BLACK BAYOU LAKE (13) near Monroe, and BAYOU DE SIARD (14), which flows through the city, are good for big bass, bream and crappie among the cypresses.

Moving south again, near Natchitoches, at the junction of State Highways 1 and 6, there are a number of good lakes around CANE RIVER LAKE (15).

Southwest Louisiana has some of the best fishing in the state, with many lakes, ponds and bayous, plus a string of big marsh lakes along the coast, many of which provide both fresh and brackish-water fishing. LAKE CALCASIEU (16) is one of the most highly developed fishing sections in Louisiana. It can be reached from Lake Charles via State Highway 27, which makes a big circle around the lake, between

Lake Charles and Sulphur. Boats and bait are available at nearly all points where secondary roads run into the lake, as well as at Lake Charles and at Cameron at the mouth of the lake. Lake Calcasieu can produce some excellent fishing for redfish, sea trout, flounder, sheepshead, croakers, catfish, and sometimes bluefish, spadefish and drum. This is excellent casting water but those going in small skiffs should remember that being shallow, the lake can blow up into big waves very fast. Another point to be checked is the condition of the water. When the Calcasieu River is high and muddy, fishing is poor. But when the opposite condition prevails, the salt water backs up into the lake and then fishing can be excellent.

Fishing for the freshwater species can be very good in three neighboring lakes, LAKE MISERE (17) can be reached by State Highway 27. LAKE ARTHUR (18) is further east on State Highway 14 at the town of Lake Arthur; and GRAND LAKE is just south of Lake Arthur. Lake Misere has a fine reputation for bass, crappie and goggle-eye. Lake Arthur and Grand Lake have some freshwater fishing but mostly the take is catfish.

Close to Morgan City, well to the east on U.S. 90, GRAND LAKE and LAKE VERRET (19) both have good freshwater fishing. In Lake Verret the best catches are made at the south end of the lake. Accommodations are available nearby.

In all these lakes fishing can vary widely with the season and from year to year. Up-to-the-minute information should always be obtained at the nearest town. Anglers can consult either the local game warden or tackle store operator at such communities along U.S. 90 as, moving from west to east: Lake Charles, Jennings, Crowley, Rayne, New Iberia, Jeanerette, Franklin, Morgan City, Houma, Raceland and Gretna. Abbeville, on State Highway 14, west of Iberia, is another fishing center.

Throughout the southwest corner of the state, the largemouth black bass is the most commonly caught freshwater species but there are also plentiful crappie and bream. Those who like to find their fishing in more remote areas should go into the Lacassine National Wildlife Area, southeast of Lake Charles. Lacassine produces some of Louisiana's biggest bass each year and there are also goggle-eye, bluegill and bream. Headquarters for the area is Lake Arthur at the junction of State Highways 14 and 26. There is a resident manager on the spot. This is for serious fishermen, because it is tough to get into, hard to fish, and there is no shade whatever. The season is from March 15 to October 15. The area is closed during the winter to protect the ducks and geese. Only entry is by boat from two launching spots, one on each side. On the east you can put in at LACASSINE BAYOU (20) and on the west at Bell Ditch. There are fishing camps along the Bayou, where you can get detailed instructions; and on the Bell Ditch you go in from State Highway 14 to the Humble Landing, open to anglers through the courtesy of the Humble Oil Company. Motors in the Lacassine Area are limited to 7 horsepower.

Immediately to the north, near the town of Vinton, some outstanding fishing can be enjoyed in old canals along U.S. 90 and on down State Highway 27 to Hackberry on Lake Calcasieu.

The Sabine Swamp National Wildlife Area along the western border of Louisiana is another choice spot for those who like to get away from the crowd. Crappie, both large and numerous, make the main catch but there are also bass and bream. Ask for instructions as to how to get into the Swamp at Lake Charles, or from the manager on Highway 27, south of Hackaberry. Like the Lacassine National Wildlife Area, it is closed in winter. While there are no full-time guides on these lakes, it is sometimes possible to obtain one by writing the Chamber of Commerce of the nearest town. Anglers planning to fish the remote bayous and swamps of Louisiana should obtain quadrangle maps, for 30¢ each, from the Department of Public Works, Baton Rouge, Louisiana. Fishing camps, filling stations and sporting goods stores also often have detailed maps of their own neighborhood.

North of this coastal area, on higher ground, there is good fishing for the fresh-water species in ANACOCO LAKE (21), southwest of Leesville at the junction of U.S. 171 and State Highway 8; CHICOT LAKE (22) north of Eunice on U.S. 190; BUN-DICK'S LAKE (23), roughly paralleled by State Highway 113, at Dry Creek, which lies north of U.S. 190 at Reeves; and LONGVILLE LAKE (24), north of State Highway 110, one-half mile west of Longville, which is reached via U.S. 190 directly south of Leesville.

RIVER FISHING IN LOUISIANA

Louisiana's rivers vary from broad, slow, often muddy rivers like the Mississippi, to a few faster-running clear streams coming out of the higher ground in the north. These are augmented by myriads of bayous, connecting links between lakes and swamps, where there is some current, but where the angler may feel he is fishing in a pond or swamp rather than a stream. The bayous provide some of the state's outstanding freshwater fishing. They are so prevalent that it would be impossible to ennumerate them, there usually being one or more adjacent to every lake or river.

The smaller, faster, clear streams are mostly in the northeast. BAYOU BARTHOLO-MEW (25) is reputed to be the purest stream in Louisiana. It winds from the Arkansas border in the northeast, down towards the town of Monroe, and can be reached from U.S. 165 and State Highway 139. Other similar rivers are BAYOU MACON (26), paralleling state Highway 17; the BOEUF RIVER (27), along State Highway 124, north of Jonesville; the TENSAS RIVER (28), reached from U.S. 84 near Jonesville, and the OUACHITA (29), reached from State Highway 124 between Columbia and Harrisonburg. All provide excellent clear-water fishing.

Rivers which have earned reputations as consistent producers are many. The LITTLE RIVER (30), in the hilly area around Lake Catahoula, can be fished from White Sulphur Springs or Fishville on State Highway 8. BAYOU COCODRIE (31), between Lake Catahoula and the Mississippi, is considered one of the nation's best streams for largemouth, bass and crappie, when it is at its peak. It can be reached from Frogmore on U.S. 84, via State Highway 129.

In the southwest, the SABINE RIVER (32), forming the western border, is good. It can be reached from many communities along U.S. 171, all the way from Mans-field to Lake Charles. Enquiries should always be made at these towns as to how the river is producing at the time.

In this southwest corner, the CALCASIEU RIVER (33), flowing into the lake of the same name, runs for miles beside a secondary road which you can reach from U.S. 165. Only a few miles east is the NEZPIQUE (34), which crosses Interstate 10 and U.S. 90 near Jennings.

Close to Baton Rouge is the ATCHAFALAYA (35), which runs more or less parallel to the Mississippi, only a few miles west of it. It can be reached from State Highway 105 off U.S. 190, west of Baton Rouge.

A good stream in the far southeast is the TANGIPAHOA (36), along U.S. 51, north of Hammond.

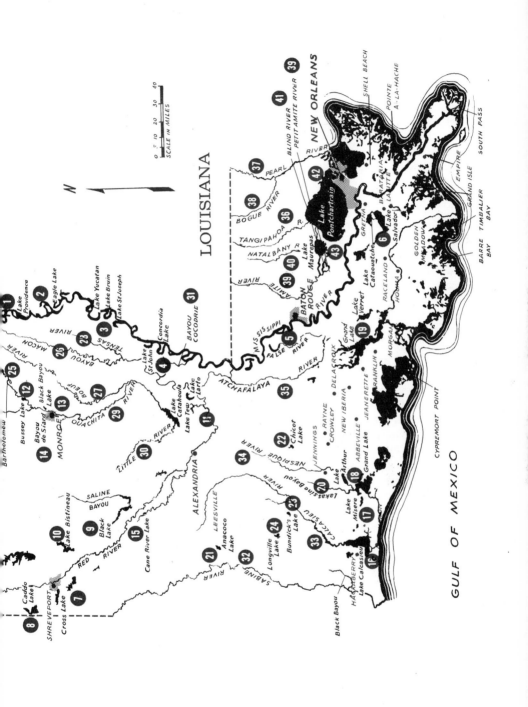

Most of these rivers flow through picturesque cypress growth and provide ideal territory for casting.

There are many good streams and bayous to the north of New Orleans including the PEARL RIVER (37), which marks the Mississippi border. In this lower part of the Pearl, the river is composed of many channels, flowing through trees bedecked with Spanish moss. Other good rivers in the same area are the BOGUE (38), immediately west of the Pearl; the AMITE and PETIT AMITE (39), which flow into Lake Maurepas and are reached by country road all the way from the Mississippi border on the north, to the outlet into Lake Maurepas. You can get instructions locally as to how to reach two other rivers close to New Orleans, the NATALBANY (40) and the BLIND RIVER (41), both good producers. Remember that heavy rains may muddy these rivers quickly and spoil the fishing for a few days.

SALTWATER FISHING IN LOUISIANA

Because of their outlet to the sea, LAKE PONTCHARTRAIN (42) and LAKE MAURE-PAS (43), near New Orleans, offer fishing for the saltwater species, plus some fresh-water fish. Largemouth black bass and sea trout can sometimes be taken in the same habitat. But the fishing is mainly for sea trout, croaker and sheepshead. Tarpon also move in, to the extent that the city of New Orleans sponsors a City Limits Tarpon Rodeo each year. The choice spot to fish is along U.S. 11, which crosses the outlet to the sea. Boats and motors may be rented at either end of the bridge. Anglers using small croakers as live bait, and also deep trollers, take some big sea trout in this area. A six-mile channel connects Lake Pontchartrain with Lake Maurepas, to the west. One of the best tarpon spots is at the Pontchartrain end of the channel.

New Orleans anglers can find some exceptional fishing in a short drive to the east and south, via State Highway 46, to Shell Beach, and to Pointe-a-la-Hache, to the south on State Highway 39. Lafitte and Barataria, on State Highway 45, a mile further west, allow outlet to Turtle Bay. All this area has excellent fishing for the shallow saltwater species and there are boats available at many points.

The saltwater fishing pretty well divides into seasons—white trout, red snapper, grouper and bluefish being taken in winter; sea trout, Spanish and king mackerel, bonito, dolphin, red snapper, tarpon, sailfish, blue and white marlin, redfish (channel bass), bluefish, spadefish and jack crevalle appearing in the summer.

Both sea trout and redfish are found in great schools around the Chandeleur Islands, which can be reached by boat or by a thirty-five minute flight into the Gulf from New Orleans, or about twenty-five minutes from Gulfport-Biloxi. The cost of the flight is about $30. Preston E. Davis, New Orleans Airport, specializes in flying parties out to the islands to wade the beaches and fish for sea trout, bluefish, ladyfish, tarpon, redfish, Spanish mackerel and pompano.

The speckled trout (sea trout) is the commonest fish taken on the Louisiana coast. Some of the best fishing for the species is found around the offshore oil rigs near the Chandeleur Islands, around Cocodrie, Cameron and Grande Isle.

The fishing around the oil rigs originated in 1948, when oilmen drilling off the coast had to set up platforms as a work base. Some are as broad as a city block. Even the smallest serves as a hideout for fish. King and Spanish mackerel, tarpon, jack crevalle, bluefish, sea trout, barracuda, sheepshead, croakers, dolphin, bonito and cobia—you can name practically any fish that swims the Gulf waters and at some time or other you may find him around an oil rig. Spadefish and pompano are the two that are probably taken in greatest numbers during the winter. Even sailfish are taken occasionally.

Fishermen usually tie up to the rig and fish with natural bait or by casting artificial lures. This method is particularly successful in winter. Trolling is more popular in the other seasons, the boats weaving in and out among the many rigs. Grand Isle is one of the top spots from which to fish the rigs, and you can usually get a guide there through Charley Sebastian or David Lee Fink. A guide is advisable if you don't know the water as the weather can blow up quickly and become quite dangerous. Night fishing is a real experience here, with the sea around each rig lighted up by the flaring gas outlets where the waste is funneled off into the air.

For all kinds of coastal fishing, Grand Isle rates as one of the top fishing ports on the Louisiana coast. Tarpon, known locally as grand ecaille, migrate to the Gulf Coast in the spring and are found off Grand Isle from May to the middle of September. June and July are the peak months. Grand Isle can be reached via State Highway 1, south from New Orleans.

Especially in August and September, sea trout can be taken from the beaches at Grand Isle. In most places the wading is excellent and the fish work quite close inshore.

About mid-June, dolphin move into offshore waters in large schools and then Louisiana anglers have great sport. They usually try to hook a fish by trolling, keep it on, and other dolphin will stay with it back of the boat and can then be taken by casting various artificial lures on fly, plug or spinning rods. The dolphin in this area are small, seldom running above 10 pounds, but they offer great sport on this light tackle.

Cobia are taken from the middle of April to the middle of September, often weighing up to 30 pounds. They are usually caught by anglers trolling or still fishing around the rigs, and it also pays to make a cast to anything that floats. Sometimes there will be a cobia underneath.

Another seasonal swimmer, the redfish or channel bass, moves in in September and from then through November some fine big fish are taken, up to 50 pounds, on bait and artificial lures.

Great concentrations of tarpon are also found at Southwest Pass, thirty-five miles southeast of Grand Isle, where the Mississippi flows into the sea, forming a strong rip at the dividing line between salt and fresh water. The water can be treacherous, with cross currents and tidal action. The Louisiana record, a 198-pound fish, was taken here. Popular baits for the big grand ecaille are artificial plugs, spoons and jigs.

South Pass is still comparatively undeveloped from the sport-fishing point of view, but is rapidly becoming better known as sailfish, dolphin, swordfish, marlin, tuna and mako sharks are found to be in these waters. It's a thirty-five to forty-mile run out there from the ports, and some boats plan to stay out several days rather than lose so much time going and coming. Captain Bob Micheltree, Box 216, Venice, Louisiana, will charter for trips of this kind.

Small boats may be rented and in many cases guides are available at Shell Beach, at the end of State Highway 46; Delacroix, at the end of State Highway 300; Empire and Bouras, on State Highway 23 below New Orleans; Golden Meadow and Leeville on State Highway 1 near Grand Isle; Cocodrie, on State Highway 79, thirty miles south of Houma; Cypremort Point, at the end of State Highway 59.

From headquarters at Houma, on State Highway 24, or Leeville, on State

Highway 1 near Grand Isle, you can fish the islands and shores of Barre and Timbalier Bay, where there is some good casting for redfish, sea trout and some other species. Offshore there are tarpon in the late summer and at other times kings, Spanish mackerel, cobia and jacks.

There are also charter boats and skiffs available for similar fishing at Empire, reached via State Highway 23, south from New Orleans. Charter boats get about $65 to $100 per day, carrying ten to fifteen anglers, which works out to less than $10 per day per person.

Far to the west there is the same kind of fishing out of Cameron. Here you can book charters through Jack Short Sporting Goods, Lake Charles, or Jepp Turner, Cameron.

Deep-sea charters on the Louisiana coast for tuna, dolphin, sailfish and marlin are available at Grand Isle and Cameron, south of Lake Charles on State Highway 27.

LOUISIANA FISHING REGULATIONS

Resident Fishing License $1.00
Nonresident Fishing License $5.00
Nonresident 7-Day Fishing License $2.00

SEASONS AND LIMITS

There is no closed season in Louisiana.

Species	Bag Limit	Size Limit
Bass	15	10"
Panfish	No limit	No limit

For complete regulations write: Wild Life and Fisheries Commission, 400 Royal Street, New Orleans 70130, Louisiana.

TEXAS

The State of Texas has an unpromising landscape from the point of view of the fisherman, with many square miles of desert country. Nevertheless, several great rivers traverse the state, and these, along with an increasing number of impoundments, provide some good freshwater fishing. The species include largemouth black bass, Kentucky spotted bass, white bass, sand bass, bream, catfish and gar.

Along the many miles of coast on the Gulf of Mexico there is some outstanding fishing for many of the saltwater species common in semitropical waters. Inshore species include sea trout, redfish, various snappers, snook, sheepshead, tripletail, ladyfish, barracuda, black drum, various groupers and cobia. Offshore waters produce bonito, king mackerel, Spanish mackerel, wahoo, bonito, sailfish, horse-eye jack, amberjack, Bermuda chub, occasional little tuna, blackfin tuna, yellowfin tuna, dolphin, blue runners, crevalle jack, bluefish and dolphin. Tarpon move into waters along the entire Gulf in early spring and summer.

The main rivers of Texas are those which form much of its borders. The Rio Grande marks the western border from El Paso to Brownsville on the Gulf. The Red River is the dividing line between Texas and Oklahoma on the north; and the Sabine forms the eastern boundary with Louisiana. The other river of major proportion is the Colorado, flowing down through the middle of the state to the Gulf at Matagorda.

The lakes are mainly man-made. Lake Texoma, created by the Denison Dam on the Red River, is the largest and is shared with Oklahoma. Also shared with another state is Lake Caddo on Cypress Creek, on the Louisiana border. In the southeast, Sabine Lake extends into both Texas and Louisiana. Directly across the state on the Rio Grande, is the great Falcon Reservoir. In the central part of the state, near Austin, the course of the Colorado is marked by a series of large impoundments: Buchanan, Granite Shoals, Marble Falls, Travis Park and Austin. These, plus a number of lesser lakes created by dams on the smaller rivers of the interior, provide Texans with considerable fishing for the freshwater species mentioned above.

Texas is more than well served by highways. U.S. 59 bisects the eastern corner from Texarkana to the Gulf of Galveston. Interstate Highway 45 connects Dallas in the north to Houston in the south; and Interstate Highway 35, only a few miles to the west, covers the whole area from the northern border through Waco and Austin to San Antonio, thence to Laredo on the Mexica border. In western Texas a similar system of excellent north-south thoroughfares includes U.S. 83 from the border through Abilene to Laredo; and U.S. 87 from the border through Amarillo and Lubbock as far south as Big Spring, then eastward to Port Lavaca on the coast. The main cross-country highway in the northern panhandle is U.S. 66. Further south, east-west transport is provided by U.S. 82 from Lubbock east, and by U.S. 80, which is partly in conjunction with Interstate Highway 20. In the south, Interstate Highway 10 and Interstate Highway 35 supply a through route from Laredo on the Mexican border to Port Arthur at the eastern edge of the state. Also following the curve of the coast, U.S. 77 and U.S. 59 serve the Gulf area. From these major routes, highways fan out like spokes in a wheel from every community, providing ready access to the various fishing areas.

Most of Texas is hot in summer. Anglers should go prepared with the coolest of fishing clothes, but sufficient to protect themselves against the sun, for in many places there is little or no shade. When you plan to wade a river, you will probably prefer to wade wet, in order to be cooler, rather than wearing waders.

Wild game will not present a problem but snakes are prevalent and should be constantly guarded against.

There's a place for almost any tackle you prefer in Texas fishing. The fly rod with poppers is ideal for much of the fishing for largemouth black bass. Streamers should be included in your box for when the fish are not feeding near the surface, and also for fishing the schools of white bass. Spinners like a 7-foot rod, and such lures as the Bomber, Whopper-Stopper, Pico Perch, Devils Horse, and jigs, eels and worms. Plug casters use pretty much the same lures on a 6-foot 1-inch rod. Bait fishermen take their share on small minnows.

The same tackle with only slight variation will do for much of the fine inshore fishing found in the saltwater shallows, with the proviso that you step the leader on the fly outfit up to 10 pounds, and add backing to take care of long runs. For saltwater spinning, a medium-weight outfit with a medium saltwater reel that will hold up to 200 yards of 10- to 15-pound-test monofilament will do. The best lures for inshore fishing are the spoons, either gold or silver, red and white minnow-type lures, and artificial shrimp.

Bait fishermen use mainly plugging rods and reels and bait up with a large hunk of mullet, though some who prefer to use lighter gear use shrimp and live mullet or shad.

For deep-sea fishing, charter boats supply the necessary tackle.

LAKE FISHING

As mentioned earlier, LAKE TEXOMA (1), on the RED RIVER (2), is the largest body of water in Texas. Two-thirds of the area actually lies in Oklahoma, but there is plenty of access from the Texas side. Denison, on U.S. 75, at the southeast corner of the lake, is the main center to obtain boats and accommodations. There is excellent fishing for black bass, white bass, crappie, bluegill and channel catfish. The largemouth-bass fishing is best in March and April, and again in October and November. White bass, however, continue to hit well all summer. Artificial worms are great fish takers, and the Bomber, Hellbender and Pico are also highly recommended by local anglers for the largemouth. Small spoons are best for the white bass.

One of the attractive features of this lake is the fishing barges, more like floating docks, with shaded decks, chairs, bait for sale, lunch counter and all conveniences. The fish are coaxed to congregate around the barges by chumming, so fishing is nearly always profitable. The main centers for the barges are Grandpa's Point, Highport Resort, Rock Creek Camp, Preston Fishing Camp, Big Mineral Camp, Island View Resort and Little Mineral Dock, all reached by the country road from Denison, which runs around the lake shore.

To the west, a group of lakes have been formed by dams on the WICHITA (3), a tributary of the Red. Lying to the southwest of Wichita Falls, they are LAKE KEMP

(4), DIVERSION LAKE (5) and KICKAPOO LAKE (6), and all may be reached from U.S. 277, between Wichita Falls and Seymour.

In the northeast corner of the state, on the SULPHUR RIVER (7), a tributary of the Red, is LAKE TEXARKANA (8), nine miles from the town of Texarkana by U.S. 67 or U.S. 59. The lake holds black bass, crappie, bream and channel catfish, and below the dam there are sometimes spectacular runs of white bass, usually in April during the spawning season.

Just to the south of this, CADDO LAKE (9) lies across the Texas-Louisiana border. Fishing is good all year for largemouth black bass, Kentucky spotted bass, sand bass, bream and catfish. This is one of the prettiest lakes in the state with many islands, bayous and stands of cypress. The largemouth bass are small to medium in size, but white bass are very plentiful and there are also many chain pickerel and lots of bream. Local anglers recommend baits such as the H & H, Torpedo and weedless spoons. The lake can be reached from Jefferson on U.S. 59, via State Highway 49 on the north and State Highway 134 on the south. Roy Butler, at Jefferson, guides on the lake, and there are other guides available at a number of fishing camps on Caddo. To the southwest of Caddo, near the town of Tyler on U.S. 69, is TYLER LAKE (10), noted for producing some exceptionally big bass, even though the lake is small.

Immediately to the west of Caddo is LAKE O'THE PINES (11), with fishing for black bass, white bass and crappies. You can reach the lake from several roads off U.S. 271 on the west, and State Highway 155 and U.S. 259 cross the lake in the upper part. There are a number of small communities offering accommodations. Tejas Village is a good place to stay, and you can get guides there through James Gross, or through Bob Perry at Jansu Landing. Both Caddo and Lake O'The Pines usually continue to produce good fishing through most of the summer, when many lakes fall off because of the heat.

One of the best lakes in the Rio Grande system is the FALCON RESERVOIR (12), on the southwest border below Laredo. Fishing for largemouth black bass and white bass can be outstanding and although the international boundary is indicated by markers strung down the lake, fishing is permitted on either side. U.S. 83 traverses the eastern shore of the lake. For accommodations and guiding write Ray Creel, Lakefront Lodges, and Roy Weathersby, both in Zapata, Texas.

Continuing up the river you come to DEVILS LAKE (13) and adjoining WALK LAKE (14). Both offer only fair fishing. Far to the north, in very dry country on U.S. 285, north of the town of Pecos, RED BLUFF LAKE (15) has produced some large bass. But remember this is hot, dry country, with no shade whatever.

On the east side of the state you will find a lake on the NECHES RIVER (16), north of Beaumont, and about ten miles west of Jasper on U.S. 190. It is known simply as DAM B (17). While the water level varies considerably because of irrigation use, it produces good fishing for bass, crappie and catfish.

The Highland Lakes, along the course of the Colorado in central Texas, hold largemouth, white bass, smallmouth, crappie, bluegills and catfish. They include TRAVIS (18), immediately northwest of Austin, and its neighbor GRANITE SHOALS (19), LAKE BUCHANAN (20), MARBLE FALLS RESERVOIR (21) and INKS RESERVOIR (22). The fishing is for bass, both largemouth and white, and lots of crappies. Lodges and fishing camps are numerous. On Granite Shoals you can get accommodations and guide service through Dave Hawk, Fishhawk Motel, Kingsland, Texas. There is a fishing pier on Granite Shoals Lake.

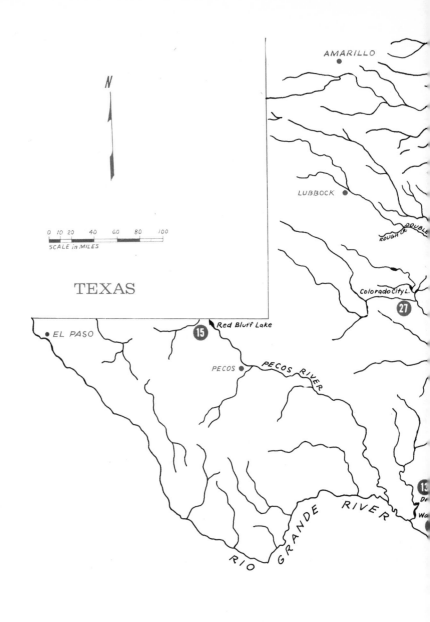

N

0 10 20 40 60 80 100
SCALE in MILES

TEXAS

AMARILLO

LUBBOCK

DOUBLE
ROUGH Cr.

Colorado City L.

27

Red Bluff Lake

15

EL PASO

PECOS

PECOS RIVER

13
De
Wa

RIO GRANDE RIVER

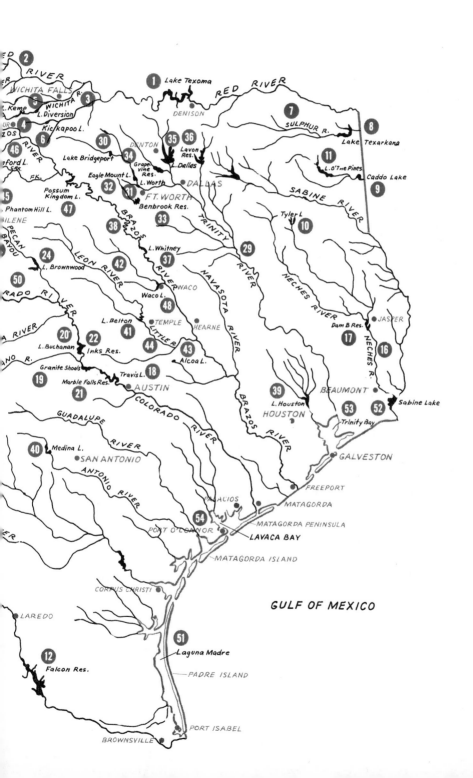

To reach these lakes, you take U.S. 290 out of Austin for a couple of miles, then turn north on State Highway 71. Or you can reach the area via U.S. 281, south from Lampasas. There are numerous motels and lodges on the lakes. Anglers planning to fish the Highland Lakes should write the Highland Lakes Tourist Association, P.O. Box 998, Austin, Texas, for a folder giving complete listings of all facilities, and a good map of the area.

On a tributary of the Colorado River, PECAN BAYOU (23), to the north, LAKE BROWNWOOD (24) can be reached from the town of Brownwood at the junction of U.S. 377 and U.S. 67. There are some cabins at the lake, and boats for hire. To the west, close to San Angelo, LAKE SAN ANGELO (25) and LAKE NASWORTHY (26) both hold the standard native fish. Boats are for hire at both lakes, and there are some cabins on San Angelo.

North of this, Interstate Highway 20 crosses the end of COLORADO CITY LAKE (27), where there are public facilities, cabins and boats for rent. OAK CREEK RESERVOIR (28) is due north of San Angelo on U.S. 277, and again there are some cabins and boats for rent.

The TRINITY RIVER (29) in eastern Texas forms the basis for another series of reservoirs. This river flows through the most populous section of Texas, including Fort Worth and Dallas, and some of the lakes on its course form the water supply for these cities. Far up on the Trinity, northwest of Fort Worth, LAKE BRIDGEPORT (30) is accessible via U.S. 81 from 287 from that city, then State Highway 24 to the lake. Practically within the limits of Fort Worth are LAKE WORTH (31) and EAGLE MOUNTAIN LAKE (32), on State Highway 199 to the northwest. South again is BENBROOK RESERVOIR (33), reached via U.S. 377, southwest from the city. All provide public facilities, cabins and boats for rent.

The GRAPEVINE RESERVOIR (34), due north between Fort Worth and Dallas, also has the same facilities. It can be reached by State Highway 114, north from Fort Worth, or U.S. 377, which touches the western end of the lake. In the same neighborhood, accessible via Interstate Highway 35 from Dallas, is DALLAS LAKE (35), or Lewisville Reservoir, between Dallas and Denton. To the northeast of Dallas is LAVON RESERVOIR (36). The best approach is via State Highway 78 from Dallas. This is a large lake with all facilities.

From this point down, there are a number of smaller impoundments on the river, all of which provide good fishing possibilities and to which there is public access, but they do not have cabins or boats for rent.

North of the city of Waco, LAKE WHITNEY (37) on the BRAZOS RIVER (38), holds lots of black bass, crappie, catfish and bream. You take State Highway 22 from Interstate Highway 35 at Hillsboro, to Whitney, where Roy Mohon operates Redwood Lodge. This is a well developed resort area, and there are other accommodations available around the lake.

LAKE HOUSTON (39), which provides the water supply for the city of Houston, can be reached via U.S. 59, north from that city, to Humble, or via State Highway 1960 from either Humble or Dayton. This is a large lake with plenty of docks where Houstonites keep their boats permanently, and there are also plenty of boats for hire. The fishing is for bass, crappie, catfish and bream.

Yet another big southern Texas city, San Antonio, has some good fishing within a few miles. MEDINA LAKE (40), only seventeen miles from the city via State Highway 16, then secondary Highway 37; or from U.S. 90 on the south, can be quite a good producer.

There are a number of other impoundments in the Brazos system. LAKE BELTON (41) on the LEON RIVER (42), a tributary of the Brazos, is reached via State Highway 36 from Interstate Highway 35 at Temple. The underbrush left in the lake when it was flooded has become a choice hideout for crappie, and the lake also produces some fine bass. There are launching areas and picnic sites.

Considered one of the best crappie and bass lakes in Texas is ALCOA LAKE (43) on the LITTLE RIVER (44), immediately to the south. FORT PHANTOM HILL (45), north of Abilene, has cabins and boats for hire. Nearby STAMFORD LAKE (46) is reached via U.S. 277 to Stamford.

About half way between these lakes and Fort Worth is POSSUM KINGDOM LAKE (47), excellent in spring and fall for bass, bream, catfish and crappie. It is on State Highway 16, north from U.S. 180; or State 254, south from Graham.

At Waco, at the junction of U.S. 84 and Interstate Highway 35, WACO LAKE (48) can also be quite good sometimes. There are cabins and boats on the lake.

RIVER FISHING

As mentioned earlier, Texas has a number of large rivers which flow the length of the state. Much of the time the larger rivers are too low or too muddy for good fishing. This is particularly true of the RIO GRANDE (49) and the TRINITY (29). Both, however, have produced world-record gar, but in general they are not in good condition for fishing for the more desirable species. The Rio Grande was for a long time confined to catfish, but the construction of Falcon Lake, Lake Walk and Devils Lake, has somewhat changed the picture and sand bass have worked into the river. During the spring run of this species and on into the summer, there is some excellent fishing for them between Falcon Lake and Del Rio. The northern part of this stretch of river can be reached from Del Rio via U.S. 277. The area just above Falcon Lake is reached via U.S. 83, and a country road which runs up the river a couple of miles above Laredo.

The COLORADO RIVER (50) winds its way from the New Mexico line, some 600 miles to the Gulf of Mexico. It is variegated in scene, from desert to the forested areas around Austin, and its tributaries vary just as much, being in full flood at times and completely dry at others. The only consistent fishing is found from Austin to the Gulf. There are many public access areas through this part of the river. The very best fishing is from Bay City on State Highway 60, down to Matagorda Bay.

The Trinity River drains the eastern side of Texas and many large cities such as Dallas and Fort Worth stand on its banks. It flows through much fine agricultural land. While there is fishing for largemouth black bass, crappie, bream and white bass in the impoundments already described, the fishing in the river itself is mostly for catfish. At the mouth there can be some fine fishing for sea trout when they move inshore and work up the river out of the salt. The Trinity is an ideal stream for floating. If you plan to fish from the bank, permission must be obtained from the landowner. However, there are public rights-of-way at most places where a highway crosses the river. These are numerous, as the river flows roughly parallel to Interstate 45, and nearly every road leading east from this main thoroughfare crosses the Trinity.

The BRAZOS RIVER (38), in the east-central part of Texas can provide some wonderful fishing in places but public access is very limited. The river is formed by three main tributaries, the Clear Fork, the Salt Fork and the Double Mountain Branch, as well as many smaller streams. Like the Trinity, it is crossed by many east-west highways from U.S. 77 from Waco to Cameron; then, on the east side of the river, from Hearne down, State Highway 6 crosses many access roads.

Because it is so widely used for irrigation, there is frequently little flow in the stream and the only fishing is in the reservoirs already mentioned. However, below Lake Whitney, fishing can sometimes be excellent. The river can be reached by county road from Waco. Permission must be obtained from the landowner, to fish the river. There are also a number of private impoundments on the lower river, where fishing is by permit only.

When you get down to tidewater, salt water backs up into the river and the saltwater species work into the channels. During the summer there is some fine fishing for tarpon, both from the banks and from boats. Accommodations of all kinds will be found around Freeport, and party boats are available.

SALTWATER FISHING

There are 1,200 miles of shoreline on the coast of the Gulf of Mexico, with a great array of estuaries and lagoons and offshore reaches, and a matching supply of the saltwater species indigenous to these waters, as mentioned earlier. From north to south, the hot spots are many. Sabine Lake, on the Louisiana border, is fine for sea trout and at the pass you can fish the jetties for tarpon, redfish, mackerel, panfish, and many occasional species that come by. Continuing down the coastal road, State Highway 87, you come to the Galveston area. Trinity Bay, the upper part of Galveston Bay, is popular with surf fishermen, working onshore from beach and jetty, or offshore from party boats. The take ranges through sea trout, redfish, flounder and mackerel, to various lesser species. Reefs, both artificial and natural, off the coast at Galveston, provide further fishing in the area. The same species are taken at Freeport, where State Highway 288 comes down to the coast, and at neighboring Port Alto. In addition, there are jewfish, snappers and cobia around the nearby reefs. This is one of the best spots for sea trout in the winter. Charters can be obtained through Party Boats, Inc., Freeport. There are also several fishing piers in the area.

From May to September tarpon are taken in the New Brazos River Channel at Freeport. Kingfishing is good from May to August at all the Texas coastal ports such as Galveston, Freeport, Port Aransas, Port Mansfield and Port Isabel. In most cases they are taken by trolling, but at Freeport many are taken while casting from an anchored boat over Ten-Mile Reef.

Continuing south from Galveston, there is excellent surf fishing during the summer on the outer side of the Matagorda Peninsula, reached by State Highway 60 from Bay City. The same is true for the entire Matagorda Island, but as there are no roads you must reach the beaches by boat. The catch will be sea trout, redfish, flounder and panfish. The bigger catches are usually made in the surf, smaller ones in the bays back of the islands. Several piers are available in protected waters, and there are boat services at Port O'Connor, at the southern entrance to Lavaca Bay, on State Highway 185; at Palacios, at the eastern entrance to the bay; and at Port Lavaca, on U.S. 87. Lavaca has an excellent pier.

From Galveston southwestward almost the entire coast is protected by a string of islands and banks: Galveston Island, Matagorda Peninsula and Island, St. Joseph Island, Mustang Island and Padre Island. This shelter provides inshore, sheltered water for small-boat fishing and also excellent territory for wading and casting. Padre Island, one of the most popular spots, is reached by causeway from Corpus Christi on the north and Port Isabel on the south. Back of Padre Island, the Laguna Madre is good for sea trout and channel bass. At the southern tip of the island there are resorts and motels, and others on Laguna Madre, many providing private fishing piers for their guests. Port Isabel is a good center for charter boats to fish offshore. There are also boats at Corpus Christi, Port Aransas, Port Lavaca and Freeport; and a pier at Port Lavaca.

Port Aransas, reached via causeway or ferry from Corpus Christi, is a renowned spot for tarpon fishermen. There is also sometimes some excellent sail fishing off-shore in July. Inshore fishing produces sea trout, redfish, flounder and panfish. There are plenty of charter boats, while several free piers and rock jetties extending far out into the gulf supply plenty of room for onshore anglers. In addition there is some twenty miles of fine beach for surf casting. Trout, redfish and croakers are taken year-round, but the offshore fishing is confined to June, July and August. Charter boats may be obtained at Mathews Store, Port Aransas, or through the Port Aransas Boatmen's Association.

There are also boats and accommodations at Rockport, on State Highway 35, immediately north of Port Aransas.

At Corpus Christi you can drive out onto the island via State Highway 358. There is $1 toll charge for the round-trip and the same if you go by ferry. On Padre Island is a 600-foot free pier, where some excellent catches are made. There is also good fishing for trout and redfish along the causeway between Corpus Christi and Padre Island. Along the beach on the outer side of Padre are many good spots for surf fishing; and to complete the picture, anglers find some good night fishing along the many lighted jetties around Corpus Christi. Charter boats and skiffs of all kinds are available.

Laguna Madre, the bay back of Padre Island, continues to offer good fishing all the way south to Port Isabel at the Mexican border. At Port Isabel there is a pass through the island, and jetties on either side make for some fine channel fishing. Surf fishing is also good all along the outside of the island. Charter boats are available at Port Isabel, and also at Brownsville.

TEXAS FISHING REGULATIONS

Resident Fishing License $2.15
Nonresident Fishing License $2.15
Nonresident 5-Day Fishing License $1.65

A $2.15 Fishing License is required of all rod and reel sportsmen in coastal waters.

SEASONS AND LIMITS

No closed season.

Species	Bag Limit	Size Limit
Black Bass	15, of which not more than 10 may be over 11 inches and the minimum length is 7 inches	
White Bass	25	None
Catfish, all kinds	25 in aggregate	None
Crappie, White Perch	25	None

For complete regulations write: Game and Fish Commission, Walton Building, Austin, Texas.

Rocky
Mountain
States

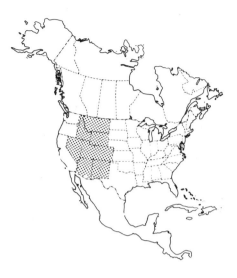

Amid scenes of wonderful beauty and in the invigorating atmosphere of the higher altitudes, the Rocky Mountain area of the western United States offers a variety of fishing that will fulfill the desires of even the most demanding angler. As the name implies, this is the rocky backbone of the West, where peaks soar to 12,000 feet and better, and the Continental Divide provides a double watershed to feed innumerable lakes and rivers. Parts of this area, such as the forests of Idaho, are green. Much of it is cattle country, with ranches spread out across the wide river valleys and running up onto the foothills. There are also vast dry areas, almost desert in character, as in Arizona, Utah and eastern Montana and Wyoming. But because of the drainage from the mountains there is always a source of water, so that even in the arid plains there are great rivers, drawing strips of vivid green across the countryside, and in the rivers there are fish.

Thus, in this Rocky Mountain area, the angler has a wide choice. He may fish high mountain lakes and small mountain streams, or if he prefers bigger water he can drop down to the valleys where mighty rivers, swelled by many tributaries, play host to fish of a size to challenge his tackle and technique. In these waters the angler will find rainbow, cutthroat, the rainbow-cutthroat hybrid, brown trout, Dolly Varden, golden trout and grayling, augmented in many places by Rocky Mountain white-fish, largemouth black bass, walleyes, northern pike, sauger, and the two landlocked silver salmon, the kokanee and the silver. To these, in a few instances, are added such seasonal visitors as the steelhead and the Chinook salmon.

357

NEW MEXICO

Except for a small strip along the western border beside Arizona, all of New Mexico is on the eastern side of the Divide. It borders on Colorado on the north, Texas and Oklahoma on the east, and Arizona on the west, while the southern boundary is Texas and the Mexican line. The largest mountain range is the Sangre de Cristo, in the north-central part of the state but two other major mountainous areas add altitude. These are the Sacramento Range in the Alamogordo region, and the Mimbres Mountains in the southwest. The highest peaks reach 13,000 feet, while the lowest point in New Mexico is 2,850, in the southeast. The eastern third of the state is part of the Great Plains formation.

The climate is semiarid, with constant moderate humidity, plenty of sun, and very little rain—ideal for vacationing. The temperature can vary widely with altitude, and the angler's clothing must vary accordingly.

Mule deer are found in almost every part of the state. Grizzly bear are now extinct but there are some black bear in suitable habitat. Rocky Mountain bighorns occur in the north-central Sandia Mountains and Mexican bighorns in the San Andres and Big Hatchet Mountains in the south and southwest. Elk may also be seen in the Sangre de Cristo Mountains in the north and in the Apache and Gila National Forests in the southwest. Antelope are found in the east and southeastern parts of the state. Javelina are rare. The Rocky Mountain rattlesnake should be guarded against at all times.

The species of game fish found in the various waters of New Mexico are rainbow trout, brown trout, eastern brook trout, and the cutthroat, the only native trout species. Of warm-water fish there are crappie, walleye, channel catfish, yellow perch, largemouth black bass and bluegill. The trout are found mostly in the mountain areas, the warm-water species in the man-made lakes and some few rivers at lower altitude.

The Rio Grande is the main river, flowing the complete length of the state, from north to south, to empty into the Gulf of Mexico. Paralleling it for some distance in the northeastern part of the state, as far south as Conchas, the Canadian River then turns abruptly east and enters Texas, to eventually spill its waters into the Arkansas and then the Mississippi. The only other major drainage rivers are the San Juan in the extreme northwest and the Gila in the southwest.

Because of its geographic location, the waters of New Mexican trout streams become low and clear enough for good fly fishing earlier than do most of the rivers of other parts of the Rocky Mountains. Fly fishermen can find some good angling in most streams of New Mexico as early as May. The exceptions are the streams in the higher mountain sections of the north, where the runoff of some rivers lasts into June, and the best low-and-clear conditions are in July.

Since the rivers are small, correspondingly light tackle is suitable. An 8-foot fly rod, with HDH line, and 10-foot leader tapered to 4X tippet is right for fly fishing. Spinners should keep to very light tackle and use the smallest lures, except in large rivers such as the Rio Grande, where sometimes spinner and fly combinations or spinner and red bead will take the fish.

The popular flies are those with some white showing, such as the Royal Coachman, Rio Grande King, Ginger Quill, Brown and Gray Hackle. As in other parts of the Rocky Mountains, wet-fly men like the wooly worm.

RIVER FISHING

There is some interesting trout fishing in the RIO GRANDE (1), which enters New Mexico from Colorado. The canyon near the border is so deep and dangerous as to be both impassable and unfishable, and perhaps as a result some very large trout develop in these waters and occasionally move downstream. In the immediate downstream waters, from Arroyo Hondo down, some substantial rainbows and browns have been taken. Smallmouth black bass have also been introduced and catches run up to 6 pounds, which is excellent for this species.

The most readily fishable parts of the river can be reached from U.S. Highway 64 between Taos and Espanola, and there are plentiful accommodations at these towns. In the lower part of the river the trout are mostly in deep holes and must be taken on bait or deep spinners, but the chances are good for a big fish.

North of Taos accommodations are available at the Singing River Ranch, four and a half miles from the town of Questa on State Highway 3, on the Cabresto Lake Road, and the Tall Pine Resort at Red River, on State Highway 38. Fishing in the Rio Grande is open year-round.

To the west of the Rio Grande, one of its tributaries, the CHAMA RIVER (2), enters the river at Espanola. Its headwaters, above the El Vado Dam, and to a point twelve miles below, hold rainbows and browns. The upper reaches also produce occasional natives. The same is true of its tributary, the BRAZOS RIVER (3), which comes in from the northeast. All this fishing can be reached via U.S. 84 to feeder roads. On U.S. 84, on the headwaters, the Elk-horn Lodge and Cafe at Chamas, and the Brazos Lodge and Ranch and El Vado Ranch, a few miles south at Tierra Amarilla, all are situated on the river, and the latter also has lake fishing in El Vado Reservoir. All three provide cabin-type accommodation. Guides are available at the Elk-horn. There are also accommodations at Espanola and Cebola.

Some very large browns, including one that weighed 20 pounds 8 ounces, have been taken from the Chama, and catches up to 6 pounds are made every season. The fishing is best in early spring and in the fall.

Much of New Mexico's best trout fishing is within the influence of the Sangre de Cristo Mountains, in the north-central part of the state, in the headwaters of the RED RIVER (4), the CANADIAN (5), the PECOS (6) and the CIMMARON (7). In the upper waters of the Pecos, in particular, there is some very good rainbow, cutthroat and brown-trout fishing, and along the stream remains of Indian pueblos may be seen. The area is reached from Santa Fe by following U.S. 84 and 85 east to State Highway 63, which runs north along the Pecos. The road ends at the entrance to the Pecos Wilderness. There's a store, service station, and saddle horses are available for trips further upstream.

Much of the good fishing water in the Pecos is fairly fast so that wet flies and spinners are widely used, but the dry-fly man can find enough water to keep him interested.

East of this area, the Canadian River also produces some good trout fishing in its headwaters. Just before it turns east to flow into Texas the Canadian has been dammed at Las Conchas, north of U.S. Highway 54, to form the Conchas Reservoir (see under Lakes).

Other good trout streams in the northern part of the state can be reached from Questa, on State Highway 3, west on State Highway 38 to the Red River Trout Hatchery; and from Santa Cruz on U.S. 258 (twenty-three miles north of Santa Fe) by State Highway 76 to Penasco. From there a Forest Service road leads in to the Santa Barbara. You can also reach this one from State Highway 3, south from the Ranches of Taos, on U.S. 64. Throughout the mountains there are a number of lodges which provide accommodations, and, in some cases, guides. An annually compiled list of guest ranches, giving description of accommodations provided, may be obtained from the Department of Development, Tourist Division, State Capitol, Santa Fe, New Mexico.

Another concentration of streams will be found in the Jemez area, west of Los Alamos. They can be reached from State Highway 44 to San Ysidro, then State Highway 4 to Jemez Springs. From there you can fish about six small streams, and there is good camping on them all. These and many other camping-fishing sites are listed in a booklet "Recreation Spots Where Fishing is Fine," issued by the New Mexico Department of Game and Fish, State Capitol, Santa Fe, New Mexico. It gives location and facilities for many streams and lakes suitable for family fishing vacations. Two guest ranches in the area also offer stream fishing: the Lazy Ray Guest Ranch, address, Mr. Howell Gage, Korber Building, Albuquerque, New Mexico; and the Tent Rock Ranch, Pena Blanca, New Mexico.

In the southwestern part of New Mexico some good trout waters can be found out of Silver City, on U.S. 180 and 260, northwest of Las Cruces. Here the head-waters of the SAN FRANCISCO and the GILA (8) yield fairly good fishing for rainbows in spite of the fact that it is one of the most heavily fished areas in the state. A few browns are also taken. To get to the really productive water in this rugged section it's advisable to pack in with guides, from Silver City. Fishing in the Gila Wilderness is available at Bear Mountain Lodge, four miles north of Silver City. The address is Mr. and Mrs. Fred McCormick, P.O. Box 1163, Silver City, New Mexico.

Further north, the same kind of fishing is available at Willow Creek Ranch, on State Highway 12, between the town of Reserve on U.S. 180 and Datil on U.S. 60. The operator, Jim Vance, Box 325, Reserve, New Mexico, provides cabins for fishermen who bring their own supplies.

In the south-central region the Sacramento Range of mountains provide the setting for a small, much fished but productive trout fishery, roughly marked by the Carrizozo on the north and the Orogrande on the south, along U.S. 54; and a line drawn between Tinnie on U.S. 70 and 380, and Elk on U.S. 83. There are several winter sports establishments in these mountains where anglers can stay, and there are also accommodations at Ruidoso.

LAKE FISHING

A few smaller lakes in New Mexico have been planted with trout. STORRIE LAKE (9), on State Highway 3, north from Las Vegas, is a good producer; and so are the LATIR LAKES (10), northwest of Pecos, off State Highway 63. In the northeast corner of the state, fourteen miles east of Colmer, near Springer, on U.S. 85, the CHARETTE LAKES (11) have been stocked with rainbows and browns. From

NEW MEXICO

Springer it is possible to fish six other small lakes with a variety of species from trout to the warm water fishes. In the northwest, near Gallup, is BLUEWATER LAKE (12), on Interstate Highway 40 between Gallup and Grant. The fishing here is for rainbows.

North of this, twenty-six miles east of Farmington off State Highway 17, the NAVAJO RESERVOIR (13), completed in late 1962, has been stocked with trout and is expected to produce well shortly. This will be the largest lake in New Mexico. In the southwest, the BEAR CANYON DAM and WALL LAKE (14) have limited trout fishing. Both can be reached from San Lorenzo.

It should be noted that on most of the smaller lakes in New Mexico boats are permitted but not motors.

Aside from the above mentioned, and a few stocked lakes currently being developed by the New Mexico Department of Game and Fish, most of the lake fishing in the state is for the warm-water species. Of the larger lakes, ELEPHANT BUTTE (15), formed by the damming of the Colorado River near the town of Truth or Consequences, is the most productive to date. The lake is forty-five miles long and two to five miles wide, well supplied with bass and crappies, and you can take walleyes by trolling or fishing with minnows. There are also channel catfish. It can be reached from U.S. 85, which runs along the western side of the lake. The same species are found in the CABALLO RESERVOIR (16) to the south; and just below the Caballo Dam in the fast water there are some rainbow trout. For the bass and crappie the fall season is best, when the fish come to the surface and can be taken on top-water lures of all kinds.

Besides accommodations at Truth or Consequences there are motels, cabins, restaurants, boats, and boat-launching facilities at the reservoirs.

The lower reaches and the dammed portions of many of the rivers mentioned in the trout information above have been developed as suitable for the warm-water species. On the Canadian River in the northeast, CONCHAS LAKE (17) has been stocked with largemouth black bass, walleye and bluegill, crappie and channel catfish. Catfish can also be taken in the river just below and just above the lake. For this fishing you can stay at the town of Tucumcari; and there are camp sites and boats at the lake. There are also extensive facilities for trailers and for camping at the lake; several stores for supplies, and one lodge. There is no charge for camping for the first seven days, after that $1 per day.

A number of small, deep lakes near Santa Rosa on U.S. 66 (Interstate Highway 40) offer good bass fishing and others which hold warm-water species in fishable numbers are the BOTTOMLESS LAKES (18) southeast of Roswell on U.S. 380; JACKSON LAKE (19) in the northwest, eight miles north of Farmington on State Highway 17; ALAMOGORDO RESERVOIR (20), ten miles north of Fort Sumner on U.S. 84, then nine miles west on State Highway 203.

NEW MEXICO FISHING REGULATIONS

Resident Fishing License $5.50
Nonresident Fishing License $10.00
Nonresident 5-Day Fishing License $5.25
Nonresident 10-Day Fishing License $8.00
All persons 14 years of age or over must have a license.

SEASONS AND LIMITS

Species	Open Season	Daily Bag and Possession Limits
Trout	May 4–Nov. 30 North of U.S. 66 April 1–March, following, South of U.S. 66	12
Walleye	April 1–March 31	12
Black Bass	April 1–March 31	12
Crappie	April 1–March 31	40
Northern Pike	April 1–March 31	6
Catfish, except Bullheads	April 1–March 31	15

No limit on perch, bullheads, bluegills and other sunfishes.
No size limit on any species except northern pike, 14 inches.

Fishing is permitted all day and all night, except with some exceptions which must be checked at the time you purchase your fishing license.

For complete regulations write: Department of Game and Fish, State Capitol, Santa Fe 87501, New Mexico.

ARIZONA

While Arizona is best known for the semiarid and desert topography of the southern area of the state and the Grand Canyon in the north, certain parts of the state have enough high, timbered slopes to provide watersheds which can support a considerable amount of fishing.

One belt of green country, much of it fortunately devoted to national forests, runs across north-central and eastern Arizona, with mountains and plateaus from 6,000 to 9,000 feet. There is similar territory in the Kaibab National Forest in the north-central part of the state. These belts provide suitable habitat for some trout, including a few scattered remnants of the "yellow-bellied Arizona native trout," the only original trout of Arizona. It somewhat resembles the California golden, and is found most commonly in the headwaters of the Little Colorado. More often caught are the rainbow and the brown, both of which have been stocked by the Arizona Game and Fish Department in suitable waters.

The two great river-drainage basins, the Colorado in the north and west to southwest; and the Salt in east-central Arizona, with their many impoundments, also provide suitable water for bass, channel catfish, crappie and sunfish.

With such a diversity of topography and altitude, the climate can vary from very warm to cold enough to freeze over some of the high mountain lakes on winter nights. But aside from these higher altitudes, the climate is uniformly warm and dry.

Like the rest of the country Arizona is enjoying a population boom, but nevertheless there are vast areas of the state which are relatively undeveloped, and naturally these are the best from the angler's point of view. Highway access to most such areas is good. Interstate 40 traverses the entire northern part of the state, bisected at Flagtaff by U.S. 89, while further south Interstate 10 provides the same cross-country access to side roads leading to the fishing in the Phoenix-Scottsdale vicinity.

Arizona has no closed season on any fish species found in its waters, but a few lakes and streams are posted one year or another by the Arizona Game and Fish Department, and regulations must be checked accordingly.

Those who fish the mountain sections of Arizona may occasionally encounter black bear, but the grizzly, once common here, is now extinct. In high mountain prairies elk are occasionally seen. Deer are common. If you are lucky you may see a bighorn sheep. In the desert country there are javelinas.

Throughout Arizona it is always well to watch for rattlesnakes. If you should hear the warning rattle of this snake, stop in your tracks and try to locate him before stepping off. Remember that rattlers sometimes lose their rattles; others just don't rattle. Keep your eyes open all the time, and never step into a clump of sagebrush or other shady shelter.

COLORADO RIVER RESERVOIRS

Lake fishermen in Arizona will find most of their sport in the great impoundments of the Colorado and the Salt and Gila. The Colorado lakes include LAKE

MEAD (1), formed by the Hoover Dam and shared with Nevada. Lake Mead has 550 miles of shoreline, some of it within Arizona. Best access to the lake, however, is on the Nevada side. The lake has good fishing for crappie, bluegills and catfish, and some excellent fishing for largemouth black bass. There are rainbows below the dam, in the Colorado River; but again, this is best reached from the Nevada side.

Further south, the Davis Dam has backed up another reservoir, LAKE MOHAVE (2), again featuring bass, bluegills and crappie. Arizona anglers can go in from Kingman on State Road 68 to Davis Dam or Bullhead City, both at the extreme south end of the lake. There is also some very fine rainbow-trout fishing in the cooler waters at the top of Lake Mohave, where the influence of the river is still felt. There are now some deluxe motel accommodations at Davis Dam. Boats are available; there are boat-launching ramps and camp sites.

Following south from Lake Mohave to Lake Havasu, which is the next large impoundment of the Colorado, there is a series of sloughs and overflows, sometimes accessible, sometimes not, depending on the water level. When you can get to them, this area, known as the Topock Swamp, can produce some fine fishing for both bass and crappie, and is particularly popular with bait and fly casters. To reach the swamps you go in to the town of Topock, south on U.S. 66 from Kingman.

LAKE HAVASU (3), above the Parker Dam, is the southernmost of the lakes of the Colorado chain to have a good reputation for consistent fishing. There are largemouth black bass, channel and blue catfish, bluegills and crappie. Casters have good luck by casting in to shore from skiffs.

Below this, the visitor may have a hard time locating really good fishing, but native Arizonians manage to come up with some excellent catches from CIBOLA LAKE (4) and MITTRY and MARTINEZ LAKES (5), just outside Yuma. Martinez, just above the Imperial Dam a few miles north of Yuma, boasts big channel catfish, bass to 6 pounds, and crappie to 3.

Throughout the length of the Colorado system there are boat docks and skiff rentals at the end of nearly every road which leads in to the river. Cabins or motel accommodations are not plentiful but there are lots of camp sites. As in all desert areas, carry water, cooking facilities, and plenty of supplies.

GRAND CANYON AREA

In the Grand Canyon area of the Colorado River, up near the Utah border, there is a considerable amount of trout fishing, most of it requiring a pack trip or at least a long hike. Page and Marble Creek are the only two towns in the area. Just south of the Utah border is NORTH CANYON CREEK (6) with plentiful 6- to 8-inch rainbows. Don't be put off by the size, as the stream is small, very clear, and the fishing calls for expert use of a fly rod, with suitably fine leader tippet and tiny flies.

From Jacob Lake, to the west, you can reach BRIGHT ANGEL CREEK (7), one of the best trout streams in Arizona; or you can pack in from the Canyon to explore a good ten miles of fishing. CLEAR CREEK (8), to the southeast, is known for slightly larger fish, but is less consistent as a producer than Bright Angel. Both are ideal dry-fly streams.

From the town of Fredonia, some thirty miles north of Jacob Lake, you can pack in to the THUNDER RIVER (9), a fast-flowing stream with long stretches of white water. You want weighted flies, heavy spoons for spinning, and plenty of

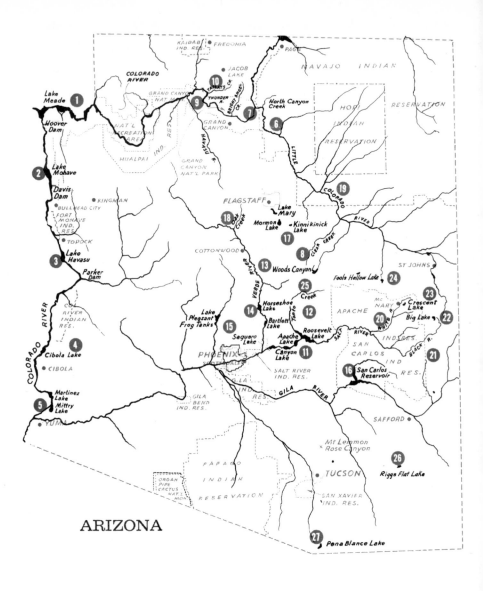

ARIZONA

N

0 5 10 20 30 40 50

SCALE IN MILES

weight in your sinkers if you are using bait. The TAPEATS (10) is another good stream in the area.

SALT RIVER RESERVOIRS

The damming of the Salt River in east-central Arizona has resulted in four major lakes, SAGUARO, CANYON, APACHE and ROOSEVELT (11) on all of which the angler will find both camping facilities and boat-rental agencies. Roosevelt and Apache are regarded as the best fishing lakes, the other two being used extensively for water sports. Many creeks in the surrounding area also offer some good fishing. TONTO CREEK (12), flowing into Lake Roosevelt from the north, has fifty miles of fishing for brown and rainbow trout of moderate size.

A third river system which has been dammed to produce reservoir fishing is the VERDE (13), a tributary of the Salt, flowing south through central Arizona. The river has smallmouth bass, largemouth bass, and is renowned for its catfishing, this last being especially good between the town of Cottonwood and HORSESHOE LAKE (14). This lake, and Bartlett to the south, both offer good fishing for the warm-water species and are easily reached from Scottsdale or Phoenix via the Cave Creek Road, north.

Good bass fishing can also be found to the north and west of Phoenix at LAKE CARL PLEASANT and FROG TANKS (15), though these two are not as productive as Bartlett and Horseshoe. To the southeast of the city the SAN CARLOS RESERVOIR (16) on the Gila River also has good largemouth-bass fishing and catfish.

FLAGSTAFF AREA

The city of Flagstaff has mostly warm-water fishing to offer its visitors, in LAKE MARY and MORMON LAKE (17), but KINNIKINICK, to the south, has some cutthroat. The fly fisherman will find some good trout fishing in streams, however. OAK CREEK (18), only fifteen miles south of the city, is the major one, but also the most heavily fished. It has both rainbows and browns. The West Fork yields mostly rainbows. In Lower Oak Creek you'll find smallmouth, panfish and catfish, not to mention carp and suckers—in fact, these are found throughout the above-mentioned streams.

EAST CENTRAL AREA

Accessible from the town of McNary in the east-central part of Arizona, or from the larger town of St. Johns, is the headwaters of the LITTLE COLORADO (19), and also the WHITE (20) and the BLACK RIVERS (21). This is a very popular area, all three rivers and several lakes producing good trout fishing, including some of the Arizona natives, particularly in the upper Little Colorado. Throughout its length, till it empties into the Canyon, there is good rainbow and brown-trout fishing.

Many Arizonians consider the Black River very good, and BIG LAKE (22) at the top of the river has been stocked with cutthroat. Nearby CRESCENT LAKE (23), yields browns, rainbows and some natives.

Some of the lakes most recently constructed by the Arizona Game and Fish Department, and which will probably be currently producing good fishing, are FOOL HOLLOW LAKE (24), WOODS CANYON (25), RIGG'S FLAT (26) and PENA BLANCA

(27), all of which have been stocked with trout. The last two are readily reached from Tucson. Riggs Flat Lake is near the town of Safford, at the junction of Interstate Highway 10 and U.S. 666. Being a little further away from Tucson it is not as heavily fished and also has the advantage of better water conditions throughout the summer. Pena Blanca Lake, about seventy miles south, has some rainbow fishing in the months from November to May, on a put and take planting basis. There are also some medium-sized bass which hit best in the evenings on small flies and popping bugs, and large catfish which are taken on chicken livers and other "stink baits."

ARIZONA FISHING REGULATIONS

There is no general closed season on any species in Arizona waters, but certain waters are periodically closed for fishing for various species; current fishing regulations should always be checked.

Resident Fishing License $5.00
Trout Stamp (Resident) $2.00
Nonresident Fishing License $15.00
Trout Stamp (Nonresident) $6.00
Nonresident 5-Day Fishing License $5.00
Trout Stamp (5-Day Nonresident) $3.00
One-Day Fishing License, good for all fish, except in Colorado River, resident and nonresident $2.00
Colorado River License, all species $10.00

LIMITS

The limit on trout, kokanee salmon, black bass and channel catfish (all catfish with forked tails) is 10 per day of each species, or in possession; except the limit on channel catfish taken from the waters between Nevada and Arizona is 25 per day in possession. The bag and possession limit for striped bass, found only in the Colorado River, is three, and the minimum length is 16 inches. No live or cut bait in trout waters is permitted, except in the Colorado River.

For complete regulations write: Game and Fish Commission, Arizona State Building, Phoenix, Arizona.

UTAH

Utah lies on the backbone of the Rocky Mountains with drainage to Salt Lake on the northwest, to the Colorado River on the southeast, and added cross-drainage running north and south as a result of the transverse Wasatch and Uinta Ranges in the northern part of the state. On its northern and eastern borders it shares the topographical features of Wyoming and the Colorado Plateau, while in the south and west the main outlook is one of arid plains and desert lands of the Great Basin. Throughout the state the scene is varied with such wonders of nature as Monument Valley, Cathedral Valley, Zion Canyon, Bryce Canyon and, of course, Great Salt Lake.

The two largest rivers in Utah, the Colorado and the Green, both in the south and east, are suitable only for catfish. Salt Lake itself, the largest lake, is too briny to support fish life. But there are many small rivers and lakes in the mountain ranges which hold trout, bluegill, walleye pike, kokanee salmon and whitefish; and an increasing number of reservoirs provide the same kind of fishing.

The summer season in Utah is dry, except for the month of August when there are usually heavy showers of short duration. There is a general difference of 40 degrees between daytime temperatures and those of the night and the fisherman should carry suitable clothing, especially as he is likely to be fishing at an altitude of from 4,000 to 8,000 feet.

Eight major U.S. highways lead into the state and there are four interstate railways and five major airlines operating to its major cities, thus bringing Utah within a few hours of many of the populous cities of the country. Accessibility of towns from which the angler will take off into the better fishing areas is further augmented by numerous bus and train excursions to the many scenic wonders, which are often located in the same general regions as the good fishing.

This same situation makes it possible to find plentiful accommodations in these areas. The primitive parts of the state are well supplied with camp sites maintained by the state. In traveling to remote areas, however, complete supplies and emergency provisions should be carried.

At higher altitudes elk may be encountered. In some sections mule deer and antelope are very numerous, and in certain specific areas there are mountain lions and bobcats. As throughout the Rockies, there may be rattlesnakes.

Fishing in the State of Utah is limited by two disadvantages: much of the state is arid, and many of the waters which originally held a sizable head of fish have been dammed to supply power and irrigation, or to prevent erosion, with the result that fishing is diminishing. However, this has been somewhat offset by the creation of man-made lakes, some of which are producing increasingly good angling. In the offices of the Utah Fish and Game Department, you may see a 28-pound cutthroat from Strawberry Reservoir in central Utah. It rivals the lake trout of the same weight taken from Utah's greatest natural body of fishing water, Fish Lake, further south near Koosharem. In spite of the fact that Utah is not generally regarded as a top fishing state, it did produce an American record brown trout, a 37-pound 4-ounce fish taken from the Logan River in the extreme northern part of the state near the Idaho border.

Those lakes and rivers which are the best producers are also the most heavily fished, since they are closest to the large centers of population. These are the waters of the Uinta Mountains in the northeast, just east of Salt Lake City. Fortunately much of this mountainous area has been set aside as a National Forest Primitive Area and will be preserved in its wild state, thus also preserving the fishing. There are hundreds of miles of crystal-clear streams and more than 1,000 lakes, about half of which contain trout of one kind or another. Access to this high country can be made from Lonetree, Wyoming, on the north, from Mirror Lake on the west (east of Kamas), and also from Roosevelt, on U.S. 40, on the south. From all these towns passable roads lead up to a central trail which parallels the backbone of the range from Mirror Lake as far as King's Peak.

NORTHERN AREA

Throughout the area the fishing is in the upper waters, the lower streams being heavily tapped for irrigation. There are rainbow, brown and cutthroat trout in the PROVO (1) and WEBER RIVERS (2), both of which head up near Mirror Lake.

Here, as throughout the high-altitude areas of the West, the streams are high and muddy early in the season. This is the time for bait fishermen, the fly man coming into his own when the water is low and clear.

From Hanna, on state road 35, off U.S. 40 at Duchesne, fishermen can go into the GRANDADDY LAKES BASIN (3), where there are approximately 300 small lakes in a ten-mile-square area. To the southeast, from Roosevelt, the angler can reach the headwaters of the UINTA RIVER (4). Several of the lakes in this basin have been stocked with grayling. There are cutthroat trout in many of the small streams which unite to form the Uinta; and other lakes in the basin hold grayling, cutthroat, rainbow and some brook trout, usually two or more species to a lake.

To simplify getting in to the mountain streams it should be noted that all streams of the southern slope of the Uinta, from Whiterocks River westward, flow to the Duchesne River, while those east of Whiterocks River flow to the Green, near Vernal. Access is therefore easiest from the drainage area of the river you are to fish, rather than across the range. Roads of a sort lead up most of the streams toward the crest.

The WHITEROCKS (5), ASHLEY CREEK (6) and its forks, and BRUSH CREEK (7), as well as numerous lakes in the basin, provide excellent fishing and can be reached via Vernal, the gateway to the Dinosaur National Monument.

The BEAR RIVER (8) rises in the western slopes of the Uinta and flows north into Wyoming, then into Idaho near Bear Lake, which is shared by Idaho and Utah. The river almost completely circles the lake as it turns south again and eventually empties into Great Salt Lake. There are some trout in the headwaters, and bass, walleye and catfish in CUTLER RESERVOIR (9), which dams the river in northern Utah. Below the dam there is some good spring walleye fishing. From there down the stream produces good catfishing. The twenty-mile-long lake provides some of Utah's best fishing for cutthroat, rainbow and lake trout; and there are three species of whitefish.

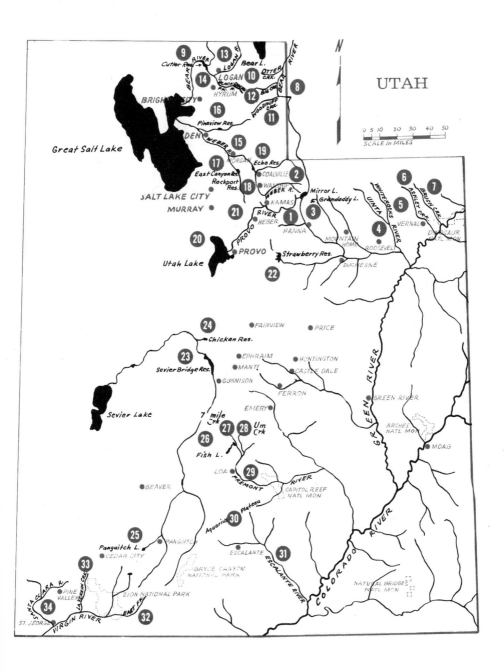

While not to be classed as "fishing" from the sporting point of view, there is a season for Bonneville cisco, unique to this lake, when the fish come in to spawn at the shores around the middle of January. The fish are only 6 to 8 inches in length and the mouths so small they cannot be taken on hook and line. Holders of a Utah fishing license may take fifty per day with dip net.

Several small streams which enter Bear River to the south of Bear Lake also have trout. These are the OTTER (10), WOODRUFF CREEK (11) and BIG CREEK (12).

To the southwest of Bear Lake lie the two streams which have the greatest appeal to the trout fisherman in Utah: the LOGAN (13), which produced the state's biggest brownie to date, and which annually turns up a considerable number of this species from 10 to 20 pounds, as well as rainbows and cutthroats of substantial size; and the BLACKSMITH FORK RIVER (14), which many rate as high as the Logan, especially for brown trout on flies in late summer. The Logan is a small stream, with many cottages along the banks, not prepossessing looking from the fisherman's point of view. Dams set here and there seem to furnish the water needed to hold the big brown trout. Both of these rivers, and the northern reaches of the WEBER RIVER (15), another good trout stream, can be reached from the town of Logan, via State Highway 242 from Hyrum.

From headquarters at Ogden, just east of the midsection of Salt Lake, the angler can reach the Ogden River for stream fishing and can add some excellent rainbow-trout fishing in PINEVIEW RESERVOIR (16). This is also a good point from which to work the Weber and its tributaries, with the several dams which have produced EAST CANYON RESERVOIR (17) near Morgan and ROCKPORT RESERVOIR (18) at Wanship, both providing trout fishing; also ECHO RESERVOIR (19) at Coalville, with good fishing in late August and September for California goldens.

Further south, readily reached from Salt Lake City via the town of Murray, on Alt. 50, there are a number of natural lakes which have trout. They are Martha, Catherine, Lillian, Mary, Blanche, Silver and Twin Lakes. The adjacent canyon streams also offer fishing for small trout.

Using Provo as headquarters, you can fish UTAH LAKE (20) for bass, walleye and catfish, and the PROVO RIVER (21) for trout and whitefish. The river has been dammed at Heber and below the dam is some of the best brown-trout fishing to be found in Utah. Above the dam, in the headwaters of the river, there is excellent rainbow and cutthroat fishing. The reservoir itself holds rainbows and browns.

Not far to the east, up Daniel's Canyon, is the STRAWBERRY RESERVOIR (22), well known for its rainbows and cutthroats and also producing some browns. As mentioned earlier, the largest cutthroat ever taken in Utah came from the Strawberry Reservoir.

Those who want to try some "wild-country fishing" in Utah should take the Skyline Drive for 100 miles along the crest of the Wasatch Plateau, which can be reached from Highway 10 on the east, via Price, Huntington, Castle Dale, Ferron or Emery; or from the west via feeder roads from U.S. 89 at Fairview, Ephraim, Manti and Gunnison. The drive lies at high elevation, much of it between 9,000 and 11,000 feet, producing a good watershed; and the lower valleys and meadows on both sides are well supplied with small lakes which hold rainbows, brook trout and cutthroat trout of modest size.

SOUTHERN AREA

To the northwest of Gunnison is SEVIER BRIDGE RESERVOIR (23), noted for its walleye pike. The river of the same name offers very little fishing as most of the waters of this system are used for irrigation. There is some bass fishing in the small CHICKEN RESERVOIR (24) on one of the tributaries of the Sevier, and Otter Creek has some brown-trout fishing.

Still further south on U.S. 89, you find PANGUITCH LAKE (25), southwest of the town of Panguitch in the Dixie National Forest. There is excellent rainbow fishing and the Kokanee salmon has done very well in Panguitch.

You'll be one of a crowd if you go to FISH LAKE (26) in south-central Utah, but it may very well be worth it. About 40,000 anglers visit Fish Lake annually, to try for some immense lake trout, to 30 pounds and better, as well as to enjoy its consistently good rainbow fishing, spiced with a few brooks and browns. The lake is seven miles long by one mile wide, and you reach it via State Highway 24, north of Loa.

Nearby SEVEN-MILE (27) and UM CREEKS (28) and the FREMONT RIVER (29) also have trout fishing. The latter is open year-round for both rainbows and browns.

An ideal area for a pack trip lies south of Loa (or north of Escalante), where the road to the AQUARIUS PLATEAU (30) passes Big Lake, Posie Lake and Cyclone Lake. The heavily forested plateau is from 10,000 to 12,250 feet high. Many of the lakes are scarcely ever fished. Guides can be obtained at the village of Boulder, on dirt road 117 south from Teasdale on State Road 24.

Further south, the ESCALANTE RIVER (31) also has some good fishing for cutthroat up to 1 pound.

The extreme southwestern part of the state of Utah is drained by the Colorado and San Juan Rivers but their attractions are limited mainly to scenery and the plentiful catfish. The construction of the Glen Canyon Dam on the Colorado has resulted in a new Lake Powell, so recent in formation that at this writing there is little definite fishing information available. However, since this was the location of the famous Colorado River boat trips through Glen Canyon, undoubtedly fishing will be developed and current information can be obtained from Art Green's Canyon Tours, Inc., Page, Arizona; Jackson Scenic Tours (also arranges fishing), Fremont, Utah; and Cross Tours and Explorations, Inc., 860 South 1000 East, Orem, Utah.

Moving to the more western part of the state, you will find some trout fishing east of the town of Beaver, on Interstate 15. West on State Highway 21 to Kent, LeBaron, Anderson Meadows and Puffer's Lake are found. Following Interstate 15 south to Cedar City, the angler can turn west on State Highway 56 to find some waters that are particularly attractive to the trout addict, and especially to the fly fisherman who likes to make his leisurely way through fine countryside, fishing clear water. Such an angler will enjoy fishing for rainbow and brook trout in Duck Creek, Navajo and Aspen-Mirror Lakes. This is park-like country with pleasant forests and the spectacular Cedar Breaks. The many small waters call for delicate presentation of your fly. Nearby Minersville Reservoir, VIRGIN RIVER, EAST FORK (32) and LAVERKIN CREEK (33) all hold trout, too.

Moving into the extreme south of the state, from St. George on U.S. 91 (future Interstate 15), you can branch out to SANTA CLARA RIVER (34), Baker's Reservoir and Newcastle Reservoir, above Pine Valley, for good rainbow and brown-trout angling. Upper and Lower Enterprise Reservoirs are stocked with rainbows.

Those who plan to fish in Utah should write for the current list of "Guest Ranches, Lodges, Resorts, Camps in Utah" issued by the Utah Tourist and Publicity Council, State Capitol, Salt Lake City, Utah. This list indicates which of the establishments features fishing, and what type, in most cases. A list of "Hunting, Fishing, Exploring and Sightseeing Guides" issued by the Utah State Department of Fish and Game, gives similar information. A third list, "Utah River Guides," also available through the Tourist and Publicity Council, covers most of the floatable rivers of the state. Emphasis is on sightseeing, but undoubtedly some of these guides could provide fishermen with accommodations on the streams that are fishable.

UTAH FISHING REGULATIONS

Resident Fishing License $3.50
Nonresident Fishing License $10.00
        5-Day $4.00
        6-Day $5.00
        7-Day $6.00
        8-Day $7.00
        9-Day $8.00
       10-Day $9.00

Less rates for children, depending on age.

SEASONS AND LIMITS

In general, the Utah fishing season is from June 1–November 30, during the hours from 4 a.m. to 9 p.m. Some waters are open year-round, and there are numerous exceptions to the open season.

Species	Limits
Trout and Salmon	10 fish or 7 pounds and 1 fish. For Bear Lake only, the limit is 7 pounds and 1 fish, but not to exceed 15 pounds.
Grayling	15 fish
Black Bass, White Bass	In aggregate, 10 fish or 15 pounds and 1 fish
Walleye Pike	5 fish
Whitefish	25 fish, except 10 from Weber River
Bonneville Cisco	50 fish (Bear Lake only)

For complete regulations write: Department of Fish and Game, 1596 W. North Temple, Salt Lake City 16, Utah.

NEVADA

In spite of the fact that much of the State of Nevada is arid or desert country, there are numerous waters which provide a wide variety of fishing. Several varieties of trout are found in the fresh, cold streams and lakes along the eastern slopes of the Sierras in the western part of the state. Crappie, bluegill, perch and largemouth black bass are found in the warmer waters of central and eastern Nevada.

The Colorado River, forming part of the southeastern border between Arizona and Nevada, is the only large stream. The state contains several of the most famous lakes on the continent, however, namely Pyramid, Walker, and part of Lake Tahoe, as well as many miles of shoreline on Lake Mead.

In the dry parts of Nevada, the climate is very warm, but the fisherman going to the high mountains for stream fishing, or to the slopes of the Sierras, will find warm clothing necessary at night; and in the peaks of the Owyhee and Ruby Mountains, he will often find snow in midsummer.

As in much of the central area of the west, there are rattlesnakes at low altitudes, but seldom at the higher levels. Game is not a problem, though the fisherman may see deer, elk, antelope and bighorn sheep, as well as thousands of waterfowl, depending on where he is fishing.

Because of the many desert areas of Nevada, anglers should always carry water, emergency rations and a plentiful supply of gas if they plan to go off the beaten path. And trips away from well-established roads should be made by horse, jeep or pickup truck.

The following dry flies, in sizes 12 and 16, will take fish in Nevada waters: Black Gnat, Royal Coachman, Dark Hendrickson, Cowdung, Light Cahill, Ginger Quill, Quill Gordon, Rio Grande King, Adams. In wet flies, you should go provided with the Black Gnat, Coachman, Royal Coachman, Light Cahill, Black and Yellow Nymph, Black and Orange Nymph, and Gray Nymph, all in sizes 12 and 14. Bucktails and streamers should be on size 8 long-shanked hooks, and basic patterns are the Gray Ghost, Red and White, Black and White, the Muddler, and the Edson Tiger.

Spoons and spinners for spin casters should be in weights of ⅛ and ¼ ounces; and for patterns it is best to consult the local tackle stores for the best item on the waters you will fish.

WESTERN AREA

Of the natural lakes in Nevada, WALKER (1), PYRAMID (2), TOPAZ (3), CATNIP (4) and SUMMIT LAKE (5) all hold the Lahontan cutthroat, the only trout native to western Nevada. The world's largest cutthroat was a 41-pounder taken in Pyramid Lake in 1925. At present Walker is the best cutthroat producer, with fish running from 3 to 16 pounds. There are also brook trout in the lake.

U.S. 95 skirts the western shore of Lake Walker, providing ready access, and boat-rental agencies will be found at many points. There are accommodations at Babbitt and Hawthorne at the southern end of the lake. The season never closes at Lake Walker, but the peak catches are made in April and May.

Pyramid and Walker Lakes are both close to the western border of Nevada, and famous Lake Tahoe lies exactly on the border between Nevada and California. LAKE TAHOE (6) was once a prime source of cutthroat trout until the unhappy combination of commercial fishing and water pollution almost destroyed the fish population. Today it has been restocked and there is good fishing for brook trout, rainbows, browns, some lake trout, and kokanee salmon. This being one of the most highly developed tourist spots in the country, there are abundant accommodations at Carson City, Reno and Minden, as well as along the shores of the lake.

Pyramid Lake, which is thirty-one miles from Reno, is the remnant of a great inland sea, which once covered an area 550 miles east and west, and 300 miles north and south. Today this desert lake is thirty miles long and is still shrinking in size each year. Visitors to Pyramid will see white pelicans, as this is the largest rookery for this now-rare bird in the United States.

When first discovered in 1844, the lake teemed with giant cutthroat and was a favorite spot for Indians to gather to get fish for food. The most common catch today is the rainbow; they average 14 to 18 inches but can go much larger, some having been taken up to 12 pounds. Cutthroat average 4 to 9 pounds with top catches of 13 pounds. Eastern brook trout have also been planted but have not fared well and are rare catches. Browns are sometimes taken, these fish working in from the TRUCKEE RIVER (7) which feeds the lake. Other occasional catches are the kokanee salmon and the Sacramento perch. There is still another fish, the cui-ui, which is very common in Pyramid Lake and is unknown elsewhere in the world, but this species is usually taken only in the spring by snagging.

Anglers can drive up almost the entire east shore of Pyramid Lake on either paved or improved highway and unimproved road the balance of the way. Much of the fishing is done by casting along 100 miles of shoreline, the casters locating the drop-offs where the fish like to prowl. Those who plan to use bait should check the state regulations as only bait taken from the lake or the Truckee Drainage may be used. In addition to the Nevada angling license, fishermen need a Reservation Permit, obtainable at sporting goods stores in Reno and the Sparks area as well as at Nixon and Sutcliffe. One day, $1, season, $3. An Indian boating permit (for fishing purposes) is $1 per day, or $5 per season. Possession limit is five fish.

There are boat landings at Sutcliffe on the mid-western shore and at the southwest end of the lake. Those who bring their own boats should use these established landings because of the danger of launching along the sandy shore where there are no facilities. Restaurants, stores and accommodations can be found at Nixon at the south end of the lake and at Sutcliffe.

In this general area, RYE PATCH RESERVOIR (8), on U.S. 40 northeast of Pyramid Lake, has fairly good fishing for largemouth black bass, rainbow and cutthroat trout. Boats and lodging may be found at Humboldt and several other towns along U.S. 40.

LAKE MEAD

LAKE MEAD (9) provides the best bass fishing in the state. The lake is formed where the Hoover Dam backs up the Colorado River on the border between Nevada and Arizona. The lake is 246 square miles in area, with 550 miles of shoreline. Besides largemouth black bass there are crappie, bluegill and catfish. As the bass usually lie very deep, the most successful way of taking them is with mudpuppies

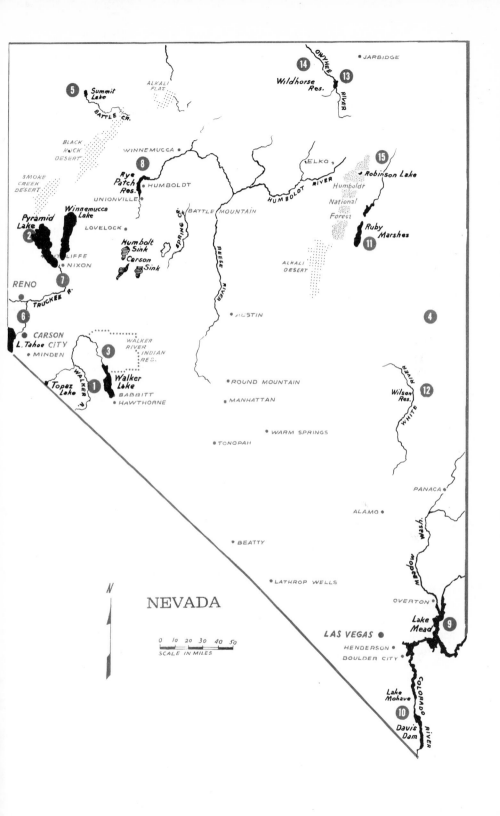

NEVADA

SCALE IN MILES
0 10 20 30 40 50

N

or artificials of the same. However, when you catch the bass on the surface, Lake Mead can produce some wonderful angling for plug, fly or spin casters.

Boulder Beach, Las Vegas and Echo Bay are the main centers from which anglers fish the lake. There are tackle stores, boat-rental agencies, and restaurants at all of them. There are accommodations available at Overton, Boulder City and Las Vegas, which is only twenty miles away. At Boulder Beach there is a free public campground for either tents or trailers. Cabin and camping accommodations can also be found at Overton Beach, Temple Bar, Willow Beach, El Dorado Canyon and Searchlight Ferry. Those who wish to use several more remote camping sites along the shores of the lake must be sure to be completely outfitted and have all necessary supplies.

There is good fishing for rainbow trout in the Colorado River below the Hoover Dam. On occasion they can be taken by all the casting methods, and by trolling with conventional lures, but the popular local bait is the doughball, formed by rolling dough completely around the hook. Some inventive fishermen flavor the dough with such exciting ingredients as anacin, banana oil and garlic, and one manufacturer makes a special cheese lure called "dynamite." Clusters of salmon eggs, single salmon eggs and worms are also successful, and even roasted marshmallows have been reported as good bait.

The state stocks fish from 8 to 14 inches, but you may take some from 15 to 20 inches, and now and again some lucky angler hangs a buster of 6 or 8 pounds. A few years ago two 18-pounders were caught on doughballs. The season is open year-round, twenty-four hours a day. During the hot summer weather, many anglers go out early in the morning and again at dusk. At such times, in the rocky, dry hills that form the river canyon, you may see bighorn sheep coming down for a drink and occasionally wild burros.

Fishermen should go with a guide on the Colorado, at least until they know the river. The water level varies considerably as the outlet at the dam is changed. Since the river runs between high walls, quite a current is formed, in some places as fast as forty-three miles per hour. The usual schedule is to release water from the dam at 7 a.m., stop it at 3 or 3:30 p.m., and resume releasing at 7 p.m., but this schedule is not always followed.

Guides can be found usually at boat-rental agencies such as Willow Beach, where, incidentally, the most famous guide is a woman, Minnie McFarland, who used to be a waitress, went fishing, and liked it so much she started guiding.

The Davis Dam, further downstream on the Arizona-Nevada border, also backs up the river to form LAKE MOHAVE (10). This far down the river bass take over as the main fish, with only occasional rainbows, mostly in the upper waters of the lake. There are also crappie and bluegill. On the Nevada side of the lake there are accommodations at El Dorado Cover, Cotton Wood Cover, Searchlight and Nelson.

In both Lake Mead and Lake Mohave, the states of Arizona and Nevada each honor the other's license, requiring only the addition of a stamp.

ELKO REGION

In another part of Nevada the angler can combine trout fishing and bass fishing, too, in totally different surroundings. This is in the Elko region, in the northeast corner of the state. Here in the Ruby Mountains, close to the trail which the pioneers followed on their way to California, there is both lake and stream fishing of exceptional interest. High in these mountains the spring-fed RUBY MARSHES (11) provide a perfect habitat, the right conditions being maintained by the establishment of a Fish and Wildlife migratory-bird refuge. In the potholes and canals of the marshes, rainbows, brooks and brown trout grow big and healthy. The heaviest fish ever known to have come from the Ruby Marshes was a 13-pound rainbow. A 6¼-pound brook trout and a 6-pound brown have also been recorded. The average runs between 2 and 3 pounds.

The canals are collecting ditches put in in 1950 to pick up all the water from the springs and regulate the water level in order to have more water for nesting and molting birds.

In 1940 largemouth black bass were stocked from Lake Mead. These bass average 2½ pounds and some are taken annually to 7 and 8 pounds.

This is beautiful country, with unexpected and unexpectedly productive fishing. Those who wish to pack in should contact Claude E. Gerber, Mountain View Ranch, Starr Valley, via Deeth, Nevada.

About eighty miles from Elko, the WILSON RESERVOIR (12), although only about a mile square, has produced some fine trout. This is an irrigation lake, but rainbows were planted in it, and the average catch is 2½ pounds. The biggest recorded went 5 pounds 12 ounces.

Sixty-five miles from Elko, in northern Nevada, famous WILDHORSE RESERVOIR (13) lies at an altitude of 5,400 feet. Wildhorse was formed by damming the Owyhee River. The lake is three miles long and half a mile wide at its widest point. After squawfish and other coarse species got into the lake, it was poisoned, in 1955, and the following year was stocked with rainbows and kokanee salmon. Since then the production has been good, and rainbows are being taken with an average weight of 3 pounds. A few years after the first stocking of the reservoir, three rainbows taken there had a combined weight of 16 pounds.

Fishermen troll with "Christmas trees," also called "Ford fenders," with worms and sometimes plugs behind. The woolly worm is the best fly, while spinners use ¼-ounce spoons with telling effect.

Wildhorse Reservoir is open all year but the best time is from April 1st to the middle of December, when ice forms. After a suitable thickness has been established, there is good ice fishing until the breakup in March.

The OWYHEE RIVER (14), flowing out of Wildhorse Reservoir, has some fast rainbow fishing. Most of the fish are small, but in the fast water these 12- to 15-inch fish provide plenty of sport. When I was there I found that very few people fished it, and it's well worth a try.

Those anglers who would like to combine some excellent fishing for brook trout from 6 to 16 inches, with a trip to some extremely beautiful high country, should pack in to ROBINSON LAKE (15). It lies at 9,000 feet, with constant ice fields to serve as refrigerators for your catch. Outfitters from Elko will take you in.

Those who want to explore mountain fishing on their own can get a map of the Humboldt National Forest in Elko County from the Forest Supervisor, Post Office Building, Elko. This map shows the myriad creeks of the Forest, the roads over which they may be reached, and the campgrounds. For instance, a loop road out of Elko to the north and west will carry you past Taylor Canyon, Jack Creek, Bull Run Basin, Trail Creek, along the Owyhee River below Wildhorse Dam, to Jack Creek Campground and North Fork Campground. Fishing is generally good in the neighborhood of all the campgrounds and permission to reach farther waters can usually be obtained from ranchers.

Another loop which circles north from Elko towards the Idaho border crosses many small mountain streams, with fishing for small trout. Lodging can be obtained at Mountain City, Jarbidge, Jack Creek and Lamoille, meals at Jack Creek, Mountain City, Owyhee and Lamoille. There are gas stations at Taylor Canyon, Tuscarora, Jack Creek, Wildhorse, Mountain City, Owyhee, and Jarbidge; and at Lamoille, Rock House in Ruby Valley, Jiggs and Lee on the southern loop.

NEVADA FISHING REGULATIONS

Resident Fishing License $5.00
Nonresident Fishing License $10.00
Nonresident 5-Day License $3.50
No license required for children under 14, but only half limit allowed.

LIMITS

With some exceptions, which must be checked when you purchase your license, the following limits apply:

Trout: 15 fish or 10 pounds, whichever is reached first. However, at least 5 trout may be taken, regardless of weight.
Salmon: 5 fish, no weight limit.
Bass: 10 fish, no weight limit.
Catfish and other game fish not mentioned above, 25 fish in aggregate, no weight limit.

Exceptions: Lakes Mead, Mohave and Colorado River, daily possession and bag limits: 10 trout, 10 bass, 25 catfish, no limit on bluegill or crappie.

Walker Lake, daily bag and possession limit: 5 trout, 5 perch, 5 salmon.

Lake Tahoe, daily bag and possession limit: 5 trout, 5 kokanee salmon, 5 mountain whitefish, or combination thereof.

Topaz Lake, bag and possession limit: 10 trout or 10 pounds and one fish, provided that, irrespective of weight, 5 trout may be taken.

Pyramid Lake, daily bag limit, including cui-cui: 5 game fish. Possession: one day's limit.

For complete regulations write: Fish and Game Commission, P.O. Box 678, Reno, Nevada.

COLORADO

When you hear Denver, capital city of Colorado, referred to as the "mile-high city in the Rockies," you get a fairly accurate idea of the terrain the fisherman may expect in this mountain state. In the range which slices through the central part of the state there are more high peaks than in any other state, and the fishing reflects this condition. In general the valleys are deeper and narrower than those of comparable areas and the streams are smaller and more rushing in character. There are innumerable mountain brooks and hundreds of crystal-clear mountain lakes. Almost every high meadow reveals a small stream winding back and forth in ox-bows, with here and there a beaver dam backing up the water to form a pond. These meadow streams invariably contain table-size trout, while the beaver ponds often harbor fish of substantial size, as large as 2 to 4 pounds.

Colorado's rivers flow from both sides of the Rocky Mountain range, the eastern waters reaching the Mississippi and the western ones the Pacific. The major rivers in size are the Rio Grande, South Platte, Colorado and Arkansas, but the major ones from the angler's point of view are the slightly smaller streams such as the Gunnison, the upper drainage of the North Platte, the Animas, the White and the Yampa. The fish are rainbow, native, brown and brook trout, according to the location and nature of the stream; and in the cold-water lakes and reservoirs there are sometimes lake trout and kokanee salmon. In other reservoirs in the lower altitudes, and in warm-water natural lakes, particularly in the eastern part of the state, there are walleye, largemouth black bass, perch, catfish, crappie and drum.

Since Colorado has long been one of the most heavily fished states, the annual depletion of fish is very great. This is compensated for by extremely heavy stocking by the Colorado Game and Fish Department, especially in those streams which bear the brunt of summer fishing: the Taylor Fork and East Fork of the Gunnison, the Frying Pan, the Roaring Fork and the streams of Estes Park.

While it is possible to drive to many spots where good fishing is available, the very nature of mountainous Colorado makes it a top state for packing or hiking in to the more remote waters where fishing is likely to be less crowded. The state provides many exceptionally fine camp sites, usually with mountain springs to supply water, wood readily available, and good fishing nearby. The Colorado Game and Fish Department, Box 720, 1530 Sherman Street, Denver 1, publishes a brochure, "A Guide to the Major Fishing Waters of Colorado," which indicates the highways that lead to the major fishing spots. A list of resorts and dude ranches which offer fishing as an attraction can be obtained from the same source. Many of these ranches will outfit pack trips to some of the high streams and lakes for one day, overnight or longer.

In general the summer climate of Colorado is one of bright, sunny days with an occasional afternoon thunderstorm, and distinctly cool nights. The fisherman should be equipped with woolen slacks, a cotton shirt topped by a woolen one, and a Windbreaker or rainjacket for evenings. Campers will need the addition of woolen underwear and warm sleeping gear. Chest-high waders are a necessity for adequate fishing of the larger rivers, but on many of the small mountain streams hip boots are sufficient.

The State of Colorado is also renowned for its hunting. Consequently, the angler who fishes in the less-populated areas may see deer and bear almost anywhere. In the higher altitudes there will be bear, elk, antelope, and if you are lucky you may spot a bighorn sheep. There are also mountain lions, but it is a rare treat to sight one of these shy creatures.

Since most of the fishing is in fairly high country, rattlesnakes are not as much of a threat as in some other areas of the Rockies. However, in the dry, more arid regions of the foothills the angler should always keep an eye out for them.

TROUT STREAMS

The GUNNISON RIVER (1), one of the major trout streams of North America, leads Colorado rivers in the size of fish and quality of the fishing. This river regularly turns up fish in the 1- to 2-pound class, and annually giants of 10 pounds spark the angler's interest. The brown is the predominant variety but rainbows and cutthroats are also taken, with a scattering of brook trout.

While there is some fishing in the upper waters of the Gunnison where it parallels U.S. 50 down from Monarch Pass, the best fishing starts near the town of Almont where the Taylor River and the East Fork add their waters to the river. Conditions are ideal from there down to Sapinero; and below, the more adventurous fisherman will find the famous Black Canyon of the Gunnison. A narrow, one-way road is passable but not good.

The Gunnison is a big, fast-flowing river, its level controlled somewhat by the Taylor Dam at the top of its tributary, the Taylor River. But it can be waded in most places, with care, even when the water is high. Fly fishermen find that streamers and bucktails take the bigger fish, the Muddler and the Spruce Fly being two good producers. The latter was first tied in Idaho as a wet fly, then made into a streamer. Wet flies and nymphs also pay off, the Gray Nymph being particularly good. And there are times when a dry fly will do deadly damage on the Gunnison, though mostly when the river is low. Local anglers pretty well limit their dry-fly fishing to the fall when the water has been shut off up at the Taylor Dam. This is a great bait river, with hellgrammites, nightcrawlers, bunches of smaller worms, and live minnows all producing their share of big fish. Fishing in the Gunnison is usually at its best in late August and early September, but good catches are made throughout the season.

The Gunnison is heavily fished but even so there is lots of water that is seldom hit, and the ambitious angler who makes his way to such spots can expect some extra-good fishing. In this regard, many Colorado ranches are posted, but if asked, the owners will often grant permission to fish. In such cases, be sure to leave all gates exactly as you find them—open or closed, as the case may be. Treat the cattle with respect, and don't litter the river banks. Then the rancher will welcome the next fellow, too.

The TAYLOR RIVER (2) is the major tributary of the Gunnison. It enters the river near the town of Almont, flowing down from the Taylor Dam twenty one miles higher. Though handicapped somewhat by the varying volume of water released from the dam, the whole twenty one miles is good trout water. The altitude at the dam is 9,000 feet, and towards evening the air becomes quite cold and occasionally there are snow flurries. Yet even under such conditions the trout will hit dry flies, the main problem being to keep from snapping your fine leader tippet, as it becomes brittle with the cold air and cold water. Much of the river is fast and for this reason, especially when there is a heavy flow being released from the dam, dry-fly men must use a short line to avoid drag and keep their fly floating properly. But once this is managed, a good catch is practically assured. The Taylor is also highly regarded by spinners, who use small spoons, or flies with a bubble. The river produces rainbows and browns from 8 to 14 inches, and occasionally to 17 inches.

The EAST RIVER (3), which also enters the Gunnison near Almont, is smaller than the Taylor, more of a meadow stream in character, and calls for a more careful approach and a lighter delivery. The angler must keep well hidden from the fish if he hopes to take many trout from the East. The same is true in the TOMICHI CREEK, close to the town of Gunnison. This stream, winding through hay meadows, holds some nice brown trout. It is also inhabited by hordes of mosquitoes. They are called "blind" mosquitoes and luckily do not bite, but each time you put your foot down as you walk through the meadow grass, a swarm flies up in your nostrils.

From Interstate Highway 70, at Glenwood Springs, the Colorado angler has access to three famous trout streams, the FRYING PAN (4), the ROARING FORK (5) and the CRYSTAL (6), which pour their waters into the Colorado River at the Springs. Much of the Roaring Forks and Frying Pan can be fished with Aspen as headquarters, but there are accommodations available at most of the small towns along the course of the rivers.

The Crystal joins the other two near Carbondale. Above, there are accommodations at Redstone, a small town near McClure Pass. The Crystal is well named, one of the clearest streams the writer has ever seen, flowing over the beautiful white blocks from the abandoned marble mines. There are some good-sized rainbows in the upper reaches near the ghost town of Marble, site of a quarry which has been abandoned for many years.

The Colorado River itself, near Glenwood Springs, provides twenty five miles of good rainbow and brown trout fishing from the town down to Rifle, on Interstate 70; there are also channel catfish.

Northwest of Glenwood Springs, the WHITE RIVER (7) offers excellent summer fishing for rainbow, brown and brook trout. Fishermen can headquarter at the town of Meeker, and there is an unimproved road all the way up the river to Trappers Lake. Unfortunately, a great deal of the land is posted.

From Steamboat Springs, on U.S. 40, just west of the Continental Divide, anglers can reach the YAMPA RIVER (8) and its tributaries, and there are also quite a number of lakes and reservoirs in the general area. Besides Steamboat Springs there are two other sizable towns, Oak Creek and Yampa; and accommodations can also be found in the smaller centers of Mad Creek, Hayden, Glen Eden, Hahns Peak and Columbine Lodge.

In the Rocky Mountain National Park Area, the LARAMIE RIVER (9), one of Colorado's better trout streams, flows north into Wyoming, and as it is not close to a major highway is not too heavily fished. Much of the stream is posted, however, but near Glendevey, the Lazy W Cross Ranch has fourteen cabins with twelve miles of river to fish. The trout are willing, and some up to 5, 6 and 7 pounds are taken each year. Flies produce best in this fine stream. The peak of the runoff of high water is in mid-June, so fly fishing is good by June 25th. The season closes

October 31st. The first three weeks in July are tops. Go in from U.S. Highway 287 north from Fort Collins to State Highway 14 at Ted's Place, then follow the signs for Glendevey.

To the south, near Loveland on U.S. 34, stream fishermen find rainbows and browns in the BIG THOMPSON (10), the NORTH FORK OF THE THOMPSON (11), the FALL RIVER (12), and NORTH and SOUTH ST. VRAIN CREEKS (13). There is also good fishing in Estes Lake, Horsetooth, and Rattlesnake and Carter Reservoirs. Accommodations are available at the towns of Estes Park and Lyons, and also along the Big Thompson and Vrain Creeks.

In the extreme southern part of Colorado, the RIO GRANDE (14), though affected by the extensive use of its water for irrigation, nevertheless offers good trout fishing in that part which traverses the San Luis Valley along U.S. 160 near Del Norte. Parts of the river here have been set aside for fly fishing only.

The UPPER ARKANSAS RIVER (15), almost square in the middle of the state, also has some excellent trout fishing, the best waters being from the town of Leadville down to a few miles above Pueblo.

The number of small trout streams is legion, and in addition there are many places where rivers which are not top trout streams as a whole have stretches where you can find excellent fishing locally. An example of this is the waters of the SOUTH PLATTE RIVER (16), just southwest of Denver, and the NORTH PLATTE (17), above Steamboat Springs, where occasional good catches are made.

LAKES AND RESERVOIRS

Almost every lake and reservoir in the mountainous part of Colorado will have trout of one kind or another. Certain ones have established reputations for producing. Some of these are the TWIN LAKES (18) near Leadville, SWEETWATER LAKE (19) near Glenwood Springs, TRAPPERS LAKE (20) at the head of the White River, east of Meeker, GRAND LAKE (21) on U.S. 34 in Estes Park, SHADOW MOUNTAIN and GRANBY RESERVOIRS (22), near Granby, in the same area as Grand Lake; and in the west and south, VALLECITO RESERVOIR (23) near Durango, the LAKES OF THE GRAND MESA (24) near Grand Junction, and MONUMENT LAKE (25) near Trinidad in the southeast are all good. TAYLOR PARK RESERVOIR (26) at the top of the Taylor River, is good for rainbows. Other trout lakes which yield sizable catches regularly are WILLIAMS CREEK RESERVOIR (27) near Pagosa Springs and the WILLIAMS FORK RESERVOIR (28) near Parshall; the RED FEATHER LAKES (29), west of U.S. 85 and U.S. 87, northwest of Fort Collins; LAKE JOHN (30), near Walden; ELEVEN MILE CANYON (31) and ANTERO RESERVOIRS (32), near the towns of Hartsel and Lake George off U.S. 24; and VEGA RESERVOIR (33) near Collbran.

Many of the ponds in back of beaver dams high in the Colorado Rockies hold tackle-busters, mostly brook trout but also some cutthroat and rainbows. Usually the waters holding the trout are shallow and the fish extremely shy. If you suddenly step up to full height on top of the dam you will panic them, so make your approach carefully, stay low and drop the fly lightly. Care is still needed on the retrieve. If you are camping up in the meadows, fish early and late, shunning the time when the sun is bright on the water.

Usually small flies are the payoff at dams. Size 14 and 16, and even 18, will get you 2- and 3-pounders. Good patterns are the Blue Dun, Flying Black Ant, Iron Blue Dun, Light Cahill, Black Gnat, Ginger Quill and the Black Jassid size 18.

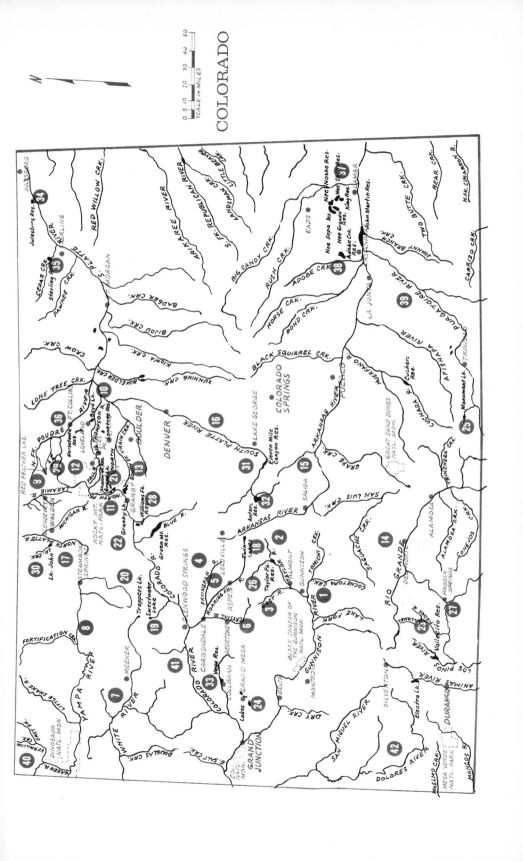

COLORADO

SCALE in MILES
0 5 10 20 30 40 50

The standard nymphs in black and yellow, black and orange and gray, in sizes 12 and 16 are good. One of the most successful flies I've ever used in these high waters is the size 12 Phillips Red and Black Ant. Once you use this fine fly you will always find a place for it in your fly book.

The warm-water species are found mostly in the reservoirs which lie in the plains sections of eastern and southern Colorado. JULESBURG RESERVOIR (34) near Julesburg and STERLING RESERVOIR (35) near the town of Sterling hold crappies to 2½ pounds and 1½-pound perch. BOYD, LONE TREE and HORSETOOTH LAKES (36) in the Loveland area; and further south the RESERVOIRS NEAR EADS (37), and ADOBE CREEK RESERVOIR (38) north of Las Animas, are also productive. Some warm-water fishing is also to be enjoyed in parts of the Arkansas and PURGATOIRE (39) Rivers, in the Yampa, White and GREEN (40) Rivers, and in the COLORADO (41) and DOLORES (42).

In Colorado, fly fishing has always been the most popular method of taking trout, and the purist is given some special consideration in this regard. In Parvin Lake in Larimer County, Butts Lake in Delta County, Bull Creek Reservoirs No. 1 and 2 in Mesa County, Woods Lake in San Miguel County and the East River in Gunnison County for three miles upstream from its confluence with the Taylor River at Almont, only artificial flies may be used, or artificial lures with a single-shank hook. Artificial flies only may be used in the Roaring Fork northwest of Aspen from Hallum Lake to Upper Woody Creek in Pitkin County; in the Rio Grande River from the lower end of Masonic Park to the American Legion Bridge in Mineral and Rio Grande Counties; in the Rio Grande River from the eastern fence line of the 4UR Ranch below Wagon Wheel Gap upstream for a distance of approximately seven miles.

A fairly complete selection of flies to cover all your Colorado fishing should include the following:

Dry flies, sizes 10 to 16—Rio Grande King, Iron Blue Dun, Flying Black Ant, Ginger Quill, Brown Hackle, Peacock Body, Adams, Mosquito, McGinty, Trude, Irresistible, Gray Wulff, Royal Wulff, Red Variant, Goofus Bug.

Wet flies, sizes 8 to 12—Adams, Black Gnat, Brown Hackle, Cahill, California Coachman, Leadwing Coachman, Gray Hackle, Yellow Body, Light Cahill, Mosquito, Professor, Red Ant, Phillips Red and Black Ant, Western Bee, Royal Coachman.

Nymphs, sizes 12, 14 and 16—Gray, Yellow May, Dark Olive, Black and Yellow, Black and Orange, Brown May Nymph.

Streamers and Bucktails, sizes 6, 8 and 10—Black-Nose Dace, Gray Ghost, Black Marabou, Yellow Marabou, Edson Light Tiger, Royal Coachman, Black and White Bucktail, Brown and Yellow Bucktail. Also the Muddler Minnow fly, in sizes 10, 4 and 2.

COLORADO FISHING REGULATIONS

Resident Fishing License $4.00
Nonresident Fishing License $10.00
Nonresident 5-Day License $3.50

SEASONS AND LIMITS

The fishing season in Colorado is described by the Game and Fish Department as "open year-round." This innovation is planned to provide for a longer period for both local and visiting anglers to enjoy their sport, and it is believed it will also make for better management of the waters of the state through eliminating opening-day pressure and early-season pressure in general, by permitting longer periods of stocking. The exceptions to the "open" regulations, however, are numerous enough that anglers should check the particular water in which they plan to fish.

Fishing is open on all lakes or reservoirs any time of the day or night. On all streams and beaver ponds, the fishing hours are from 4 a.m. until 9 p.m.

Use of live minnows as bait is forbidden in most waters above 7,000 feet.

The season in Rocky Mountain National Park, commonly called Estes Park, is from June 15 through September 30, and the hours are from 4 a.m. to 8:30 p.m.

Bag and possession limit for trout is 10 fish daily in the summer and 6 fish daily in the winter. Juveniles (under 15) not holding a license may have only half daily limit.

For complete regulations write: Department of Game, Fish and Parks, 6060 Broadway, Denver 1, Colorado.

WYOMING

Lying just south of Montana, the State of Wyoming shares its general topography. The Continental Divide runs from the northeastern corner across Wyoming in a southeasterly direction, so that some rivers flow to the Atlantic, some to the Pacific. In the Wind River Range, waters are shed to the Missouri, Colorado and Columbia Rivers.

Consequently the state has a tremendous variety of fishing waters, from high altitude lakes and rushing mountain streams to the broad, slower-moving rivers of the eastern plains. In addition, Wyoming offers the unique terrain of Yellowstone Park, with its several famous streams and vast Yellowstone Lake. As in Montana, a majority of these waters are readily accessible from first-class highways, and because of the long-time popularity of the state as a sportsman's haven, there are many guide services to take fishermen in by pack trip or jeep to the more remote lakes and streams.

The major species of fish are brown trout, rainbow trout and the native cutthroat of the Rockies. The record brown trout ever taken in Wyoming weighed 16½ pounds; the largest rainbow, 18½ pounds, and the heaviest cutthroat went 14 pounds 10 ounces. California golden trout have been stocked in a few remote, high-altitude lakes, and while in general this species runs small, the world-record golden, weighing 11 pounds 4 ounces, was taken in Cook's Lake, in northwestern Wyoming, on August 5, 1948, by Charles Reed.

Eastern brook trout have also been stocked in high mountain lakes and have developed well, producing fish which ordinarily go from 8 to 10 inches but on occasion run as high as 3 pounds. The largest ever known to have been taken from Wyoming waters was a hefty 10-pounder.

In some of the high-altitude lakes there are substantial populations of grayling, often weighing in at 2 pounds. A very few lakes add the Mackinaw (lake trout) to the list, and in those waters where this species is found it seems to do very well, several having been recorded to weights of 35 pounds.

There are also a few coarse fish in Wyoming, mostly in impounded waters such as Lake de Smet and other reservoirs. However, even in those waters in which coarse fish thrive, trout generally also seem to be able to hold their own; consequently many of Wyoming's reservoirs provide outstanding trout fishing. Lake de Smet is a good example of this. It is one of the very best rainbow lakes in the state. Occasionally the angler may also find kokanee salmon reaching a top weight of 3 pounds.

In all, twenty one species of fish are listed as found in Wyoming. Besides the sporting species mentioned above, there are Rocky Mountain whitefish, grayling, western sauger (sand pike), walleye pike, yellow perch, pumpkinseed (common sunfish), black crappie (calico bass), northern rock bass, largemouth black bass, southern channel catfish, northern black bullhead, stonecat, burbot (ling), carp and suckers.

Wyoming's human population is small, its animal population large. In many areas there is "open range," where stock roam at large, and therefore the motorist must exercise care in driving for fear of hitting cattle which have strayed onto the highway. The same applies with regard to deer and antelope, which may leap across the road in front of you unexpectedly. There are also elk, moose and mountain sheep. These will likely be encountered only by the angler who goes into the more remote areas by pack or jeep, though the writer once passed three bighorn sheep sedately walking along the edge of the road, at the foot of the Big Horn Mountains.

Bears are common everywhere. The writer has seen one crossing an open field beside the highway with the nearest trees in the foothills a couple of miles away. Your behavior with regard to animals must be especially considered when you enter Yellowstone Park, and this matter will be dealt with later in this chapter.

The altitude in Wyoming varies from 3,125, where the Belle Fourche River leaves the state, to the towering height of Gannett Peak, 13,785 feet. The mean altitude is 7,000 feet. Therefore, in spite of the fact that, especially in the more arid regions, the days can be very hot, evenings are invariably cool or even cold, and the fisherman must go prepared for a quick drop in temperature at sunset. Light-weight woolen underwear under cotton pants will not be too uncomfortable even on warm days, and will provide the necessary protection against the evening chill. A cotton shirt for daytimes, and a heavier one plus a sweater to don at dark, are also perfect for an all-day fishing junket.

A great deal of Wyoming's fishing is in streams which traverse ranches and in most cases the angler must obtain permission to fish. Sometimes he must pay a small "trespass fee." In other instances, motels and guest ranches control stretches of river for the use of their guests.

Most of the streams are at their best in the foothills, since the topography drops off to sandy flats which are generally dry except immediately along the rivers. In some sections there is very low water after the spring runoff. Occasionally this has its advantages; for instance, in the southeastern area both the Platte and the Encampment Rivers become ideal fly-fishing streams in the late summer, when the water is low and clear.

Light- and medium-weight spinning rods, and medium-sized reels capable of holding 200 or 300 yards of 4-, 6-, or 8-pound-test-monofilament line, are more than big enough for any Wyoming fishing. An 8-foot fly rod with HDH line and a 9-footer with GBF will do the job for all types of fly fishing, from small stream to lakes. Leaders should be 7 to 12 feet long, and tapered down to 2, 3, 4 and 5X tippets depending on how big the water is and how big the fish are. Some anglers also use a plug-casting rod and reel with 10- or 12-pound-test line. This is the most popular outfit for bait fishing.

I could give a long list of flies, lures and bait which will take fish in Wyoming at one time or another. On the whole, the list would be the same as those given in the Montana chapter, and, indeed, for most Rocky Mountain fishing. But it always pays to ask at local tackle stores what is the hot lure, bait or fly of the moment—often there is something which will take fish, or more fish, when other lures will not.

NORTHEASTERN AREA (MAP #1)

This part of Wyoming is easily reached via U.S. 16 or U.S. 14 from Rapid City, North Dakota. From the south it can be approached via U.S. 87 from Casper. Using

Kaycee as a jumping-off point you can fish the NORTH FORK OF THE POWDER RIVER (1), the MIDDLE FORK (2), and the RED FORK (3). The North Fork contains browns, rainbows and cutthroats, generally in the 8- to 12-inch size, but the lower reaches have turned up some lunkers. The Middle Fork has browns and rainbows plus some very small brookies in the headwaters. The Red Fork offers good brown and rainbow fishing. In all, the various forks of the Powder provide about sixty-two miles of fishable water, most of it readily accessible, with the exception of the Powder River Canyon, where considerable hiking is necessary.

Out of Buffalo, north of Kaycee on U.S. 87, LAKE DE SMET (4) has some excellent rainbow fishing as well as some browns, averaging 15 inches and occasionally reaching 4 pounds in weight. There's no limit on the perch and rock bass that abound in the lakes. A number of resorts along the shore offer boats and accommodation, and there are good camping facilities.

From either Buffalo or the nearby town of Story, the angler who is willing to rough it a bit can reach a number of lakes, either by packhorse provided by outfitters at these towns; or in a few cases, on foot. Six of the string of lakes called the SEVEN BROTHERS (5), can produce rainbow and lake trout, while the seventh was planted with cutthroat in 1957 by the Wyoming Game and Fish Department. Another cutthroat lake available by horse trail only is FLORENCE LAKE (6), which lies at an altitude of 11,200 feet, offering a fairly rugged trip.

In north-central Wyoming the Big Horn Mountains thrust down from Montana to form a watershed quite separate from the Continental Divide. Fishing in northeastern Wyoming benefits therefrom because of the fact that myriads of mountain streams come plunging down from the Big Horns. Near the town of Buffalo, CLEAR CREEK (7), and its tributaries provide good fishing for small browns, rainbows and 6-inch brookies, as do NORTH PINEY and SOUTH PINEY CREEKS (8).

Small cutthroat and some rainbows are found in FRYING PAN LAKE (9) and FLAT IRON LAKE (10). In CLOUD PEAK RESERVOIR (11) they run much larger, 3 pounds being fairly common, and some hitting the 9-pound mark. KEARNEY LAKE (12), which can be reached by pack horse, has good rainbow-trout fishing and a number of lake trout, which, on occasion, have been registered at 20 pounds.

Continuing north on U.S. 87 to the Sheridan area, an angler will have a choice of small streams flowing down from the Big Horn Mountains. Most are accessible by car in their lower reaches, by jeep as you go higher, but in many cases the headwaters can be reached only by horseback or hiking. Throughout the creeks, a 12-inch fish is a good one, but nearly all produce 7- to 10-inch trout in abundance.

BIG GOOSE CREEK (13), LITTLE GOOSE CREEK (14), EAST FORK OF LITTLE GOOSE CREEK (15), WEST FORK OF LITTLE GOOSE CREEK (16), and EAST BIG GOOSE CREEK (17) are all small-fish producers. The TONGUE RIVER (18) above Ranchester to the Canyon gets a little better, with browns and rainbows to 12 inches, plus whitefish. Catches made in the North and South Tongue run slightly smaller.

A fairly good bet for a fisherman passing through, without time to seek permission to fish on a ranch, is SAND CREEK (20), reached via U.S. 14 in the extreme northeast, adjacent to Cook Lake. Six miles of the stream is controlled by the Fish and Game Commission, to insure public access. An adjoining club, the Belle Fourche, will permit added fishing for $1 per day. The fish are brown trout, 6 to 12 inches, and there are plenty of them. In Cook Lake the rainbows run to 10 inches.

Further south, around Newcastle, where U.S. 16 enters the state, LAKE RESERVOIR (21) has rainbows averaging 12 inches. Nearby STOCKADE BEAVER CREEK (22) adds brook trout. Just north of Moorcroft, where U.S. 14 and U.S. 16 come together, KEYHOLE RESERVOIR (23) changes the picture with fairly good fishing for walleye pike and channel catfish.

Throughout Wyoming, access to most reservoirs is good and in most cases there are camping areas and boat-launching facilities.

EAST-CENTRAL AREA (MAP #1)

The main fishing in this area is provided by the numerous reservoirs resulting from the damming of the Platte River. In nearly all cases there is good road access, boat-launching facilities, and camping facilities but with the exception of the Glendo and Guernsey Reservoirs, close to the towns of the same names, hotel or motel accommodation is usually from ten to fifty miles distant. The Wyoming Game and Fish Commission cautions visitors to bring their own drinking water and to carry emergency food rations, extra gas and oil and motor parts because of the hazards of sudden storms, which are common on large reservoirs. Water fluctuations may also cause some inconvenience, though these are usually slow enough to cause no difficulty. Occasionally at Pathfinder Reservoir the water is so low as to make boat launching difficult; and at Guernsey the water fluctuation is so great as to make for poor fishing.

GLENDO (24) and GUERNSEY (25) RESERVOIRS are reached from U.S. 20 on the north or U.S. 26 on the south. The main attraction is rainbows, 12 to 15 inches, but there are also a few brook trout.

Continuing on U.S. 20 and U.S. 26 to Casper, then turning south on U.S. 220, the angler can reach PATHFINDER (26), SEMINOE (27) and KORTES RESERVOIRS (28), all offering rainbows, and the latter two adding browns. The fish run from 12 to 20 inches. Access to Kortes is available just below the Seminoe Dam. The best boat-launching spot is in the Cold Creek and Red Hills areas on the western shore. Much of the shoreline cannot be reached except by boat.

Several other smaller reservoirs, namely the McDONALD (29), BURLINGTON (30), CHRISTINE (31) and WILD HORSE #2 (32), are reached from Highways 20 and 26, west from Casper. Burlington and Christine have rainbow trout while McDonald has rainbows and silver salmon. Wild Horse Reservoir has been stocked with largemouth black bass.

The NORTH PLATTE RIVER (33, 34), in its passage through this dammed area, has a number of stretches where there is good river fishing. From the Kortes Dam to the backwaters of the Pathfinder Reservoir, the fluctuations of the stream make fishing hazardous and uncertain, as the water level varies from almost no flow to bank full, and the level is changed on no set schedule. But when you find river conditions right, which is rarely, fishing can be good for browns and rainbows from 12 to 16 inches. The browns co-operate better in the fall.

From the Alcova Dam, down north, the North Platte parallels U.S. 220 most of the way to Casper. Throughout the stretch there is good rainbow fishing for fish from 9 to 15 inches. The river can be floated in small boats. You'll have best luck in spring and fall, out of irrigation season.

From Casper the river turns east towards Glendo. Here again it is floatable and there's nearly 100 miles of good rainbow fishing; and the same situation prevails between Glendo and Guernsey. From Guernsey to the Nebraska line, however, the river fluctuates so greatly during the summer irrigation season that fishing can be poor. However, the river here is stocked by the Fish and Game Department with both rainbows and browns, so you can have some good luck, with fish from 8 to 15 inches.

In this same area, BATES CREEK (35), DEER CREEK (36) and SMITH CREEK (37) all produce fair catches of small brook, rainbow and brown trout.

SOUTHEASTERN AREA (MAP #1)

The main centers of population in this area are the historic towns of Cheyenne and Laramie. Around Cheyenne the fishing is limited to CRYSTAL (38) and GRANITE (39) RESERVOIRS and LODGEPOLE CREEK (40); the reservoirs producing rainbows to about 10 inches, while the creek has also small brook trout. For those who wish to use boats on the reservoirs, permits must be obtained from the City of Cheyenne.

Heading across Interstate Highway 80 to Laramie the picture changes. There are plenty of 10- to 12-inch browns and rainbows in both the BIG LARAMIE (41) and the LITTLE LARAMIE RIVERS (42), but permission must usually be obtained from the ranchers who own the land adjacent to the streams. There are also innumerable good fishing creeks pouring out of the Snowy Range Mountains just to the west, and these usually offer brook trout in the 8-inch class plus 9- and 10-inch browns in the lower reaches. Accommodations, and directions to these many streams, can be obtained at either Laramie or Saratoga. Via State Highway 230 southwest from Laramie, then a dirt road up the Laramie River into Colorado, you can find good trout fishing and accommodation at Charles Wagnild's Lazy W Cross Ranch, Glendevey, Colorado.

Just to the south lies the Medicine Bow National Forest, where the Snowy Range Mountains supply the drainage for many brooks and lakes. Brook trout are most common, and there are cutthroat in a few lakes. Grayling and California goldens have also been planted. Most of the lakes lie at 9,500 to 11,000 feet. Roads are often not open until the end of June and the higher lakes are not clear of ice till the first of July.

There is a good road to Big Brooklyn Lake at the east end of the area. This lake is fished hard, but is large enough to take a good deal of pressure. Most of the other lakes in the range are smaller. You can walk to East and West Glacier Lakes—a three-quarter-mile hike. Big and Little Telephone Lakes, where there is good fishing for small brook trout and some cutthroat, can also be reached by comfortable trail; and beyond that a footpath leads right on up to the foot of Medicine Bow Peak.

The best lakes in the string are probably Brady Lake, Lost Lake, Scott Lake, North and West Klondike Lakes, but nearly all of them along this trail have pan-size brooks and some cutthroat. In most cases you can drive within half a mile, then hike in, and good camping spots are generally available.

There are also several good fishing lakes in the Laramie area. BIG GELATT (43) and LITTLE IONE (44) have rainbows and browns to 14 inches. These two lakes are on private property and may be fished by owner's permission only. In nearby LAKE HATTIE (45), the fishing is better, as to size, and there's a public fishing area. The same is true in LAKE CARROLL (46), where there are brooks as well as rainbows and browns.

LEAZENBY LAKE (47) is accessible by paved road, and has fishing for rainbows to 15 inches. No boats are allowed on Leazenby.

North of Laramie, the WHEATLAND RESERVOIR (48) can be reached via dirt road off U.S. 30 and 287. Wheatland offers public fishing for walleye pike. There is fair boat launching.

From U.S. 30 and 287 you can drop down to the Saratoga area or you can reach this town from the Colorado border on Highway 120 and 230. Either way, you're in one of the choicest fishing spots in southern Wyoming. The NORTH PLATTE (49) and the ENCAMPMENT (50) are the standout streams. At Saratoga there are plentiful accommodations, ranging from the luxurious Saratoga Springs Inn, with its golf course and excellent dining room, to numerous motels and housekeeping cabins. There are several excellent guides at Saratoga for jeep trips to inaccessible areas or for floating the North Platte.

This part of the North Platte is a fine river to fish and the water above Saratoga is full of fish. As there are no dams up here, the flow is constant. The best fishing is from August 1st through to the end of the season on October 31st. Both browns and rainbows average 12 to 14 inches in the heavily fished spots but by jeeping or floating to less readily reached water you can up your catch a great deal, with quite a few 3½- and some 4-pound fish. And you never know what you may come up with. The biggest brown ever taken from the Platte weighed 18 pounds 9 ounces. In August 1962 I jeeped from Saratoga Inn to a couple of remote spots where a single morning's fishing produced two-dozen browns to 2 pounds and I tied into a couple of bigger ones. The Brown Wulff, Royal Wulff and Red Variant dries, and the Muddler Minnow Number 4 took them.

Floaters use rubber rafts or small boats, putting in at the several county bridges. It is possible to go as much as forty miles in a day, but your success will be much greater if you stop frequently to thoroughly fish the most promising pools. Some of them, in this big river, are large enough to require a couple of hours for complete coverage.

The North Platte is quite shallow in spots, and grassy, too, which makes it tough for spinners, but if you watch carefully you will find plenty of spots where either the spin caster or the bait fisherman can have a field day.

Float trips can be arranged through the Saratoga Inn and through Verg Teter's Guide Service, Saratoga, phone 7-3054 and 7-3011. They will also supply information as to the best fishing places at the moment, and the flies which are taking. As a basis in dry flies you should have the Gray Hackle, Yellow Body; Red Variant; Silver Blue Dun; Light Cahill; Royal Coachman; Gray Wulff and Black Gnat. The best wet flies are the Muddler, Red Squirreltail, Edson Tiger, Gray Ghost and White Ghost.

The Encampment River, near Saratoga, is forty miles long, and Bill Walker of the Saratoga Inn claims that thirty-nine miles of it is fishable. It is a great dry-fly river. The largest trout ever taken from the Encampment weighed 15 pounds, not quite as big as the largest from the Platte. But those who fish both consistently claim that the average will run higher in the Encampment than in the Platte. At any rate, this beautiful trout stream, named from the fact that the Indians used to hold their spring encampment here, is one of the most pleasant in the West. It's the kind of river where you can fish your way upstream, looking for and casting only to risers. The size of the fish will fool you. A small dimple may mean a 12-incher or a 4-pounder. But it calls for careful approach and a gently dropped fly. There are numerous bends with deep holes and overhanging brush where the lunkers can hide. The river is good from June 15th to the end of October, with the hottest time around the 10th or 15th of June, when the river begins to drop.

At the town of Encampment, about eighteen miles up Highway 230 towards the

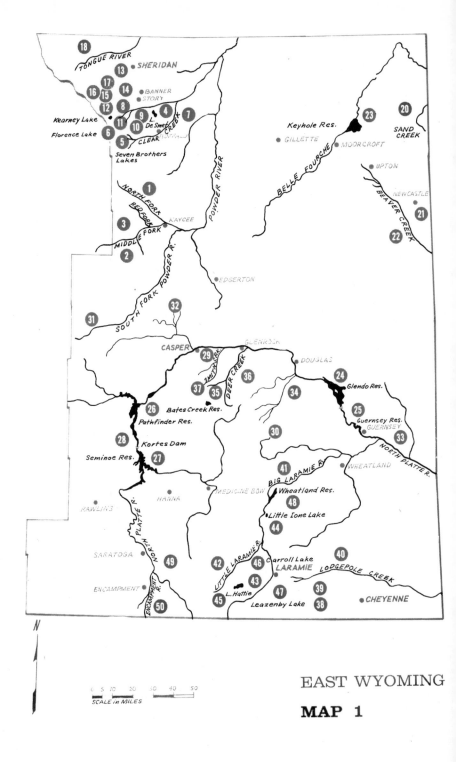

EAST WYOMING

MAP 1

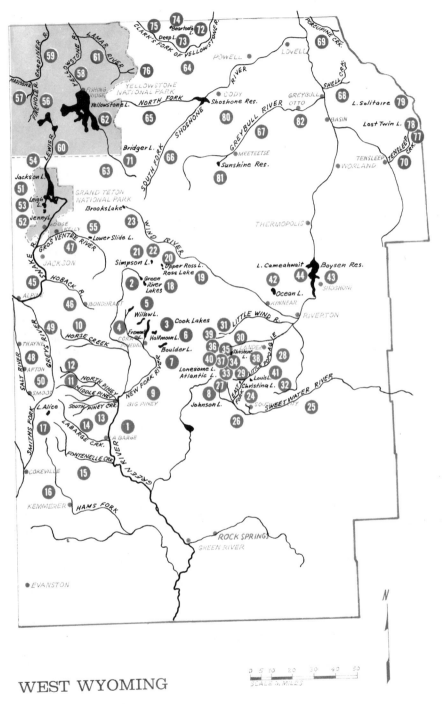

WEST WYOMING

MAP 2

mountains, D. M. Alsop, at the Pine Motor Lodge Cafe, can furnish guides to take anglers to the many small streams, such as Hell Creek, Miner Creek, Willow Creek, the North Fork of the Encampment, Hasking and Soldier Creeks, all full of brook trout, small, but wonderful eating. There are several small motels at Encampment, and good camp sites in the general area.

SOUTHWESTERN AREA (MAP #2)

This section of the state gets the full benefit of the flow of water that is shed from the western front of the Great Divide. A lot of this water ends up in the GREEN RIVER (1), one of the best trout streams in Wyoming. Fishing is good in the Green River from the GREEN RIVER LAKES (2), high up against the Divide, all the way down to about forty miles below Pinedale. Following the Cora Road, about fifteen miles west of Pinedale, off U.S. 187, you can drive twenty miles up towards the Green River Lakes on a good dirt road and find rewarding fishing all along the way. You seldom catch a brown this far up but there are lots of rainbows, mostly small, though the writer took a few considerably better than the 12-inch average.

In the lower Green, the angler will catch much larger fish. There are plenty of rainbows in the 2-pound class; and some really big ones in that stretch of river that curves eastward away from U.S. 187, southwest of Pinedale. There are 4-, 5- and 6-pounders in the twenty miles downstream from here and there is always the possibility of coming up with a 10-pounder.

Unfortunately it is difficult to get to the Green River to fish it properly. To the writer's knowledge there is only one public access area, and that a very small one on a poor-grade country road just out of Pinedale. When I asked permission to fish the water on the adjoining ranch, I was turned down. If the State of Wyoming could arrange for a few more public access areas on the Green, they'd have an outstanding fishing attraction, especially in September when the water level drops. The river harbors some fine fish. Meantime, there are numerous dude ranches around Pinedale with access to fishing, and some of the motels in the town also have entry to various ranches and can send their guests there to fish. Jim Campbell of the Pine Creek Motel can arrange your fishing and obtain guides for you.

One of the best flies for the Green River is the Muddler Minnow. This will take plenty of browns. The White Muddler seems best for rainbows. For big browns, the muddler should be in hook sizes 10, 4, 2 and 1/0. The white muddler is best for rainbows in sizes 10, 8, 6 and 4. As a rule, rainbows like a smaller fly than do brown trout. For those patterns which are popular at the moment, anglers should call at Jim's Sporting Goods Shop (Jim Prather) in Pinedale; or see Herbert D. Molyneux, Molyneux Sporting Goods, Pinedale. They can also set up guided trips, both on the Green and to mountain lakes, in some of which the angler will find golden trout. Packers at Pinedale or Cora can take you to the COOK LAKES (3), where goldens go to 15 inches.

The record for lake trout in Wyoming was taken at FREMONT LAKE (4), north of Pinedale, in 1953, when Monte Wight, trolling a spoon, hooked and landed a 38-pounder. In 1961, fifty lake trout taken there averaged out at 20 pounds apiece.

There is good lake trout and rainbow fishing in WILLOW LAKE (5), north of Pinedale, while HALF MOON LAKE (6), to the east of Fremont Lake, has rainbow fishing. BOULDER LAKE (7), a little to the south of Half Moon, has been known to produce 4- and 5-pound rainbows. JOHNSON LAKE (8), further south along U.S. 187, and reached via a rough road through Big Sandy Opening, is a meadow lake, with grayling to 15 inches. Two nearby smaller streams well worth fishing are the NEW FORK RIVER (9) and HORSE CREEK (10). The New Fork, which empties into the Green, produces 5- and 6-pound brownies. Horse Creek is full of brook trout in early spring and late fall.

South of Pinedale, on U.S. 189, anglers can find some motel accommodations at Big Piney and LaBarge; and there are many lakeside forest camps. Here the streams come from the mountains to the west, and at their headwaters are numerous mountain lakes. Of these, MIDDLE PINEY LAKE (11) is accessible by dirt road from the town of Big Piney. There are Mackinaw trout to 17 inches, as well as rainbow and brook trout. NORTH PINEY LAKE (12) is accessible by several miles of trail from roads on North and Middle Piney Creek, and the cutthroat in the lake range from 10 to 15 inches. NORTH, MIDDLE and SOUTH PINEY CREEKS (13) are all particularly appealing to fly fishermen as they are mountain streams, with occasional beaver ponds, meadows and open water. The fish will be brook and native trout, from 8 to 12 inches.

Further south, on U.S. 189, LaBARGE (14) and FONTENELLE (15) CREEKS are readily reached from the highway and there are accommodations as well as good camping at LaBarge. Several tributaries of the creeks are also fishable. The rainbows and brook trout go to a top of 12 inches.

Continuing down U.S. 189, you come to Kemmerer, where the HAMS FORK (16) is a stream similar to the LaBarge and Fontenelle, with rainbows and cutthroat to 15 inches; and brook trout in many of the tributaries. Hotels and motels are available at Kemmerer. There are also rainbows to 15 inches in the Hams Fork Reservoir.

If you take U.S. 30N from U.S. 89, west of Kemmerer, you can reach the SMITHS FORK and LAKE ALICE (17). The last one and a half miles from the forest camp site at Lake Alice is steep and rough and calls for pack horses, or at least a sturdy hiker. Pneumatic boats can be packed in for use in the lake, which produces cutthroat trout from 10 to 15 inches. The Smith and its tributary streams offer cutthroat and brooks to 12 inches. There are some accommodations at Cokeville.

WEST-CENTRAL AREA (MAP #2)

The largest river in west-central Wyoming is the Wind River. While there are many whitefish in the Wind, and they take a fly readily, the browns and rainbows are scarce. However, there is excellent fishing in its tributaries and in the high mountain lakes of the headwaters. Dubois is the main town for accommodations, and there are several good tackle stores where arrangements can be made for trips to outlying waters. Arrangements also can be made through Duane Redman, Fishing Guide, P.O. Box 51, Dubois, Wyoming. A number of lakes to which Dubois guides have access hold good-sized rainbows and cutthroats, as well as eastern brook trout.

ROSS LAKE (18) is noted for lunker rainbows, while UPPER ROSS (19) is loaded with small cutthroat. HIDDEN LAKE (20) on Torrey Creek, has both rainbows and cutthroat, as does the creek above Trail Lake. There is good brook-trout fishing in SIMPSON LAKE (21), SOAPSTONE LAKE and BLANKET LAKE (22), and in WIND RIVER LAKE and BROOKS LAKE (23) to the northwest of Dubois.

Some of the high lakes near Dubois hold grayling, and one of them, Lake of the Woods, will produce fish up to 2 pounds. It's a rough trip in, but you can do it by jeep, through Duane Redman, of Dubois. It's a very interesting journey. You'll see the remains of the corrals and runways built many years ago by the Sheepeater Indians, who used to stampede and trap the bighorn sheep.

Many of the tributaries of the Wind are good fly-rod streams. The EAST FORK

OF THE SWEETWATER (24), which can be reached (with caution) on a dirt road from Highway 28, will produce brooks, rainbows and browns of about 10 inches. The SWEETWATER RIVER (25) itself, south of South Pass City, has some larger ones. The UPPER SWEETWATER (26) and LARSEN CREEK (27) have pan-sized brooks in plentiful numbers.

The LITTLE POPO AGIE (28), which crosses Highway 287, is a first-rate trout stream, but since it flows almost entirely through posted land, it must usually be fished from the canyon upstream in the National Forest, and this requires the use of a jeep or pickup truck. There are brook trout and rainbows in the higher waters and rainbows and browns lower down.

SILAS CREEK (29) and SAND CREEK (30) are well known for brook-trout fishing, while the SOUTH FORK OF THE LITTLE WIND RIVER (31), lying west of Dickson Park, has substantial numbers of golden and rainbow trout, only about 9 inches long, but providing excellent fly fishing.

Several lakes in the headwaters of the Little Popo Agie are also known as good fishing spots. CHRISTINA LAKE (32) is good for lake-trout fishing in late spring and early summer. It can be reached by jeep only. ATLANTIC LAKE (33), two miles further up, has cutthroat and brook-trout populations. Nearby TOMAHAWK LAKE (34) does have some cutthroat, but is rated as only fair and is not open until July 15th. It can be reached by a forest trail from Fiddler's Lake. VALENTINE LAKE (35) and WASHAKIE LAKE (36), west of Dickson Park, and DEEP CREEK LAKE (37) in the same area, all produce goldens. The lakes can only be reached by horse or foot trail. The same applies to SHOSHONE LAKE (38), which offers fishing for brook trout (season closes Aug. 15 in this lake), GRAVE LAKE (39), where there are lake trout, and LONESOME LAKE (40), which is stocked with cutthroat.

Continuing south out of Lander, on the Loop Road which runs from Lander down to U.S. 28, FIDDLER'S LAKE (41) offers fair-sized brook trout, and Louis Lake has rainbows, brooks and lake trout.

Moving north of Lander to Riverton, the angler will find himself in an area where the water lends itself to the propagation of warm-water fish. OCEAN LAKE (42), north of Highway 26 near Kinnear, produces some outstanding crappie fishing during the summer, good largemouth black bass fishing in May and June, and fair bass fishing on into the summer. BOYSEN RESERVOIR (43), near Shoshone, offers rainbow and brown trout, walleye pike, perch and sauger, with moderately good fishing all summer, and good fishing in spring and fall. LAKE CAMEAHWAIT (44), to the northwest, has a record of outstanding bass fishing.

NORTHWESTERN AREA (MAP #2)

This is one of the most attractive fishing areas in America, sharing much of the topography of Yellowstone Park, which occupies a large square in the extreme northwest corner. This whole section is well supplied with dude ranches, resorts and camping spots, readily reached by car.

The fishing derives from the watersheds of the Continental Divide and the Tetons, which range down from the southern boundary of Yellowstone. Approximately sixty miles of the SNAKE RIVER (45) may be reached via U.S. 26, 89 and 187 south of Jackson Lake. The Snake is justly rated as one of Wyoming's top rivers, producing some very large rainbows each year up to 8 pounds, and adding cutthroat, whitefish, and a few browns to the angler's catch. The best time is from mid-July through October.

The Snake is a big river, and crystal clear. Most of the fishing is done by floating, anglers covering about twenty miles in the hours between 9 a.m. and 5 p.m. Float trip arrangements can be made through Boots Allen, owner of the Fort Jackson, a fine tackle shop in Jackson, where accommodations are available. He will also advise on trips to neighboring lakes, and tell you where to fish, either with guides or on your own. The telephone is 907. There are all facilities in Jackson. Float trips can also be arranged through Marvin Dabel, at Alpine, a few miles south of Jackson.

Spinning and bait fishing are both very successful in the Snake, but as in so much of the West the emphasis is on flies. Mrs. Boots Allen ties a fly, the Humpy, that is so good that many fishermen don't bother with anything else, as far as dry flies go. Best sizes are 8, 10 and 12. However, the Light and Dark Variant, the Rev. Lang and the Adams are all good producers, too. In wet flies the Royal Coachman, Blue Dun, Rio Grande King and the Muddler are all top rated.

To the southeast of Jackson, the HOBACK RIVER (46) parallels U.S. 189 from well east of the town of Bondurant to the Junction with U.S. 187 (and the Green River) at Hoback Junction. Much of the stream can be seen from the road. This is a fair cutthroat river, with fish averaging 10 to 14 inches. To the north of Jackson, near Moose, the GROS VENTRE RIVER (47) is the same type of stream, crystal clear, but it has more volume than the Hoback and many deep pools which hold cutthroat and rainbows to 15 inches. It can be reached via an unimproved gravel road from U.S. 187 to Kelly, then east.

In the southern part of this sector of Wyoming, the SALT RIVER (48) and the GREYS RIVER (49) roughly parallel U.S. 89, the Salt to the west, almost on the Idaho Border, and the Greys River to the east. Both these streams have been gaining a reputation lately for pleasant fishing for fairly substantial trout. The Salt is a meadow stream, fed by spring creeks, and can be reached from the towns of Afton and Thayne. Since it flows mostly through private land, it is necessary to obtain permission to fish the Salt. Your catch will be cutthroat, brown and brook trout to 15 inches and sometimes considerably larger. Accommodations are available at Doyle Medus' Corral Motel and Ted Hale's Silver Stream Motel in Afton. They will also arrange float trips on the Salt, as will Hy Herchin's Tackle Shop staff. The Greys is a cutthroat stream with some fish up to 16 inches, and can be reached by a fair gravel road which runs its entire length south of Alpine. There are occasional runs of 1½- and 2-pounders out of Lake Palisades.

Near Smoot, on U.S. 89, just north of the Salt River Pass, the COTTONWOOD RESERVOIR (50) produces cutthroat and brook trout to 15 inches.

JACKSON LAKE (51) is the largest body of water in the northwestern part of Wyoming (again excepting Yellowstone Park). It is probably the most popular camping and fishing lake in Wyoming, accessible by U.S. 26, 89 and 287 where they join to lead into Yellowstone Park. In Jackson Lake there are lake trout, cutthroats and browns up to 18 inches. This lake and neighboring Jenny Lake lie in one of the most scenic spots in North America, with breathtaking views of the Tetons. JENNY LAKE (52), also reached via paved road, holds cutthroat, brooks, rainbows and lake trout to about 16 inches.

LEIGH LAKE (53), just above Jenny, can be reached by a one-mile hike or by horse trail. The cutthroats here measure up to 16 inches, and the lake trout go as high as 25 inches. Rental boats are available at the lake.

Further north, GRASSY LAKE (54) is also regarded as very productive, holding cutthroat trout and rainbows to 16 inches in length. The lake can be reached by a gravel road from the main highway, and there are cabins available about nine miles from the lake.

These lakes all lie to the west of the Snake. To the east, in the Gros Ventre area, LOWER SLIDE LAKE (55) can be approached by the same dirt road which parallels the Gros Ventre River. There is good camping and the fish are substantial cutthroat, rainbow and lake trout to 14 inches.

YELLOWSTONE PARK (MAP #2)

The extreme northwestern corner of Wyoming comprises almost the entire area of Yellowstone National Park, only a small part of which reaches into Montana and Idaho. A license is not required to fish in the Park but special seasons, limits and restrictions apply. (See Wyoming Regulations at end of this chapter.)

Every angler who fishes in Yellowstone Park should remember that there are bears, elk, moose and, in some places, rattlesnakes. If he meets a wild animal of any kind he should avoid disturbing it. Sometimes they are unpredictable. As you enter the Park you see signs everywhere advising you to stay in your car and not to feed the bears. You are handed more such warnings when you go through the entrance gate. You should take them seriously. I've seen many pictures of bear bites and heard many authentic stories about people being bitten or mauled by bears. Some were seriously disfigured, others died. The bears in the park are cute and comical and fuzzy and you do want to pet them, but don't. Take pictures of them from the safety of your car, but do not walk up close to try for a picture, do not stick your arm out of the car to pet or feed a bear. A sudden move might cause a bear to slap you. They are wild animals and you never know what they may do. This applies to all wildlife. A buffalo might charge and gore you. A deer, elk, antelope or moose might rear up and strike you with its sharp hooves. A coyote might bite. Any wild animal is best left alone.

Nearly all Park waters provide fishing of one kind or another, for cutthroat, rainbow, brown and lake trout, Montana grayling, and Rocky Mountain whitefish. In some waters the hybrid cutthroat-rainbow is found, a fish combining the best qualities of both species.

Some of the most popular streams, such as the FIREHOLE (56), MADISON (57), YELLOWSTONE (58), GARDINER (59), LEWIS (60) and LAMAR (61) can be fished immediately adjacent to the road with good success. But the angler who walks back a half mile or so will discover much better fishing. The less frequented waters hold some good fish.

YELLOWSTONE LAKE (62) is one of the most famous spots for cutthroat in the Rocky Mountains. Fishermen go on the lake in boats to troll or cast, and there is also good casting from shore in many places. Where the lake pours out to form the Yellow-stone River, anglers gather by the score to fish from Fisherman's Bridge, a hot spot for cutthroat. Although it's crowded, every day hundreds of trout are taken. If you fish there and don't see fish rising, cast blind, and you'll probably get some.

From there down, all the way through the Park, and on into Montana the Yellow-stone is excellent fishing water. (See Montana) Within the Park the fish are mostly cutthroats and in some places it is very difficult to reach the river, but everywhere it approaches the road, fishing is very good, so there's really no need to go too far back. Hayden Valley is one of the good spots and can be reached by only a short walk. There are plenty of cutthroat there which will go from 1 to 2½ pounds.

There is some good brown-trout fishing in the Madison River within the Park, in either direction from Madison Junction. The Gardiner is a great river in the fall when there is a run of big brown trout and many anglers come up with fish from 2 to 5 pounds. It's a small stream and provides plenty of fun when the hefty browns run and jump and fight up a fit.

The Firehole is another good park stream and, true to its name, you can fish one part of it right at the foot of a falls from a hot spring, and catch trout with the water hissing and steam rising around you.

To reach some really great high-lake fishing in the northeast corner of Yellowstone Park, you must go to Cooke City, Montana, on U.S. Highway 212, from Yellowstone to Billings. Along the Montana-Wyoming line there is lake after lake to which you can pack in and where you can tent and catch brook trout, cutthroat and rainbow till they come out of your ears. Gene Wade of Cooke City, and Elmer Larson of Silver Gate, three miles down the mountain towards the Park, both outfit and guide trips to these lakes.

Fishing is good in the Park all summer, but there is a notable pickup in fishing in the fall because of the runs of big browns. Some wonderful fishing can be enjoyed there in September and October. There is a good tackle shop at Gardiner, Montana, the northern entrance to the Park; and Merton Parks, the proprietor, will bring you up to date on flies, lures and bait that are successful at the moment. He can also guide you on float trips or wading the various rivers in the Park, and arrange trail or pack jaunts to more remote spots.

All visitors to the Park should obey the regulations and retain only fish they can use. It is a scandal among sportsmen that many of the beautiful fish from these waters end up at night in camp garbage cans. Such thoughtless and wasteful people should not be fishing, and certainly not in a national park.

NORTH-CENTRAL AREA (MAP #2)

The headwaters of the YELLOWSTONE RIVER (63) run north through the southwest corner of this sector of the state, offering cutthroat trout to 18 inches. Parts of the river can be reached by the Valley Road southwest from Cody and then west to the borders of Yellowstone Park. Other rivers in the area can also be fished. All of these require the services of an outfitter, and there are many in the area to serve the angler.

Via Route 120 north from Cody, fishermen can reach the CLARK'S FORK OF THE YELLOWSTONE (64), to cover about seventy-five miles of fishing for cutthroat, rainbow and brook trout averaging 10 to 16 inches. There's great variety of water in this stream, from heavy rapids to slow-moving stretches, and one five-mile canyon is accessible only on foot in a few places.

The NORTH FORK OF THE SHOSHONE RIVER (65) parallels U.S. 14 and 20 between Cody and Yellowstone Park for a distance of about forty miles. There are rainbows and cutthroat trout from 10 to 18 inches, and the water is suitable to all types of fishing. Motels and dude ranches in the area offer accommodations.

The SOUTH FORK OF THE SHOSHONE (66), where rainbow, cutthroat and brown trout average about 14 inches, is more difficult to reach, necessitating a twenty-five-mile drive on the Valley Road (gravel) from Cody, then a pack trip for another twenty-five miles. Arrangements can be made with dude ranchers on the lower river, and from Cody.

There are several attractive mountain streams in north-central Wyoming, usually requiring an outfitter's service to provide access and equipment for camping. From headquarters at Meeteetse the angler can fish the lower ten miles of the GREYBULL RIVER (67) from an oiled road, but above that there's another twenty-five miles of good water which must be reached by dirt road, then trail. Cutthroats run from 11 to 13 inches, and fly fishing is most successful here because of the steep drop of the stream.

Near Greybull, where U.S. 20 crosses U.S. 14, SHELL CREEK (68) is accessible in its lower reaches by oiled road which gives way to dirt and eventually to trail. There is about twenty-five miles of fishable water containing browns to 14 inches, rainbows to 11, and brook trout to about 8 inches. There are numerous dude ranches along the lower stream and some motels nearby.

Another mountain stream, PORCUPINE CREEK (69), runs through the picturesque Devil's Canyon in the Lovell area, on U.S. 310, north from its juncture with U.S. 14 and 20. There are brown, rainbow, cutthroat and brook trout, from 9 to 14 inches. To reach this river you must make a good ride or hike through rugged country in the lower part; then hike on a fair forest-service road for the middle section. The top waters, where the small brookies are the catch, is accessible by car. The nearest accommodations are at Lovell, but there are several camp sites available.

Easily reached from paved Highway 16 between Worland and Ten Sleep is TEN SLEEP CREEK (70), with twenty-five miles of brown and rainbow-trout fishing. There are plenty of accommodations along the way.

BRIDGER LAKE (71) is the largest of the numerous natural lakes in north-central Wyoming. It covers about 300 acres in the beautiful wilderness area known as the "thorofare country." Bridger can be reached via the Valley Road out of Cody, then by a ten-hour pack trip, which can be outfitted by any of the numerous dude ranches in the Cody area. The lake provides fishing for cutthroat trout from 15 to 18 inches.

More readily accessible are BEARTOOTH LAKE (72), DEEP LAKE (73), T LAKE (74) and UPPER CLAY BUTTE LAKE (75), which lie to the northwest of Cody. Beartooth is on a paved road out of Cody and there are tourist accommodations right at the shore as well as at nearby dude ranches. The rainbows, cutthroat and brook trout run from 9 to 13 inches. Deep Lake calls for a five-mile trip over poor dirt road and then a mile hike up a steep grade. There are camp sites at the end of the road, dude ranches nearby. The fish are cutthroats, to 12 inches.

T Lake lies at a 10,000-foot elevation. Since the trout are small—brook trout run about 8 inches—the limit at this lake is placed at 10 pounds rather than a number limit. T Lake and several others are within a pleasant two-hour hike from the highway. Beartooth Lodge and several dude ranches supply accommodations nearby.

Like many other lakes where grayling are to be found, Upper Clay Butte Lake can be reached only over a difficult trail, either on foot or on horse. The grayling go to 14 inches, and there is good camping along the shore. Dude ranches in the Cody area can outfit fishermen for this lake.

The fisherman who would like to combine a try for cutthroat and goldens can follow Highway 120 between Cody and Badger Basin to a gravel road which takes off near Pat O'Hara Creek, and then goes up Sunlight Creek. From the end of the road a steep hike will take you to COPPER LAKE #1 (76), where there are good cut-throat, running from 16 to 20 inches. A further hike to COPPER LAKE #2 will usually produce the goldens. Horses for this trip can be obtained from outfitters and dude ranches in the Cody area.

Via U.S. 16 east from Worland, anglers can reach MEADOWLARK LAKE (77), where there are plentiful accommodations and good fishing for rainbows to 13 inches. Boats may be launched or rented here. LOST TWIN LAKE (78) is near as the crow flies, but calls for a half-day ride or hike. The lake has been planted with golden trout but the catches are spotty—sometimes very good and sometimes very poor.

Another lake in the same area, which must be reached by horse or by hiking, is LAKE SOLITAIRE (79), a very pretty lake, high among the peaks. Outfitters go in from Shell, Hyattville, and various ranches along the road. The fish are very small —brook trout from 8 to 10 inches (10-pound bag limit)—but there are several other lakes which can be fished en route; and the scenery makes it a worthwhile trip.

Eight miles west of Cody is the SHOSHONE RESERVOIR (80), also known as the Buffalo Bill Reservoir, 7,000 acres in size, with good fishing for rainbows and cut-throat to 16 inches, browns from 14 to 17, and lake trout averaging 18 inches. A few have been taken that went to 20 pounds. There are boat-rental agencies and boat-launching facilities at the lake, and one outfitter on the north shore provides restaurant service.

Another reservoir, the SUNSHINE (81), which can be reached via dirt road fifteen miles west of Meeteetse, also has launching facilities, but no other services. Some cutthroat are taken by lures and bait from the shore, but most of the fishing is by trolling. The fish are from 16 to 24 inches.

Those who are looking for walleye pike can find them at WARDELL RESERVOIR (82), eight miles south of Otto. The fish run to 20 inches. There are also black bull-heads to ¾ pound. The changing water level of the reservoir sometimes makes boat launching difficult. There are accommodations at the nearby towns of Otto, Basin and Greybull.

WYOMING FISHING REGULATIONS

Resident Fishing License $3.00
Nonresident Fishing License $12.00
Tourist Five-Day Fishing License $4.00

Many lakes and streams in Wyoming are open to year-round fishing. The bulk of the trout fishing season opens as early as May 1 or as late as June 1, depending on area. Closing date is usually October 31. Special regulations apply in many streams, lakes and areas; and particularly in Yellowstone and Grand Teton National Parks. These regulations should be checked on entry to either park, as changes occur annually.

In general: There is no license requirement in Yellowstone National Park. The general open season is from sunrise, May 30 to sunset, October 15. Possession limit of game fish at any time is five; except the limit for Yellowstone Lake and Yellowstone River upstream from Canyon Junction is three game fish. Some waters are reserved for fly fishing only.

A Wyoming State Fishing License is required for Grand Teton National Park and the general Wyoming regulations apply, with several exceptions. Notable is the banning of fish eggs or fish for bait, except on Jackson Lake where *dead* fish for use as bait is permissable.

For complete regulations write: Game and Fish Commission, P.O. Box 378, Cheyenne, Wyoming.

IDAHO

The State of Idaho stretches from the Canadian border to the northern borders of Nevada and Utah. Almost its entire eastern border is composed of picturesque mountain ranges: the rugged Bitterroots along the Montana border, and the towering Teton Range in Wyoming, where Yellowstone Park touches the corner of Idaho. The mountains extend across most of the state, providing a tremendous expanse of country suitable for outdoor recreation. The whole of the state is greener in character than its neighbors to the east, partaking of some of the characteristics of its western neighbors, Washington and Oregon. It is estimated that 73 percent of the total acreage of Idaho is publicly owned, either by state or federal agencies.

As a result of the several watersheds from the different mountain ranges, there are a number of major river drainage systems: the St. Joe, Pend Oreille and Coeur d'Alene draining to the west; the Kootenai to the north; the Clearwater westward to join the Snake at the Washington border. The Snake itself, which carries a tremendous volume of water as it traverses the widest part of the state, increases its flow from numerous other rivers which come down from the mountains and the high plains. In the central part of the state the Salmon, Payette and Weiser form still another drainage area.

All of these rivers have numerous tributaries, providing a vast network of fishable water. In addition, there are hundreds of lakes hidden among the peaks, as well as several of America's most famous large lakes—Pend Oreille, Bear Lake, Coeur d'Alene Lake and Priest Lake and a number of reservoirs.

The lowest elevation in the state is 738 feet, at Lewiston on the western border, where the Snake River leaves Idaho. The highest peak is Mount Borah, 12,655 feet high. Between these extremes the major part of Idaho ranges from 2,000 to 3,000 feet in altitude.

During the summer season the days are warm, occasionally going above 80 degrees, so that the Idaho angler will find cotton shirts comfortable at this time. But evenings are always cool. Especially in the mountainous country and at higher altitudes, woolens are necessary even on a summer evening. For the early spring and late fall fishing, when the salmon and steelhead runs are on, extra-heavy clothing is required, as temperatures fall into the 40's and even to freezing.

As would be expected from the mountainous, wooded nature of the terrain, game is plentiful in Idaho. Fishing along a stream, the angler may see deer, both mule and whitetail. In the wilder sections he may encounter moose, black bear, occasionally cougar and, at high altitudes, elk. There are antelope in the more arid areas, while bighorn sheep and mountain goats are found at the very high altitudes. There are also a few caribou.

In the Selkirk Mountains, near the headwaters of the Pack River, there are some grizzly bear, but they are comparatively few in number, to the point that there is no open season on them. But grizzlies are mean and unpredictable and should be given a wide berth. If one is encountered, make off in the opposite direction, quietly and slowly.

The trouts and salmon constitute the major fishing attractions of Idaho. Some idea of the magnitude of the sport fisheries can be gained from figures issued by state authorities indicating that the catch of trout is better than 10 million per year. The trouts include the seagoing rainbow, called steelhead, resident rainbow, cutthroat, brown, Dolly Varden and Mackinaw. The Pacific Chinook salmon run all the way from the sea up the coastal rivers to provide spectacular fishing in the Salmon River and its tributaries.

In addition to the trouts and salmon there are smallmouth black bass, largemouth black bass, perch, crappie, sunfish, bullhead and channel catfish in the warmer waters, especially reservoir impoundments, of which there are now many on the larger rivers of the state.

Since so much of Idaho is publicly owned, there is probably more water open to fishermen than in any other state in the Union. For the same reason there are many camp sites with ready access to good fishing.

Rail, road and air service is available to the principal cities of Idaho, and from these the sportsman can readily work into the wilderness areas by private plane to small airfields, or by jeep or pack trip, and in many cases by hiking. Hotel and motel accommodations are found at most communities and there are numerous dude ranches and resorts.

Idaho divides naturally into four specific areas: the northern panhandle adjoining the Canadian border; the Clearwater River drainage basin; the Salmon, Payette and Weiser River Drainage Basin; and the Snake River Drainage Basin.

NORTHERN PANHANDLE

There are a number of famous rivers in this area, such as the St. Joe, the Coeur d'Alene, the Pend Oreille and the Kootenai. At the extreme northeastern corner of the state, the Moyie enters Idaho from Canada. These rivers can be reached via U.S. 2 to Bonner's Ferry, then north on U.S. 95 to fish the Kootenai, or north on the Moyie Falls Road to fish the Moyie. Both streams have good rainbow-trout possibilities and are especially popular with fly fishermen in late summer and early fall. In the same neighborhood there are a number of fine fishing lakes nestling among the heights of the Selkirk Mountains. Numerous roads follow the beds of the many creeks which drain into the Kootenai. Some are passable by car while others require horse or jeep. Bonner's Ferry is the best jumping-off place for such trips; while Sandpoint is the nearest major town with numerous motels, and all associated services. The high lakes offer a variety of cutthroat trout, eastern brook trout and rainbow trout and occasionally kokanee, the landlocked sockeye salmon.

Further to the east the terrain is more rugged, with stands of virgin timber, beautiful scenery and some pleasant high meadows. The fisherman must either pack or hike in to these lakes, with U.S. 95 as a starting point. To obtain lists of guides and packers in Idaho, see addresses at the end of this chapter.

PRIEST LAKE (1), which lies in this area, has good kokanee, cutthroat and Dolly Varden fishing and is famous as the home of a substantial population of hefty lake trout. The largest one ever taken there went 51 pounds and many between 25 and 40 pounds are on the records. As in most water where lakers are found, the fishing for this species is best in May and again in late October and November. In hot weather the fish go very deep and can only be reached by deep trolling. Many of the streams that flow into the lake have substantial populations of eastern

Some of Idaho's mountain lakes can only be reached by horseback, but the catches of hefty trout make the trip worthwhile.

brook trout. Hill's Resort is a good spot to get equipment and information as well as accommodations.

Just south of Priest Lake several other smaller bodies of water have the happy combination of trout and largemouth black bass. These are SPIRIT (2), TWIN (3), HAUSER (4) and HAYDEN (5) LAKES. All have rainbow, cutthroat and kokanee, and bass in the shallower parts.

Immediately east of Priest Lake a number of smaller lakes can be reached via Myrtle, Snow and Ruby Creek roads, from the Pack River Road, and on several roads from Priest Lake itself.

At the bottom of the panhandle of Idaho lies one of the nation's most famous fishing lakes, PEND OREILLE (6). This forty-three-mile-long lake regularly produces whoppers of rainbow trout, called Kamloops, because the fish were stocked with rainbows from the Kamloops area of British Columbia. The eggs were obtained there because of the extremely healthy fish of the Kamloops area, were raised in the state hatchery in Idaho and planted in the lake when they were 7 to 8 inches long. As soon as they had grown big enough to start feeding heavily on the small landlocked kokanee salmon they began to blow up to fantastic size. The world record for the species was raised three times in as many years, with fish weighing 21, 23½ and 37 pounds.

The top fishing time for these Kamloops is during the months of May and early June and again in October and November, when the fish move nearer the surface and can be taken on casting tackle. The fall fishing is more certain than that in May and June because the spring runoff affects conditions.

During the summer months the fish are taken by trolling with Monel or leaded line or extremely heavy weights to get down to the depths where the fish are sitting it out in cool water. Lines used vary from 10- to 30-pound test and the lures are big spoons, plugs and wobblers. This tackle can be rented at most tackle shops in the area and is also often available at resorts for nominal rent.

Although most of the fishing is conducted by trolling from large boats, charter boats or smaller private craft, some good rainbows are taken each year by casters working the shallower parts of the lake. The writer was with Jim Parsons of Sandpoint, Idaho, and Joe Bates in early October, 1948, when Joe used spinning gear at the point where the Clark Fork River pours out into the lake to take a Kamloops that went 31 pounds 12 ounces. This was a four-year-old fish, already blown up to blimp size.

Lake Pend Oreille is also plentifully supplied with cutthroat trout, kokanee, also called blueback, the fish which supplies the bulk of the food for the rainbow; and there are also Dolly Varden, perch, crappie, bluegill, whitefish, and largemouth black bass. The kokanee can be taken either trolling or handlining, the latter being most popular in February and March while the fish are schooling. Then the boats anchor over the schools by the hundred and use bait on handlines to take the generous limit of fifty fish per day. Later in the season the kokanee are taken by slow trolling. Though this species is small, it is eagerly sought because of its fine flavor, especially when smoked. The world-record Dolly Varden, weighing 32 pounds, also came from this lake.

Pend Oreille is reached via U.S. 10A from the east to Sandpoint at the northern end of the lake, or from the west via U.S. 2 and U.S. 195. Alternate 10 parallels the western shore, with access to the lake on a number of good dirt roads. There are several excellent resorts along the lake shores, though they are few enough in number that reservations should be made early if you plan to be there at the height of the fishing.

Sandpoint, the major town, and headquarters for nearly all the resorts, is on the main line of the Northern Pacific and Great Northern Railways. Commercial airlines serve Spokane, Washington, only seventy-six miles away and there is an excellent municipal field for private planes at Sandpoint. Greyhound buses also run north and south on U.S. 95 and east and west on U.S. 2 or 10A.

In Lake Pend Oreille, the season is open year-round for bass, perch, bluegills, crappie and kokanee. For the trouts the fishing extends from May 1st to the end of November. Talache Lodge and the Wheel Inn and Marina are two of the largest resorts in the area. Information as to others can be obtained through the Sandpoint Chamber of Commerce, Sandpoint, Idaho.

The stream fisherman will also find much to interest him in the eighty or more creeks and rivers which empty into Lake Pend Oreille. The larger ones have good populations of cutthroat and also Dolly Varden. From these rivers many small trails lead up to primitive areas where there are many small creeks.

Moving south we come to the COEUR D'ALENE RIVER (7), which flows into the lake of the same name, and offers some good cutthroat and rainbow fishing. It is happily at its best at that most convenient time for the angler—midsummer—as well as in early fall. Finding its source in the same mountain range, the Bitterroots, is the ST. JOE RIVER (8). There are rainbows and cutthroat, some fine dry-fly fishing; and the lower river has largemouth black bass. East of St. Maries it is popular for float trips, especially in the lower waters where good catches of cutthroat and Dolly Varden are made.

Coeur d'Alene Lake (9) is 125 miles long, second in size in Idaho only to Pend Oreille. It has excellent cutthroat fishing, and there are some smallmouth black bass and kokanee salmon. There are many resorts in the area with boat rentals and every convenience for the angler. Arrow Point Lodge is one of the most fully equipped. Numerous smaller lakes may also be fished from headquarters at Coeur d'Alene.

CLEARWATER DRAINAGE BASIN

Where Idaho bulges out as the Bitterroot Range bends eastward into Montana, the angler finds himself in a vast, heavily timbered area drained mainly by the Clearwater River (10) and its tributaries. To the fisherman this is one of the most appealing river groups in the United States for it is on the route of the unique steelhead and Chinook salmon spawning run. Pacific coast fish, traveling all the way across Oregon and into Idaho, find their way to the very headwaters of the Clearwater, the Snake, the Salmon, the Weiser and their tributaries.

The best period for this fishing is from July 1st to mid-August, and the best time of day is early morning or evening. Regulations must always be carefully checked before fishing for Chinook as certain waters are prohibited after mid-July. The average weight of these fish is 15 pounds, but many small males are taken early in the season. The largest recorded have been females, in the 45-pound class.

Orofino and Grangeville are the two major towns, while Kooskia, Greer, Pierce and Weippe offer limited accommodations. There are Ranger Stations on all three branches of the Clearwater, the North Fork, Middle Fork and South Fork.

Roads to the North Fork, the Lochsa River and the Selwayd River, all headwaters of the Clearwater, are often snowbound until mid-July. For a short period after that it is possible to drive via State Highway 9 from Kooskia all the way up the Lochsa valley and over the Lolo Pass into Montana, along the same route followed by Lewis and Clark.

The Elk Track Lakes, in the Clearwater country of Idaho, are popular for their scenic beauty and superb fishing.

SALMON RIVER AREA

South of the Clearwater area the mighty SALMON RIVER (11) bisects the state, flowing all the way from the town of Salmon, almost on the Montana border, to join the Snake on the line between Idaho and Oregon. For a full 300 miles upstream from the Snake there is excellent steelhead fishing in spring and fall. There are also rainbow, cutthroat and Dolly Varden trout, and, as in the Clearwater, Chinook salmon, the latter fishing being at its best from late June to early September.

Parts of this river run through inaccessible, rugged country that can be reached only by boat or pack train, and much of it is best fished with a guide. A current list of Idaho Outfitters and Guides can be obtained from the Idaho Fish and Game Department, 518 Front Street, Boise, Idaho. It is a very complete list, made up annually, and gives the rivers upon which the individual guides work, and their town address.

Through various guides float trips can be arranged for two days to a week or more, the price running in the neighborhood of $30 per person per day. Many remote parts of the Forks of the Salmon can be reached by plane, to the numerous small airfields throughout Idaho, and such trips will run correspondingly higher.

There are also several combination float-sight-seeing-fishing expeditions available on the Snake and Salmon through Western River Expeditions, Inc. The address is Jack Currey or Jerry Morgan, 1699 East 3350 South, Salt Lake City, Utah.

Below the Salmon, where the state bulges westward into Oregon, the WEISER (12) and PAYETTE RIVERS (13) and their headwaters, provide good trout fishing. In the same general area, the sloughs along the lower Boise River and at the mouth of the Weiser also have a population of bass, crappie and perch.

The South Fork of the Payette, near Lowman, on Highway 21 north from Boise, is particularly well known for good catches and there are good camping facilities.

The BOISE RIVER (14) and its North and South Forks provide fair to good rainbow trout fishing; as do the reservoirs close to Boise such as Lucky Peak, and Arrow Rock Reservoir, northeast of Lucky Peak. Both can be fished either from boat or from the bank.

The most satisfactory fishing on the Boise watershed, however, is on the three forks, the North, Middle and South, which are accessible from dirt roads paralleling the streams. Fly fishing especially is at its best in September and October.

SNAKE RIVER DRAINAGE BASIN

The SNAKE RIVER (15) one of the outstanding streams of the Rocky Mountain area, enters Idaho from Wyoming and crosses the state in a great, southern curve, heading north just beyond Boise, and then, along the Idaho-Oregon border, plunging through the notorious Hells Canyon.

Much of the Snake traverses semiarid country, and this, along with the dams and reservoirs which are now constructed along it here and there, makes for such diversity of conditions that fishing varies greatly. Generally speaking, the best areas for trout are below the Minidoka Dam near Burley; from Twin Falls downstream to Hagerman; and in a few spots downstream from there, sometimes seasonally. For instance, the C. J. STRIKE RESERVOIR (16), southwest of Mountain Home, is usually good in the early spring, but not so good later; while in ISLAND PARK RESERVOIR (17), in the headwaters of the Henrys Fork, the fishing is best in late summer. This

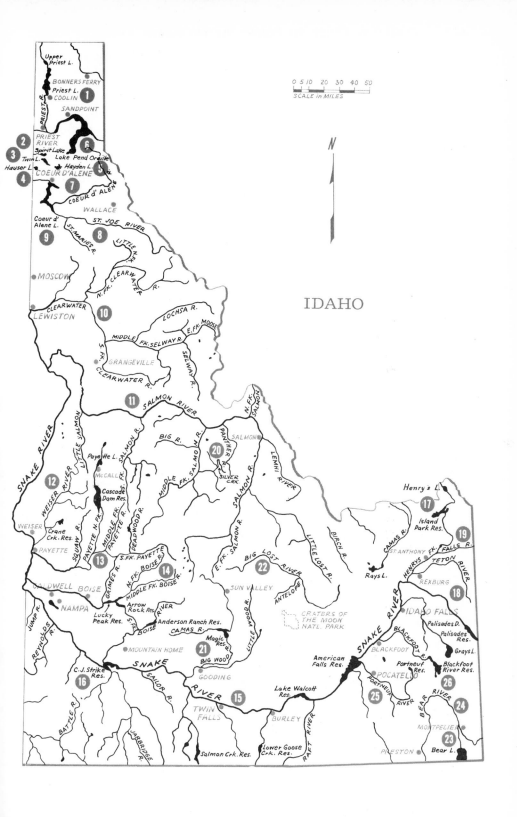

0 5 10   20   30   40   50
SCALE in MILES

N

IDAHO

Upper
Priest L.
BONNERS FERRY
Priest L.   ①
COOLIN
SANDPOINT

PRIEST
RIVER
②
③   Spirit Lake   ⑥
Twin L.   Lake Pend Oreille
Hauser L.   Hayden L.
④ COEUR D'ALENE
⑦ COEUR d'ALENE

WALLACE

Coeur d'
Alene L.   ST. JOE RIVER
⑨   ⑧
St. MARIES R.   LITTLE N. FK.

MOSCOW
N. FK. CLEARWATER R.

CLEARWATER   ⑩
LEWISTON   LOCHSA R.
S. FK.   E. FK. MOOSE
MIDDLE FK. SELWAY R.
GRANGEVILLE
CLEARWATER R.   SELWAY R.

SALMON RIVER   ⑪
N. FK. SALMON

SNAKE RIVER
LITTLE SALMON   BIG R. MIDDLE FK. SALMON R. PANTHER R. SALMON
Payette L.   ⑳ SILVER
McCALL S. FK.   CRK.
Cascade   LEMHI RIVER
Dam Res.
WEISER RIVER
⑫
SQUAW
WEISER   PAYETTE N. FK.
Crane   MIDDLE FK.
Crk. Res.   PAYETTE   DEADWOOD R.
PAYETTE   S. FK. PAYETTE E. FK. SALMON R. BIG LOST RIVER ⑳
⑬   GRIMES R.   N. FK. BOISE R. ⑭   ⑫
CALDWELL BOISE MIDDLE FK. BOISE   SUN VALLEY   ANTELOPE
NAMPA   Arrow   RIVER
Lucky   Rock Res.   Anderson Ranch Res.
Peak Res.   S. FK. BOISE   CAMAS R.
⑯   Magic
JUMP R.   C.J. Strike Res. ⑳
REYNOLDS R. Res.   SNAKE   BIG WOOD
⑯   ⑳
MOUNTAIN HOME   GOODING   SNAKE
BATTLE R.   RIVER
SAILOR   ⑮
JARBRIDGE R.   RIVER   TWIN
                FALLS   BURLEY
Salmon Crk. Res.   Lower Goose
                Crk. Res.   RAFT RIVER

Henry's L.   ⑰
Island
Park Res.   ⑲
CAMAS R.   HENRY'S FK. FALLS R.
St. Anthony   TETON
              RIVER
Rays L.   REXBURG   ⑱
BIRCH R. LITTLE LOST R.
CRATERS OF
THE MOON
NATL. PARK   SNAKE RIVER IDAHO FALLS
LITTLE WOOD R.   Palisades D.
            Palisades
BLACKFOOT R. Res.
American   BLACKFOOT   Grays L.
Falls Res.   Portneuf   Blackfoot
PORTNEUF RIVER Res.   River Res.
POCATELLO   ⑳
⑳   BEAR   ⑳
Lake Walcott   RIVER
Res.   MONTPELIER
                ⑳
PRESTON   Bear L.

Island Park District on Henrys Fork, or North Fork of the Snake, is one of the best-known fishing areas, with good accommodations, and boats available for fishing both the Reservoir and HENRYS LAKE, to the north. Henrys Lake is famous for its big rainbows, cutthroat and eastern brook trout. Many fish from 5 to 10 pounds are taken each year. Much trolling is done, but nymph fishing pays off heavily. One of the most effective flies on this lake was tied especially for it by Dan Bailey of Livingston, Montana. It is called the Henrys Lake Nymph and is an outstanding fly. Fishing at Henrys Lake is best in September and early October, although fine catches of trout are made earlier in the summer, either at dawn or dusk. Night fishing is also permitted, and it can be rewarding. Gary Howells, who guides in the area, can be reached in summer at Staley Springs Lodge, Mack's Inn, Idaho, phone North Henrys Lake 8153; and in winter at 655–33rd Street, Richmond, California. Phone Beacon 3-0960.

Some of the best fly fishing in Idaho is on the North Fork of the Snake below the dam at Ashford Reservoir. This water has produced 10-pounders with regularity and is highly regarded by fly fishermen. From early July to the end of the season is the best time to fish.

Sturgeon are at best an occasional fish, but interest in this species is growing on the main Snake River, where fish up to 400 pounds have been taken on rod and reel. Anglers who go for them use heavy surf-casting outfits with 90- to 20-pound-test line and chunks of meat for bait. The best months are May, June, September and October.

There's a limit of two fish, but where the Snake forms the boundary between Idaho and Washington and Idaho and Oregon, three fish are permitted. Minimum length is 36 inches and none over 72 inches may be kept.

As further evidence of the diversity of fishing in the Snake, smallmouth black bass, channel and flathead catfish are found in the stretch of water from Swan Falls (due south of Boise) to Lewiston where the Snake turns into Washington.

Lying to the north of the Snake, on the eastern border of Idaho, the TETON RIVER (18) holds some excellent rainbows and cutthroat trout. The average will run from 2 to 3 pounds and fishing is good throughout the season. The town of Driggs on State Highway 33 serves as headquarters. The Teton is a good dry-fly river, with the Whitcraft, Red Variant, Light Cahill, Quill Gordon, Mosquito, Adams, Ginger Quill, Blue Dun, Iron Blue Dun and Irresistible all producing well.

At Ashton, on U.S. 20 and 191, a few miles north of Driggs, the angler can get instructions on how to reach the FALLS RIVER (19), not as well known or as well fished as it should be. The Falls River is best right after the spring runoff, about July 1st. Its tributary, the Bechler, running close along the border and on into Yellowstone Park, is difficult to reach but offers great rewards in some exceptional dry-fly fishing, especially in September. Trout of 5 pounds are there for the taking. The best way to go in is from Warm Springs, Idaho, about five miles north of Ashton. The mosquitoes and deer flies are extremely bad, so go prepared.

There is excellent fishing in the Sun Valley area, where, with Ketchum as head-quarters, anglers can readily fish SILVER CREEK (20) to the south on U.S. 93. This beautiful stream, reminiscent of the English chalk streams, is crystal clear and demands considerable finesse in handling the fly if you are to catch fish. But it's well worth the effort; there are some good trout in the Silver.

An hour from Sun Valley, the BIG WOOD RIVER (21) is at its best in September and October. Just to the east the well-named BIG LOST RIVER (22) is equally good.

This river disappears eventually into the big lava formations south of Highway 88 between Arco and Mud Lake.

That triangle of Idaho which lies south and east of the Snake also has some excellent angling possibilities. BEAR LAKE (23), lying across the Idaho-Utah border, offers good cutthroat-trout fishing, especially at midsummer, as well as some fair lake-trout fishing. The BEAR RIVER (24), which parallels U.S. 30N between Montpelier and Soda Springs, is good later in the season; and the PORTNEUF RIVER (25), south of Pocatello, is also worthwhile. Outstanding lake fishing can be had at the BLACKFOOT RIVER RESERVOIR (26), which is reached via Highway 34 to Henry from Soda Springs. Trout up to 20 pounds have been taken and fishing is consistently good. The various smaller reservoirs in the same general area vary in productivity from fair to excellent, requiring that local enquiries be made to check on the fishing at any given time.

MOUNTAIN LAKES

As might be inferred from the topography, there are scores of small mountain lakes in Idaho, many of which can be reached only by footpath or pack trail. According to location, they may contain rainbows, brook trout or cutthroat. In a number of lakes there are grayling and Dolly Varden, and there has been extensive planting of the California golden trout.

For those who want to try for this latter species, Calahan Lake is probably the best bet. This lake lies in the Cabinet Mountains, which can be reached via US 10A, then over a new logging road from Troy, Montana, rather than from the Idaho side. White Sand Lake in the Powell Area was stocked with goldens many years ago and in 1958 produced a record 5-pound 2-ounce golden; but in 1960 the lake appeared to be barren. However, it was stocked again and, as it has excellent food conditions, should be producing. North Three Links Lake was also stocked with both goldens and cutthroats in 1961.

Other lakes which have been planted with golden trout are: in the McCall area to the east of Payette and Upper Payette Lake—Bill's Lake, Ann's Lake, North Lake, Buckhorn Mountain Lake. In the Bighorn Craggs area—Big Clear Lake, Pothole Lake, Gooseneck Lake, Crater Lake, Glacier Lake. In the Sawtooth Wilderness Area—Brown's, Rock Island, Heart, P. S. Everly, Alpine, Regan and Coney. In the White Cloud area—Big Boulder #1 and #2, Chamberlain Lakes #1, 2, 3, 7, 8, 9. And in the Copper Basin area—Bella's Lake #1, Golden Lake, and North Fork.

Since nearly all the mountain lakes of this rugged terrain call for detailed plans for either hiking or packing in, and often require the services of a guide, it is recommended that the reader write the Idaho Fish and Game Department at Boise for a very fine and unusually comprehensive booklet, "Mountain Lakes in Idaho."

IDAHO FISHING REGULATIONS

Resident Fishing License $4.00
Nonresident Fishing License (season) $15.00
Nonresident 5-Day Fishing License $5.00
Nonresident First-Day Fishing License $2.00
Nonresident Additional 1-Day License $1.00
Shipping Permit $.50

SEASONS AND LIMITS

The Idaho general fishing season is open from June 4 until October 31, with local exceptions which must be checked with each year's current regulations. There are also restrictions as to methods of fishing for certain species at certain times. Fishing hours are from 4 a.m. until 10 p.m., again with local exceptions.

Trout:	7 pounds and one fish, but not to exceed 15 fish. Includes kokanee-brook, Dolly Varden, mackinaw. (Some exceptions)
Steelhead:	Two fish per day or in possession. Not more than four fish in 7 consecutive days or more than 20 per calendar year. Steelhead under 20 inches are classed as trout and trout regulations apply.
Salmon:	Two fish over 20 inches in length of either Chinook or sockeye or in aggregate. Salmon under 20 inches in length are classed as trout and trout regulations apply.
Bass:	Largemouth or smallmouth, 12 of either or in aggregate.
Cisco:	50 fish.
Whitefish:	50 fish per day. No possession limit.
Sturgeon:	Two fish except in Snake River which forms boundary between Idaho and Oregon or Idaho and Washington, where limit is 3. Minimum length limit is 36 inches. Maximum length limit is 72 inches.

For complete regulations write: Fish and Game Department, 518 Front Street, Boise 83701, Idaho.

MONTANA

Montana rates as one of the top fishing states of this western area. The standard fish taken in Montana waters are brown, rainbow and cutthroat trout and Rocky Mountain whitefish. In some of the higher lakes golden trout have been stocked and in certain lakes and rivers you may also find eastern brook trout and grayling. In a few of the lakes silver salmon have been introduced, while in the warmer waters of the more shallow lakes found in the northern part of the state, and above some of the man-made dams, besides the trouts there are walleyes, northern pike, largemouth black bass, sauger, and, on occasion, crappie.

Through the mountains, foothills and valleys of middle and western Montana run many of the greatest fishing rivers of our country: the Yellowstone, Big Blackfoot, Bitterroot, Big Hole, Gallatin, Jefferson and Madison, the last three joining at Trident to form the mighty Missouri. In many of these streams the average trout will run more than a pound and in some as high as 2 pounds; 4-, 5- and 6-pounders are taken each week from the Yellowstone and Madison rivers and these, along with others in the state, produce an annual high quota of 10-, 12- and even 15-pound fish. Montana is also loaded with smaller rivers and so great is their fishing potential that even these streams will yield a more than occasional 4-pounder.

Augmenting the fishing possibilities of the rivers are countless lakes. Such large bodies of water as Flathead Lake, Georgetown Lake and Duck Lake turn up some tremendous fish, as well as producing in quantity. There are also innumerable smaller lakes, some mere mountain potholes, all of which produce trout of one kind or another, and some of which add bass, pike, walleyes, perch and kokanee salmon.

With few exceptions the bigger and better waters in Montana are easy to reach. Good roads parallel the Yellowstone on either side of the river from Big Timber all the way down to Gardiner, which is the northern entrance to Yellowstone Park and Wyoming. You can drive for miles along the banks of the Madison. Main roads skirt the Missouri, the Gallatin and the Jefferson, around Three Forks. In the Missoula area, fine roads approach close to the Big Blackfoot, the Bitterroot, Clark Fork of the Columbia, Rock Creek and others. Good main highways and secondary routes traverse the state north and south, east and west, reaching into even remote areas. In many cases it is possible to fish right where you park your car alongside the river, while in others a short walk will put you in a good pool. In places where it is necessary to leave main roads and walk or drive on private property, the angler should treat that property with the same care he would give his own, taking care not to damage fences or frighten cattle. He should close each gate behind him —or if he finds the gate open, leave it open. Most ranchers are willing to allow fishermen on their property when asked, and the exceptions are usually those who in the past have suffered damage at the hands of thoughtless visitors.

The more remote spots on the larger rivers can be reached by float trip. Most float fishermen use big rubber life rafts, although occasionally skiffs are also used. The anglers cast as they float downstream, working the shorelines, one man at the oars to control the boat, the others doing the casting. When a good pool is reached, they beach the boat at the head of the pool, get out and fish it thoroughly at their leisure, then get back into the boat and go on downstream to new water. This is an effective way of fishing and enables the angler to reach water that is seldom fished, but a float trip should not be attempted without a guide unless you know the river thoroughly. Float guides are available at almost any town near good floatable water throughout the state. The cost of a float is approximately $25 per day, and as the number of guides is limited, the angler who plans to be on the river at the height of the season should make his reservation early. Names of guides, outfitters and people able to advise on floating in the various rivers will be listed with the detailed descriptions of those rivers.

Montana is famous for the many pack trips available to high mountain and wilderness areas, most of which offer exceptional fishing. In some of the rivers and lakes far back in the high country you can take 1½- to 2-pound cutthroat on nearly every cast. In others you'll find Dolly Vardens running from 5 to 15 pounds. Again you may choose a lake where the dazzling-hued golden trout has been stocked, or where your offerings bring up brilliant-colored eastern brook trout. Back in this high country you will listen to a serenade at night as cautious coyotes, a half-mile from your campfire, bark and yodel, hitting a note higher than high C, telling in their own inimitable way how wonderful is nature among the peaks.

The Western Montana Outfitters and Guides Association publishes a folder which lists the areas where such trips are available and supplies the names of those outfitters who serve each area. This folder may be obtained by writing Jack Holloday, Montana Advertising Commission, Helena, Montana.

The price of such a back-country trip may run as high as $50 per person per day, but it is well spent with these men who have been packing into the hinterlands for many years, are equipped with good horses, tents, bedding, cooking utensils, and who know the trails and the fishing thoroughly. They are alert, competent men who see to the comfort, safety and enjoyment of those they guide.

Because of the altitude, even summer nights will be chilly and the camper needs warm clothing. In really high areas the pack-trip season is also limited by snow to July, August and early September.

Throughout Montana, summer temperatures rise into the 80's and very occasionally into the 90's, but late afternoons, early mornings and evenings are cool and fishing clothes should be chosen accordingly. Blue jeans are a more or less standard uniform, with a cotton shirt for midsummer, wool for spring and fall, and a Windbreaker or sweater for warmth when needed. For comfortable fishing, hip boots are necessary on the smaller streams and for lake-shore angling, while to fish the larger rivers effectively, chest-high waders are essential. In all cases felt soles or hobnails will provide added safety on slippery rocks.

Montana is basically a fly fisherman's country, but spinners and bait fishermen take their full share of fish. The 8½-foot rod is ideal for fly casting on Montana lakes and rivers when the angler expects to be throwing the larger, wind-resistant dry flies or streamers and bucktails. A GBF line matches this rod and the leader should be soft nylon, tapered down from a 30-pound-test butt section through lengths of 20-, 15-, 12- and 10-pound test to the smaller X classifications. The heavy butt section allows for better casting, acting like a continuation of the fly line, while the lighter tippet provides better fly placement and less visibility to the fish, an important consideration in most of Montana's crystal-clear mountain waters. A 9-foot rod, matched with a GAF line, is also used on the bigger waters; while for the small rivers, and when using small flies, an 8-foot rod with HDH line will prove efficient.

While there are always special flies which have proven themselves on the individual streams or lakes, there are also certain basic patterns the angler can stock in his fly box and be prepared for almost any eventuality. A generous assortment for Montana fishing should include the following:

Dry flies, hook sizes 8 to 20—Adams, Black Gnat, Light Cahill, Royal Coachman, Gray Hackle, Yellow Body, Light Hendrickson, Hendrickson, Iron Blue Dun, Ginger Quill, Mosquito, Tup's Indispensible, Gray Wulff, Grizzly Wulff, Sure Strike Special, Red Trude, Donnelly's Light Variant, Red Variant, Multi-Colored Variant, Black Spider, Ginger Spider, Blue Dun spentwing, Adams spentwing, Light Cahill spentwing. Hook sizes 18 and 20—Black Jassid, Black Flying Ant, Gray Midge hackle fly, Blue Dun spentwing, Humpy, Sofy Pillow.

Wet flies, hook sizes 8 to 16—Gray Hackle, Yellow Body, Brown Hackle, Coachman, Royal Coachman, Black Gnat, Western Bee, Cowdung, Blue Dun, Leadwing Coachman, March Brown, Professor, Mosquito, Ginger Quill, Black Woolly Worm, True Woolly Bear, Black and Orange.

Nymphs, sizes 10, 12, 14, 16—Gray Nymph, Ed Burke, Caddis Fly, March Brown, Phillips Black and Yellow, Phillips Black and Orange, Large Stone-Fly Nymph, Ginger-Quill Nymph, Yellow May, Brown May, Black May, Cream Mayfly nymph.

Ants, hook sizes 8 to 16—black, red, white, black and red.

Beetles, hook sizes 10 to 14—black, brown, bronze, green.

Streamers and bucktails, hook sizes 6 to 12, long shank—Black Ghost, Gray Ghost, Black-Nosed Dace, Red and Yellow, Red and White, Black and White, Muddler, Mickey Finn.

Big Bucktails, hook sizes 1 and 1/0—Platinum Blonde, Honey Blonde, Red and White, Red and Yellow, Muddler.

Marabou, hook sizes 6 to 12—Black, Yellow, Black and Yellow, White.

Montana spin casters usually find that a 6½- or 7-foot rod and a good reel, either open or closed face, equipped with 200 yards of 4- or 6-pound-test monofilament line will see them through all their lake and stream fishing. The choice lure of the moment in any given location can readily be ascertained at the local tackle shop and besides these, the spinner should have a basic assortment of ⅛-, ¼- and ½-ounce spoons and spinner-type lures such as the Mepps, size 0 through 4, with the 2's and 3's proving most popular; Thomas Cyclone; Goldfish in small sizes and also in the ½-ounce, which has proven very good for big trout; Flatfish; and Daredevil. The smaller lures are used in small rivers, the larger ones in the bigger rivers and in the lakes. Many anglers never think of using a ½-ounce lure for trout, considering them too large. But big trout like a mouthful, and many a lunker is brought up from the deeper pools on a ½-ounce lure.

Baits which are fine producers all over Montana are grasshoppers, dead or alive, the live being best; live sculpin minnows; red worms; shiner minnows; hellgrammites; stone-fly nymphs; and maggots. Eggs are illegal, as are live sucker minnows, though suckers with the heads cut off may be used. Bait fishermen should check the Montana Fish Laws carefully, as minnows are not allowed in many waters and it is the angler's responsibility to know the law on the water he is fishing. These regulations are supplied in brief at the end of this chapter, but annual changes should be checked with the Montana Fish and Game Department, Helena, Montana.

Fishing is good in Montana throughout the open seasons listed by the Fish and Game Department. However, the bigger rivers are subject to a runoff of snow water from the mountains and this comes later than the easterner usually expects. For instance, the water in these rivers will be low in May before the snow has really started to melt in the high country, and there will be good fishing then. But when the snow begins to melt on the higher slopes the runoff swells the rivers and gives the water a dingy color. When the runoff really gets going there is often so much force to the current that it is almost impossible to fish. The smaller streams run off quickly, so there is usually good early-summer angling in these, but some of the larger rivers stay high until mid or late August.

For all Montana rivers, then, the best fishing period is from July 15th to October 15th. Throughout this period the weather is usually fine, and especially after August 15th, when the big rivers become low and clear, you can get in some fantastic fishing. Boiling it down still further, the most productive thirty days for big fish would be from September 20th to October 20th.

As mentioned previously, fishing in the high mountain lakes is at its best earlier, as September and October will be on the cold side in the high altitudes.

Montana is big-game country and the angler may expect to see antelope in the drier sections, deer almost anywhere in ranch country and in the willows along the rivers. Bear and moose are common in many sections, particularly those adjacent to National Forests and Parks, and both animals should be treated with respect. The fisherman need have little fear, however, as long as he minds his own business, quietly goes his way and allows the animal to do the same. In a few wilderness areas there are grizzly bears, which are always potentially dangerous. The angler who is going into such areas must exercise extreme caution.

Elk may also be encountered in the high country. They are very shy of human beings and rarely present any problem.

The Rocky Mountain rattlesnake, which is the least venomous of the rattlers and rarely causes death, is common in parts of Montana and anglers should always be on the alert, even though these snakes tend to keep to the high, dry land and only occasionally are seen along a river. In fifteen years of Montana fishing the writer has seen only four rattlers and these were all on dry, rocky terrain. Nevertheless, in any area where snakes may occur the outdoorsman should always watch where he steps.

LAKE FISHING IN MONTANA

There are a number of large lakes in Montana which have earned special attention from anglers. In recent years DUCK LAKE (1), just a few miles south of the Canadian border, near Glacier National Park, has blossomed forth as one of the really great rainbow lakes. The fishing rights here belong to the Blackfeet Indians, on whose reservation the lake is located, and the visiting angler pays a daily fee of

$1 in addition to the cost of his regular Montana State Fishing License. (See Montana Fish and Game Regulations at end of this chapter.)

To encourage fishing in Duck Lake, the Blackfeet Indians conduct a three-day fishing tournament over the July 4th weekend. Last year's winners were rainbows that weighed 15½, 15 and 14½ pounds. All were taken on trolled spoons, but fly fishermen, spinners and bait fishermen all have good luck at Duck Lake. Rainbows up to 12½ pounds have been taken by the casting methods, the spinners using large spoons, and the fly men leaning heavily to the tan Woolly Worm and the Duck Lake Special. Anglers fishing with bait favor nightcrawlers, barnyard worms and maggots, often fastening the latter on the hook of a woolly-worm fly and trolling it behind the boat. Spring is the best time at Duck Lake, March in particular producing many monsters in the 15-pound class.

Anglers who fish Duck Lake stay at the small town of Babb, where there are two motels, or drive thirteen miles to St. Mary at the entrance to Glacier Park, where there is an excellent hotel, many cottages and a fine restaurant.

Another large Montana lake which has a history of producing big fish is GEORGETOWN LAKE (2), near Anaconda. The majority of fish taken at Georgetown now will be cutthroats averaging about 1½ pounds, augmented by some eastern brook trout, Montana grayling and silver salmon which have been stocked. But there are also some enormous rainbows that reach 14 and 15 pounds.

Wall of Fame in Dan Bailey's Fly Shop, Livingston, Montana, displays plaques of trout over 4 pounds caught on flies in Montana waters.

Georgetown produces well all summer, on standard flies, nymphs and spinning lures, as well as bait, but the peak of the fishing for the big rainbows is in late September and through October. One angler took a string of big rainbows there on spin tackle on November 11th—eight fish that weighed from 8½ to 14 pounds. For this late-season, big-lake angling, spin fishermen use fairly large spoons, while fly fishermen use big streamer flies on 2 or 1/0 hooks, and, when weather conditions warrant, big dry flies.

It should be remembered that this lake is at an altitude of 7,000 feet, and it can be very cold, so the angler should come prepared with plenty of warm clothing. Sometimes in the fall, when snow flurries blow across the lake, you will find the fishermen wearing gloves.

Accommodations for anglers are provided in several good motels right at Georgetown or you may stay at either Anaconda or nearby Phillipsburg. Accommodations at the lake include the Brown Derby Motel and Restaurant; 7 Gables Motel and store; Ray Denton's Denton's Point Trailer Camp and Restaurant and Boat Livery; and Jack's Place, cabins. Proprietors Fritz and Elsie Bjorkland, Box 68, Georgetown Lake, via Anaconda. Phone 563-5062.

FLATHEAD LAKE (3), in the northern part of the state, is an immense body of water. Some years ago a "sea monster" was reported to have been seen there. The consensus of opinion is that the monster was a giant sturgeon, but who knows? Perhaps some lucky angler will discover what it was one of these days, but in the meantime the lake provides plenty of good sport with cutthroat, lake trout, and Dolly Varden trout and kokanee. This being one of the most scenic areas of the state, there are numerous motels along the way as well as at the towns of Ronan, Polson and a little further north at Kalispell.

In the drier parts of Montana, where the state slopes off eastward into wheatlands and dry grazing country, there are a number of dams for power and irrigation, which have created lakes. These are mostly on the Missouri River. CANYON FERRY RESERVOIR (4), near Helena, has good trout and bass fishing, and FORT PECK RESERVOIR (5), also an impoundment of the Missouri, has all types of fish, from trout to bass, walleyes, pike and sauger. There are some paddlefish there, too, but these are not classed as game fish and are taken mostly by snagging.

Smaller impounded lakes occur here and there throughout the state, ranging from the TIBER (6), FRESNO (7) and NELSON (8) RESERVOIRS in the north, which offer such warm-water fish as bass, walleyes and sauger, to the RUBY RESERVOIR (9), HEBGEN LAKE (10) and ENNIS or MEADOW LAKE (11). These last three, in the heart of the trout country, give up good-sized rainbow and brown trout.

Most lake fishing is done from boats, but in places it is possible to work these waters from the shore, or even wade, with reasonable success.

There are innumerable mountain lakes in Montana, most of which offer good fishing. DAILEY'S LAKE (12), thirty-five miles south of Livingston, turns out some good rainbows, although heavy fishing has reduced their numbers somewhat, as this lake can be reached by car. To reach most of the high mountain lakes, however, it is necessary either to make a major hike or use a jeep or pack horse and carry a rubber life raft in order to fish the lakes adequately. This kind of fishing is best arranged through a guide service; then you can take your pick of lakes with rainbows, cutthroat, eastern brook trout or goldens. Some of the favorite areas into which anglers like to make these pack trips are the Hell Roaring Country accessible from

Livingston or Gardiner; the Red Lodge area, accessible from Silver Gate, Red Lodge and Cooke City; the Ruby Mountains, accessible from Laurin, Alder, Sheridan, Twin Bridges or Virginia City; the Gallatins, which can be reached from Bozeman; the Madison Range, reached from Ennis or West Yellowstone; and the Glacier Park area, which will be covered separately in this chapter. Several lakes in which golden trout have been stocked can be reached by pack trip from the 320 Ranch, south of Bozeman, through arrangement with Jim Goodrich, the proprietor.

The standard Montana spoons and baits are successful in these high lakes. Best-producing flies are the Phillips Black Ant, Black and Red Ant, both on #12 hooks; the big dry flies such as the Royal or Gray Wulff; Red Variant; a big Spider skipped across the surface; and the black and yellow, the brown and the gray nymphs.

RIVER FISHING IN MONTANA

The YELLOWSTONE RIVER (13) is the best known of all Montana Rivers. It runs from headwaters in Yellowstone Lake within Yellowstone National Park, "down north" for fifty-five miles to Livingston, where it makes a big bend westward and traverses the entire state to join the Missouri on the Montana-North Dakota border. The best fishing is in the first hundred miles outside the Park, where the river runs through rocky gorges and Yankee Jim Canyon, then through the luscious ranch country of Paradise Valley. The fishing extends for about fifty-five miles below Livingston, to Reed Point, where the water has warmed sufficiently that trout fade out and trash fish take over.

The Yellowstone has always been one of the great trout rivers of America. Indians once gathered along its banks to catch fish. Early mountain men, roaming its reaches, saw cutthroat as long as their legs. Pioneer settlers took them by the hundreds. Today's fish population is slightly different. The cutthroat is still common in the higher reaches, especially within the boundaries of Yellowstone Park, but the rainbow and the brown are the most common catches now in the balance of the river. Brown trout were first introduced in 1906 by the state authorities, and so well has the brown fared in the Yellowstone that in spite of the fact that there has been no further stocking of browns, this fish is today the most plentiful one in the river.

Shortly after the browns were first planted, the state began to stock fingerling rainbows and they still annually plant 500,000 of the species. They do reasonably well for a year and provide a lot of good sport. Some few survivors grow to bumper size, so that during the course of a season rainbows in the 4-, 5- and 6-pound class are taken from the Yellowstone, with an occasional one even larger.

An interesting development resulting from the stocking of rainbows has been the appearance of the hybrid rainbow-cutthroat. Of course this fish cannot reproduce, but the hybrids grow to big weights and combine the best qualities of both ancestors. They fight harder than the cutthroat or the rainbow, jump more than the cutthroat, and seem to survive better than the rainbow. They have added immensely to the angling scene in the Yellowstone River.

Because of a sudden descent of muddler or sculpin minnows into the Yellowstone from feeder streams, the size of the brown trout in the Yellowstone has jumped a pound in average weight within the last two years. Almost every brown trout you open will have at least one of these minnows in it. As a result of its great natural potential, plus these developments, the Yellowstone offers probably the best trout fishing in America today.

Add to the trouts the Rocky Mountain whitefish and you have the fish population of the Yellowstone. The whitefish, which reaches top weights of about 4 pounds, is regarded as a nuisance by some anglers, but it is a great taker of flies, spinning lures and bait and puts up a fair fight. It provides good sport on a dry fly as this fish has a very small mouth and is hard to hook. For this reason the whitefish is a good "practice fish" for the fly man. They taste excellent in the cold season, or when taken from really cold water, and are regarded as the finest fish for smoking.

The best fishing period on the Yellowstone is from April until the runoff of snow water from the mountains discolors the water, usually in June; and again from late July until the weather becomes too cold for comfortable fishing or for the fish to feed well. The top period is usually from September 20th to October 20th.

In the fishable stretch there are many pools, rapids and flat runs, offering great variety of fishing. Wading is good throughout and in some parts of the river float trips are feasible. Two major towns, Gardiner, the northern entrance to Yellowstone Park, and Livingston, fifty-five miles downstream, offer motels, laundries, restaurants, churches, grocery stores, garages and service stations. There are also a few dude ranches within reasonable access of the river, and Chico Hot Springs, half way between Livingston and Gardiner, offers the combination of dude ranch and spa.

In Gardiner, Park's Fly Shop offers complete anglers' supplies, and Merton Parks guides anglers on trips into the Park and to high mountain lakes as well as on float trips on the Yellowstone. He will also arrange pack trips to remote areas for lake and stream fishing.

Livingston is the most central point from which to fish the Yellowstone. The town, besides offering all the facilities mentioned above, is a main station on the Great Northern Railway, and there is bus service from Butte, Billings and Bozeman. The nearest major airport is thirty-five miles away at Bozeman, but there is an excellent small-plane landing strip, recently paved, at Livingston. Billings and Butte both have fields which carry transcontinental plane traffic, and many anglers fly into either of these ports, rent a car and drive the 116 miles to Livingston. U.S. 89 parallels the river from Gardiner to Livingston and the new Interstate Highway 90 and U.S. 10 follow the river below the town.

In Livingston there are two excellent tackle stores, Dan Bailey's Fly Shop, one of the most famous in the country, and Dick's Pack Sack. Float trips can be arranged through Bailey's and either shop can supply information about the fishing in the surrounding area.

A number of guides work out of Livingston, providing a variety of services from daily fishing-guide service to pack and float trips. These are: Jim LaValley, Harold Shanstrom, John Adams, Larry Adams, Mel Ingram, Don Williams, Paul Christiansen of the 63 Ranch, and LeRoy Fatouros of the Black Otter Guide Service.

Of the numerous tributaries of the Yellowstone, the BOULDER (14) is the best known. This river enters the Yellowstone on the east bank near Big Timber. The Boulder is formed by the confluence of the East and West Boulder, the latter a good fishing stream in itself. The Main Boulder has cutthroat, brown and rainbow trout plus the ever prevalent Rocky Mountain whitefish. The average catch will be from 1 to 2 pounds but browns up to 7 pounds are taken annually. The West Boulder is a smaller stream but offers excellent angling for cutthroat rainbows and an increasing number of browns. Both these rivers are at their best in the fall, during late September and October when the big browns move in to spawn. These fish are hungry and hit hard and fight like fiends.

The SHIELDS RIVER (15) enters the Yellowstone about five miles downstream from Livingston and can be reached via U.S. 89 to Wilsall. The river holds some good brownies and also gives up the odd rainbow.

A number of other fishable streams are tributaries of the Yellowstone. BIG CREEK (16) flows in on the west side a couple of miles south of Emigrant, upstream from Livingston. This is a fine mountain stream and holds cutthroat, rainbows and some browns in the lower reaches. EIGHT MILE CREEK (17), across the river from Emigrant, offers some good cutthroat fishing and, though it is a small stream, occasionally 2 pounders are taken. Well downstream, entering the Yellowstone near Columbus, the STILLWATER RIVER (18) provides occasional good fishing for moderate-sized browns.

Along the Yellowstone and its tributaries, the stand-out fly patterns are: dry flies—black, gray and grizzly Wulff in size 12; Light Cahill, size 14; dry Grasshopper, size 12. Wet flies—all black or orange and black Woolly Worm, size 12. Nymphs—gray, black-and-yellow, all brown, sizes 12 and 16; and the bigger mossbacks, sizes 8 and 10. The best all-round fly is the muddler fished an inch below the surface, although on the Yellowstone some anglers use a sinking line and reap a rich harvest along the bottom with both this and other flies. Aside from the Muddler, the Edson Tiger, Black Prince, brown and yellow bucktail and multiwing streamers on 1/0 hooks are good for big trout, and in the fall the platinum and honey blondes, on 1/0 hooks should not be overlooked.

The BIG HOLE RIVER (19) rises in the Bitterroot Mountains and runs through the great "Valley of 10,000 Stacks" in western Montana, one of the greatest hay areas of the West. Early settlers referred to such wide valleys as "holes," hence the name Big Hole. Up in this meadow country in the top reaches of the river there are rainbows, some eastern brook trout, and a great many grayling. The stream is small, winding, and easily fished with hip boots. Since it travels mostly through ranch land, permission to fish should be requested from the ranchers, both out of respect for their privacy rights and because of the fact that when irrigation is in progress, your car may well get bogged down if water has been let in across the path on which you entered. In the lower part of this Upper Big Hole, the river parallels Highway 278 and there is good angling beside the road.

At Divide the Big Hole enters a Canyon and from here down it is a much bigger river. The best fishing is from Divide all along the way for seventy miles to where the Big Hole joins the Jefferson River just below Twin Bridges. There are miles of wonderful pools, making this a particularly attractive river for fly fishermen, especially in the late summer.

Below Divide there are many brown trout, some few 5-pounders being taken, and lots in the 3- and 4-pound class. The largest brown ever to come from this river went 17 pounds. Rainbows are also stocked and provide good dry-fly fishing. The largest on record to date was a 7-pounder.

Whitefish are plentiful in the larger pools and some grayling have worked down from the Upper Big Hole, especially into the canyon, so the angler may expect to augment his catch with an occasional fish of this species.

Fly men fishing the Big Hole use all the standard Montana flies, but the Red Variant has proven particularly good as have large Spiders skipped across the surface. In the late fall, some tremendous fish are taken on big streamer flies, particularly the Muddler.

Spinners find smaller spin lures more successful in the low, crystal-clear water than larger spoons, which take fish in a murky stream. Best baits are grasshoppers, minnows, night crawlers and smaller worms.

Anglers fishing the Big Hole may stay at Twin Bridges, where there are several motels, grocery stores, drug store, service stations and two restaurants. At Frank's Tackle Shop the angler can get up-to-the-minute information about what's going on both in the Big Hole and other streams such as the Beaverhead, Ruby and various small creeks in the area, such as the Alder, which runs from Virginia City down into the Ruby.

Accommodations are limited at Twin Bridges, but Dillon, only forty miles away, has plentiful motels and all the services of a larger town. The small towns of Glen, Melrose, Divide and Wise River offer limited accommodations, and Biltmore Hot Springs, on the road between Twin Bridges and Dillon, has limited cabin accommodations, light meals and a swimming pool. There are excellent accommodations at the Sportsman Motel, at Melrose. Reservations should be made through Mr. or Mrs. Danny Pendergast, phone Melrose 835-2141. Meals are also available at the Quack Quack Cafe next door. The Pendergasts have horses available for trips to mountain lakes (about $20 a day per person) and jeep trips can also be arranged. On the Upper Big Hole the town of Wisdom has several motels, restaurants, a grocery store and service stations, and still further up, at Jackson, there is a grocery store and an excellent modern inn, complete with hot springs.

There are many excellent camping spots along the Big Hole, and usually you need only to request permission of the rancher to pitch your tent at some convenient spot by the river. There are also public campsites (see map), and one particularly pleasant one at the famous Big Hole Battleground, a few miles above Wisdom.

During the time when there is sufficient water in the Big Hole to make float trips feasible, floats may be arranged through Swede Olsen at Silver Star on Highway 41 between Dillon and Whitehall; and through Ray Rathie 4 Mile Vue, Butte, Montana, Phone 723-3546; and Jack Atcheson, 2309 Hancock Street, Butte, Montana. Phone 792-3498.

The JEFFERSON RIVER (20) is formed about three miles below Twin Bridges by the confluence of the Big Hole and the Beaverhead Rivers, with the added waters of the Ruby, which enters the Beaverhead only a short distance higher. The Jefferson is a fairly large, shallow and slow-moving river. It flows through the hay meadows and pastures past Whitehall to Cardwell and Jefferson Island, and on to LaHood, paralleling U.S. Highway 10 to Three Forks, and on to Trident where, along with the Madison and the Gallatin, it pushes its waters into the Missouri.

There are few rainbows in the river and it holds multitudes of Rocky Mountain whitefish and even some trash fish such as carp, but the brown-trout fishing is better than average and at times the pools are alive with rising fish. When the Jefferson is low and clear, it is one of the best rivers for brown trout in Montana. The average catch will go a pound and a half, with 3- and 4-pounders taken every day. Some 5-pounders are caught annually, and the biggest known to come from the Jefferson weighed in at 12 pounds.

Many of the pools are long and flat, furnishing great evening angling for cruising trout. There is a good fly hatch throughout the summer, and when the water is low and clear it is a good fly-fishing river. The low and clear state can be expected in late August and throughout September, though even then it can be affected by storms in the Ruby Mountains, which cause mud to pour into the Ruby and then

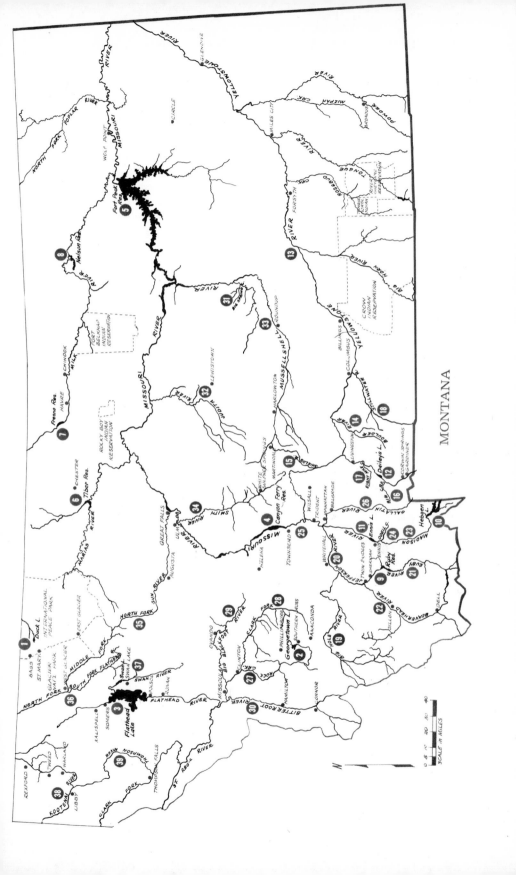

down into the Jefferson. This condition usually clears up a few days after the storm. All in all, the best fishing period on the river is from July 15 through October.

Jefferson browns will hit all the popular Montana dry flies, streamers and bucktails, the standard spoons, and bait of all kinds. The river may be fished from Twin Bridges, already described under the material on the Big Hole River; or the angler may stay at Whitehall or Three Forks, both providing complete accommodations; or at LaHood, where there are cabins and a restaurant.

The RUBY RIVER (21) rises in southwestern Montana in the mountains of the same name, flows down into the Ruby Reservoir, then continues below the lake to run down through the meadows in back of Alder, Laurin and Sheridan. A few miles north of Sheridan it joins the Beaverhead. This is a very good river, easily reached from Highway 287 between Ennis and Twin Bridges, and carries a good head of trout. There is good fishing in the river above the reservoir for browns and some rainbows, with fish from 14 to 16 inches being not unusual. This is high-meadow fishing with plenty of space for the angler, but the trout are easily frightened and even heavy footsteps along the bank will send them scurrying. The careful, quiet angler is the one who will come in with a true picture of what the Ruby has to offer.

There is some fishing from the lake shore and, below the reservoir, all the way along to the Beaverhead there is good fishing in the Ruby. In some of the hard-to-reach stretches you are apt to have a rise from a crooked-jawed old brownie that will scare you. Nine- and 10-pound browns have been taken from the Ruby.

The BEAVERHEAD RIVER (22) is another meadow stream which holds some good fish, and stretches of this river are seldom fished. The Beaverhead is a continuation of the Red Rock Creek, which flows down from the Lima Reservoir in the extreme southwestern part of the state. Red Rock itself is a narrow, winding stream and holds plenty of brown trout in the 1- to 2-pound class. It traverses ranch land for almost its entire length and permission to fish must always be obtained. Near Dell it joins Sheep Creek and together with waters from several other small creeks forms the Beaverhead. The best stretch of the Beaverhead is from this juncture down to a short distance above Dillon, and there are many places from which you can reach the river along Highway 41 out of Dillon. Pound fish are the average and 4- and 5-pounders are taken each year. This river is often murky in color and is therefore regarded more as a bait-fishing stream. However, fly and spin casters take their full share of fish; in fact, in the late season flies produce extremely well.

The MADISON RIVER (23) has long been recognized as one of the great trout streams of America. It rises in the Yellowstone National Park, entering Montana at the extreme southwest corner and flowing due north to Trident, where it joins the Gallatin and Jefferson to form the Missouri. Several dams on the Madison have changed its character somewhat so it does not have the crystal clarity of its original state, and the raising and lowering of the water level in these dams causes fluctuations in the fishing, but it is still one of the top rivers, turning up many huge rainbows and browns each season. Contrary to prognostications at the time, the earthquake of 1959, which caused part of the river bed to be dry for several weeks, did not harm the fishing; on the contrary, it seems a little better since then, with an increasing number of big fish being taken.

The fish life of the Madison is comprised of browns and rainbows. Although the river was originally renowned for its rainbow fishing, it is the brown you will now take most often. There are also a few grayling.

The best fishing is during early July when there is a phenomenal hatch of stone flies on the Madison. The big-eyed browns go wild for these tasty morsels and fish of 4, 5 ,and 6 pounds are caught on artificials which match the hatch. Then good fishing continues throughout the summer, except when too much water is let out of the dams and the water level rises. This situation may last for a few days or a week, at which time it is well for the fly angler, at least, to spend his time on neighboring streams or visit some of the high mountain lakes.

Large flies are usually the most successful on the Madison, the most popular being the Sofa Pillow, size 10 Gray Wulff and the Trude, in dries; and the #4 and #2 Muddler in wets. Spinners lean to spoons with telling effect. Minnows, grasshoppers and nightcrawlers are all popular with bait fishermen, and there is a great natural supply of crawfish in the river.

The Madison River can be fished from headquarters at West Yellowstone or Ennis, much of the river running close to Highway 287. In West Yellowstone either Bud Lilly or Pat Barnes Tackle Shop can arrange float trips on certain sections of the river (part of it is closed to floating), and has all information as to the best flies and lures of the moment. In Ennis, Tom Morgan's Tackle Store supplies the same services. Both these shops can also arrange pack trips to high lakes or small streams in the immediate area. Both towns have numerous motels, service stations, and restaurants. Two of the large motels are El Western and Sportsman's Lodge. The latter also has a restaurant and a landing strip for planes.

One tributary of the Madison which is particularly worthy of note is ODELL CREEK (24). Odell holds some substantial trout, 2-pounders being taken with great regularity. Permission to fish Odell, except in the immediate vicinity of the highway, must be obtained from the ranchers. Once close to the stream, the angler must work very circumspectly because this is a small and narrow river and the fish hear the slightest noise.

The MISSOURI RIVER (25), carrying all the waters of the Gallatin, Jefferson and Madison, is a big river, necessitating chest-high waders in most places. Parts of the river offer good fishing, notably the twenty miles from Toston Dam to Townsend. From Hauser Dam to the Gates of the Mountains is probably the best stretch for fly fishing. Between Canyon Ferry and the Hauser Dam there is good trolling or casting from boats. Boats may also be used below Canyon Ferry, but there are none below Hauser until Beaver Creek because of rocks and shallows. From there to the Gates of the Mountains it is again possible to use a boat.

Brown trout and rainbows comprise the fish in the Missouri, with the addition of some bass below the bridge at Townsend and in some of the reservoirs. From Wolf Creek all the way to Ulm there is excellent trout fishing, and from Ulm to Great Falls it continues fair.

Highways 287 and Interstate 15 parallel much of the river, but in some sections to reach the river it is necessary to drive about five miles off the hardtop on dirt roads. There is also entry via a secondary road which runs from U.S. 90 near Three Forks, up through Clarkson, Lombard and Toston.

Anglers fishing the Upper Missouri will find accommodations at Townsend, Helena or Three Forks. Three Forks has motels and the usual small-town services of restaurants, service stations, churches and grocery stores. Helena, being the state capital, has all the facilities of a big city, including many motels. Townsend has a few motels, restaurants and service stations. The River Inn Motel, Mr. and Mrs. Les Goodwin, Proprietors, at the intersection of U.S. Highways 287 and 12, is a good place to stay. The Mint Cafe puts up a really substantial fisherman's lunch for $1. Fishermen who are working the northern section of the Missouri must camp or stay in Helena or Great Falls and drive to the fishing each day.

Like so many rivers which have been dammed, the Missouri is not as clear as most of Montana's trout streams and this determines the choice of flies and lures. Big spinning lures and the larger flies, streamers and bucktails pay off. Again the Muddler comes through as a mighty good fly on the Big Mo. Best baits are night crawlers and minnows, while grasshoppers do well in the late summer.

Like the Yellowstone, the Missouri is open to fishing year-round. Late July and August are regarded as the slowest fishing months of the year; the best fishing is in September and October, and from April into July.

The GALLATIN RIVER (26) is formed by many small rivulets in Yellowstone Park, and continues to be swelled by numerous small tributaries until it reaches a good size by the time it approaches U.S. Highway 191 between West Yellowstone and Bozeman. It flows north as far as Gallatin Gateway, then turns westward to flow past Manhattan. Just below Logan, at Trident, it joins the Madison and the Jefferson to form the Missouri.

The top part, along Highway 191, holds rainbows and cutthroats. As the river comes out of the canyon at the foot of the mountains and hits the valley floor, brown trout appear and some good ones are caught there every year. The average size of the rainbows is about ¾ of a pound; the browns go 1¼ pounds. However, rainbows up to 3 pounds and browns of 4 and even 5 are caught occasionally. The largest rainbow known to have come from the Gallatin weighed 4½ pounds; the largest brown 9½ pounds.

Small dry flies are good on this river, both the upper and lower stretches. Back of Belgrade the Gallatin winds slowly through hay meadows, fed here and there by a smaller, incoming stream, usually a spring creek, and the rainbows through here have a decided liking for size 16 and 18 dry flies. The best patterns are the Blue Dun, the Iron Blue and the Light Cahill. The browns in this lower section go for bigger dries, the Royal Wulff, Grizzly Wulff, the Pink Lady and the Grasshopper fished dry. The Muddler does yeoman duty, too, especially in the lower reaches.

Spin fishermen on the Gallatin River generally use small spoons and some use a bubble with a fly. Both presentations take fish. Bait fishermen use the same steady producers commonly popular throughout Montana—night crawlers, minnows, and grasshoppers.

There are many places to stay while fishing the Gallatin. Dude ranches in the area are equipped to put the angler on the Gallatin as well as take him to some of the high mountain lakes of the Gallatin range. Gallatin Gateway has modern cabins and a grocery store, and seven miles away is Bozeman, a large town with every facility. For anglers who wish to stay on the lower Gallatin, Bozeman is also convenient, and there are cabins at Belgrade, Manhattan and Three Forks, and restaurants and service stations in each of these towns.

ROCK CREEK (27) starts high up in the mountains of Deer Lodge National Forest and comes tumbling down through Lolo National Forest till it debouches into the Clark Fork of the Columbia at Clinton, on U.S. Highway 10, about twenty-two miles east of Missoula. In all, this beautiful mountain stream provides sixty-five miles of wilderness fishing for rainbows. They average under a pound but it is not unusual to take them to 3 and 4 pounds, and the largest on record went a hefty 6 pounds. In the lower reaches brown trout have moved up from the Clark Fork to spawn and while they are not taken in great numbers, they come big, averaging a good 4 pounds, and a 10½-pounder has been recorded. There are also Rocky Mountain whitefish. The stream is crystal clear with well-defined pools, calling for careful fishing. This is an area where the angler may expect to see moose and bear, and caution should be taken accordingly.

All the standard flies listed for Montana in general are good, with emphasis on the Blue Dun and Red Variant, in sizes 12, 14 and 16. The best fly for the big brownies in the lower reaches is the Muddler, size 4. Spinners use small spoons for the rainbows but go to half-ounce lures for the browns in the lower stretches. Grasshoppers and worms are used by bait fishermen and these account for some big fish. Rock Creek is at its best from July 1st through October 31st.

There are good accommodations at Bruce Elliott's Rock Creek Lodge on Highway 10, a scant 100 yards from where Rock Creek empties into the Clark Fork, and guide service and tackle can also be obtained there. Or the angler may stay at Missoula, where there is every type of accommodation and convenience.

The CLARK FORK OF THE COLUMBIA (28) may be fished from the same headquarters. This stream rises in the hills near Anaconda and flows westward along Highway 10. However, due to irresponsible dumping of waste, both vegetation and fish have been destroyed along a great deal of its length. A clean-up program, instituted by the mines at the instigation of sportsmen and the state authorities, has resulted in considerable improvement. Now some good browns are being taken from the Clark Fork just west of Missoula and twenty-two miles east of Clinton, where Rock Creek adds its pure waters to the Clark Fork. The average brown in the Clark Fork will weigh 2 pounds and the largest known to have been taken weighed a hefty 10 pounds.

The best time to fish this river is from August 1st to October 31st, and while many flies will produce, the #4, #2 and 1/0 Muddler are outstanding. Spinners use all the large spoons, and bait fishermen are successful with all the conventional baits.

The BIG BLACKFOOT RIVER (29) is formed by the joining of many small streams which flow down from the mountains of Lewis and Clark County in west-central Montana. The Blackfoot joins the Clark Fork of the Columbia at Missoula and can be reached by U.S. 20 east from Missoula towards Ovando. As there is very little accommodation along U.S. 20, the angler should stay in Missoula, where he will find plentiful accommodations, as well as several tackle shops where he can readily obtain advice as to the best fishing spots along the river.

The Blackfoot is one of the most beautiful rivers in Montana, its crystal-clear water pouring over many wide gravel beds and through rolling hills and pleasant pasture lands. The angler who works back from the road will see mule deer and an occasional black bear. It is also a big river, and chest-high waders are necessary in order to reach the best positions for fishing many of the pools.

Rainbows in the Blackfoot average a pound, with an occasional 2- to 2½-pounder and the odd one up to 5 pounds. There are also a few browns in the lower Blackfoot, near Missoula.

The river is fishable all along the line. The best time is from August 1st through October. Dry flies, small bucktails and nymphs do well, and the smaller spinning spoons are effective, rather than the big half-ounce spoons used for browns. Rainbows like their flies and lures served up in smaller doses. Bait fishermen take their limit with nightcrawlers and grasshoppers.

The BITTERROOT RIVER (30) parallels U.S. 93 from the Idaho border to Missoula. The main part of the stream is formed at Connor where the east and west branches join and from there, till it joins the Clark Fork of the Columbia at Missoula, it continues for sixty-five miles, gathering water from the myriad feeder streams which pour down out of the Bitterroots, the mountain range which forms this part of the border between Montana and Idaho.

In the upper part of the Bitterroot River there is good fishing for eastern brook trout as well as rainbows, and as you work further down the browns put in their appearance. The brook trout average ¾ of a pound, with 1- and 2-pounders taken now and again and the biggest going 4 pounds. The average rainbow will go 1 pound, while 2- and 3-pounders turn up occasionally. The biggest on record weighed 6 pounds. The browns grow big in the Bitterroot, with a fine average of 2 pounds, 3- and 4-pounders taken frequently, and the largest known a hulking 10-pounder.

All the standard Montana flies are successful, with emphasis on the Royal Coachman and Red Variant dries, and the small bucktails and streamers in the brook-trout area. When they reach brown-trout waters, anglers go to slightly larger flies such as the Muddler and Spruce Fly. Spinners vary their offerings in the same way, the small spoons for the upper stretches, the larger ones where they may expect to find the big browns. Bait fishermen take their fish on nightcrawlers and minnows, and grasshoppers are particularly good in the late summer.

Missoula offers all conveniences and services for fishermen on the Bitterroot and there are some motels and smaller town services at Hamilton.

BIG SPRING CREEK (31), near Lewistown, lies considerably to the east of the major river-fishing area of Montana, yet it is one of the really great trout streams of the state. This gigantic spring rises from the ground some ten miles southeast of Lewistown and flows northwest to join the Judith River, which in turn runs northward to the Missouri. In the ten miles above the town there is terrific fishing in crystal-clear water. Fish are rising most of the time, both rainbows and browns, ranging from ¾ pound to 2 pounds, and this part of the river yielded the largest fish ever taken in Spring Creek, a gigantic 18-pound brown. While this fish was taken on a worm, the upper part of Spring Creek is a dry-fly man's ideal stream. Because of the clarity of the water it pays to go down to a 4X or 5X tippet when dry-fly fishing. The most common hatch can be matched with a size 16 or 18 Blue Dun and the same fly with a spent wing does well. However, sometimes a size 16 Light Cahill or a Red Variant is the fly that will do the trick.

Below the town, Spring Creek also offers fine rainbow and brown-trout fishing though the water is not so clear here. But the fish on the whole average a pound bigger, rainbows going 1½ to 2 pounds and browns a bit heavier. Three- and 4-pound fish will often be taken in the same day from the same pool. Down here the best flies for browns are the large streamers and bucktails and the Muddler, but they will also take the standard dry flies, the Gray Wulff and Royal Wulff being perhaps the best. The rainbows prefer the smaller flies, particularly the Red Variant and size 12 Blue Dun, and occasionally a size 16 Blue Dun or Light Cahill.

The ranchers along Spring Creek at Lewistown have gone all out in co-operating with anglers, providing parking places and putting stiles over the fences to make access to the river easy. Visiting anglers should be careful to use these stiles and not damage fences, and to observe the signs which indicate that certain fields should not be entered. The co-operation of the ranchers in this area is an outstanding example of landowner-sportsman relations, and the fisherman should do his full share to preserve such a situation.

Lewistown offers every accommodation, from motels, hotels, restaurants, launderies, grocery stores and service stations to tackle shops where the visitor will find ready advice on the best fly, bait or lure of the moment. The same shops are equipped to supply directions for reaching the best portions of WARM SPRING CREEK and the JUDITH RIVER (32) in the same area, which offer some angling for browns and small rainbows. Guide service on Big Spring Creek, as well as on the Big Hole River, Madison, Beaverhead, Rock Creek, Duck Lake and Wade Lake can be obtained through Vern Field, 514 East Broadway, Lewistown, Montana, phone 538-3254.

The MUSSELLSHELL RIVER (33) also lies in the drier, eastern slopes of the foothills. It can be reached via U.S. Highway 12 from White Sulphur Springs to Harlowton and the good fishing does not extend much below this point. However, in the higher waters brown trout of 2 and 3 pounds are caught regularly. A great deal of this area is posted, and permission to fish must be obtained from the ranchers.

The SMITH RIVER (34), lying a little further west and fed by streams from the Jefferson National Forest on one side and the Helena National Forest on the other, has a reputation for some exceptional fishing. It can be reached by dirt road from White Sulphur Springs on the south or from Ulm on the north where the Smith joins the Missouri. However, as with the Mussellshell, a great deal of land along the Smith is posted and access is difficult. Some few anglers float the river while others obtain permission to fish from some of the ranchers. Two- and 3-pound browns and rainbows make the fishing and it is not too exceptional to come up with a 5-pounder.

Visiting anglers will find accommodation and services at White Sulphur Springs, or further away, at Helena. Local tackle stores will supply detailed fishing information.

The NORTH FORK OF THE SUN RIVER (35), lying just northwest of Helena, in the Lewis and Clark National Forest, provides some very fine rainbow-trout fishing. The fish average about 1 pound, with a goodly dividend of 2- and 3-pounders. The fishing is best suited to the fly and very little spinning or bait fishing is done. Best flies are the Red Variant, Blue Dun, Light Cahill, Ginger Quill and the Iron Blue Dun, in sizes 14 and 16. A size 12 dry of any of the standard Montana flies will also take its share of fish.

The best part of the river lies north of the Gibson Dam and is only accessible by jeep or pack trip to Klick's Dude Ranch. The nearest town is Augusta, which offers good accommodation.

Lower down the Sun, in the Gibson Dam and in the big water below, there are some rainbows, but the water is often muddy and what fish are taken are usually caught on bait or big spoons.

The FLATHEAD RIVER (36), in the northwestern corner of Montana, near the Canadian border, is made up of three branches, the Middle Fork, the South Fork and the North Fork. The Middle Fork lies north and east of Flathead Lake, forming the southern border of Glacier National Park, while the South Fork is to the south and east of Flathead Lake and pours into the reservoir formed by Hungry Horse Dam. This reservoir, in turn, spills its waters into the North Fork of the Flathead, which is then further swelled by its conjunction with the Middle Fork about twenty miles above Hungry Horse. This North Branch then parallels the western boundary of Glacier National Park right to the Canadian line. The waters of the Flathead are chiefly famous for the fine cutthroat fishing they provide, but Dolly Vardens are also taken. Where the river runs within the boundaries of Glacier National Park, special fishing regulations apply.

Spring creeks in Montana are gentle, quiet streams set against a background of magnificent mountains. Here the author casts a fly in Paradise Valley, the valley of the Yellowstone River.

The Middle Fork is readily reached from U.S. Highway 2, between West Glacier and East Glacier, but access to the South Fork is only by pack horse and consequently provides some wonderful wilderness fishing, with cutthroat to 2 pounds rising to almost every cast. Like most of the Flathead waters, it offers ideal dry-fly fishing. When you are trying especially for Dolly Vardens, deep-swimming flies or spoons are more successful.

The South Fork lies within grizzly country and anglers should go in only with competent outfitters. These are located at Ronan and Polson on U.S. 93 from Missoula to Flathead Lake, or at Swan Lake, Big Fork, Seeley and Creston, on U.S. 326.

The SWAN RIVER (37) parallels the course of the South Fork of the Flathead, just to the west, lying between it and Flathead Lake. The Swan has long been recognized as a fine rainbow and cutthroat river and is particularly noted for a run of brilliant, crimson-sided cutthroats in the fall. The average fish will run 1 pound, the largest 4, and the rainbows are about the same weight.

This is a fairly narrow river with much brush and crystal-clear, sparkling cold water, and requires careful fishing. Flies of the standard Montana patterns are more successful than spinning lures or bait, except in some of the deeper pools.

Access is by U.S. 326, which runs north from U.S. Highway 20, about forty miles east of Missoula. There are some accommodations available at Seeley Lake, Swan Lake, Lairds and Creston, and there are a number of good camping spots as well as established camp sites.

Several smaller streams in the area also furnish some fishing, and Swan Lake, into which the Swan River empties, holds both rainbow and cutthroat trout.

The KOOTENAI RIVER (38) makes a big loop through the extreme northwest corner of Montana. It is paralleled by U.S. 37 throughout most of its length, providing easy access for fishermen. This river offers good fishing for rainbows and cutthroats which run up to 2 pounds. It is particularly good fly water, with all the standard dries paying off, but spinners take their share with small spoons, and bait fishermen are most successful with grasshoppers.

The town of Libby has some motels, restaurants and a service station, while Warland, Tweed and Rexford offer minor services.

The THOMPSON RIVER (39), just south of the Kootenai, is accessible via secondary road from Thompson Falls; or via pack or foot trail in its northern limits, from U.S. Highway 2 about fifty miles west of Kalispell. The Thompson holds the same fish as the Kootenai.

YELLOWSTONE PARK

While Yellowstone Park is almost entirely within the State of Wyoming and the fishing is described in the chapter dealing with that state, the main northern entrance is at Gardiner, Montana, on U.S. 89. Here you can find numerous motels, and there is an excellent tackle shop, Parks Fly Shop, where arrangements can also be made for float trips on the Yellowstone and guided fishing trips within the Park.

Further to the east U.S. 212 comes down through Montana from Billings, loops into Wyoming briefly, then back out to Cook City, Montana, and then back into the Park and crosses the northern sector. This is wild and scenic country and there is some excellent fishing in the high lakes both within and outside the Park's borders. Arrangements for pack and jeep trips can be made through Gene Wade, Hiland Guide Service, Cooke City, Montana.

GLACIER NATIONAL PARK

Glacier National Park is more renowned for its beauty than for its fishing, but nevertheless there is plenty of excellent fishing within reach of the highway anywhere in the park, and pack or hiking trips can be arranged to less frequently fished lakes far from the beaten path. Some of the better known lakes are Two Medicine, Swiftcurrent, Josephine, Grinnell, Cracker, Gunsight, Red Eagle, St. Mary, Bowman, Kinta, Elizabeth, Glenns and McDonald. Nearly all have the beautiful native cutthroat trout, and many also have rainbows and/or lake trout. The Cutbank River and the Belly River are also good cutthroat producers, while the Flathead River, the Middle Fork of which forms much of the western boundary of the park, is famous for its husky cutthroats and Dolly Vardens.

Because of the high altitude and consequently heavy snow runoff, the fishing is not usually good until fairly late in the season, which, however, opens in May and closes in mid-October. No license is required to fish in Glacier National Park, but there is a limit on the fish that may be kept. The daily catch must not exceed 15 pounds of fish or a total of ten fish. Possession of more than one day's limit is prohibited.

Most of the fishing is by fly, and the use of live bait or multiple spinning lures is outlawed. The favorite flies are the standard Montana variety listed earlier, and the casual angler may purchase these as well as rent complete equipment at Glacier Park Lodge, Lake McDonald Hotel, Many Glacier Hotel, Two Medicine Lake, and also at Rising Sun and Swiftcurrent campgrounds.

MONTANA FISHING REGULATIONS

Resident Fishing License $3.00
Nonresident Fishing License $10.00
Nonresident 5-Day Fishing License $3.00

SEASONS AND LIMITS

Most rivers are open from May 24 to November 30, some are open all year. Check for special annual exceptions when you purchase your license. Fishing hours are 5 a.m. to 10 p.m. Mountain Standard Time, in all waters unless otherwise specified.

No person shall take or possess more than the daily bag limit of fish unless otherwise specified. Generally, for trout, the limit is 10 fish not to exceed 10 pounds and 1 fish.

For complete regulations write: Department of Fish and Game, Helena, Montana.

Pacific
Coast
States

The three states bordering on the Pacific Ocean, Washington, Oregon and California, share the benefits of both mountains and sea to produce a widely varied sport fishery. Still more variety is added through the great distance covered latitudinally, from the cool climate of the Canadian border to the desert along the Mexican border on the south.

The Rocky Mountains extend the entire length of the Pacific coastal states, widening and narrowing here and there. Watersheds are provided not only to the Pacific but in many cases to the interior and, because of the form of the mountains, occasionally to the north and south. On the eastern slopes there are some arid regions, and the Great Basin of southeastern California, which includes Death Valley, can truly be termed desert. Yet close by there is interest for fishermen in the high mountain country and in the drainage basin of the great Colorado River, which empties into the Gulf of California just south of the U.S.-Mexico border.

The species of fish the visitor will find on the Pacific coast are as varied as the topography and climate. Rainbow, brown and cutthroat trout are found in most mountain areas and in some of the cooler waters of the lower altitudes. In the alpine lakes of California there are California golden trout, native only to this area; and in yet others there are Lahontan trout, now almost extinct, but still found in a few waters.

Most of the sporting warm-water species have been introduced to the man-made lakes and some natural lakes and lagoons

435

throughout Washington, Oregon and California, so that now there is excellent fishing for largemouth black bass, walleye, crappie, bluegill and catfish, as well as limited opportunity to take smallmouth black bass.

The most striking feature of Pacific coast fishing is the seasonal runs of certain fish from the salt into the freshwater streams to spawn. The Pacific salmon is the major one of these fish. There are two species, the king salmon, also called Chinook, and the smaller Coho, also called silver salmon. Dog salmon, humpback and sockeye are other salmon also found in the Pacific coast area but they are not important as sport fish. Yet another salmon, the kokanee, is believed by many persons to be a stunted sockeye that never leaves fresh water and seldom reaches more than a pound in weight. These fish provide some sport in coastal lakes where they have been stocked.

Some rainbow and cutthroat trout of the Pacific coast states also run out of the coastal rivers into the salt to feed, then return to the rivers to spawn. These seasonal runs provide some fantastic fishing, particularly in the case of the rainbow, the famous "steelhead" of the Pacific coast. Angling for these, as well as the salmons, is not confined to the immediate coastal area. These adventurers often run up to the headwaters of the stream of their choice and branch off into tributaries. They can be taken in rivers and creeks far in the interior of Washington, Oregon and California.

Besides the river fishing, anglers go for them in the ocean, adding to the salty sport already provided there by many sea species. These latter range from the giant swordfish and marlin of the Southern California coast to sea perch and small species which can be taken on hook and line from rocky promontories or sandy beaches all along the Pacific shores.

As if these waters were not already well supplied, two anadromous fish which were not native to the Pacific have been added. These are the striped bass and the shad, planted in the 1800's. Today they are found in great numbers, from central California northward, and provide some of the greatest sport fishing to be found along the Pacific coast.

CALIFORNIA

The State of California offers fishing for almost every game fish known in the United States. With 1,200 miles of coast along the Pacific, there is a variety of oceanic fishing for such species as yellowtail, albacore, marlin, black sea bass, white sea bass, barracuda, surfperch, kelp bass, sculpin and Pacific mackerel. Into the northern rivers run the anadromous Pacific salmons, the Chinook, or king, and the silver, and these are augmented by striped bass and shad transplanted from the Atlantic seaboard. These two species thrive in California waters from San Francisco north, and together with the salmons provide offshore fishing as well as great sport in rivers during their seasonal spawning runs.

Providing watersheds to produce habitat for many species of freshwater fish, several great mountain ranges run north-south through California: the Coastal Range on the west; the Cascades and Sierra Nevada in the interior; and the Santa Inez Mountains in the south just above the Mexican border. In the many lakes and streams of these mountains and foothills are found, according to location, rainbow, brown, brook, lake and California golden trout; and in warmer waters at lower elevations there are largemouth bass, a few smallmouth bass, walleye, sturgeon, bluegill, catfish, crappie, perch and carp. There are also Rocky Mountain whitefish in some lakes and streams.

In spite of the formidable barriers of the two mountain ranges, there are many excellent highways providing access from the eastern states. U.S. 299 crosses the entire state in the north, from the Oregon border to Arcata, near Eureka, on the coast. U.S. 40 (Interstate 80) comes in from Reno in the central part of California, offering approaches to several north-south highways through the middle of the state as well as to the San Francisco area on the coast. Further south, Interstate Highway 15 leads from Las Vegas into the complex of routes to the Los Angeles area; as do U.S. 40 from Kingman and U.S. 10 from Phoenix, Arizona. In the extreme south, U.S. 8 comes out of Yuma, Arizona, and skirts the Mexican border across the state to U.S. 80 leading to San Diego.

The major north-south highways are U.S. 101, skirting the coast from the Oregon border to Mexico; Interstate 5 and U.S. 99, which follow the same course, but inside the Coastal Range, from Oregon as far south as Los Angeles; and U.S. 395, which runs down the eastern side of the Sierras, cutting into Nevada at Reno, then back to head southwest for San Bernardino and thence south to San Diego. From these main highways almost any part of California can be reached by feeder roads.

Because of the complex topography of California, as well as its variety of climate from north to south, fishermen must judge their clothing requirements according to the fishing they will be doing. For instance, when steelheading, or fishing for salmon in the coastal rivers, it can be very cold and wet; while in the High Sierras, days will be bright and hot but nights can be very cool. A lot of the good fishing is in areas where such conditions prevail, so the fisherman must go prepared.

Tackle requirements also depend on the type of fishing. Deep-sea tackle can range from the giant outfits used for tuna to the light trolling outfits preferred for smaller fish by many sports fishermen. Freshwater tackle varies from the light 7-foot Rocky Mountain fly rod for small Sierra streams, to the big spinning rods and 9½-foot fly rods and plug-casting outfits generally used for warmer-water species in the numerous man-made lakes and the sloughs in the lower reaches of rivers. This tackle is also being used increasingly by those who like to cast for stripers in the bays, inlets and sloughs of those rivers into which these fish run. Flies, baits and lures vary as widely and will be dealt with individually with the fish concerned.

According to locale, the angler may encounter deer, both mule and whitetail, elk, black bear and cougar. In the high mountains he must watch for grizzly in certain areas; and if he's lucky the coastal fisherman may see seal. In many parts of California there are rattlesnakes. Anglers should keep alert, not crowd a bear or any other wild animal, and at all times walk carefully and keep a sharp eye for snakes.

OCEAN FISHING IN CALIFORNIA

Your choice of how you will go for the saltwater species found along the California coast is varied. Surf casters take surfperch regularly off the northern beaches, and striped bass during the seasonal runs, from San Francisco northward. On the more southern beaches they catch surfperch, spotfin, corbina and yellowfin croakers. Others use surf-casting gear to fish from the rocks of the many rugged promontories, to take cabezon, kelp bass, rockfish, opaleye and bottom swimmers such as flounder. In many places piers have been constructed for fishing, the main ones being located at Crescent City, Arcata, Eureka, Trinidad, Princeton, Santa Cruz, Capitola, Aptos, Monterey (3), Cayucos, Avila (2), Pismo, Gaviota, Goleta, Santa Barbara, Ventura, Paradise Cove, Malibu, Santa Monica, Ocean Park Manhattan Beach, Hermosa Beach, Redondo Beach, Belmont Shore, Seal Beach, Huntington Beach, Newport Beach, Balboa, Capistrano Beach, San Clemente, Oceanside, Del Mar, Pacific Beach, Ocean Beach and Avalon. A license is not required to fish from a public pier.

In the more northern California waters, pier fishermen may expect to catch surfperch, jacksmelt, kingfish and rockfish. Further south you may take halibut, queenfish, corbina, spotfin or yellowfin croaker, surfperch, smelt and kingfish.

Surf and rock fishermen use line testing anywhere from 8 to 45 pound on spinning or surf-casting reels which hold 250 yards of line. The rods run from 6 to 12 feet in length. Among bait fishermen, the "California Special" sinker in common use is a small tobacco sack filled with sand. This sinker does not snag the way a metal one will when moved by the current among the rocks. Favorite natural baits are shrimp, abalone chunks and squid. Artificial lures of all kinds are also used.

Big-game fishing is popular in the San Diego area where there is some outstanding trolling for marlin and swordfish out of Coronado Islands and Mission Bay, from April through October. In addition to the billfish, anglers take yellowfin, bluefin tuna, albacore, white seabass, bonito, barracuda, and lesser species.

Current records of the International Game Fish Association show that three records are held by marlin taken from California ports. These are a 692-pound striped marlin taken out of Balboa by A. Hamann, in the 80-pound line test class in 1931; the same fish holds the 30-pound line test class; and a 332-pound striped marlin holds the top place in the 50-pound line test class. It was taken by Ruth DeLamar, fishing out of Catalina in 1961.

A record swordfish has also been taken in California waters. This was a 365-pounder taken out of Catalina by J. W. Jump, in 1928, and it still is the top fish in the 30-pound line test class.

Charter boats for this kind of fishing run from $75 to $125 per day, which includes tackle and bait. Of course, many marlin fishermen are old hands at the game and prefer to bring their own tackle.

Other types of sea fishing are considerably cheaper, the cost of going out on a party boat ranging from $5 to $10 per person. Both party boats and individual charter boats may be found at almost every seaside town or village; but the main fishing fleets are at San Diego, Oceanside, San Clemente, Balboa, Huntington Beach, Newport, Long Beach, San Pedro (the latter three fishing the Santa Catalina Island area), Seal Beach, Wilmington, all the towns on Santa Monica Bay, Port Hueneme (boats fish Santa Cruz and Snacapa Islands), Santa Barbara, Avila, Morro Bay, Cayucos-San Simeon, Monterey, Moss Landing, Santa Cruz and Capitola, Princeton, San Francisco, Berkeley, Oakland, Richmond (boats go to the Farallon Islands), Sausalito, San Rafael, Bodega Bay, Noyo, Eureka, Trinidad, Crescent City.

The species of fish caught are barracuda, yellowtail, albacore, bluefin tuna, bonito, kelp bass, mackerel, rockfish, black sea bass, white sea bass and, as previously described, swordfish, marlin and bluefin tuna in the Santa Catalina and San Clemente Islands.

Of eleven world records for black sea bass listed on the charts of the International Game Fish Association, ten were taken in California, the hot spots being the Coronado Islands, San Clemente and Catalina. The All Tackle Record, a fish weighing 557 pounds 3 ounces, was taken at Catalina Island in July, 1962, by Richard M. Lane. Many others in the 400- to 500-pound class have been taken. Several record white sea bass have also been taken in California waters.

Many large albacore are taken off the California coast, especially in the San Diego and Santa Catalina Island areas. Back in the 1920's, this species was occasionally taken up to 50 pounds and better; a good fish these days will be between 30 and 40. For instance, the two most recent International Game Fish Records for this fish are a 28-pound 12-ounce fish taken in July, 1961, by Pearl E. Dudley, which tops the 12-pound line test records; and a 39-pound 2-ounce fish caught August 15th, 1962, by Karen Ann Batemen, which leads the 20-pound line test class. The all-time heavyweight of the species in California waters weighed 66 pounds 4 ounces, and was taken on 30-pound-test line in 1912 by P. Kelly. It was within 3 pounds of the all-tackle world record.

Varying with the species and the latitude, the ocean fishing season extends roughly from March to mid-November; the best months, over-all, being April to October.

Along the south coast, from Santa Monica south to San Diego, almost every port has party boats which fish all year. The spring months are best for yellowtail and the San Diego area the best location. About forty-five miles off shore, Catalina and San Clemente Islands have occasional schools of bluefin tuna. About July 1st schools of albacore also appear and when these move inshore they provide terrific sport for both charter-boat and skiff fishermen. Mostly they are fished by chumming and using anchovies and sardines for bait. The fish soon become smart and won't hit a line heavier than 15-pound test. Much of this fishing can be done without a guide, and any of the sporting goods stores in port can give you the lowdown on what is the best location at any given moment.

Northward from Monterey, the salmons start to show, and only a few miles beyond that, the striped bass and shad are added to the list. Striped bass were introduced into California coastal waters in 1879, took hold phenomenally and have developed to the point of providing an outstanding sport fishery. The State of California has been extremely progressive in handling the species, placing it on the sport fish list in 1935 and outlawing netting. About fifty charter boats cater almost exclusively to striped-bass fishermen in the "Delta" area of San Francisco Bay, during the season. Boats may be chartered for $65 while party boats are much lower, about $5 to $10 per person.

The striper may be fished year-round throughout its West Coast range, but the measure of an angler's success depends on where and when he fishes. Stripers feed in the salt during the summer and migrate into fresh water and the salty shallows to spawn either in the fall, to hold over till spring, or in the spring, when they move in to spawn during April, May and June. The peak of the season is July, August, September and October. Fishing starts to get good in late August in the San Francisco Bay, San Pablo Bay, Carquinez Strait and Napa River. Occasionally the peak is reached much later—inland at Port Chicago it is November—but in general fishing is not good during the winter months, as the bass feed very little in cold water. However, it is known that many stripers winter in the Delta area and there is considerable fishing for them there in winter, using bait and a sliding sinker which can be adjusted to be sure the bait gets down to the bottom where the fish are lying. Action usually picks up again in March, when the fish really get on the move and are taken by anglers as far up the Sacramento and Feather Rivers as Marysville and Colusa. Once they start to spawn, however, they do not feed. In June they go back to the salt and few are taken in fresh water.

Increasingly, light-tackle anglers are taking stripers by fly fishing and spinning. Larry Green, writer for the outdoor magazines, has had wonderful fly-rod fishing in San Francisco Bay, taking stripers on streamers, bucktails and popping bugs. His biggest striper on a fly was a 15½-pounder taken on a fly-rod popper I sent him— a bug which has taken many on the East Coast and a 29-pound 6-ounce fish I took at Coos Bay, Oregon, in September, 1948. This is believed to be the biggest striper ever taken on fly.

Striped bass are also taken from the beaches, 1958 having been a banner year. Beach fishermen used to use sardines for bait, but increasingly spin casters are adopting artificials.

In the deep water around Alcatraz Island, at Raccoon Strait, anglers troll for stripers, using jigs, spoons or white bucktails with very heavy weights, and some big fish have been taken. With striped bass, the lighter the tackle used, the greater the sport; but whenever the fish is found in deep water it is usually necessary to go down to him, with weight, and this cancels out the light tackle. Frequently, as at Raccoon, only a very heavy weight will go down through the current that flows through the Straits.

Sardines, either fresh or frozen, are the favorites with bait fishermen. Many use two sardines on 4/0 to 7/0 hooks, two on each leader, with 2 to 6 ounces of lead to get the baits down. One point which should be observed by bait fishermen is the size of the hook. In order to avoid catching undersized fish, the hook should be at

Surf fishermen cast for stripers in the shadow of the Golden Gate.

least an inch across between shank and point—this prevents the smaller fish from swallowing the hook and being hurt.

The legal size limit of a striped bass which may be taken in California is 16 inches, this length being stipulated because the fish do not spawn until they are 20 to 24 inches in length, and the effort is made to prevent the loss of too many brood fish.

The Department of Fish and Game, 722 Capitol Building, Sacramento 14, California, issues an excellent "Striped Bass Fishing Map" for the San Francisco Bay and Delta areas, which is invaluable to the newcomer to these waters. Boat-launching spots and harbors where charters can be obtained are shown, and complete information is supplied on all phases of striper fishing.

Shad were introduced into California waters in 1871. Like the striped bass, they are anadromous. They begin their annual spawning run in April and continue on through July. The best runs are in the Sacramento, the Russian, the American and the Feather Rivers. In the summer months it is possible to get in on some fine fly fishing for shad in the lower American, Yuba and Feather Rivers.

In the lower reaches of the rivers "shad bumping" is legal—this is hand netting, the name coming from the peculiar bump the fisherman feels as a shad hits the net which is held below the boat.

SALMON AND SEA-RUN TROUT

There are two salmon and two sea-run trout in California coastal waters. The king salmon, called Chinook, has black spots on its back and on both lobes of the tail. The inside of the mouth is dark. The silver salmon, also called Coho, has spots only on the back and the upper lobe of the tail. Its gums are white, the balance of the mouth dark.

The king salmon is found in the ocean all along the California coast from Monterey northward. It migrates only into the larger streams from San Francisco north. But from these large streams it will make runs into some remarkably small ones. King salmon have been known to reach 100 pounds. Fifty-pounders are occasionally taken by anglers, but the average weight is about 20 pounds except in the Klamath River, where they run smaller. Those taken in the ocean are generally smaller than those taken in the rivers, because of the fact that the river fish are spawners.

In the ocean kings sometimes stay close to the river where they were spawned, and move into it again when their spawning time comes. Yet king salmon do make long forays both off and along shore, and fish from the Sacramento area have been taken in northern California. Nevertheless, when spawning time comes, they almost inevitably return to the parent river, to spawn and die.

Some fish start into the rivers early in the spring, the date varying with the runoff of snow water, but usually in May in the Sacramento area. The big run is in the fall, again the date varying with weather conditions, for the fish wait for the water to cool. If a river is too warm all summer to hold fish, that river will not have a spring run at all; the fish will wait till fall. This is the case, for example, in the Tuolumne and Stanislaus Rivers.

The silver salmon is smaller, averaging 7 to 12 pounds. Although there is a record of a 30-pounder, fish of even half that size are rare indeed. The silver swims the ocean all the way from the Mexican line northward, but in fresh water is taken only in those rivers above Monterey. This species prefers slightly smaller streams than does the king salmon, but the two are often found in the same waters. All young silvers stay in the river a full month before going to sea, and once in the sea they do not travel as far from the home river as do the kings.

The silver salmon does not make a spring run, coming into the rivers only in the fall, waiting for the rain to swell the rivers enough to provide them with the water and the temperature they require. Generally, the runs are during the period from October to January. They do not go into the San Francisco Bay area.

Ocean fishing for salmon is limited by the distance from port of the fishing grounds and the roughness of the sea, and thus is done mostly on charter boats or party boats, with experienced skippers. But there are some areas where skiff fishing is possible, for anglers who are also good boatmen.

During the summer, party boats operate out of Crescent City, up near the mouth of the Smith River, near the Oregon line. Just outside the harbor there is good skiff trolling for kings and silvers. Further south, Trinidad Head offers protection for small-boat fishermen. There are party boats as well as a skiff rental agency at Trinidad, and also boat-launching sites. The peak of the season comes in July and August and both salmons are frequently plentiful close inshore.

Launching sites, rental agencies and charter boats are also available at Buhne Point at the entrance to Humboldt Bay immediately south of Eureka, and the summer months can bring some outstanding fishing there. But the tide can be very treacherous and the harbor entrance should be fished only on an incoming tide. On the outgoing, breakers form in the channel, creating real danger for small boats. And if you're caught outside the harbor on an outgoing tide, you may find rough seas building up very quickly. Another danger spot for strangers is at Nick's Cove, near Inverness. The outgoing tide makes the bay very dangerous.

Again to the south, anglers may reach Shelter Cove to launch their own skiffs by traversing a narrow, rough road from Redway on U.S. 101. Moving on down the coast, spots which provide skiff launching, rentals, and party-boat services are Noyo Harbor, at Fort Bragg, Bodega Bay, where there is a good launching site in Doran Park on the east side of the harbor entrance. At Fort Bragg trolling is usually done quite close inshore with bait or spoon. At Bodega most anglers troll very deep with a 2-pound weight. They often pick up good catches of rockfish as well as the salmon they are after.

Next we come to San Francisco Bay, probably the steadiest producing waters along the whole coast. Fishing is mostly done from charter boats or party boats operating out of Fisherman's Wharf, Sausalito Yacht Harbor, and Gas House Cove in San Francisco, the Berkley Yacht Harbor, and various smaller docks. Boats are heavily booked here during the season, particularly on weekends, and early reservations should be made. This can be done through all the local bait and tackle shops.

The approved method of fishing is to troll with bait or artificial lure plus a heavy sinker, from 1 to 3 pounds. When a fish strikes, a sinker release lets go of the weight and the angler can then play the fish with some sport. It is advisable to rent a glass or steel rod from the skipper, rather than use your own good bamboo, if you have one, because the heavy weight will soon wreck it.

Party boats are also available at Princeton, Santa Cruz, Capitola, Moss Landing, Monterey, Morro Bay and Avila, but as far as salmon are concerned, the fishing this far south is sporadic. The exception would be in the spring, when there is occasional fair salmon fishing.

For a very comprehensive folder and map entitled "Salmon and Steelhead Fishing," write the California Department of Fish and Game, 722 Capitol Avenue, Sacramento 14, California.

STEELHEAD, CUTTHROAT, SALMON

Famous everywhere that fishermen gather is the steelhead trout, a rainbow that goes to sea and returns to the freshwater streams to spawn. This fish is seldom taken at sea but is found in almost every suitable river along the coast from Northern California on up. The steelhead will usually weigh from 2 to 10 pounds, and uses much smaller streams than does the salmon. In the sea they are silver in color but once back in the fresh water they regain the red stripe of the rainbow and are readily identifiable.

The run of spawning fish into the rivers usually takes place in the winter and spring, although in some few of the larger rivers, such as the Sacramento, the Eel and the Klamath, they are often working in throughout the year. Unlike Pacific salmon, steelhead do not die after spawning.

The cutthroat trout also performs a spawning migration into the rivers of the Pacific. Found in California from the Eel River northward, this species is readily identifiable from the steelhead by the bright red slash under each side of the jaw. Few of them grow to more than 4 pounds, and they are inclined to stay closer to the salt for their spawning than are the steelhead. These sea-going members of the family put up a very hard fight, and most anglers prefer them to the resident cut-throat. They are also called bluebacks and harvest trout.

The best cutthroat fishing usually occurs after the first heavy rains of the fall and fishing continues through the winter, and, in some rivers, such as the Smith and Klamath, as late as April. As well as those just mentioned, the Redwood Creek and the Mad River are excellent cutthroat streams.

In recent years this species has been planted in some lakes and lagoons along the coast with excellent results. In March of 1963 cutthroat up to 10 pounds were being taken in Freshwater Lagoon near Arcata on Muddler Minnow flies. Consistent catches of fish up to 6 pounds were being made. Nearby Big Lagoon also has fishing for steelhead.

Starting from the north, some of the best rivers are as follows:

The SMITH RIVER (1), whose North Fork parallels U.S. 199, offers good fly fishing for steelhead in December and January. There are sea-run cutthroat from March to May; and silvers come in in October and are taken all winter. King salmon are taken at the mouth of the river by trolling in late September and October.

Just to the south, the KLAMATH RIVER (2) gets the earliest steelhead run in the state, sometimes in late July, nearly always in early August, and the fishing picks up from then on. The Klamath is famous for its "half pounders," as the early fish are called. This is a misnomer, as the steelhead run up to 2 pounds. King salmon also come into the Klamath, and there's excellent fishing for them at the mouth and in the lagoon in August and September. In the lower waters the fishing is by trolling spoons and spinners, and salmon eggs are also used. About three miles upstream better light-tackle water starts, and all the standard fly patterns, in large sizes, will take fish.

You can get boats and guides to fish the lower part of the river at Klamath, but it calls for a roundabout trip to reach the upper part. Take U.S. 101 to Arcata, then go to Willow Creek on Highway 299, then north on the Hoopa Valley Indian Reservation road to the junction of the Klamath and the Trinity. There is excellent fly fishing in the riffles from there downstream, known as the Johnson District. In the upper part of the Klamath, fishermen must be very very careful when wading because of the violent fluctuations of the water level, resulting from changes at the Copco Dam.

There are resorts and cabins at Klamath and some accommodations at Weitchpec, but in general this is camping country. You can get fishing directions at the small town of Orleans where there are two hotels, several stores and, in the neighborhood, about fifteen miles of fishing.

The TRINITY RIVER (3), a tributary of the Klamath, has a spring run of king salmon and in summer they can be taken as far up as Lewistown, west of Redding. There are a few silver salmon. During the summer there are also a few steelhead, but the bulk of the run comes after the first autumn rains, and fishing is good all winter. In the fall there is sometimes some excellent fly fishing in the upper Trinity as long as it stays clear.

REDWOOD CREEK (4), again to the south, has good fishing for sea-run cutthroat in its lagoon, in fall and winter, and sometimes into early spring. Steelhead, silvers and kings also come in in the fall.

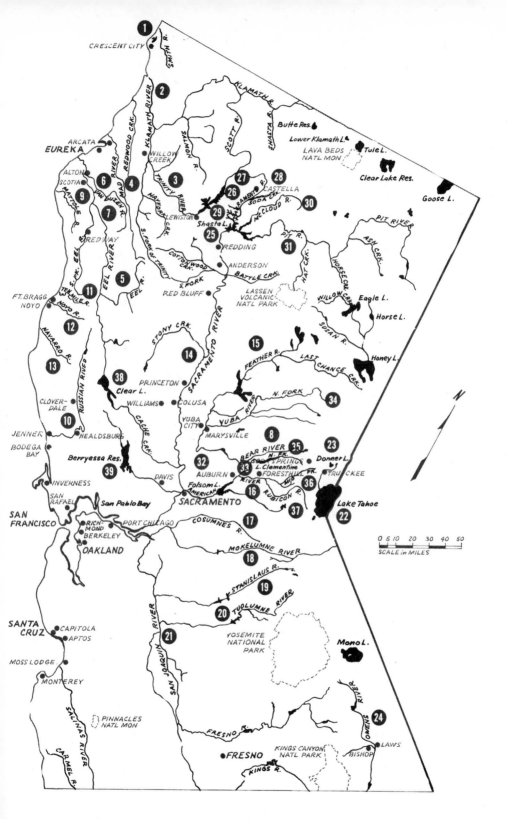

CALIFORNIA

The EEL RIVER (5) is one of the best West Coast rivers for large steelhead. It is also one of the most attractive from the fly fisherman's point of view, and you can reach a great deal of it from the highway, as much of it parallels U.S. 101. The best fly fishing is from Scotia down to just above the mouth of the river, and the steelhead are in there winter-long. In tidewater, trollers go for king salmon in late August and on through the winter, and the same species can be taken further upstream throughout the winter. Anglers who wade the tidal pools must watch for water fluctuations due to the tide.

The MAD RIVER (6), the VAN DUZEN (7), the BEAR (8) and the MATTOLE (9) offer the same kind of fishing, the runs usually starting after the first fall rains. To reach the Mattole, which can be very good, go to Alton, where a road turns east and crosses both the upper part of the Mad River and the Van Duzen.

The RUSSIAN RIVER (10), emptying into the Pacific at Jenner near Bodega Bay, has fall and winter runs of steelhead and silver salmon, the best fishing being on the lower forty miles. When you get low water during the winter there is good fly fishing in that stretch from Cloverdale to Healdsburg, right along U.S. 101. Below Healdsburg there are several resorts, with access to a lot of good fishing.

Several other smaller streams, such as the TEN MILE (11), the NOYO (12) and the NAVARRO (13) also have fall and winter runs of silver salmon and steelhead, and a few kings.

Within range of the San Francisco Bay area, the SACRAMENTO RIVER (14) has good runs of king salmon, both spring and fall, and steelhead the year-round. Some of the best fishing for steelhead is in midwinter, far upstream, near Redding and Red Bluff and Anderson, below the Shasta Dam. There are also some big kings up here, spring and fall. Salmon are mostly taken on big spoons, the steelheads on salmon-egg clusters.

The Sacramento's many tributaries also offer much fishing. The FEATHER RIVER (15) is best known for steelhead, but has a few fall-run king salmon, and an even smaller spring run. The AMERICAN RIVER (16) has some steelhead in May and June, and a fall run of king salmon and steelhead starting in October and going through December. The COSUMNES (17) and MOKELUMNE (18) have fall runs of king salmon, too, but water conditions are unreliable.

Two rivers which flow into the San Joaquin River southwest of San Francisco, the STANISLAUS (19) and the TUOLUMNE (20), have late-run king salmon, usually coming into the rivers from October through December. The Tuolumne gets the largest salmon of any river in the San Joaquin system. The SAN JOAQUIN (21) itself plunges through a gorge for most of its length and has little fishable water.

LAKES AND STREAMS IN THE INTERIOR

With its many natural and man-made lakes, and its countless alpine streams, the interior of California offers almost as much variety in its fishing as the coastal area. LAKE TAHOE (22), one of the most spectacular of the lakes, is twenty-two miles long, twelve miles wide, and has seventy-one miles of shoreline, two-thirds of it within California. It lies at an altitude of 6,229 feet, and is spectacularly clear. Originally this lake was the home of a species known as the Lahontan cutthroat trout. They were so plentiful that a commercial fishery was operated on the lake, with foreseeable consequences. The lake was almost completely fished out. In the 1880's there were also "silver trout," which may have been a rainbow or another color phase of the cutthroat, but these also disappeared before the heavy netting. As a result of overharvesting and pollution, damage to spawning beds in tributary streams by lumbering operations, the construction of dams which interfered with fish migrations, plus the planting of non-native species, the fishing fell away to almost nothing and the Lahontan became almost extinct. Since 1949, however, Kokanee salmon, Lahontan trout, Yellowstone cutthroat, Kamloops trout, rainbow and brook trout have been planted, and fishing has improved considerably.

Because of the depth and clarity of the water in Lake Tahoe, "deep lining" is the best method of fishing so that boat and angler are not visible to the fish. Deep lining calls for a stout rod, large-capacity reel, and a long Monel, copper or lead-core line. A large spinner or spoon is used with a 3- to 4-foot leader made of heavy nylon or wire, at the end of which the lure, or a hook baited with a minnow, is attached. This gear is trolled very slowly so the lure or minnow is kept within a foot of the bottom. Since the depth of the lake ranges from 100 to 500 feet, and constant adjustments must be made, it is exacting fishing. Occasionally a rainbow is taken in this way, but usually the catch is Mackinaw trout.

Top lining, on the other hand, entails trolling fairly close to shore, where there is gravel or rocks, and using conventional spinning or plug-casting gear with mono-filament line and artificial lures. This method takes rainbows and an occasional brown. During the fall, winter or early spring, it may also produce a Mackinaw.

Otherwise the conventional fishing methods are used—casting bait or lures from the shore, and using flies when the fish are feeding on the surface.

There are plenty of facilities of all kinds around the lake, and boats may be rented almost everywhere. There are public boat landings at Lake Tahoe and at Cave Rock on the Nevada side.

DONNER LAKE (23), near the town of Truckee, is a fairly consistent producer of rainbows and browns from 12 to 18 inches in length, sparked by an occasional 9- or 10-pound fish. Mackinaw from 10 to 20 pounds are caught fairly regularly. Donner is the only lake in the area which is open in April and is very good early in the season. There are a number of resorts on the lake, and it is one lake where fishing from the shore is feasible. In addition there are a number of piers.

If you go into Nevada from Lake Tahoe and go south on U.S. 395, you can reach some of the best stream trout fishing on the eastern slopes of the mountains in the OWENS RIVER (24), from below Lake Crowley to Lone Pine. Though heavily fished, it is an excellent producer of browns and is especially attractive to fly fisher-men. Some of it can be floated in rubber rafts. You can go in from Tom's Place, Bishop or Laws. Trout up to 9 pounds have been taken, and there are plenty of 2-pounders.

LAKE SHASTA (25), the largest man-made lake in California, has a variety of year-round fishing. Located almost squarely in the middle of the northern half of the state, Shasta is easily reached by U.S. 299 east and west, and Interstate 5, north and south. Browns average 2½ pounds and are taken up to 12 pounds, and there are also Kamploops trout, rainbows, largemouth black bass, smallmouth black bass and kokanee salmon. Shasta is much used as a recreational lake; there are several recreational areas and plenty of boat rentals and resorts. But because the lake is so big, with 365 miles of shoreline, it can take care of a lot of fishermen. One of the likely spots to pick up a good brownie is on the Sacramento arm of the lake; another is at the Salt Creek Inlet.

On Shasta the fishing is all done from boats as the shores are generally steep.

Since the water is deep, the favorite lures are deep-running plugs, although poppers sometimes pay off for largemouth. For the smallmouth, anglers troll large white flies or occasionally have good luck with poppers. Trout are seldom taken on flies, as they are in deep water and come best to the small wobbler-type spoons.

In the Sacramento River above the lake there is some very good fly fishing in the canyon, with a variety of water suitable for spinning or bait fishing as well. Lower down, near Castella, the Fish and Game Department makes very heavy plantings of fish. Quite a few of these fish are holdovers, with the result that you may get a good one every now and again. Like most big fish, especially brown trout, they are hard to take.

Tributaries of the Sacramento which also produce some good fly fishing are FLUME CREEK (26), CASTLE CREEK (27), SODA CREEK (28) and SHOTGUN CREEK (29). The McCLOUD RIVER (30) and the PIT RIVER (31), to the east of Shasta, can produce some excellent rainbow fishing, but a great deal of the water is private.

Moving west from Lake Tahoe towards Sacramento, the fisherman will find a complex of lakes and streams. FOLSOM LAKE (32), a man-made lake on the American River, produces rainbows to 5 pounds, largemouth black bass to 4. It is open year-round and is regarded as one of the best warm-water lakes in California. There are many boat-launching ramps. The lake can readily be reached from U.S. 50 and 40.

LAKE CLEMENTINE (33), accessible by narrow road from U.S. 49 east of Auburn, offers trout and bass fishing. In the same area the BEAR RIVER (8) is good, and the NORTH FORK OF THE YUBA (34) is fair. The approach road from Soda Springs is seldom passable until the end of the first week in July.

The town of Foresthill is a good center from which to make forays into the North Fork Canyon and the Middle Fork Canyon. The going is rough but there is good water for fly fishermen in the NORTH FORK (35) and MIDDLE FORK (36) of the AMERICAN RIVER and in the RUBICON RIVER (37) French Meadows on the Middle Fork has a good camping area from which to fish the more inaccessible lakes and streams in the peaks. Some of the most spectacular places to fish are the Upper and Lower Hell Holes of the Rubicon, and the Royal Gorge on the North Fork of the American. Late in the season you can pick up trout from 20 to 30 inches.

California waters have been uniquely receptive to introduced species of fish. Just as the striped bass and shad took so well to the coastal waters, so the basses and breams now thrive in many waters which did not have natural populations of the species. Largemouth black bass are found in many of the lakes and reservoirs as well as in some sloughs and rivers at lower altitudes. CLEAR LAKE (38), on State Highway 20 west of Yuba City and Williams, is an outstanding example. Lucky Lloyd, who lives at Lower Lake, at the south end of Clear Lake, has made some fantastic catches there. He took 14 largemouth that totaled 76 pounds in one day. One hundred a day is regular fare. Lucky, who has fished there for forty-five years, says he seldom takes anything under 3½ pounds. The best fishing is from 4 P.M. till midnight. At night Clear Lake anglers also fish for crappies by shining a spotlight on the water. This brings the crappies to the surface and nearly every cast gets a strike. The fish weigh up to 3 pounds. This is nearly all fly-rod popper fishing.

Smallmouth black bass have also been stocked, mostly in colder waters, and are doing very well in the BERRYESSA RESERVOIR (39), and parts of the Colorado

River, in the Merced, American, Consumnes and Feather Rivers. Sunfish are found in the lowland lakes, reservoirs, ponds and sloughs.

Lying south of U.S. 10, just north of the Mexican border, is one of the great natural phenomena of the continent, the Salton Sea. In this lake, which is 235 feet below sea level, you can fish for saltwater species inland, for the corvina has been stocked here. Specimens up to 25 pounds are taken, and there are also sargo, a species similar to perch. These run to about 2 pounds and are excellent on the table.

U.S. 99 parallels the west side of the lake from Coachella on Interstate 10, and State Highway 111 runs along the east coast. While there are very few settlements, facilities are available at Desert Shores on the west and Durmid on the east. There is a state park at the north end of the lake with camping facilities.

Also in desert country, Lakes Havasu and Mohave on the Colorado River, where it forms the border between California and Arizona, offer a variety of fishing. In Mohave there is good year-round angling for largemouth black bass. Poppers will take them in the shallows, February through April, when they are spawning. After that the best catches are made on deep-running plugs fished in the deeper water where the current of the river is still felt. Bait fishermen take them on waterdogs and mudsuckers.

For accommodations you must go to the Arizona side, out of Searchlight, or to Nevada, where there are good accommodations at Davis Dam, and boats, camp sites and boat ramps will be found. There is some excellent rainbow fishing at the head of Lake Mohave and in the coves at the northern end of the lake. The same is true of the water just below the Davis Dam. Trout to 17 pounds have been taken here. You can fish from an anchored boat or in some cases from the shore. At Lake Havasu the fishing is much the same except that the water is too warm for trout.

MOUNTAIN LAKES AND STREAMS

The possibilities of high-country trout fishing in California are so great that the fisherman must necessarily make his selection first of the general area in which he wishes to fish, then narrow it down to more specific spots. The rewards in the high country can be wonderful, if not in size of fish, certainly in quantity, and in the scenery. In an effort to direct anglers from the heavily fished, accessible waters to the more remote wilderness areas, the California Department of Fish and Game issues a set of "Anglers' Guides to the High Sierras," with maps and very complete details. They cover the French Canyon and Humphreys Basin and Mono Creek, Fish Creek, Bear Creek, the Huntington-Shaver-Dinkey Lakes Area and the Crown Valley and Blackcap Basin, all in Fresno County, to the northeast of Fresno; the Granite Creek area in Madera County, just to the northwest; the Mineral King Area of Tulare County, east of Tulare; the Trinity Divide, covering Trinity, Siskiyou and Shasta Counties in the Cascades of north-central California; the Trinity Alps in the same area; the Salmon and Scott Mountains in the same general area; and the Marble Mountains in Siskiyou. In planning trips to any of the high country it is well to remember that there will be snow in the peaks until mid-May. Fishing is best from June 1st on.

One species which attracts anglers to the high country of California is the golden trout, discovered some fifty years ago in Volcano Creek, now named Golden Trout Creek, at the headwaters of the South Fork of the Kern River, and in the upper reaches of the Little Kern River. Plantings have now spread the species widely in a number of lakes in the High Sierras, from Alpine County, east of U.S. 395, just inside the Nevada-California border, southward. Since most of the plantings have been made in the high waters these trout like, from 9000 to 13,000 feet, most of these lakes must be reached by pack trip. Those who go to these high lakes usually like to take a 7-foot fly rod, a bullet-tapered line, and very fine leaders. Wet and dry flies, sizes 8 to 12, in patterns such as the Royal Coachman, Red Ant, Gray Hackle with yellow body, Mosquito, Grizzly King, Professor and Black Gnat, are all successful.

Information regarding licenses, regulations and outfitters for packing into the High Sierras should be obtained from the National Park Service, 180 New Montgomery Street, San Francisco, or the U.S. Forest Service, 630 Sansome Street, San Francisco.

Goldens do not grow to any great size, and the sport of catching them is in the unusual nature of the fish, their beauty and rarity. Even so, the average weight will be 1½ pounds, and some few have been taken up to 8 pounds. They have been transplanted from California to a number of high lakes in Montana and Wyoming, but nowhere can you fish for them with the certainty that you can in California.

Also in Alpine County, the angler may be fortunate enough to encounter another species known only to California, the Piute trout, found in the upper drainage of Fish Valley in Alpine County.

COLORADO RIVER

Forming part of the border between California and Arizona, in the extreme southeast, the Colorado River provides its own brand of fishing. Man has changed the character of the river from a stream subject to extreme flood and low water, in which were found only a few species of minnows, to a well-controlled series of reservoirs and channels. Into these have been introduced largemouth black bass, smallmouth black bass, bluegill, sunfish, crappie, catfish and, in a few sections, rainbow trout. The last are stocked in the cooler water of the Needles area below the Davis Dam, just at the point where Nevada, Arizona and California come together. Feeding on the threadfin shad, they put on weight in a hurry, and although extremely heavy fishing in the area keep the numbers down, occasional catches of big fish are made. Some largemouth and smallmouth bass are also found in this part of the river, where the temperature is cooled by subsurface release of water from the dam. There are also channel catfish.

For those who want to explore some unusual bass fishing, there is the Topock Swamp, inaccessible by road, but producing some fine casting possibilities once you get in. You go by boat from Topock to fish this series of sloughs and swamps. In November through January there is also excellent angling for crappie. From that point down to Lake Havesu, mentioned earlier, the river is accessible only by boat and the fishing is pretty well limited to catfish.

From this point on down the river the series of dams produce water conditions favorable to the same kind of fishing—bass, crappie and bluegill in the eddies and sloughs, and catfish the most prevalent species in the river. Probably rating as one of the West's hot spots for catfish is the Colorado below Headgate Rock Dam, where it runs for 100 miles through a wide valley to the Imperial Reservoir. The summer months are the best time.

There is also some exceptional catfishing in the fast water below the Palo Verde Diversion Dam. Like so much of the lower Colorado this area can only be reached by boat. The nearest launching site is at the Sixth Avenue Landing above Blythe, at the Junction of U.S. 95 and Interstate 10.

South to the Mexican border and Yuma, Arizona, the river is paralleled in California by a passable dirt road. At Palo Verde, on this road, there are several fishing camps, and there are several more at Davis and Three Finger Lake.

In the southeastern tip of California, seventeen miles north of Yuma, the Imperial Dam backs the water up into a series of sloughs and overflows which often form lakes to which entrance can be obtained from the river. They produce excellent bass fishing in spring and fall, crappie fishing in late winter and early spring. The catfishing is good throughout the summer.

There are boat landings at Imperial Dam on the Arizona side, and at Martinez Lake, further north on U.S. 95. Both have camping facilities, cafes, provisions, and boat rentals. There are some cabins at Martinez. On the California side of the river, accessible by dirt road, the hamlet of Picacho, north of Winterhaven, has camping facilities and boat rentals. Further south, the only place which provides any facilities whatever is Haughtelin Lake, three miles north of Winterhaven, where boats are available for bass and bluegill fishing.

CALIFORNIA FISHING REGULATIONS

Resident Fishing License $3.00
Nonresident Fishing License $10.00
Special 10-Day Nonresident License $3.00
Special 3-Day Citizen License, Pacific Ocean $1.00
Sport-Fishing License Stamps $1.00
Colorado River Special Use Stamp (for boat fishing only) $2.00
Nevada license is valid for all waters on Lake Tahoe and Lake Topaz.

SEASONS

Trout, Salmon, Mountain Whitefish	
North Coast area	May 29–Oct. 31
Southern California	All year
Rest of state	May 2–Oct. 31
All other fish	All year

Note: There are closed seasons to protect salmon spawning. There are numerous local regulations, and special winter seasons, in designated waters.

For complete regulations write: Department of Fish and Game, 9th and O Streets, Sacramento 95814, California.

OREGON

The topography of the State of Oregon is dominated by two famous ranges of the Rocky Mountains, the Coastal Range and the Cascades. In the central and southwestern part of the state there is a large arid region, which, however, gets some water from the Malheur and Owyhee River systems. The state's entire western border fronts on the Pacific Ocean. The result of this wide variety of terrain, with water everywhere, is an equally wide variety of fishing.

Five species of Pacific salmon come into Oregon coastal waters: the Chinook, silver, sockeye, dog, or chum, and humpback. The Chinook, or king, and the silver, or Coho, are the ones of main interest to the angler. The Chinook is named for the Indians who used to live along the Columbia River, which forms the border between Washington and Oregon. The Columbia used to play host to tremendous numbers of Chinooks on their annual spawning runs. The most commonly taken size today will be from 10 to 45 pounds, but the record for rod and line, taken in the Umpqua River, weighed 83 pounds. In Oregon Chinooks come into almost every river along the Pacific coast. They make two spawning runs, one in the spring and one in the fall. A few are taken in the rivers year-round.

The silver salmon is a smaller fish, averaging about 8 pounds in these waters. The silver makes its spawning run in late summer and early fall. They often spawn quite close to the salt and are frequently taken in brackish water as well as further upstream. The silver also usually prefers the slower, smaller and shallower streams for its spawning.

Not as sporting as either the Chinook salmon or the silver, the sockeye nevertheless provides some good fishing in inland lakes. It is believed that originally this species spawned only in rivers which had their source in a lake. The fish come in from the sea in June or July, making their first run at the age of three to four years. When the young fish hatch they move into the lake and stay there for about a year, then migrate to the ocean. On occasion they become landlocked and are forced to remain in the lake. As the sockeye feeds entirely on plankton, and the supply in a lake is limited compared to the ocean, the result is a stunted fish. In such lakes a sockeye seldom grows to more than a couple of pounds, and is generally called kokanee.

The chum salmon averages about 10 pounds, with a top fish going 20 pounds. This species is more common further north and is taken only occasionally in Oregon waters. The humpback seldom weighs 10 pounds and is more likely to go 3 to 5 pounds. Like the chum, it is rare in Oregon, and even when there is a reluctant lure-taker.

The trouts of Oregon include the rainbow, cutthroat, brown, brook, Dolly Varden, lake and some golden. The rainbow is the most widely distributed, occurring in hundreds of lakes and rivers. Wherever it can find an outlet to the sea it heads out to feed and comes back as the sturdy steelhead. In Oregon, this rainbow which has been to sea is variously called steelhead, redsides, silversides and silver trout. The redsides of the McKenzie and Deschutes Rivers, and the silversides of the Klamath, are widely renowned among Oregonians as especially sporting fish. While the steelhead runs are mainly from November through March, some rivers also have a summer run, usually of smaller fish, so that in some cases the steelhead may be taken year-round.

Next in importance among the Oregon trouts is the cutthroat, the native trout of the West. The main fishing for cutthroat in Oregon is in the Wallowa Mountains, but the species is taken in many other places. When this fish makes a journey to the sea and returns to spawn, it is called blueback or harvest trout, and provides wonderful sport not only in the rivers into which it makes its spawning run but also in brackish-water lagoons along the coast, and in the bays and estuaries. The cutthroat in Oregon runs up to 3 pounds, though a few larger ones are taken each year.

As in so many other places where the species have been stocked, brown, brook and lake trout have done remarkably well in these western waters. Very large browns, up to 8 pounds and better, are taken from the Deschutes River, Paulina Lake and East Lake. The Wickiup Reservoir is a top spot. Being especially suited to cold water, brook trout are found mostly in the lakes of the high country, often are small in size, but occasionally are taken up to 3 pounds. Lake trout have been introduced to a few lakes and some of them, Lake Odell in particular, have produced fish that weighed 15 pounds and better. The Dolly Varden trout, which has been known to reach weights of better than 20 pounds in Oregon waters, is most common in the Minam-Wallowa Mountain area. In many rivers where there are trout, anglers will also take the Rocky Mountain whitefish.

There is considerable good fishing for largemouth black bass, notably in the shallower parts of Lake Tahkenitch and Lake Siltcoos, on the coast near U.S. 101. They are also found in the backwaters of the Columbia and Willamette Rivers, in Lake Mercer, on the coast south of Waldport; and in the Owyhee Reservoir in the east-central part of Oregon. Most of the warm-water lakes also contain crappie, yellow perch, warmouth bass and bluegills.

Saltwater fish which are taken along the Oregon coast include the sea perch, ling cod, kelp bass, flounder and red snapper. The sea perch, which is the most attractive to anglers, is readily taken from beaches and rocky shores and is an excellent table fish.

Two additions by stocking have increased the sport-fishing possibilities of the Oregon coastal waters. The striped bass, introduced to the California coast in 1879, has worked its way northward, and today one of the most famous spots to fish for this sporty species is at Coos Bay, Oregon. The average striper in Oregon waters will be about 10 pounds, but fish up to 40 pounds and better are taken. Being anadromous, striped bass make seasonal spawning runs into some of the coastal rivers, notably the Coquille and Umpqua.

Shad were also transported to the Pacific coast from the Atlantic and now occur in Oregon in runs into the Columbia, Willamette, Sandy, Coos, Coquille, Siuslaw and Umpqua Rivers. They usually weigh between 2 and 3 pounds but occasional catches are made up to 12 pounds, and a few larger.

Wildlife is plentiful in Oregon. Deer and bear are frequently seen, elk are in the higher areas, and mountain sheep are in the northeast corner of the state. East of the southern Cascades, Cougar may be found, and seal are often seen along the coast. Fishermen should also watch for rattlesnakes. They are thick in some of the remote fishing places. They will usually "buzz" you but don't count on this. Keep your eyes busy searching the ground in front of you. Never step into a clump of bushes or across a log if you cannot see the other side. Few outdoorsmen are struck by rattlers, but vigilance pays off.

COLUMBIA RIVER SYSTEM

While the State of Oregon seems to divide naturally into three zones—the coastal, the mountain and the central and eastern area, the fishing does not divide so easily. This is because the Columbia River extends its influence almost entirely across the northern border, and it has many large tributaries—the Willamette in particular—running relatively north and south. In the southern part of the state the same is true, coastal rivers providing the means by which the anadromous species go far inland during their spawning runs. At one time tremendous runs of salmon and steelhead used to travel to the headwaters of the Columbia, but today fishing is limited to the lower reaches below the Grand Coulee and other dams.

Some saltwater trolling for salmon is done at the mouth of the Columbia, but the good fishing is really from Rainier upstream. The spring run of Chinooks can start in February, but usually it is March before a substantial number of fish are in. Anglers trolling in this area fish out of Astoria or Warrenton at the south side of the inlet. In July the fall run of both Chinooks and silvers starts, the peak of the run coming in the last half of August through the first two weeks of September. At this time the casters come into their own, using spoons, spinners, flatfish and the inevitable cherry bobber. By late season, fish can be taken far upstream in such tributaries as the JOHN DAY (1), WALLA WALLA (2), GRAND RONDE (3) and IMNAHA (4), the last two flowing into the Snake, also a tributary of the Columbia. The Columbia also has some runs of summer steelhead in June and July and these fish can readily be taken from the banks as well as from boats.

WESTERN OREGON

The WILLAMETTE RIVER (5) is the Columbia's largest tributary within its lower reaches. Cradled between the Coastal Range and the Cascades, and emptying into the Columbia at Portland, the Willamette drains a large part of the western interior of the state, with tributaries reaching far south. The salmon come into the Willamette in mid-March and there is usually a good run throughout April; then the fish move into the tributaries. One of the best known is the CLACKAMAS (6), entering the main river at Gladstone, paralleled for much of its length by State Highway 211. Two small towns, Estacada and Three Lynx, offer very limited accommodations. The next tributary to the south is the MOLALLA (7), entering the river at Canby. There is no highway along the lower part of the river, but State Highway 211 crosses it east of the town of Molalla. Continuing upstream, the SANTIAM (8) can also be reached from Highway 213, in its lower part, and from State Highway 22 in the upper part. In this upper part anglers will find some accommodations at Detroit Lake and Mill City.

The McKENZIE (9) and the MIDDLE FORK OF THE WILLAMETTE (10), both entering the mainstream at Springfield on Interstate 5, complete the picture as far as tributaries from the Cascades are concerned. The fish start to show in Santiam and McKenzie in early June, and throughout June and July these are two of the most popular streams. The Santiam is especially good for those who want to fish from the shore. Casters use spinners and wobblers. There are many resorts and docks where anglers can rent boats along the lower Willamette. Fishing in this area is more or less stylized. For instance, from the mouth of the river up to Portland, most of the fish are caught by trolling with artificials or cut bait. From there up to Oregon City anglers usually go in for "lining," anchoring their boats side by side across the river and waiting for the fish to come to their baits.

In the Willamette drainage area there is a winter run of steelhead from January to June in some of the upstream tributaries of the river. Most of them also harbor rainbows and cutthroat, the rainbow fishing being best in the Clackamas, McKenzie and Middle Fork of the Willamette, already mentioned. Many streams around Mount Hood, off U.S. 26 east of Sandy, hold both species. The rivers coming down from the eastern slopes of the Coastal Range are good for cutthroat trout.

From the Columbia south, every river has its run of either salmon or steelhead or both, varying in size and in time. The NEHALEM RIVER (11) has a good run of Chinook salmon in August and on through September. Silver salmon come in just behind the kings, about the middle of August, and are usually caught up until the middle of October. Fall rains also bring a run of small jack salmon to this river, and there is a winter run of steelhead from November to March. For most fishing in the Nehalem, anglers use spinners with feathered treble hooks but for the jacks the popular method is fresh-egg bait on any kind of light tackle, as the fish run only from 3 to 5 pounds. The lower Nehalem can be fished from Wheeler, on the coast, or from Elsie, upstream, where U.S. 26 crosses the river. A dirt road runs along the stream.

To hit the peak of the salmon fishing in the nearby Tillamook Bay area, you should be there from mid-April to mid-May, or from mid-September to mid-October, as these are the two periods of strong runs. However, the silvers that come in the fall run continue on into December. There are five good rivers in the general neighborhood, the TRASK (12), WILSON (13), TILLAMOOK (14), KILCHIS (15) and MIAMI (16). During the summer there is good offshore trolling for salmon, and there are numerous boats available for this. Anglers fishing either sea or river stay at the ports of Rockaway, Garibaldi or Tillamook on the coastal road, U.S. 101; or for those fishing higher in the river there is Lee's Camp, on State Highway 6, between Tillamook and U.S. 26 out of Portland.

Among the most popular and productive salmon rivers of Oregon are the NESTUCCA (17) and the Little Nestucca. King salmon are taken in the tidewater area in June and July, and the fall run really gets going in the river in August, continuing through September. Silver salmon come in late September to add to the fishing, and they are taken up until the first of December. The steelhead are there in numbers from late fall to late spring. There are boats and guides available at Hebo, Beaver or Blaine, on U.S. 101. From nearby Pacific City, on the coast, deep-sea fishermen go out for summer-long angling for silver salmon in the salt. Mooching is one of the most popular ways to fish, but wobblers, spinners, plugs and fly-rod streamers all take their share. A few king salmon are also taken at this time.

Entering the ocean at Kernville on U.S. 101, the SILETZ RIVER (18), a few miles further south, also offers two types of fishing: casting from the banks in the upper waters, and trolling from boats in the lower. The king salmon come into the Siletz in August and are at their best in September. The silvers start in late in September and continue through October and November. To add to the salmons, this river has a nice run of sea-run cutthroats from early July right through into fall, and the summer run of steelheads from March to November. State Highway 229 parallels the river for about half its course, but there are no towns on the upper section.

Just south of the Siletz, at Depoe Bay, there is an excellent port for deep-sea fishing boats, and from here you can get party-boat fishing, or individual charters, to go not only for salmon, but also perch, bass and red snapper. This is a good bet for tourist-fishermen, because half-day trips can be arranged.

Both Chinook and silver salmon run into the YAQUINA RIVER (19) in August; and from May to September they are taken offshore by fishermen working out of Newport, where there is a fleet of deep-sea boats. The river can be reached via U.S. 20 between Corvallis and Newport.

At the same time, the fish come into the ALSEA RIVER (20), a small stream entering the ocean near Waldport. The silvers run a little later into October. Sea-run cutthroat can also be taken from July to November, and the steelhead from March to November. There are plenty of boats available in the tidewater section of the river; and there is good bank fishing above. State Highway 34 parallels the Alsea for almost its entire length.

Some of the most varied fishing of the coast can be had around the SIUSLAW RIVER (21), which enters the Pacific at the town of Florence, on U.S. 101. The spring run of salmon comes into the river in late May and continues through August. The best fishing is in midsummer, and local fishermen highly recommend the Bear Valley spinner at this period. The fall run seems to come right on the heels of the other, the king salmon showing from September 1st to about the middle of October. The silver salmon start right after the first heavy autumn rains and are taken right through to January, though the best months are October and November. The stretch of river between Florence and Cushman, a couple of miles upstream, on State Highway 36, is very good. At the small village of Swisshome the river turns south, away from Highway 36, and access is through a dirt road. Silver salmon also run into the two coastal lakes just to the south, SILTCOOS and TAHKENITCH (22), in October and November. Besides the salmons, the Siuslaw has a good run of steelhead from March to November.

Further south lies the UMPQUA RIVER (23), draining the western slopes of the Cascades over a wide area, through its two branches, the SOUTH FORK and the MAIN UMPQUA (23). This has long been one of the best steelhead rivers of the west, especially attractive to fly fishermen. It enters the ocean near Reedsport at Winchester Bay, and inland it runs right beside State Highways 225 and 38 for many miles. Nowadays fishing is best below the point where the two forks come together, as above that, at Roseburg, there is a dam. There is a spring run of Chinook into the river from the middle of March through June. The silver come after the fall rains.

There are accommodations at Reedsport and Winchester Bay on the coast, at Roseburg and some of the small towns in its neighborhood, and on the North Fork there are several resorts.

In early summer there is good dry-fly fishing for rainbow and eastern brook trout in the North and South Forks of the Umpqua, with June the top time.

In Winchester Bay, king salmon and silvers are taken all summer by trolling, mostly with herring. At Salmon Harbor there are boats, guides and tackle shops. You can get detailed information from Harry Ludwig, Salmon Harbor.

The next major river to the south is the Coos (24), which has a good run of Chinooks, starting in July and lasting through September. The silvers start in September and the run lasts through November. During the summer they are taken offshore. Empire and Charleston Harbor on Coos Bay are both embarkation points for this fishing.

Just north of the Coos, the TEN MILE LAKES (25), at Lakeside on U.S. 101, are known for very good runs of silvers at the end of October. And just south of Coos Bay the COQUILLE RIVER (26) has a fair run of silvers from mid-September to the end of November. There are also a few king salmon at this time. The Coos and Coquille both have winter-run steelhead.

The lower waters of the Coquille can be reached from State Highway 42S, between Bandon on U.S. 101, and Myrtle Pt., on State Highway 42, which then runs along some miles of the upper waters. There are several small towns but most anglers find accommodations at Coquille on State Highway 42 near the coast, or at Roseburg, where State Highway 42 meets Interstate 5.

Since striped bass were introduced into California waters in 1879, this species has gradually extended its range northward. Today some of the best striper fishing to be found on the coast is at Coos Bay as the fish move inshore to spawn in fresh and brakish water and make runs into the Coos and Coquille Rivers. Summer and fall is the best time although there are fish around for most of the year. Much of the striper fishing is done by trolling deep, but there is some fine casting to be had in Coos Bay. The writer was fortunate enough while fishing there in 1948, on Captain James Christiansen's boat, out of the Sportsman's Dock, to take a 29-pound 6-ounce striper on a popping bug. However the average fish in this area will go about 6 pounds. Many are also taken fishing from shore on artificial plugs. Bait fishermen use sculpins, frozen herring and pilchards.

One of the most famous of our western streams, the ROGUE RIVER (27), forms the backbone of the drainage system of the southern part of Oregon, between the two mountain ranges. Chinook salmon come into the mouth of the river at Gold Beach in April and the spring run is usually strong through May and June. There is a second run in September. The silver salmon also come in in late September and are taken until December.

The peak fishing for the Chinook varies as you progress upstream. At Grants Pass, May is the best month, and above that there is good fishing in June. The season closes in July. Along the lower thirty miles of the river, anglers use boats to fish the riffles. At Grants Pass and up, there is some bank fishing, some boats and several resorts, and residents have constructed piers, locally called "salmon boards," from which to cast. Silver and copper spoons are the popular lures, and red beads seem to add a little special allure.

The steelhead fishing in the Rogue varies in the same way, starting at the coast in late August and being at its best at Grants Pass in October. The river has a famous summer run of steelhead, which draws fly fishermen from all parts of the U.S.A. Gold Beach and Grants Pass are fishermen's headquarters. Local fishermen will tell you that fly fishing and trolling will get the steelhead in September and October, but that after that fresh eggs are called for.

There are plentiful accommodations along the Rogue at various small towns, and guides can also be found at most resorts for floats of a day or longer on the river. The limit is two salmon per day and you can have them canned for you on the spot. Guides get about $30 per day, two fishermen per boat, and will supply tackle and bait.

Several small rivers close to the southern boundary of Oregon offer some good casting for both salmon and steelhead, as well as tidewater trolling. The CHETCO (28) has a good run of Chinook salmon in the middle of August, continuing through October. It overlaps the silver-salmon run which starts in late September and continues through December. There's a gravel road for some miles up the stream from the town of Brookings on the coast.

The WINCHUCK RIVER (29), the PISTOL (30) and the SIXES (31) all are very short rivers but provide some Chinook and silver salmon in September and October. In the summer there is little water, but when things pick up in the fall these small rivers have excellent runs of big steelhead. The Winchuck crosses the coastal highway, U.S. 101, just south of the Chetco. The Pistol and the Sixes are both marked by small villages of the same names, on U.S. 101 between the Coquille River and the Chetco.

DESCHUTES RIVER SYSTEM

Many of the tributaries of the Columbia which lie to the east of the Cascades also have seasonal runs of salmon and trout. One of the most popular fishing rivers in Oregon is the DESCHUTES (32), which drains northward from the Cascade Mountains to enter the Columbia about seventeen miles east of The Dalles. The Deschutes has a run of salmon in the lower reaches in April, May and June, but it is for its excellent steelhead fishing that the river is so widely known. The best months are from July through September, and the best fishing area is from the juncture of the Deschutes and the Columbia south to Maupin on U.S. Highway 197. This is bank fishing, but as you go further upstream (south) towards Bend, there are some opportunities for boat fishing. The Deschutes is frequently muddy, at which time anglers have most success with spinning lures, but when you find it clear it is a fine river for fly fishing.

Trout fishing goes on all summer in the Deschutes, from May through October, with the bigger catches in the fall. In the river around and above Redmond, the rainbow is the most common catch, with some brook trout also being taken. Lower down you will find more browns.

Several of the tributaries of the Deschutes are also popular. The LITTLE DESCHUTES (33), METOLIUS (34), WHITE RIVER (35) and the CROOKED RIVER (36) all provide excellent fishing at one time of the year or another for spring Chinook salmon, summer steelhead, kokanee, or one of the trouts.

Of these, the Metolius is probably the most interesting. A portion of the top part of the stream, where it emerges as a full river from beneath Black Butte, is reserved for fly fishing only. Here as well as further down the fishing for rainbow is good.

The Crooked River, which is accessible from Redmond via U.S. 97, going north, then on a dirt road to Cove, has about six miles of good rainbow fishing from the mouth of the river upstream. Higher in the Crooked River drainage some of the tributaries provide fishing for small rainbows, and there are slightly larger ones in

OREGON

SNAKE RIVER
IMNAHA RIVER
JOSEPH
WALLOWA
WALLOWA L.
MINAM R.
GRANDE RONDE
ELGIN
LA GRANDE
UMATILLA RIVER
PENDLETON
BUTTER CREEK
WILLOW CREEK
ROCK CREEK
THIRTY MILE CRK.
EAGLE CREEK
POWDER RIVER
BURNT RIVER
BAKER
SUMPTER
MIDDLE FK.
N. FK.
Olive L.
Magone L.
JOHN DAY RIVER
CANYON CITY
Strawberry L.
BEECH CREEK
S. FK.
MALHEUR RIVER
WILLOW CREEK
BULLY CREEK
Beulah Res.
N. FK.
JUNTURA
S. FK.
CALAMITY CRK.
SILVIES RIVER
Malheur L.
Harney L.
BURNS
SILVER CRK.
MIDDLE CRK.
BLITZEN RIVER
TROUT CRK.
CROOKED CRK.
OWYHEE RIVER
SUCKER CRK.
ANTELOPE RES.
RATTLESNAKE CRK.
LITTLE OWYHEE RIVER
OWYHEE
Owyhee Res.
Dalrymple
BOYES RIVER
OCHOCO
CROOKED RIVER
REDMOND
Prineville Res.
BEND
DESCHUTES RIVER
LA PINE
East L.
Paulina L.
Silver L.
Thompson Valley Res.
Summer L.
L. Abert
Hart L.
Crump L.
Pelican L.
LAKEVIEW
GOOSE CREEK
SYCAN RIVER
SPRAGUE RIVER
Upper Klamath L.
KLAMATH FALLS
LOST RIVER
KLAMATH RIVER
KLAMATH NAT'L WILDLIFE REFUGE
Four Mile L.
Lake of the Woods
SPRING CR.
Crater L.
CRATER LAKE NAT'L PARK
Diamond L.
WOOD RIVER
DIAMOND LAKE
WILLIAMSON RIVER
ROGUE RIVER
GRANTS PASS
APPLEGATE RIVER
ILLINOIS RIVER
CHETCO RIVER
BROOKINGS
GOLD BEACH
PISTOL RIVER
SIXES RIVER
BANDON
COQUILLE RIVER
MYRTLE POINT
S. FK. COQUILLE
COOS BAY
COOS RIVER
EMPIRE
CHARLESTON
LAKESIDE
Ten Mile Lakes
REEDSPORT
Tahkenitch L.
Siltcoos L.
UMPQUA RIVER
NORTH UMPQUA RIVER
SOUTH UMPQUA RIVER
ROSEBURG
COW CREEK
FLORENCE
SIUSLAW RIVER
CUSHMAN
SWISSHOME
MAPLETON
LONG TOM RIVER
EUGENE
SPRINGFIELD
McKENZIE RIVER
MIDDLE FORK
N. FORK
Clear L.
Waldo L.
Cougar Res.
Blue R.
WILLAMETTE RIVER
Detroit L.
SANTIAM RIVER
NORTH SANTIAM RIVER
SOUTH SANTIAM RIVER
CALAPOOYA RIVER
MARION FORKS
MILL CITY
SALEM
ALBANY
CORVALLIS
ALSEA RIVER
YAQUIN RIVER
ELK CREEK
WALDPORT
NEWPORT
DEPOE BAY
PACIFIC CITY
ROCKAWAY
GARIBALDI
TILLAMOOK
WHEELER
NEHALEM RIVER
NESTUCCA RIVER
TRASK R.
WILSON RIVER
HEBO
BLAINE
NESKOWIN
PORTLAND
GLADSTONE
CANBY
MOLALLA RIVER
CLACKAMAS RIVER
ESTACADA
SANDY RIVER
SANTIAM R.
THREE LYNX
WARM SPRINGS INDIAN RESERVATION
METOLIUS RIVER
SISTERS
SQUAW CREEK
WHITE RIVER
MAUPIN
MT. HOOD
THE DALLES
COLUMBIA
DESCHUTES RIVER
N. FK.

0 5 10 20 30

N

the OCHOCO RESERVOIR (36). The upper waters can be best reached from Prineville at the Junction of U.S. 26 and 126.

While the White River, another tributary of the Deschutes, is usually too discolored by the runoff of snow water to provide good angling during the early season, it is a good stream for rainbows in late July, August and September. Access is via State Highway 52 or U.S. 197. The White joins the Deschutes near Sherar.

The many lakes in the Deschutes system nearly all provide fair to good angling for small rainbows, cutthroats, and in some cases browns, lake trout and kokanee. WICKIUP and CRANE PRAIRIE RESERVOIRS (37), which can be reached by dirt road from U.S. 97 south of LaPine, are two of the largest. These, as well as DAVIS and ODELL LAKES (38), reached from State Highway 58, just north of its junction with U.S. 97, produce (on occasion) lake trout up to 25 pounds and kokanee up to 20 inches, as well as rainbows and cutthroat. Nearby SUTTER LAKE (39), near Sisters, is good kokanee water. PAULINA and EAST LAKES (40), east from U.S. 97 about thirty miles south of Bend, have good rainbow fishing. The fish hit flies well and many are also taken on trolled worms.

This is a popular resort area and you will find accommodations on Paulina Lake, Mud Lake, East Lake, South Twin, Big Lava, Elk, Little Cultus, Suttle, Blue, Three Creeks, and the Ochoco and Rock Creek Reservoirs. Early reservations should be made because of the popularity of the region. Further information about fishing in the area can be obtained from the Region Office of the Oregon Game Commission at 222 East Third Street, Bend, Oregon. Inquire about Mud Lake, which is the only water in this part of the world that is stocked with Atlantic salmon.

SOUTH-CENTRAL WATERS

Although much of the state south of the Deschutes drainage area is semiarid, there are nevertheless a number of rivers which supply some surprisingly good fishing. This is basically the headwaters of the Klamath River and as that river has been dammed on its course through California towards the sea, there are no sea-run fish, but the KLAMATH (41), WILLIAMSON (42), WOOD (43) and SPRAGUE (44) RIVERS all support trout, the Williamson being particularly noted for its big rainbows. A number of creeks are excellent except when the water is being used for irrigation. To make the best of these—Deep Creek, Honey Creek, Dairy, Silver and Spring—the angler should get in on the early-season angling.

A number of lakes also provide fair to excellent rainbow fishing. UPPER KLAMATH LAKE (45) has some good-sized rainbows which run into the Williamson River.

Just north of the California line, LAKE OF THE WOODS (46) is a popular spot, with rainbows and some warm-water fish. Nearby FOUR MILE LAKE (47) adds kokanee and eastern brook. There are cabins and boats at Lake of the Woods, boats only at the Four Mile, which is reached over a rough road. As far as accommodations are concerned, the best bet is Lakeview at the Junction of U.S. 395 and State Highway 66, and Klamath Falls, at the lower end of Upper Klamath Lake, about 100 miles further west.

Further north, DIAMOND LAKE (48), which can be reached by road up the south fork of the Umpqua from Roseburg, was poisoned and replanted with trout in 1958 and since then has been producing fish weighing 3 and 4 pounds, and full

Oregon has thousands of high mountain lakes which offer exciting fishing for those who are willing to make the rugged trip.

daily limits. The fish are rainbows and Kamloops. Little guide service is needed, but is obtainable through Joe DeBernardi, Diamond Lake Resort. There are also camp sites and a Forest Service Headquarters. Weekends are very crowded.

EASTERN AREA

As might be expected, the eastern part of Oregon is the least attractive from the fisherman's point of view. Nevertheless, because of the migratory species which make their way up the Columbia and into its many tributaries, far inland, there is some unexpected fishing to be had. As already mentioned, from late winter into spring, steelhead and spring Chinook move into the JOHN DAY RIVER (1) in small numbers. This river enters the Columbia some twenty miles east of The Dalles, flowing down from far up country to the south and east. Some of the steelhead run all the way up as far as the town of John Day at the junction of U.S. 395 and U.S. 26. The upper waters also provide good trout fishing from May to October and there are three trout lakes in the headwaters. LAKES OLIVE and MAGONE (49) may be reached by dirt road off U.S. 395 south of Beech Creek; STRAWBERRY LAKE (50) by hiking in from U.S. 395 near Canyon City.

Moving east along the Columbia, the outlet of the UMATILLA RIVER (51) provides some good fishing for the migratory species. It can be reached via U.S. 30 west of Pendleton. Heavy irrigation use limits the trout fishing in most of the streams in this area, and a considerable part of the Umatilla lies within the Umatilla Indian

Reservation and may be fished only by special permit. The season is from May to the early part of October.

In the extreme northeastern corner of Oregon a substantial run of salmon comes through the Snake River from the Columbia, and into the WALLOWA (52) and GRAND RONDE (3). Steelhead also come into these rivers and into the IMNAHA (4) POWDER (53) and EAGLE (54), further east, in sufficient numbers to make interesting fishing. The Wallowa and Grand Ronde can be reached via State Highway 82, northeast from La Grande. This road crosses the Grand Ronde at Elgin and the Wallowa at the town of Wallowa, then runs parallel to the Wallowa River up to Wallowa Lake. A dirt road which leaves State Highway 82 at Enterprise runs across country to the headwaters of the Imnaha, then follows the river all the way down to the Snake River. The small village of Imnaha is the only settlement in the area. State Highway 86 from Baker to Richmond on the Snake parallels the Powder River, and just above Richland a dirt road leads up Eagle Creek. This is all sparsely settled country, but with a little exploring and asking questions of anglers at Pendleton, Baker or La Grande, you can find both salmon and steelhead on occasion in these and many of the small creeks of the area.

Rainbow-trout fishing is also good in many of the lakes, the better ones being accessible only by trail. Wenaha, Minam, Lostine and Imnaha are the better known lakes. The lakes of the Wallowa Mountains provide especially attractive fishing for those who want to pack in to a spot where they know that, though the fish may be small the supply will be plentiful. There are about thirty lakes in this group, with either rainbows or eastern brook trout or both. They can be reached via U.S. 30 to La Grande, then east on State Highway 82; or from Baker via State Highway 203. Packers are available at various places along the road. All lakes above 5,000 feet are open year-round, although usually, because of snow conditions, they can only be reached in June, July and August. Indicative of the numbers of fish, the daily limit is thirty per person. Fly fishing is the choice of most anglers on these lakes; and it's a good idea to pack in a rubber boat or life raft, in order to be able to thoroughly cover the water.

Those planning to fish in northeastern Oregon would be well advised to contact the Chamber of Commerce at La Grande, Enterprise or Baker; and the Oregon Game Commission Office at Box 226, La Grande, Oregon, for current regulations as well as the right time for the migratory fish.

The southeastern quadrangle of Oregon is mainly comprised of desert and range but there are several streams and a number of lakes and reservoirs where there is some good fishing to be found. The season in general extends from May to early October but, again, current regulations must be checked.

The Steens Mountain area (west of State Highway 78 and U.S. 95) offers rainbow fishing, and though the streams are small the fish are surprisingly good. Access is difficult but can be made from the French Glen Road, south from Burns on State Highway 205. There is also trout fishing in the BLITZEN RIVER (55), to the east of this road, flowing north to Lake Malheur. The SILVIES RIVER (56) is also good and can be reached by a hike from a dirt road north from Burns. Further west, small DELINTMENT LAKE (57), near Suntex, which in turn is near Riley at the junction of U.S. 395 and U.S. 20, is one of the best trout lakes in Oregon. Further east, BEULAH RESERVOIR (58), north of U.S. 20 at Juntura, has fair rainbow fishing. Neither boats nor accommodations are available at the lakes but there are camp sites.

The OWYHEE RESERVOIR (59), at the top of the Owyhee River, has no accommodations either, and anglers should take their own drinking water. There are no boats available. Anglers fishing the river below the reservoir sometimes take rainbows of fairly good size. Several dirt roads give access to the Owyhee from U.S. 20 on the north and State Highway 78 on the west, or you can go in from U.S. 95 in Idaho.

OTHER LAKE FISHING

In order to avoid confusion, with so many migratory species to deal with, I have not described the many lakes, both large and small in the various watersheds which have excellent fishing of one kind or another. Because of their inaccessibility except by trail, many Oregon lakes offer better than usual fishing. Usually they can be fished from the shore, but when possible, it is wise to pack in a life raft or rubber boat.

Accessible from Detroit, on State Highway 22, about sixty miles east of Salem; or from Wapinitia, on State Highway 216, which turns west from U.S. 197 at Maupin, are the OLALLIE LAKES (60). The largest, Lower Olallie, is about sixty acres in size, and carries both eastern brook and rainbow trout. The others are regularly stocked with eastern brook and one, Fish Lake, has cutthroats. There's similar fishing in the surrounding lakes throughout the Olallie Meadows—Brietenbush Lake, Jefferson Park and the Firecamp group.

The MARION LAKES (61), which can be reached from the Marion Forks Guard Station on the North Santiam Highway, offer similar fishing, as do the adjacent Duffy Lakes, Scar Mountain, and the Square Lakes group. In Square Lake itself, which is about fifty-five acres in size, there are also lake trout.

South of the Three Sisters, you can reach the Mink Lake Basin area, either from North Century Drive or South Century Drive at Bend; or from U.S. 97. From Elk Lake on the Century Drive, you can take a fairly good road to Wickiup Plains, and from there hike in to several good lakes. Nash is particularly good. There is a commercial pack outfit at Elk Lake each summer.

Similar lake fishing is found in the Taylor Burn group of lakes in Willamette and Deschutes National Forests, in the Rogue River headwaters area, and the Mountain Lakes Wild Area, near Medford and Klamath Falls.

One of the finest backcountry lakes in Willamette Pass area is Bobby Lake, five miles by trail from the Gold Lake Forest Camp. The Yoran Lake group lies further south and can be reached via Odell, where there is a pack outfit stationed each summer.

Because of altitude, snow often blocks the trails in the Mount Hood National Forest until some time in June, but after that there is access to a limited number of the lakes by road, many more by trail, especially those on the western slope of the Cascades. There are camp grounds at most lakes. Detailed information about this area can be obtained from the Regional Office of the Oregon Game Commission, Route 1, Corvallis, Oregon.

The Game Commission also published a booklet entitled "Oregon's Back Country Lakes," which gives details invaluable to those planning such fishing in Oregon. You can order it from the Commission at P.O. Box 4136, Portland 8, Oregon.

OREGON FISHING REGULATIONS

Resident Fishing License $4.00
Nonresident Fishing License $10.00
Nonresident 7-Day Fishing License $5.00

SEASONS

In general the trout season opens about the middle of April and closes early in October. Warm-water species such as bass, catfish, perch and crappie may be fished all year. Fishing for the salmons and sea-run trouts varies according to district. In some cases the season will be open on the lower end of a river and not in the headwaters, and vice versa. There are also some special closed seasons on inland waters.

For complete regulations write: Oregon State Game Commission, P.O. Box 4136, Portland 8, Oregon.

WASHINGTON

The State of Washington has two topographical features which produce good fishing: the waters of the Pacific Ocean along its shores, and the Cascade Range with its many lakes and streams. The seacoast has much protected water in the Puget Sound area and south of the Olympic Peninsula where several large bays and inlets provide shelter and afford good harbors for fishing craft. One of these is Grays Harbor, on which are located the towns of Aberdeen and Hoquiam, and the town of Westport at the south side of the inlet. Farther south, Willapa Bay is protected by the North Beach Peninsula, and just below is the great inlet of the Columbia River, which forms 300 miles of the border between Washington and Oregon.

The most important fish in Washington waters is the salmon. The salt waters of the ocean produce all the Pacific salmons: the Chinook, or king; the silver, or coho; the humpback; the dog salmon, or chum; and the sockeye, or red salmon or blueback.

Though all the salmons run upstream to spawn, the major fishing for them is offshore and in the mouths and inlets of rivers, since Pacific salmon die after spawning and are therefore not in prime condition in the rivers. Seasonal runs of one variety or another enter nearly every freshwater stream along the coast, and in some cases they travel across almost the entire state in their search for spawning headquarters. As in the other Pacific states, the Chinook salmon is the prime target for sportsmen. Chinook salmon range up to 60 pounds along the Washington coast, the average taken by anglers being about 25 pounds.

During the spawning migrations the fish come down the coast, heading for the Columbia and other West Coast rivers. The first fish usually reach the northern, Juan de Fuca area of Washington in May. From there some work into the Puget Sound-Skagit Bay area, while others go on down the coast, each seeking its parent river. Meanwhile fresh schools keep coming in on the same paths, to provide increasingly good fishing till September.

Silver salmon, also called coho, and sometimes referred to in Washington as salmon trout, come in in October and December. A mature fish, three years old, will weigh between 8 and 10 pounds. Sometimes the young feed in the rivers and sounds for a full year before migrating to the salt, and quite a few remain in Puget Sound till ready to spawn. Because the food is limited, these fish do not grow large, but in spring and summer there is quite a bit of good fishing for these small residents of the Sound. Then in the fall the larger, mature, hook-nosed silvers come in from the ocean and are taken in quantity.

The humpback, which is found only occasionally further south, is abundant in some Washington waters. The fish, which weigh from 6 to 8 pounds when mature, migrate into the Puget Sound area in August and September. For some reason these Puget Sound runs come only in odd years, even though the same species makes annual runs in Alaska.

The humpback runs into the Stillaguamish, Skagit, Snohomish, Puyallup and Nooksack Rivers. In the salt the best fishing areas are around Whidbey Island, Port

465

Susan and Port Gardner, and in the spring some good catches of immature fish are made at Port Defiance, near Tacoma.

The dog salmon, also often called chum or fall salmon, usually weighs between 10 and 12 pounds. Because they are latecomers in the migration schedule, not as many are taken as the other sporting salmons. They migrate into the Puget Sound area in October, November and December, and the best fishing grounds for them there are in the Admiralty Inlet, San Juan Island region. Some dog salmon are also taken along the coast and in the Columbia River.

The sockeye salmon is often called red salmon and blueback in Washington; when it is landlocked it is called kokanee, sometimes redfish or silver trout. In Puget Sound they average about 6 pounds, while those taken in the Columbia River run smaller, from 3 to 4 pounds. This species runs into the rivers from June through August. Since they do not hit lures readily, anglers rarely fish for them in the salt. But they will take a fly in fresh water, and then the sockeye is an acrobatic handful.

Second only to the salmon in importance to the sport fisherman, and, indeed, regarded by many as of first importance, is the steelhead, a rainbow trout which has run out to sea to feed, then returned to the coastal river of its birth to spawn. The major influx is the winter run from January to June, but many rivers have an additional summer run in July. These are usually prime fish, full of fight. The winter run will average 10 to 14 pounds with a few as heavy as 20 pounds. The state record is 28½ pounds. Five to 8 pounds is a good size for summer steelhead, with an occasional fish reaching 15 pounds. Steelhead are found to some degree in almost every stream which has an outlet to the Pacific.

To some extent the brown and brook trout, but notably the cutthroat, also perform these salty migrations. In Washington you'll hear fishermen talking about the harvest trout, or blueback. This is a sea-run cutthroat that hangs around the estuaries in spring and early summer, then in the fall moves into the rivers to spawn. This species provides wonderful fishing in the rivers from August through March, and in the sea year-round. The strongest runs usually take place in September, with a second good run occurring in February, but this may vary greatly with the individual river.

The cutthroat like fairly deep water with rocks, boulders or overhanging brush for protection. They are good fly takers and the bright flies are usually the best— but not always!

Other saltwater species which are taken along the Washington coast are sole or flatfish, flounder, turbot, sandsole, rockfish, which in Washington you will hear called sea bass and rock cod, though it is not related to either. A limited number taken by sportsmen run in the 3-pound class, though some up to 20 pounds have been taken. Black rockfish, also known as black sea bass, are common in the shallower waters. Albacore appear in the warmer waters alongshore in July, and fishing for this species in weights up to 30 pounds is good. The average will go between 9 and 15 pounds.

The shad, while not native to Pacific waters, has done extremely well since it was introduced in California in 1871, and in the Columbia River between Washington and Oregon in 1886. Now strong runs follow the Pacific coast as far north as Washington. The fish are taken in the Columbia River commercially, mostly in the month of June. Very few are caught by sport fishermen.

Freshwater fishing in Washington is as widespread and varied as that found in the salt. The Cascade Mountains run the entire length of the state, creating two watersheds, the one through the West Coast rivers flowing to the Pacific, and the other shedding waters eastward to the Okanogan River, the Upper Columbia, far inland, and the Snake. All of these rivers, of course, also make their way to the Pacific through the Columbia.

The Cascade Mountains rise to tremendous heights and many of them are capped with glaciers which feed numerous streams. Among the peaks are hundreds of small lakes, ideal homes for trout. Much of the terrain has been designated National Parks, National Forests and Wilderness Areas, thus preserving the natural conditions of this range, which is probably the most beautiful in North America. There are numerous camp sites throughout, under control of the U.S. Forest Service. A list of these sites may be obtained by writing the Forest Service, Box 4137, Portland 8, Oregon.

Species found in the freshwater lakes and streams of the Cascades include brook trout, rainbow trout, brown trout, Dolly Varden and Rocky Mountain whitefish. In the lower-lying fresh waters to both east and west of the Cascades, there are also some largemouth black bass, smallmouth black bass, crappie, bluegill, perch and catfish.

Taken mostly commercially, and under stringent protection regulations, are the white sturgeon and the green sturgeon of the Columbia River. One taken on the Pacific coast many years ago is reputed to have weighed 1,800 pounds. Much smaller sizes are taken nowadays in the Columbia, but very rarely.

Because of the mountainous terrain, the means of access in Washington are comparatively limited. Travelers coming from the east and heading for the northern interior or coastal areas travel on U.S. 2, west from Spokane. In the South, U.S. 410 from Lewiston, Idaho, leads across to the Columbia River. From there you can continue west on U.S. 410 to Tacoma and Seattle, or follow the Columbia on State Highway 8 to Vancouver, then north on U.S. 830 to Kelso. There U.S. 99 will take you to Chehalis, where you can turn west to the Olympic Peninsula or proceed north to Tacoma and Seattle. The major north-south highways are U.S. 99, which parallels the coast, and U.S. 97, coming in from Okanagan Falls in British Columbia, to the north. On the southern border two highways lead in from Oregon: U.S. 97 at the Dalles, and U.S. 395 from Pendleton, Oregon.

The summer climate throughout Washington is uniformly cool compared to other areas. Along the coast, boat fishermen need a jacket and rainjacket. Beach fishermen will be comfortable during the day in cotton pants and shirt, with a heavier overshirt for evening. In the mountains and farther inland, heavier clothing is in order. And for those who go for the salmons and steelhead in the early spring, fall and winter, quite heavy clothing is required.

In the mountainous areas of Washington the angler may encounter black bear and possibly grizzly, the latter only in the country along the Idaho border. Deer are numerous and there are some elk, bighorn sheep and mountain goats. Mountain lions are widespread but seldom seen. Along the coast there are seals.

Washington anglers in the salt use every type of tackle from big, ocean-going trolling outfits to fly rods. Salmon fishing offshore is mostly by trolling, and "mooching" is the approved method, whether fishing from charter boat or skiff. A double-handed rod, 7 to 9 feet in length, is used, and a level-wind saltwater reel with 15- or 20-pound-test monofilament line. Herring is used for bait, with enough weight to get down close to the bottom, and slow trolling is the rule.

Ocean charters for salmon usually cost between $12 and $15 per person per day. Boats carry from three to eighteen anglers and furnish tackle. You can also mooch from your own or a rented skiff, boats from 14 to 17 feet in length renting for about $5 per day. Motors are expensive and many anglers bring their own. Ten horsepower is about right and 18 would be the outsize limit for these skiffs. Those who stay inside the sounds and bays could get along with a smaller motor.

The popular outfit for freshwater trout fishing in Washington is the fly rod. An 8-foot rod, HDH line and a leader tapered to a 4X tippet will serve for most of the rivers and lakes. For bigger streams and lakes an 8½- or 9-foot rod is called for, and these should be fitted with a forward-tapered fly line to allow for a long "shoot" of the line.

Most steelhead rivers call for long casts, and many anglers use a "shooting head" of 28 or 30 feet of fly line in front of 20-pound-test nylon or monofilament, called the shooting line. It does a good job. However, the standard forward-tapered fly lines purchased in tackle stores are hard to beat.

The standard nymphs, wets, dries and bucktail-streamers will do the job for resident trout in Washington waters. The best steelhead flies are the Thor, Princess, Kalama Special, Skykomish, Sunrise, Siwash Special, Van Luven, Harger's Sea Shrimp and Drain 20. These can all be used in sizes from 6 to 1/0.

Trout-fishing leaders should be tapered from a heavy butt section where the leader is joined to the fly line, down through lengths of 20-, 15-, 12-, and 10-pound-test nylon to whatever breaking strength is desired for the tippet. Because the steel-head is usually taken in fairly big water, anglers generally use an 8- or 10-pound-test tippet for this species.

For trout fishing, spin fishermen use light outfits with 4- or 6-pound-test mono-filament line, and small spoons and spinners. For steelhead and salmon they go heavier, using lines of 8- to 12-pound-test breaking strength. During heavy water runoff they go to 15 and even 20. The larger spoons, cherry bobbers and salmon eggs are all used by spinners.

SAN JUAN ISLANDS

In the San Juan Islands, between Vancouver Island and the north Washington coast, there is some kind of salmon fishing year-round. Very large king salmon come in the spring and are caught from June through September. There are some resident fish, immature kings which are called blackmouth locally, and fishing for them is at its best from December through March. These fish can run as big as 20 pounds.

About the middle of April a run of silver salmon starts and there's good fishing for weights up to about 6 pounds until the middle of July. At that time the whoppers of the species appear and the fishing for these bigger fellows is good until the end of September.

The humpback salmon appears about July 15th, coinciding with the run of big silvers, but ends a couple of weeks earlier. As elsewhere in its range, the humpback runs occur every other year, rather than annually.

The San Juan Islands and Anacortes, Lummi and Bellingham Islands, nearby, all share in this general good fishing, and consequently this is an area of numerous fishing camps and boat-rental docks. There is a car ferry from Anacortes to Orcas; one from Anacortes to Guemes; and yet another from Gooseberry Point, near Bellingham, to Lummi Island.

The resorts on Orcas Island, near Eastsound, will also arrange trout fishing for anglers who want to go over to the Cascade waters on the mainland.

PUGET SOUND AREA

Almost every seaside community along the Puget Sound Coast can outfit a fisherman in one way or another, but certain ports cater especially to the sports fisherman. They are usually near waters which have proven favorite feeding grounds or travel routes for salmon. Many of them also offer good bottom fishing for other species, such as sole, flounder and rock cod.

Whidbey Island, which stretches for fifty miles parallel to the coast north of Seattle, can be reached by ferry in fifteen minutes from Mukilteo, off U.S. 99 at the south end of the island; or by bridge at Deception Pass at the north end of the island via State Highway 1. There are many resorts on Whidbey, and the surrounding waters seem to hold fish longer than those of any other part of the Washington coast. Humpbacks, Chinook and silvers are all found at one time or another, and all three are taken consistently from early spring throughout the summer off the southwest coast of the island. Possession Point, Holmes Harbor, Langley, Mutiny Bay and, further north, Bush Point, are all top fishing spots. Fifty-pound salmon have been taken off the south coast of Whidbey Island.

From Whidbey or Seattle boats run over to Hope Island, where there is trolling for exceptionally big Chinook which average 40 pounds and, on occasion, have gone as high as 70 pounds. For some reason, mooching, so popular elsewhere, is not as successful here as trolling with big spoons.

Hope Island lies off the delta of the Skagit River. Tackle, guides and accommodations will be found at the Hope Island Resort on the mainland north of LaConner on State Highway 1, as well as at Seattle and Whidbey.

At Stanwood, which is just off Interstate 5, south of Mount Vernon, there's a free bridge to Camano Island. Most of the resorts on Camano are on the west side of the island, where the fishing is for Chinook and silvers passing through on their way to rivers up the coast. Some of the best fishing is around Polnell Point. The spring run of cutthroat trout, good in much of Puget Sound, is probably at its best right here. And on the mainland near Everett there is standout fishing for Chinooks and silvers in the mouths of the Skokomish and Stillaguamish Rivers, as well as for the smaller resident silvers or blackmouths. Tulalip, Stanwood and intermediate points provide accommodations of all kinds.

Anglers in the Seattle area have easy access to practically year-round fishing along the mainland facing the southern tip of Whidbey Island. This area is noted more for its "feeders" than for its runs of adult fish, but the feeders are there in such numbers that there is usually excellent fishing, especially during the period from March 1st through September. This is a popular spot with everyone because there's good charter-boat water, good water for trolling, casting or bait fishing. As the tide moves around Whidbey Island, spinners are particularly successful in the eddying current at Point No Point and Foul-Weather Bluff. There is also good fishing along the shore around Mukilteo.

A charter boat docked in Westport harbor with a day's catch of salmon.

Throughout the coastal district winter fishing is good for blackmouth going to 14 pounds, Point No Point and Port Gamble Bay being two of the hot spots. The numerous resorts in the area offer accommodations and all services.

Within the environs of Seattle there is just about as good salmon fishing as you will find anywhere in the Sound. The top season runs from August 1st to November 15th for silvers, August 1st to September 15th for Chinooks. Blackmouth stay around all winter. While most Washington anglers go for salmon with heavy gear, this is one area where fly fishermen have their day. Some very good catches are made with flies, during October and November, near Ballard.

From Tacoma the angler can reach excellent trolling for salmon at Dash Point and Brown's Point on the north, and around all the islands in front of the city, as well as at Point Defiance. There are boats and a hotel at Gig Harbor, and you can also get boats at Warren, near Wollochet Bay, facing Fox Island. Both Wollochet and Gig's are good for winter fishing for blackmouth, with the fish hitting well for moochers as well as on spinning lures. Gig Harbor is one of the few spots where dog salmon are taken on light tackle. Spinners should also try their luck at Anderson Island.

Salmon of all kinds are taken year-round at the Narrows and at Point Defiance. Summer and fall are best for Chinooks and silvers at the mouth of the Puyallup River, which empties into Puget Sound at Tacoma. Unfortunately, the area southwest of Tacoma, around Olympia, has been virtually ruined for sport fishing by the illegal taking of spawning stock in streams, and by pollution. Today what little fishing there is can be found around Steamboat Island.

Across the bay from Tacoma, Bremerton is the center for those who want to go for silvers and blackmouths. They feed in all the bays and inlets along this shore, including the Suquamish, Yukon Harbor and Poulsbo. There are boats at Manchester, Poulsbo and Bremerton. The Chinook salmon will run anywhere from a pound to 15 pounds. Best catches are made in the winter.

Many of the rivers along the Bellingham Bay-Puget Sound coast have runs of steelhead as well as salmon. The Nooksack, Skagit, Pilchuck, Stillaguamish, Skokomish, Snoqualmie, Tolt, Green and Puyallup all have winter runs, usually entering the streams about December and lasting through March in this part of Washington. The Stillaguamish and Snoqualmie also have summer runs, usually from about June 15th to the end of April.

The NOOKSACK RIVER (1), entering Bellingham Bay north of the city of Bellingham at Lummi Bay, is one of Washington's largest rivers. It is discolored with glacial water all summer but there is good fishing for cutthroat and Dolly Varden trout early and late. Then in the fall and winter both salmon and steelhead move in. Some sea-run cutthroat also come in. The river has three forks, the North Fork, Middle Fork and South Fork, and all offer good fishing for cutthroat, Dolly Varden, sea-run cutthroat and steelhead. The lower river access is from U.S. 1 and Alternate U.S. 99, as well as via many secondary roads. Accommodations are plentiful around Bellingham and at Marietta at the river mouth, as well as along State Highway 1A which runs up river for a considerable distance.

The SKAGIT RIVER (2) enters Skagit Sound to the south of this, near the city of Mount Vernon. The river is easily approached through its entire length via State Highway 16 on the north and a paved county road along the south shore. This is generally regarded as one of the best, and possibly the best, steelhead river in Washington. It is discolored in the summer but usually clears somewhat by the time the silver salmon, Chinook and sea-run cutthroat come into the river in the fall. The steelhead usually appear in December. Throughout the season there is good fly fishing for rainbows in the higher waters of the stream. Guides are available at Hamilton, Lyman, Sedro Woolley and Mount Vernon.

There are now three dams on the upper Skagit and the top one, Ross Dam, backs up twenty-four-mile Lake Ross into Canada. There is some very good fishing for large rainbows and Dolly Varden. State Highway 16 skirts the lower end of the lake and from there in trails are the order. There is a resort on the lake, open from July to October. Inquiries should be addressed to Ross Lake Resort, Rockport, Washington.

The STILLAGUAMISH (3) is another famous Puget Sound river, reaching the bay at Stanwood on Coastal Highway 1E. The Stillaguamish can be an excellent river, but most of the main part and much of the North Fork are frequently disturbed by mud slides. Nevertheless, there is some fishing all the time and good fly fishing after September 1st in the downstream waters, from Sylvana to Arlington, when the sea-run cutthroats come in. The North Fork is now restricted to fly fishing only during the summer and fall, and this is a top time for steelhead. During the winter there is another run and at this time, when the river is usually muddy, bait is widely used and some good catches are made. There are also sea-run cutthroats in the fall. The South Fork also gets both summer- and winter-run steelhead, up as far as Granite Falls. Above that the fishing is for rainbows, on a put and take basis.

The SNOQUALMIE RIVER (4) comes into Puget Sound at Everett and much of the river runs alongside State Highway 15B and U.S. 10. This river is very high till late July but then has good fishing for resident cutthroat and rainbows. Later in the season the sea-run cutthroat come in, followed by steelhead. Some steelhead stay around the river mouth all summer. Some cabins are available both along the main river and its forks, and there are plenty of accommodations at Duvall, Carnation, Snoqualmie and North Bend. Where its tributary, the Tolt, joins the Snoqualmie is one of the most famous steelhead holes in the west. Another tributary, the PILCHUCK (5), is only open in the lower reaches around Snoqualmie, where there is a fair run of winter steelhead.

The SKYKOMISH RIVER (6), another tributary of the Snoqualmie, is also an excellent river for steelhead, best liked by anglers in the summer, especially by fly fishermen, as the water is low and clear at this time. Atlantic-salmon techniques such as the greased-line method of fishing a fly are successful in the Skykomish. From the town of Monroe, a couple of miles above the outlet, up to the forks at Index, U.S. 2 runs very close to the river. The towns of Monroe, Sultan and Gold Bar all provide accommodations.

The GREEN RIVER (7), which flows to Elliott Bay at Kent, is subject to special regulations to protect the young steelhead in the summer, and the annual fishing laws should always be checked before fishing this river. In the fall there is excellent steelhead angling and there are some good resident rainbows.

The PUYALLUP RIVER (8), at the south end of Puget Sound, is probably the top stream of them all for winter-run steelhead, with the possible exception of the Skagit. The Puyallup is big, generally discolored, and difficult to wade. It joins the WHITE RIVER (9) at Puyallup. In both streams, in the lower river, there are rainbows and cutthroat. Sea-run cutthroat come in in the fall and there is a good run of steelhead from December through February. Below Puyallup, the White is generally known as the Stuck River.

Entering the bay west of Tacoma is the NISQUALLY RIVER (10), formed by glacial streams from Rainier National Park. It offers fishing for cutthroat, Chinook salmon and silver salmon, steelhead and sea-run cutthroat. The lower part of the river, which can be reached by State Highway 51 from Olympia and State Highway 5H from Tacoma, is very heavily fished. Upstream from the town of McKenna, where the river is not so accessible, is where you'll find the best fishing.

OLYMPIC PENINSULA

The large block of land separated from the main body of the state by Puget Sound is known as the Olympic Peninsula, named for the range of mountains which form its backbone. To reach the Peninsula you can go around the southern end of Puget Sound at Olympia, and from there follow U.S. 101 along the coast. There are very few roads to the interior. A ferry also provides service from Port Townsend on the northeast corner to Keystone on Whidbey Island.

The north shore of the Olympic Peninsula, facing the Straits of Juan de Fuca, is today's outpost as far as the Washington salmon fisherman is concerned. The fish come in here fresh from the sea and raring to go, providing some wonderful fishing. Pillar Point at the mouth of the Pysht River is good, and to the west,

Sekiu and Clallam Bay are noted for their runs of silver salmon in September and October. All along here you can get good fishing for some kind of salmon from early May when the Chinooks first put in an appearance, all through the year, as one migration follows another. Even in the winter, for those anglers who are hardy enough to brave the weather, there is outstanding blackmouth fishing at Neah Bay and Sekiu.

You can stay at Port Angeles, on U.S. 101 at the northeastern corner of the Peninsula, and in ten minutes be into excellent salmon fishing for either silvers or Chinook, the latter being taken up to 50 pounds as recently as June, 1963. Most of the fishing is done by trolling with flasher and herring combination. Salmon can be taken year-round but the peak months are June, July and August.

As well as the accommodations to be found at Port Angeles, there are resorts at Neah Bay, Sekiu, Clallam Bay, Dungeness and near Port Ludlow, all with adequate facilities to take care of quite a number of fishermen. Charters can be arranged through Mel's Resort at Neah Bay, Al Alson at Sekiu, as well as at other resorts along the coast. At Port Angeles you can get charters through Chick's Marina and at the Port Angeles Salmon Club, a nonprofit organization which operates the Thunderbird Boathouse there. The club also sponsors an annual $10,000 fishing derby on August 31st and September 1st.

Steelhead fishing is extra good in the winter in a dozen streams on the Olympic Peninsula, some fish running as heavy as 15 pounds. In summer there is good fishing for resident rainbows and cutthroat. Early-season anglers generally use spoons, worms and salmon eggs but flies are good in late summer.

Following the coast westward along the Straits of Juan de Fuca, anglers find winter steelhead in the DUNGENESS RIVER (11), between Port Townsend and Port Angeles, and in the ELWHA RIVER (12) to the west. The Dungeness is good all winter from early December on, and there is a lighter, summer run in May and June. There is a dam on the Elwha, which river crosses U.S. 101 about nine miles west of Port Angeles. From the Straits up to the dam there is good winter steelhead fishing, and in the lake above the dam some fine rainbow fishing. Boats can be obtained at the Elwha Resort where U.S. 101 crosses the river.

Further west the PYSHT RIVER (13) enters the Straits at Pillar Point. This is a good river for sea-run cutthroat as well as steelhead. A county road connecting the coastal highway, State Highway 9A, and U.S. 101, further inland, runs up along the river from the small town of Pysht at the mouth.

The longest road should end in the best fishing, and in many ways the La Push area on the northwest coast of the Olympic Peninsula bears this out. U.S. Highway 101 will take you there, either by circling north from Olympia, around the north shore along the Straits of Juan de Fuca, then south again; or via Aberdeen east, then north. There is top-rated salmon fishing from early May to late September. Boat rentals in the Quillayute River supply skiffs and motors, while the resorts which cluster around the river mouth provide charter-boat service to the fishing waters, which are only a few minutes from the dock. In addition, there are several Indian reservations along the coast, and many anglers obtain the services of an Indian guide, with his dugout canoe, and go for salmon in this way.

The Quillayute is only four miles long, formed by the conjunction of the SOLEDUCK, BOGACHIEL and CALAWAH RIVERS (14). It has a good run of steelhead in late July and early August. The Quillayute also has resident cutthroat, rainbows

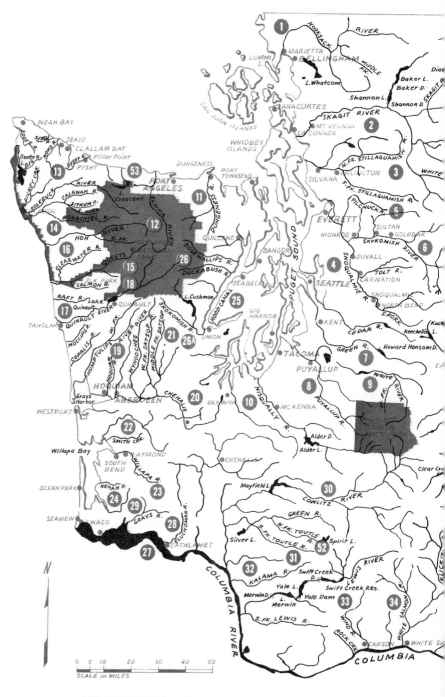

WASHINGTON

SCALE in MILES
0 5 10   20   30   40   50

N

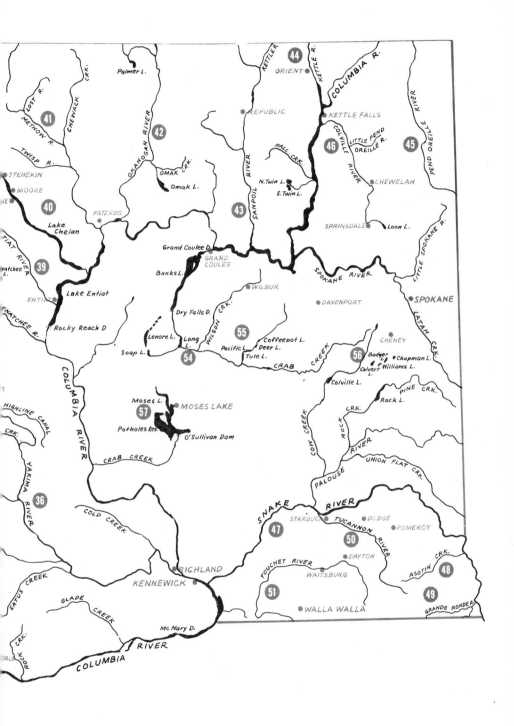

and Dolly Varden. Later the fish move up to the tributaries, and consequently the Soleduck, Calawah and Bogachiel all have long seasons for steelhead, as well as good fishing for resident cutthroats and rainbows.

The Forks Motel at Forks, just south of where the road into La Push leaves U.S. 101, is a good place to stay and can provide guides on request. This is a very popular spot during the spring run of steelhead, so early reservations are necessary. At the Forks you can follow U.S. 101 around to the east to the Soleduck Hot Springs road, and in summer time you can get a pack string there to go deep into the Olympic National Park.

South of La Push the QUEETS RIVER (15) can be fished out of the coastal town of the same name. A county road runs up along the river to the hamlet of Elk Park. The Queets also has a good late-July, early-August run of steelhead and sea-run cutthroat. This river is not usually clear and is therefore fished mostly with bait or heavy lures rather than flies. There are also resident cutthroat and Dolly Vardens. At the town of Queets there is an inn and cabins, and pack horses and guides are available for inland fishing.

Some tributaries of the Queets have excellent fly fishing for rainbows and cutthroats. The CLEARWATER RIVER (16), especially, is good summer-long for cutthroat. The sea-run cutthroat come in in the fall and the steelhead in the winter. There is a fishing camp at the town of Clearwater about three miles upstream.

In the same general area, the QUINAULT RIVER (17) comes down from Lake Quinault to Taholah on the coast. U.S. 101 runs inland here, to touch the shores of the lake. To reach the lower part of the river you go in from Hoquiam on State Highway 9C. Steelhead fishing is best in the Quinault in July and August, just below the Forks. There is some excellent fishing for cutthroat, Dolly Varden and rainbows, and there are seasonal runs of sea-run cutthroat.

Above the river, LAKE QUINAULT (18) has the same fish plus some silvers and sockeye. There is a large resort on the lake, and Indian guides are available for canoe trips downstream. There are also pack horses for upstream fishing trips. There are numerous camping spots around the lake.

Prices for the various services vary widely and information should be obtained from either Bergman's Resort, Quinault, or the Quinault Mercantile Store. At either place anglers can also purchase the special permit required to fish the lake and those parts of the river which are within the Indian Reservation.

The Westport area, at the mouth of Grays Harbor, near the towns of Aberdeen and Hoquiam on the west shore of the Olympic Peninsula, is one of the best sport-fishing ports. There are many resorts, just as many fishermen, and 200 charter boats to take them out for big Chinook and silvers. The cost of a party boat here as in most West Coast ports is about $10 per person per day. Fishing is mostly by mooching, the boats drifting one area then moving to another and drifting again.

Those who plan to go out in skiffs must remember that this is very dangerous water. Storms blow up in a hurry and there is a tremendous tide and frequently big rollers. At the slightest sign of bad weather, small-boat anglers should put in to shore.

Around Westport the early season sees feeder fish moving around the jetties, and these can go anywhere from 6 to 40 pounds. Towards the end of June the run is on and August sees fishing for Chinook and silvers close inshore. The fish that come in late are headed for the rivers that flow into Grays Harbor, the Humptulips, Hoquiam, Wishkoh, Wynoochee and Chehalis, and these are often very big fish, some going to 80 pounds.

Besides salmon fishing, there is good casting for sea perch along the beaches near Westport. The fish average about 2 to 3 pounds.

The Grays Harbor rivers all have runs of sea-run cutthroat, starting in early July and continuing on through the fall; and on their way in they can be taken in the tidal areas. Early in the season they like single salmon eggs and light lures such as the flatfish. In tidewater some big ones are taken by trolling deep.

The HUMPTULIPS RIVER (19), which enters North Bay at Grays Harbor, and the Wynoochee River, which joins the Chehalis at Montesano, are two of the better steelhead rivers of the state, with excellent winter runs. The Humptulips can be reached from State Highway 9 at several places, and a county road roughly parallels much of the lower course, from Copalis Crossing to the town of Humptulips. There are accommodations available at both places. The lower part of the river is very large and most of the fishing is by boat, trolling for Chinook and silver salmon, sea-run cutthroat and steelhead. Upstream there is fishing for resident cutthroat and rainbows.

The CHEHALIS RIVER (20) comes into the harbor at Aberdeen. It is badly polluted in the lower waters but from Montesano up there is some good fishing. The steelhead season is from December through February, while silver salmon and sea-run cutthroat are taken in August and September. State Highway 9 follows the Chehalis for most of its length and there are accommodations at all the towns. An excellent tributary, the SATSOP (21), is reached by county road from either Grady or Satsop on State Highway 9. This is a renowned winter steelhead stream, and in summer has good fly fishing for resident rainbows and cutthroats in all of its four forks.

To the south, SMITH CREEK (22) and the WILLAPA RIVER (23), both entering Willapa Bay, have good fishing for sea-run cutthroats. They are especially good for fly fishing in mid-August, when these sea-run cutthroats will fall all over themselves for a red fly or bucktail shrimp. Lures that are successful are the 3/16 ounce Spin Wobbler, Andy Reeker spoon, ¼-ounce Highland Fling and the ¼-ounce Canadian Wonder. The Smith can be reached from State Highway 13A west of Raymond. The Willapa follows the road to Chehalis, State Highway 12, from Raymond.

If you follow U.S. 101 south from Raymond you cross the NEMAH RIVER (24), where there is also some good fishing for sea-run cutthroat trout and a winter run of steelhead. The nearest town is South Bend to the north; or anglers can stay at Seaview to the south or find accommodations at the head of North Beach Peninsula.

Running for seventy miles almost due north and south along the eastern side of the Olympic Peninsula, the HOOD CANAL (25) lives on its past reputation to a certain extent. However, it is to be hoped that future good management may return it at least somewhat to its former position as a producer of good fishing. Even as it stands there are some feeding blackmouths around all year and runs of adult fish in July and August, and of silvers in September to December. Along the lower half of the canal there are many resorts and every boating facility. Further north there are fewer facilities but better fishing, as there is an unusually large concentration of blackmouths in March, plus good cutthroat trout fishing in the fall and good silver salmon runs in September and October.

Accommodations are to be found on the western shore of the Hood Canal at Brinnon and Quilcene. On the eastern shore anglers stay at Bangor or Seabeck or go across the peninsula to Bremerton.

The DUCKABUSH and DOSEWALLIPS RIVERS (26), entering the western bank of the Hood Canal at Dabon Bay, are two top steelhead streams. The Duckabush is at its peak through the summer months. The Dosewallips is generally better in September and the fishing is at the Forks. You can approach these two rivers from U.S. 101 and there are accommodations at Brinnon and Quilcene to the north, or you can go still farther north to Port Townsend and Port Angeles.

The South Fork of the SKOKOMISH RIVER (26A) reaches the Hood Canal near Union. The lower water can be reached from U.S. 101 and State Highway 21, both of which cross it west of Union. The winter run of steelheads is one of the best on the Hood Canal. Sea-run cutthroat come in in September, and at this time there is some excellent fly fishing around the mouth of the river. At other times the fish are taken mostly on bait and spinners.

The North Fork of the Skokomish starts above Lake Cushman, flows through the lake and on down to meet the South Fork about twelve miles below the lake. Steelhead make their way up the river as far as the falls about seven miles below the lake, and anglers can reach this part of the river by trail from the river mouth. Although the Skokomish is frequently disturbed by the release of water from Lake Cushman, which is the power reservoir for the city of Tacoma, there is some good day-to-day fishing for resident Dolly Varden, rainbows and cutthroat.

The lake is kept stocked with silvers and there are some rainbows and cutthroat. There are camp sites on the shore, accessible by gravel road from Hoodsport on U.S. 101; and at the south end of the lake you can get boats at Berg's Resort. Boats are also obtainable at the north end at Staircase Resort. From this point you can reach the upper waters of the North Fork of the Skokomish.

COLUMBIA RIVER SYSTEM

While the COLUMBIA RIVER (27) is the passage through which many salmon make their way into the interior of Washington and Oregon, it is rapidly declining as a sport-fishing river. So many dams have been built and so many more planned that there will soon be little river left, and as a result, few spawning possibilities for the Pacific salmon. In addition, commercial fishing has been so heavy as to seriously deplete the supplies of fish. However, some salmon and steelhead still manage to ascend the fish ladders provided at various dams and make their way to the spawning beds, and are taken throughout the length of the river.

Besides the major rivers mentioned already, several small streams at the Columbia Inlet produce good salmon and steelhead fishing at times. The ELUCHOMAN (28), entering the Inlet at Cathlamet, has good steelhead fishing, plus fall runs of silver salmon and cutthroat. It is paralleled for its shore length by State Highway 12D. The GRAYS RIVER (29) is popular with late fall and winter fishermen for its fine run of steelhead. There are also some salmon. The lower river can easily be reached via State Highway 12 and 830; but the upper part calls for packing or hiking in. However, the upper waters produce some fine fishing for steelhead, rainbows and large cutthroat.

At the mouth of the Columbia the ports of Ilwaco and Megler have charter-boat services for silvers and Chinook, which are taken from late June through September, mostly by mooching with herring.

All along the north shore of the Columbia Inlet there are occasional sloughs where anglers find some good bass fishing. Brooks Slough at Skamokawa is good all summer; and Deep River, on the Ocean Beach Highway, further west, is excellent and can be fished from the banks as well as by boat. Boats are available both at Deep River and Skamokawa. There is also good fishing for the warm-water species on Puget Island, which can be reached by bridge from Cathlamet.

In the Skamokawa River, at the town of the same name, there are bass and crappie in the lower water and steelhead, cutthroat and rainbows up above.

In the Columbia River, from Longview upstream, there is steelhead fishing for much of the year, with cutthroat also taken from late July through October.

Longview is a good point from which to fish the lower Columbia, as there's year-round fishing within ten minutes' drive, in each case, in the Columbia, Cowlitz, Toutle and Kalama. There are winter steelhead in all four. The COWLITZ (30) has an excellent run of Chinook salmon in April and there are steelhead from December to April. The fall run comes in September and lasts for about three months. There are also resident rainbows and cutthroat, as well as whitefish.

The TOUTLE RIVER (31) is best from December to April for steelhead. Fishing for resident rainbows and cutthroat is good from April to July; and there's a run of sea-run cutthroat from August to October. This fall run of cutthroats, as well as some silver salmon, also goes into the South Fork of the Toutle, much of which can be reached by trail only from State Highway 1R east of Castle Rock. There are also resident cutthroat and rainbows, and steelhead in the summer.

The next major river to the south, the KALAMA (32), is considered a top summer steelhead river, too, and in addition has an excellent run of "springers" in March. The summer run comes in June and July. The river can be fished with fly, bait or spinning lure all the way from its juncture with the Columbia at Kalama, twenty miles upstream to Piegon Springs. At Camp Kalama at the mouth of the river you can get a guide for floats on the Kalama.

The fate of the Columbia necessarily affects the salmon runs in all these streams. Efforts are being made to provide salmon stairs so the spawning stock can continue to pass by the numerous dams, but, nevertheless, a lot of the damage has been done and fishing in these rivers is not what it used to be. The same is true to an even more marked degree of the rivers which join the Columbia beyond the big bend at Portland.

The WIND RIVER (33), which enters the Columbia at Carson, half way between Portland and The Dalles, is known for its summer run of fish that are heftier than average, weighing from 7 to 9 pounds. They occasionally appear in late July, but the run is usually in August and September. The best fishing is from Shepherd Falls down to the Columbia, and in the lower section there is some first-rate dry-fly fishing. The last two miles above Carson runs through a picturesque canyon and this, too, is good casting water, for either fly or spinning. There are motels and restaurants at Carson. A paved road follows the river for about fifteen miles, then gives way to a gravel road.

The WHITE SALMON RIVER (34) enters the Columbia at the town of White Salmon. State Highway 8D follows the river all the way up so it is easily reached. There are some steelhead and Chinook salmon in the lower three miles, below the dam. Above that there are resident rainbows and some eastern brook trout. There is also some good fishing for largemouth black bass in the sloughs of the Columbia at the mouth of the White Salmon.

Proceeding eastward, the next stream is the KLICKITAT (35), which has a good summer run of steelhead, has some resident cutthroat and Rocky Mountain white-fish, and is stocked with rainbows annually. The best way to reach the river is to go in on the county road from Goldendale on State Highway 8, or from Lyle on the Columbia, nineteen miles east of White Salmon.

Just before the Columbia makes a curve north to Kennewick and Richland, anglers find some fairly good steelhead fishing below the McNary Dam, from August right through the winter. Boats are available at Plymouth on State Road 8.

EASTERN SLOPES OF THE CASCADES

From this point north the Columbia skirts the eastern slopes of the Cascades, picking up water from dozens of rivers coming down from the mountains. The Columbia itself is obstructed at regular intervals by dams and consequently, because of this situation plus the many dams lower down on the river, the number of salmon and steelhead getting through is negligible compared to what it should be. However, there is some steelhead fishing in the waters below the dams, and at the mouths of several rivers, including the Entiat, Methow and Okanagan.

The largest tributary on the western shore of the Columbia is the YAKIMA RIVER (36), which comes into the Columbia above Richland. At times it can be quite good for rainbows, some cutthroat and eastern brook trout, as well as Rocky Mountain whitefish, but it is adversely affected by frequent release of water from CLE ELUM, KEECHELS and KACHESS LAKES (37), above.

Lake Cle Elum is about nine miles long and one mile wide. Fishing here and in neighboring Kachess Lake is for silvers and Mackinaw trout, rainbows, eastern brook trout and Dolly Varden. Many other smaller lakes in the same area hold all or some of the same species. Cle Elum is reached from U.S. 10 to the Snoqualmie Winter Sports Area and there are accommodations at Cle Elum, Keechelis and Easton.

From Lake Wenatchee, in the eastern Cascades, the WENATCHEE RIVER (38) flows sixty miles to the Columbia. This is a big river and can be waded only at very low water. There are cutthroat, Dolly Vardens, rainbows and eastern brook trout. Fishing for whitefish is popular in the winter. State Highway 2 follows the river up from its mouth for some miles, then U.S. 2 comes in from the south and goes on up almost to the lake. There are accommodations of all kinds along the way. The lake can be reached by State Highway 15C from U.S. 2 at Leavenworth or Nason Creek. There are several resorts on the lake and boats are readily obtainable to fish for cutthroat, rainbow and Dolly Varden.

The ENTIAT RIVER (39) enters the Columbia some sixteen miles above the Wenatchee. Although this is another glacial stream, and frequently discolored, there is good summer fishing for rainbows, cutthroat, Dolly Varden and eastern brook trout. It is paralleled by a dirt road leaving the Columbia River Highway, U.S. 97, at Entiat. The same road gives access to the lower waters of the Mad River, a tribu-tary of the Entiat. Those who work their way by trail further upstream on the Mad find some good cutthroat fishing.

As mentioned earlier, LAKE CHELAN (40) is one of the few really large lakes in Washington. Lying in the eastern Cascades, it is really just a widening of the river caused by a dam at its junction with the Columbia. The lake is fifty-two miles long and only a mile wide, hemmed in by the Chelan Range on the south and the Sawtooth Range on the north. Although it can produce some fine cutthroats, rainbows and Dolly Varden, it is not heavily fished. You go in from the town of Chelan about fifty miles north of Wenatchee, on a county road on the south side of the river. There is also a ferry running the length of the lake to Lucerne, Moore and Stehekin, where there are several cabin resorts. Pack trips into small streams higher in the mountains may also be arranged. Arrangements can be made through Camp Gettysburg, Lucerne; Moore Inn at Moore; or Golden West Lodge at Stehekin.

One of the most popular rainbow streams on the east slopes of the Cascades is the METHOW (41), which joins the Columbia at Pateros. The stream can be reached from State 16, which runs beside it for some sixty miles. Above this are several tributaries, also heavily stocked with Rainbows. In the lower part of the river, from the junction with the Columbia up to Mazama, there are numerous dude ranches.

Beyond this the Columbia once more makes a sharp turn, again heading west. On the turn the OKANOGAN RIVER (42) comes in from the north. The Okanogan has some small brown trout and it is reported that winter steelhead are beginning to appear in this river. There are also Rocky Mountain whitefish. U.S. 97 runs beside the river all the way to the Canadian border.

From this point on through eastern Washington the Columbia has been backed up by dams to form the Franklin D. Roosevelt Lake, or Grand Coulee. The level of water in this lake fluctuates so widely that it is not only poor to fish but boating is dangerous. A few good-sized rainbows are taken occasionally at the creek mouths.

The SANPOIL RIVER (43), on the north shore, east of the Coulee Dam, has a reputation for excellent fishing in spring and fall for both eastern brook trout and rainbows of better than 2 pounds average weight. The river can be reached from Republic, south on State Highway H4, which runs with the river for some sixty miles; or you can come up State Highway 2 from Coulee City to State Highway 4 at Wilbur, then north to cross the river via a free ferry.

The next major tributary on the north is the KETTLE RIVER (44). You can follow this stream down from the Canadian border on U.S. 395 to Kettle Falls. The river is stocked with rainbows and there is excellent winter fishing for whitefish. Where the river enters the Columbia there are largemouth black bass. The town of Orient, about fifteen miles up from the river mouth, is a center for a number of small resorts on the river and several neighboring small lakes.

Following State Highway 22 from the Columbia north towards the Canadian border for only half a mile, then turning left on a gravel road, anglers will find Big Sheep Creek, which has a wide variety of water, from slow runs with good deep holes, to faster runs in the lower section. This creek is reputed to turn out quite a few rainbows in the 3-pound class.

There are a number of major tributaries of the Columbia which come from the east, getting their water from the mountains of Idaho. The PEND OREILLE RIVER (45) winds through the northeast corner, cuts back north into Canada, then south and west to join the Columbia on the Canadian border south of Trail, B.C. The fishing is generally good at the mouth of every creek, for brown, rainbow and cutthroat trout, which occasionally go better than 5 pounds. There are also bass, perch, crappie and Rocky Mountain whitefish. The river is accessible throughout from State Highway 6 on the west bank and a county road on the east bank. There are accommodations at several small towns along State Highway 6.

One of the best rivers in the area, the COLVILLE (46), flows north along U.S. 395 to the Columbia at Kettle Falls. There are eastern brook trout in the Colville in the top waters, between Springdale and Chewelah, and there are browns and rainbows further down. There are also some bass in the lower waters. A tributary of the Colville, the LITTLE PEND OREILLE, is fairly good for rainbows and eastern brook trout.

The famous SNAKE RIVER (47) forms part of the southeast border with Idaho, then turns west and reaches the Columbia at Kennewick. In July and August anglers take steelhead by trolling around the juncture of the Snake and the Columbia, where boats are available at Kennewick. Upstream from Pascoe on the Snake there is some good fishing for bass, crappie and catfish below the first dam. This is also a good place to try for sturgeon. A county road follows the north side of the Snake from the junction, and State Highway 3D runs along the south bank, to a small town called Page. This area can produce some pretty good spring bass fishing. Steelhead come in in late July and continue through the winter, and reports are that the steelheading is better in the Snake than it used to be.

In the area south of U.S. 410 between Lewiston, Idaho, and Walla Walla, Washington, there is some fairly good stream fishing for rainbows in several small streams which come down from the heights around Oregon Butte and Diamond Peak. You can reach the largest of them, ASOTIN CREEK (48), from the town of Asotin, south of Lewiston on State Highway 3. This creek is kept pretty well supplied with stocked rainbows, and anglers get occasional steelhead, too. At Asotin you can obtain instructions on how to reach some of the small feeder streams, which can be quite good, especially early in the season. But lack of water can be a problem in much of this southeast corner of the state, so it's always wise to make inquiries before treking in to some remote lake or river.

The GRANDE RONDE RIVER (49), which cuts across the extreme southeast corner of Washington to enter the Snake, is a fairly good-sized river and has some rainbow fishing, a good run of steelhead, and some salmon and bass. It can be reached from State Highway 3 from Lewiston, or via a gravel road from Pomeroy on U.S. 410.

From Dayton, also on U.S. 410, you can go south to Butte Creek for both rainbows and Dolly Varden, and very occasional steelhead. The best fishing is in May or June. Much of this area is very dry in summer and the streams are too low then to support fish.

From September through the winter there is usually fair steelhead fishing in this area wherever a tributary enters the Snake. The mouth of the TUCANNON RIVER (50), which can be reached from U.S. 295 via the gravel road to Starbuck, is one of the best. In the Tucannon itself there are rainbows, steelhead and some salmon. At Dayton or Dodge, or Waitsburg, to the south, you can get directions to some small, isolated lakes constructed by the Fish and Game Department of Washington, where there is fishing for rainbow and brook trout. Out of Dayton and Dodge you can also fish the TOUCHET RIVER (51) for rainbows and some Dolly Vardens. This is good camping country.

LAKE FISHING

The fishing in Washington rivers is so spectacular as to overshadow the fact that in literally hundreds of lakes in the state there is excellent fishing for trout and some warm-water species. In both the Cascades and the Olympic Mountains you can hike from the highway to a secluded mountain lake only a few miles from the road, or you can pack in for longer trips to lakes which are in true wilderness country. Much of this lake fishing requires steep climbing, and you must pack in a rubber raft if you want to get away from shore at all. On many lakes there are rafts, but you can never be sure that someone else will not be using them when you arrive.

Most of the mountain lakes have been stocked with rainbows, some with brook trout, and a few with California goldens. Since the productivity of these mountain lakes varies from year to year, it's always wise to check with someone in the nearest town or village as to the condition of the lake in which you plan to fish.

Many of the choice lake areas have been developed as recreational and winter-sports areas, or are in National Forests or Parks. In western Washington the Sno-qualmie Pass area has many good lakes, with rainbows, brook trout and some native cutthroat, in pan sizes. This area can be reached via U.S. 10 from Seattle.

The same types of lakes are found to the north in the Skykomish area, reached via U.S. 2 from Everett. Still further north the Glacier Peak and Skagit River area near the Canadian border offers a selection of rainbows and cutthroat amid primitive surroundings.

Anglers can follow Interstate Highway 5 north from Portland, Oregon, to the town of Castlerock to find several good fishing lakes. Further to the northeast, on State Highway 5, the town of Packwood is a good entry point for the White Pass District and Blankenship Meadows. SPIRIT LAKE (52), at the head of the North Fork of the Toutle River, has early-season fishing for rainbows and some large cutthroat. You can troll or fish from shore. There are also eastern brook trout in the river, as well as rainbows. You can drive right to this one via State Highway 1R.

In the Olympic Peninsula the lake-fishing possibilities are endless, but there is one lake in particular which makes interesting fishing because anglers may take two species of trout not known elsewhere. CRESCENT LAKE (53) is on U.S. 101 west of Port Angeles on the north shore of the Peninsula. The two species are known as the Beardesley and the Crescenti trouts, the former a rainbow and the latter a cutthroat. Trolling with heavy weights is the method used for the major part of the lake, which is very deep. But there is some fly fishing and light lure casting along the shores. The Beardesley trout in Crescent Lake will average 6 pounds and go as high as 20 pounds. Lake fishing in this area starts in May and continues through October. You can stay at either Rosemary Lodge or Fairholm, one at each end of the lake.

In the eastern Cascades there are also many lakes which are stocked with rainbows and some cutthroat. Around Chelan Lake, already described, there are innumerable such small bodies of water, both in the Chelan Range to the south and the Sawtooth Range to the north. In most cases they are reached by rugged trail or by packing in. Outfits are obtainable at the resorts on Chelan Lake, as mentioned earlier. The same situation holds in the Okanogan River area, where many pothole-sized lakes are stocked with rainbows.

There are many small lakes west of Spokane which can range from only fair to very good, where anglers can find a variety of fishing for both bass and trout. LONG LAKE RESERVOIR (54) at Stratford on State Highway 7, is good for bass, and the perch fishing is outstanding. There are no boats available but you can fish from shore. Southwest of Davenport on U.S. 2, and then State Highway 7 to Odessa, anglers will find some excellent fishing for largemouth black bass in PACIFIC LAKE (55), fish reaching the hefty weight of 8 pounds. There are also crappie, catfish and perch. Throughout this area there are a number of lakes which hold crappie and some bass, and a few are annually stocked with rainbows. You can usually get information about their current productivity at the towns of Davenport, Odessa and Wilbur.

One spot where there is some fairly good fly fishing in this area is BADGER LAKE (56), fifteen miles south of Cheney, on U.S. 90 south from Spokane. The lake is well stocked with cutthroats and rainbows, and fly fishing is good early in the season and again late in the summer. There are several resorts right on the lake. Nearby CHAPMAN LAKE (56) adds fishing for largemouth and smallmouth bass, and silvers.

MOSES LAKE (57), a much larger body of water, is on U.S. 10 southwest of Spokane. This lake is highly developed residentially but there is fishing for crappie and bluegills, and some bass. Boats are available at the town of Moses Lake. To the southeast of the O'Sullivan Dam on Moses Lake there are a number of small lakes which have good rainbow fishing. Access to them is fairly easy via county roads out of the town of Othello.

WASHINGTON FISHING REGULATIONS

Resident State Fishing License $4.50
Resident County Fishing License $3.00
Nonresident Fishing License $15.00
Nonresident 7-Day Fishing License $4.00

SEASONS

All fish, lowland lakes and designated streams   April 25–Oct. 31
High lakes and all other streams   May 31–Oct. 31

Note: Opening date is July 1 in numerous important coastal steelhead streams, to give protection to immature steelhead.

For complete regulations write: Department of Game, 600 North Capitol Way, Olympia, Washington.

Alaska
and the
Canadian
Provinces

ALASKA

Because of its remoteness from the rest of the continent, as well as the nature of its climate and terrain, Alaska has remained the least developed area in North America, with the exception of the barren lands of the Northwest Territories. But its thousands of lakes and rivers hold fish in untold numbers for those who are fortunate enough to be able to reach them.

The species to be taken include king (Chinook) salmon, silver (coho) salmon, kokanee, sockeye (blueback) salmon, dog salmon, humpback salmon, rainbow trout and steelhead, cutthroat trout, lake trout, Dolly Varden trout, eastern brook trout, northern pike, whitefish, Arctic grayling, Arctic char, burbot or freshwater ling, and that rare species of the far north, the sheefish.

The Yukon is the main river, splitting the state in half in its progress from east to west. The Tanana, one of its tributaries, is almost as large, flowing northwest from the Yukon border through Fairbanks to join the Yukon at Tanana, almost square in the middle of Alaska. In the north, many smaller rivers flow down north to the Arctic Ocean from the Brooks Range of Mountains, while in the south and central areas several mountain ranges such as the Kuskokwim in the south-central area, the Talkeetnas above Anchorage, and the Wrangell Mountains to the east, shed streams in all directions.

There are few very large lakes. The largest, Lake Iliamna, lies southwest of Anchorage near the top of the Alaska Peninsula. A group of smaller lakes is located immediately to the west and Lakes Naknek, Becharof and Ugashik, also fairly large, are out on the Peninsula. But the number of small lakes is legion.

For many years Alaska was cut off from the rest of the continent except for the occasional coast-wise steamers plying up the British Columbia coast to Ketchikan, Juneau and Anchorage. Then, during the last war the Alaska Highway was built, from Dawson Creek in British Columbia across the southern corner of the Yukon and into Alaska, ending at Fairbanks. Another road known as the Mayo Road, was put through from Whitehorse in the Yukon to Dawson and on down to join the Alaska Highway at Tetlin Junction. These roads, and a few arteries running down to Anchorage, Spenard, Seward and Homer on the Kenai Peninsula, south of Anchorage, plus two short stretches of highway running northeast and northwest of Fairbanks, are the only roads in the vast 586,400 square miles that make up Alaska. The main method of transportation is the airplane; and for years Alaskan bush pilots have been renowned for their skill.

To reach Alaska, you can go by daily flights from Seattle to Fairbanks via Alaska Airlines and Pan American World Airways, the rate being approximately $100 each way. Daily flights are also available from Seattle to Anchorage on Northwest Orient Airlines and Pacific Northern Airlines. There is steamer service up the coast from Vancouver to Skagway, details of which can be obtained from the Alaska Steamship Company, Seattle, Washington; Canadian National Steamship Company, Vancouver, British Columbia; and Canadian Pacific Steamship Company, Vancouver, British Columbia.

Canadian Coachways operates a bus service from Edmonton, Alberta, to Dawson Creek, British Columbia, where you can make connections with Alaska Motor Coaches to Fairbanks. There is also bus service between White Horse, Yukon and Fairbanks. Information about schedules may be obtained from Canadian Coachways Limited, 10805-120th Street, Edmonton, Alberta; Greyhound Lines of Canada, Limited, 222-1st Avenue West, Calgary, Alberta; Northern Stages, Limited, 1189-4th Avenue, Prince George, British Columbia; Alaska Motor Coaches Inc., P.O. Box 1048, Fairbanks, Alaska; White Pass & Yukon Route, 508 Standard Building, 510 West Hastings, Vancouver 2, British Columbia; Alaska Highway Tours, Joseph Vance Building, Seattle 1, Washington.

The spring breakup in Alaska starts in late April. May is slightly warmer, but the real summer weather doesn't come until June. From then, through July and August temperatures will range from 55 degrees Fahrenheit to 70 degrees. Fishermen should bring plenty of warm clothing and also remember that the coastal zone is subject to much rain and you will want suitable gear for that. Always take warm underwear for especially cool days and for fishing in the higher altitudes. Sturdy boots are a necessity for hiking.

Wild animals are very much in evidence and particularly the grizzly bear. In some places it is not safe to fish without a rifle at hand. Depending on your location there are also moose, deer, black bear, brown bear, goats, caribou, sheep, elk, musk ox, polar bear, wolves, wolverine, bison as well as many small animals.

Because of the great variety of fishing in Alaskan waters anglers usually like to carry several kinds of gear. An 8½-foot fly rod with GBF line, and a leader tapered down to 6-pound-test tippet will fill the bill for most fly fishing for steelhead, silver salmon and larger trouts. For smaller trout and grayling the angler should go to 3, 4 and even 5X.

While all the classic patterns are good, to the point that sometimes you can't find a fly that the fish will *not* take, the dull shades seem to be best. The Coachman, Silver Doctor and Mosquito are all popular. The flies should include the above patterns plus any of the standard U.S. patterns in sizes 10 to 16. Popular bucktails are the famous Muddler Minnow, red and white bucktail, all-white bucktail, all-yellow bucktail. Most of the standard streamers used in other parts of the United States are good in Alaska, and these should be augmented by the multi-wing streamers tied by the Phillips Fly and Tackle Company of Alexandria, Pennsylvania.

A medium-action spinning rod with flatfish, spoons and plugs will serve for spinning. Big spoons seem to take a notable number of big northern pike, king and silver salmon, lake trout and sheefish. Since you may tie into a really big fish, your reel should be large enough to hold a couple of hundred yards of 15-pound-test monofilament line.

Whatever your choice of gear, be sure to take a plentiful supply because there will be very little available, except at Anchorage and Juneau.

The difficulties of transportation in Alaska are so great that it is best to book your fishing trip through a competent guide service which has planes, camps and guides at its command. Outdoor Vacations, Inc., Columbia, Missouri, and Northwest Airlines, Anchorage, Alaska, operate such services, with flights to ten great fishing spots. One of these trips takes you to the renowned Brooks Range in the extreme north, where, in the streams flowing from the north side of the range into the Arctic, and in the many lakes, there is some of the state's top fishing for lake trout and Arctic grayling. Because of the northern latitude the season is short, from June 15 to August 15. You can manage a trip like this from Bettles Field, which is 500 miles north of Anchorage, just within the Arctic Circle, for about $600 per person per week for a party of three.

Other trips may be arranged to lakes and streams only 150 miles from Anchorage, to waters where grayling, rainbows and lake trout abound, for as little as $298 per person for a week.

The Wrangell Mountains, in the southeast corner of Alaska, are a favorite fishing area, with the Copper River and several lakes providing an abundance of grayling and some rainbows and lake trout. State Highway 1 cuts down from the Alaska Highway to a number of small communities, following the Copper River partway, then heading southwest to Anchorage.

From Anchorage flights can be arranged to Lake Iliamna, where there is excellent fishing. The Kvichak River, running out of the lake, is one of the top spots for steelhead and also holds Dolly Varden, rainbows, pike, grayling and salmon. The Newhalen and Talarie are also good.

All facilities for planning trips will be found at Anchorage, which serves as a good starting point for many trips to the interior, such as Mount McKinley, to the north, where the grayling fishing is excellent, and the Kenai Peninsula to the south, where you will find grayling, steelhead, salmon and lake trout. This is one of the few areas in Alaska accessible by road, State Highway 1 continuing from Anchorage down to the town of Homer at the point of the Peninsula.

There's an airfield at South Naknek, below Iliamna Lake, and accommodations at the little town of South Naknek. In the surrounding lakes and streams all varieties of fish may be taken. To the east, Kodiak Island also has an airport and lodging and guides can be obtained at the town of Kodiak.

From Dillingham, on the coast just to the west of the Alaska Peninsula, you can fly to the string of lakes including Tikchik, Nuyakuk, Chauekuktuli, and Chikuminuk for some fishing in an area which has been little exploited. These lakes and the surrounding streams produce rainbows up to 36 inches, and plenty from 27 to 30 inches.

There is a twenty-mile road from Dillingham to Lake Aleknagik, from which point you can go by boat to a camp on the Agulawak River. There are Arctic char, pike, rainbow and grayling in nearby rivers in great abundance.

Guide service for this area may be obtained through Jack Randall, Cooper Landing, Alaska; Ray McNutt, Empire, Alaska; and John Pearson, Dillingham, Alaska. The latter has a camp at Tikchik Lake Narrows where some trophy trout have been taken. The rates are about $250 for seven days.

Also out of Anchorage you can fly to Snowshoe Lake, about 150 miles northeast, and with that as headquarters make short hops into several other lakes and streams. The cost is about $300 per week per person, for a party of three or more.

At Chisana, just off the Alaska Highway near the Yukon border on the eastern slope of the Wrangell Mountains, pack trips can be arranged over a seven-day trail through country abounding in lakes and streams filled with grayling, rainbows and lake trout. The trip is topped off with a flight to Chitina on the Copper River for some excellent grayling fishing. This trip costs in the neighborhood of $326 per person, with a minimum party of two.

It is possible to take a more economical trip in the Copper River area if you are willing to do your own cooking. You leave from Anchorage, go to Chitina, purchase your supplies there, then go by boat to camp. Boats, guides and your plane transportation are all included in the price of about $130 per person, with a minimum party of two.

Fairbanks is the center from which to plan trips further inland. Northwest Orient Airlines flies fishermen from Fairbanks over the Mount McKinley Region to Talkeetna on the Susitna River. There is an excellent lodge there and fishing can be arranged in remote lakes and streams reached only by airboat or plane. The cost runs about $195 per person for a five-day trip.

Wien Alaska Airlines flies several routes from Fairbanks into the hinterlands, aimed mostly at tourists, but some of them make stops at spots of interest to anglers. These include Nome, Kotzebue, Point Barrow and Fort Yukon. For further information, write Wien Alaska Airlines, 3rd and Lacy Streets, Fairbanks, Alaska. Phone 3355.

Much useful information on flying in Alaska can be obtained from the Information Officer, FAA, Box 440, Anchorage, Alaska; and from the Alaska Flight Information Handbook, obtainable from the Superintendent of Documents, U.S. Printing Office, Washington, D.C.

Southeastern Alaska, that area stretching down the coast and bordering on British Columbia, is the spot to go if you are looking for salmon. From north to south, with headquarters at Juneau, Sitka, Petersburg, Wrangell and Ketchikan you can get to many fine rivers. The steelhead season is from late April to June, and at the same time there are king salmon in the salt, offshore. Dolly Varden, rainbow and cutthroat trout are also taken. The salmon start to move into the streams in July.

Around Ketchikan are many lakes which can be reached only by plane and which produce trout to 25 inches in abundance. Closer to town and accessible by car are Ward Lakes and Ward Creek, with steelhead, rainbows and cutthroat trout. Perseverance Lake, only 1½ miles from the highway, has been stocked with eastern brook trout, and some of them reach 20 inches in length. Only a few hours by boat and you can reach excellent steelhead waters in season, and take rainbows, cutthroat and Dolly Varden all summer long.

The inland waterways along this coast of many islands, abound with salmon in season. The king salmon comes in May, June and July, and they average 20 to 40 pounds. Coho or silver salmon fishing is at its best in July, August and September. These fish will run from 8 to 30 pounds. There are many salmon derbies, mostly for king salmon, and the prizes are so big that there is a heavy turnout. Juneau is the site of one of the most famous. Boats for charter are available at all the ports.

It should be remembered that even with the small populations of the towns along this coast, there is extremely heavy fishing, and the angler who wants to get into the best should engage a plane or boat to get to the least frequented waters.

One possible exception is Petersburg, where there is good trout fishing in many lakes and streams and often excellent fishing for good salmon within sight of the docks. Fishing for cohos and silvers is good in the fall. Many anglers miss a fairly good game fish by not trying for humpback salmon with flies.

Throughout July and August, silver salmon are found in the salt along the entire Alaska coastline and are taken in the inlets and bays by trolling. Then as they start up the rivers to spawn they will hit flies and spinning lures. The king salmon is more limited in his range, being taken most consistently in the waters of the southeastern part of Alaska, between Ketchikan and Juneau. However, they do range all the way west to the mouth of the Yukon River.

Often overlooked by the angler planning a trip to Alaska is the northern pike. This species grows to considerable size and provides real sport in these cold northern waters. The fish are found mostly in the northern part of Alaska, in sloughs, weedy ponds, and the upper waters of the Yukon and Tanana Rivers, near the Canadian border.

Far to the north, the Seward Peninsula, extending out into the Bering Strait, has some fine fishing for grayling in waters that are ideal for fly fishing. At mid-summer, Arctic char also move into these streams on their spawning runs to provide some excellent fishing. Just north of the Peninsula, in the Kobuk River, you will find yourself within range of the sheefish, or inconnu, a hard-hitting, silvery species known only in the waters from here north and across the top of the continent to the MacKenzie River.

THE ALASKA HIGHWAY

Many anglers dream of driving the Alaska Highway and fishing "on their own." The highway begins at Dawson Creek in northeastern British Columbia, crosses part of the Yukon Territory, and goes on into Alaska to Fairbanks. It traverses a heavily forested region with myriads of lakes and streams, many of which are the home of rainbow trout, lake trout and Arctic grayling. However, it should be remembered that those lakes and streams close to the road have been heavily fished and it is often necessary to go into the interior to find really good fishing.

The road is not paved, can be very dusty, and while it is open year-round, the best traveling is between June and October. In the summer the road is good enough for you to make good time, especially as daylight lasts for about twenty hours in this northern latitude. There are quite a few government-operated campgrounds and there are also stores, restaurants, service stations and some accommodations at convenient intervals. These are listed in great detail in the booklet "Alaska Highway," obtainable from the Canadian Government Travel Bureau, Ottawa, Canada; no one should start out on the Alaska Highway without this booklet.

ALASKA FISHING REGULATIONS

Resident Fishing License $5.00
Nonresident Fishing License $10.00
Nonresident 10-Day Fishing license $5.00

SEASONS AND LIMITS

The vast area of Alaska is divided into a great many regulatory areas where regulations vary both as to season and limits. For complete regulations write: Alaska Department of Fish and Game, Subport Building, Juneau, Alaska.

YUKON TERRITORY

The Yukon Territory has an area of 207,076 square miles, extending from the Arctic on the north to British Columbia on the south, and sandwiched between Alaska on the west and the Northwest Territories on the east. It is a land of tremendous beauty, with many mountain ranges separated by wide valleys, crowded with lakes and rivers. The mountain ranges of major importance are the St. Elias in the southwestern corner, where Mt. Logan, 19,850 feet high, marks the loftiest spot in Canada; the Selwyn and Mackenzie Ranges on the eastern border; Cassiar Range on the southern border; Pelly Range in the central area; Ogilvie Range in the northwest; and the British Mountains in the far north.

The species of fish to be found are lake trout (which grow to tremendous size), Arctic grayling, rainbow trout, northern pike, Great Lakes whitefish, Dolly Varden trout, kokanee (landlocked salmon), cutthroat trout, steelhead, king salmon, coho salmon and inconnu or sheefish, a rare species known only in a few extreme northern waters of the world.

The explored lakes of considerable size are Kluane, about 150 square miles in area; Lake Laberge, made famous by Robert W. Service; and Lakes Dezadeash, Bennett, Marsh, Aishihik, Tagish, Teslin and Frances. There are many other smaller lakes, known mostly to residents and a few exploring fishermen.

The most important river is the famed Yukon, flowing down north through the center of the Territory and on into Alaska, for a total of 1,980 miles. Other large rivers include the Teslin, Pelly, Stewart, White, Donjek, McQuesten, Nisutlin, Ross, Klondike, Peel, Porcupine, Wind and Snake.

The Yukon is truly a "last frontier," its handful of towns accessible by limited rail service and via the Alaska Highway and a few other lesser roads which serve the southern sector of the Territory, or by airplane. Most of the flying is done in float planes, utilizing the lakes and rivers as landing bases.

The 1,523-mile Alaska Highway enters the Yukon in the extreme southeast at Dawson Creek, British Columbia, and cuts across the south and goes on to Fairbanks, Alaska. It is a good gravel road, with service stations, stores, accommodations and restaurants at convenient intervals. Government-operated camp sites are also available along the route. Those who plan to tow trailers of any kind should obtain special regulations dealing with weight and size limitations from The Commander, Northwest Highway System, Whitehorse, Yukon Territory. All anglers who plan to drive the highway should also obtain a booklet "Accommodations and Roadside Facilities, Alaska Highway," from the Canadian Government Travel Bureau at Ottawa, Canada. It provides complete information on gas, oil, motor repair facilities, restaurants, campgrounds, trailer parks, fishing camps, hotels, highway junctions, etc.

Access may also be made to the Highway from Haines, on the southern tip of Alaska, via highway to Haines Junction, passing through British Columbia; and it is

492

also possible to drive to Whitehorse from Atlin, in northern British Columbia.

From the Alaska Highway at Whitehorse, a highway runs north to Dawson City and during the summer the "Sixty-Mile Road" is open from there to the Alaska border. East of Whitehorse, you may travel some seventy-five miles east and north towards the Selwyn Mountains to Chapman Lake; and further south a side artery leads to Mayo Landing and Keno. Still further south the 146-mile-long Coal Road leads off the Alaska Highway to Ross River. There are no facilities along the road, and it is open only in the summer.

Canadian Coachways, Ltd., 10805-120th Street, Edmonton, Alberta, operates bus service daily in summer between Dawson Creek, British Columbia, and White-horse, Yukon Territory; and three times weekly from Whitehorse to Beaver Creek at the Alaska border, and the same from Whitehorse to Dawson City. Complete information and schedules may be obtained from Canadian Coachways at the above address, or the Bus Depot, Whitehorse, Yukon Territory.

Another bus line, the White Pass and Yukon Route, provides service in spring and summer from Whitehorse to Beaver Creek at the Yukon-Alaska border, and makes connections there for interior points in Alaska. This company also runs buses between Whitehorse, Yukon Territory, and Haines, Alaska, to the south. The same route is more or less paralleled by the White Pass and Yukon Route narrow-gauge railway, the route of the "Trail of '98." Information as to special services and rates for fishermen who bring their automobiles and campers may be obtained from the White Pass and Yukon Route, P.O. Box 2147, Seattle 11, Washington; or White Pass Depot, Whitehorse, Yukon Territory.

Air service to the Yukon is excellent with flights daily except Sunday from Edmonton and Vancouver to Whitehorse; and twice weekly from Whitehorse to Mayo and Dawson City. There are also flights via several airlines from Seattle and Fairbanks to Whitehorse. Information about current schedules should be obtained from travel agents. Charter flights may be arranged at the airports at Watson Lake, Whitehorse, Dawson and Mayo. There is a variety of equipment available, including land- and water-based planes and helicopters.

Though summers are short in the Yukon, temperatures during July and August may range as high as 80 degrees, and have been recorded to 90 degrees. But nights are always cool to cold. Anglers need fairly heavy woolens for evenings and cool days, and should have one heavy outfit for a cold snap. There is not much rain but nevertheless, it is wise to carry a rain jacket.

Chest-high waders with felt soles are the ideal outfit, both for warmth and for wading on slippery rocks. If you own a pair of rubber-soled waders, a felt-soled sandal can be bought that fits over the boot and gives a good gripping surface. These can be bought at Dan Bailey's Fly Shop, Livingston, Montana, if you cannot find them in your local shop.

Fly fishermen will find an 8- or 8½-foot rod plenty large enough for Yukon fishing. The 8-foot rod should be matched with an HDH (DT6F) line; the 8½ with a GBF (DT9F). Leaders should be tapered down to the following strength tippet for the following fish: grayling, 4X or 5X tippet; Dolly Varden, 1X tippet; kokanee, 4X tippet; cutthroat trout, 4X tippet or 3X if you get into larger fish; steelhead, 10-pound-test tippet; king salmon, 12-pound-test tippet; coho salmon, 10-pound-test tippet; inconnu, 10-pound-test tippet.

Fishing along the Alaska Highway in Canada's Yukon Territory.

Popular dry flies for grayling are the Black Gnat, Royal Wulff, Gray Wulff, Adams, Light Hendrickson, all in size 12. Add to these the following on size 16 hooks: Red Variant, Black Gnat, Royal Coachman, Adams, Light Cahill and Blue Dun. If you wish to go lower in hook sizes, you can have fun with Jassids tied on size 18 and 20 hooks; brown and also gray hackle midge flies in size 20; and the Black Flying Ant in size 20. Small nymphs, on size 16 hooks, that take plenty of grayling are the gray nymph, black and yellow nymph, orange and yellow nymph. Small streamers are effective with grayling but this species rises so readily to a dry fly that streamers, wet flies and nymphs are seldom used.

The top steelhead flies are the Brad's Brat, Skykomish Sunrise, Polar Shrimp, Spitfire, Thor and Golden Demon.

Coho salmon will hit a red and white streamer, an all-white streamer or bucktail, and most of the standard U.S. streamers and bucktails, on hooks from #6 to 1/0. The Phillips multi-wing streamers in red and white, and red and yellow; and the strawberry blonde, tied on a 1/0 hook, are all good producers.

A medium-size spinning outfit with 8-pound-test monofilament line can be used for grayling, steelhead, cutthroat and inconnu. A larger rod and reel will prove best for salmon and larger steelhead. Spoons are about the best medicine for lake trout, either trolled or cast, and scaled according to the size of fish you expect to encounter —large spoons for big fish, small spoons for the smaller ones. The casting for this species is most profitable in spring and fall, when the fish are in the shallows of the lakes. Saltwater jigs in white, yellow, or red and white, and tied on 1/0 and 3/0 hooks, are sometimes used with the larger spinning outfit, and 10- or 12-pound-test line. The lure is dropped down to the bottom in the deeper parts of the lake, then pulled slowly upward with sharp up-and-down jigging motions of the rod tip. Some good fish are taken this way.

Anglers may see moose, deer, caribou, mountain goats, Dall sheep and coyotes. Black bear are common. Grizzlies are found in many areas. They are unpredictable and should be given a wide berth. Most fishermen carry a gun along, just in case. Elk and buffalo have been planted in the Yukon and deer are moving in gradually. There are no poisonous snakes.

LAKE FISHING

Kluane Lake, the largest body of water in the Yukon, lies along the Alaska Highway at Mile 1060. Fishing is for lake trout and grayling. Guides are available at several lodges along the lake and at nearby Haines Junction; and there are also several camp sites on Kluane. There is an airfield at the north end of the lake.

South of Haines Junction are two more large lakes, Kathleen and Dezadeash. Kathleen Lake and River can both be reached from Mile 146 on the Haines Highway (Mileage numbers from 0 at Haines, Alaska, not Haines Junction). There is excellent fishing for lake trout, rainbow trout, Arctic grayling and some landlocked salmon. Dezadeash is at Mile 134 on the same highway. It is noted for large lake trout, Dolly Varden trout, and there are also rainbows and grayling. They are taken mostly by trolling as the lake is large and windy.

Further east, near the town of Carcross, Lakes Tagish, Little Atlin, Snafu and Atlin all produce lake trout, grayling and northern pike, and Bennett Lake also has some cisco.

At Mile 837 on the Alaska Highway, Lake Teslin extends up into the Yukon from British Columbia. It produces lake trout, Arctic grayling and northern pike. Nearby Marsh Lake at Mile 883 is also good, particularly for northern pike. From Swift River, at Mile 733, on to Reflection Lake, at Mile 1160, most of the lakes produce lake trout, all have Arctic grayling, and some have northern pike. In Louise Lake, at Mile 919, there are also rainbows.

Daughney Lake at Mile 724, and Watson Lake at Mile 635 on the British Columbia border, have Arctic grayling, lake trout and Dolly Varden trout.

On the Mayo-Dawson road, the best fishing lakes are Lake LaBerge, which has lake trout, Arctic grayling, northern pike and inconnu or sheefish; Fox Lake, Braeburn Lake, Mayo Lake and Twin Lakes, all with lake trout, Arctic grayling and northern pike; Minto Lake, with lake trout and northern pike.

RIVER FISHING

The great Yukon River and its tributaries provide grayling, some rainbows, some salmon and inconnu, depending on where you fish. Right at Dawson City you can take grayling, salmon and inconnu practically in the town itself. At Otter Falls, 125 miles above Whitehorse, there is excellent rainbow fishing and a terrific concentration of grayling, some going to 18 or 19 inches in length, far better than average size. Besides being loaded with fish, this is one of the most beautiful spots in the Yukon. These are only two of the well-known spots along the Yukon River. There are many others which can be reached by following directions obtained from local sources.

Other rivers which can readily be reached from the Alaska Highway, and where anglers will find Arctic grayling and Dolly Varden trout, are Contact Creek, at Mile 588; Iron Creek, Mile 595; Hyland River, Mile 605; Upper Liard Bridge, Mile 642; Rancheria River, Miles 687 and 718; and Swift River, Mile 733.

A mimeographed sheet entitled "General Fishing Guide for Yukon Territory," and giving the species to be found in many waters along the Alaska Highway, may be obtained from the Department of Travel and Publicity, Whitehorse, Yukon Territory. The same office will supply a current list of guides and fishing camps, both on and off the road. Requests for special fishing information may be addressed to the Department of Fisheries, Box 2410, Whitehorse, Yukon Territory.

YUKON TERRITORY FISHING REGULATIONS

Resident Fishing License $1.00
Nonresident Fishing License $2.00

SEASONS AND LIMITS

Species	Season	Daily Bag and Size Limit
Arctic Grayling	No closed season	20 fish, 8″ minimum length
Lake Trout Dolly Varden	No closed season	5 in aggregate, 8″ minimum length
Kokanee (landlocked salmon)	No closed season	5
Rainbow Trout Cutthroat Trout	No closed season	5 in aggregate, 8″ minimum length
Steelhead	No closed season	2 fish, 8″ minimum length
Spring Salmon (King, Chinook) Coho Salmon	No closed season	2 in aggregate
Northern Pike	No closed season	20

For complete regulations write: Department of Fisheries, Box 2410, Whitehorse, Yukon Territory, Canada.

NORTHWEST TERRITORIES

Canada's Northwest Territories offer real frontier fishing. Stretching for more than a million square miles across the northern border of Canada, from Hudson Bay to the Yukon, the Territories have scarcely been touched by anglers. The comparative few who have penetrated this vast wilderness have found unexcelled fishing for lake trout, Arctic grayling, northern pike and walleye, plus the Arctic char and the inconnu or sheefish, both found only in extreme northern waters. Within a few years fishermen in the remote waters of the Northwest Territories have produced lake trout that crowded the 62-pound world record, have upped the Arctic-char record several times, and have established a new top weight for Arctic grayling.

The lake trout is found throughout the drainage systems of the Mackenzie, Coppermine, Back and Thelon Rivers. They commonly run in the 30- to 40-pound class and a record of 62 pounds 4 ounces has been taken. In these cold northern waters the fish are often found near the surface so they can readily be taken on casting gear, though the largest are more often taken by trolling. However, in the Northwest Territories lake-trout fishing does not call for the heavy metal trolling lines used for the species in more southern waters, because of the fact that the fish lie close to the surface except for a short time in August, when they go deep. Even then you can take them by trolling flashing spoons on nylon line.

The Arctic char is one of the least-known game species of the North American continent. This colorful fish and fine fighter is found in Arctic waters from Baffin Island to within 100 miles of the Mackenzie River mouth, and occurs both in land-locked and sea-going forms. The Tree River, near Coppermine, is one of the best spots, producing fish up to 27 pounds. Fifteen-pounders are common, and the average is 5 to 7 pounds.

Arctic grayling, more colorful than the grayling of southern waters, are found only in the lakes and streams which drain to the Arctic Ocean. They are most common in the Mackenzie, Coppermine, Anderson, Thelon and Back drainages; and in Great Bear Lake. The top weight known in the Territories is 5 pounds, the average about 2.

Northern pike are particularly numerous in the Great Slave Lake area but are also found in the Mackenzie and Anderson River drainages. Many have been taken weighing close to 40 pounds, and the average will go between 5 and 15 pounds.

Walleye are common around Great Slave Lake especially in the Yellowknife and Hay River areas, with a few further north. They will average between 3 and 5 pounds, with an occasional 10-pounder.

The inconnu or sheefish is most generally taken in the Hay, Anderson, Taltson and Big Buffalo Rivers, with the Hay River having an exceptional run in May and June right after the spring breakup. This species belongs to the whitefish family, and little is known about it to date, as it is comparatively new to anglers. Catches range from 5 to 20 pounds, but some members of this strange species weighing more than 70 pounds have been reported by commercial fishermen.

The major lakes are Great Bear and Great Slave Lakes, covering a combined area of about 10,000 square miles, and there are thousands of lesser lakes and a network of streams. The main drainage of the western portion of the Territories is through the largest of these rivers, the Mackenzie, to which flow the waters of Great Slave and Great Bear Lakes. The west-central area is drained by the Coppermine and its tributaries; while the eastern area pours its waters through several rivers to Hudson Bay.

There is only one highway in the Northwest Territories. This road, known as the Mackenzie Highway, leads north from Grimshaw, Alberta, which is around 320 miles northwest of Edmonton. It serves the Hay River and Yellowknife sections, the only populated areas in the Territories. A series of campgrounds has been constructed along the highway, with tent or trailer accommodations, fresh water supply, sanitary facilities, fireplaces, picnic tables and covered camp kitchens. There are hotels and various services available at Hay River and Yellowknife. From Yellowknife a road known as the Ingraham Trail travels eastward to Prosperous and Prelude Lakes.

On both roads gas stations are limited and an extra supply of gasoline should always be carried, particularly for that part of the highway between Enterprise and Yellowknife, a distance of about 283 miles.

There are a few boats available along the route, and those who bring their own boats will find some fishing at the roadside; but most of the really good areas can be reached only by plane. Scheduled airlines operate from Montreal, Ottawa, Toronto, Winnipeg, Edmonton and Vancouver, to various spots in the Territories. Complete information on schedules should be obtained either from the fishing camp to which the angler plans to go, or from the Northwest Territories Tourist Office, Kent-Albert Building, Ottawa, Canada. Charter planes for local flights are available at Hay River and Yellowknife.

For those who wish to go in by bus, Canadian Coachways, Ltd., 10805-120th Street, Edmonton, Alberta, provides service to Hay River and Yellowknife, from Edmonton; and also from Vancouver, British Columbia, via Prince George, Dawson Creek, Peace River and Edmonton. There are two hotels, one motel, a rooming house and a trailer park in the town of Yellowknife; and a camp site at nearby Long Lake. Similar accommodations are available at Hay River.

Charter-plane service may be obtained at Hay River to fly to the interior, through Carter Air Service, Hay River, Northwest Territories; or H. F. Courtney, 5720 Blue Ridge, Kansas City 33, Missouri. Phone Fleming 6-0273.

Extending as they do, from sub-Arctic to Arctic climate, the Northwest Territories experience a considerable diversity of climate. Nevertheless, wherever you go, even in midsummer, you may count on temperatures consistently in the 40's and 50's, and sometimes colder. Take plenty of woolens, a good windbreaker or parka, long underwear, and, although it seldom rains, a rain jacket for use in boats. For the hiking that is frequently necessary to reach good fishing waters, you need sturdy, 8"-top rubber-soled boots, and warm, wool socks.

On occasion mosquitoes and sandflies can be very bad, so take along plenty of insect repellent, and, if you can stand to wear it, a head net.

This, with gloves for cold days, and sunglasses for bright ones, will outfit you for fishing in the Northwest Territories. There is no problem of wild animals or snakes.

Arctic grayling are such willing takers of flies, that most anglers go for them with fly tackle. They put up a good fight for their size on this gear. Their large, colorful dorsal fin is a thing of beauty, and they also make very good eating. The 8½-foot rod, matched with a GBF line, and a 10- to 12-foot leader tapered to a 4X tippet is fine for grayling. Best dry flies, all in sizes 14 and 16, are the Black Gnat, Mosquito, Blue Dun, Adams and Ginger Quill. Best wet flies are the Black Gnat, Cowdung, Blue Dun, Gray Hackle, Brown Hackle, March Brown and Royal Coachman, all in sizes 12 and 14.

Arctic char will take flies and streamers and bucktails tied on #2 hooks; and the larger ones will hit a 1/0. They also hit spoons cast with a spinning outfit. Known producers are the small Dardevles, spoons and Mepps spinners, but many others are good, and anglers should always check the resort to which they are going for favorites in that area.

Large spoons such as the Husky Dardevles, Half Wave, Gibbs-Stewart, Helin Flatfish, Williams Wobbler and Guide Spoon, are top rated for lake trout, and with these you want heavy-duty snaps and swivels, and many anglers use a stout casting rod with plenty of line.

In this northern region the summer is very short, so that the season at most fishing camps extends only from June 30th to September 15th. In many cases there is still ice on the lakes except at this time. Anglers should check with the camp where they plan to fish, for the best times for the type of fishing they want.

GREAT SLAVE LAKE AREA

Yellowknife, on Great Slave Lake, is the only community in the area. Two hotels, the Gold Range and the Yellowknife, offer accommodations in town, and can arrange fishing trips. The Bay-Vu Motel, Box 454, Yellowknife, Northwest Territories, has housekeeping cabins, and will arrange for guides, boats and motors.

Twenty-two miles by air northeast of Yellowknife is Prelude Lodge, address Box 144, Yellowknife, Northwest Territories. Accommodations are about $6 per day and boats are available at $3 per hour or $18 per day. Guides may be obtained for $15 per day but are not really needed as grayling, lake trout and northern pike can all be caught within twenty minutes of camp. There is some fishing tackle available, and camp kitchens for tenters.

Also at Prelude Lake, Timber Lodge, Box 423, Yellowknife, Northwest Territories, can be reached by road, twenty-five miles northeast of Yellowknife. Boats are available; rates will be supplied on request.

From Yellowknife anglers can fly via Wardair Air Lines, about ninety miles to the east, to Great Slave Lake Lodge, on the north shore of the lake, for about $50 round-trip. Rates at the lodge average about $60 per person per day, which includes accommodations, meals, boats, guide and care of fish. Guests fish the McKinley River and several smaller lakes as well as Great Slave Lake. Reservations may be made between November 1 and May 1, by writing Walter E. Pierce, Lemont, Illinois. Phone 257-6947; and between May 1 and November 1, writing c/o Wardair Ltd., Yellowknife, Northwest Territories. Phone 4434.

On the southeast corner of the lake is Snowdrift Lodge, in a good area for light tackle, as the water in the vicinity ranges from 10 to 30 feet in depth and fishing can be done close to shore. A medium-weight spinning rod with 10- to 20-pound-test monofilament line, or a medium casting rod with 20-pound-test line is the usual gear. It's also wise to bring a light spinning outfit or a fly rod for grayling.

The flies and lures already described are suitable. Reservations at Snowdrift should be made through Mr. and Mrs. Kermit Gear, 607 Second Avenue West, Williston, North Dakota.

Frontier Fishing Lodge, on the east arm of Great Slave Lake, is reached by plane from Hay River, Fort Smith or Yellowknife. There is excellent fly fishing for grayling, and outpost trips can be arranged to other lakes and rivers. The rate is about $60 per day plus transportation. Prospective anglers should write Frontier Fishing Lodge, Box 397, Yellowknife, or 13184-114th Avenue, Edmonton. Phone 403-455-6179.

GREAT BEAR LAKE AREA

Great Bear Lake Lodge, on Great Bear Lake, is reached by private plane from Winnipeg, Manitoba. Arrangements should be made through Warren Plummer or Bud Williams, Great Bear Lake Lodge, Ltd., c/o Airport Hotel, Winnipeg, Manitoba, Canada. Phone 204-783-7035 (Winnipeg). The rates run about $75 per day with a minimum of $500. The camp operators also offer outpost trips to Coppermine, an Eskimo settlement on the Arctic Ocean, and the Tree River, to the east, both with fantastic fishing for Arctic char. These trips run about $75 to $100 per person per day, or the two can be combined for about $115 per person, including overnight stay at Tree River. There are also accommodations at Plummer's Tree River Char Camp, 250 miles north of Great Bear Lake Lodge, at $100 per person for two days and one night.

Also on Great Bear Lake is Great Bear Lodge, not to be confused with Great Bear Lake Lodge just described. Reservations may be made through Arctic Enterprises, 833 South Phillips Avenue, Sioux Falls, South Dakota. Rates are about $645 per week, including transportation to the lodge from Edmonton, Alberta. Side trips will be arranged to the Arctic coast for Arctic char.

Branson's Cameron Bay Camp, on Great Bear Lake, near Port Radium, offers a seven-day package trip from Edmonton for $645, for the same kind of fishing as the other lodges just described. They also have a daily rate of $100 with a $300 minimum.

MACKENZIE RIVER AREA

Anglers may arrange trips to the lower waters of the Mackenzie River by writing the Mackenzie Arms Hotel, Box 1115, Inuvik, Northwest Territories. Hotel rates are from $7.50 to $14.50 per day for rooms, and meals are extra. The fishing is in the Mackenzie River in the Delta area.

NORTH-CENTRAL AREA

There are some accommodations available in the north-central part of the coast at Arctic Islands Lodge, Cambridge Bay, on Victoria Island. Reservations may be made direct, or to 10336 Villa Avenue, Edmonton, Alberta. Charter planes are available for the flight in. Rates for meals and room are about $24 per person per day, and this includes transportation to the fishing. Boats, motors and guides are extra.

SOUTHERN AREA

There are several spots in the southern part of the Northwest Territories where anglers will find some accommodations. Near the Alberta-Saskatchewan Border, at Fort Smith, the Pinecrest Hotel provides rooms at $6 to $14 per day. Meals, guides, boats and charter air service to inland spots may be arranged through the hotel.

Twenty miles north of Fort Smith, Burnt Lake Cabins has accommodations available at $25 per day without meals. The camp can be reached by charter plane from Fort Smith or Hay River. Boats and motors are available, and the catch will be lake trout and walleye.

Similar fishing may be found in the southwest corner of the Territories, around Fort Simpson and Liard, near the confluence of the Liard and Mackenzie Rivers. Accommodations are at the Fort Simpson Hotel, about $6 single, $10 double, without meals. Again, guides, boats, motors and charter air service are available.

Immediately to the west is Nahanni Butte. Nahanni Safaris, Ltd., Box 33, Fort Nelson, British Columbia, will arrange the 160-mile flight in, in float plane. The cost per week is about $675, with everything provided, except that the guests do their own cooking on camp stoves. The price includes a boat trip through the canyons of the Nahanni River. Fishing is for lake trout and grayling.

In the south-central area, at Hay River, anglers will find accommodations at the Hay River Hotel, Box 40; the Hay River Motel, Box 1; and the Ace Motel. There is fishing in the immediate area for grayling, lake trout, pickerel and inconnu. Carter Air Service Ltd., Box 128, Hay River, Northwest Territories, operates a camp at Nonacho Lake, 230 miles to the north. Boats, motors, gas, oil and camping equipment are supplied for fishing for northern pike and lake trout; guests bring their own food. The rate is $20 per day.

NORTHEASTERN AREA

Far to the northeast, well above Hudson Bay, is Baffin Island, also a part of the Northwest Territories. It is reached only by air, via Nordair from Montreal. East Coast Lodge, located near Frobisher Airport, at the settlement of Frobisher Bay, provides rooms for $12 to $15 per person per day. The cost of meals is $2.25 for breakfast, $3 each for lunch and dinner. Boats, motors and guides are available for fishing for Arctic char, and the resort has a cold-storage plant to take care of the catch.

Also on Baffin Island is Ikhaluvik Arctic Camp, addressed at: Bryan R. Pearson, Ikhaluvik Camp, Frobisher Bay, Northwest Territories. Tent accommodations are supplied but guests must bring their own sleeping bags, fishing gear and guns, if they plan to take part in a seal hunt. The fishing is for Arctic char, within 100 feet of camp. The rate of $1,000 for seven days, includes transportation from Montreal and return, and all facilities, including guides.

Anglers planning to visit the Northwest Territories should write the Northwest Territories Tourist Office, Kent-Albert Building, Ottawa, Canada, for the current issue of "Inn and Igloo," which lists all available accommodations in the Territories. Those who plan to drive should also ask for "The Mackenzie Highway to Canada's Northwest Territories."

NORTHWEST TERRITORIES FISHING REGULATIONS

Resident Fishing License $1.00
Nonresident Fishing License $2.00

SEASONS AND LIMITS

Species	Season	Daily Bag Limit
Trout Grayling	No closed season	Not more than 20 trout and grayling in aggregate and not to include more than 10 trout of any variety.
Arctic Char	No closed season	10 per day, 20 in possession
Pike, Walleye, Yellow Pike, Perch	No closed season	10 per day

No one shall use any bait or line capable of giving off light either by natural or artificial means. Guides are not compulsory but are recommended when fishing unfamiliar waters.

For complete regulations write: Department of Fisheries, Hay River, N.W.T.

BRITISH COLUMBIA

British Columbia is Canada's most western province. The states of Washington, Idaho and Montana border it on the south, the Yukon and Northwest Territories on the north. Its eastern boundary is the high ridge of the Rocky Mountains along the Province of Alberta, while the entire western edge lies along the Pacific Coast, marked by so many bays, inlets and channels that one can scarcely tell which is island and which is mainland. Elevation varies from sea level to 12,972 feet, at Mount Robson, the loftiest peak in the Canadian Rockies.

Since most of the eastern border is marked by the Continental Divide, the greater part of the province lies in the Pacific watershed. But north and northeast of the town of St. George, in mid-province, the rivers flow down north and eventually find their way to the Arctic Ocean via the MacKenzie River. In the southeastern corner of the state the Kootenay River system flows to the south to the Columbia Basin.

These north-draining waters produce Arctic char, Arctic grayling and northern pike, as well as some of the species found in the waters flowing to the Pacific: brown, rainbow and brook trout, plus the cutthroat, native trout of the west, lake trout, kamloops trout, Dolly Varden, smallmouth black bass, largemouth black bass, yellow perch and Rocky Mountain whitefish. The Pacific coastal rivers play host to an annual migration of the Pacific salmons, Chinook and coho, while the landlocked salmon, known as the kokanee, is taken in inland lakes. The rainbow and cutthroat also go to sea and return at certain seasons to the coastal rivers to provide some outstanding fishing.

While there are no lakes of tremendous size in British Columbia. there are many smaller ones plus river widenings which provide lake type of fishing. Similarly, because of the steep mountain terrain, the rivers are numerous rather than large.

Accessibility is limited by the mountainous terrain. Motorists may come in from Alberta on the east via Highway 1 at Lake Louise or Highway 93 a few miles further south. Once in the state, Highways 93 and 95 provide a path south, or you can go west on Highway 1 to Kamloops, in the south-central area. Entry from the United States is via some fourteen ports of entry, of which the main ones are on U.S. 91 in Montana, becoming Highway 4 in British Columbia; U.S. 89 in Montana, becoming Highway 2 in British Columbia; U.S. 93 in Montana, becoming Highway 93 in British Columbia; U.S. 95 in Idaho, connecting with British Columbia Highways 3 and 95; Washington Highway 6, continuing as 6 in British Columbia; U.S. 395 in Washington, connecting with Highway 3 in British Columbia; U.S. 97 in Washington, becoming 97 in British Columbia; and U.S. 99 on the Washington coast, becoming Highway 1 in British Columbia.

In the southern part of the province there are a number of cross-country highways in the area south of Kamloops, but north of that road travel is limited to Highway 97, running up the middle of the province to Prince George. From there Highway 97 continues north and east to Dawson Creek, thence back into Alberta; and also from Prince George Highway 16 travels west to the ocean at Prince Rupert.

Trout fishing at Gold Creek near Revelstoke, British Columbia.

The Alaska Highway cuts across the northeast, from Dawson City to Watson Lake in the Yukon.

Both Canadian Pacific and Canadian National Railways provide excellent service in southern British Columbia, and as far north as Prince George and Dawson Creek. Trans-Canada Airlines also serves the entire south through the larger cities, and there are several charter services available for flights to the interior.

British Columbia Air Lines serve the major part of the south coast with service from Vancouver to Victoria, Babaimo, Tofino, Port Alberni, Campbell River, Zeballos, Tahsis, Chamiss Bay, Port Hardy, Ocean Falls and Bella Coola. Out of Prince Rupert the same line flies to Masset and Sandspit on the Queen Charlotte Islands. Flight information may be obtained at Vancouver Airport, Phone Cr 8-8466.

Pacific Western Airlines has regular service in the Vancouver area to Vancouver Island; and in the Prince Rupert area to Stewart and Alice Arm; and provides charter service to almost any point in British Columbia, and north into the Northwest Territories as well as east into northern Alberta and as far north as Uranium City, Saskatchewan.

Ferries to Vancouver Island will be found at Tsawwassen, twenty-four miles south of Vancouver; Horseshoe Bay, eighteen miles north of Vancouver; Seattle, Washington to Victoria; Port Angeles, Washington to Victoria; and Anacortes, Washington to Victoria.

Cottons are usually sufficient for basic summer wear in the lower altitudes, but in the mountains one should go prepared for cooler weather, and possibly even snow flurries. Flannel or lightweight wool jackets are always needed, and on occasion anglers will be glad to have woolen underwear. Canvas sneakers or loafers with rubber soles are practical for boat fishing but those who plan to hike in to lakes will need strong, ankle-height boots. For stream fishing, waders are essential.

Big game may be seen almost anywhere except in the most populated areas. Bears are numerous and high in the mountains you may be fortunate enough to see mountain sheep or goats. In between these are all the game animals of the Rockies. As is usually the case, they will not bother you if you do not bother them, the grizzly bear being the exception.

While not common in most places, the western rattler may be encountered in British Columbia.

Tackle used in British Columbia varies as widely as the species. The most popular outfit for trout is the fly rod, an 8-foot length, with HDH line, and any of the standard flies. But many other outfits are used and even for the trouts—the kamloops, for instance—all types of tackle take fish. The largest kamloops fall victim to deep trolling with vari-colored beads strung on wire along with revolving spinners and a large silver wobbler at the end.

Standard dry-fly patterns are the McGinty, Ginger Quill, Brown and Gray hackle and bi-visibles; and all the common wet flies. Streamer flies which are popular are the Silver Doctor, Parmachene Belle, Montreal, Royal Coachman, Professor and Jock Scott.

For salmon fishing, much heavy boat tackle is used, and anglers generally depend on the recommendations of their boatmen.

VANCOUVER ISLAND

Vancouver Island, off the extreme southwest coast of the British Columbia mainland, can be reached via ferry and plane service as described earlier in this chapter. On the island, Highway 19 runs up the inshore coast and several cross-country roads traverse the southern sector. However, there are few traffic arteries in the north. Many streams rushing down from the mountains to the sea provide migration routes for steelhead, sea-run cutthroat trout, and salmon. The hilly terrain is dotted with lakes which offer good trout and bass fishing, the bass having been stocked.

One of the best producing rivers is the Cowichan at the south end of the island. The twenty-eight-mile-long river can be reached by the Gibbons Road from Duncan on Highway 19, and accommodations are available at the same town. Boats and guides will be found at Lake Cowichan at the head of the river. There is good fishing for salmon, cutthroat and steelhead year-round except at midsummer, when action can be slow. Brown trout up to 5 pounds have also been taken in the headwaters.

There is some smallmouth black bass fishing in Elk and Beaver Lakes near Victoria, and in St. Mary and Rosemary Lakes on Salt Spring Island in the Georgia Straits, just north of Victoria. The island is reached via ferry from Pt. Roberts on the mainland, south of Vancouver.

Further north, on Highway 19, at Qualicum Beach, anglers will find all services while they fish the Little Qualicum River, an eight-mile long stream with kamloops, rainbows, steelhead and cutthroat trout of good size. The best fishing seems to come in the paired months of January and February, April and May, September and

October. Brook trout are found throughout this southeast part of the island, particularly in the tributaries of the Cowichan, as well as in Spectacle, Round and Semenos Lakes. And practically anywhere along the coast you may encounter sea-run cutthroat trout, which move in and out of the larger streams throughout the year.

Continuing north on the island, the Ash River is reached from Highway 4 off Highway 19 at Parksville. This river is twenty-eight miles long and has summer runs of both steelhead and cutthroat, from June through October. Winter runs of steelhead come in from December to March. There are plentiful accommodations of all kinds at Alberni. The Stamp River, nearby, can be reached from Alberni by car, and while there are no accommodations on the river, there is a grocery store nearby and camping in the Stamp Falls Provincial Park. Steelhead run into the Stamp from July through September and from December through March.

The renowned Campbell River is still further north on Highway 19, ninety miles from Nanaimo, by car or bus. Although only three miles in length this river attracts fishermen from all over the world for its fine angling for tyee salmon and steelhead. Fly fishing is very popular at the Campbell though spinning gear is most used for the big fish. There is also some excellent water for resident cutthroat, one of the best spots being Upper Campbell Lake, reached via good gravel road seventeen miles from Campbell River. The lake is fifteen miles long and one and a half miles wide. There are also rainbows and Dolly Varden trout. Boats are available at the lake, but Strathcona Lodge at Campbell River has the nearest accommodations.

Buttle Lake, tributary to Upper Campbell Lake, also produces cutthroat and rainbows up to 6 pounds and Dolly Varden to 12 pounds. It is thirty-two miles by gravel road southwest of Campbell River. You can camp there and there are boat-launching facilities.

LOWER MAINLAND

The lower mainland of British Columbia offers somewhat the same variety of fishing as is found on Vancouver Island. The Vedder River, near the towns of Chilliwack and Hope, a short distance east of Vancouver on Trans-Canada Highway 1, is easily the best steelhead river on the lower coast. The fishing is best in late fall and early spring, and deep fishing rigs like the cherry bobber on spin casting or heavier outfits are preferred. The river also plays host to coho salmon, Dolly Varden and cutthroat trout.

At Port Coquitlam and Haney, on Highway 7, just inland from Vancouver, the Coquitlam, Chehalis and Alouette Rivers have good steelhead runs from December until March, and also have cohoes and resident trout. The Alouette also holds Dolly Varden and kokanee. Eastern brook trout are common throughout the area, especially in Stave Lake, north of Mission City on Highway 7. Also reached from Mission City, Chehalis Lake is noted for both Kamloops and Dolly Varden trout. There are no accommodations at the lake, which is reached via a logging road eight miles west of Harrison.

Highway 101 runs up the coast from Vancouver as far as Bliss Landing. Some ferry trips are necessary to reach the Powell Lake area, to the east of Bliss Landing. There, Black, Cranberry, Dodd, Duck, Emily, Florence, Freda, Goat and a score of other small lakes have fishing for cutthroat trout. Anglers must find accommodations at the various small communities on Highway 101.

The Powell Lake area also has five streams, the Brem, Phillips, Theodosia and Vancouver Rivers and Wolfson Creek, in all of which steelhead and cutthroat may be taken. Brem River also plays host to coho salmon. Most of these streams must be reached by boat, and arrangements can be made through Clarence Tatlow, Box 21, Squamish, British Columbia. The best season on the Brem is from May to September. The Phillips is fair all season and January to May is the best time for steelhead in the Theodosia and Vancouver Rivers. Wolfson Creek, the only one of the group which can be reached by road, is best fished in January, May and in the fall.

CENTRAL COASTAL AREA

Ragged with inlets and river mouths, this area is best reached by steamship from Vancouver, or by charter plane. Rivers Inlet, about 250 miles north of Vancouver, and about the same distance south of Prince Rupert, is good tyee-salmon water, having the reputation of producing the best-conditioned and largest tyee on the Pacific coast. An 82-pounder was taken in 1951 by Frank Piscatelli of Vancouver. Many others in the 70-pound class have been caught, and commercial fishermen have taken them to 100 pounds. As there are neither accommodations nor boat rental services, most sportsmen reach this section in their own or chartered yachts.

The tyee run peaks at two seasons, one about one week at the end of July and again at the end of August. But they are taken from mid-July to mid-September. Cohoes follow them, but little fishing is done for this species in this remote area. Those who plan to fish here must register with the special fisheries officer at Rivers Inlet, at no charge, but to keep track of the harvest. There are also some annual special restrictions in this area, and sport-fishing regulations should be checked carefully.

To the north of Rivers Inlet is Bella Coola, where the river of the same name and the Atnarko are both good bets for salmon and steelhead anglers. The steelhead run starts in late October and continues through April, though the peak months are January, February and April. The town of Bella Coola has a Rod and Gun Club Derby which has recorded the heaviest steelhead at 19 pounds 11 ounces. It is seldom that an angler does not take his limit in these waters.

During May, June and July the spring salmon enter the Bella Coola River and fish up to 40 pounds have been taken. However, the spring run off affects the fishing very much so that it is impossible to predict when the fishing will be best.

Bella Coola can be reached by Highway 20 through the lower part of Tweedsmuir Provincial Park. This highway is generally kept open in winter but it is best to check in advance with highway authorities. It starts at the town of Williams Lake on Highway 97 from the south. The Northland Navigation Company offers a sea route via steamer from Vancouver to Bella Coola.

For information about accommodations, write A. Elsey or W. Stiles at Bella Coola, British Columbia. For guiding, contact Alfred Bryant, Bella Coola.

QUEEN CHARLOTTE ISLANDS

The Queen Charlotte Islands, lying off the coast of British Columbia, off Prince Rupert, can be reached by steamer from that city. Trolling, bait casting, spinning and fly fishing are all popular with anglers who go to these islands, and they take coho running from 21 to 24 pounds, and grilse in lesser weights. Most of the fishing is done in open water from a boat, so lots of line on the reel is important, and a net for landing is essential. Many anglers use a 6- to 8-inch piece of wire on their leader to prevent the male coho from cutting the line with his front teeth when hooked on the corner of the mouth. Trolling rigs used generally consist of a light saltwater rod and reel that will hold 75 yards of 18-pound-test nylon or monofilament line backed by 350 yards of 8-pound-test line.

Spinners will find that nickel, copper, brass or pearl lures all take fish, in sizes from No. 2 to No. 5. Coho polar bear flies are the most popular for fly-rod men, and these are also used for trolling. The popularity of the fly is shown by the fact that a number of local residents tie them for sale. There is a tackle shop in the village of Sandspit, and a hotel at Charlotte City as well as several cabins at Copper Bay. Guides get $15 per day to handle two fishermen. Boat, motor and gas cost another $15 per day. Contacts are Jack Fraser, Sandspit, British Columbia; Edward Williams, Sandspit, British Columbia; and Ronald Stewart, 205—8th Avenue West, Prince Rupert, British Columbia. The season is September 1 to October 15th, with the peak around the last week in September.

NORTHWEST AREA

Northwestern British Columbia, including roughly that area traversed by Highway 16 which connects Prince Rupert on the west coast to Prince George on Highway 97 in the interior, is generally a land of rainbow trout, lake trout, Dolly Varden and eastern brook trout. The northern wilderness can be penetrated by a road leading north from Vanderhoof on Highway 16, to Fort St. James on Stuart Lake, then to points north. Vanderhoof is some sixty-two miles west of Prince George. Stuart Lake is one of the largest lakes in the province, approximately sixty miles long. There are several camps on the islands in the lake, which provide modern service, and there are cabins, boats and motors available on the mainland. Trolling is very good for rainbow trout and char, while fly fishermen find good sport in the streams entering the lake. The midsummer months, July through September, are best. Char run up to 20 pounds, rainbows to as much as 10, though a 5- or 6-pounder is a good one.

This is the general picture of hundreds of lakes both large and small around the Prince George-Vanderhoof-Burns Lake and Smithers area. At the town of New Hazelton on the upper Skeena River, on the northern loop of Highway 16, the steelhead, coho salmon, Dolly Varden, cutthroat trout and Rocky Mountain whitefish are added to the roster. Near here is the Kispiox River, one of the most popular steelhead rivers of the west. It flows in a southerly direction to enter the Skeena about eight miles north of Hazelton. An unimproved road runs up the road for about fourteen miles. There is camping, or anglers may stay at modern hotels in New Hazelton and South Hazelton. The best fishing in the Kispiox is from August through October. Steelhead weighing over 20 pounds are taken on flies, while spinners use cherry bobbers for steelhead, and the "Tee" spoon for casting for coho and Dolly Vardens. Anglers should always be equipped with waders, regardless of what method of fishing is planned.

The Cloyah River, further west on Highway 16, about sixteen miles east of Prince Rupert, can also produce good fishing from December to April. Nearest accommodations are at Prince Rupert. There are also several lakes in the vicinity which offer good fishing for cutthroat trout. These include Fisherman's Cove Lake, Kahtada Lake, Leverson Lake, Lowe Inlet Lakes, Prudhomme Lake and Rainbow Lake.

NORTHEAST AREA

Looking back inland to Prince George, we find the northeast section of British Columbia accessible via Highway 97, north from the town. A number of small lakes and streams close by offer fishing for rainbows from 1 to 3 pounds. Some of the better known lakes are Bednesti, Six Mile, Summit, Tudyak and Trapper. Eighty miles further north is McLeod Lake, twelve miles long, and with good accommodations at several tourist resorts. The fishing is for char up to 12 pounds and rainbows to 2 pounds. The Parsnip River, which flows into the lake, has good fishing for grayling and Dolly Varden throughout the summer and into October. A guide is recommended in this whole area in order to reach several other streams well worth fishing and especially popular with fly and spin fishermen. Contact Harry Chingy, McLeod Lake; or Joseph Berghammer, Box 874, Prince Rupert, British Columbia.

Highway 97 winds northeastward to Dawson Creek, in which vicinity a number of lakes offer fishing for lake trout and northern pike, locally known as jackfish. The largest is Moberly Lake, reached by dirt road, north from Highway 97 at Chetwynd. Others are Swan, Azouzetta and Rocky Mountain Lakes. Directions must be obtained at Dawson Creek.

Out of Dawson Creek, the Alaska Highway runs to Fort St. John on the border between British Columbia and the Northwest Territories. At Fort St. John the angler in search of remote places can reach the Peace River over a graded road running southeast. The Peace is a large, slow-moving stream, flowing north into the Arctic. There are limited accommodations except at Fort St. John, and guides with river boats should be employed. These can be obtained through Leo Rutledge Jr., or Jack Powell, at Fort St. John. Fishing is fair for Dolly Varden and rainbows during July and August. The main attraction, however, is the Arctic grayling, which run to 4 pounds in this river. They rise readily to flies.

There is some good fishing country southeast out of Prince George, reached via Highway 16. Parts of this road are closed during the winter but in summer it can be travelled clear to Robson Provincial Park and on into Jasper National Park in Alberta. Much of the road parallels the Fraser River. The best center of operation is the town of McBride, about three quarters of the way down the road towards the Alberta border. From here you can fish Yellowhead and Moose Lakes, Moose River, Grand Brook and Ghita Creek, as well as the Fraser River. There are cabins and boats at Yellowhead, which is just four miles from the Jasper Park boundary. Yellowhead and Moose Lakes can also be reached on the Canadian National Railway. The species of fish are rainbow and brook trout and Dolly Varden, and the fishing is best after August 1st.

CARIBOU DISTRICT

A vast **wilderness** area lying roughly between the Fraser River and Highway 16 on the east to **Tweedsmuir** Provincial Park on the west; and Quesnel on the north to Ashcroft on the south is known as the Caribou District. Highway 97 traverses it, and several offshoots of gravel highways lead east and west to the more remote fishing spots. This is rainbow trout country, with also some good fishing for lake trout and Dolly Varden. It is also an area of unlimited accommodations. Boats and guides are available everywhere. Access on the west is via Highway 20, from the Caribou Highway or Highway 97, whichever you wish to call it. Highway 20 proceeds west to Tweedsmuir Provincial Park, some 250 miles away, and then clear on through to Bella Coola. As mentioned under the Bella Coola section, earlier, there are rainbow and cutthroat trout in Atnarko Lake in the Park, and the rivers hold coho and Chinook salmon, and steelhead to 10 pounds. Anahim Lake, just east of the Park, has good rainbow fishing and boats and accommodations are available.

SOUTHEAST AREA

Other lakes in the area west of Williams Lake are Chilko, Clearwater, Elkin, Konni and Verdan Lakes. All are between 150 and 200 miles west of Highway 97. Chilco has rainbow trout to 6 pounds, and some Dolly Varden. There is fair fly fishing for rainbows in Clearwater but they only average about 1 pound. At Konni Lake, Konni Lake Lodge has cabins, boats, and an air strip about 2,000 feet long. Nearby lakes, including Elkin, have produced rainbows up to 6 pounds. Small rainbows and Dolly Varden trout are found in the Blackwater River, forty-five miles north and west of Quesnel, on the Blackwater Road.

Turning east from Williams Lake on gravel roads, anglers can reach Horsefly Lake, Quesnel Lake, and Caribou Lake. Lodges, cabins and swimming are featured along with fair fishing for rainbows, lake trout and kokanee. Most of them are taken by trolling, and the season is May to October. A good stream in this area is the Quesnel River running from Quesnel to Likely. There are reputedly rainbow trout to 10 pounds, spring salmon to 35 and Dolly Varden as well. This is good spinning water from May to October. There are hotels, resorts and guides at Likely. Contact Herman Nielson, Likely, British Columbia.

Using the city of Kamloops as the focal point, anglers will find themselves within easy reach by road, rail and float plane, of a variety of fishing from Wells Gray Provincial Park, (due east of Williams Lake), south to the U.S. border, and from Vancouver on the west to Alberta on the east. Within this area are many lakes with fair to good fishing for kamloops and kokanee. In the extreme southeastern section Dolly Varden and cutthroat trout become more prevalent, and along the border with Washington, Highway 3 touches many lakes and streams in which kamloops, Dolly Varden, cutthroat and kokanee are found, as well as eastern brook trout, in some cases. To add to this, the Columbia River winds for eighty miles through the province before it leaves British Columbia and enters the state of Washington. In its drainage are found largemouth black bass ranging to 6 pounds, the only members of this species found in British Columbia.

The largemouth are in the Vaseux, Osoyoos and Shannon Lakes in the Okanagan Valley, where the towns of Kelowna and Vernon have accommodations of all kinds, on Highway 97. Bass may also be taken in Christina Lake near Grand Forks on Highway 3, close to the Washington border and Kootenay Lake, which Highway 3 crosses, also produces fair catches of largemouth bass near the town of Kaslo.

Further east on Highway 3, at its junction with Highway 5, the town of Princeton is the center of some good eastern-brook fishing, in Wolf Creek, ten miles north of the town. Similar fishing may be reached from Princeton via the Coalmount-Tulameen Road to Otter Creek and Otter Lake.

A notable feature about the fishing in the area around the town of Kamloops at the junction of Highways 5 and 97, has to do with the succession of the seasons during the summer. The lower lakes warm up early in the season and fishing consequently falls off. But all the angler needs to do is travel to waters in the same area but at a slightly higher altitude, to find his good fishing again. Most of the lakes in this area are between 3,000 and 4,000 feet above sea level, and are stocked annually. Face, Pasca and Wyse Lakes, twenty-eight miles southwest of Kamloops, are good and there is a lodge nearby. Contact Mile High Fishing & Hunting Lodge, Box 250, Kamloops, B.C.

Another lodge, Le Jeune Lodge, Box 8, Kamloops, British Columbia, offers fishing on Lac Le Jeune, one of the most consistently productive lakes through the season. Kamloops run to 4 pounds. Very small dry flies are successful.

Kamloops is served by two trains daily on the Canadian Pacific Railway and those who come by this means will find outfitters there to arrange plane trips to the interior. D. F. Robertson, Squilax, British Columbia, can outfit small parties for Kamloops trout up to 10 pounds in weight, in Little River, nearby; and to remote rivers further from headquarters.

For further information regarding points accessible by rail, write General Tourist Agent, Canadian Pacific Railway, Montreal 3, Quebec.

BRITISH COLUMBIA FISHING REGULATIONS

Resident Fishing License $2.00
Nonresident Fishing License (Alien) $7.00
Nonresident Fishing License (Canadian) $3.50
No license required for fishing in tidal waters.

SEASONS AND LIMITS

No closed season except as defined annually in Game & Fish Regulations, which should be checked at the time you purchase your license. Catch limits vary greatly, and your annual regulations must be checked for each species, according to the area in which you are fishing. Overall, 3-days' catch limit is the possession limit.

For complete regulations write: Fish and Game Branch, 567 Burrard Street, Vancouver, British Columbia.

ALBERTA

The Province of Alberta is the "in between" land of western Canada, marking the change from the moderate altitude, lake-and-river-marked plateau of Saskatchewan to the high-soaring mountains of British Columbia. On its northern borders is the Arctic landscape of the Northwest Territories; and on the south it shares the variegated landscape of Montana, from the dry wheatlands of the east to the Glacier National Park-Waterton Lakes area on the west. Much of Alberta is foothill country. However, the Rocky Mountains, where they form the southwestern border, jut into the Province, to form one of the loveliest regions of natural beauty on the North American continent.

The slower streams of the lakes of the farm belt and prairies teem with northern pike, perch, walleyes and goldeye. Some of the lower rivers produce large specimens of Rocky Mountain whitefish, grayling and rainbow trout. However, it is the more than 3,000 miles of clear, fast-water streams on the slopes and foothills of the Rockies that attract the greatest number of sportsmen. The principal species in these waters are the cutthroat trout, native of the west; rainbow and brown trout, both stocked; Rocky Mountain whitefish; and Dolly Varden, also known as bull trout. Some lakes produce lake trout as well. Arctic grayling are plentiful in the Peace and Athabaska systems that drain into the Arctic Ocean.

In that part of Alberta that lies south and east of Edmonton, the flow of water is to the South and North Saskatchewan Rivers and the Red River, all traveling eastward into the Province of Saskatchewan. In the north the drainage is to the Arctic through the Athabaska and Peace Rivers to Lake Athabaska and hence to Lesser Slave Lake in the west. These last two are the only two lakes of real size in Alberta although there are many beautiful smaller lakes, especially in the mountains.

Some Alberta streams, especially in the higher parts of the mountain range, are fed by glacier waters and consequently are discolored; anglers look for streams which start, rather, in a lake, as these are usually clear. An example is the Maligne River which starts in Maligne Lake high in the mountains of Jasper Park. Lake and river both have excellent speckled-trout fishing.

Alberta is served by the east-west Trans-Canada Highway 1, crossing the southern portion through the cities of Medicine Hat on the Saskatchewan border, to Calgary and Banff, thence into British Columbia. A single route, Highway 2, is the major north-south artery, entering the province on the Montana border at Carway, and being an extension of U.S. 89 through Glacier National Park. This route extends far into the northern part of Alberta to Edmonton and 129 miles beyond. At Edmonton, Highway 43 branches off and proceeds through the extreme northwest to become the MacKenzie Highway into the Northwest Territories and on to the north shore of Great Slave Lake. From Valleyview, on Highway 43, another road goes west into British Columbia, and in turn becomes the Alaska Highway.

From Edmonton a loop road also travels west; when it reaches the mountains it turns south and curves down along the range to the south and east to Banff and

Calgary. There are passes across the mountains into British Columbia at Lake Louise, via Highway 1, and at Crows Nest, well in the south, west of Lethbridge, via Highway 3.

Rail transportation is excellent, Canadian National and Canadian Pacific Railways transcontinental lines serving all the major cities and as far north as Peace River. Airplane service is provided by Trans-Canada Air Lines to the larger cities and towns; and at Edmonton there is charter service available to many parts of northern Alberta as well as the Northwest Territories and Alaska.

During July and August the fisherman will be comfortable in summer clothing plus sweaters for morning and evening. During spring and early fall the weather can be quite cool and heavier clothing is advisable. Rain coats and waterproof boots are essential; and waders or at least hip boots should be part of your equipment.

For the northerns, walleyes and such species, all types of tackle are used; but Alberta is a trout-fishing province, and those who go for the trouts usually use fly rods. An 8-foot 4-ounce rod and a single-action reel with HDH fly line is more or less standard, and a 10- to 12-foot leader should be tapered down to a 3X or 4X tippet, depending on the general size of the trout in a given lake or stream. All the standard flies will take fish, but those running to browns and grays seem most popular. The muddler and squirrel-tail streamers are both popular.

There is no closed season in Alberta. Trout of all species, as well as grayling, Rocky Mountain whitefish, pike, pickerel, perch and goldeye may be taken year-round.

However, special fishing licenses are required in the several national parks, and special fishing regulations prevail in some cases. Complete information in this respect should be obtained when you purchase your license.

Alberta is big-game country. There are black bear, grizzly bear, cougar, elk, moose, mule deer, whitetailed deer, bighorn sheep, mountain goats and caribou, among the larger animals, and many smaller ones. While most of them will not bother you unless you bother them, this is not the case with the grizzly, and in fact, all bears should be treated with great respect. Southern Alberta is within the range of the western rattlesnake.

SOUTHERN AREA

The fishing in south-central Alberta north to Calgary, is limited to pickerel, northern pike and perch, found in all the lowland streams on both sides of Highway 2. There are also dozens of lakes on either side of this highway which contain the same species, all readily available over the many roads that traverse this populated area. Accommodations of all kinds are also plentiful, principally in motels and hotels, as resorts are not numerous here.

In the southwest section the Bow River and Oldman River systems produce some good trout fishing. The Bow originates near Calgary and flows southeast to the South Saskatchewan River, seventy-five miles west of Medicine Hat. The Oldman joins the South Saskatchewan at the same point. Directions as to where to fish the headwaters of both rivers should be obtained from tackle stores at Calgary, at the junction of Highway 2 and Highway 1; at High River, on Highway 2A, off Highway 2 at Nanton; and at Lethbridge, further south, at the junction of Highways 4 and 3, as well as at all intermediate points. This is an area of plentiful accommodations and excellent roads all within short drives of good fishing.

The larger rivers such as the Elbow, the Highwood, the Sheep and Jumping Pond have good populations of fair-sized Dolly Varden and Rocky Mountain whitefish. These streams are fast, may be torrential, and are not too easy to fish. Fly and bait produce about equal results.

Below Calgary rainbows and cutthroats from 4 to 8 pounds are sometimes taken in the Bow River but because of pollution from the city these are not good to eat. Most anglers prefer to go to the upper tributaries where, although the catch will be only cutthroats of a pound or less, the water is pure and the fishing more pleasant.

The Spray Lakes in the headwaters of the Bow River can produce some fine cutthroat fishing, and there are both cutthroats and rainbows in the Kananskis Lakes. The favorite method of taking these lake swimmers is by trolling.

Those who particularly want to fish for cutthroat trout should try Racehorse Creek, Dutch Creek, Livingston Creek, Willow Creek, and the Crowsnest and Belly Rivers. They are best reached out of Fort MacLeod at the junction of Highways 2 and 3; at Pincher Creek on Highway 3; and at Claresholm, on Highway 2. There are motels throughout the area, and the streams are fairly heavily fished, especially in midsummer.

Throughout the North and South Saskatchewan River drainage, the goldeye is found, running up to a pound in weight, about 12 inches in length. They rise readily to a fly, and are an extremely popular table delicacy.

JASPER AND BANFF PARKS

To the north and west of Calgary, reached by Highway 1 to Lake Louise, and then 93 on northward, are two famous parks, Banff National Park and Jasper National Park. A park motor vehicle license must be obtained at the entrance, and is good for all National Parks in Alberta for the entire season. The cost is $2. A Park fishing license is also required, and costs $2 for the season or $1 for one month. The licenses are obtained at Park Information Centers and from Park wardens. Banff has been highly developed as a vacation rather than a fishing resort, but there is some angling for rainbow, eastern brook trout, lake trout and splake, a cross between brook trout and lake trout.

Jasper Park has quite extensive fishing for lake trout, rainbow, brown, eastern brook and Dolly Varden trouts, Rocky Mountain whitefish, pike and splake. Near Jasper, in the north-central part of the park, the best lakes are Lake Edith, for rainbows; Lake Annette, for eastern brook trout; First Trefoil Lake, for eastern brook; Second Trefoil Lake, for eastern and rainbows; Lac Beauvert, for almost all species indigenous to the area plus some splake; and Mildred Lake, which has eastern brooks and browns.

Those who are willing to hike can probably find less heavily fished and therefore more productive waters by following the well-marked trails which lead up towards the mountains to the west of Jasper. In Pyramid Lake, directly to the north, there is good lake-trout angling in the shallows in spring and fall, and the fish are taken deep trolling in the summer. There are also rainbows, splake, eastern brook trout and Rocky Mountain whitefish.

Many other lakes are located within hiking distance of the highway north from Jasper. Some provide good fishing while others are barren, and the stranger planning to find his own fishing in this area should obtain a copy of a pamphlet published by the National Parks Branch, Department of Northern Affairs and National Resources,

Ottawa, Canada, entitled "Angler's Guide to Jasper Park." It gives the location of the trails, and indicates which lakes do not have fish . . . a situation which can change from year to year. Therefore you want the current pamphlet. There are some twenty streams in the Park which also offer fair to good fishing, and the pamphlet contains information about these.

Maligne Lake is the largest and best-known lake in the Park. It holds some fine, bright-colored speckled trout up to 4 pounds. They are mostly taken by trolling with bead-chain spinners. However, just before the lake drains into the river, where the outlet narrows the current builds up and in this area fly men take some nice fish, mostly on a No. 6 squirrel-tail streamer, allowed to sink well.

WEST-CENTRAL AREA

In west-central Alberta there is some good fishing for brown and brook trout in waters accessible by several county and secondary roads running west from Highway 2, between Calgary and Red Deer; and from Highway 9, north to Drumheller from Highway 1, east of Calgary. Some of the more northern ones can also be reached from Highway 47 (unpaved), which runs south from the town of Edson on Highway 16, west of Edmonton.

Those rivers to the east of Highway 2 are generally in the system of the Red Deer River, and include the Raven River, Alford Creek, Dogpound Creek and Schrader Creek. All of them offer good dry-fly fishing. There are some Dolly Vardens in these streams, too, and in the higher reaches rainbows are taken.

To the west of Highway 2, a good spot can be reached via Highway 11 out of Red Deer to Nordegg. In this area there are quite a few beaver dams which have been stocked with brown trout and can produce some excellent fishing. It is particularly attractive to fly fishermen. The small Spiders on No. 12 hooks are good, and so are the Royal Coachmen, Ginger Quill, Parmachene Belle, and McGinty—in fact all the conventional trout flies will take fish. This whole area just described is about the most popular in Alberta with trout fishermen.

There are accommodations at Red Deer, Ponoka and Wetaskiwin on Highway 2, and at Rocky Mountain House, half way to Nordegg on Highway 11. At the Diamond Cross Ranch, east of Banff, you can arrange guided fishing excursions to the mountain streams through Al Nordlund, Diamond Cross Ranch, Seebe, Alberta. Pack trips to the headwaters of many of these streams can also be arranged at Red Deer on Highway 2.

To the north of this general area, Highway 16, already mentioned, runs west from Edmonton to Edson, where Highway 47 then leads south. Beyond Edson, at Hinton, a dirt road leads northwest to the fringes of Wilderness Provincial Park, a part of Jasper Park, then turns north again to eventually reach Highway 34, far to the north, just west of Valleyview. In its wanderings it crosses the headwaters of the Berland, Simonette and Laterneil Rivers, all excellent rainbow streams which have produced fish up to 5 pounds. There is excellent dry-fly fishing. Several lakes which can best be reached by pack trip also offer some good rainbow fishing. Dolly Vardens have been reported to 10 pounds in the more remote streams and some of the lakes. The McLeod and Sakwatamau Rivers, near Whitecourt on Highway 43, have grayling and rainbows.

Accommodations are always at a premium and it is a good idea to make reservations in advance. At Edson there are the Commodore Hotel, Edson Auto Court,

Edson Motor Hotel, Jasper Highway Tourist Camp, McLeod River Inn and Sunset Motel. At Whitecourt there are the Whitecourt Hotel, Rivers Hotel, Glenview Hotel, Hannigans Motel and Jack Pine Motel.

From Edmonton northward, the majority of the waters are in the Athabasca and Peace River systems. Much of the area is accessible only by pack trip from such towns as Whitecourt, Fox Creek, Little Smoky and Valleyview on Highway 43. And further north the highway crosses the Little Smoky, which along with its tributaries the Waskahigan and Iosegun Rivers, can be quite good.

ALBERTA FISHING REGULATIONS

Resident Fishing License $2.00
Nonresident Fishing License $2.00

SEASONS AND LIMITS

There is no closed season on any fish in Alberta.

Species	Possession Limit	Daily Bag Limit
Trout and Grayling	15 in aggregate	10 fish of one species only or 10 fish in aggregate
Kokanee Salmon	10	10
Rocky Mountain Whitefish	30	15
Lake Trout	10	5
Lake Whitefish	8	8
Perch	50	25
Pike, Walleye, Sauger, Goldeye	30 in aggregate	15 fish of one species only or 15 fish in aggregate

For complete regulations write: Director of Fish and Wildlife, Edmonton, Alberta.

SASKATCHEWAN

The lower half of the Province of Saskatchewan is geographically very much like the grasslands and rich agricultural areas of western North Dakota and Montana which border this Canadian province on the south. As you proceed north the country becomes less rolling, with more outcroppings of rock, until in the far north it is similar to the flat barrenlands of the Northwest Territories which form the northern boundary on the 60th parallel of latitude. On the east the boundary is Manitoba, and on the west the land begins to rise to the higher country of the Province of Alberta. Saskatchewan is slightly wedge-shaped, 393 miles wide at the south tapering to 277 miles wide along the northern border. It has a total of 251,700 square miles, nearly as large as Texas. The altitude slopes gently from southwest to northeast, the highest point being the Cyprus Hills Provincial Park at 4,546 feet, while the lowest is about 1,500 feet.

Saskatchewan has three major river systems which drain its thousands of lakes and their equally numerous streams. The North and South Saskatchewan Rivers originate in Alberta and flow east and northeast to join a network of lakes near the town of The Pas in northeast Manitoba. The Churchill River also flows eastward into Manitoba, crossing Saskatchewan's north country in a necklace of blue lakes, bays and connecting waterways, to the north of Lac La Ronge. Lac La Ronge, near the end of the road north in Saskatchewan, is the largest of the well-known fishing lakes, but there are dozens more of tremendous size and innumerable smaller ones where fishing is good. All together there are 10,000 lakes and streams in Saskatchewan offering a wide variety of fishing opportunities.

The species of fish to be found are northern pike, walleye, Arctic grayling, lake trout, brook trout, rainbow trout, yellow perch, goldeye and whitefish. The heaviest lake trout known to have been taken was a 72-pounder. Northern pike range up to 30 pounds, Arctic grayling to 2 and 3 pounds, with the odd one slightly larger. Walleye run between 4 and 6 pounds. Brook and rainbow trout are good sized at around 3 pounds occasionally, and in some few places there are brown trout which come regularly in the 2-pound class and have been taken to 14 pounds. The trout fishing is pretty much confined to the southeastern part of the province. Yellow perch and goldeye will average a pound, but the fine-tasting Great Lakes whitefish reaches 5 pounds.

As far north as Prince Albert the fisherman-motorist will have no trouble getting around. Highway 39 enters from North Dakota at Portal and proceeds northwest to the main cities of Moose Jaw and Regina, from which roads spread out throughout the southern part of the province. There are also several lesser highways providing entry from North Dakota and Montana at some fourteen other points across the southern border. Such ports of entry are marked on highway maps with small crossed flags.

North of Prince Albert the fisherman will be confined to Highway 2, running northward to Lac La Ronge, the end of the road. Just north of Prince Albert Highway 55 crosses Highway 2, providing east-west traffic at this northern latitude, which, however, ends about 100 miles short of the Manitoba border, where the road peters out. Halfway along the eastward progress of Highway 55, at Smeaton, another road, known as the Hanson Lake Road, turns north and makes a big loop north and east into Manitoba at Flin Flon, turns south to The Pas, then westward into Saskatchewan again and joins Highway 3 which eventually reaches Prince Albert.

Similar access to more remote areas is provided from Highway 55 west of Prince Albert. At Green Lake anglers may follow a gravel road north for many miles to Lake Churchill and Peter Pond.

Northwest Airlines, Western Airlines, Braniff Airways and Trans-Canada all fly to Lac La Ronge, in the northern part of the province. Other vast areas in the far north of the province must be reached by charter float planes. To serve sportsmen, two airline companies operate regular schedules. Pacific Western Airlines flies from Edmonton, Alberta to outlying areas in Saskatchewan; and Saskatchewan Government Airways flies the same service out of Prince Albert.

Accommodations in Saskatchewan are keeping pace with the ever increasing traffic to these remote areas. Camps with variable services dot the highways and there are now many fine camps at fly-in lakes.

Throughout the Province of Saskatchewan the climate is temperate. While cotton clothing will serve on the warmest summer days, every evening is pleasantly cool and woolens are needed. Sometimes it can be really cold even in midsummer, and anglers should go suitably equipped. Rainwear should also be carried.

There is no game more dangerous than the bear in Saskatchewan, and he will not bother you if you leave him alone. If you are fortunate you may see antelope in the grasslands, and deer and moose roam the Churchill River area in great numbers. In the extreme northwest section in the Lake Athabasca and Tazin Lake area there are caribou, again not dangerous. Mosquitoes and flies of all kinds are present in large numbers, and you should have plenty of insect repellent to deal with them. A head net is a good idea.

Standard lightweight plug- and spin-casting rods are suitable for most fishing in Saskatchewan, except for lake trout, which except in spring and fall usually have to be taken by deep trolling. However, this far north the fish stay within reach of light tackle for longer than in more southern waters and many anglers like to go for them with fly rods, preferably a 9-foot 6-ounce rod, matched with a GAF line that will lay out long casts and handle large streamers and bucktails. For trout fishing in the more southern waters, an 8-foot fly rod weighing 4 ounces, and fitted with an HDH line is heavy enough. Use a 4X tippet in the slower streams.

The big lake trout can also be taken on spin-casting gear, with line testing 8 to 10 pounds. Plug casters use 12- to 15-pound-test line, and it's advisable to carry an extra reel so you won't lose time if one goes bad on you. For those who prefer to troll for the big lakers, camps usually supply big boat reels loaded with copper or Monel line.

Fishing is limited by climatic conditions in much of northern Saskatchewan to June through September. Nevertheless, for those willing to face possible snow and cold, there is fishing from May 5 to the following March 31st.

THE FAR NORTH

Dozens of excellent fishing lakes and rivers, many scarcely known, are found in the far northern part of Saskatchewan, the area between the Manitoba boundary on the east and Alberta on the west; and from the southern end of Reindeer Lake in the east across the province to the upper ends of Peter Pond and Churchill Lake in the west. Top waters for giant lake trout, northerns and walleyes are Lake Athabasca, in the extreme northwestern corner, Black Lake and the Fond du Lac River, slightly to the east; Cree Lake, almost due north of Lac La Ronge; the Foster Lakes between La Ronge and Cree; Reindeer, already mentioned; Wollaston, north of Reindeer, neighboring Waterbury Lake; and Tazin Lake, north of Lake Athabasca. Tazin Lake is one of the surest bets for big lakers and northern pike. All those mentioned and many others in the general area have wonderful fishing for Arctic grayling.

The only accommodation on Tazin Lake is Tazin Lake Lodge, operated by Vince and Bill Pullar (address Uranium City). They will make complete fly-in arrangements for guests, who come via Saskatchewan Government Airways on a regular schedule of flights Monday, Wednesday and Friday from Prince Albert to Uranium City, then a twenty-minute flight to Lake Tazin by float plane. Prices at the camp run about $275 per person per week, and this includes the float plane trip from Uranium City to camp.

There are several camps in the Stoney Rapids area at the eastern end of Lake Athabaska. Morberg's Camps, located twenty-five miles west of Black Lake on the Fond du Lac River, offers fishing right at camp and other outposts developed each year, all with excellent fishing for lake trout and Arctic grayling. Rates here are about $35 per day per person.

Also headquartered at Stony Rapids is Walt Shaeffer's Grayling Lodge on Black Lake, with excellent Arctic grayling fishing, and some fine fly-casting possibilities for Great Lakes whitefish, as well as big pike and walleyes. During the winter write him at Box 151, Rockglen, Saskatchewan.

Plane fare from Prince Albert to Stony Rapids is about $100; from Lac La Ronge, about $75.

Closer to the eastern boundaries of this northern part of Saskatchewan, there are modern camps on Wollaston Lake and Waterbury Lake, and there's fine fishing for lake trout, northern pike, walleyes and Arctic grayling. From this camp, either by canoe with guide, or by float plane, anglers can go in to many other lakes, and are within reach of the Fond du Lac, Geikie and Cochrane Rivers. Wollaston Lake Camp can be reached by Parsons Airway Charter service out of Lynn Lake, Manitoba, on the Canadian National Railway out of Winnipeg. Or you can drive to Lac La Ronge and fly in via Saskatchewan Government Airways charter service.

At Waterbury Lake, west and slightly south of Wollaston, Jim Jackson operates a lodge. His winter address is 115 Woodward Avenue, London, Ontario; summers he is reached at Jackson Lodge, Lynn Lake, care of Trans Air, Manitoba. A good highway connects Winnipeg, Manitoba, to Flin Flon, where there is plane service to Lynn Lake. From Lynn you fly in on Parsons Airway charter service. Besides the excellent lake trout, northerns and Arctic grayling in Waterbury Lake, the camp gives access to a number of rivers with fine fishing for the same species. The lakers run to 40 pounds, the northerns to 30, the grayling really trophy fish that go over 3 pounds. This is a very scenic country, with plenty of fish.

LAC LA RONGE AREA

Further south in Saskatchewan, but still very much the north country, is the vast band of lakes and streams accessible from Highway 2 to Lac La Ronge, the

Hanson Road on the east, and the gravel road to Churchill Lake on the west. Cabins and camp sites are fairly numerous along this road and the fishing is fair to good in the easily accessible lakes. There are lake trout, northern pike, pickerel and Great Lakes whitefish. Arctic grayling can be found in nearby fly-in lakes.

Lac La Ronge itself is a 500-square-mile body of water containing 1,192 islands and is usually free of ice by late May. Early season fishermen take the lakers for which La Ronge is famous on fly and light spinning tackle, but later in the summer most of the fishing is by trolling. In bays and around islands there can be some excellent fly fishing for whitefish when this species rises to feed at evening. There are also northern pike and walleyes. A small but good modern hotel provides accommodation at Lac La Ronge and there are several outfitters who can arrange to take parties to fly-in lakes, such as Black Bear Island, northwest, near the Churchill River; McKay Lake, a few miles north of La Ronge; McIntosh Lake, northeast of La Ronge; and Nemeiben and Nipew Lakes, to the north. These are all particularly recommended for lake trout, northern pike and walleyes. The last are also numerous in Besnard, Drinking, Emmeline, Little Deer, Nistowiak, Otter and Wapawekka Lakes and the Churchill River, all in the environs of Lac La Ronge.

Wilson Sanderson, Lac La Ronge, can supply guide service for Lac La Ronge and surrounding waters. In the Churchill River area, Tom Pierce, P. O. Box 7512, Oklahoma City 16, Oklahoma, operates Sportsman's Lodge on the southern end of Lake McIntosh, which is fifty miles by air, north of Lac La Ronge.

NORTHWEST

To the south and west again, from the city of North Battleford, anglers can drive to Meadow Lake Provincial Park via either Highway 26 or Highway 4. Lake trout are not as numerous in this area as they are further north but northern pike are there in both size and quantity, and there are lots of walleyes. Ring perch can be taken on any type of tackle, and are highly regarded for their food value.

Meadow Lake Park can also be reached from Prince Albert via Highway 55; and en route there is a gravel road turnoff going north to Churchill Lake, Peter Pond Lake and Buffalo Narrows. Still another goes in at Green Lake to Lac La Plonge and Lac Ile a La Crosse, then continues on up to Churchill Lake. And twenty-five miles east of this another gravel road leads to Sled, Mirasty, Smoothstone and Dore Lakes. All through this area there are fine camp sites, and there are some camps and resorts too.

Northern pike and walleye enthusiasts will find some fine sport in the North Saskatchewan River near North Battleford. You go northwest on Highway 26, to Highway 3, near St. Walburg, then south to the river. You can also continue on north on 26 for about fifty miles to the Beaver River, which crosses the road south of Meadow Lake Provincial Park. This is a good pike and walleye stream.

PRINCE ALBERT AND NIPAWIN PARKS

On its way north to Lac La Ronge, Highway 2 leads through Prince Albert National Park, 1,496 square miles in area. Its three major lakes, Kingsmere, Crean and Waskesiu, all hold lake trout, northern pike and pickerel. To the east is Nipawin Provincial Park, smaller, but perhaps with slightly better fishing because it is not so highly developed as a summer resort. The best approach to Nipawin Provincial

Park is over the Hanson Lake Road starting at Smeaton on Highway 55, running north through the park, then turning northeast and ending at Creighton, across the border from Flin Flon in Manitoba.

White Gull Creek, which flows southwest from the lower corner of Nipawin Park and enters White Gull Lake, has been stocked with brook trout. Both the creek and the lake can be reached via gravel road out of the Park. McDougal Creek, at the northeast corner of the Park, is also rated as a good stream for stocked brook trout.

SOUTHERN AREA

The angler who is willing to do a little exploring and to question local fisher-men can find some surprisingly good trout fishing in southern Saskatchewan—sur-prising because of the fact that although the fish often average out at 2 pounds apiece, very little is known about this fishing except among a few of the "local boys" —and they aren't always telling. The best of it is in the southwest corner in the Cypress Hills area, in a number of tributaries of the South Saskatchewan. These streams were stocked away back in the 1920's, and have remained good producers ever since, with some subsequent stocking but considerable natural reproduction. Battle Creek, Bone Creek, Farewell Creek, Belanger Creek and Frenchman Creek all have fishing for either browns, rainbows or brooks. Bear Creek, which flows north into Crane Lake on Highway 1, is another stream that is usually productive. There are some accommodations at the small town of Maple Creek, which is more or less headquarters for this fishing; and lots of accommodations at Swift Current. Anglers planning to fish these creeks should get directions as to how to reach them from tackle stores or the hotel owner at Maple Creek. In most cases they are accessible at some spot by country road. The proper gear is an 8-foot fly rod, with HDH line and you must go down to a 4X tippet, as the streams are generally clear. Some are difficult to fish because of the high grass and overhanging bushes, but the fish are good-sized.

There is good fishing for northern pike, walleyes and perch throughout the course of the Qu'Appelle River, which crosses southeastern Saskatchewan. Crooked Lake is reached via Highway 47 off Highway 1 at Grenfell; Round Lake via High-way 9 off Highway 1 east of Broadview. Further east is a group of lakes at Fort Qu'Appelle, known as the Fishing Lakes, all good producers. Going north on High-way 11 at Regina, you come to the largest lake in the system, known as Last Mountain or Long Lake, and it has the reputation of turning out big pike. Smaller Buffalo Pound Lake, on Highway 2, north from Moose Jaw, also rates high for pike.

SASKATCHEWAN FISHING REGULATIONS

Resident Fishing License (any person residing
  in Canada) $2.00
Nonresident Fishing License (for waters not
  frequented by trout or grayling) $5.00
Nonresident Fishing License (all waters) $10.00

SEASONS AND LIMITS

Species	Open Season	Size Limit	Daily Bag Limit
Grayling	May 4–March 31	None	10
Trout, Bass	May 4–March 31	None	5
Lake Sturgeon	May 4–March 31	None	1
Yellow Perch	May 4–March 31	None	No limit
All other fish	May 4–March 31	None	8

For complete regulations write: Director of Fisheries, Department of Natural Resources, Prince Albert, Saskatchewan.

MANITOBA

Like the fertile farmlands of northern Minnesota and North Dakota, which border it on the south, southern Manitoba is a vast agricultural area, with wide, flat expanses of green in spring turning to the gold of the crops as the fall season approaches. As you progress north the terrain becomes more rolling with outcroppings of rock among thick stands of poplar, birch and spruce. There are thousands of lakes of all sizes, with equally numerous streams joining them. Nowhere in the province does the altitude go above 3,000 feet.

Sporting species of fish found in Manitoba are northern pike, walleye (pickerel), lake trout, brook trout, rainbow trout, brown trout, smallmouth black bass, largemouth black bass, Arctic char, Arctic grayling, Great Lakes whitefish, splake, goldeye and mooneye, silver bass (sheepshead), sauger, sturgeon, perch and muskellunge.

Of these the lake trout, northern pike, walleye and Arctic char are the most widely taken. The heaviest lake trout known to have come from Manitoba waters was a 63-pounder taken in Lake Athapapuskow, between the towns of The Pas and Flin Flon, off Highway 10 in the northwest-central part of the province. Lakers are regularly taken up to 40 pounds in this area. Average weights of other species can be judged by the entry standards of the Manitoba Master Angler Awards. To win the Master Angler badge a northern pike must weigh at least 18 pounds; muskellunge, 20 pounds; walleye pike, 8 pounds; lake trout, 20 pounds; brook trout, 4 pounds; rainbow trout, 4 pounds; largemouth and smallmouth black bass, 3 pounds; grayling, 2 pounds; Arctic char, 4 pounds; splake, a cross between brook and lake trout, 4 pounds; brown trout, 4 pounds; whitefish, 4 pounds.

The largest lakes are Lake Winnipeg, Lake Manitoba and Lake Winnipegosis, slanting like great inland seas across the entire south-central part of the province. The waters picked up by these lakes flow south through the Red River of the North, eventually to reach the Mississippi. North of the lakes, drainage is to Hudson Bay by a network of lakes and streams, some scarcely mapped as yet.

Almost all of Manitoba's highways are found in the south. From the capital city of Winnipeg, some seventy miles from the southern border, roads fan out to provide transport throughout this area via the main east-west route of Highway 1, which as a continuation of Ontario Highway 17 from Kenora, becomes the Trans-Canada Highway at this point; and a network of feeder roads. A series of roads also fans north from the city to the southeastern corner of Lake Winnipeg; while Highway 6, the major part of it still gravel, extends northward between Lake Winnipeg and Lakes Manitoba and Winnipegosis to Grand Rapids on the northwest shore of Lake Winnipeg. This marks the farthest point north, except one, that the motorist can travel in Manitoba. The road which reaches farthest north is Highway 10, which leaves the Trans-Canada Highway at the city of Brandon, and proceeds northward close to the western border of Manitoba to Flin Flon, on the border with Saskatchewan. There the road hooks southward and eventually will make connection with Highway 6 to Regina, Saskatchewan.

From the south, motorists may enter via Minnesota Highways 313 or 89, in the southeast corner of Manitoba; U.S. 59 a little further west; and U.S. 8 (Interstate 29) on the Minnesota-North Dakota border. There are border entry points on North Dakota Highways 18, 32, 1, 20, 28, 30, 3, 14 and 83.

Anglers who plan to camp or travel with trailers should obtain the pamphlet "Manitoba Campgrounds" from the Travel and Publicity Branch, Department of Industry and Commerce, Legislative Building, Winnipeg, Manitoba.

Beyond the reach of roads, transportation is by float plane, with the many lakes providing landing bases in even the most remote spots; and by rail via the Canadian National Railway route to Churchill on Hudson Bay; and the same company's Lynn Lake line, running directly north from the Pas.

Air transportation may be arranged through Trans Air Ltd., Box 5, St. James, Manitoba; Aero Trades, Winnipeg International Airport; Northland Airlines, 660 Washington Avenue, Winnipeg 15, Manitoba; Island Lake Airways, c/o Bristol Aero Industries, Winnipeg International Airport; Riverton Airways, 411 Childs Building, Winnipeg 2, Manitoba; Selkirk Air Service, Selkirk, Manitoba; Falcon Aviation, Caddy Lake, Manitoba; Thomas Lamb Ltd., The Pas, Manitoba; Parsons Air Service, Channing, Manitoba; Ilford Airways, Ilford, Manitoba; Chiupka Airways, Lynn Lake, Manitoba; and R. Parsons, Churchill, Manitoba.

Those who operate their own planes should obtain the Official Air Navigation Map of Manitoba from the Travel and Publicity Branch of the Department of Industry and Commerce, Legislative Building, Winnipeg. It is a very complete brochure, with listings of many services, as well as navigation information.

The climate in Manitoba can be simply defined as cold in winter, cool in summer, except in the extreme south. Daytime temperatures in midsummer range between 70 and 85 degrees, while the summer-night average is about 55 degrees. Cotton shirts will suffice for daytime fishing, with a sweater for early morning and evening, but should be supplemented by light woolen underwear and waterproof clothing for cool, rainy days. Such clothing is fine for the southern and central part of Manitoba during the months of June, July and August. At other seasons, and at all seasons further north, the angler should be equipped with heavy woolens, a good windbreaker and waterproof, strong boots.

There is plenty of wild game in Manitoba and except in the most southern area the angler is likely to see deer, moose, bear and in the far north, possibly caribou. In Riding Mountain National Park, just west of Winnipeg, there are elk. If the animals are not disturbed there is usually no danger to an angler.

While the 50th parallel of Latitude is generally regarded as the northern limits of the rattlesnake (Manitoba's southern boundary is the 49th Parallel), there could be a few members of this family up into south-central Manitoba.

Black flies and mosquitoes are prevalent, and anglers should always be equipped with net headgear and plenty of insect repellent.

SOUTHERN AREA

In southern Manitoba, Highway 1 follows the course of the Winnipeg River, noted for its fine smallmouth black-bass fishing. One of the favorite spots is at Pointe du Bois in Whiteshell Provincial Park on the eastern border with Ontario. The Park is reached via Highway 4, north from Highway 17 at the border, or the same highway east from Selkirk, north of Winnipeg; in both cases to Highway 11,

Typical of the many lakes in south-central Manitoba, Falcon Lake offers superb fishing for walleye, northern pike and smallmouth black bass.

then by dirt road at Lac du Bonnet to Pointe du Bois. There is good walleye and northern pike fishing in Echo Lake just to the east. The best-rated smallmouth lakes in the park are West Hawk and Falcon, both readily accessible from Highways 4 and 17 in the southeast corner; and these and nearby High Lake also have populations of lake trout. Lac du Bonnet has all services and there are several resorts on the river. They should be addressed as follows: Eagle Nest Lodge, 76 Crestwood Crescent, St. Boniface 6, Manitoba; and Pine Island Lodge, Pointe du Bois, Manitoba; winters, 515 Ferry Road, Winnipeg 12, Manitoba.

Guide service in the park and information as to accommodations may be obtained from Vic Burgess, Pointe du Bois, Manitoba. Early July is the best time to go into this area, as then the bass can be taken on all types of casting lures, both surface and underwater. Fly-rodders should have an 8-foot 4-ounce rod with plenty of backbone, and an HCH line with leader tapered down to a 6-pound-test tippet. Any dark streamer fly, predominantly brown or black, slashed with red, on a No. 4 hook, is regarded as good, and so is the Colorado Gold Spinner.

Early in the season the lake trout may also be taken near the surface by the casting methods, but as summer comes on they go deep and then the deep-trolling methods with spoons on wire lines are most successful. Northerns are taken on all types of tackle.

Northern pike and walleyes are the most common species in Lakes Winnipeg, Manitoba and Winnipegosis. Because of the fairly extensive network of highways already described in this area, it has been highly developed as a family vacation spot. Along these lakes and on those of Riding Mountain National Park, to the west, accommodations are plentiful. Motels cost about $6 per day single, $9 double. Resorts will run about $25 per person per day, including cabin, meals, boat, motor, gasoline and one guide per each two guests. Fishing-camp seasons usually run from May to mid-October.

While most of the fishing in Riding Mountain National Park is for northern pike, there are also some eastern brook and rainbow trout, notably in Katherine Lake, off Highway 10 near Washagaming, on Clear Lake. A special license required for fishing in the Park may be obtained from Park attendants.

In the comparatively undeveloped country to the east of Lake Winnipeg the angler has a chance for some fine, back-country fishing for walleyes, northerns and trout at Fishing Lake Lodge, 170 air miles from Winnipeg. It's seventy-five miles from the nearest road and 110 miles from the nearest railway. Flights in and accommodations should be arranged through Reg. Treacy, Box 403, Winnipeg 1, Manitoba. Rates are about $375 per person per week, including the flights. You can get your fishing licenses at the lodge.

NORTHWESTERN AREA

From the upper section of Lake Winnipeg to the Arctic Circle, much of northern Manitoba is wild, wide-open country, with many distant lakes known only to the pilots who fly over them and the occasional Indian who may go through in his canoe. Only a narrow strip here and there is also accessible through two lines of the Canadian National Railway, the one going to the shores of Hudson Bay at Churchill, the other north from Flin Flon to Lynn Lake, as previously described.

Those who want to travel as far north as possible by road will find accommodations and access to Lake Winnipegosis at Swan River and Overflowing River, on Highway 10; and some facilities at several other small communities en route and on the shores of the lake. There are northerns, walleyes and goldeyes. Enquiries should be addressed to Myrtle Burrell, Dawson Bay Post Office, Manitoba.

The Pas, a town of some 5,000 people, is sixty-six miles north on Highway 10, a total of 475 miles from Winnipeg. This is the terminal point for the Canadian National Railway, and Trans-Canada Air Lines has service to The Pas six days a week. Clearwater Lake, fifteen miles from town, is popular with lake-trout fishermen, while other nearby waters produce walleye and northern pike. Information as to fishing in the area can be obtained at Hill's Store and Service Station, as you enter The Pas on Highway 10; or by mail through the Chamber of Commerce, The Pas, Manitoba. Continuing north towards Flin Flon, Lake Athapapuskow has the same species plus smallmouth black bass.

Highway 10 ends at Flin Flon, a town of 12,000 inhabitants. Anglers travel from here to the interior via the Hudson Bay Line of the Canadian National Railway, on a three-days-a-week service—Monday, Wednesday and Friday. In summer they also go by plane, canoe or pack trip. In winter the only other methods of transportation in this remote country are snowmobile or tractor, and occasionally planes on skis.

Flights via Trans Air Limited can be arranged in the summer from Winnipeg to Flin Flon every day except Sunday; and the same line charters to take anglers to inland lakes and streams. Details should be obtained from Trans Air Limited, Post Office Box 5, St. James, Manitoba.

The town of Flin Flon conducts a Trout Festival each June, with a $1,000 prize for the top fish and several other cash prizes. For information anglers should write The Trout Festival Association, Flin Flon, Manitoba. Clearwater Lake and Cranberry Portage, both to the south of Flin Flon, both offer access to a number of good fishing lakes, including the three Cranberry Lakes, Elbow, Iskwasum, Reed and Tramping Lakes. These last four can now be reached by car over a dirt road from Simonhouse on Highway 10.

For reservations at Reed Lake Lodge write Box 1265, The Pas, Manitoba; winter address: Box 156, Gilbert Plains, Manitoba.

There are several lodges in the area around Flin Flon as well as at The Pas and Cranberry Portage, and to the west of the road on Lake Athapapuskow. For further information anglers should write F. W. Constable, Cranberry Portage, Manitoba, or the Flin Flon Chamber of Commerce, Flin Flon, Manitoba.

Prospective fishermen should also obtain a copy of the current "Where to Stay in Manitoba," issued by the Travel and Publicity Branch, Department of Industry and Commerce, Legislative Building, Winnipeg 1, Manitoba. It lists not only the accommodations in the parts of the province accessible by road, but also those to which the angler must fly. And the material is brought up to date annually, which is important with the great strides being made in opening up remote areas of northern Manitoba.

Following the line of the Canadian National Railway north from Sherritt Junction, near Flin Flon, there are two lodges at Elbow Lake: two more at Kississing Lake, reached by the railway. They can be addressed as follows: Thompson's Kississing Lodge, Sherridon, Manitoba, winter address 555 Lyndale Drive, Winnipeg, Manitoba; Cambrian Lodge, Sherridon, Manitoba; Elbow Lake Lodge, Cranberry Portage, Manitoba, winter address Box 187, Hurley, South Dakota; and Ashdown's Camp, Cranberry Portage, Manitoba.

On the spur line running east from Optic Lake, outfitting can be arranged through Stan Millan at the Snow Lake Hotel, Snow Lake, Manitoba, a very modern hotel in the wilderness. From here fly-in fishing trips can be arranged to even more remote waters. Other outfitters in the The Pas area are Lloyd Wasylkoski, 903 Constant Avenue, The Pas, Manitoba; and Alex Green, 335 LaRose Avenue, The Pas, Manitoba.

Herbert Unger, 913 Sargent Avenue, Winnipeg, Manitoba, also outfits for the Reed Lake and Snow Lake area, as well as in the less remote Whiteshell area.

There is very little fishing in the immediate vicinity of Lynn Lake which town has about 1,200 inhabitants, but there are several fly-in lodges easily reached from here. Information can be obtained from Harry Davies, Box 128, Lynn Lake. His winter address: 866 North Wabash Avenue, Chicago 11, Illinois. North of this, only forty miles out of Le Pas, there is excellent pike fishing at Cormorant Lodge, camp on McGavock Lake offers lake trout, northern pike, walleye and Great Lakes whitefish. Wolverine Lodge, thirty miles north of Lynn Lake on Vandekerckhove Lake offers fishing for lake trout, northerns and walleye, both at headquarters and outpost camps which they service by truck or air as the need may be.

NORTHEASTERN AREA

The vast reaches of northeastern Manitoba are served by the Hudson Bay Line of the Canadian National Railway, leaving the main line at The Pas and proceeding northeastward through wild country laced with lakes and rivers. At Cormorant, the village of Wekusko can also be reached by road from Snow Lake. There is a lodge nearby. Continuing up the railway, Thicket Portage is a good spot from which to start canoe trips, but outfitting must be done at Le Pas, as there is no service at Thicket Portage.

Just before the line turns north at Amery, there is a hotel at the small village of Gillam. Guides and supplies can be obtained here to go north to the Limestone and Weir Rivers. The Limestone is particularly good for fly fishing, being shallow, and with clear banks. Both have good fishing for speckled trout. The Nelson River is also good, and the Angling River, to the south of the railway line.

God's Lake, far to the south, can only be reached by plane. Anglers seeking the big brook trout for which this area is justly famous, board a chartered seaplane at Winnipeg on Saturdays and fly directly to camp. The cost of a seven-day trip, including the plane flight is about $550. Brook trout from 4 to 7 pounds are common and fly fishing is excellent, from June 1 to September 15. There are also lake trout, with the fish staying near enough to the surface to be taken on light tackle throughout the season. Arrangements to reach the camp should be made through Ruminski Brothers, Box 714, Winnipeg, Manitoba.

Arctic grayling in Manitoba are taken in those streams which flow to Hudson Bay. Deer River, on the Hudson Bay Branch of the Canadian National Railway is a good spot, only a few miles south of Churchill. The Owl River, Silcox River and Harriet Creek are also accessible by rail. Others which are good but must be reached by plane or canoe are the Seal River, North Knife and the South Knife, immediately above Harriet Creek. August and September are the top months for this species. The fish congregate in the rapid parts of the rivers, and are also found in some lakes. They rise readily to flies, preferring the small, dark patterns.

The Arctic char is found in the estuaries of streams flowing into Hudson Bay, and in such rivers as the Churchill, Seal, Caribou and others further north. They are taken on flies and on spinning gear using silver spoons and wobblers, and like the lake trout, must sometimes be taken by deep trolling. Guiding and outfitting arrangements can be made at Churchill to reach these rivers. There are two hotels at Churchill, one with dining room.

MANITOBA FISHING REGULATIONS

Resident Fishing License $2.25
Nonresident Fishing License $6.50

SEASONS AND LIMITS

Species	Open Season	Daily Bag Limit
Northern Pike, Walleye, Sauger	May 18–March 31	8
Sheepshead, Bass, Goldeye, Mooneye, Whitefish	May 18–March 31	6
Muskellunge	May 18–March 31	
Lake Trout, Rainbow Trout, Brown Trout	Designated waters: April 15–March 31 Other waters: May 18–March 31	5
Arctic Char	Designated waters: April 15–March 31 Other waters: May 18–March 31	6
Arctic Grayling	June 15–March 31	6
Sturgeon	June 15–March 31	1

There are no size limits on fish caught by angling.

For complete regulations write: Department of Mines and Natural Resources, Room 1003, Norquay Building, 401 York Avenue, Winnipeg, Manitoba.

ONTARIO

Because of its accessibility to the highly populated eastern United States, Ontario has probably been visited by more sportsmen in quest of good fishing than all the other Canadian provinces put together. Yet much of its northern reaches remain a vast wilderness, known only to trappers, lumbermen and Indians. Of the million square miles that is Ontario, with its 250,000 lakes and countless streams, there are still thousands of square miles of forest.

While the Province of Ontario is laced with rivers, it is its lakes which provide the bulk of the fishing, the rivers being more or less an adjunct to the lake fishing. Some, such as the St. Lawrence in the Thousand Island section, the St. Mary's at Sault Ste. Marie, the French River near North Bay, the Nipigon River in northwestern Ontario and the Albany and Ogaki in the Hudson Bay area, all have earned special names for themselves. But they will be treated along with the lakes in the following pages because of the fact that the rivers and lakes are so interwoven.

The fish found in Ontario are the largemouth and smallmouth black bass, with emphasis on the latter, great northern pike, walleye, speckled trout, splake (a cross between speckled and lake trout), rainbow trout, lake trout, brown trout, muskellunge, landlocked salmon, aurora trout (a species reputed to be indigenous only to a few lakes in the Sudbury area) and kamloops trout. The greatest propagation efforts are carried out in connection with the muskellunge, which has been introduced with very good results in some of the lakes and streams of southern Ontario. They are found elsewhere throughout many waters of the province but are probably best known to anglers in the Lake of the Woods area on the western border, and in the Rice Lake waters of the Kawartha chain in southeastern Ontario.

The smallmouth black bass, lake trout, northern pike and walleye (generally known in Ontario as pickerel) are the most widely distributed species and the angler will find them in most lakes and many streams. Lake trout will run to a maximum weight of 50 pounds, with an average closer to 10. Northerns reach weights of 40 pounds, and even occasionally heavier, but 10- to 20-pounders are more the going weight. The walleye is found in sizes from 3 to 15 pounds, the latter being a lunker. Of these three, the walleye and the lake trout are regarded as the best table fare (though their fighting qualities are not up to those of the northern), with the exception of the lake trout when taken on light gear on a surface lure, as is sometimes possible in the spring and fall.

In Ontario there are close to 100,000 miles of good highways leading to highly productive fishing waters and in many cases to resorts and fishing camps in remote places. There are fifteen key entry points from the United States into the province, so that access is easy all the way from New York State to Minnesota; and there are also entrance points from the Province of Quebec on the east and Manitoba on the west. Of major interest to fishermen is the famed Trans-Canada Highway, which crosses the entire Province and in doing so touches on some of the most renowned fishing areas, particularly in the more northern reaches.

Ontario is well served by railways, the Canadian National and Canadian Pacific having extensive routes throughout the province in a more or less east-west direction, while the Ontario Northland Railway serves the James Bay area from North Bay northward, and the Algoma Central serves the otherwise rather remote section north and west of Sault Ste. Marie.

Plane service is by scheduled flight to all the big cities and by charter plane to almost any hamlet you name. Much of the Ontario northland was opened up by float planes and every northern lake still serves as a landing field for dozens of planes that ply the country catering to fishermen. Those who plan to fly private planes into Ontario should obtain Aeronautical Charts from The Surveyor General, Legal Surveys and Maps Service, Labelle Building, Ottawa, Canada. The charts are 25¢ each (subject to change).

The Ontario Department of Travel and Publicity, Parliament Buildings, Toronto, Ontario, will also provide a list of Air Fields and Air Harbors in Ontario, and a current list of Non-Schedule Charter Services, of which there are many.

In Ontario warm, summer days are interspersed with cool, rainy days and if you are far enough north there can be frost even in August. Lightweight cotton clothing is generally sufficient for daytime but should be supplemented with sweaters and light wool jackets for cool evenings and good waterproof clothing for rainy days. Rain hats and waterproof shoes or hunting pacs are a necessity when boats get partly filled with water while you fish in a summer shower; or for trekking over wet trails from one lake to another. A two-piece rainsuit is best for cool, rainy days of spring.

Because of the vast distances encompassed in Ontario, open and closed seasons vary widely. Fishing for some species is open earlier in southern Ontario than further north, and there are also local differences, east and west.

In general the trout season opens about the last weekend in April, the bass season about June 23rd in southern Ontario and June 30th in Northern Ontario. Similarly the muskellunge season opens ten days earlier in the south than the north. There is no closed season on any species in most Great Lakes waters—but not all. Therefore anglers should always consult their current Ontario Fishery Regulations before fishing.

SOUTHERN AREA

The southeastern part of the Province of Ontario encompasses a number of vacation areas each having somewhat the same attractions to the fisherman, and yet each with certain individual attributes, too. The Thousand Islands of the St. Lawrence have long been famous for smallmouth bass fishing; and this area produced the world record muskellunge. The area is most easily reached via New York State Highway 12E out of Watertown, N.Y., to Kingston, Ontario; or over the bridges that leave Highway 12E near Alexandria Bay and hop across the Thousand Islands to Ivy Lea near Gananoque on Ontario Highway 2. This has always been one of the most highly developed areas in Ontario, from the tourist's point of view, but nevertheless there is still some fine fishing to be had. Kingston, Gananoque and Brockville are three good centers from which to work, and there are all types of accommodations, boats and some guides available. Coming from more westerly points, motorists entering at Niagara Falls or Fort Erie travel the Queen Elizabeth Way along the north shore of Lake Ontario to Toronto, then on Highway 2, eastward.

Those most interested in angling usually prefer to go further north over Highways 32 and 15 to the Rideau Chain of Lakes. The small town of Chaffey's Locks on Highway 15 is in the heart of the best fishing and there are other accommodations easily accessible in the area. Hundreds of spring-fed lakes in the Rideau Chain offer smallmouth, northern pike, some lake trout and walleyes, as well as panfish. A strict code of conservation prevails in the Rideau Lakes area and visiting anglers are encouraged to limit their catches to what they can eat during their stay there. Guides are available at many resorts such as the Opinicon, at Cheffey's Locks, and bait in the form of minnows is usually available. However, although minnows are the favored bait for midsummer, at all other times excellent catches can be made on artificials of all kinds.

Moving west along the north shore of Lake Ontario we come to the city of Belleville, on Highway 2, where Highway 14 leads south onto the Isle of Quinte, with walleyes, large and smallmouth black bass, muskellunge and northern pike. Accommodations are plentiful around Picton and Wellington as well as at Belleville. The Isle of Quinte may also be reached via Highway 33 from Kingston, then by ferry from Adolphustown to Glenora. Skiffs are available at all the lakeside towns.

Following Highway 14 north from Belleville, then Highway 7 west to Peterborough, the angler will find himself at the entrance to the famed Kawartha Lakes where chances for walleyes, pike, muskellunge and bass remain consistently good despite heavy fishing by a great influx of summer vacationers. There have been tremendous catches of walleyes in the 6- to 8-pound class in Pigeon and Sturgeon Lakes, near Bobcaygeon, a resort town at the junction of Highways 36 and 500 and good catches of both walleyes and bass are made every day on plug-casting lures, except at midsummer, when minnows are the best producers. There are many resorts in the area, and several, including The Rockland House and Pine Beach Lodge in the town itself. These two are good contacts for information as to current fishing conditions.

In the Kawartha Lakes, the angler will find some of the finest muskellunge fishing in Ontario. The Sturgeon, Pigeon, Buckhorn and Lovesick Lake Chain has been heavily stocked with this species and many are also taken, up to 40 pounds, in the Pigeon River, near Burleigh Falls, at the junction of Highways 28 and 36. At Forest Hill Lodge on nearby Lovesick Lake anglers will find guides who know the waters well. Muskies here are taken by casting large pike minnows and other large plugs and spoons on 12-pound-test line; the majority of the fish, however are caught by trolling. Trollers use a stiff-action casting rod and a strong reel such as the Pflueger Supreme and 20-pound-test monofilament line.

Rice Lake, lying only about twenty-five miles north of Lake Ontario, is the largest and shallowest of the group and produces some of southern Ontario's top fishing. The lake may be reached via Highway 28, north from Port Hope, on Lake Ontario; Highway 45, from Cobourg, to the east; or from Highway 7 to the north of the lake. The shallow, warm lake, filled with aquatic growth, is a natural breeding spot for largemouth black bass and walleye. The average walleye will weigh 5 pounds, and a big one will be 10 pounds. While muskies do not grow to tremendous sizes, there are many taken each year in the 20-pound class. The largemouth rise readily to cast lures of all kinds, and this is a fine spot for those who like to fish top-water lures of all kinds, from popping bugs on fly rods, to spinning or plug-casting lures.

The last half of September and all of October are the best times to get action with casting plugs. It is also the best time for fly-rod fishing with streamers and popping bugs for bass and panfish.

Anglers planning to fish the Rice Lake area should contact Burl Chadwick, owner of Deer Head Lodge, Bailieboro, Ontario; or the Bewdley Hotel, on the west end of the lake, at the same address.

There are many other excellent fishing lakes in the Kawartha group. Information will be obtained as to the numerous resorts on such lakes through the towns of Bobcaygeon, already mentioned, and Lindsay, at the junction of Highways 35 and 7, and Fenelon Falls, reached via Highway 35, north from Lindsay.

Immediately to the north lie the Haliburton Highlands, which although some-what similar in nature, are higher in altitude and therefore the fishing leans to smallmouth bass, some lake trout and also a few speckled trout. The Haliburton Highlands are reached via Highway 121 off Highway 35 at Minden; or north from Peterborough on Highway 28 to Bancroft. From Bancroft, anglers may follow Highway 62 further north to Barry's Bay, another center from which to fish a series of lakes and streams in the Madawaska Valley. Several lakes in this district have earned wide reputations for bass to 5 pounds, big lake trout and walleyes, among them Weslemkoon, off secondary road 500, east of Bancroft, Trout Lake at Barry's Bay and Baptiste Lake, off Highway 127, north of Bancroft.

To anglers who wish to travel by boat, there is particular interest in south-eastern Ontario, in the fact that two of the oldest water routes on the continent traverse this region. The modern boatman may follow the same routes and find good fishing along the way. From Kingston he may travel north and slightly east through the Rideau Lakes to Ottawa, via the Rideau Canal, completed in 1832, and still in service. Coming thus by boat, he will reach waters not readily available to those who travel by road. And those who make the trip by canoe rather than power boat can portage to many lakes not frequently fished by others. Navigation routes are well marked, and charts may be obtained from the Chief Hydrographer, Canadian Hydrographic Service, Department of Mines and Resources, Ottawa, Canada. Ask for Chart No. 1575, Rideau Lakes Route, Kingston to Narrows Lock; and Chart No. 1576, Rideau Lakes Route, Narrows Lock to Ottawa. There is a charge of 25 cents per chart, and the remittance must be by money order or New York Draft.

The second route by which anglers may explore the fishing of southeastern Ontario is the Trent Canal, connecting Lake Ontario with Georgian Bay, via Trenton on Lake Ontario, to Rice Lake, to Peterborough, through the Kawarthas to Fenelon Falls and then out to Lake Simcoe. The course from there north to Georgian Bay will be mentioned later in this chapter. Charts of this Canal may also be obtained from the Canadian Hydrographic Service.

From the Haliburton Highlands northward, the landscape begins to take on a more rugged character. One of Ontario's most attractive Provincial Parks is located in this area. Algonquin Park contains 2,700 square miles of wilderness preserved as much as possible in wilderness state, with game being totally protected, and fishing by special license in addition to your regular Ontario license. Fishing is fair to good for smallmouth black bass and lake trout, and this is one of a limited number of spots in southern Ontario where there is some good stream fishing for speckled trout.

The lake trout are mostly taken by deep trolling with pearl and metal wobblers and wire line. Spin casting and plug casting with various lures will take the small-mouth. Speckled trout are best fished with light-weight fly rods (about 4 ounces) and HDH line with tapered leaders and wet flies tied on No. 10, 12 or 14 hooks.

Only one road, Highway 60, touches the Park, travelling from Huntsville, on Highway 11, eastward to Highway 17 at Arnprior, north of Ottawa, and traversing a small corner of the Park in doing so. Train service is also available to Huntsville or Arnprior, and bus from there in. There are two resorts, many young people's camps and dozens of excellent camping spots along the canoe routes which enable anglers to reach into the remote corners of Algonquin. Complete information can be obtained from the Department of Lands and Forests, Parliament Buildings, Toronto, Ontario, Canada.

The best fishing in southwestern Ontario is found along the shores of Lake Erie; and there is some angling also on Lake St. Clair and the southern tip of Lake Huron. Points of entry are Niagara Falls, Buffalo-Fort Erie, Detroit-Windsor and Port Huron-Sarnia. The species include large and smallmouth black bass, pike, walleye, muskellunge and panfish, with very occasional lake trout. Long Point, reached over Highway 59, south from Tillsonburg on Highway 3, about halfway along Lake Erie between Buffalo and Detroit, offers some of the world's best smallmouth bass fishing; and the prospects can be almost as good at Point Pelee, well to the west, off Highway 3 at Leamington. Walleye are also taken, especially in the spring. Most bass and walleyes are caught by trolling feathered spinners or by drifting with live minnows or worms, but in October there is some exciting sport for fly fishermen and plug casters who work the shoals with which the shallow lake abounds.

Accommodations are plentiful, as this is the most thoroughly urban area in Ontario; and boats are available at most lakeside towns, such as Port Dover at the end of Highway 6; Port Rowan, off Highway 59 near Long Point; Port Stanley, on Highway 4, south of St. Thomas; and Leamington and Kingsville, on Highway 3 near Point Pelee.

There is also some fishing for brown trout, stocked speckled trout, large and smallmouth black bass in both ponds and streams in southwestern Ontario, but this is so spotty that it is necessary to have some local contact in order to be able to find productive waters.

North of this section, however, there is a better opportunity to take a typical Ontario variety of bass, walleye, lake trout, brown trout, rainbows, speckled trout and pike in the waters of Bruce Peninsula. The Peninsula juts out into Lake Huron to form the enclosing arm of Georgian Bay and consequently provides access to much of its fine bass fishing. Many roads lead from the southern, urban sectors to Owen Sound, at the southern end of the Peninsula, and from there Highway 6 leads northward to the tip of land at Tobermory. Here an auto ferry will take you to South Baymouth on Manitoulin Island, dealt with later in this chapter.

Travelling from Toronto, on Lake Ontario, northward over Highway 11, anglers come to southern Ontario's largest inland body of water, Lake Simcoe and its small northern attachment, Lake Couchiching. These two lakes provide some excellent fishing for walleye, lake trout, muskies, smallmouth bass and pike, with emphasis on the good catches being early and late in the season; the lakes are among the most highly developed in the Province from the point of view of use for water sports. During the winter Lake Simcoe is the ice-fisherman's haven and exceedingly good catches are made. The towns of Barrie and Orillia on Highway 11 provide accommodations of all kinds on the western shore. Atherley and Beaverton, on Highways 12 and 48 provide the same services on the eastern shore, and the town of Washago marks the northern tip of Couchiching.

North again lie two of the most highly developed vacation areas in Ontario, the Muskoka Lakes and Georgian Bay. The Muskoka Lakes and their adjoining streams hold some of the indigenous species of fish, but the area is mostly devoted to holiday resorts rather than fishing camps. The situation is considerably different in the Georgian Bay area, with Parry Sound on Highway 69 as its hub. Georgian Bay, with its 30,000 Islands and many miles of rocky shores, is great water for smallmouth black bass, and there are also walleyes, pike, some lake trout and panfish in most of the inland waters as well. Especially in the spring, there is excellent walleye fishing in the Magnetawan River, reached via Highway 124 from Parry Sound. Fishing camps are numerous, and details can be obtained from the Parry Sound Board of Trade, Parry Sound, Ontario, Canada.

There are also many resorts along Highway 69, and also on Highway 103 between Footes Bay and Waubaushene, which highway skirts part of the shores of Georgian Bay. From camps in this latter area guides take anglers out into the bays and islands of Georgian Bay for muskies, and up the numerous streams for walleyes and bass.

Information as to individual camps may be obtained from the Parry Sound Chamber of Commerce, Parry Sound, Ontario.

EAST-CENTRAL AREA

Sprawling above this, across the narrowest portion of Ontario, is Lake Nipissing, which, with the French River which provides its outlet to Georgian Bay, has long been a great fishing center. The lake is reached via Highway 11 north from Toronto (300 miles), then west on Trans-Canada Highway 17, skirting the north shore of the lake. Both the Canadian Pacific and Canadian National Railways also serve North Bay.

The French River provides a migration route for walleye and muskellunge from Georgian Bay to Lake Nipissing, and the latter has long been one of the best-known walleye spots in Ontario. The fishing is usually best wherever a stream enters the lake, forming swirls and eddies and some current. A list of places to stay along the lake shore, and many neighboring resorts may be obtained from the North Bay Chamber of Commerce, North Bay, Ontario.

The French River is most easily reached by highway via the comparatively new Highway 69, leaving Highway 11 at Gravenhurst. The French, one of the routes of the explorers, is some seventy miles long, and its neighbors the Wolsley, Murdock and Pickerel at times offer equally good fishing. The French is best known as a muskellunge stream, at one time producing some outstanding catches. Although the size and quantity are both smaller than in earlier days, there is still good fishing for this species as well as walleyes and northern pike, both of which reach top weights in this river. Anglers will also find some of Ontario's finest smallmouth black-bass angling in the French. Some of the best-known lodges catering to anglers and providing guide service are Sand Beach Lodge, Rutter, Ontario; Lift-the-Latch Lodge, French River, Ontario; French River Chalet Bungalow Camp, French River, Ontario; and Wolsley Lodge, Noelville, Ontario.

From Rogerson's Hotel and Camps at Port Lorig, Ontario, fishermen can drive to the Pickerel River and several lakes connected by it. The resort is reached over a feeder road, Highway 522, which leaves Highway 11 at Trout Creek and runs west to Lake Wauquimakog at the headwaters of the Pickerel River. Camps in this area have facilities for getting fishermen into remote waters by float plane or canoe. There are muskies, northern pike and smallmouth bass.

The city of North Bay, on the northeastern corner of Lake Nipissing, has long been regarded as the gateway to the north. From here Trans-Canada Highway 17 leads west to Sudbury, Sault Ste. Marie and points west; while Highway 11 leads northward to Timagami Provincial Forest, then on north for many miles, and eventually turns westward to serve the vast reaches of remote northwestern Ontario. The Timagami Provincial Forest lying north of the towns of North Bay and Sudbury is like Algonquin Park, in that there is very little access by road. Highway 11 touches the southeast corner; while Highway 560 crosses the midsection of the Forest, leaving Highway 11 at Englehart. These are the only means of highway access. The town of Timagami, the only community providing accommodations and services, is also served by the Ontario Northland Railway; and from the town a daily steamer plies between the resorts and private camps on Lake Timagami. From these resorts, anglers can make their way by canoe or hiking into the interior. The same is true, to a lesser degree, at the small towns of Shining Tree, O'Brien and Gowganda, on Highway 560, but these are basically lumbering rather than resort towns. The species taken are northern pike and walleyes, and some fair-sized speckled trout.

Highway 560 extends out the western side of Timagami Provincial Forest and makes a loop north and slightly east again to the small town of Gogama, also on the Canadian National Railway. In nearby Chrysler Lake, some twenty-two air miles to the southeast, splake, a cross between speckled trout and lake trout, are taken. One weighing 22 pounds 12 ounces was once netted out of this lake.

NORTHERN AREA

Continuing north on Highway 11, you enter the famed mining district of Northern Ontario, but in almost every lake and stream there is some kind of fishing, and wilderness camps and other resorts are fairly plentiful. Those in the South Porcupine, Porcupine and Timmins area are close enough to the northern boundary of Timagami Provincial Forest to be able to send their guests in to some wild and unexploited country in the forest. In the Porcupine district, Arctic Tourist Outfitters, Ltd., Box 1107, South Porcupine, will arrange such trips. One of their better camps for fine speckled-trout fishing is Ominuk Fishing Camp.

The town of Cochrane is popular with sportsmen as the last jumping-off place for James Bay, via the Ontario Northland Railway; and those who do not wish to drive across the entire northern part of the Province leave their cars here and proceed by Canadian National Railways to Nipigon and other points west.

Those who do drive west on Highway 11 will find accommodations and services in a series of small towns, and two larger settlements, Kapuskasing and Hearst; then for 130 miles to Longlac and another nineteen to Geraldton there are no communities of any kind.

Lake trout in the Geraldton area run to 45 pounds and many trophy fish have come from lakes and streams in the neighborhood. Walleye and northern pike also reach top sizes, while speckled trout from 2 to 8 pounds are found. Austin Airways,

Ltd., P.O. Box 627, Geraldton, Ontario, provides fly-in service for fishermen to the more remote camps.

Twenty-nine miles west of Geraldton, Highway 11 turns south at the town of Beardmore and runs through Nipigon Provincial Forest to the north shore of Lake Superior, where it joins Highway 17. Beardmore, Jellicoe, Macdiarmid and Orient Bay, all on Highway 11, are regarded as speckled trout meccas of Northern Ontario. The Lake Nipigon Fish Derby, held the third week in June each year, has produced lake trout to 60 pounds, northern pike to 43 pounds and speckled trout to 10 pounds. Walleyes generally run only about 2½ pounds but have been taken up to 12 pounds.

The curve of Highway 11 across the eastern and northern part of Ontario encloses a vast area that is crowded with lakes and streams which have been well-preserved by the fact that until fairly recently there were comparatively few ways to get to the interior. Now Highway 17 extends from Sudbury, only eighty-nine miles west of North Bay, to Sault Ste. Marie and then north along the entire shore of Lake Superior; and Highway 129, another new road, connects Highway 17 at Thessalon, with Chapleau, far in the interior. From Chapleau a secondary road crosses this vast area to join Highway 101 at Folyet and hence permit traffic back through Timmins to Highway 11. Even so, there are untold miles which are completely inaccessible except by air, canoe, or rail. The Canadian National Railway provides service to the most northern part of this sector from Cochrane via its transcontinental line; and also from North Bay and Sudbury via a supplementary line. The Canadian Pacific offers the same service on a slightly more southerly route; and the two are bisected by the Algoma Central and Hudson Bay Railway from Sault Ste. Marie to Hearst. Nearly every flag-stop and town on these lines has its quota of fishing camps and information may be obtained from the railways concerned.

Those who come from the southeast will enter this vast area at Sudbury, and make their further journeys from there according to their means of travel. Via Highway 17 westward to Sault Ste. Marie, known as "The Soo," there are many resorts and motels, often on lake or stream, and there is some fishing available, although as is always the case, roadside fishing is never as good as that in more remote waters. Charter planes are available at Sudbury for transportation to such waters; since most of the flying in this area is by pontoon plane, every lake serves as a landing field. Sudbury-based planes fly anglers to the most remote areas, including the Chapleau Game Preserve, dealt with later in this chapter.

Further west similar air service will be found at Algoma Mills, on Highway 17, home base of Fluronian Air Service and Lauzon Air Service, both equipped for flying into remote lakes. Fluronian also has a base at Wawa on Highway 17, 144 miles north of Sault Ste. Marie, thus bracketing the entire area. In most cases these flying services will set up their own camps to accommodate fishing parties of any size. And while you may choose your own lake, it is well to follow their suggestions as they know the country thoroughly and can judge where you will get the best fishing at the time concerned.

Algoma Mills, where this charter plane service is available, is situated on Lake Lauzon, a top-rated smallmouth black-bass lake which also has some excellent walleye fishing.

MANITOULIN ISLAND

Branching off Highway 17 about forty miles west of Sudbury, Highway 68 leads southward to Manitoulin Island, which although geographically an extension of the Bruce Peninsula to the south, is more aligned with the northern part of Ontario, from the fisherman's point of view. Manitoulin has a rugged landscape with many lakes and streams as well as coves and inlets of Georgian Bay and North Channel waters. There are many rocky shoals and promontories, all making for ideal fishing waters for those who like to cast. Smallmouth black bass, northern pike, walleye and muskies are all found, plus some extra-large-sized rock bass. There are also lake trout in some lakes, and rainbows have been imported from the Pacific coast and stocked on the island.

Gore Bay and Little Current are the principal towns and the Chambers of Commerce in these two centers will supply information as to specific camps and resorts, which are very numerous.

It is also possible to reach Manitoulin via car ferry from Tobermory at the tip of the Bruce Peninsula, to South Baymouth, and from there good roads lead to all parts of the island.

CENTRAL AREA

From the town of Thessalon, some thirty-five miles further west on Highway 17, Highway 129 leads north to Chapleau through 150 miles of true wilderness along the valley of the Mississagi River. Several resorts along its course include Limberlost Lodge on Kegos Lake, and Appleby Resort, both of which have housekeeping cottages at reasonable rates; and others are The Outpost, Demers Lodge, Wakomata Camp and Snowshoe Camp. All can be addressed at Thessalon. The fishing is for northerns, walleyes and lake trout, and best of all, speckled or brook trout, which increase in size as you move north along the road.

At Chapleau you can fly into wilderness camps for prices as low as $45 per person per week, including the flight in and out, staying at tent camps operated by the Teriault Air Service on some of the finest speckled trout and lake trout waters, with the additional attraction of good walleye and northern pike fishing.

From Chapleau it is possible to go via Canadian Pacific Railway to more northern points which cannot be reached by road. One of these is Camp Missanabie, about fifty miles north of Chapleau. Here the lake trout, northern pike and walleyes are about as plentiful and as large as you will find anywhere in Ontario.

Similarly, you can travel via the Canadian National Railway, to the north, to reach one camp after another in the Elsas area. Whiskey Lake, near Camp Kenogaming at Elsas, operated by Jim Thurston, has produced speckled trout up to 6 pounds, and smaller ones are plentiful.

At Chapleau you can also arrange wilderness trips by canoe with competent guides, into Chapleau Game Preserve, where hunting is forbidden but fishing is superb. Speckled trout fishing is excellent in dozens of lakes and nearly every lake in the sector has outstanding fishing for either trout, walleyes or northern pike. There is one hint worth passing along—make your choice in favor of a lake specifically known for lake and brook trout, if that is what you are after. Lakes containing walleyes and northerns are usually not so good for brookies as are those which contain only the trouts.

Another way to get into the Chapleau district is to fly via scheduled flights on

Trans-Canada Airlines from Cleveland, Chicago, New York, Boston, or Detroit to Timmins. From there pontoon planes operate to Kapuskasing Lake at Elsas, where George Glazier of Go-Send-A-Lodge will get you into some of the best speckled trout, walleye and northern pike waters in the Chapleau Game Preserve.

Just above the town of Sault Ste. Marie there is some good fishing for rainbow trout in the Soo Rapids of the St. Mary's River. There are also some speckled and brown trout in these waters. It is difficult fishing, calling for boats and guides who know the dangerous water thoroughly, but on occasion good catches are made.

Anglers who travel from Sault Ste. Marie northward on Highway 17 around the north shore of Lake Superior should take time out to fish the coves and bays for coasters, big rainbows that run up to 8 pounds in weight. Though not plentiful they do occasionally provide some sensational fishing. About sixteen miles out of the Soo there is a gravel road, Highway 556, heading northeast up the Goulais River Valley. It leads to many lakes and streams with rushing waterfalls and good fishing, and at its northern end is Ranger Lake, with excellent fishing for speckled and lake trout. At some future date this road will go through to Highway 129 between Thessalon and Chapleau, but at present Ranger Lake is the jumping-off place for canoe and plane trips into rugged, undeveloped country.

Turning the opposite direction along the Goulais River where it crosses Highway 17 at Mile 19 (from the Soo) you follow the lower course of the river to Goulais Bay on Lake Superior. There are a number of resorts along both river and bay, and during the walleye-run in the spring there is exceptional fishing.

Anglers wishing detailed information as to resorts throughout the Algoma Region surrounding Sault Ste. Marie should write the Chamber of Commerce, Sault Ste. Marie, Ontario, Canada.

The next important spot on Highway 17 is Batchawana Bay. This is a good place to rent a boat and fish the wild, rocky shoreline for coasters and lake trout, usually of large size, that lie in holes and pockets of shallow-water beaches around Lake Superior. In the spring rainbow trout move into the mouths of some of the rivers in this area and run upstream to spawn. Some remarkable catches are made at that time. One of the favorite spots is Pancake Bay, just north of Batchawana, where spring-run rainbows go into the Chippewa, Harom and Griffin Rivers. Spinners and flies take them at this time. Later in the summer trolling with deep-running spinners and silver wobblers is more effective when the fish are in the quiet bays of Lake Superior from Batchawana Bay on north to the Nipigon River and beyond.

Another important point north is the Montreal River, a mighty stream crossed by trestle and providing an unforgettable scene. A power dam located at the base of the trestle forms a huge lake for many miles upstream. Just above the dam are some of the biggest northern pike to be found in the province. Below the dam are both rainbows and speckled trout. L. Patton operates the Dam-Site Lodge at this point. Address: Montreal River, Mile 92, Algoma Central Railway, Ontario, in summer; and 6387 Hatchery Road, Pontiac, Michigan in winter.

Throughout this northward turn of Highway 17, it is fairly closely paralleled by the Algoma Central and Hudson Bay Railway. Via this means it is possible to reach Sand Lake, at Mile 138, where there is good speckled and lake-trout fishing, and a nearby lake offers smallmouth bass. A lodge is operated by Norm Berg, address: 91 Bellevue Avenue, Sault Ste. Marie, Ontario. A few miles further north, at Franz, the Canadian Pacific Transcontinental line crosses the Algoma Central and provides a connection to other fishing camps just a few miles to the east and west. And from Mile 206 on the Canadian Pacific anglers can start an exceptionally pleasant canoe trip all the way from Wabatongushi Lake, just east of Franz, down to Lake Superior at Michipicoten. The course covers some excellent walleye, northern pike and speckled-trout waters.

Continuing on northward on the Algoma Central and Hudson Bay Railway, anglers can find accommodations at Oba, where there are several lodges fronting on Oba Lake, with opportunities for pike and walleye fishing; and speckled trout in nearby waters. Camps on Lake Kabinakagami, to the west, specialize in canoe trips. Write Paul Goulet, or R. A. Watson, Oba, Ontario. This lake is renowned for its limitless supply of walleyes and northerns. Lauri Vihonen, Oba Hotel, at Oba, also outfits for wilderness trips.

NORTHWESTERN AREA

The extreme northwestern part of Ontario is most easily reached from Minnesota, via U.S. 61 to Port Arthur and Fort William; via U.S. 71 via the bridge between International Falls and Fort Frances; and at the Baudette-Rainy River Bridge on U.S. 11, south of Lake of the Woods. From Port Arthur, Highway 17 extends across the province to the western border, and is closely paralleled by the Canadian Pacific and Canadian National Railways. To the south, Highway 11 extends for 120 miles west from Port Arthur to Atikokan, and again is paralleled by a branch of the Canadian National Railway. Aside from these there is no means of travel in a vast expanse stretching between the head of the Great Lakes and Lake of the Woods. The area is crammed with lakes and streams, many with outstanding fishing.

Some of these lakes are in the Quetico Provincial Park on the Minnesota border, where no roads are permitted. Entry is from Highway 588 west from Fort William to North Lake, and from there travel is by canoe over a chain of lakes and rivers that extends completely across the province to Lake of the Woods. Anglers can also go in from Atikokan, where there are accommodations at Sylvan Lake Cottages, run by Ben Eyton, Box 1390, Atikokan, Ontario.

There are brook trout in small numbers, but the first are mainly northern pike, walleye and lake trout.

While you could choose almost any lake in the vast network which spreads out on either side of Highway 17, and have a fair chance of finding good fishing, there are certain areas where the lakes are known producers. Two such places have only recently been opened up to motor approach.

The farthest point north to be reached by auto in Ontario is Central Patricia, north of Ignace on Highway 17. It leads from Ignace to and beyond Savant Lake, formerly served only by rail. The road leads into wilderness country of lakes and streams that produce northern pike and walleyes at nearly every cast. There are also lake trout, sturgeon and Great Lakes whitefish along this route, which is unpopulated except by Indians and construction crews.

From Dinorwic, thirty-five miles west of Ignace, another unimproved road, Highway 72, leads north to Sioux Lookout, near Superior Junction, where the two branches of the Canadian National Railway come together. There are many lakes well-supplied with lake trout and northern pike; and this is the area where smallmouth black bass are said to have first been stocked in northwestern Ontario. A note to the Sioux Lookout Chamber of Commerce will get you up-to-date information as to fishing camps in the area.

Immediately to the west is Dryden, close to several lakes which are famous among fishermen, notably Eagle and Wabigoon, noted for muskies, walleyes, northern pike, trout and bass. Walter Pierce, Vermilion Bay, Ontario, operates one camp and there are many more, whose addresses may be obtained through the Chamber of Commerce at Dryden. In all, there are fifty fishing camps in the neighborhood, as well as hotels and motels in the town itself.

From Vermilion Bay on Highway 17, another unimproved road of considerably greater length leads to the Red Lake District. This Highway 105 taps vast Lac Seul to the east, as well as innumerable smaller lakes, and along its length are several towns where air service is available to fly anglers in to the remote waters of this most northerly outpost area. Trans Air, Ltd., operates daily between Red Lake and Winnipeg; Green's Airways works out of Red Lake; and Lac Seul Airways has bases at Perrault Falls about halfway up Highway 105, and at Ear Falls a little further north. There are also some sixty new licensed camps in the Red Lake District which can be reached by car.

LAKE OF THE WOODS

Probably no area in Ontario has been more widely publicized than Lake of the Woods. The name has become synonymous with muskellunge in the minds of American sportsmen. Yet it is actually the very fine fishing for smallmouth black bass that brings the masses of fishermen to this lake. The bass run to 5 and 6 pounds, which is very high for this sporting species, and the fishing is much more certain than that for muskies, which come few and far between. In this regard, it is important for the angler to know that this is the case. Because of their temperament and elusiveness, muskies are taken with comparative infrequency and it takes a dedicated muskie man to keep at it day after day without getting a hit. But the bass are always there and usually willing. However, the muskies are there too, and when taken are extremely hard-fighting fish, and specimens up to 56 pounds have come from Lake of the Woods.

The lake trout is also found in quite considerable numbers throughout most of the Lake of the Woods area. Fishing is best for them in spring and fall when they can be taken by casting in preference to deep trolling, as is usually required in summer. Lake trout to 20 pounds are taken.

Two other good catches will fill-in between muskie hits—northern pike run to 20 pounds and better, and will take almost anything you throw at them. And walleye in the Lake of the Woods run to the unusually large weight of 10 pounds.

There are many American Plan camps as well as housekeeping accommodations along Highways 17 and 71. (The latter comes up the eastern shore of the lake from the border.) Many more are hidden away on some 14,000 islands, to which the guests are transported by boat or plane from Kenora.

One of the finest resorts in the area is Minaki Lodge at the junction of Sand and Gun Lakes on Highway 596, northwest of Kenora. At one time this resort could only be reached by the Canadian National Railway. You can make reservations and plan for guides and boats through A. Pascoe, Manager of the Lodge, Minaki, Ontario.

On the English River, north of this, Doug Hook operates Separation Camp, reached by a thirty-five-mile seaplane flight from Kenora. He can be reached at Box 610, Kenora. His brother, Keith Hook, Box 128, Kenora, operates Nooks Muskie Camp, a fishing lodge on Lake of the Woods, which is reached by launch or seaplane out of Kenora.

From the shores of Hudson's Bay, west to the Manitoba border, there is a vast expanse of Northern Ontario still untouched by road. Planes based at the various centers mentioned in this chapter will fly anglers into many lakes in this area, but due to the shortness of the season and the remoteness of the terrain, plans must be made early. The Albany River Basin, north of the Canadian National Railway trans-continental line, has many fine fishing waters. The Albany rises in Lake St. Joseph, well to the northwest of Lake Nipigon, and flows eastward to Hudson's Bay. Anglers go by Canadian National Railway to Nakina, or can now drive there via the new road, Highway 584, north from Highway 11 at Geraldton. From Nakina the river is reached by canoe or plane. In planning such a trip, and similar ones to the Little Current River, Drowning River and the Ogoki, all to the northeast of Nakina, all famous for their speckled trout fishing, contact Emile Cote, Nakina P.O. Ontario. Lakes in the area also produce lake trout, pike and pickerel.

Reached only by Canadian National Railway or by air is Grey's Camp, on the Ombabika River, ten miles west of Tashota Station. The mailing address is Manataree P.O., Ontario. Bruce's Camp, at nearby Willet P.O. on the railway, can also be reached by boat up Lake Nipigon from Orient Bay.

Because of the tremendous area of the Province of Ontario, and the almost incredible number of fishing resorts, camps and lodges as well as the opportunities for camping, it would be impossible for one publication to list all such accommodations. Therefore prospective anglers should give some idea of the area in which they plan to fish, when writing for such details. The Ontario Department of Travel and Publicity, Parliament Buildings, Toronto, will then supply regional information. Reception centers at many border points can also supply both information and folders descriptive of many camps and resorts. Such centers are found at all the major entry points.

ONTARIO FISHING REGULATIONS

Resident Fishing License $3.25
Nonresident Fishing License $6.50
Nonresident 3-Day Fishing License $3.25

SEASONS AND LIMITS

Seasons and limits vary according to area. For complete regulations write: Fish and Wildlife Branch, Department of Mines and Forests, Parliament Buildings, Toronto 2, Ontario.

QUEBEC

The 600,000 square miles of forest, clear lakes and streams that comprise the Province of Quebec are bounded on the west by Ontario and the waters of James and Hudson Bay. While most of the province is north of the St. Lawrence River, a slice of it lies to the south, thus making its southern neighbors the states of New York, Vermont and New Hampshire. In the east and southeast, Maine and New Brunswick touch Quebec, while to the northeast lies Newfoundland's Labrador, stretching up to the icy waters of the Arctic which comprise Quebec's northern boundary.

The altitude rises from sea level to as much as 4,000 feet in the great Laurentian Plateau which covers most of Quebec. Drainage is mostly to the St. Lawrence, except in the far north where rivers flow to Ungava Bay, and in the extreme south, below the St. Lawrence River, where the streams empty their waters to the Bay of Chaleur.

The major species of fish found are the eastern brook trout, which is widespread; ounaniche, or landlocked salmon, which is more prevalent here than anywhere else in Canada; lake trout; walleye, known locally as pickerel and dore; northern pike; largemouth and smallmouth black bass; and perch. There are also Atlantic salmon and sea-run trout in some coastal rivers.

A system of excellent highways serves the southern part of the province but as you move north the roads thin out and much of the far north is accessible only by float plane or canoe.

The summer climate is pleasant, cottons usually sufficing from May through August for daytime wear, with lightweight wool sweaters for evening. Those who go early in the spring or late in the fall will need heavier woolens as these seasons can be quite cool. Raingear is also essential, and those who plan to wade the rivers for their fishing should have chest-high waders, both for warmth and to reach the best spots.

For general lake fishing, every angler has his choice of tackle, but those who go for salmon and trout usually use fly rods. For salmon a 9-foot rod weighing 6 ounces, and equipped with a single-action fly reel and 200 yards of 15-pound-test nylon backing is about right. The leader should be tapered from a 30-pound-test monofilament butt section down to 6- or 8-pound-test tippet. Wet and dry flies of all the standard patterns are usually most successful in sizes 6, 8 and 10. For speckled trout the rod should be 8 feet, weighing 4 ounces, and carry an HDH line and a leader tapered down to 4X or 5X tippet. Flies should be No. 12 to No. 16.

It is natural that the more northerly parts of Quebec should have a good population of bear, deer and some moose, but as elsewhere, the angler who leaves these animals alone will seldom be bothered by them. The province is outside the range of any poisonous snakes. Probably its greatest pest, as far as the fisherman is concerned, are the blackflies, which can be very bad in June and later, the further north you go. Insect repellent and mosquito netting are an essential part of the fisherman's gear in Quebec.

EASTERN AREA

Fishing in Quebec is made available to visiting anglers through a well-organized system of licensed outfitters, clubs and parks. Nearly every promising area can be reached through these sources. The best bet for fishermen making the long trek to eastern Quebec is to locate where there is a combination of speckled trout and salmon, with possibly the addition of ouananiche, or landlocked salmon. A camp which offers this choice is the Fortier Tourist Club, licensed to outfit fishermen on Lake Vacher, in territory fourteen miles from Schefferville on the Labrador border. The camp, which has a capacity for sixty people, can be reached only by plane or by the Quebec North Shore Railway, north from Sept-Iles at the mouth of the famous Moisie River, on the north shore of the St. Lawrence. In addition to the main lodge there are eight outlying camps with speckled trout, ounaniche and pike fishing. For reservations write Albert Fortier, Box 28, Schefferville, Quebec.

Schefferville is also the jumping-off point for salmon, trout and Arctic char fishermen heading for the George River flowing into Ungava Bay close to the Labrador border in northern Quebec. For details about this camp, see the Labrador chapter.

Further west along the St. Lawrence River is the Matamec Salmon Club, under the management of W. E. Gallienne, Box 248, Sept-Iles, Quebec. The nearby Reed's River Club is under the direction of T. C. Richardson, Fergus Farms, P.O. Box 670, Fergus, Ontario. Both camps have modern accommodations and outpost camps with fishing for salmon, speckled trout and sea trout. The Godbout River and others in this same general area can be fished for Atlantic salmon, sea trout and speckled trout from the Comeau Hunting and Fishing Club, Noel M. Comeau, Proprietor, 380 East Laurier Avenue, Quebec, Quebec. The phone is 418-529-7755.

At Sept-Iles, the Quebec North Shore Railroad, Ltd., operates a passenger train on Tuesday and Friday at 8 a.m. to Knob Lake, near Schefferville where there are no public accommodations but where top brook-trout fishing can be enjoyed by making accommodations in advance with the Iron Ore Company, of Canada, Ltd., at Knob Lake, Newfoundland. Lakes and streams between can be fished if you have your own camping gear.

From Sept-Iles it is also possible to take a plane sixty-five miles to Manitou Fishing Camp on Lake Manitou where brook trout run to 8 pounds, probably the largest in Quebec. For accommodations at this camp write the Baie Comeau Company, Baie Comeau, Quebec. From this headquarters planes can be hired to fly you to other fine speckled-trout fishing both in eastern Quebec and in the remote interior of Labrador.

The St. Lawrence Hunting and Fishing Co., Inc., has territory under lease ninety-five miles east of Sept-Iles. From their hotel at Mingan all points of the Mingan Park are easily reached by air. A paved road leads to Patterson Lake, five miles from the hotel, where fishing is good. There are four main camps, seventy miles by air, and three secondary outposts where you can fish for speckled trout, rainbow trout, ouananiche, Atlantic salmon and even cod, mackerel and flounder.

Sept-Iles can be reached by Trans-Canada Air Lines from Montreal and by steamship from Quebec City and Montreal.

CENTRAL AREA

In central Quebec is the renowned Laurentide Park, directly north of Quebec City, one of the best spots in the province for speckled trout. The total area of the park is more than 4,000 square miles, most of it in the Laurentian Mountains, with an altitude up to 2,500 feet. Its hundreds of lakes and white-water rivers make it a favorite spot for canoe trips. Highway 54 and its branch, 54-A, run through the center of the park, leading to luxury resorts such as Le Relais, L'Etape and Le Gite; and to less pretentious but equally popular camping grounds where independent sportsmen may pitch their tents, park their trailers or use a shelter with stove and running water. The western part of the park and the adjacent Kikissink area is reached only by train from Montreal, Quebec or Chicoutimi. Anglers wishing to fish this section, particularly the unfrequented wilderness adjoining the park borders, can do so through the Club Panache, Club Homano or Club Touladi, all of which have good accommodations and guides to take you to the best speckled trout, lake trout and ouananiche waters. Reservations can be made through Bert Hamel, C.P.400, Roberval, Quebec. The areas fished can be the shores of the La Croche River, and two more distant territories, one 100 miles northeast of Roberval and the other sixty miles west of Roberval, the latter reached only by plane.

North of Laurentide Park is huge Lake St. John, one of the largest lakes in Quebec, and with its tributary streams the home of great ouananiche and speckled-trout fishing. Arrangements for accommodations can be made through Robertson & Son, Pointe Bleue, Roberval, Quebec. They are located in the Indian Fish and Game Territory, which they have under lease, 180 miles north of Lake St. John on the shores of the Serpent River. They are fully equipped for canoe trips under canvas, and have excellent guides, a legal requirement in this area.

In this area the best fishing is from mid-July on, as until that time the ouananiche stay in Lake St. John where they are difficult to catch. When they start to move upstream in the tributary rivers, the fun begins. In some of the rivers, such as the Ashuapmuchuan, the migrating ouananiche do not reach the best fishing spots until late August and early September. For springtime fishing, the best spot is Lake Tchita-gama on the big Peribonca River, when the catch will include speckled trout, lake trout and northern pike as well as ouananiche.

Rates in this area are about $50 per day for a ten-day trip for two people, with two guides. Take your own sleeping bags but Robertson & Son will supply everything else. The same trip can be made at a slight saving with only one guide, but this cuts down on your fishing time because of the time required for the sole guide to set up camp and prepare meals every day.

Continuing northwest through the wilderness of central Quebec you come to the Chibougamau Reserve, which is traversed by a highway out of St. Felicien just north of Lake St. John. Although there are pike and walleyes in the many lakes and streams of this preserve, the greatest attraction is lake trout, which can be caught on the surface with artificial flies from ice-out until the second week in June. After that deep trolling is usually necessary, with wire line and silver wobblers or spoons. When the fish are deep it usually requires a guide to find the best spots. The fish often run up to 20 pounds.

In addition to the non-resident fishing license, a fee of $2 per day is charged all adults using the park for camping and fishing. There are many well-established camp sites.

At Lake Aigremont, sixty-six miles from St. Felicien, there is an inn while at Lake D'Argenson there are camping shelters with wood-burning stoves, the shelters being 12 feet square, not large but enough for those who bring their own camping gear, except tents. There is a good supply of water from a deep well here and at the filling station and at Lake Aigremont. Elsewhere in this area you have to use lake or river water.

Reservations for these and other accommodations in this reserve should be made in advance through F. de B. Gourdeau, General Superintendent of Parks, Department of Game and Fisheries, Quebec, Canada. Make your reservations early as both shelters, inns and camp sites are much in demand.

Accessible only by air are the outcamps of the Broadback River Fishing Camps around Chibougamau. Information about the fishing, which is for lake trout, speckled trout, pike, walleye and whitefish, according to location, can be obtained from Ronald A. Thierry and Rene Demers, Box 454, Chibougamau, Quebec.

NORTHERN AREA

If you continue north on the secondary road through Chibougamau you will wind up at Lake Waconichi in the Mistassini Reserve. The lake is twenty-three miles long, in the midst of remote, wild country where Cree Indians live in the manner of their forefathers. Lake Mistassini, a vast lake to the north, can be reached by plane. It and its small neighbor to the south, Lake Waconichi, are part of the Hudson Bay drainage, their outlet being the Rupert River. This area is far enough north that trout fishing remains good all summer, though the best catches are made between the middle of June and the middle of July. The brook trout are plentiful and run up to 8 pounds in Lake Mistassini, while the lakers go to 20 and more. They can readily be taken on flies. Arrangements to visit this area should be made through Roland Simard, Club Jacques, 336 East Scott Street, Alma (Roberval), Quebec, who has airplane service to the lakes, and log cabin accommodations available there.

WESTERN AREA

Farther west from Amos on Highway 45, another gravel road reaches northward to isolated Lake Mattagami. Along these roads, and as far west as the Ottawa River, which forms the western boundary of Quebec, there are innumerable outfitters who have leased territories on lakes and streams in which trout, walleyes, northern pike, bass and muskellunge can be taken. A list of such outfitters, detailing what they have to offer can be obtained by writing the Quebec Outfitters' Association, 380 East Laurier Avenue, Quebec 6, Quebec.

Lying to the south of this region is La Verendrye Park, traversed by highway 58, which becomes Highway 11 at Mont-Laurier, some 150 miles northwest of Montreal. La Verendrye ranks second only to the Laurentide Park as the natural habitat for the speckled trout and there are also great numbers of northern pike, walleye and lake trout. There are many fishing camps along Highway 58 and many areas in which anglers may pitch a tent or park a trailer. Canoeing is good in the numerous large lakes and guides are available at most of the fishing camps. Reservations may be made by writing the Parks Service, Department of Game and Fisheries, Quebec, Canada.

Beyond the limits of the park the Jesmer North Club, operated by Jacques Berube, Clova, Quebec, can arrange trips to waters containing speckled trout, pike, walleyes and muskellunge. The club can be reached either by Highway 58 north from La Verendrye, or via Canadian National Railway.

To the southwest of Val d'Or on Highway 59, which leaves Highway 58 about twenty-five miles north of the limits of La Verendrye Park, you can drive to three camps on the shores of the Ottawa River at Carriere Bay, where there is good walleye and pike fishing. For information write H. W. Daoust, 1015 Brebeuf Street, Val d'Or, Quebec.

Those who are looking for smallmouth black bass along with pike, lake trout and walleyes, will find them most plentiful in the extreme southwest corner of Quebec, particularly in the Lake Kipawa area. Highway 46 from North Bay, Ontario, skirts the western edge of Kipawa Reserve and a secondary road runs into the town of Kipawa at the southern end of Lake Kipeawa. Here accommodations can be found at White Pine Lodge, from which it is also possible to fish many other lakes in the area.

Continuing on north on Highway 46, anglers can drive far into the northwest part of Quebec, and at the small town of La Sarre get a plane to fly in to otherwise inaccessible lakes where tent and cabin camps are maintained by the La Sarre Air Service, Ltd., G. E. Pronovost, Operator, Box 418, La Sarre, Quebec.

GASPE PENINSULA

The Gaspe Peninsula, on the southern shore of the St. Lawrence, can be reached by Highway 2 out of Quebec City, or via Trans-Canada Air Lines from either Montreal or Quebec to Gaspe on the tip of the peninsula. Cars may be rented there. While salmon move up most of the rivers of the Gaspe Peninsula, probably the best bet is to contact the Hotel Restigouche, Matapedia, Quebec, which is Highway 6 at the northeast corner of the New Brunswick border. This hotel has thirty miles of the Patapedia River under lease, and as this is a tributary of the renowned Restigouche, it is a good producer. The hotel operates several modern camps and in all can put its guests on some sixty salmon pools.

The Little Cascapedia River, to the east, is accessible to public fishing, and there is also some open water on the Matane, which flows north into the St. Lawrence River at the town of Matane on Highway 6. While there are not many salmon rivers other than these that are open to the public, a little enquiry will sometimes turn up such a stream. Accommodations are no problem on the Gaspe, as this is the most highly-developed tourist travel area in Quebec. For those who want some good speckled and lake-trout fishing, Isidore Lechasseur, Box 880, Mont-Joli, Quebec, has eighty-three square acres near Rimouski under lease. It can be reached via Highway 6 or by rail.

At Ile-aux-Grues, reached from Montagny on Highway 2, on the south shore of the St. Lawrence, some thirty miles east of Quebec, there is some striped-bass fishing. The island must be reached by ferry. There is a lodge for twenty-five persons, operated by Gabriel Vezina, Ile-Aux-Grues, Quebec.

ANTICOSTI ISLAND

Not to be overlooked on the Quebec fishing scene is Anticosti Island at the mouth of the St. Lawrence River. There are six really good salmon rivers, but the fishing is private and any arrangements must be made through D. J. Wallace, Consolidated Paper Corp., 1643 Sun Life Bldg., Montreal, Quebec. Guides are compulsory on the island; and complete accommodations are available.

A complete list of Outfitters in Quebec may be obtained from the Outfitters' Division, Department of Fish and Game, Parliament Buildings, Quebec City, Quebec.

QUEBEC FISHING REGULATIONS

Resident Fishing License $1.10
Nonresident Fishing License (all species except salmon) $5.25
Nonresident Fishing License (including salmon) $15.50
Nonresident 3-Day Fishing License (including salmon) $5.25
Dependent's Fishing License (wife, and children under 16) $2.10

SEASONS AND LIMITS

Seasons and limits vary widely in Quebec according to area. For complete regulations write: Department of Tourism, Fish and Game, Parliament Buildings, Quebec City, Province of Quebec.

LABRADOR

Labrador is that part of Newfoundland lying on the mainland of the continent. The closest contact with Newfoundland is at the northern tip of the island, where it is separated from Labrador by the Strait of Belle Isle. The Province of Quebec forms the balance of the southern border of Labrador, and all of the western border. The east is entirely on the Atlantic ocean, and is marked by deep, ragged bays. There are many wonderful salmon and trout streams, but all are difficult to reach. The easiest way is by chartered plane from Eastern Provincial Airways at Gander, Newfoundland. The fare can run from about $350 for some of the more southern points of call in Labrador, to over $500 for the more northern ones. The Canadian National Railway operates a steamer service during the summer with stops at many ports, including Battle Harbour, Cartwright, Goose Bay Airport, Rigolet, Makkovik, Davis Inlet and Nain but there are no guides or accommodations and the angler would have to carry his own complete camping kit. Those wishing to do so could write the Canadian National Railway, St. John's, Newfoundland, for further information.

Licensed guides (not less than one per two anglers) must accompany all non-resident anglers in Labrador; and a permit is required from the Department of Mines and Resources, St. John's, Newfoundland, to carry fishing gear in an aircraft and to travel in restricted areas. Visitors should check carefully.

The summer is short, with the open months only June to September, but mid-summer days may be quite warm, though evenings always call for wool clothing. A large supply of insect repellent and net head coverings are recommended.

The Forteau is the most southerly and best known salmon river in Newfoundland, entering the Strait of Belle Isle on the south coast. The river is fifteen miles long and has some fine pools. The salmon run to 20 pounds and 7-pound trout have been taken. You can reach the Forteau via chartered three-passenger plane from Wellon's Flying Service, P.O. Box 789, Corner Brook, Newfoundland, for a charge of $165 round-trip. The rate from Gander is $336 each way, for a five-passenger plane. Cabin accommodations can be obtained through A. H Parsons, Rocky Harbour, Bonne Bay, Newfoundland, but early reservations are recommended. In the same area and through the same agency, fishermen can get on the Pinware and County Cat Rivers.

Located southeast of Goose Bay, the Eagle River is 150 miles long, emptying into Sandwich Bay. It can be reached by boat to Cartwright or by charter launch from Gander, which is expensive. There are no accommodations and all equipment must be taken in. The contact is Warden F. S. Brown, Separation Point, Labrador, and the best fishing is from July 15 to August 31. The fish can run up to 15 pounds.

Other rivers in coastal Labrador which are known to have good fishing but on which there are at present no facilities are the Gilbert, St. Mary's and Sinneys Brook. Information on these may be obtained from John Acreman, Fisheries Officer, St. Mary's Harbour. The best time is from July 10 to August 10.

Well to the north, arrangements for excellent fishing for Arctic char, brook trout and lake trout may be made through Mrs. Evely Tilier, Nain, Labrador.

In the interior of Labrador there is some outstanding fishing for speckled trout, ouananiche, lake trout, some splake, pike and whitefish. The majority of the waters which can be reached lie along the branch of the Quebec North Shore and Labrador Railway which runs between Sept-Isles on the Quebec coast of the Gulf of St. Lawrence, and Schefferville, on the northern boundary between Quebec and Labrador. There is a twice-weekly train, leaving Sept-Iles at 8 a.m. on Tuesdays and Fridays and leaving Schefferville for the return trip on Wednesdays and Saturdays. You can also fly from Montreal to Schefferville, daily except Sundays.

Several fly-in fishing resorts along this route offer accommodations. There is a lodge and cabins operated by Frontier Fishing and Hunting Limited, P.O. Box 249, Station H, Montreal, Quebec, on Lake Ashuanipi, at mile 224 on the railway. A base for both land and seaplanes is also available, and guests can fly directly from Sept-Isles to camp. There is room for about twenty-four guests. Rates, including the flight in and out run about $300 to $400 for a five-day trip.

A similar arrangement for junkets further to the interior may be made through Great Northern Fishing Camps, 562 Union Street, Bangor, Maine; or Box 1887, Schefferville, Quebec, the latter address being the one to use from June 11 to September 9th.

There is a resort on Fremont Lake, operated by Elmer Wilson, Shin Pond, Maine; and another on Sandgrit Lake, operated by Roger Holt, Holt's Flying Service, Greenville, Maine. Both work on a seven-day trip basis, at about $400 per trip.

Although geographically located in the Province of Quebec, the George River is generally referred to as being in Labrador. It is reached by plane from Schefferville due north to Arctic Anglers Camp on Ungava Bay. Currently it is producing some of the best salmon, brook trout and Arctic char fishing in Canada. Prices, including the flight from Schefferville run about $775 to $950 per week, according to how near you are to the peak of the salmon run. The season extends only from July 15 to September 10 unless weather conditions permit later closing. For complete information and reservations, write Mr. Bill Littleford, Arctic Anglers, P.O. Box 942, Setauket, Long Island, New York.

While the bulk of the attention in Labrador fishing is given to salmon and the trouts, there is also excellent northern-pike fishing, the weights going as high as 15 pounds. The fish hit ferociously, and are found almost anywhere in inland waters where there is a little eddy. One angler reported them as "pests" because they occasionally swallowed a 2-pound brook trout he was playing.

Lake trout also grow to exceptional weights, the record being in the 50-pound class. This far north they are more often found in water where they can be reached with flies than is the case farther south. Yet another species to be found in some of the lakes is the Great Lakes whitefish, a wonderful table delicacy and great sport on small flies.

NEWFOUNDLAND

Newfoundland is an island lying in the mouth of the St. Lawrence River, and since 1949 has been a Province of the Dominion of Canada. Politically it includes a part of Labrador on the mainland, on the north shore of the St. Lawrence River. This sector has been dealt with in the previous chapter. Geographically, the island is similar to that of this part of the mainland, with a rocky, much eroded terrain whose low-altitude mountains are crumbling remnants of some of the oldest formations in the world. The country is marshy, with many bogs among upjuttings of rugged rock, thousands of lakes and ponds and intricate patterns of rivers and brooks. A map of Newfoundland looks like a network of veins in an anatomical drawing.

The major fish is the Atlantic salmon, which comes into most of the rivers and is often found far inland. There are also eastern brook trout, brown trout, rainbows and some landlocked salmon or ouananiche. The eastern brook trout is the main "sea-run" trout of Newfoundland, going to the salt in great numbers and returning to many of the same rivers as the salmon, to provide some fantastic fishing. Sea-run brook trout average 2 pounds and 14-pounders have been taken. The brown also goes to sea, and although angling for the sea-run members of this species is not as well known in Newfoundland as that for brook trout, there are reports of 14-pounders taken on the Avalon Peninsula near Argentia. Browns in inland waters average 2 pounds and reach a maximum of 7 pounds.

The main ocean fish sought by sport fishermen is the bluefin tuna. Within recent years some spectacular members of this species have been taken off Newfoundland. A few swordfish have also been taken. Fishing for cod is also becoming popular, although the majority of people go for the Newfoundland cod by jigging rather than by sport-fishing methods.

There are three major-sized rivers in Newfoundland—the Humber, draining the northern area in a southwestern direction, from the heights near White Bay to the Bay of Islands at Corner Brook; the whole of central Newfoundland feeds its waters to the Exploits River, emptying into Notre Dame Bay on the northeast; to the south of this is the renowned Gander River, flowing to Bonavista Bay. These are by no means the only salmon rivers; there are literally hundreds around the complete shoreline of the island.

The largest lakes are Grand Lake and Deer Lake in the Humber system, Red Indian Lake on the Exploits River and Gander Lake on the Gander; but again there are many other fairly large lakes and a multitude of ponds throughout the island.

One thing which long held Newfoundland back economically and at the same time helped to preserve the angling possibilities, was the difficulty of transportation to the island and on it. In recent years this problem has been much eased and it is now only a few hours by air from various points on the Canadian and U.S. mainland to some of the best fishing waters in Newfoundland. Trans-Canada Air Lines operates regular services to Canadian cities on the mainland from Tampa, New

York, Boston, Chicago and Cleveland; and from Montreal there are direct flights daily to Stephensville, Gander and St. John's. Pan American operates flights from New York, Baltimore and other East Coast cities to Gander, Newfoundland.

For those who prefer to go by boat, the Furness Warren Line, 10 State Street, Boston, has limited passenger and freight service between Boston and Halifax, Nova Scotia and St. John's, Newfoundland. Reservations may be made at the above address or at 1 Upper Water Street, Halifax, Nova Scotia. A ferry leaves Sydney, Nova Scotia, daily at 11:55 p.m., completing the 100-mile trip at 6:55 the following morning. The fare is about $30 round-trip. Steamers and ferries also carry trailers at a charge of about 75¢ per foot.

Steamer service also operates from St. Anne des Monts, Quebec, a six-hour trip for about $18, permitting connections with Newfoundland, Labrador, twice a week.

The salmon season in general begins June 5th and ends September 15th, but as with salmon waters everywhere, each stream has its own timetable and the salmon fisherman must always check thoroughly to be sure he will be on the river of his choice when the salmon are in. Write for current information on Newfoundland salmon rivers to the Newfoundland Tourist Development Office, Confederation Building, St. John's, Newfoundland.

You can fish for some kind of trout, too, from January 15th to September 15th, but the season varies with each species of trout, and with the sea-run varieties. Complete angling regulations for these should be obtained annually, but the resumé at the end of this chapter will give a general idea of the seasons.

In the salt, the bluefin tuna and occasional swordfish are taken from August until the end of September. Cod jigging goes on all the time.

Fairly good unpaved roads now circle much of the Newfoundland coast with the exception of the southern shores, where there is a considerable expanse unapproachable by road. Eastern Provincial Airways, based at Gander on the north coast, on Highway 1 at its junction with Highway 40, will fly fishing parties to this south coast. They also operate daily except Sundays between St. John's, on the southeast, Gander in the east-central zone, and Deer Lake on the west-central coast.

The Canadian National Railway offers extensive service, with rail connection from Port Aux Basques to many points such as Corner Brook, Deer Lake, Grand Falls, Gander and then south and east to St. John's on the Avalon Peninsula. The railway also operates coastal steamer service to drop anglers off along the southern coast. In such cases it is necessary to take all your own equipment, tote it yourself and set up camp yourself, unless dealing through a licensed outfitter.

For a mimeographed sheet showing current methods of reaching the island, and timetables on trains and passenger ferries, write the Newfoundland Development Office, St. John's, Newfoundland.

There are a number of other coastwise steamers, stopping at many small ports, where again, however, anglers must remember there will be no accommodations available except by previous arrangement. Full description of this steamer service, and the routes, is contained in "Hunting And Fishing Guide To Newfoundland," issued by the Newfoundland Tourist Development Commission, St. John's, Newfoundland.

Daytime temperatures in Newfoundland average 65 degrees. Wool clothing is always a necessity and in the early season woolen underwear should be included. Rain gear is also essential as is comfortable, waterproof footgear for tramping the often boggy terrain.

Moose are plentiful in the interior and should be given a wide berth, although they are not dangerous if you do not disturb them. There are also some caribou, and bear are fairly numerous. No poisonous snakes are found on the island. If you are fortunate you may see seals in the bigger salmon rivers—though many anglers do not regard this as good fortune. The seals feed on salmon and the sight of a seal in your salmon pool may end your fishing for some time.

Mosquitoes, black flies and deer flies are an ever present menace in Newfoundland, and anglers should go well prepared with insect repellent and netting.

WEST COAST

The Grand Codroy and its two branches, the North Branch and the South Branch Rivers, are three of the best salmon streams in the province. Access to them is singularly easy. The Grand Codroy is twenty-five miles from Port aux Basques and can be reached via Highway 1 and by Canadian National Railway. There are twenty very good pools in the eighteen miles which is readily accessible. Fishing is best from June 1st, when the salmon first enter the stream, until June 30th, when fishing begins to taper off in the lower pools as the fish move upstream. These rivers host a fairly good run of fish ranging from 4 to 20 pounds, and very occasional 40-pounders are taken.

There are several spots where cabin accommodations are available; Dennis Ryan, Sandy Ryan and J. T. Farrell, operators, can all be addressed at O'Regan's via Doyle's, Newfoundland. A. L. Gillis can be contacted at Codroy.

From July 1st on, it is better to locate at South Branch as the upper pools of the Grand Codroy and the North and South Branches can be best fished from here. About ten pools on the South Branch are accessible by road, while seven pools on the North Branch can only be reached by rail. Mrs. Mike Wall, 67 Station Road, Humbermouth, accommodates sportsmen on the South Branch.

The Little Codroy, to the south of the Codroy, can also only be reached by train, and involves a thirteen-hour train trip from Gander; or by steamer from Sydney, Nova Scotia, an overnight trip. The river is worth it. There's plenty of big water, as well as smaller pools. Fish average about 6 pounds and go up to 20. The fishing is from June 15th on, the peak of the run coming between July 1st and September 15th. One of the attractions of this river is that fresh fish keep coming in right up until the very last day of the season.

North from the Codroy, on the coast of St. George's Bay, is a group of three rivers, the Robinson's, its tributary the North Feeder, and the Barachois to the south. The Robinson's can be reached by train or Highway 1 to Cartyville. A. P. Legge and George Shears, Cartyville, offer accommodations at reasonable rates. Guides cost about $10 per day. From Cartyville it is possible to drive or walk to the Barachois. The fishing starts about the end of May and is at its best by mid-to-late June and continues until nearly the end of August. The average weight is close to 6 pounds and there are occasional large fish. The Barachois is also very good for sea trout.

Close by, to the north is the Fishels River, which gets the earliest salmon run in Newfoundland, the first salmon coming in at the end of May. For the first three weeks there is usually good fishing in the lower part of the river, then the salmon go upstream, making very few stops en route, with the result that fishing is unsatisfactory. There are also sea trout. Mrs. E. Young, Fishels, has limited accommodations. There is no road above Highway 1 and the going is tough. Continuing north you come to Harry's River, one of the best and one of the most highly developed. The fish come in around June 20th and there's both wading and fishing from canoe. Accommodations are available through Ray Doucette, P.O. Box 203, Corner Brook. Highway 1 crosses the river twice. Mr. John Samms also has cabins and housekeeping cabins at Black Duck on Highway 47, east of Stephenville, and can provide guides.

The Fox Island River comes to the Gulf of St. Lawrence just above the Port au Port Peninsula. A secondary road running north from the village of Port au Port on Highway 47, crosses the lower stream. The salmon come in about June 15th and the best fishing period is from July 15 to September 15th. But from the middle of May through July there is consistently good sea-trout fishing. For some years Atlantic salmon fishing fell off in this river, but recently has been improving again. For guides, who are available at Stephenville and Port aux Basques, contact Fred Pelley, Stephenville.

Proceeding up the west coast, the next good salmon river is the Serpentine, a great favorite because of the size of both its salmon and trout. The salmon can run to 33 pounds, the trout to 12. The river is very clear and lends itself to wading as well as boat fishing. Salmon come in about June 20th and fishing usually continues good until the season closes on September 15th. There is also good sea-trout fishing in several brooks in the neighborhood.

The Serpentine can be reached over an eighteen-mile private woods road between Corner Brook on Highway 1 and Serpentine Lake, then by boat across the seven-mile lake to the "Home Pools" of the river. Here Ray Doucette, operator of Dhoon Resort at Black Duck on Highway 47 has a fishing camp and also has several outpost cabins from which the best pools on the river can be fished. Eastern Provincial Airlines will fly parties in five-passenger planes from Gander to the Serpentine.

At this point we reach the Humber, one of the largest in Newfoundland and probably the best for big salmon. The average fish taken is around 14 pounds and top weight runs to 40 pounds. The best fishing is from August 1 to September 1. You can reach the lower Humber by Highway 1 from Port aux Basques, or by train, a distance of 135 miles. Or you can fly into Stephenville Airport, a distance of fifty-two miles via Highway 47 then Highway 1. And it can also be reached by train from Gander, or by charter plane from Gander Airport.

Ray Wellon, Wellon's Lodge, Box 456, Corner Brook, operates a lodge and cabins on the river; and a single cabin is available through Reg. Coombs, Sportsman's Haven, Box 278, Corner Brook.

The Upper Humber can be reached by train to Deer Lake, then by car twenty-three miles to Big Falls, and Highway 1A crosses the river a mile below that at Little Falls. The Big Falls Pool is famous. Fishing starts there around June 20th and continues good until July 10th. The first run will be fish averaging about 6 pounds, with an occasional one up to 25 pounds. In the upper reaches of the Humber several smaller streams have good salmon and trout fishing.

You can get guides at Deer Lake by contacting Chesley Nichols, John Nichols and Kenneth Campbell. There are no accommodations on the river but if you bring your own sleeping bags the guides can set up camp near the river.

Traveling north from Corner Brook on Highway 44, then Highway 73 near Wiltondale, you can reach the town of Portland Creek thence by boat to the river of the same name, where there is a good chance for extra big fish. Forty-pounders have been taken occasionally, though the run is more between 4-to-20 pounds. Eastern Provincial Airways will charter a five-passenger plane from Gander to the creek, and you can also come by Canadian National Steamer out of Corner Brook to Daniel's Harbour, then by small boat to the river. Fishing starts about July 1 although some of the feeder streams are earlier. Fishing continues good till the end of August.

From Portland Creek you can continue up Highway 73 to Western Brook, above Bonne Bay. Sea-run brook trout go very large here, some to 8 pounds, and salmon have been taken up to 30 pounds. Accessibility is difficult and there are no accommodations of any kind, but it's worth a little effort for such good fishing. The trout come in to Western Brook in late June, salmon around the middle of July.

In the same area, slightly to the north, River of Ponds can also be reached via Highway 73 It offers some exceptional fishing at times. It can also be reached from the railway, which touches Port Saunders, ten miles from the river; or, of course, by air. The first salmon come in around July 1 and the peak fishing is from July 10 to August 10, though there is some fishing until mid-September. The weights run from 4 to 42 pounds. Sea-run brook trout come in early in August.

Anglers must take their own camping equipment and make arrangements through Mr. T. Sheppard, River of Ponds, Newfoundland, who is the warden.

EAST COAST

The next important salmon river lies well-around on the northeast coast. The Exploits is the longest river in Newfoundland. It can be reached via Highway 1, west from Gander to Windsor, then Highway 1A follows the river upstream for several miles. At Badger you can go still further upstream by Highway 50, to its outlet at Red Indian Lake. The railway follows the river for some forty miles. The best fishing is from July 1 to August 31, with the average fish about 5 pounds, and an 18-pounder a big one. Accommodations are available at Paragon Hotel, Baird's Hotel, Monte Rose Hotel and Mrs. Noble's Tourist Home, as well as several other establishments at Grand Falls, near the mouth of the river. Several other streams in the area also offer fishing. They are the Peter's River, near Bishops Falls, below Windsor; the Campbellton River to the east; and Point Leamington River off Highway 42 north from Windsor.

The Gander River empties in Bonavista Bay on the northeast coast of Newfoundland. It can be reached by taxi from Gander at slight cost, at Glenwood, where Highway 1 crosses the river. Good fishing begins around July 1 and continues until September 15. The average fish will be about 5 pounds but some are taken up to 20 pounds. Fishing is usually done in river boats powered by outboard motors but some of the pools can be fished from the bank. The pools are wide and deep and you seldom find low water in this river. Saunders Camp (P.O. Box 435, Gander, Newfoundland) provides accommodations fifteen miles from saltwater, with good fishing both upstream and down. There is a good hotel at Gander.

The Gambo River, just to the south, can also be good and you can usually find boarding house accommodations at the village of Gambo on Highway 1. The Terra Nova, still further south on Highway 1, runs through Terra Nova National Park, where you can camp and where there is also a twenty-four-unit bungalow camp. There is some salmon fishing and considerable trout fishing in the interior. The Avalon Peninsula is all but an island, joined to the mainland of Newfoundland only by a narrow neck of land between Trinity Bay on the north and Placentia Bay on the south. The salmon rivers on the peninsula carry runs of fish that are small but numerous, in late June and through July. Sea trout appear in May and are taken at the mouths of the many brooks, most of them within easy driving distance of St. John's. This is the most heavily-populated part of Newfoundland, and roads skirt the entire shore and cross the peninsula in several places. You can drive to the Samonier River from St. John's via Highway 1, then Highway 6, a distance of sixty miles. There are cabins near St. Catherines on the river. Highway 6 continues on to the Placentia River on the west, and parallels the river for some distance. While the fish are small, there is fair fishing through July and August. By following Highway 5, the coastal road, south from St. John's, anglers will come to the Trepassey River, on the extreme south of the Avalon Peninsula, where again there is good summer fishing for small fish, in this and several other small rivers nearby. Boarding house accommodations will be found at Trepassey.

SOUTH COAST

On the south coast of the mainland the Conne River, which flows into Bay D'Espoir, offers fishing in one of the most beautiful spots in Newfoundland. You can fly in from Gander or come by Canadian National Railways steamer from either Port aux Basques or St. John's. Take your own sleeping bags, and get guide service through Stephen John, Conne River, Newfoundland. The fishing is from early June through July. Although the salmon are plentiful, they seldom go over 4 pounds; but there is good trout fishing to add to the sport in the mouths of the many small brooks which flow into the bay.

Directly to the west is the Salmon River and at its head is Long Pond, which has some good fishing for lake trout. The lake can only be reached by a long hike up the river, or a boat trip, which would have to be arranged by competent guides. Anglers can obtain guiding service through Fred Lushman, Thomas Young or Henry Rose, Grey River, Newfoundland.

The Port aux Basques steamer calls at Ramea, an island nine miles from the mouth of the Grey River, and the lower river is navigable by boat for about eight miles up. But it is a wild and rugged trip, with the fishing doubtful until well up one of the tributaries, the Salmon River, where some fine catches have been made. Mosquitoes are very bad in this area.

For some really remote fishing, Fred Lushman will also take anglers to the White Bear River, to the west of the Salmon. Much of it has not been fished, as far as is known, but the lower waters have produced quite good catches, though none of great size to date. The season starts in early June and continues well into July. There is a Canadian National Railways steamer service about every ten days, after June 4th, from Port aux Basques to Ramea; or occasionally a motor launch may be chartered for the run. At Ramea it is necessary to go to the mainland by boat, which can be obtained from John Penney & Son at Ramea. They will also outfit for food. The trip in to the mainland costs about $15. Guides get about $10 per day plus their keep.

There are thousands of rivers and ponds throughout Newfoundland whicn can offer good trout fishing in season for eastern brook trout, speckled trout, rainbows and browns. Often this angling can be combined with that for salmon and sea trout. The rainbow season extends from June 15 to September 15; that for the other trouts (sea trout excepted) from January 15 to September 15. Trout fishing trips can be arranged out of Corner Brook through Reg. Coombs, Sportsman's Haven, P.O. Box 278, Corner Brook, in lakes which can be reached by small plane. There is also reputedly some excellent trout fishing for good-sized fish in the Buchansto Badger area, in central Newfoundland. You can go to Badger by rail or Highway I A, then High 60 to Bucans Junction; or write Charles Perrier, Pine Falls Camp, Buchans Junction.

In the St. John's area of the Avalon Peninsula there are many ponds within twenty-five miles of the city where there is good fishing, although it is advisable to choose those which are at least a mile from the highway, as they will be less heavily fished.

SALTWATER FISHING

While tuna have not been fished much in these waters by sport fishermen, some bluefins weighing 1,200 pounds have been harpooned by commercial men and there is good possibility of a first-rate future sport fishery. Huge schools have been seen regularly in Conception Bay off the Avalon Peninsula, where tuna boats report an abundance of large schools of herring, squid and mackerel on which the tuna feed. The heaviest tuna taken so far on rod and line weighed 871 pounds. The Newfoundland Tuna Club is now affiliated with the International Game Fish Association and all catches are recorded officially. Every effort is being made to increase the number of boats fishing for tuna, in order to develop the sport.

Swordfish have been taken in southwest coastal waters and efforts are being made to develop this possibility, too.

NEWFOUNDLAND AND LABRADOR FISHING REGULATIONS

Nonresident Fishing License, Salmon
    Season $30.00
    Two Weeks $20.00
    Daily $5.00
Nonresident Fishing License, Trout
    Season $5.00

SEASONS AND LIMITS

Species	Open Season	Bag Limit
Salmon	June 5–Sept. 15	6 per day, not more than 21 per week
Rainbow Trout	June 1–Sept. 15	
Other Trout	Jan. 15–Sept. 15 (in unlicensed rivers) May 24–Sept. 15 (in licensed rivers)	36 trout or 15 pounds plus 1 trout, per day

Nonresident fishermen on scheduled rivers must be accompanied by a licensed guide. Nonresidents traveling in a Forest Restricted Area must be accompanied by a licensed guide. (Labrador is such an area each summer.)

For complete regulations write: Wildlife Division, Department of Mines, Agriculture and Resources, St. John's, Newfoundland.

NOVA SCOTIA

The Appalachian Mountains that lend lofty coolness and rugged variety to much of eastern North America find their terminus in Nova Scotia. Here they level out to altitudes that nowhere are in excess of 1,200 feet above sea level. The low, gentle slopes invite a growth of green forests to their summits, framing a landscape dotted with hundreds of blue lakes connected by clear streams, and the whole encircled by the waters of the Atlantic Ocean, making this the most truly maritime of Canada's Maritime Provinces. Interspersed amid the forests and spread along the coastal plains are many farms.

The coastline is characterized by a kind of ragged beauty with capes and points of land extending out into the sea and long fingers of the ocean reaching inland to the heart of forest and farmland. This irregularity increases the actual length of the shoreline to more than 4,500 miles.

This mixture of forest and marine landscape provides the setting for an equally varied fishing. The fresh waters yield speckled or brook trout, which are native to the province and consequently are widely distributed. They run very small in size, often only 6in ches in length, and a consequent generous limit allows the angler to take twenty per day. Rainbow trout have been imported from the Pacific coastal waters to which they are native, and have done well in some Nova Scotia waters. Five-pounders are sometimes taken. They rise to flies well in the early and late seasons, but during midsummer they are mostly taken by trolling with spinners, in water 15 to 30 feet deep. The brown trout has also been imported and from first plantings in Milford Haven and Guysborough Rivers has spread to many other waters. Browns have been taken up to 11 pounds, and sea-run individuals to even greater weights, but not in numbers.

Lake trout, also called grey trout and togue, are native to Nova Scotia but are not widely distributed. They will average 3 to 6 pounds with a very occasional one going as high as 12 pounds.

Yet another import, the black bass, has done fairly well in a few lakes where the species has been stocked. The maximum size would be 4 pounds.

Saltwater species include pollack, mackerel, tautog, haddock, cod, halibut and wolf-fish (catfish), as well as the big game species of tuna, and swordfish. In addition there are runs of striped bass and Atlantic salmon, working into the rivers from the salt; and conversely some browns and brook trout go out from the rivers to feed in the sea and return to provide extra-special sport.

The tuna is the glamor fish of Nova Scotia, being the giant of the mackerel family, with tremendous power and speed. Although some fish over 1,000 pounds are believed to have been taken in Nova Scotia waters, the official record is a 977-pounder taken by Commander M. Hodgson, a Canadian Naval Officer, in St. Ann's Bay, Cape Breton Island, on 130-pound-test line. Captain Jack Carpenter of Miami holds the 80-pound-line-test class with an 880-pound tuna taken in Nova Scotia waters, and the all-tackle women's record is also a Nova Scotia fish, an 882-pounder taken by Mrs. A. D. Crowninshield.

Angling for giant tuna requires special tackle. Some specialists in the sport prefer medium-weight tackle, but those less skilled in this type of fishing stick to the heavy gear. Tuna boats are equipped with swivel chairs and foot wells, and captain and crew must be competent to play an important part in landing the big fish.

The accepted practise is to chum at dawn with fresh herring and pieces of other fish, to attract the tuna to the angler's boat. The bait is usually fresh mackerel sewn on the hook, then offered to the bluefin and allowed to sink a few feet. The tuna generally strikes hard, taking the bait in a torpedo-like rush. Then he is off on a long, high-speed run. The angler's boat follows as fast as possible to avoid extra strain on the tackle, and to keep the fish from stripping the reel. Run after run follows and the fight sometimes goes on for hours. Finally the tuna breaks water and begins to circle the boat. If the angler then maintains continual pressure and gives the fish no chance to get a second wind, the contest may soon be over. But it's a gruelling game, calling for good muscle on the part of the angler, and co-operation by captain and crew.

Another Nova Scotia fish which calls for specialized tackle is the Atlantic salmon. Fish of this species average 6 pounds, but many much larger ones are taken. Fishing is limited to fly rod only. In the old days rods were 10 and 12 feet long, but the modern angler is more inclined to use an 8½- or 9-, or at most 9½-foot rod, along with a single-action reel and a GBF forward-tapered line for the 8½-footer, a GAF for the others. With this he uses 200 yards of 18-pound-test backing, and a 9-foot leader tapered from a 30-pound-test butt section to a 6-pound-test tippet.

The flies which take the most salmon vary with the river and the advice of guides or other local authorities should always be heeded. A good assortment to start with should include the Silver Doctor, Jock Scott, Black Dose, Dusty Miller, Fiery Brown, Brown Hackle, all in wet flies; and in dries, the Brown Hackle, Gray Hackle, Cinnamon Sedge, Pink Lady, and the Deadly McIntosh, a native Nova Scotian. Also the Wulff hair-wing dries.

Many of the streams in which the best salmon fishing is found do not lend themselves to wading or casting from shore. Therefore you should count on a guide with boat—the guide being required in most cases, anyway, to get you to the best lies, especially near the mouths of rivers, where the stream is wide.

While Nova Scotia, by its very shape, is isolated even from its neighboring Canadian Provinces, travel has been made easy and inviting over the years. Those who travel by car will find a modern auto ferry operating daily in summer and tri-weekly in other seasons from Bar Harbor, Maine, to Yarmouth on the western end of Nova Scotia. Another steamer ferry carrying fifty cars each trip operates between Saint John, New Brunswick, and Digby, in western Nova Scotia. Or you may come in by Highway 2 from New Brunswick on the west.

Canadian National Railways operate three trains daily between Montreal and Halifax, the capital city of Nova Scotia. The Canadian Pacific operates steamer ferry service between Saint John, New Brunswick and Digby.

There are also frequently scheduled air flights between New York, Boston, Toronto, Montreal and various points in New Brunswick, Prince Edward Island and Newfoundland, to Halifax. Some flights make stops at Yarmouth on the western end of the peninsula, and Sydney on the southeast coast of Cape Breton Island.

From Yarmouth, Highway 1 funnels traffic along the west coast to Digby, continues on more than half the length of the Province, then turns east to Halifax. Highway 3 provides a similar Yarmouth to Halifax route on the east coast. From Halifax, Highway 7 continues on around the coast and west at Liscomb to Antigonish, whence a network of roads leads up through the narrow neck of land which joins Nova Scotia to New Brunswick. From Antigonish, Highway 4 leads north and east to Cape Breton Island. On the Island itself, Highway 4 services the southern half, to Sydney, while Highways 5 and 19 serve the northern half. From both Halifax and Sydney there are ferries to Newfoundland; and there is also steamer service between Halifax and New York.

Though July and August are the favorite vacation times, they are not the best months for inland fishing. Water levels tend to be too low and air temperatures too high. Better results will be had in midsummer, however, if there has been an early rainy season.

Services of a licensed guide must be engaged for each three members of a party fishing in lakes and streams lying within the wooded areas of Nova Scotia. The fee for a licensed guide varies from $7 to $15 per day plus board. Many of the streams, however, flow through open country and in such case a guide is not required. Nor is a guide required for saltwater fishing, and boats can be chartered at many points along the 4,500 mile coastline.

Guides may be located through tackle stores and through the offices of the Department of Lands and Forests, or through hotel managers.

Before planning to fish in Nova Scotia, anglers should check whether a license is required. This is one of the few places where such a license is necessary to fish for striped bass; and a license is also called for when fishing for the sea-run trouts, as well as freshwater trout.

Complete details for the year in which you plan to fish should be obtained from the Department of Fisheries, Halifax, Nova Scotia.

Summers in Nova Scotia are tempered by the closeness of the sea—and so are the winters. The mean annual temperatures range between 40 and 45 degrees and those for the month of July between 62 and 66 degrees. There are higher temperatures in the interior of the southwestern part of the province but it is rare that the thermometer anywhere goes above 90 degrees. Light cotton clothing is sufficient for daytime fishing in most cases, but a wool sweater will be needed always, morning and evening; and for occasional cool days the angler may very well wish for some lightweight woolen underwear. Raincoats and waterproof hats and boots that turn water are standard equipment.

Those who fish the wooded areas may encounter deer, which, of course, are not dangerous. There are some moose, and if these are avoided in the fall and at any time when there is a young calf along, the angler may expect no trouble. There are also bears and wild cats, along with lesser fur-bearing animals such as the red fox and the raccoon, but like most other creatures of the wilderness, they are harmless unless cornered and molested by man. Nova Scotia has no poisonous snakes.

SOUTHERN AREA

Nova Scotia's most outstanding fishing in the past has been found at the extreme southern end of the Province at Wedgeport. For years an International Tuna Cup Match was held here during the seasonal runs of tremendous bluefin tuna, starting in July and reaching a peak in September. Teams from many nations competed each year for the Alton B. Sharp trophy. In 1949, however, less than seventy-two tuna were boated by five competent teams in three days of angling, and since then, for unknown reasons, the number of tuna taken has decreased anually. In 1960 the matches were discontinued until the fish return in greater numbers. Nevertheless, there are still some fish taken every year, and the past record is so good that there is plenty of hope for a future resurgence.

Tuna boats are available at Wedgeport and also at several other points around the coast of this southern part of the peninsula. There is usually only one boat to a port, so reservations are necessary if the tuna are in. Such ports are Shag Harbor, Clarks Harbor, and Barrington Passage, all on Highway 3 near Shelburne; Churchover and Birchtown in the same neighborhood; Stonehurst, Pleasantville and Lunenburg; and Marriott's Cove and East Chester, just to the east, on Highway 3. There is also one at White Point near Liverpool, near the junction of Highway 8 and Highway 3, the coast road. On the west shore there are boats at Cape St. Mary, on Highway 1, north of Wedgeport; at Digby and Annapolis Royal in the Annapolis Basin; at Halls Harbor where Highway 12 comes out to the Minas Channel on Bay of Fundy.

At all these same points boats may be obtained to fish for pollack, mackerel, haddock, cod and tautog; and striped bass when they are in these waters. The pollack average 4 or 5 pounds and are occasionally taken up to a whopping 35 pounds. Party boats bring in as much as 600 pounds of fish a day, and being listed as commercial fish, they are readily sold in the markets. Sport fishermen in general, however, prefer to remove the hook and put the fish back, beyond those they want for their personal use. While most of the fishing is from party boats and skiffs, many light-tackle men also take pollack from shore, using plug- and spin-casting rods. The fish take lures as well as bait.

The season for pollack fishing is July through October, and the best catches are made early in the morning and in the evening. While the fish are taken almost universally along the coast, the hot spots are at Long Island, the peninsula running south from Digby, and traversed by Highway 17; and its neighboring Brier Island. Also the Tusket Islands off Wedgeport; Cape Sable Island, at the turn of the peninsula; and quite a few are even taken around Halifax.

Throughout the coastal waters anglers take mackerel, cod, haddock, flounder and other small fish, working from rowboats and fishing the waters not far from shore. The tautog, on the other hand, seems to be pretty well confined to the extreme southern tip of Nova Scotia, in the mouths of rivers in the general area of Wedgeport. This fish, locally called tautog, is the same as the blackfish of the Chesapeake Bay, and the oyster fish of more southern waters.

The mackerel move inshore in May and are found throughout the summer. When they are feeding near the surface the schools may be spotted and can then readily be fished with flies and shiny metal lures. In flies, a white bucktail is the best taker.

Light-tackle men also take flounders and cunners from many wharfs along the coast, and even come up with haddock, cod, halibut and catfish, locally called wolffish. However, these species are more commonly taken by bottom fishing with bait, either using a rod or handline.

Striped bass come into coastal waters and the mouths of rivers all along the coast from Shelburne on the southeast, up and around the curve and along the Bay of Fundy. In the more exposed areas they are taken mostly alongshore, but when they round the curve into the Bay of Fundy they seem to work more into the rivers. The mouth of the Bear River just across the bay from the town of Digby is a hot spot, and another is the Annapolis River in the same area. They also like the many sandy beaches along this coast. Surf casting and wharf fishing for the species is good long the shores of Minas Basin and Cobequid Bay, reached via Highway 15. All kinds of gear are used, from casting outfits to bait-fishing tackle, and the catches are best at dawn and dusk, and at any time on a high tide.

A license is required to fish for striped bass in Nova Scotia, and can be obtained from the Department of Fisheries, Halifax, Nova Scotia or from local tackle stores.

Fishing for sea-run brook trout and sea-run brown trout along Nova Scotia's shores is more or less novelty angling. The trout are usually taken at the mouths of rivers which have populations in the fresh water. The sea-run brook trout do not run large, a 2-pounder being a pretty good fish. The sea-run brown, on the other hand, strays a little more from his native river and they grow larger. Brown trout weighing 25 pounds have been caught near Guysborough, but the average weight is 8 to 10 pounds. All the trouts are caught usually by trolling or casting from the shore with spinning outfits and artificial lures. A fishing license is required.

In general, the sea-going trouts are found in all streams flowing into the Atlantic from Lunenburg on the east coast, although a few come into the more southern rivers, notably the Medway and LaHave Rivers.

The Medway originates far inland in Stony and Long Lakes and enters the Atlantic Ocean at Liverpool. It can be reached throughout much of its length by county road and there are accommodations at Liverpool or Lunenburg; and Mr. Clarence Lowe, South Brookfield, Nova Scotia, operates a camp on the river, with canoes and guide-service provided.

The LaHave River originates in Cloud Lake, also far in the interior and enters the Atlantic at Bridgewater near Lunenburg. There are plentiful accommodations at Lunenburg, and the river can also be reached from Sunny Brook Lodge and Cottages, R.R. 3, Lunenburg, Nova Scotia.

Most attractive fish of all to many anglers is the Atlantic Salmon, and these too come into the Medway and LaHave, and indeed, to nearly every stream along the coast to some extent. The season is open through most of June and all of July and August, but as is usually the case, there are many variations which must be checked locally. Accommodations are available at many places along the coastal highways 3 and 7. Some of the rivers which enjoy special reputations are the La-Have, already described, and the Gold, reached from Chester Basin and Beech Hill on county road from the coastal Highway 3, north of Lunenburg; and on the western shore of this southern part of Nova Scotia, the Annapolis river which runs along Highway 1, parallel to the coast; and the Gaspereau, which enters Minas Basin near Wolfville, further up the coast. In the south the Tusket River, entering the sea near Wedgeport, gets a good run. Many other streams have salmon in season too, and sometimes good fishing can be located simply by making local enquiries.

In the southern sector of Nova Scotia there is some good rainbow fishing in Rumsey Lake, Kedgemakoogie and Sunken Lakes, all of which can be reached from Merrymakedgie Cottages at New Grafton, off Highway 8, either north from Liverpool or south from Annapolis Royal. There are lake trout in Lake Pochwock, on Highway 1, north of Halifax, and in Sherbrooke Lake, reached by county road from Lunenburg. The fish will weigh between 3 and 6 pounds, and are taken mostly by trolling, except in early spring when they are near the surface and may be taken on flies.

Lake Shubenacadie, a few miles north of Halifax via Highway 2, is the only water in Nova Scotia which has fishing for landlocked salmon.

There is some fair stream-trout fishing in the southern part of Nova Scotia in the Tobeatic Game Sanctuary, which has an area of 200 square miles and includes part of Lake Rossignol, the largest inland body of water in this part of the province. Sanctuary regulations require that a non-resident be accompanied by a guide unless he is merely passing through by road. A permit must also be obtained from the Forest Ranger.

While the smallmouth black bass was not native to these waters, the species has been introduced in an effort to provide more freshwater fishing. They will be found in Milo Lake in the extreme south, near Carleton, off Highway 40; Elliott Lake, reached from Annapolis Royal; and Lily Lake, west of Halifax via county road. Streamer flies, spinning lures, spinners and small bass plugs on casting outfits are effective tools.

CENTRAL AREA

Salmon come into many of the rivers of the Nova Scotia coast north of Halifax. Some of the top catches are made in the Musquodoboit River, entering the sea at Musquodoboit Harbor, on Highway 7; and in the West River, Sheet Harbour, along Highway 24, which runs west from Highway 7 at Sheet Harbour. Another excellent salmon river is the St. Mary's, running along beside Highway 7 where it turns west to Antigonish. Between these two are two others which have good reputations, the Moser and the Ecum Secum, east of the Liscomb Game Sanctuary. Liscomb Lodge, Liscomb Mills, Nova Scotia, on the ocean road, Highway 7, provides accommodations close to all these streams. The lodge also has charter-boat service for saltwater fishing.

Fishing for speckled trout is good in Liscomb Game Sanctuary and a county road crosses the area from Sheet Harbour on the coast to Trafalgar on the north edge of the Sanctuary. No guide or entrance permit is required at this game preserve unless you plan to camp there.

Local trout anglers like the Parmachene Belle, Silver Doctor, Stone Fly, March Brown, Brown Hackle, Cowdung, Montreal, Scarlet Ibis, Yellow Sally, Professor, Queen of Waters, Black Gnat, Coachman, Jenny Lind, Nixon and Drummer, in wet flies. For dries they go to the Brown Hackle, Gray Hackle, Parmachene Belle, Black Gnat, and the various duns and bi-visibles. The trout will also hit all the salmon flies.

Rods should be not more than 8 feet in length, weighing about 4 ounces, with slow, wet-fly action. With this, an HDH tapered line and a leader trimmed down to 4X or 5X tippet.

In many of these east-coast streams the brook trout go to sea and re-enter the rivers in two annual migrations or "runs," the first in April or May and the second in late June or early July. Some of the better streams for these sea-run fish in the central part of Nova Scotia are the Moser, Salmon and Ecum Secum, all close together, as described earlier; and the Musquodoboit and St. Mary's also already described; and all reached from Highway 7 along the coast. Speckled trout are also found in the streams flowing into the Northumberland Straits between Nova Scotia and Prince Edward Island.

Sea-run brown trout are found in summer in Chedabucto Bay and Guysborough Harbour on the coast opposite Cape Breton Island; and they are also taken further west in Merigomish Harbour on the shore of Northumberland Strait, at several points off the coastal highway which runs east from Glasgow.

CAPE BRETON ISLAND

The northern part of Nova Scotia is an island, known as Cape Breton Island, separated from the mainland by the Strait of Canso. Its rugged 700 miles of beautiful shoreline offer many attractions to the fisherman. The island is reached via Highway 5 from Auld Cove on the mainland, by bridge to Port Hastings on the island. There is car ferry service between Sydney, the largest city on the island, and Prince Edward Island, and to Port aux Basques, Newfoundland. There is also plane service from several U.S. cities, by scheduled airlines.

The island is the locale of Nova Scotia's most famous Atlantic salmon river, the Margaree, on the west coast, running from Lake Ainslie north to the Atlantic. The largest salmon ever taken in Nova Scotia, weighing 52½ pounds, came from this river. It also has a late summer run of speckled trout. Fishing camp accommodations can be arranged through James A. Bennett, N. E. Margaree, Nova Scotia.

The Chéticamp River, to the east, in the Cape Breton Highlands National Park, rates as the second most important salmon river on the island.

Tuna and swordfish are taken occasionally off the coast of Cape Breton, during early July to mid-September. Stripers work into the coastal waters to some degree and are taken fairly regularly in the Framboise River which comes down to the coast at Framboise, south of Louisbourg.

The Kilkenny and Mira Rivers, just to the interior of this, also offer brown-trout fishing, which can be located through guides out of Sydney.

Vast Bras d'Or Lake, in the heart of Cape Breton Island, is really an arm of the ocean, with bore-type outlets at either end, and consequently it provides tide-water fishing for all the smaller saltwater species indigenous to the area, including some particularly good pollack fishing.

Charter craft are available for saltwater fishing at Big Bras d'Or on Highway 5, west of North Sydney; at Ingonish Beach and Ingonish, on the Cabot Trail which circles the north cape; and Neils Harbour and Dingwall, further north on the same road. The same species are taken as from the mainland ports.

A very complete list of charter boats available for fishing Nova Scotia waters may be obtained from the Nova Scotia Travel Bureau, Department of Trade and Industry, Halifax, Nova Scotia. The cost of such charters varies according to location, but in general will run about $25 to $50 per day, depending on the boat and the number of persons in the party. Boats for tuna fishing and swordfishing run much higher. Anglers will also find much informative material in another publication of the same department, entitled "Outdoors in Nova Scotia."

A mimeographed sheet, prepared annually, gives up-to-the-minute information on licensed guides and various facilities available for fishermen.

Nonresident Fishing License $5.00
Resident Fishing License (salmon only) $2.00

SEASONS AND LIMITS

Species	Open Season	Size and Bag Limit
Salmon	According to area	3 per day, 15 per week
Trout	Generally April 15–Sept. 15	20 per day, 6" minimum
	Lakes stocked with rainbow trout: July 1–Oct. 31	
Landlocked Salmon	April 15–Sept. 15	10 per day, 15" minimum
Black Bass	July 1–Oct. 31	10 per day, 9" minimum

Nonresident fishermen must be accompanied by a licensed guide. One guide may accompany three fishermen.

For complete regulations write: Wildlife Conservation, Department of Lands and Forests, Halifax, Nova Scotia.

PRINCE EDWARD ISLAND

Prince Edward Island, Canada's smallest province is only 140 miles long and varies from four to forty miles in width. It lies in the southern arm of the Gulf of St. Lawrence, cradled between the curve of the New Brunswick and Nova Scotia coasts. The highest point is only 500 feet above sea level and its low-lying, sandy shores are indented with many bays and arms of the sea, running far inland. Rivers and ponds are numerous.

The freshwater fish include brook trout, brown trout and some sea-run members of the same species. While the average is small, they have been taken up to 5 pounds. Rainbows have also been stocked in a few lakes and ponds. These introduced-fish have done well enough to produce some in the 7-pound class. In a few places they are also occasionally taken in tidal waters.

Atlantic salmon make a fall run into many of the rivers of the island; and offshore saltwater fishermen take mackerel, haddock, cod and hake.

While there are no lakes of major size, ponds are myriad throughout the island; and rivers are almost as numerous.

Prince Edward Island is liberally laced with highways, including a section of the Trans-Canada Highway (No. 1), which runs along the south shore. There is also rail service to most major towns of the island and branch lines to several smaller communities. Commercial air transportation is available to Summerside and Charlottetown, the capital. Ferry services operate between Cape Tormentine, New Brunswick and Borden, on the south coast, a distance of nine miles; and Caribou, Nova Scotia, and Charlottetown, a distance of fourteen miles.

The island is highly developed agriculturally and there are no remote areas with wilderness fishing, the angling being readily reached via highway, throughout. There are no dangerous wild animals and no poisonous snakes.

Prince Edward Island enjoys an extremely mild climate, with the summer heat seldom going above the high 70's. Light cotton clothes are suitable for daytime wear, light woolens for evening. Anglers will find hip boots sufficient for most rivers, though those who plan to try the estuary fishing for sea trout and those who fish for salmon in the fall will find the chest-high waders more satisfactory.

For trout and salmon an 8½-foot fly rod is ideal, in the latter case with an added 150 yards of backing to the line to take care of the salmon's long runs. The famed Parmachene Belle and Dark Montreal are probably the most widely-used trout flies, but the angler should also add the Silver Doctor, White Miller, Dusty Miller, Cowdung, Stone Fly, Jock Scott, Mosquito, Ibis and Orange Shrimp, in sizes 8 to 12. All the standard salmon patterns are good.

Many sea-run trout are taken by spinners using a medium-weight outfit with ¼-ounce spinners. The same gear will do nicely for fishing the lakes and ponds.

In general, there is freshwater fishing available from April 15th to the end of October. However, it must be remembered that the sea-run fish are migratory and enter the rivers only at certain times and for limited periods. So it is most important for anglers going to Prince Edward Island for such fish to make a careful check as to the schedule of the runs. Otherwise you may lose time and money by reaching the rivers when the fish are just not there. Most of the trout run from the salt into the freshwater streams occur in June but in some rivers they do not appear until July or even August. Anglers should make enquiries specifically about the stream they plan to fish. The dates are usually approximately the same each year in each river.

The salmon seldom come into Prince Edward Island rivers until fall, the peak season being late September and October. In these waters, possibly because of the mud and sand bottom, Atlantic salmon do not rise as well to a fly as they do elsewhere in their range.

Almost every mill pond and lake has its population of trout, usually brook trout and browns. Rainbow trout will also be found in Glenfinnan Lake, about fifteen miles from Charlottetown, the capital city. They have also been stocked at Keefe's Lake, about sixteen miles from Charlottetown, and in Scales' Pond at Freetown. In these lakes a few specimens up to 7 pounds have been taken. The season does not open until July 1st.

Ponds which have produced good trout fishing include Arsenault Pond, near Tignish, at the extreme northwestern tip of the island; Bank's Pond, near Freeland on Highway 12; Brander's, Found's and Campbell's Ponds, near Kensington, on Highway 2; Barlow's Pond, near Wellington, on Highway 2; Hunter River Pond and Stream, northwest of Charlottetown, on Highway 2; MacDonald's Pond near Crapaud, off the Trans-Canada Highway (Highway 1) on the south-central coast; MacLeod's and Stewart's Ponds, near Vernon, on Highway 3; Jerome Lewis Pond, near St. Peters, on Highway 2 along the north shore; several ponds near Souris, off Highway 2, at the eastern tip of the island; several more near Murray Harbour on Highway 4 and Annandale on Highway 5 in the same area; and Morrison's Pond and MacDonald's Pond, off Highway 5 near Cardigan. At Elmira, on Highway 16, at the northeastern tip of the island, fishing can be very good in East Lake and North Lake when the fish are running.

You can fish Cousin's Pond, Carr's Pond and Dalvay Lake in Prince Edward Island National Park on the north-central shore, without a license.

Popular rivers with fishermen are the Tignish, Kildare, Brudenell, Marchbank's Stream and Mill River East, all of which can be reached from Alberton, via Highway 2, at the northwestern end of the island. Other highly regarded streams in this area, and all accessible from Highway 2 are the Little Pierre Jacques, Big Pierre Jacques, Foxley, Sheep, Sunnyside Stream and Grand.

In the central part of the province Hunter River Stream and Campbell's Stream are along Highway 2. Wheatley River Stream is reached from Highway 7. From Highway 1 (Trans-Canada Highway) you can fish the West River at several places, and the North River near Charlottetown. The Vernon River and Vernon River Stream are reached from Highway 3.

Fishable rivers in the eastern part of the island include the Hay River, near St. Peters, reached via Highway 2; the Montague and Cardigan, reached from Highway 3; the Belle River, from Highway 4; and the Grand from Highway 5.

The rivers which have the best runs of sea trout are the Brudenell, Montague, Vernon, Murray, Mill, Kildare, Cardigan and its tributaries, the Seal and Mitchell. Salmon move into many of the same rivers in the fall, but in limited numbers, and as mentioned earlier, do not readily rise to a fly.

Saltwater fishing in Prince Edward Island is pretty well limited to handlining for such edible species as the haddock, hake, cod and mackerel, but a few anglers now go out for mackerel with fly rods and spinning gear, taking fish up to 5 pounds. Charters are obtainable at Alberton Harbour, Stanley Bridge Wharf, Rustico Harbour, Covehead Harbour, Savaga Harbour, North Lake and Launching Harbour. The price is usually from $3 to $10 per person for a day or half-day trip.

The booklet "Where to Fish on Prince Edward Island" is obtainable from the Prince Edward Island Travel Bureau, Box 1087, Charlottetown, Prince Edward Island. It lists many ponds and streams you won't find on any map, but the province is small enough that with this book and a few local inquiries, you can find them readily. Prospective visitors should also obtain "Prince Edward Tourist Accommodations," as the details given about the resorts usually supply information as to whether there is fishing available in the area.

PRINCE EDWARD ISLAND FISHING REGULATIONS

Resident Fishing License	$1.00
Nonresident Fishing License	$3.00

SEASONS AND LIMITS

Species	Open Season	Size and Bag Limit
Trout	April 15–Sept. 30	20 per day
Rainbow Trout in Glenfinnan and O'Keefe's Lakes	July 1–Oct. 31	3 per day, 10″ minimum
Salmon	June 5–Oct. 31	6 per day, 21 per week

Above regulations do not pertain to National Park.

For complete regulations write: Travel Bureau, Charlottetown, P.E.I.

NEW BRUNSWICK

Roughly rectangular in shape, the Province of New Brunswick has an even division of the geographic attributes of piedmont and sea. In the west it borders on the State of Maine, in the north on the Province of Quebec, and the contiguous country partakes of their hilly, evergreen country with its lakes and streams. On the south and west the Atlantic Ocean washes the shores, broken by land only where a neck runs southeastward to join it with the Province of Nova Scotia. That Province, hooking around to the southwest, forms the great Bay of Fundy, further enhancing the seacoast of New Brunswick. With this double-natured topography, New Brunswick has a variety of fishing opportunities. The Atlantic salmon is the quarry of the majority of fishermen who come to New Brunswick, but there are also speckled or eastern brook trout, smallmouth black bass, landlocked salmon, lake trout, eastern chain pickerel and perch in the fresh waters; while the salt offers some big-game fishing off the northeast coast for tuna, as well as angling for the nomads of the east coast, the striped bass and the shad. There are also lesser bottom feeders such as pollack and cod.

In the northwestern highlands of the Maine and Quebec border area, in some cases the altitude rises to more than 2,000 feet, and from these heights the rivers flow south and east at every angle. The two main streams are at absolute variance with each other, the St. John flowing from the northwest border, southward through the entire western part of the province to enter the Bay of Fundy; while the Miramichi rises in the south-central section and flows northeast to the Atlantic Ocean. The many lesser rivers follow the same pattern, dividing the drainage equally between south coast and east coast, from the high central dome of the interior.

While lakes are numerous there are none of great size, and they are of minor importance in the fishing scene.

Some 3,400 miles of good paved roads, with many secondary offshoots, provide access to the coastal areas of New Brunswick. Roads from many entrance points along the Maine border lead to Highway 2, which runs along the St. John River south to the sea at the city of St. John, then cuts eastward along the coast to Moncton, turns south and leads into Nova Scotia. In the north, from the Van Buren, Maine, point of entrance, Highway 17 traverses the northern part of the Provice to meet Highway 11 at Campbellton, from which Highway 11 goes down the east coast; while also from Campbellton, Highway 8 goes inland and cuts across the central part of the province to Fredericton. Entrance from Quebec is at Matapedia, Quebec, to Highway 11, which then follows the east coast, as mentioned, down to the southern extremity at Moncton. While many of the roads cross rivers, by ferry, all ferries are free.

There are three major airports, at Moncton, Fredericton and St. John. Both the Canadian National and the Canadian Pacific Railways serve the province.

Light cotton clothing is usually sufficient for daytime wear during summers in New Brunswick. The occasional cool day will call for lightweight underwear, and woolens are good to have at night. Those who come early in the season will need plenty of wool; and of course, every angler should have a waterproof jacket and hat. Moccasins or light hiking boots are suitable when traveling or fishing from a boat, but for hiking over rough trails in the backwoods, strong boots with 6- to 10-inch high leather tops and heavy soles will make the going easier.

Since the Atlantic salmon is the top sporting species in New Brunswick and since fishing for this gamefish is limited to fly rod and artificial fly only, anglers generally lean to this method in all their freshwater fishing. Although some salmon anglers still prefer the old-time 10- to 12-foot salmon rods, most modern fly men use an 8½- to 9½-foot rod weighing five to seven ounces. These are designed to carry the torpedo-tapered GAF and GBF lines which make for longer casting with greater ease, and long casts are required more than is the case in trout fishing. Leaders for these outfits are tapered from a 30-pound-test butt section to 8-, 6- or sometimes even 4-pound-test tippet, the choice being usually determined by the nature of the water plus the ability of the fisherman to handle a heavy fish on light tackle.

The same outfit can conveniently be used for bass fishing. For this species, it is also permissible to use other methods, and spinning and plug casting are both popular and successful.

In addition to the standard 35 yards of fly line, the salmon fisherman should use at least 200 feet of backing, of 14- or 18-pound-test nylon squidding line. Salmon may run in the 30-pound class or larger, on occasion, but even the average 6- to 10-pounder will give a good fight and take out plenty of line.

In New Brunswick, according to many guides and outfitters, there is a decided preference for the single-hook flies, in sizes from No. 2 to No. 10. Some anglers have individual preferences for non-standard patterns but usually the old stand-bys get good results. These include the Silver Doctor, Parmachene Belle, Jock Scott, Montreal, Brown and Gray Hackle, and the Black Gnat. The Wulff dry flies, and the Brown Bivisible, Pink Lady, all on size 8, 10 and 12 hooks, are also popular. When the water is low, the standard low-water salmon flies are used; sparsely tied, small flies, on size 10 and 12 hooks. Best patterns are the Silver Doctor, Black Doctor, Black Dose, Silver Gray, Thunder and Lightning, Jock Scott, and Blue Charm.

The outfit used for Atlantic-salmon fishing is heavier than you need for speckled-trout fishing, as the brookies run much smaller. An 8-foot rod, weighing 4 ounces, that will handle an HDH line is about right. Leaders should be long, 10 to 12 feet, and tapered down to 4X or 5X. The fish also like their flies in size 12 or smaller.

The salmon season opens in some places as early as April 1st and continues through the summer, generally until September 15th but in some cases till October, early openings and late closing being by special permit. In fact the whole sport of salmon fishing is rigidly regulated to protect the sport and assure everyone partaking of their fair chance at fish. No one is permitted to fish other than by fly fishing, and the number of rods per mile of stream is limited. Not more than four salmon per day, including grilse (young salmon of 3½ to 5 pounds) may be taken by any angler, or a total of twenty-one per week.

Many of the salmon rivers are under lease to operators of fishing camps, who limit the fishing there to their guests, and again, regulate the number of rods per mile of stream, in order to assure no overcrowding.

When fishing for Atlantic salmon from a canoe or any type of water craft, the holder of a non-resident fishing license must employ the services of a licensed guide. Also, under regulations of the Forest Fire Act, non-residents must be accompanied by a guide when traveling through forest land. One guide may accompany up to three non-residents, in this case.

Anglers will hear of "spring angling" for black salmon, meaning early season fishing from ice-out to about the end of May; and also of "bright fishing," which means the fishing for new-run salmon, just in from the salt, and which usually occurs from early July to the end of September, depending on the river.

New Brunswick is a great hunting province, and in the interior bears are quite numerous, but need not be feared if you leave them alone. Deer will also frequently be seen. There are no poisonous snakes.

NORTHERN NEW BRUNSWICK

Practically all streams in the northern sector have access to the sea, insuring good movement of salmon. Thus, Northern New Brunswick includes most of the best salmon waters in the province. The famed Restigouche River rises inland a short distance northeast of Edmunston on Highway 2, in the northwestern corner. It flows southeast for a considerable distance, then turns northeast and forms part of the border between New Brunswick and Quebec before emptying into the Bay of Chalheur at the Quebec town of Matapedia, west of Campbellton, New Brunswick. Five and one-half miles of the main Restigouche is Crown Reserve Water where permission to fish must be secured each year by writing the Deputy Minister, Department of Lands and Mines, Fredericton, New Brunswick. This stretch of water is limited to eight rods per day from June 5 to August 31, Sundays excepted. Applications to fish these exclusive waters are given preference in order of their receipt. Anglers are accommodated at government-approved camps.

The Upsalquitch River rises in the north-central interior and flows north to the Restigouche at Robinsonville. This rivers and its branches, the Northwest Upsalquitch and the Southeast Upsalquitch, have excellent salmon fishing in July. Tulley Asbell runs a small camp for Atlantic salmon fishing near the mouth of the river. He can be addressed care of Austin Harris, Upsalquitch, New Brunswick.

There are thirty-one miles of Crown Reserve waters on the Upsalquitch. Fishing is limited to ten rods per day for the season from June 15 to August 31. Reservations are accepted and allotted by official drawing on March 15th. Crown Reserve angling licenses for the Upsalquitch are not refundable or transferable. For more information and for reservations, write Director, Fish and Wildlife Branch, P.O. Box 1024, Department of Lanes and Mines, Frederickton, New Brunswick.

Robert S. Firth, Manager of Ingeland Camp, has eight freehold pools on the Upsalquitch and takes care of fishing for six rods from June 15 to August 31. Address him at Robinsonville, New Brunswick.

Another famous stream in the northern sector is the Tobique. It has its headwaters in tributary streams rising in northwest New Brunswick, more or less on the back of the height of land which sheds water to the Upsalquitch. The Tobique flows southwest into the Saint John River at Perth, located on Highway 2, north from Fredericton. To fish the picturesque Tobique near its source, write James Black at Plaster Rock, R.R. 1, Victoria County, New Brunswick. His camp is situated at Nictau, some sixty-four miles by good road above Perth.

Rising directly east of the headwaters of the Tobique, the Nepisiguit flows from the Nepisiguit Lakes near Mount Carleton, the highest point in the province, at 2,690 feet, and flows northeast to Nepisiguit Bay at Bathurst on the extreme north-eastern coast. Its many tributaries include the Little Southwest, and South Nepisiguit Rivers and Forty-Four Mile Brook, all good trout and salmon streams. George Gray, Box 62, R.R. 5, South Bathurst, Gloucester County, New Brunswick, controls seven salmon pools on the Nepisiguit River, and caters to canoe-trip parties as well as those who wish to stay put for their fishing. The best times for salmon are July, August and September; while trout fishing is at its peak in June and July.

Marking the southern edge of the wilderness area of northern New Brunswick is the Miramichi River, with its many arms and tributaries. The river is easily approached via Highway 8 which touches the stream at many points from Boiestown to where it enters Miramichi Bay on the north-central coast. Some of its branches include the Bartholomew River, Dungarvon, Renous, North Pole Brook, Sevogle, as well as the Southwest and the Northwest Miramichi Rivers. All are well-served by camps offering fishing for speckled and sea trout as well as some of the best fly-rod angling for Atlantic salmon in Canada.

One of the most outstanding salmon runs in Canada occurs in the "Mountain Pool" on the Miramichi. Boyd's Fishing Lodge, located there, can be queried as to possibilities on this. The address is Tom Boyd, 65 Carleton Street, Fredericton, New Brunswick.

A good location on the lower Miramichi is Amos Munn Camp (a string of three), Renous, R.R. 1, Northumberland County, New Brunswick. There is good trout and salmon fishing. A second lodge at Renous is Nobconcli Lodge, Manager Don Paul Cliver, Renous, New Brunswick.

The Northwest Miramichi, a branch of the river running south to join the mainstream at Highway 8, south of Newcastle, is a good stream in itself and has several good tributaries, notably the Sevogle River. At Red Bank, on secondary road from Highway 8 at Derby Junction, anglers can stay at a camp operated by Murdock Sutherland, Box 205, Red Bank, R.R. 1, New Brunswick.

In addition to these streams, the Cains River is a top rated stream with salmon fishermen. The river has its origin in a game refuge south of the Southwest Miramichi River, and enters the main branch of the Miramichi at the town of Howard, reached by secondary road off Highway 8 at Blackville or Upper Blackville. At Howard the Neil Allen Camps has the principal accommodations and provides guide service for both the Cains and the Southeast Miramichi. The address of the camp is 8 Princess Street, Marysville, New Brunswick. Angling starts right after ice-out in April, but the best run is around early June. At the same time trout fishing is good.

Wendell V. Allen operates Poplar Camps four miles from the mouth of Cains River and another camp eight miles from the mouth. Both cater to those fishing for spring salmon, from ice-out until May 24th. The same outfit has three camps at the mouth of the Cains where fishing is for Atlantic salmon from October 1st to 15th. The address is Penniac, York County, New Brunswick. This late-season fishing can be combined with deer, bear and grouse shooting, which is good in this area.

Following either the coastal Highway 11, or the inland Highway 8, north from Miramichi Bay, you come to the outlet of the Tabusintac River, another beautiful stretch of salmon water. A secondary road leaves Highway 11 at Wishart Point on the coast, and leads to the river. Accommodations and guiding can be arranged through John L. Wishart, Wishart Point, New Brunswick.

While the Atlantic salmon overhadows all other species, there is some excellent trout fishing to be had in the same rivers that play host to the salmon. The speckled or brook trout is the most common species, and several of the rivers have some exciting fishing for the sea-going members of this species, the runs occurring around the end of May and in early June.

SOUTHERN NEW BRUNSWICK

Southern New Brunswick also contains many good salmon streams, though not of quite the caliber of the northern ones, and also has some good trout fishing, smallmouth bass in some lakes, and some pickerel, lake trout (togue) and perch.

The major river is the St. John, its entire length easily reached by the network of highways which laces this southern area. The river itself is bracketed by Highways 2 and 21, and most of the other major roads of the province come in to these two, at one point or another. In the St. John there is fair-to-good salmon fishing above Fredericton, which is at the junction of Highways 8 and 2. The best-known pools are Hartt's Island Pool, five miles above the city; the pools at Hartland, Bristol and Bath, the latter three near the Juniper Road, about 100 miles above Fredericton.

Arrangements for fishing the St. John and many lakes along its length can be made through M. McGann, Hillcrest View Lodge, Debec, R. R. 3, Carleton County, New Brunswick. There is good trout fishing in this whole area during May and June. Black bass, yellow and white perch are taken in June, July and August, pike from May through September, and Atlantic and landlocked salmon from June through August.

On a secondary road off Highway 2 at Junioer, anglers will find access to much excellent water in Little and Big Taegue Brook, Elliot Brook and the North and South Branches of the Miramichi, through Maurice Biggar, Junioer, New Brunswick.

The best smallmouth black-bass fishing in New Brunswick is found in the Chiputneticook chain of lakes on the southwest border between New Brunswick and Maine. Landlocked salmon are also found in fair quantity in this area. Magaguadavic Lake and its surrounding smaller lakes, are also good, and the St. Croix River, flowing from Chiputneticook Lake south to Passamaquoddy Bay is a good bass stream. Weldon Leeman, Forest City, Maine, U.S.A., operates camps on the Chiputneticook Lakes, with access to waters producing landlocked salmon, togue (lake trout), brook trout and smallmouth black bass, and George Welock has a lodge at Loon Bay, about twenty miles north of St. Stephen, where there is good early- and late-season fishing for smallmouth black bass and landlocked salmon in the lakes and trout fishing in the St. Croix River.

At the opposite extreme of this southern sector of Maine, on the far-east coast, in the Richibucto River, where Highway 34 comes out to the ocean, there is fishing for Atlantic salmon, trout, striped bass and perch. The best season is May and June. A camp on Richibucto is operated by Havelock Robertson & Son, Robertson, Route 2, Rexton, New Brunswick.

Most of the seaside towns in New Brunswick offer some fishing for saltwater species. Pollack fishing is attracting growing numbers of anglers to the Passamaquoddy Bay area on the southwest coast. Pollack, relatives of the cod, are taken on feathered jigs trolled with best results when the tide is rising or falling and the fish are chasing schools of herring. The pollack range up to 25 pounds in weight. Charter-boat fees will usually run about $20 for five hours fishing, with a minimum of two in the party. At Passamoquoddy Bay there is ferry service to Deer, Campobello and Grand Manan Islands, and boats are available on all three for saltwater fishing ventures. On the mainland there are accommodations at two large fishing camps at McDougall Lake, which offer their patrons a chance at both saltwater fish and freshwater varieties. The lake is reached via secondary road from St. George on the coastal Highway 1. From these camps you can reach the Magaguadovic and Digdeguash Rivers, coming in from the northwest, both of which have good runs of salmon in season. Write George Matheson, Bonny River, Charlotte County, New Brunswick.

Kent Ross, of St. Andrews, New Brunswick, at the extreme southwest tip, where Highways 1 and 41 come down to Passamoquoddy Bay, can arrange for boats for salt water fishing throughout the Grand Manan Island, Passamoquoddy Bay and Bay of Fundy area.

There is ferry service to the islands and accommodations are available on the mainland nearby at Chamcook Lake Fishing Camp, Charlotte County, New Brunswick. At the camp there is landlocked salmon and lake-trout fishing. A little further north on Highway 3, there are also accommodations at Alex Hovey's Camp, Moore's Mills, with access to the St. Croix River and several small lakes and streams for smallmouth black bass, pickerel, landlocked salmon and trout.

About fifty miles northeast of St. John, Highway 14 leaves Highway 2 and leads down to the coast to Fundy National Park. Here there is salmon fishing in the Wolf River and several smaller streams. Boats can be rented at Bennett and Wolfe Lakes. No license is required to fish either trout or salmon waters within the park boundaries, and the season is open on both species from June 15 to September 15.

There are some motel and housekeeping cabin accommodations, but reservations should be made early, through George Marks, Havelock, New Brunswick, until May 1st; after that Alma, Albert County, New Brunswick; through Windsor Hotel, Moncton, New Brunswick, till May 1st; and through Robert Friars, Fundy Park Chalets, Alma, Albert County, New Brunswick.

NEW BRUNSWICK FISHING REGULATIONS

Resident Fishing License $2.50
Nonresident Fishing License (including salmon) $15.50
Nonresident Fiishing License (except salmon) $7.50
Nonresident 3-Day Fishing License (except salmon) $5.50

SEASONS AND LIMITS

Species	Open Season	Bag Limit
Salmon	May 15– Aug. 31, with exceptions	4 per day, 21 per week, with exceptions
Landlocked Salmon	April 15–Sept. 15, with exceptions	
Striped Bass	No closed season	No limit
Black Bass	April 1–Sept. 30	Local option
Trout	April 15–Sept. 15, with exceptions	Local option

Fishermen in forested areas and in waters holding Atlantic Salmon must be accompanied by a guide.

For complete regulations write: Fish and Wildlife Branch, Department of Lands and Mines, Fredericton, New Brunswick.

Mexico,
Bahamas,
Bermuda

MEXICO

Mexico, forming the southern end of the continent, has remained comparatively undeveloped as far as the fishing possibilities go. Only along the west coast have such spots as Guaymas, Mazatlan, Manzanillo and Acapulco become known to anglers as centers of tremendous fishing for the big-game species. With roads rapidly improving, plus increased access by air, conditions are changing, New saltwater areas are opening up, and fine bass and trout fishing is becoming available in the fresh waters of the interior. But anglers are looking more and more to the really exceptional fishing to be found along the coast. One of the most promising developments is the opening up of the peninsula of Baha California, the long arm of land which encloses the Gulf of California. A paved road now leads down from San Diego, California, some 200 miles to Rosario. From there down, the road is very dusty and bumpy. About halfway down there is intermittent ferry service from the small village of Santa Rosalia on the east coast of the peninsula, across the bay to Guaymas. Below that the dirt road continues for a few miles, then again you run into pavement to La Paz. A secondary road runs out around the end of the Peninsula and circles back to La Paz. It must be emphasized that this is a road for jeeps and pick-up trucks rather than low-slung cars, and that anyone attempting it should have complete supplies for camping if necessary and for car repairs, as well as a good supply of fresh water.

Access to the important fishing towns on the west coast of the mainland of Mexico is easy. State Highway 15, a good, paved road, extends from Nogales on the Arizona border to Guaymas, then follows the coast all the way down to Mazatlan. From there it gradually works inland to Guadalajara, thence east to Mexico City. There you can take Highway 95 to Acapulco. Air service is also excellent. Three airlines, from Tiajuana, Nogales and Juarez, serve Guaymas. Mazatlán has the second busiest airport in Mexico; and there's good service to Puerto Vallarta and Acapulco. Consult your travel agent for up-to-date schedules. There are also train connections and bus service to most parts of Mexico, but progress can be very slow. For instance the 250-mile train trip from Nogales to Guaymas takes eleven hours.

In the coastal fishing areas of Mexico the climate is tropical. You will want light cotton clothing, plenty of sunburn lotion, sunglasses, and a wide-brimmed hat. Also come prepared with something to counteract "tourists' disease" and NEVER drink tap water or eat raw vegetables. Carry plenty of insect repellent, and particularly if you go into the interior beware of ticks. There are several kinds which can make your life almost unbearable. However, few are found in the north-central zone or at higher altitudes.

GULF OF CALIFORNIA

The Gulf of California is often referred to as the world's greatest fishtrap because the northward-migrating fish move into it in such tremendous numbers. Somewhere along its coasts there is fishing for almost any Pacific species you can name.

576

On the mainland at the head of the Gulf you can reach the small town of Puerto Peñasco via Arizona Highway 85 to the border, then Mexico Highway 8 to the coast. There is good surf fishing for sea trout, sea bass, pompano and Sierra mackerel. You can rent a skiff at Puerto Peñasco but bring your own motor. Charter boats are available for trolling offshore waters for sailfish and dolphin.

Guaymas is probably the easiest of the Mexican coastal towns to reach. It's a two-hour flight from Nogales by air, or you can drive the 250 miles on Highway 15, south from Nogales, a good paved road. There is also twice-daily bus service; and the already-mentioned train service, which takes 11 hours, and is not to be recommended. The town is highly developed as a sport-fishing center with a great variety of accommodations, ranging from the Playa de Cortes, a first-rate luxury Hotel to an excellent trailer court right on the beach. Rates at the Playa run about $12.50 per day with meals. At the Miramar Hotel next door, rates are considerably lower and it's a pleasant spot to stay. A fine fleet of fourteen fishing craft, equipped with ship-to-shore radio is docked at the Miramar and serves both hotels. Rates for fishing are from $6.50 to $7.50 per hour, depending on the size of the boat. Capacity is six persons and the minimum charter is 6 to 8 hours. There are also two party boats which leave the pier at 8 a.m. and return at 2 p.m., then go out again until 7 p.m. The cost is $8.50 per person and the number is limited to seven persons per boat. The fare includes tackle, bait and all equipment. Outboards and skiffs may also be rented by those who wish to fish the bay waters on their own.

For overnight cruises a 48-foot diesel-powered boat, the Nautilus, is available. The capacity is six people, at a rate of $100 per 24-hour day. Cruises can go as far as Mazatlan down the coast, or across the bay to La Paz.

Arrangements for all the above hotel and boat accommodations should be made through Tom Jamison, Hotel Playa de Cortes or Hotel Miramar, Guaymas, Mexico, by airmail, phone or telegraph. Phone 36 or 121.

The fish working into the Gulf of California pretty well follow a schedule. At Guaymas, the best fishing for the various species is as follows: January and February: yellowtail, totoaba, grouper, sea bass, sierra, pompano, corvina, rock bass, red snapper. March and April: striped marlin, yellowtail, totoaba, grouper, sea bass, sierra, pompano, corvina, rock bass, red snapper. May, June and July: striped marlin, blue marlin, black marlin, sailfish, dolphin, sierra, giant grouper, white sea bass, jewfish. August, September and October: striped marlin, black marlin, blue marlin, sailfish, dolphin, sierra, roosterfish, corvina, yellowtail. November and December: striped marlin, yellowtail, totoaba, grouper, barracuda, pompano, corvina, rock bass, red snapper, bonefish.

Throughout the year there is good onshore fishing for casters who work the piers, bridges and beaches at Guaymas, or wade the beach at San Francisco Bay, only a few miles drive from the town. The writer, fishing the off-season, was lucky enough to take a 12-pound corvina on spinning tackle off the rock jetty right in front of the Playa de Cortes. The bay to the north of the town, where there is a nice sandy beach, can also be productive in season. Bonefish come in in tremendous numbers, but they are very small, seldom reaching two pounds, apparently a subspecies of the great sporting fish we catch in Florida and the Bahamas. But in season, casters working this beach may take any of the inshore species.

Following Highway 15 southward you reach Mazatlan, an equally famous fishing port. At Mazatlan the height of the sailfish season is from the middle of April to

December. These Pacific sails average about 100 pounds and a world record weighing 198 pounds was caught there in 1955 by George Anglem. The striped marlin come in about the middle of November and stay around until May. The largest known to have been taken at Mazatlan went 330 pounds, but the average will be about 145 pounds. Black marlin are also taken, in May, June and July, although they are not as numerous as the striped marlin. But they make up for it in size, the top fish taken being a 662-pounder, and plenty being caught weighing between 300 and 400 pounds. Mazatlan is the site of an Annual Deep Sea Fishing Tournament, usually in November. Those wishing to compete should bring their own tackle as the local fleet of charter boats supply only Class "C" tackle.

Charter-boat rates are from $55 to $75 per day. Skiffs and outboards are available for inshore fishing. There are several first-rate hotels at Mazatlan, including the fine new Hotel de Cima; and there are quite a number of camping areas.

Beside the marlin and sailfish already mentioned, Mazatlan waters include dolphin, red snapper, mackerel, yellowtail, bonito, roosterfish, sea bass and snook. In the harbor there are red snapper, grouper and Sierra mackerel. A little more than a mile to the south of the entrance to the port there are some fine sand flats where you can usually find roosterfish in conditions ideal for casting.

SOUTHERN COASTAL AREA

Manzanillo, well south of Mazatlan, can be reached by highway 80, leaving Highway 15 at Guadalajara, or by rail from that city. Sailfish and marlin seem to be in this area almost year-round and there are many species of smaller fish but sport fishing has been little developed. The best time is from December to May, when the climate is pleasant and there is not too much rain. The Hotel Playa de Santiago can provide more complete fishing information.

Acapulco has long been the most popular fishing resort in Mexico. The city has grown to considerable size and has taken on all the aspects of a tourist town but the fishing is still there and, as is all too-seldom true of most Mexican fishing ports, there are good charter boats available. You can reach Acapulco either by plane or by Highway 95 from Mexico City. Sailfishing is as good here as anywhere in the world. There are also marlin and they are of considerable size, though not in as great numbers as further north. Dolphin are plentiful and follow their usual custom of hanging about anything that floats in the water. Yellowfin tuna, pargo, jack crevalle, skipjack, roosterfish and Sierras are also taken. However, on this more open coast, the smaller fish are not as plentiful as they are farther north in the Gulf of California.

BAJA CALIFORNIA

The newest and most promising sport-fishing area to be developed in Mexico is the Peninsula of Baja California. Although most of it is still in extremely primitive condition, nevertheless it is possible to fly in to one or two spots where there is exceptional fishing to be had. By Aeronaves de Mexico Airlines from Tijuana, Guaymas, Mazatlan and Los Angeles, you can fly to La Paz, and from there it's a two-hour taxi ride to Rancho Buena Vista Lodge. Sometimes air taxis are available and in that case the trip will take only 30 minutes.

The fishing is so close to shore that you hardly have time to bait up before you are into fishing water. But the best fishing is around the group of islands offshore. There are black marlin, striped marlin, sailfish, roosterfish, mackerel, tuna, dolphin, skipjack, chiro or ladyfish, albacore, cabrilla, wahoo, snappers and needlefish. Broadbill swordfish are taken occasionally. Deep fishing brings up groupers, snappers and jewfish. Dolphin have gone as high as 77 pounds 12 ounces, and a 35 pound 3 ounce dolphin was taken on 10-pound-test spinning tackle. Yellowtail run regularly in the 20-pound class and a 42-pounder was taken on 10-pound-test spinning tackle. These are only a few of the fish that have earned La Paz its fast-growing reputation. There are also yellowfin tuna believed to be in the 200-pound class, and needlefish have been seen 6 feet long. April through June are the best months weather-wise, as winds can be bad at other times. For full details contact Charles M. Walters, P.O. Box 1486, Newport Beach, California. Phone 3-4638.

EAST COAST

There is also some excellent and mostly undeveloped fishing along the east coast of Mexico, on the Gulf. Access is fairly easy by Highway 101 south from Brownsville, Texas, at the mouth of the Rio Grande River which forms the international border here. Tarpon move well up into the Rio Grande early in the spring and remain until October or even November. Those who fish the river for them have discovered that these river tarpon often lie deep, coming up to roll for air only occasionally, and that most times you have to fish deep to get them, using a jig or other heavy lure to go down where the fish are lying. Trolling will pick up a few but more will be taken by casting a jig into the deep holes cut by the current around the river bends.

Baby tarpon, on the other hand, behave just like they do in Florida waters. Make your cast in against the mangrove limbs and the chances are a baby will come out and sock it.

One disadvantage about the Rio Grande is that it is frequently muddy for weeks at a time, making fishing very uncertain.

You can stay at Brownsville, but bring your own boat as there are few available on the river. Casting from the banks is sometimes successful and those who work their way down to the mouth of the river often find snook and channel bass in the surf.

Immediately to the south, the Laguna Madre, enclosed by a peninsula and a string of islands, although heavily fished commercially, is still one of the best spots for the casting fraternity as there are flats with weakfish, channel bass, snook and ladyfish. Unfortunately seining is rapidly spoiling this fishing.

The Soto la Marina River, flowing into the Gulf about halfway between Brownsville and Tampico, provides much the same conditions as are found throughout the Gulf States and the same species of fish: tarpon, redfish and sea trout. There is one hotel, but the area has not been developed.

Tampico, on the other hand, provides everything for the fisherman in the way of accommodations and boats and tops it off with some excellent fishing for tarpon, snook, channel bass or redfish, sheepshead, jewfish, sea trout, pompano, mackerel, pargo, catfish and perch. There are also sailfish and marlin offshore, but to date little fishing has been done for these species.

The Panuco River enters the Gulf at Tampico and the whole situation makes for good light-tackle fishing. There's good casting for snook, with some tarpon thrown in, and if you work up into the tributaries of the Panuco you eventually come to black bass country.

The Panuco River, running through the city, offers exciting tarpon fishing. The best season is from early spring to July, at which time the river is likely to become muddy from heavy rains. Even then you can sometimes take tarpon at the mouth of the river. A big annual tarpon rodeo is held in April, indicating the peak of the season.

If you have the urge to do battle with a monster jewfish, this is the spot. Around the jetties on the Panuco, they have been taken up to 700 pounds. All the lagoons down this coast offer the same kind of fishing, much of it scarcely touched by sport fishermen.

The Tamiahua Lagoon, to the south of Tampico, is very good for sea trout and "corbina." You can get boats at Tampico to make the run down via canal which connects with the lagoon.

Reefs around the islands lying off Tampico offer excellent barracuda fishing, and also produce jacks, tarpon, pargo and sometimes wahoo.

Continuing south from Tampico, via Highway 180, you come to Tuxpan. This is a very good stretch of coast. Bring your own motor, but it is possible to rent a skiff. You can get into some good fishing for tarpon, barracuda, mackerel, snapper, snook and many other fish around the mouth of the Tuxpan River. Reefs offshore provide ideal grounds for a great variety of fish including jack crevalle, jewfish, barracuda, pargo, tarpon, wahoo, mackerel and groupers. Boats and guides may be obtained through the several hotels in the city, which incidentally, can be reached by both air and rail, as well as road.

May, June and July are the best months to fish Gulf waters, as later in the season there can be a great deal of wind, making it hazardous to venture out.

Just south of Veracruz, at the town of Alvarado, there is excellent opportunity for casting for snook and tarpon, but the area has not been developed in any way and you pretty much have to find your own fishing.

The Bay of Campeche, formed by the big curve of Mexico up to the Yucatan Peninsula, promises to be one of the country's top fishing areas of the future. A big lagoon, Laguna de Terminos, shelters the village of Ciudad del Carmen, where some accommodations are available. The best fishing is in April, May and June. The tarpon fishing is outstanding, big barracuda are plentiful, as are big pargo, and there are great schools of ladyfish. Sea trout are everywhere and the snook will break you up. While local accommodations are limited, there is an excellent fishing camp, El Tarpon Tropical, located on the peninsula of Aguada. It can be reached by a 700-mile flight from Galveston. The camp is set in a region of creeks, flats and mangrove swamps that make ideal territory for snook and tarpon. The tarpon range all the way from babies of 5 pounds up to monsters of 190 pounds. The smaller ones seem to stay in the creeks and alongshore, while the bigger ones hang out in the Laguna de Terminos, the bay enclosed by an island along which Highway 180 runs. Inshore fishing also brings snapper, jacks, sea trout, mackerel, ladyfish, grouper and barracuda. For reservations write Hal Hassey, Apartado Num. 40, Carmen, Campeche, Mexico.

FRESHWATER FISHING

Mexico's inland waters are even more difficult to reach than the salt. In general, it can be said that the tropical rivers of the south hold bass, while the mountain lakes and streams hold trout, mostly rainbow.

Around Veracruz there is some good fishing for black bass, black trout and catfish. the bass season is open year-round. There is a limit of twenty-five per day. The trout season extends from March 1 to October 31, and the limit is fifteen per day. There is no closed season and no bag limit on catfish.

Between Mexico City and Guadalajara there is some fine fishing for bass in Lake Patzcuaro, or the Lake of the Humming Birds, second in size of all Mexican lakes only to Lake Chapala. The latter, nearby, has some bass but very few. Anglers who have fished both claim it's a draw whether Lake Patzcuaro or Don Martin Lake near Nuevo Laredo, far to the north, is the best bass lake in Mexico. Lake Patzcuaro is very weedy, so take plenty of weedless lures.

Lake Tequeuzquintengo, south of Mexico City, has some good-sized bass, but the lake is greatly used for pleasure boating, which usually puts the damper on the fishing.

Between Mexico City and Guadalajara there are a number of small rivers and lakes which can be fished from the road. The largest one, the Salitre, and the lake of the same name, can be quite good from October to May, but at other times are too muddy to fish. Some of the tributaries hold brook trout.

In general it can be said that Mexico's rivers are clear from October to May, which is the dry season. Float trips are possible on many at this time, and you can vary your fishing from bass or trout in the upper waters to snook and sea trout as you come down to tidewater.

Mexico's trout fishing is mostly on the high plateau in the Mexico City area and is the result of the stocking of rainbows and brook trout. The country is usually high enough in altitude that you will need warm clothing and the roads are often narrow, rough and treacherous. But you may find 5-pound rainbows in some of the dams on the higher rivers.

For further information about fishing in Mexico, anglers should write the Direccion General de Turismo, Avenida Juarez, Num. 89, Mexico, F.D.

MEXICO FISHING REGULATIONS

No passport or visa is required, but pick up a Tourist Card at the border.

Nonresident Fishing License, yearly	$20.00
Nonresident 3-Month Fishing License	$10.00
Nonresident 1-Month Fishing License	$4.00

THE BAHAMAS

The Bahamas consist of a chain of islands lying in the Atlantic Ocean, starting directly east of Palm Beach, on the Florida coast, and extending southward to within fifty miles of Cuba. The nearest point in the Bahamas to the United States is Bimini Island, only fifty miles from Miami. The outer islands face on the Atlantic, the inner ones on the Straits of Florida and the Old Bahama Channel between the islands and Cuba.

The Bahamas are formed by upjuttings of coral and sandstone. In many cases the islands are surrounded by vast "banks," shallow flats which are navigable only with small boats, but through which are channels giving access to the land. The topography thus offers suitable habitat for almost every variety of saltwater fish, from deep-water to shallow-water swimmers, from cruisers to reef dwellers.

The species available include Allison tuna, blackfin tuna, bluefin tuna, amberjack, barracuda, bonefish, blue marlin, white marlin, sailfish, bonito, dolphin, grouper, kingfish, tarpon, wahoo, snapper, yellowtail, permit, mackerel, horse-eye jack, crevalle jack, the odd black jack, blue runners, oceanic bonito, kingfish, mako shark, mutton snapper or muttonfish as it is called locally and a few of the extremely rare spearfish have been taken in Bahama waters.

The islands are served by such major airlines as Pan American World Airways and British Overseas Airways, as well as a number of smaller but well-established local lines. Pan American and BOAC operate between New York and Nassau, the capital, on New Providence Islands; BOAC also flies between Nassau and Montreal, Toronto, Bermuda, London and Lima, Peru.

Local airlines which provide service from the Florida coast are Mackey Airlines, Bahamas Airways, Chalk's Flying Service, and such charter services as Cat Cay Airlines. Most may be contacted at Miami International Airport, West Palm Beach Airport and Fort Lauderdale Airport. Chalk's Flying Service is headquartered at 368 NE 57th Street, Miami 37; and Midet Aviation Company at International Airport, West Palm Beach.

From Nassau, Bahamas Airways and Mackey Airlines fly regularly scheduled flights to many of the "out islands," as the more remote cays are called; and the non-scheduled lines offer charter services to the same areas. There are airstrips at West End, Grand Bahama Island, Marsh Harbour, Andros Island, Eleuthera Island, Great Exuma Island, San Salvador, which is the most eastern island and Columbus' first landfall, and Little Inagua and Great Inagua Islands, the most southern in the group. Some resorts also operate seaplane service exclusively for their guests.

Many anglers fly their own planes to the Bahamas. Persons wishing to do so should obtain a copy of "Private Plane Facilities in the Resort Islands of the Bahamas," from the Ministry of Tourism, Nassau in the Bahamas. It lists all facilities in detail, giving the times when the various airstrips are open for traffic and provides information as to regulations governing plane entry.

Steamship service to the islands is via the S.S. Italia and the S.S. Nassau, weekly, from New York; and via overnight steamer from Miami to Nassau, twice weekly. Reservations may be made through any travel agent.

582

The islands are a favorite area for cruising, and, in fact, there are still many choice spots which can only be adequately fished from a base aboard a cruiser. Charter-boat services are available at Miami, West Palm Beach and Nassau marinas. Current lists of such services may be obtained from the Ministry of Tourism, Nassau in the Bahamas. Prices vary greatly according to the type of transport and the area to which you wish to travel. $300 to $400 per week, plus food and fuel, is a good basis on which to figure costs.

Daily offshore and reef fishing trips aboard charter boats operating out of resorts and public docks, run from $45 to $125 per day, with bait, fuel and tackle supplied. Inshore guides for bonefish and other light-tackle species, charge from $25 to $50 per day, and the angler usually brings his own tackle.

The Bahaman climate is pleasantly warm and humid. The average January temperature is 71 degrees; the lowest on record for that month is 51 degrees. The average temperature in mid-summer is about 82 degrees, with a maximum in the very low 90's. Throughout the year the percentage of humidity remains in the low 70's. Light tropical clothing is in order for fishing. Newcomers to the sun should wear long-sleeved shirts and long slacks to avoid a painful sunburn. Wide-brimmed hats are also a necessity, and may be purchased in the colorful native straw markets. To this, add rubber-soled sneakers and a rain jacket, preferably the long "boat-length" type, a plentiful supply of suntan lotion, and you are ready to fish Bahaman waters. It's also wise to bring some insect repellent.

While informal clothing is nearly always in order, many resorts request that guests wear a jacket and tie at the dinner hour. For ladies, Bermuda-length shorts are suitable for daytime wear, and light cotton dresses for evenings.

Charter boats supply the angler with suitable tackle for offshore trolling for the big-game species, and for reef fishing. Except at Nassau, experienced anglers may find the equipment a little limited, and if you like to fish with balanced tackle it is well to bring your own 12-, 20-, and 80-pound-test outfits.

Casters should also bring their own tackle and a plentiful supply of good-producing lures and flies, as few will be available in the islands.

For such shallow-water swimmers as the bonefish, one of the most popular species, a light saltwater spinning outfit is good, a 6½- or 7-foot, medium-action rod, weighing from 5 to 7 ounces, and a reel that will hold 400 yards of 6- or 8-pound-test monofilament line. For offshore fishing, and for bigger, inshore fish, a 7½- or 8½-foot rod, weighing 7 to 10 ounces, and a reel big enough to carry 400 yards of 10- or 12-pound-test line is better.

Fly fishermen use a 9- or 9½-foot rod with GAAF (WF10F) or GAF (WF9F) line, and leader tapered down to 8-pound-test tippet for bonefish and other small inshore fish; for larger fish, the same rod and line, with leader tippet of 12-pound-test strength.

Plug casting is not widely practised in Bahaman waters, but plenty of fish can be taken by this method. Heavy plug-casting gear is particularly good for deep jigging for big groupers and snappers and for casting to 40- to 50-pound tarpon and other larger fish. The best outfit is a 6 foot 2 inch long-plug rod, usually glass, weighing 4 or 5½ ounces. This stout stick is required to cast lures weighing 1 to 3½ ounces and also for lifting and pulling a big fish your way. The Pflueger Supreme plug-casting reel with level wind and cub drag matches the rod perfectly. The reel holds 205 yards of 15-pound-test monofilament.

In order to counteract the sharp teeth and rough scales of many of the big-fish species, many anglers use a length of 40-, 50-, 80- or even 100-pound-test nylon at the end of the line.

Casters will find all the standard lures and flies used in other saltwater areas are good fish takers in the Bahamas. Most inshore species will also take bait, usually finny crabs or cut pieces of conch. Small live fish such as grunts are also used.

For offshore trolling, captains use feathers, strip bait, mullet and small bonefish for blue marlin.

While there is no "season" and no license is required for fishing in the Bahamas, there are certain periods when different species are found in these waters in greatest numbers. For the more important species, these are the seasons and areas:

Allison tuna: Some throughout the year in all deep-water areas. Best in June, July and August.

Barracuda: Year-round throughout area.

Blackfin tuna: All deep-water areas, especially numerous around Nassau. May through September, best months.

Bluefin (giant) tuna: May 7 to June 15th. Bimini, Cat Cay and West End, Grand Bahama.

Bonefish: Year-round throughout the islands. Best period, March through early July, slack off during heat of summer. Fishing picks up again in late October through early December, slacks off again during January and February.

Blue marlin: Some throughout the year. Best months, June and July. Most common on western side of the northern islands, Bimini to Walker Cay. Also Tongue of the Ocean off Andros and Berry Islands; Exuma Sound; and in the Atlantic from Exuma northward to Green Turtle Cay.

Bonito: Very plentiful around Nassau but found in all deep-water areas. May through September, best time.

Dolphin: Some all year in all deep-water areas. Best time, winter and spring.

Grouper: Year-round in almost all reef areas. Spring months best.

Kingfish: Found throughout the islands, with the Berry Islands and Bimini the recognized hot spots. Peak season is May through July but schools may be found year-round.

Permit: Found throughout the islands. Best times, March through June; and October through December.

Sailfish: Hot spots are the Berry Islands, Cat Cay, Bimini, Walker Cay, West End, Exuma Sound and Tongue of the Ocean. Season is from fall through winter and into spring.

Tarpon: Not plentiful, this species will run about 40 pounds. Some are taken year-round in scattered areas throughout the islands. Many of those taken are caught at night.

Wahoo: November through April in most deep-water areas. Exuma Sound, near the southern end of Eleuthera is a top spot; also Northeast and Northwest Providence Channels, north of Nassau.

White marlin: Fall through spring, from Bimini eastward to Eleuthera; and from Walker Cay south to Exuma Sound, in the ocean and channels.

The famous "blue holes" of the Bahamas, dotted here and there throughout the islands, furnish some great sport at all times of the year. These holes are usually

100- to 300-foot circles of brilliant blue in the midst of the green-hued inshore waters. They harbor tarpon, jacks, snapper and grouper, and often bonefish as well. When you first fish a blue hole you think you've found the jackpot, for strikes are fast and furious. But like fish in any confined area, they eventually get on to you, and then you have to move on to the next hole.

There is no wild game in the Bahamas and there are no poisonous snakes. Sand flies, mosquitoes and a few deer flies are the only hazards. Anglers who wade the beaches in search of their fish should wear canvas sneakers to guard against stepping on sharp shells, coral and sea urchins, any of which can inflict a nasty wound. On a few of the keys there are poisonwood trees, similar to those of Florida, and visitors should learn to recognize this tree in order to avoid an unpleasant, poison-ivy-like infection.

Waders should also avoid going into very deep water. Although there are few, if any, reports of shark attacks in these islands, large sharks often cruise close in and it is well to avoid them. There are lots of barracuda inshore, too, but they seem merely curious, and while they will often swim in close for a look-see, as far as I know none has ever attacked a wader.

The Bahamas divide geographically into several groups: the western Bahamas, including Cat Cay and Bimini; the northern Bahamas, including Grand Bahama Island, the Abaco Cays, Green Turtle Cay and Great Abaco; the Central Bahamas, encompassing Nassau on New Providence Island, Andros Island, the Joulter Cays and Berry Islands; and the Eastern Bahamas, including Eleuthera and the Exuma Cays.

WESTERN BAHAMAS

The islands of Cat Cay and Bimini, lying between the main body of the Bahamas and the Florida coast, are only fifty miles from Miami, and have long been regarded as one of the great fishing spots of the Atlantic coast. There is excellent fishing for blue marlin, white marlin and other species taken by deep-water trolling; and fine bonefish flats which have produced many record bonefish and permit. One of the world's greatest bonefish guides, Bonefish Sam Ellis, fishes out of Bimini.

Bluefin tuna make an annual migration past Bimini and Cat Cay between mid-May and mid-June, to provide some of the world's most exciting fishing as boats gather here from all parts of the Florida coast to try for the big tuna.

Hotels are available on Bimini and fishing trips will be arranged by the management. The hotels include the Compleat Angler, Ocean View and Seacrest, Anchors Aweigh Hotel, Bimini Big Game Fishing Club, Bimini Marina Cottages and Brown's Hotel. Reservations may be made directly with the hotels at Bimini, or through Chalk's Fly Service, 368 NE 57th Street, Miami 37, Florida. Reservations at the Avis Bimini Club can be made through Walter Scheff, Box 1446, Coral Gables, Florida, or at the hotel itself.

CENTRAL BAHAMAS

Nassau, on New Providence Island, is the capital city of the Bahamas. It is a major seaport and airport and a large fleet of charter boats is located there, to fish the surrounding cays and channels and charter for trips to more distant waters. Close to Nassau will be found excellent fishing for albacore, Allison tuna, oceanic bonito, wahoo, kingfish and barracuda. The all-tackle world-record wahoo, weighing 133½ pounds, was taken at Little Green Cay near Nassau in 1943. Wahoo fishing is best in the Nassau area during the winter months. During this period large Allison tuna also run along the Tongue of the Ocean, the channel between Andros and the Exumas. As the wahoo-run dwindles in the spring, kingfish appear in great numbers. During the summer there are tremendous schools of oceanic bonito and albacore in the offshore waters around Nassau.

Further afield are the vast bonefish flats of the Berry Islands, Joulters Cay and Andros Island, the latter offering bonefish, reef fish, tarpon and ladyfish in the channels; marlin, sailfish and amberjack in the deep water; and snappers and groupers in the blue holes. Generally it calls for an overnight trip from Nassau to fish these islands. Daily charters out of Nassau run between $40 and $50 in the summer; $50 to $75 in the winter. As mentioned earlier, longer charters will cost about $300 to $400 plus food and fuel, per week.

Andros is the largest of the Bahama Islands. There are facilities at Fresh Creek, with many miles of excellent trolling water available. There are marlin, both blue and white, sailfish and mako sharks. Tarpon are found in the Fresh Creek area and the blue holes produce fine fishing for groupers, snappers, jacks, ladyfish and tarpon. The same species are found in the many reef and channel areas. For accommodations at Fresh Creek, anglers should write The Lighthouse Club, Box 758, Nassau, Bahamas; the Andros Island Fishing Club, Nicholls Town, Andros, Bahamas; Small Hope Bay Lodge, Fresh Creek, Andros, Bahamas; and the Andros Fishing Camp, Mrs. Clifford Johnson, Nicholls Town, Andros Island, Bahamas. On Pot Cay, in North Bight, on Andros, the Bang Bang Club is one of the oldest fishing clubs in the Bahamas. The camp may be reached via Nassau Overseas Operator, or through P.O. Box 1125, Nassau, Bahamas.

Just ten miles north of Andros are the famed Joulter Cays, an area of vast sand and marl flats, sometimes underwater, sometimes high and dry. It's ideal territory for bonefish, schools of which may often be seen milling along the edge of the flats waiting for high tide to put sufficient water on the banks so they can swim up in search of food. Channels through the banks also offer fishing for barracuda, jacks, muttonfish and tarpon. On the eastern side of Joulters there are reefs and coral heads, adding to the fishing possibilities, with grouper, snapper, cuda and jacks.

Immediately to the north of Joulters the Berry Islands form a curve where the Northeast Providence Channel and the West Providence Channel come together, to the north of Nassau. Anglers fish these waters by charter from Nassau; and there is a resort at Frazer's Hog Cay, one of the southern islands of the group. Reservations may be made through Mel Borne, Manager, Frazer's Hog Cay Club, Limited, c/o 9750 SW 63rd Court, Miami, Florida. The catch may include blue marlin, white marlin, wahoo, sailfish, kingfish, false albacore, bonito, Allison tuna, blackfin tuna and dolphin in the trolling waters, and many other species along the reefs. Tarpon are found in the channel along Frazier's Hog Cay and there are bonefish on most of the flats. In some cases casters can take amberjack, horseye jack, barracuda, snapper, yellowtail, groupers and blue runners while casting from shore. In the blue holes there are tarpon.

The northern Bahamas include three large islands, Grand Bahama, Little Abaco Island and Great Abaco, as well as many other smaller cays such as Walker Cay in the north and a string of islands along the outer (eastern) shore of the Abacos, including Spanish Cay, Great Guana Cay and Man of War Cay. This is one of the most highly developed areas in the islands, with a number of airstrips and a variety of resorts, from the large Grand Bahama Club, Hope Bight Lodge and Angler's Club at West End on Grand Bahama, to small inns which take anywhere from four to a dozen people.

The Walker's Cay Club is one of the Bahamas' oldest resorts. There is excellent deep-water trolling for wahoo, sailfish, marlin and tuna, as well as reef fishing and bonefishing. Reservations may be made through The Manager, Walker's Cay Club, Walker's Cay, Bahamas.

At West End, on the western tip of Grand Bahama, only seventy miles across the Gulf Stream from Palm Beach, there is a fine marina, a charter-boat fleet, skiffs and skiff guides and a party boat for drift fishing. Accommodations are available at the Grand Bahama Hotel, Box 59-2375, International Airport, Miami, Florida. Also at the Buccaneer Club and Hope Bight Lodge, West End, Bahamas. At nearby Freeport are the Caravel Club and the Fishing Hole. At the east end of Grand Bahama, the Deep Water Cay Club caters especially to fishermen, and there are excellent bonefish flats, and also fishing for cuda, snappers and grouper; and a charter boat available for deep-water trolling. Reservations may be made through Gilbert Drake, Deep Water Cay Club, P.O. Box 1829, West Palm Beach, Florida. The resort can be reached by taxi from Freeport and West End, both of which are served by Mackey Airlines and Bahamas Airways; or by charter plane direct to Deep Water.

In the Abacos, most of the development of resorts has been along the lesser cays on each side of the main islands of Little Abaco Islands and Great Abaco Island. Many are small resorts with perhaps one or two deep-sea trolling boats and several skiffs and inshore guides available. On Green Turtle Cay on the east side of Little Abaco are several such resorts. These include Bluff House, Lowe's Beach Cottages, The Other Shore and Pimlin Bay Cottages, all addressed at Green Turtle Cay, Abaco, Bahamas; and the New Plymouth Inn, P.O. Box 645, Nassau, Bahamas. A little further south there are a few resorts at Hope Town. The Elbow Cay Club, Hope Town Harbour Lodge and Seaview Cottage may all be addressed at Hope Town, Abaco, Bahamas. Coral Cottage is reached through P.O. Box 1688, Nassau, Bahamas; and White Sound Club through Elbow Cay, Abaco, Bahamas.

At Cherokee Sound, fishermen will find facilities available through P.O. Box 645, Nassau, Bahamas; and Eastern Shore Cottages, March Harbour, Abaco, Bahamas.

Among the larger resorts in the area, Treasure Cay Club, Treasure Cay, Abaco, Bahamas, offers excellent bonefishing, and has good guides available. Other large resorts which cater to fishermen are the Guana Harbour Club, Gordon O'Gara, Manager, 169 S. Country Road, Palm Beach, Florida, or direct to Great Guana Cay, Abaco, Bahamas; and the Great Abaco Club, Marsh Harbour, Abaco, Bahamas.

EASTERN BAHAMAS

The eastern Bahamas include the "out islands" of Eleuthera, the Exuma Cays,

Long Island and the surrounding smaller cays. Eleuthera is well-developed, with several flights weekly via Bahamas Airways to Harbour Island, Governor's Harbour and Rock Sound, all of which provide resorts with facilities for fishermen. There are also charter boats at Spanish Wells, which is a flag-stop for the planes, but accommodations there are limited to boarding houses. There is good bonefishing in inshore waters, tarpon in the channels and creeks, and also jacks. In the northwestern part of Eleuthera and the southwest, there is good reef fishing and trolling in offshore waters, particularly in Northeast Providence Channel, to the north of the island. The species include wahoo, kingfish and dolphin in winter, and albacore and bonito in summer. There are also some Allison tuna, marlin and mackerel.

Harbour Island, at the northern end of Eleuthera, has a number of resorts where fishing guides may be obtained. These include Pink Sands Lodge, Allen Malcolm, Manager; Picaroon Cove Club, Basil Albury, Manager; Little Boarding House, Miss Hattie Thompson, Manager; and Bottom Harbour Cottages. All may be addressed at Harbour Island, Bahamas.

There are a number of larger resorts at Governor's Harbour on Eleuthera, including the Belmont, Buccaneer Club, Balara Bay Water Sports Center, Cleartide Inn, French Leave and Potlach Club, all addressed at Governor's Harbour, Bahamas. Other clubs, reached through Nassau, are the Hatchet Bay Yacht Club and Cottages, Harrisville Company, Box 677, Nassau Bahamas; and the Cotton Bay Club and Rock Sound Club, Albert Moser, Box 8, Nassau, Bahamas. The latter has access to a good fleet of deep-sea and reef-fishing boats based at nearby Davis Harbour.

Two small resorts which cater to anglers are the Current Club, Hugh Young, Manager, Box 343, Nassau, Bahamas; and Moontide Cottages, Current Island, Eleuthera, Bahamas.

Southeast of Nassau lie the Exuma Cays, with a great variety of water offering all types of fishing because of the fact that on the east, Exuma Sound falls away to great depths suitable for deep-sea species, while on the west are the shallow Bahama Banks, for inshore species. There are few resorts. The major one is Peace And Plenty, William J. Thomson, Manager, George Town, Exuma, Bahamas. This is the home of the annual "Out Island Regatta" and provides excellent accommodations in modern, motel-type buildings with all facilities, including bonefish guides and a crusier for offshore trolling. There are widespread bonefish flats and sandy shores, where bonefish, permit, gafftopsail pompano, snappers and cuda are taken. Offshore catches are wahoo, mackerel, bonito, kingfish, dolphin and some billfish. A small resort, Hoppers Bay Cottages, George Town, Exuma, Bahamas, also provides some accommodations.

Also in the central area of the Bahamas, Reginald Pinder operates the St. George's Hotel, Spanish Wells, Bahamas; and on Long Island, Mr. and Mrs. Leslie Knowles operate the Santa Maria Club. It may also be reached through Jane Wallen, Rootes Building, Nassau, Bahamas.

Lying between Long Island and San Salvador is Rum Cay, where Grantwood Lodge also caters to fishermen. It can be reached through Grantwood Enterprises, 7920 W. Drive, Harbor Island, Miami Beach, Florida.

Many of the islands throughout the Bahamas can only be fished by chartered or private boat and arrangements must be made in advance to assure obtaining food and fuel en route, and to provide clearance papers. The islands are well set-up in this regard. Complete information regarding charters may be obtained through the Nassau Yacht Haven, P.O. Box 1216, Nassau, Bahamas; Brown's Boat Basin, P.O. Box 716, Nassau, Bahamas; Chamber of Commerce Docks, 1310 Fifth Street, Miami Beach 39, Florida; Chamber of Commerce Docks, Fort Lauderdale, Florida; West Palm Beach Fishing Club, West Palm Beach, Florida.

Many new resorts are currently being planned and constructed in the Bahamas and anglers planning to fish there should write for further information to Don McCarthy, Fishing Information Bureau, Ministry of Tourism, Nassau in the Bahamas.

BERMUDA

The islands of Bermuda, lying only 750 miles east of New York City, present a salty fishing ground much easier to reach from the congested areas of the United States than is any comparable water. While we speak of Bermuda, in the singular, actually over a hundred islands comprise the Bermudas, a series of sandstone and coral formations rising some 15,000 feet from the ocean floor. This reef area covers about 300 square miles, and in addition there are banks lying to the southwest, known as the Challenger Banks. It is an area where tropical and cooler waters mingle, and this, along with the conformation of the ocean bottom makes it an ideal habitat for fish, ranging all the way from pan-sized sergeant-majors to the giant mako shark. Inshore, in shallow water easily reached by light-tackle casters are bonefish, gray snappers, gafftopsail pompano, barracuda. On the reefs, groupers, Bermuda chub, rockfish, snappers, yellowtail and bonito will keep you busy all day. Offshore trolling brings wahoo, dolphin, Allison tuna, blackfin tuna, the oceanic or Bermuda bonito, mackerel, which is also called little tuna or false albacore, and occasional white and blue marlin. Some of the biggest amberjack in the world are found in Bermuda waters. Wahoo are also extra-big while blackfin tuna, Allison tuna and bonefish run to good size. White and blue marlin are caught each summer.

The island is readily reached via daily flights from New York on Pan American World Airways, BOAC, Eastern and several other airlines. Flights operate from other East Coast cities such as Miami, Florida, via Nassau in the Bahamas; and from Montreal and Ottawa, in Canada, as well as a number of European cities. There is a twice-weekly steamer service between New York and Hamilton, the capital city of Bermuda. While at dock in Bermuda the ship serves as passengers' hotel. The steamship is operated by the Furness Bermuda Line, 34 Whitehall Street, New York, N.Y.

Only small cars are permitted on the island, and the speed limit is twenty miles per hour—which you will find fast enough on the narrow roads which wind between high rock walls festooned with lush-flowering shrubs and vines. Bicycles are widely used, especially the English motor bike, with a small motor. If you're adept at riding one of these, you can spend many a pleasant day exploring the fishing at remote corners of the islands. Otherwise, it is a good idea to hire a cab driver to show you the fishing spots onshore. It seems that nearly every cab driver in Bermuda is a fisherman, and he'll take you to the right spots. The bridge at Flatts, right beside the Bermuda Aquarium is one. There are some tremendous snappers there, very hard to take, but worth the try. Whale Bay is the place to try for bonefish.

The bonefish is sought here in a slightly different way than in Florida or the Bahamas. The water is much deeper, so you seldom see a tailing fish. But from a high bluff at Whale Bay you can often see them swimming, standing out clearly against the white sand. All the angler has to do is clamber down the hill, wade out, make his cast, and with proper co-operation get a hit from a bonefish.

The climate in Bermuda varies from cool and damp in winter, to very warm in summer. The best fishing is from early spring to late fall when you can generally expect fine weather with the exception of a possible blow as the hurricane season nears. In the early spring you may want long trousers to fish in, and a sweater for warmth. This, topped with a rain jacket to break the wind, is all you will need. As summer comes on, shorts are worn almost exclusively, and you scarcely ever need anything for warmth, although it's always wise to have a rain jacket. Use plenty of sunburn lotion and wear a long-billed or wide-brimmed hat. Insect pests are nonexistant. Be sure you wear rubber-soled shoes for in the boats, and take an extra pair for the times you may want to wade the beaches for some casting.

The tackle you will need in Bermuda varies widely according to the fish you seek. Spinning is the most popular of the casting techniques, because of the fact that the monofilament line is less readily seen in the phenomenally clear water of Bermuda, and also because in most cases the water is too deep for successful fly fishing. With a spinning outfit you can fish artificials which pop along the surface, use jigs that sink deep, or use bait. A 6½- to 7-foot rod and a large reel capable of holding 400 yards of 6- or 8-pound-test line is ideal for most circumstances. But for fishing the reefs, where you may tie into something of a real scale buster, a rod measuring 7½ to 8½ feet, and weighing from 7 to 12 ounces will give you more lifting power. This rod calls for a larger reel, loaded with 10-, 12- or even 15-pound-test line.

The jig-type bucktails with hook riding up are hard to beat. In ¼-ounce weight they can be bounced along a sandy bottom in a way that a bonefish finds irresistable. For deep jigging over reefs, the ½-ounce jigs are better.

Many Bermuda anglers like to cast at night, and at such times you should use the heavier outfit described above. The shrimp, Salty Cisco, Nylure and Barracuda lure are all good in ¼-ounce sizes. The Upperman bucktails are tops.

The Phillips Big Boy, a lure that dives and pops and in general kicks up quite a commotion is excellent for barracuda, which with his little brother the sennet, will often be found in sandy bays.

Those who use bait must seek out the greenworm if they want to take bonefish. It's about the only thing he'll look at. For other species, hogmouthed fry, pilchards and sometimes a whole live fish about 6 inches long will fill the bill.

While most of the water along Bermuda's shores is too deep for successful fly fishing, there are a few exceptions. Gafftopsail pompano work into the surf along many of the bathing beaches and can be taken on small spoon-type fly-rod lures or small bucktails. Occasionally snapper and yellowtail also come within range of a fly, as for instance, in Harrington Sound, near Flatts, where sometimes schools of the fish can be seen breaking. But in general, if you want to use a fly rod you must resort to chum to raise the fish to your level. But when you do so, you have the privilege of trading punches with some sensational tackle busters, as all kinds of fish work into the chum line.

You'll need a 9- or 9½-foot fly rod weighing about 6 ounces, and this calls for a GAF (WF9F) line, because you need that weight not only to balance the rod, but to get out into the wind which is usually present to some degree on the ocean. The fly reel should be big enough to hold 200 yards of 18-pound-test squidding line backing, as well as the fly line, to take care of the long runs made by such fish as the bonefish, false albacore and bonito.

The leader should be 12 feet long and tapered from a 30-pound-test butt section next the line, through shorter lengths of 25-, 20-, 15-, 12-, 10- and 8-pound-test.

When you go for some of the bigger reef fish, you can stop at the 12-pound-test.

One fly every fly fisherman should have on his trip to Bermuda is a small white bucktail known as the "Fry Fly," because it was tied to match the hogmouthed fry used as chum. Many fish which will not touch an ordinarily cast fly, will sock a Fry Fly that is floating casually with some of the real thing. This special fly may be obtained from the Phillips Fly & Tackle Company, Alexandria, Pennsylvania.

For inshore barracuda, you can't beat a popping bug on a 2/0 hook, and the popper should be played fast.

For offshore trolling, Bermuda has charter boats berthed at St. George's and at Hamilton, Paget, Warwick and Somerset. They may be reached as follows:

GUIDE	BOAT	PHONE
St. Georges		
Capt. Roy Taylor	Wally III	9371
Capt. Gerald Pascoe	Escort	9424
	Captain Bink	
Capt. Walter Pascoe	Sea Scout	9424
Capt. Edric Pearman	Swordfish	9511
Capt. Campbell O'Connor	Diane	9549
Hamilton		
Mr. Musson Wainwright	Melby	2218
Paget		
Mr. Leslie Martin	Sharlee II	4348
Warwick		
Capt. Chris Smith	Valiant II	2645
Mr. Bert Darrell		2294
Somerset		
Capt. Russell Young	Sea Wolf	8234
	So What	
Capt. Milton Pitman	Salty Too	8302

For further additions since this list was compiled, consult the Fishing Information Bureau, 50 Front Street, Hamilton, Bermuda.

Bermuda Captains are light-tackle minded, keenly aware that the feel of a good fish on light tackle has transformed many an indifferent angler into an enthusiast. So they are equipped with a variety of tackle to suit the occasion. For instance, while a beginner might use 130-pound-test line when trolling for big wahoo, Allison tuna or marlin, a fisherman with wide experience may go down to 50-, 30- or even 20-pound-test line. It is this pitting of his skill in handling the delicate tackle against the power of the fish that helps to make the game. Many such anglers prefer to bring their own tackle, and for these, the following table will serve as a guide.

HEAVY TACKLE

Tip weight	Reel	Line
16-20 ounces	12/0	39 thread linen, wet test 117 lbs. or 130-lb.-test dacron
12-16 ounces	10/0	24 thread linen, wet test 72 lbs. or 80-lb.-test dacron
10-12 ounces	6/0	15 thread linen, wet test 45 lbs. or 50-lb.-test dacron

LIGHT TACKLE

6-8 ounces	4/0	9 thread linen, wet test 27 lbs. or 30-lb.-test dacron; or 25-, 30-lb.-test nylon monofilament
4-6 ounces	3/0	6 thread linen, wet test 18 lbs. or 20-lb.-test dacron; or 15- 20-lb.-test monofilament

EXTRA-LIGHT TACKLE

2¾-ounces-4 ounces	3/0	10- 12-lb.-test monofilament

Penn Senator, Ocean City Big Game and the Fin-Nor Reels are all first-class.

Some trollers use big saltwater spinning outfits, loaded with 12- or 15-pound-test line. This calls for real skill in handling some of the fish you'll encounter in Bermuda waters, and should be left in the hands of the experienced.

One of the most ardently sought species in offshore trolling in Bermuda is the wahoo, a member of the mackerel family—long, stream-lined, with a beak-like snout and vertical bars on its dark blue-gray sides. They seem to be more common in Bermuda waters than elsewhere, and also grow to some exceptional sizes. The average is 45 pounds, and plenty are taken between 70 and 90 pounds. There are some fish around all year but the peak of the fishing for this species comes in May, August and September. Small sennet, small gar and strip bait are all used. Anglers who favor 20- or 10-pound-test line use a 6/0 hook, well-sharpened; while those using heavier tackle go to a 7/0 hook, as the wahoo has a large mouth. Baits are usually trolled from the outriggers and the wahoo strike to the bait is a soul stirring one. He splashes water all over the place, then takes off on a run that may be as much as 600 feet. Do not strike until the line becomes tight between rod and fish. Then get set for a fight that will keep you busy for a good long time with a fish that acts like a torpedo.

Both the white and the blue marlin are taken in Bermuda waters though not in great numbers. However, a white weighing 128 pounds 14 ounces was taken in Bermuda, and this is a very large fish for the species. Blues are a little more plentiful, and some boats have raised as many as four in a day. The top weight known to have been taken was 370 pounds, well above the average in any waters. The season for both blue and white marlin is from May to October, with July and August being the top months.

The yellowfin tuna, known in Bermuda as the Allison tuna, is one of the most widely-sought game fish. The Bermuda record weighed 265 pounds, and many almost as large are taken. The peak season for Allisons is from October to June. They particularly like a bait that skips along the surface and the same is true of the smaller blackfin tuna. The blackfin will hit a bait traveling ten miles an hour. It is only within recent years that this species has been added to the lists of the International Game Fish Association and as a result the records are wide open. The Bermuda record is a 36-pound fish taken by Joseph E. Baptiste, Jr., in 1963. This is a substantial weight for the blackfin, which does not grow to the size of his fellow tunas.

Another species which seems to reach outsizes in Bermuda waters is the amberjack. For years the all-tackle world record on sport fishing gear was a 120 pound 8 ounce fish taken in Hawaii. But commercial men in Bermuda have handlined in amberjacks much larger—a 146-pounder, and one which weighed 171 pounds after it had been dressed. Whether an angler will ever be able to land one of these tough hombres on sport-fishing gear was a moot point, until 1964, when Peter Simons of Bermuda took one that weighed 149 pounds, on 27-pound-test line, thus becoming the new all-tackle world record holder.

The mako shark, one of the fiercest fighters in the sea, puts in his appearance in October, and may be taken until March. Oceanic bonito are on hand almost continuously, but are more commonly taken from April through June. The horse-eye or Madregal bonito, also called the common bonito, occurs often enough to provide extra sport.

Certain other species which are more or less occasional visitors to these waters can spark the fishing at many an unexpected time. The cobia, though rare, can reach enormous size, one having been landed that weighed 110 pounds. Dolphin are usually picked up when you are trolling for other species but once you hook one, if you are light-tackle minded you can have a lot of fun casting to other dolphin which invariably follow a hooked fish in. While in general they run small, from 3 to 10 pounds, quite a few are taken up to 25 pounds, and the Bermuda record is a thumping big 52 pounds.

FISHING THE REEFS AND CORAL HEADS

You could look over miles of ocean around the islands of Bermuda, and think that you saw nothing but flat water—but beneath that water is a landscape of reefs and coral heads that make perfect hide-outs for all sorts of deep-dwelling fish. Some of the reefs lie only 60 feet from shore. Others may be ten miles out at sea. Bermuda guides have them pin-pointed, from the Challenger Banks to St. George's. They know right where to take you, to assure fish.

The guide usually anchors over the reef, and starts to chum, tossing over handfuls of small minnows known as hog-mouthed fry because of the size of their mouths. Sometimes sand is mixed with the fry, to take it down faster. If the reef is very deep down, pilchards are used, these 5-inch minnows being likewise crushed into a handful of sand, to help them sink down. Whatever your chum, in very short order fish start to appear, snappers, porgy, the saltwater bream, the trigger fish and a dozen brightly-colored species you seldom see elsewhere. As the chum drifts away with the tide, it attracts still others, and these are often yellowtail, Bermuda bonito, sennet, monkey rockfish, coney, squirrel fish, the rock hind and all sort of groupers. As the chum continues to drift out it reaches far-ranging schools of everything from the racy ocean robin to the mackerel. Even a wahoo may swim leisurely in for his share of the free feed.

For this reef fishing, many anglers bait with the same thing they are using as chum—whole hogmouthed fry, or whole pilchards. The spinning outfit is ideal, because of the invisibility of the monofilament line. Artificial lures are used, too, and especially when the fish are feeding avidly, they will hit one readily. Some fine catches can also be made on a fly rod, by using a long leader and a small white bucktail tied to resemble the fry. The fly should not be given any motion, but be allowed to drift with the chum. When the fish are feeding on chum they will seldom hit a lure that is moving.

The gray snapper, one of Bermuda's smartest fish, will give you a fit in a chum line, rushing your fry fly with mouth wide open, then stopping at the last moment and turning away to grab a bit of the real thing. However, on occasion you can outwit him by watching the black line which runs through the eye and up the back of the head. The more excited he gets about his feeding, the blacker that line gets— and when you figure he's really carried away by his appetite, that's the time to drop your fly in front of him and you may get him.

One of Bermuda's strongest fish is the Bermuda chub, and he's one of the hardest to catch. The thing to remember is that lobster is his favorite dish, so when you locate a spot where the captain says there are Bermuda chub, start chumming with bits of lobster. Again, as with the snapper, let them gobble it up till their bellies bulge, and then throw a lure among them and you'll find yourself hooked to one of the toughest fish in the ocean. You can't fish for chub with too light an outfit because he'll break you up and you don't want too heavy an outfit because you may pull the hook out of his soft mouth. The ideal gear is a 5- or 6-ounce rod, a reel with a good even drag and 100 yards of 15- or 20-pound-test monofilament line. Use a strong 1/0 hook, but neither leader nor weight. The sharp-eyed chub would spot anything that phony in a minute.

In 1949, the writer was lucky enough to take two chub on a small Brown and White bucktail fly, dropped into the chum and allowed to drift motionless. We managed to land the fish without gaffing them, and to this day they are swimming around in the Bermuda Aquarium, looking out at curious tourists.

INSHORE FISHING WITH CASTING TACKLE

The main fish which an angler may expect to take inshore in Bermuda are the bonefish, gafftopsail pompano, snapper and barracuda. But you never really know when some other species such as a yellowtail, mackerel or Bermuda bonito may stray a little off-course, and hit your lure.

The gray snapper will be found around all bridges and pilings and rocks. As mentioned previously, he's so smart he's been dubbed the "sea lawyer" and you have to catch him when he's feeding avidly and has forgotten his caution. Even when you hook him under such circustances, your chances of landing him are still slim because he'll head for the rocks and cut you off. However, some of the species as big as 14 pounds have been taken from the bridge at Flatts, one of the favorite spots for onshore anglers.

Barracuda will be found in all the sandy bays and coves and they too are smart. You can usually see them lying log-like near the surface apparently dreaming, but always with a weather eye out for something worth eating. They seem to move inshore in April and stay throughout the summer, usually frequenting the same waters day after day, so that if you've once located their hang-out you can usually depend on finding them there the next time you go back. They'll respond to almost any fast-moving bait, be it fly, spoon or jig, but a surface lure, one that pops, dives and cuts a herringbone pattern on the water is one of the best. The one thing to remember is that in very shallow water, a loud-popped lure will frighten a cuda, where in deeper water it will attract him.

Plug and spin casters generally use an 18-inch wire or vinyl-covered leader to circumvent the long, sharp teeth of the cuda.

The cuda will also respond to a fly-rod popper worked along the edge of a drop-off. In shallow water a streamer or bucktail is best, preferably with a touch of silver tinsel winding on the body. Red Hackle with yellow wings or All Yellow are both good, and they should be tied on 1/0 and 3/0 salt-resistant hooks.

From November to May anglers will often find large schools of sennet, a small cousin of the barracuda, and they will hit almost anything you offer them. While they seldom go above two pounds, they can provide some good light-tackle sport.

One of the greatest thrills to a Bermuda beach fisherman is to get into a school of gafftopsail pompano. When you first spot them they are often quite close to shore, picking up sand fleas in the froth of the breaking waves. They will take fly or spinning lures readily. Then after a few have been caught, they begin to develop caution and move out, and your casts must be longer. Still they keep moving out, and before long you find yourself shoulder deep, still casting to the silvery little pompano as they dash through the crest of breaking waves. Frequently chumming with hogmouthed fry or even bread will tempt them back closer inshore. So when you see a Bermuda angler walking down the beach with a rod in one hand and a loaf of bread in the other, you can be pretty sure he's not going on a picnic, he's going pompano fishing.

Part of the fascination of Bermuda fishing is the fact that you may come up with almost anything. Scientists using long-line fishing methods have found such rarities as the lancet fish, the oil fish or tapioca fish, the New York dog fish and the Berumda catfish, and dozens of other species seldom encountered.

Though most of the following species may be taken year-round in Bermuda waters, the best runs are in those months indicated.

SPECIES	BEST MONTHS
Amberjack	Sept. to May
Amberjack (horse-eye)	Sept. to June
Barracuda	March to October
Bermuda chub	All months
Bonefish	April to December
Bonito (Bermuda, or madregal)	Sept. to June
Bonito (common, or mackerel)	All months
Bonito (oceanic)	April to June
Dolphin	Nov. to May
Grouper	All months
Jack crevalle	Oct. to April
Jack (horse-eye)	Oct. to February
Mako shark	Oct. to March
Marlin (blue)	Feb. to Oct.
Marlin (white)	Jan. to Nov.

Pompano (Gafftopsail)	May to Oct.
Rockfish	All months
Sennet	All months
Snapper (gray)	All months
Tuna (Allison or yellowfin)	Oct. to June
Tuna (blackfin)	Sept. to June
Tuna (bluefin)	June, July, Nov., Dec.
Wahoo	Sept. to June
Yellowtail	All months

No passport is required to enter Bermuda for visits of less than eight months. U.S. and Canadian citizens require proof of citizenship on their return to their countries. All but U.S. and Canadian citizens must obtain an exit permit from the Currency Control Board on leaving Bermuda at which time passport must be shown. No visa is required.

For further information about fishing in Bermuda, write Peter Perinchief, Director, The Fishing Information Bureau, 50 Front Street, Hamilton, Bermuda. Telephone 1223.

INDEX OF WATERWAYS

INDEX OF WATERWAYS

Key to Abbreviations

L — Lake   B — Bay
R — River   C — Canal
S — Stream   Br — Brook
P — Pond   Cr — Creek
Re — Reservoir